D0753772

UNIVERSAL
DICTIONARY
LANGENSCHEIDT
DICIONÁRIO
UNIVERSAL

DICIONÁRIO UNIVERSAL
LANGENSCHEIDT

INGLÊS-PORTUGUÊS
PORTUGUÊS-INGLÊS

LANGENSCHEIDT

LANGENSCHEIDT'S
UNIVERSAL DICTIONARY

ENGLISH-PORTUGUESE
PORTUGUESE-ENGLISH

LANGENSCHEIDT

Contents
Indice

Author: Claudina Marques Coelho

© 1984 Langenscheidt KG, Berlin and Munich
Printed in Germany

Abbreviations
Abbreviaturas

The sign of repetition (~) or, with capital initial letter (≙), replaces either the whole heading: abandon; **~ed** = abandoned; or that part of it which precedes the stroke (|): abbreviat|e; **~ion** = abbreviation; alp; the ≙**s** = the Alps.

*O til (~, com inicial alterada ≙) substitui o título inteiro ou a parte dele que precede o traço vertical (|); p.ex. civil; **~idade** = civilidade; abert|o; **~ura** = abertura; natal adj: ≙ = Natal m*

---

a and, *e*
abbr abbreviation, *abreviatura*
adj adjective, *adje(c)tivo*
adv adverb, *advérbio*
anat anatomy, *anatomia*
arch architecture, *arquitectura*
art article, *artigo*
auto automobilism, *automobilismo*
avi aviation, *aviação*

bot botany, *botânica*
Braz Brazilian, *brasileiro*
chem chemistry, *química*
com commerce, *comércio*
conj conjunction, *conjunção*
contr contraction, *contra(c)ção*
dem demonstrative, *demonstrativo*

eccl ecclesiastical, *eclesiástico*

elect electricity, *ele(c)tricidade*

f feminine, *feminino*

fam familiar, *familiar*

fig figurative, *figurativo*

GB Great Britain, *Grã-Bretanha*

geol geology, *geologia*

gram grammar, *gramática*

int interjection, *interjeição*

jur juridical, *jurídico*

m masculine, *masculino*

mar maritime, *marítimo*

mec mechanical, *mecânico*

med medical, *medicinal*

mil military, *militar*

min mineralogy, *mineralogia*

mus music, *música*

naut nautical, *náutica*

pers personal, *pessoal*

pl plural, *plural*

poss possessive, *possessivo*

pres present, *presente do indicativo*

pron pronoun, *pronome*

prp preposition, *preposição*

s substantive, *substantivo*

sg singular, *singular*

thea theatre, *teatro*

US United States, *Estados Unidos*

v/aux auxiliary verb, *verbo auxiliar*

v/i intransitive verb, *verbo intransitivo*

v/r reflexive verb, *verbo reflexivo*

v/t transitive verb, *verbo transitivo*

zo zoological, *zoológico*

A pronúncia inglesa

1. Vogais e ditongos

símbolos	pronúncia	
	som semelhante em português	exemplo inglês
ɑː	c**a**ro	father
ø	c**a**ma	mother
æ	t**e**nho	fat
ɛə	—	care
ai	**vai**	my
au	**mau**	cloud
e	f**é**	get
ei	**lei**te	name
ə	d**e**pois	about
əː	—	bird
əu	**vou**	boat
i	part**i**	city
iː	aqu**i**	tea
iə	**ti**a	fear
ɔ	n**ó**	not
ɔː	far**o**l	law
ɔi	b**ói**a	point
u	p**o**rque	book
uː	f**á**c**i**l (Braz)	few
uə	**u**va	poor

2. Consonantes

símbolos	pronúncia som semelhante em português	exemplo inglês
b	**b**ebedeira	but
d	**d**ar	dear
f	**f**eira	food
g	**g**ato	give
h	—	ahead
j	**i**ate	yes
k	**c**omo .	come
l	qua**l**	call
m	**m**ão	mean
n	**n**ão	night
p	**p**asta	top
r	—	right
s	**s**entir	song
t	**t**omar	take
v	**v**i	of
w	**ué!** (Braz)	wait
z	**z**ebra	rose
ŋ	—	bring
ʃ	**ch**á	she
tʃ	**t**eatro (Braz)	rich
dʒ	a**dj**etivo	join
ʒ	**j**á	usual
θ	—	think
ð	—	lather

O acento tónico (ˈ) é sempre indicado antes da sílaba tónica: por exemplo about [əˈbaut]

Sílabas finais sem transcrição fonética

Por falta de espaço, não se inseriram no vocabulário alfabético a transcrição fonética das terminações seguintes:

-ability [-əbiliti]
-able [-əbl]
-age [-idʒ]
-al [-əl]
-ally [-əli]
-an [-ən]
-ance [-əns]
-ancy [-ənsi]
-ant [-ənt]
-ar [-ə]
-ary [-əri]
-ation [-eiʃən]
-cious [-ʃəs]
-cy [-si]
-dom [-dəm]
-ed [-d; -t; -id]*
-edness [-dnis; -tnis; -idnis]*
-ee [-i:]
-en [-n]
-ence [-əns]
-ent [-ənt]
-er [-ə]

-ery [-əri]
-ess [-is]
-fication [-fikeiʃən]
-ful [-ful]
-fy [-fai]
-hood [-hud]
-ial [əl]
-ian [-iən; -jən]
-ible [-əbl]
-ic(s) [-ik(s)]
-ical [-ikəl]
-ily [-ili]
-iness [-inis]
-ing [-iŋ]
-ish [-iʃ]
-ism [-izəm]
-ist [-ist]
-istic [-istik]
-ite [-ait]
-ity [-iti]
-ive [-iv]
-ization [-aizeiʃən]

-ize [-aiz]
-izing [-aiziŋ]
-less [-lis]
-ly [-li]
-ment(s) [-mənt(s)]
-ness [-nis]
-oid [-ɔid]
-or [-ə]
-ory [-əriɪ]
-our [-ə]
-ous [-əs]
-ry [-ri]
-ship [-ʃip]
-(s)sion [-ʃən]
-sive [-siv]
-some [-səm]
-ties [-tiz]
-tion [-ʃən]
-tious [-ʃəs]
-trous [-trəs]
-try [-tri]
-y [-i]

* [-d] quando segue vogais e consoantes sonoras; [-t] quando segue consoantes surdas; [-id] quando segue d e t finais.

Portuguese Pronunciation

1. Vowels

			Nearest English Equivalent
a	unstressed:	o	as in mother
	stressed:	a	as in father
e	ê – closed:	—	
	é – open:	e	as in get
	weak stress:	a	as in about
i		i	as in city
o	closed		resembles English aw in "law", but closer and short
	ó – open:	o	as in not
u		oo	as in book

All vowels may be nasalized, as for example in American long, language, Fr rendez-vous.

Diphthongs: each of the two vowels in a diphthong retains its independent quality.

Nasalized diphthongs: the stressed first element and the unstressed second element are nasalized as one sound.

2. Consonants

			Nearest English Equivalent
b		b	as in but
c	before a, o, u:	c	as in come
	before e and i:	s	as in sing
ç	(only before a, o, u)	s	as in song
ch		sh	as in shine
d		d	as in door
f		f	as in first
g	before a, o, u:	g	as in give
	before e and i:	s	as in pleasure
gu	before e and i:	g	as in gate
h	silent		
j		s	as in measure
l		l	as in silver
lh		—	
m		m	as in mean
n		n	as in night
nh		—	
p		p	as in people
qu	before a:	qu	as in frequent
	before e and i:	c	as in cat
r		as	Scottish rolled r

2. Consonants

		Nearest English Equivalent
s	at the beginning of a word or syllable: in medial position between vowels: in final position	s as in sail s as in used sh as in ship
x		as in **sh**oe, la**z**y **race**, bo**x**
z	in initial and medial position: in final position:	z as in zero s as in usual

Peculiarities of Brazilian pronunciation

Before the nasal consonants *m* and *n* the vowels *e* and *o* in the tonic syllable are closed (as opposed to being open in Portugal) and bear a circumflex (ˆ) as opposed to an acute accent (ˊ):

Port	género antónimo	*Braz*	gênero antônimo

A

a [ei; ə], **an** [æn, ən] um *m*, uma *f*

aback [ə'bæk]: taken ~ desconcertado, surpreso

abandon [ə'bændən] *v/t* abandonar; entregar, -se; **~ment** abandono *m*

abase [ə'beis] *v/t* humilhar, rebaixar

abate [ə'beit] *v/t*, *v/i* abater; *jur* anular; diminuir; **~ment** diminuição *f*

abb|ess ['æbis] abadessa *f*; **~ey** ['-i] abadia *f*; **~ot** ['-ət] abade *m*

abbreviat|e [ə'bri:vieit] *v/t* abreviar; **~ion** [-'eiʃən] abreviatura *f*

abdicate ['æbdikeit] *v/t*, *v/i* abdicar, renunciar a

abdomen ['æbdəmen] abdome *m*, abdómen *m*

abduct [æb'dʌkt] *v/t* sequestrar, raptar

abet [ə'bet] *v/t* incitar, instigar; **~tor** cúmplice *m*, *f*

abeyance [ə'beiəns] suspensão *f*; **in** ~ (em) suspenso

abhor [əb'hɔ:] *v/t* aborrecer, detestar; **~rence** aversão *f*; **~rent** repugnante

abide [ə'baid] *v/t* aguentar, suportar; *v/i* morar

ability [ə'biliti] habilidade *f*; capacidade *f*; aptidão *f*

abject ['æbdʒekt] abje(c)to

abjure [əb'dʒuə] *v/t* abjurar; renunciar a

able ['eibl] apto; hábil, capaz; **be** ~ **to** poder, ser capaz de

abnegate ['æbnigeit] *v/t* abnegar

abnormal [æb'nɔ:məl] anormal

aboard [ə'bɔ:d] *adv* a bordo

abolish [ə'bɔliʃ] *v/t* abolir

abominable [ə'bɔminəbl] abominável

abominate [ə'bɔmineit] *v/t* abominar, detestar

abortion [ə'bɔ:ʃən] aborto *m*

abound [ə'baund] *v/i* abundar; ~ **in**, ~ **with** ser rico em, estar cheio de

about [ə'baut] *prp* em volta de, sobre, acerca de; *adv* pouco mais ou menos; quase; **be** ~ **to** estar a ponto de

above [ə'bʌv] *prp* sobre, por cima de, acima de; *adv* acima, em cima; ~ **all** sobretudo

abreast [ə'brest] de frente; lado a lado

abridge [ə'bridʒ] *v/t* abreviar, resumir

abroad [ə'brɔ:d] no (ao) estrangeiro

abrupt [ə'brʌpt] abrupto; brusco

abscess ['æbsis] abcesso *m*

absence ['æbsəns] ausência *f*;

falta *f*

absent ['æbsənt] *adj* ausente;
v/r [æb'sent] ausentar-se;
~ -minded distraído

absolve [əb'zɔlv] *v/t* absolver

absorb [əb'sɔːb] *v/t* absorver

abstain [əb'stein] (**from**) *v/i* abster-se (de)

abstemious [æb'stiːmjəs] abstémio, sóbrio

abstract [æb'strækt] *v/t* abstrair; resumir; ['æbstrækt] *adj* abstra(c)to; *s* resumo *m*; extra-(c)to *m*

absurd [əb'sɔːd] absurdo

abundan|ce [ə'bʌndəns] abundância *f*; ~t abundante

abus|e [ə'bjuːs] *s* abuso *m*; *v/t* [ə'bjuːz] abusar; insultar; ~ive abusivo; insultante

abyss [ə'bis] abismo *m*

academic [ækə'demik] *adj, s* académico *m*

academy [ə'kædəmi] academia *f*

accede [æk'siːd] *v/i* aceder

accelerat|e [ək'seləreit] *v/t, v/i* acelerar; ~or acelerador *m*

accent ['æksənt] *s* sotaque *m*; acento *m*

accentuate [æk'sentjueit] *v/t* acentuar

accept [ək'sept] *v/t* aceitar; ~able aceitável; ~ance aceitação *f*; *com* aceite *m*

access ['ækses] acesso *m*; admissão *f*; ~ible [æk'sesəbl] acessível; ~ory *adj* acessório; *s jur* (*pl* **-ries**) cúmplice *m*; *pl* acessórios *m/pl*

accident ['æksidənt] acidente

m, desastre *m*; **by** ~ por acaso; ~al [·'dentl] *adj* acidental

acclaim [ə'kleim] *v/t* aplaudir, aclamar

acclimatize [ə'klaimətaiz] *v/t, v/i* aclimatar (-se)

accommodat|e [ə'kɔmədeit] *v/t* acomodar; ~ion [ə.kɔmə'deiʃən] acomodação *f*; alojamento *m*

accompan|iment [ə'kʌmpənimənt] acompanhamento *m*; ~ist *mus* acompanhante *m*; ~y *v/t* acompanhar

accomplice [ə'kɔmplis] cúmplice *m, f*

accomplish [ə'kɔmpliʃ] *v/t* efe(c)tuar, realizar; completar; ~ed acabado, perfeito; consumado; ~ment conclusão *f*; realização *f*

accord [ə'kɔːd] *v/t, v/i* concordar; conceder; *s* acordo *m*; **of one's own** ~ de moto próprio, **with one** ~ de comum acordo; ~ing to segundo, conforme, de acordo com; ~ingly em consequência; conforme(mente)

accost [ə'kɔst] *v/t* abordar

account [ə'kaunt] *v/t* considerar; *s* conta *f*; ~ **for** dar conta de; justificar, explicar; **on** ~ **of** por causa de; **on no** ~ de modo algum; **take into** ~ levar em conta; **turn to** ~ tirar lucro; ~able responsável; ~ancy contabilidade *f*; ~ant contabilista *m, f*

accredit [ə'kredit] *v/t* acreditar

accrue [ə'kruː] *v/i* acrescer; provir

accumulat|e [əˈkjuːmjuleit] *v/t, v/i* acumular(-se); **~or** acumulador *m*

accura|cy [ˈækjurəsi] exa(c)tidão *f*, precisão *f*; **~te** exa(c)to, preciso

accusation [ˌækjuː(ˈ)zeifən] acusação *f*

accuse [əˈkjuːz] *v/t* acusar; **~d** *s* réu *m*; ré *f*

accustom [əˈkʌstəm] *v/t* acostumar

ace [eis] ás *m*

ache [eik] *s* dor *f*; *v/i* doer

achieve [əˈtʃiːv] *v/t* executar, realizar, conseguir; **~ment** realização *f*, proeza *f*

acid [ˈæsid] *adj,* s ácido *m*

acidity [əˈsiditi] acidez *f*

acknowledge [əkˈnɔlidʒ] *v/t* reconhecer; confirmar; admitir; **~ment** reconhecimento *m*; confirmação *f*; aviso *m* de recepção

acorn [ˈeikɔːn] bolota *f*

acoustics [əˈkuːstiks] acústica *f*

acquaint [əˈkweint] *v/t* familiarizar; informar; **be ~ed with** conhecer pessoalmente; **~ance** conhecimento *m*

acquiesce [ˌækwiˈes] *v/i* aquiescer; **~nce** [ˌækwiˈesəns] aquiescência *f*

acqui|re [əˈkwaiə] *v/t* adquirir; **~sition** [ˌækwiˈzifən] aquisição *f*

acquit [əˈkwit] *v/t* absolver; ilibar; liquidar; **~tal** absolvição *f*

acre [ˈeikə] acre *m*

acrid [ˈækrid] acre, picante

acrimony [ˈækriməni] acrimónia *f*

acrobat [ˈækrəbæt] acrobata *m, f*; **~ics** acrobacia *f*

across [əˈkrɔs] *prp* do outro lado de; através de

act [ækt] *s* lei *f*, decreto *m*; a(c)ção *f*, a(c)to *m*; *v/t, v/i* representar; agir, a(c)tuar; funcionar; **~ion** a(c)ção *f*

active [ˈæktiv] a(c)tivo

activity [ækˈtiviti] (*pl* **-ties**) a(c)tividade *f*

actor [ˈæktə] a(c)tor *m*

actress [ˈæktris] a(c)triz *f*

actual [ˈæktjuəl] verdadeiro, real; a(c)tual; **~ly** na realidade; presentemente

acute [əˈkjuːt] agudo; penetrante; **~ness** agudeza *f*; acuidade *f*

adage [ˈædidʒ] adágio *m*

adapt [əˈdæpt] *v/t* adaptar; **~ation** [ˌædæpˈteifən] adaptação *f*

add [æd] *v/t, v/i* acrescentar, juntar; somar, adicionar

adder [ˈædə] víbora *f*

addict [ˈædikt] *s* viciado *m*; **~ed** [əˈdiktid] (**to**) adi(c)to (a); apegado (a)

addition [əˈdifən] adição *f*, soma *f*; **in ~** em aditamento a, além de; **~al** adicional

address [əˈdres] *s* endereço *m*; alocução *f*; *v/t* dirigir-se a; endereçar; **~ee** [ˌædreˈsiː] destinatário *m*

adduce [əˈdjuːs] *v/t* aduzir

adept [ˈædept] *adj,* s perito *m*

adequate [ˈædikwit] adequado

adhe|re [ədˈhiə] *v/i* aderir;

~sion [ǝd'hiːʃǝn] adesão f

adhesive [ǝd'hiːsiv] adj adesivo; **~ tape** adesivo m

adjacent [ǝ'dʒeisǝnt] adjacente, contíguo

adjective ['ædʒiktiv] adje(c)tivo m

adjoin [ǝ'dʒoin] v/t, v/i confinar (com)

adjourn [ǝ'dʒǝːn] v/t adiar, diferir

adjudicate [ǝ'dʒuːdikeit] v/t, v/i adjudicar

adjunct ['ædʒʌŋkt] adjunto m, auxiliar m

adjust [ǝ'dʒʌst] v/t ajustar; consertar

administ|er [ǝd'ministǝ] v/t administrar; **~ration** [-'treiʃǝn] administração f; **~rative** [-trǝtiv] administrativo

admirable ['ædmǝrǝbl] admirável

admiral ['ædmǝrǝl] almirante m

admiration [ˌædmǝ'reiʃǝn] admiração f

admire [ǝd'maiǝ] v/t admirar

admirer [ǝd'maiǝrǝ] admirador m

admiss|ible [ǝd'misǝbl] admissível; **~ion** admissão f; entrada f

admit [ǝd'mit] v/t admitir; **~tance** admissão f; entrada f

admoni|sh [ǝd'moniʃ] v/t admoestar; **~tion** [ˌædmǝ-'niʃǝn] admoestação f

ado [ǝ'duː] tumulto m, alarido m, barulho m; **much ~ about nothing** muito alarido por nada

adopt [ǝ'dopt] v/t ado(p)tar; **~ion** ado(p)ção f

ador|able [ǝ'doːrǝbl] adorável; **~ation** [ˌædoː'reiʃǝn] adoração f; **~e** v/t adorar

adorn [ǝ'doːn] v/t adornar

adroit [ǝ'droit] destro

adult ['ædʌlt] adj, s adulto m

adulter|ate [ǝ'dʌltǝreit] v/t adulterar; **~er** adúltero m; **~ess** adúltera f; **~y** (pl -ries) adultério m

advance [ǝd'vɑːns] s avanço m; adiantamento m; **~d** avançado; adiantar; progredir; **~d** avançado, adiantado

advantage [ǝd'vɑːntidʒ] vantagem f; **take ~ of** tirar vantagem de; **~ous** [ˌædvǝn'teidʒǝs] vantajoso

adventur|e [ǝd'ventʃǝ] aventura f; **~er** aventureiro m; **~ous** aventuroso

advers|ary ['ædvǝsǝri] adversário m; **~e** adverso; **~ity** adversidade f

ad(vert) ['ædvǝːt] s GB abbr of advertisement

advertise ['ædvǝtaiz] v/t anunciar; v/i pôr anúncios; **~ment** [ǝd'vǝːtismǝnt] anúncio m; **~r** anunciante m

advertising ['ædvǝtaiziŋ] publicidade f

advice [ǝd'vais] aviso m; conselho m

advisable [ǝd'vaizǝbl] aconselhável

advise [ǝd'vaiz] v/t aconselhar;

prevenir, avisar; **~r** conselheiro *m*

advisory [əd'vaizəri] consultivo

advocate ['ædvəkit] *s* advogado *m*; defensor *m*; ['ædvəkeit] *v/t* advogar

aerial [ɛəriəl] *adj* aéreo; *s* antena *f*

aero|drome ['ɛərədrəum] aeródromo *m*; **~dynamic** ['ɛərəudai'næmik] aerodinâmico; **~dynamics** aerodinâmica *f*; **~nautical** ['-'nɔ:tikəl] aeronáutico; **~nautics** aeronáutica *f*; **~plane** ['-plein] *GB* aeroplano *m*

aesthetic [i:s'θetik] estético

affable ['æfəbl] afável

affair [ə'fɛə] questão *f*, assunto *m*; aventura *f* amorosa; **that's my ~** isso é comigo

affect [ə'fekt] *v/t* afe(c)tar; aparentar; **~ation** afe(c)tação *f*, **~ed** afe(c)tado; **~ing** comovente; **~ion** afeição *f*; **~ionate** ['-ʃnit] afe(c)tuoso

affiliate [ə'filieit] *v/t*, *v/i* (a)filiar

affinity [ə'finiti] afinidade *f*

affirm [ə'fə:m] *v/t* afirmar; **~ation** [.æfə:'meiʃən] afirmação *f*; **~ative** [-'mətiv] *s* afirmativa *f*; *adj* afirmativo

afflict [ə'flikt] *v/t* afligir; **~ion** aflição *f*

affluence ['æfluəns] afluência *f*

affluent ['æfluənt] *adj*, *s* afluente *m*

afford [ə'fɔ:d] *v/t* ter recursos para; dar-se ao luxo de, permitir-se

afforestation [æ.fɔris'teiʃən] florestação *f*, reflorestamento *m*

affront [ə'frʌnt] *v/t* afrontar; *s* afronta *f*

afloat [ə'fləut] *adv* à tona

afoot [ə'fut] *adv* em progresso, em a(c)ção

afore|said [ə'fɔ:sed] sobredito; **~thought** premeditado

afraid [ə'freid] amedrontado, assustado; **be ~ of** ter medo de; recear

afresh [ə'freʃ] de novo, outra vez

African ['æfrikən] *adj*, *s* africano *m*

after ['ɑ:ftə] *adv* depois, em seguida; *conj* depois que; *prp* depois de, após; **~ all** afinal, no fim de contas; **~ noon** tarde *f*; **~wards** [-wədz] depois

again [ə'gen] outra vez, de novo; **~ and ~** repetidamente; muitas vezes; **now and ~** de vez em quando

against [ə'genst] contra

age [eidʒ] *s* idade *f*; era *f*; **of ~** de maioridade; *v/t*, *v/i* envelhecer; **~d** *adj* idoso

agency ['eidʒənsi] (*pl* **-cies**) agência *f*

agent ['eidʒənt] agente *m*

aggravate ['ægrəveit] *v/t* agravar; incomodar

aggression [ə'greʃən] agressão *f*

aggressive [ə'gresiv] agressivo

aghast [ə'gɑ:st] aterrado; embasbacado

agil|e ['ædʒail] ágil; **~ity** [ə'dʒiliti] agilidade *f*

agitat|e ['ædʒiteit] v/t agitar; **~ion** agitação f; **~or** agitador m

ago [ə'gou] adv há, faz; antes; **long ~** há muito tempo

agoniz|e ['ægənaiz] v/t, v/i torturar; agonizar; **~ing** angustioso, atroz

agony ['ægəni] agonia f; angústia f

agrarian [ə'grɛəriən] adj, s agrário m

agree [ə'gri:] v/t, v/i concordar; convir; combinar; entender-se; **~ to** consentir em; **~able** de acordo; aprazível, agradável; **~d** combinado; **~ment** acordo m, ajuste m

agricultur|al [ægri'kʌltʃərəl] agrícola, agrário; **~e** agricultura f

ague ['eigju:] sezão f

ahead [ə'hed] a frente, avante, adiante; **straight ~** sempre em frente

aid [eid] s ajuda f, auxílio m; v/t ajudar, auxiliar

ail [eil] v/t afligir, doer; **~ing** doente; **~ment** mal m, doença f

aim [eim] s obje(c)tivo m; mira f, alvo m; v/t, v/i (at) almejar; apontar (para); visar (a); **~less** sem obje(c)tivo

air [ɛə] s ar m; aspecto m; **in the open ~** ao ar livre; v/t arejar, ventilar; **~-base** base f aérea; **~-brake** freio m pneumático; **~-conditioned** com ar m condicionado; **~craft** avião m; **~craft carrier** porta-aviões

m; **~ force** força f aérea; **~ hostess** hospedeira f de bordo, Braz aeromoça f; **~ing** ventilação f; **~line** linha f aérea; **~liner** avião m de carreira; **~-mail** correio m aéreo; **~-plane US = aeroplane**; **~port** aeroporto m; **~ raid** ataque m aéreo; **~-sick** enjoado; **~tight** hermético

aisle [ail] nave f lateral; coxia f

ajar [ə'dʒɑ:] adj entreaberto

akin [ə'kin] aparentado; análogo

alarm [ə'lɑ:m] s alarme m; rebate m; v/t alarmar; **~-clock** despertador m; **~ing** alarmante

alas! [ə'lɑ:s] ai!

albatross ['ælbətros] albatroz m

alcohol ['ælkəhɔl] álcool m; **~ic** alcoólico

ale [eil] cerveja f inglesa

alert [ə'lə:t] adj, s alerta m

alibi ['ælibai] álibi m

alien ['eiljən] adj estranho; alheio; s estrangeiro m

alienate ['eiljəneit] v/t alienar

alight [ə'lait] v/i apear-se; adj aceso, em fogo

alike [ə'laik] adj parecido, semelhante; adv do mesmo modo

alimony ['æliməni] pensão f alimentícia

alive [ə'laiv] vivo, com vida

all [ɔ:l] adj, pron todo(s), toda(s); tudo; adv inteiramente; **~ at once** de repente; **~ right!** está bem! muito bem!; **~ the**

better tanto melhor; **not at ~** de modo nenhum; não tem de quê

allege [ə'ledƷ] v/t alegar

allegiance [ə'li:dƷəns] fidelidade f

allegory ['æligəri] alegoria f

alleviate [ə'li:vieit] v/t aliviar

alley ['æli] álea f; viela f

All Fools' Day [ɔ:l'fu:lzdei] (1° de Abril) dia m dos enganos, Braz dia m dos bobos

allot [ə'lɔt] v/t destinar; repartir, distribuir; **~ment** lote m, quinhão m

allow [ə'lau] v/t permitir; conceder; admitir; **~ for** levar em conta; **~ance** subsídio m; subvenção f; autorização f; desconto m

alloy ['ælɔi] v/t liga f (de metais)

allude [ə'lu:d] v/i **~ to** aludir

allure [ə'ljuə] v/t, v/i aliar(-se); **~ment** engodo m

ally [ə'lai] v/t, v/i aliar(-se), unir (-se); ['ælai] (pl **-lies**) s aliado m

almanac ['ɔ:lmənæk] almanaque m

almighty [ɔ:l'maiti] adj todo-poderoso

almond ['ɑ:mənd] amêndoa f; amendoeira f

almost [ɔ:l'məust] quase

alms [ɑ:mz] s (sing, pl) esmola f

alone [ə'ləun] adj só, sozinho; adv só, apenas; **leave ~** deixar em paz

along [ə'lɔŋ] prp por; ao longo de; adv para diante; **~side** adv, prp ao lado (de)

aloof [ə'lu:f] adj afastado, à parte

aloud [ə'laud] em voz alta

alphabet ['ælfəbit] alfabeto m; **~ical** [-'betikəl] alfabético

Alps [ælps] s/pl Alpes m/pl

already [ɔ:l'redi] já

alright [ɔ:l'rait] = **all right**

also [ɔ:lsəu] também

altar [ɔ:ltə] altar m

alter [ɔ:ltə] v/t, v/i alterar(-se); **alternate** [ɔ:l'tə:nit] v/t, v/i alternar(-se); **~ive** [-nətiv] s alternativa f; adj alternativo

although [ɔ:l'ðəu] posto que, embora, se bem que

altogether [ɔ:ltə'geðə] adv completamente

always [ɔ:l'wɔz] sempre

am [æm; əm] 1ª sg pres of **be**

a.m. ['ei'em] abbr of **ante meridiem** antes do meio-dia, de manhã

amass [ə'mæs] v/t acumular, juntar

amateur ['æmətə] adj, s amador m

amaze [ə'meiz] v/t espantar, assombrar; **~ement** espanto m; assombro m; **~ing** espantoso, estupendo

ambassador [æm'bæsədə] embaixador m

ambigu|ity [æmbi'gju(:)iti] ambiguidade f; **~ous** [-'bigjuəs] ambíguo

ambit ['æmbit] âmbito m; **~ion** [-'biʃən] ambição f; **~ious** [-'biʃəs] ambicioso

ambulance ['æmbuləns] ambulância f

ambush ['æmbuʃ] s emboscada

f; v/t, v/i emboscar(-se)

amen ['ɑ:'men] *int*, s amém *(m)*, ámen *(m)*

amend [ə'mend] v/t, v/i emendar(-se); ~**ment** emenda f; ~**s** s/pl inde(m)nização f

amenity [ə'mi:niti] *(pl -ties)* amenidade f

American [ə'merikən] *adj*, s americano m

amiable ['eimjəbl] amável, afável

amicable ['æmikəbl] amigável, amistoso

amiss [ə'mis] *adj* impróprio; *adv* mal; **take ~** levar a mal

ammonia [ə'məunjə] amónia f

ammunition [ˌæmju'niʃən] munições s/pl

amnesty ['æmnisti] s a(m)nistia f

amok [ə'mɔk] = **amuck**

among (st) [ə'mʌŋ(st)] entre, no meio de

amorous ['æmərəs] enamorado; amoroso; carinhoso

amount [ə'maunt] s montante m; quantia; ~ **to** v/i importar em, montar a

amphitheatre ['æmfiˌθiətə]; *US* -ter anfiteatro m

ample [æmpl] amplo, extenso; ~**ifier** [-ifaiə] amplificador m; ~**ify** [-ifai] v/t ampliar, amplificar

amputate ['æmpjuteit] v/t amputar

amuck [ə'mʌk]: **run ~** correr em frenesi

amuse [ə'mju:z] v/t divertir; entreter; ~**ment** divertimento m

amusing [ə'mju:ziŋ] divertido

an [æn, ən] *art* um, uma

an(a)emia [ə'ni:mjə] anemia f

an(a)esthesia [ˌænis'θi:zjə] anestesia f

an(a)esthetic [ˌænis'θetik] anestésico m

analogous [ə'næləgəs] análogo; ~**y** [-dʒi] analogia f

analyse ['ænəlaiz] v/t analisar

analysis [ə'næləsis] *(pl -ses)* análise f

anarchist ['ænəkist] anarquista m, f; ~**y** anarquia f

anatomy [ə'nætəmi] anatomia f

ancestor ['ænsistə] antepassado m; ~**ral** [ænˈsestrəl] ancestral; ~**ry** *(pl -ries)* linhagem f

anchor ['æŋkə] s âncora f; v/t, v/i ancorar

ancient ['einʃənt] *adj* antigo

and [ænd, ən(d)] e

anew [ə'nju:] de novo

angel [ˈeindʒəl] anjo m

anger ['æŋgə] s ira f, cólera f

angle ['æŋgl] s ângulo m; v/i pescar à linha

Anglican ['æŋglikən] *adj*, s anglicano m

Anglo-Saxon ['æŋglou'sæksən] *adj*, s anglo-saxão m

angry ['æŋgri] zangado

anguish ['æŋgwiʃ] angústia f

angular ['æŋgjulə] angular

animal ['æniməl] *adj*, s animal m

animate ['ænimeit] v/t animar; ~**ion** [-'meiʃən] animação f

animosity [ˌæni'mɔsiti] *(pl -ties)* animosidade f

ankle ['æŋkl] tornozelo *m*

annex ['æneks] *s* anexo *m*; dependência *f*; [ə'neks] *v/t* anexar

annihilate [ə'naiəleit] *v/t* aniquilar

anniversary [ˌæniˈvəːsəri] (*pl* -ries) aniversário *m*

annotate ['ænəuteit] *v/t* anotar

announce [ə'nauns] *v/t* anunciar; ~**ment** anúncio *m*; aviso *m*; ~**r** locutor *m*

annoy [ə'nɔi] *v/t* aborrecer, incomodar; ~**ance** aborrecimento *m*; ~**ing** aborrecido

annual ['ænjuəl] *adj* anual

annuity [ə'nju(ː)iti] (*pl* -ties) anuidade *f*

annul [ə'nʌl] *v/t* anular

anomal|ous [ə'nɔmələs] anómalo; ~**y** anomalia *f*

anonymous [ə'nɔniməs] anónimo

another [ə'nʌðə] *adj, pron* outro; um outro; mais um

answer ['aːnsə] *v/t, v/i* contestar, responder; *s* resposta *f*

ant [ænt] formiga *f*

antagoni|sm [æn'tægənizəm] antagonismo *m*; ~**st** antagonista *m*

antarctic [ænt'aːktik] *adj* antár(c)tico

antechamber ['ænti,tʃeimbə] antecâmara *f*

antelope ['æntiləup] antílope *m*

anthem ['ænθəm] hino *m*

anti-aircraft ['ænti'ɛəkrɑːft] *adj* antiaéreo

antibiotic ['æntibai'ɔtik] *adj, s* antibiótico *m*

anticipat|e [æn'tisipeit] *v/t* prever; antecipar; ~**ion** [æn,tisi-'peiʃən] expectativa *f*; previsão *f*; antecipação *f*

antidote ['æntidəut] antídoto *m*

antipathy [æn'tipəθi] antipatia *f*

antiquated ['æntikweitid] antiquado

antique [æn'tiːk] *adj* antigo; *s* antigualha *f*

antiquity [æn'tikwiti] antiguidade *f*

antiseptic [ˌænti'septik] *adj, s* anti-séptico *m*

anvil ['ænvil] bigorna *f*

anxiety [æŋ'zaiəti] ansiedade *f*

anxious ['æŋkʃəs] ansioso

any ['eni] *adj, pron* todo, toda; qualquer; algum, alguma, alguns, algumas; *adv* de qualquer modo; **is he ~ better?** ele está melhor?; ~**body** qualquer pessoa; alguém; ~**how** de qualquer modo; ~**one** qualquer um, alguém; ~**thing** qualquer (alguma) coisa; ~**thing but** tudo menos; ~**way** de qualquer maneira; em todo o caso; ~**where** em qualquer parte; em parte alguma

apart [ə'paːt] *adv* à parte

apartment [ə'paːtmənt] aposento *m*; apartamento *m*

apath|etic [ˌæpə'θetik] apático; ~**y** ['æpəθi] apatia *f*

ape [eip] *s* macaco *m*; *v/t* imitar, macaquear

apéritif [ə'peritif] aperitivo *m*

aperture ['æpətjuə] abertura *f*; diafragma *m*

apiary ['eipjəri] (*pl* -ries) colmeal *m*

apiece [ə'pi:s] por peça; por cabeça; cada (um)

apolog|ist [ə'pɔlədʒist] apologista *m*, *f*; **~ize** *v/i* pedir desculpa; **~y** (*pl* -gies) desculpa *f*; satisfação *f*; apologia *f*

apoplexy ['æpəupleksi] apoplexia *f*

apostle [ə'pɔsl] apóstolo *m*

appal(**l**) [ə'pɔ:l] *v/t* espantar, aterrar; **~ling** horroroso, apavorante

apparatus [,æpə'reitəs] aparelho *m*; aparato *m*

apparent [ə'pærənt] evidente; aparente

appeal [ə'pi:l] *s* jur apelação *f*; apelo *m*; petição *f*; atra(c)ção *f*; *v/i* apelar; atrair

appear [ə'piə] *v/i* parecer; aparecer; *jur* comparecer; **~ance** ar *m*, aspecto *m*; aparência *f*; aparição *f*; *jur* comparência *f*

appease [ə'pi:z] apaziguar; *v/t* aplacar

append [ə'pend] *v/t* apensar; **~icitis** [ə,pendi'saitis] apendicite *f*; **~ix** [-iks] apêndice *m*

appertain [,æpə'tein] *v/i*: **~ to** pertencer

appetite ['æpitait] apetite *m*

applaud [ə'plɔ:d] *v/t*, *v/i* aplaudir

applause [ə'plɔ:z] aplauso *m*

apple ['æpl] maçã *f*; **the ~ of one's eye** a menina *f* dos olhos; **~-pie** torta *f* de maçã; **~-tree** macieira *f*

appliance [ə'plaiəns] utensílio *m*, ferramenta *f*, instrumento *m*

applicant ['æplikənt] candidato *m*

application [,æpli'keiʃən] aplicação *f*; candidatura *f*

apply [ə'plai] *v/t*, *v/i* (to) referir-se a; requerer, concorrer; dirigir-se a; aplicar(-se a)

appoint [ə'pɔint] (**to**, **for**) *v/t* designar; nomear; marcar; **~ment** nomeação *f*; encontro *m* marcado

apportion [ə'pɔ:ʃən] *v/t* repartir; partilhar; **~ment** partilha *f*

appraise [ə'preiz] *v/t* avaliar

appreciate [ə'pri:ʃieit] *v/t* estimar, avaliar; prezar

apprehen|d [,æpri'hend] *v/t* prender; apreender; temer; **~sion** apreensão *f*; receio *m*; **~sive** receoso, apreensivo; perspicaz

apprentice [ə'prentis] *s* aprendiz *m*; *v/t* pôr de aprendiz; **~ship** aprendizagem *f*

approach [ə'prəutʃ] *v/t*, *v/i* aproximar(-se); abordar; *s* aproximação *f*; acesso *m*; **~able** acessível

appropriat|e [ə'prəupriit] *adj* apropriado; [ə'prəuprieit] *v/t* apropriar-se de; usurpar; **~ion** [ə,prəupri'eiʃən] apropriação *f*

approv|al [ə'pru:vəl] aprovação *f*; **~e** *v/t*, *v/i* aprovar

approximat|e [ə'prɔksimit] *adj* aproximado; [ə'prɔksimeit] *v/t*, *v/i* aproximar(-se); **~ely** aproximadamente; **~ion** [ə,prɔksi'meiʃən] aproximação *f* apricot ['eiprikət] damasco *m*

April ['eiprəl] Abril *m*

apron ['eiprən] avental *m*

apt [æpt] apto

aptitude [æptitju:d] aptidão *f*

aquarium [ə'kwεəriəm] aquário *m*

aquatic [ə'kwætik] *adj* aquático *m*

aquiline ['ækwilain] aquilino

Arab ['ærəb] *adj, s* árabe *m, f*; ~ian [ə'reibjən] *adj* árabe; ~ic *adj, s* arábico *m*

arbitrary [a:'bitrəri] arbitrário

arbitrat|e ['a:bitreit] *v/t, v/i* arbitrar; ~ion [a:bi'treiʃən] arbitragem *f*

arbo(u)r ['a:bə] caramanchão *m*

arcade [a:'keid] arcada *f*

arch [a:tʃ] *arch, s* arco *m*; abóbada *f*; *v/t* arquear

archaeologist [a:ki'ɔlədʒist] arqueólogo *m*

archaic [a:'keiik] arcaico

arch|bishop [a:tʃ'biʃəp] arcebispo *m*; ~deacon ['-'di:kən] arcediago *m*; ~duke ['-'dju:k] arquiduque *m*

archer ['a:tʃə] arqueiro *m*; ~y tiro *m* de arco

architect ['a:kitekt] arquiteto *m*; ~ure [-tʃə] arquitectura *f*

archives ['a:kaivz] *s/pl* arquivo *m*

arctic ['a:ktik] *adj* ár(c)tico

ard|ent ['a:dənt] ardente, fogoso; ~o(u)r ['a:dɔ] veemência *f*; ardor *m*; ~uous [-djuəs] árduo, difícil

are [a:] *pres pl a.* 2.nd *sg of* be

area ['εəriə] área *f*, zona *f*

arena [ə'ri:nə] arena *f*

Argentine ['a:dʒəntain] *adj, s* argentino *m*

argu|e [ə'gju:] *v/t, v/i* arguir, argumentar; discutir; ~ment argumento *m*; discussão *f*

aria ['a:riə] ária *f*

arid ['ærid] árido

arise [ə'raiz] *v/i* levantar-se, erguer-se, surgir

aristocra|cy [æris'tɔkrəsi] aristocracia *f*; ~t ['æristəkræt] aristocrata *m, f*; ~tic [ærista'krætik] aristocrático

arithmetic [ə'riθmətik] *s* aritmética *f*; ~al [æriθ'metikəl] aritmético

ark [a:k] arca *f*; Noah's ⌂ Arca *f* de Noé

arm [a:m] *s* braço *m*, arma *f*; *v/t, v/i* armar(-se); ~ in ~ de braço dado; child in ~s criança *f* de colo

armament ['a:məmənt] armamento *m*

arm-chair [a:m'tʃεə] poltrona *f*; cadeira *f* de braços

armful ['a:mful] braçada *f*

armistice ['a:mistis] armistício *m*

armo(u)r ['a:mə] armadura *f*; ~y arsenal *m*

arm-pit ['a:mpit] sovaco *m*

arms [a:mz] *s/pl* armas *f/pl*

army ['a:mi] exército *m*

aroma [ə'rəumə] aroma *m*; ~tic [ærəu'mætik] aromático

around [ə'raund] *adv* em volta, em redor; *prp* em volta de, em redor de, ao redor de, à roda de

arouse [ə'rauz] *v/t* despertar;

excitar; provocar

arrange [ə'reindʒ] v/t, v/i planear; chegar a acordo; arranjar; **~ment** arranjo m; disposição f; combinação f; pl preparativos m/pl

arrears [ə'riəz] s/pl débitos m/pl; **in ~** atrasado

arrest [ə'rest] s prisão f, captura f, detenção; v/t deter, capturar, prender

arriv|al [ə'raivəl] chegada f; **~e** v/i chegar

arrogan|ce ['ærəgəns] arrogância f; **~t** arrogante

arrow ['ærəu] flecha f, seta f

arson ['ɑ:sn] jur fogo m posto

art [ɑːt] s arte f; jeito m; destreza f

artery ['ɑːtəri] artéria f

artful ['ɑːtful] manhoso, ardiloso

artichoke ['ɑːtitʃəuk] alcachofra f

article ['ɑːtikl] s artigo m

articulate [ɑː'tikjuleit] v/t, v/i articular(-se); [-lit] adj articulado

artifice ['ɑːtifis] artifício m; **~r** [ɑː'tifisə] artífice m

artificial [ɑːti'fiʃəl] artificial

artillery [ɑː'tiləri] artilharia f

artist ['ɑːtist] artista m, f; **~e** [ɑː'tiːst] artista m, f; **~ic** [ɑː'tistik] artístico

artless ['ɑːtlis] natural; simples

as [æz, əz] adv como; **~ ... ~** ... tão ... como; conj como; porque; enquanto; quando; **~ if** como se; prp como; **~ soon ~** assim que, logo que; **~ such** como tal; em si; **~ well** também; **~ well ~** tanto como, assim como

asbestos [æz'bestəs] amianto m

ascend [ə'send] v/t, v/i ascender, subir

ascension [ə'senʃən] ascensão f

ascent [ə'sent] subida f, ascensão f

ascertain [æsə'tein] v/t averiguar, verificar

ascetic [ə'setik] adj ascético

ascribe [ə'skraib] v/t **~ to** atribuir, imputar

ash [æʃ] cinza f

ashamed [ə'ʃeimd] envergonhado; **be ~ of** ter vergonha de

ashen ['æʃn] acinzentado

ashore [ə'ʃɔː] adv em terra; **go ~** desembarcar

ash-tray ['æʃtrei] cinzeiro m

Asia ['eiʃə] Ásia f; **~n** adj, s asiático m

aside [ə'said] adv de lado; à parte; **~s** parte m

ask [ɑːsk] v/t, v/i interrogar, perguntar; pedir; convidar; **~ after** perguntar por; **~ for** pedir

ask|ance [əs'kæns] de soslaio; **~ew** [-'kjuː] adv de través

aslant [ə'slɑːnt] adv obliquamente

asleep [ə'sliːp] adormecido; **fall ~** adormecer

asparagus [əs'pærəgəs] espargo m

aspect ['æspekt] aspecto m

asphalt ['æsfælt] s asfalto m

aspire [əs'paiə] *v/i* aspirar

ass [æs] asno *m*, jumento *m*

assail [ə'seil] *v/t* assaltar; **~ant** assaltante *m*

assassinate [ə'sæsineit] *v/t* assassinar

assault [ə'sɔːlt] *v/t* assaltar; *s* assalto *m*

assembl|e [ə'sembl] *v/t*, *v/i* ajuntar; *mec* montar; reunir (-se); **~y** (*pl* **-lies**) assembleia *f*, reunião *f*; *mec* montagem *f*

assent [ə'sent] *s* consentimento *m*, assentimento *m*; *v/i* consentir, assentir

assert [ə'səːt] *v/t* asseverar; **~oneself** impor-se, **~ion** asseveração *f*

assess [ə'ses] *v/t* avaliar; fixar; taxar; **~ment** avaliação *f*; cota *f*

assets [ˈæsets] *s/pl com* a(c)tivo *m*; **~s and liabilities** a(c)tivo *m* e passivo *m*

assidu|ity [ˌæsi'djuː(ː)iti] assiduidade *f*; **~ous** [ə'sidjuəs] assíduo

assign [ə'sain] *v/t* atribuir; designar; **~ment** atribuição *f*; cessão *f*

assimilate [ə'simileit] *v/t*, *v/i* assimilar(-se)

assist [ə'sist] *v/t*, *v/i* assistir, ajudar; **~ance** ajuda *f*; **~ant** auxiliar *m*, ajudante *m*, *f*

assizes [ə'saiziz] *s/pl GB* sessão *f* periódica de tribunal

associat|e [ə'səuʃieit] *v/t*, *v/i* associar(-se); [... ʃiit] *s* associado *m*; **~ion** associação *f*,

sociedade *f*; **~ion football** futebol *m*

assort|ed [ə'sɔːtid] sortido; **~ment** sortimento *m*

assum|e [ə'sjuːm] *v/t* assumir; presumir; **~ed** suposto; **~ption** [ə'sʌmpʃən] assunção *f*; suposição *f*

assurance [ə'ʃuərəns] segurança *f*; seguro *m*

assure [ə'ʃuə] *v/t* assegurar; **~d** [-d] *adj* seguro, certo; *s* segurado *m*

astir [ə'stəː] *adj* agitado, em movimento

astonish [əs'tɔniʃ] *v/t* espantar, pasmar; **~ing** surpreendente, espantoso; **~ment** espanto *m*, assombro *m*

astound [əs'taund] *v/t* pasmar, aturdir

astray [əs'trei] *adj*, *adv* extraviado; **go ~** extraviar-se

astride [əs'traid] *adj*, *adv* escarranchado

astringent [əs'trindʒənt] *med adj*, *s* adstringente *m*

astro|loger [əs'trɔlədʒə] astrólogo *m*; **~logy** astrologia *f*; **~naut** [ˈæstrənɔːt] astronauta *m*, *f*; **~nomer** [æs'trɔnəmə] astrónomo *m*; **~nomy** astronomia *f*

astute [əs'tjuːt] astuto, astucioso *m*

asunder [ə'sʌndə] à parte; em pedaços

asylum [ə'sailəm] asilo *m*

at [æt, ət] de; por; em; a; **~ all** absolutamente; **~ hand** à mão; **~ home** em casa; **~ last**

enfim, por fim; **~ least** pelo menos

atheist ['eiθiist] ateu *m*

athlet|e ['æθli:t] atleta *m, f*; **~ic** [-'letik] atlético; **~ics** [-'letiks] atletismo *m*

atlas ['ætləs] atlas *m*

atmosphere ['ætməsfiə] atmosfera *f*

atom ['ætəm] átomo *m*; **~ic** [ə'təmik] atómico; **~izer** ['ætəmaizə] atomizador *f*

atone [ə'təun] *v/i* (for) expiar

atroc|ious [ə'trəuʃəs] atroz; **~ity** [ə'trəsiti] (*pl* -ies) atrocidade *f*

atrophy ['ætrəfi] *med* s atrofia *f*; *v/t, v/i* atrofiar

attach [ə'tætʃ] *v/t, v/i* ligar; unir; **~ment** afe(c)to *m*, apego *m*

attack [ə'tæk] *v/t* atacar; *s* ataque *m*; **~er** atacante *m*

attain [ə'tein] *v/t, v/i* conseguir; atingir; **~ment** obtenção *f*

attempt [ə'tempt] *s* esforço *m*, tentativa *f*; *v/t* tentar, intentar

attend [ə'tend] *v/t, v/i* assistir, frequentar; prestar atenção, atender; cuidar; **~ance** assistência *f*; **~ant** *s* contínuo *m*, servidor *m*; *adj* subordinado; assistente

attention [ə'tenʃən] atenção *f*

attentive [ə'tentiv] atento

attest [ə'test] *v/t, v/i* atestar, certificar

attic ['ætik] *s* sótão *m*

attitude ['ætitju:d] atitude *f*; postura *f*

attorney [ə'tə:ni] procurador *m*; *US* advogado *m*

attract [ə'trækt] *v/t* atrair; **~ion** atra(c)ção *f*; **~ive** atraente, atra(c)tivo

attribute [ə'tribju:t] *v/t* atribuir; ['ætribju:t] *s* característica *f*; atributo *m*

auburn ['ɔ:bən] *adj* ruivo

auction ['ɔ:kʃən] *s* leilão *m*; *v/t* leiloar; **~eer** [-'niə] leiloeiro *m*

audaci|ous [ɔ:'deiʃəs] audaz; **~ty** [ɔ:'dæsiti] audácia *f*

audible ['ɔ:dəbl] audível

audience ['ɔ:djəns] assistência *f*; auditório *m*; audiência *f*

audit ['ɔ:dit] *com* s exame *m* oficial de contas; **~or** revisor *m* de contas

auditorium [,ɔ:di'tɔ:riəm] auditório *m*

augment [ɔ:g'ment] *v/t, v/i* aumentar

August ['ɔ:gəst] *s* Agosto *m*; ♀ *adj* augusto

aunt [ɑ:nt] tia *f*

auspic|es [ɔ:'spisiz] *s/pl* auspícios *m/pl*; **~ious** [ɔ:s'piʃəs] auspicioso, favorável

austere [ɔs'tiə] austero; **~ity** [-'teriti] austeridade *f*

Australian [ɔs'treiljən] *adj, s* australiano *m*

Austrian ['ɔstriən] *adj, s* austríaco *m*

authentic [ɔ:'θentik] autêntico

author [ɔ:'θə] autor *m*; **~itarian** [ɔ:θəri'teəriən] *adj* autoritário; **~itative** [ɔ:'θɔritətiv] autorizado; autoritário; **~ity** [ɔ:'θɔriti] (*pl* -ties) autoridade *f*; **~ize** [ɔ:θəraiz] *v/t* autorizar; **~ship** autoria *f*

autobiography [ɔ:təubaiˈɔ-grəfi] (*pl* **-phies**) autobiografia *f*

autocracy [ɔ:ˈtɔkrəsi] (*pl* **-cies**) autocracia *f*

automatic [ɔ:təˈmætik] *adj* automático

automation [ɔ:təˈmeiʃən] automatização *f*

automobile [ˈɔ:təməbi:l] *US* automóvel *m*

autonom|ous [ɔ:ˈtɔnəməs] autónomo; **~y** autonomia *f*

autumn [ˈɔ:təm] outono *m*; **~al** [ɔ:ˈtʌmnəl] outonal

auxiliary [ɔ:gˈziljəri] *adj* auxiliar

avail [əˈveil] *s* proveito; *v/t*, *v/i* prestar; **~ oneself of** valer-se de; **of no ~** inútil

available [əˈveiləbl] disponível; válido

avalanche [ˈævəla:nʃ] avalancha *f*

avaricious [ævəˈriʃəs] avarento, avaro

avenge [əˈvendʒ] *v/t* vingar; **~ oneself on** vingar-se de; **~r** vingador *m*

avenue [ˈævinju:] avenida *f*

average [ˈævəridʒ] *s* média *f*; *adj* mediano; médio; **on an (the) ~** em média

avers|e [əˈvə:s] oposto, relutante; **~ion** aversão *f*

avert [əˈvə:t] *v/t* desviar; impedir

aviary [ˈeivjəri] (*pl* **-ries**) aviário *m*

aviation [ˌeiviˈeiʃən] aviação *f*

aviator [ˈeivieitə] aviador *m*

avoid [əˈvɔid] *v/t* evitar

avow [əˈvau] *v/t* declarar, confessar; **~al** declaração *f*, confissão *f*

await [əˈweit] *v/t* esperar, aguardar

awake [əˈweik] *v/t*, *v/i* acordar, despertar; *adj* desperto, acordado

award [əˈwɔ:d] *v/t* adjudicar; premiar; *s* prémio *m*

aware [əˈwɛə] sabedor, ciente; **be ~ of** ter conhecimento de, saber

away [əˈwei] *adj* ausente; *adv* embora, (para) longe; **run ~** *v/i* fugir

awe [ɔ:] *s* pavor; respeito *m*; **~struck** aterrado

awful [ˈɔ:ful] terrível; horrível; péssimo; **~ly** extremamente, muito

awhile [əˈwail] por um momento, algum tempo

awkward [ˈɔ:kwəd] embaraçoso, incómodo; desajeitado, desastrado

awl [ɔ:l] sovela *f*

awning [ˈɔ:niŋ] toldo *m*

awry [əˈrai] *adj*, *adv* de través, torto

ax(e) [æks] machado *m*

axis [ˈæksis] (*pl* **axes**) eixo *m*

axle [ˈæksl] eixo *m* (de roda)

ay(e) [ai] *adv* sim; *s* voto *m* a favor

azure [ˈæʒə] *adj*, *s* azul-celeste *m*

B

babble ['bæbl] *v/t, v/i* palrar; tagarelar; balbuciar; *s* parolagem *f*

baby ['beibi] *s* (*pl* **-bies**) bebé *m, f*; **~hood** primeira infância *f*; **~ish** infantil

bachelor ['bætʃələ] solteiro *m*, solteirão *m*; bacharel *m*

back [bæk] *s* costas *f/pl*; dorso *m*; *adv* atrás, para trás; *v/t, v/i* (fazer) recuar; fazer marcha atrás; apoiar; apostar (em); *adj* traseiro; remoto; passado; **~bone** espinha *f* dorsal; **~gammon** gamão *m*, **~ground** fundo *m*, segundo plano *m*; **~stairs** escada *f* de serviço; **~stroke** braçada *f* de costas; **~ward(s)** *adj* atrasado; retrógrado; acanhado; *adv* para trás; de regresso

bacon ['beikən] toucinho *m*

bacterium [bæk'tiəriəm] (*pl* **-ria**) bactéria *f*

bad [bæd] *adj* mau, ruim; nocivo; **from ~ to worse** de mal a pior

badge [bædʒ] *s* emblema *m*, insígnia *f*

badger ['bædʒə] *s* texugo *m*; *v/t* atormentar, ralar

badminton ['bædmintən] badminton *m*, jogo *m* do volante / *Braz* da peteca

badness ['bædnis] maldade *f*

bad-tempered ['bæd'tempəd] mal-humorado

baffle ['bæfl] *v/t* confundir

bag [bæg] *s* saco *m*, bolsa *f*; maleta *f*; *v/t* ensacar

baggage ['bægidʒ] *us* bagagem *f*

bagpipe ['bægpəip] gaita *f* de foles

bail [beil] *s* caução *f* fiança *f*

bailiff ['beilif] bailio *m*, meirinho *m*

bait [beit] *s* isca *f*, engodo *m*; *v/t* iscar, engodar

bake [beik] *v/t, v/i* assar, cozer no forno; **~r** padeiro *m*; **~ry** ['-əri] (*pl* **-ries**) padaria *f*

balance ['bæləns] *s* balança *f*; equilíbrio *m*; *com* balanço *m*; *v/t* pesar; *com* saldar; equilibrar

balcony ['bælkəni] (*pl* **-nies**) varanda *f*; *thea* balcão *m*

bald [bɔːld] calvo; **~ness** calvície *f*; careca *f*

bale [beil] *s* fardo *m*; *v/t* enfardar, empacotar

balk [bɔːk] *s* obstáculo *m*; viga *f*; *v/t, v/i* impedir, frustrar

ball [bɔːl] bola *f*, bala *f*; baile *m*; novelo *m*

ballad ['bæləd] balada *f*

ballast ['bæləst] lastro *m*

balloon [bə'luːn] balão *m*

ballot ['bælət] *s* votação *f* secreta; (boletim *m* de) voto *m*; **~ box** urna *f* eleitoral; **~ paper** boletim *m* de voto, *Braz* cédula *f*

ball-point (pen) [bɔːl ('pɔint) pen] esferográfica *f*

balm [baːm] bálsamo *m*

Baltic ['bɔːltik] *adj, s* Báltico *m*

balustrade [ˌbæləs'treid] balaustrada *f*

ban [bæn] *v/t* proibir, proscrever; *s* interdito *m*

banana [bə'nɑːnə] banana *f*

band [bænd] *s* faixa *f*; bando *m*; *mus* banda *f*

bandage ['bændidʒ] *s* ligadura *f*

bandit ['bændit] bandido *m*

bang [bæŋ] *v/t* bater; *s* pancada *f*, golpe *m*; estoiro *m*, estrondo *m*

banish ['bæniʃ] *v/t* desterrar; banir; ~ment desterro *m*

bank [bæŋk] *s* margem *f*; baixio *m*; *com* banco *m*; ~er banqueiro *m*; ~ing *s* negócio *m* bancário; ~note nota *f* de banco; ~rate taxa *f* de desconto; ~rupt *adj, s* falido (*m*)

bankruptcy ['bæŋkrʌptsi] (*pl* -cies) falência *f*; bancarrota *f*

banns [bænz] *s/pl* banhos *m/pl*, proclama *f*

banquet ['bæŋkwit] *s* banquete *m*

banter ['bæntə] *s* gracejo *m*

bapti|sm ['bæptizəm] ba(p)tismo *m*; ~st ba(p)tista *m*; ~ze [bæp'taiz] *v/t* ba(p)tizar

bar [bɑː] *s* barra *f*; faixa *f*; bar *m*; teia *f*, barreira *f*; *v/t* trancar; impedir; excluir

barbarian [bɑː'bɛəriən] *adj, s* bárbaro *m*

barbed [bɑːbd] *adj* mordaz; ~wire arame *m* farpado

barber ['bɑːbə] barbeiro *m*

bare [bɛə] *adj* despido, nu; descoberto; mero, simples; ~faced descarado; ~foot(ed) descalço; ~headed de cabeça descoberta; ~ly mal, apenas

bargain ['bɑːgin] *s* ajuste *m*, contrato *m*; pechincha *f*; *v/t, v/i* regatear

barge [bɑːdʒ] *s* barcaça *f*

baritone ['bæritoun] barítono *m*

bark [bɑːk] *s* casca *f*, cortiça *f*; latido *m*; *v/i* latir, ladrar

barkeeper ['bɑːkiːpə] botequineiro *m*

barley ['bɑːli] cevada *f*

bar|maid ['bɑːmeid] empregada *f* de bar, *Braz* garçonete *f*; ~man (*pl* -men) empregado *m* de bar

barn [bɑːn] celeiro *m*

barracks ['bærəks] *s/pl* quartel *m*, caserna *f*

barrel ['bærəl] *s* barril *m*; barrica *f*; cano *m* de espingarda

barren ['bærən] *adj* árido; estéril

barrier ['bæriə] barreira *f*

barrister ['bæristə] advogado *m*

barrow ['bærəu] carrinho *m* de mão; túmulo *m*

barter ['bɑːtə] *s* troca *f*; *v/t, v/i* permutar, trocar

base [beis] *s* base *f*; fundamento *m*; *adj* baixo, vil, *v/t* basear, fundar; ~less sem base, infundado

basement ['beismənt] cave *f*

bashful ['bæʃful] acanhado

basin ['beisn] bacia *f*

basket ['bɑːskit] cesta *f*, cesto *m*; ~ball basquetebol *m*, básquete *m*

bass [beis] *s, mus* baixo *m*

bastard ['bæstəd] *adj, s* ilegitimo *m*, bastardo *m*

baste [beist] *v/t* alinhavar

bat [bæt] *s, zo* morcego *m*

bath [bɑːθ] *s* banho *m*; banheira *f*; *v/t* dar banho a; tomar banho; **~e** [beið] *v/t, v/i* banhar(-se); **~room** casa *f* de banho; *Braz* banheiro *m*; **~tub** banheira *f*

baton ['bætən] *mus* batuta *f*

battalion [bə'tæljən] batalhão *m*

batter ['bætə] *v/t, v/i* bater; (des)gastar, demolir; *s* pasta *f* culinária

battery ['bætəri] (*pl* -**ries**) bateria *f*

battle ['bætl] *s* batalha *f*; *v/i* batalhar, combater

Bavarian [bə'veəriən] *adj, s* bávaro *m*

bawl [bɔːl] *v/t, v/i* bradar

bay [bei] *s* baia *f*; vão *m* de janela; *bot* louro *m*; *adj* baio; *v/i* ladrar

bayonet ['beiənit] *s* baioneta *f*

bay window [bei 'windəu] janela *f* de sacada

be [biː, bi] *v/i, v/aux* ser; estar; ficar; existir; haver; **~ in** estar em casa; **~ out** não estar em casa; **~ to** haver de, dever

beach [biːtʃ] praia *f*

beacon ['biːkən] baliza *f*, farol *m*

bead [biːd] conta *f*; gota *f*; **~s** rosário *m*

beak [biːk] bico *m*

beam [biːm] viga *f*, trave *f*; raio *m*; *v/t, v/i* irradiar, emitir

bean [biːn] feijão *m*; grão *m*

bear [beə] *v/t* aguentar, suportar; dar à luz, gerar; *zo* urso *m*; *com* baixista *m, f*; **~ out** confirmar

beard [biəd] barba *f*

bear|er ['beərə] portador *m*; **~ing** porte *m*; **~ings** orientação *f*, rumo *m*

beast [biːst] animal *m*, besta *f*; **~ly** brutal, bestial

beat [biːt] *v/t* bater; derrotar; *s mus* compasso *f*; ronda *f* (*polícia*); toque *m* (*tambor*); pulsação *f*

beauti|ful ['bjuːtəful] belo, formoso; **~fy** [-tifai] *v/t* embelezar

beauty ['bjuːti] beleza *f*; **~par-lo(u)r/saloon** salão *m* de beleza

beaver ['biːvə] castor *m*

because [bi'kɔz] *conj* porque; **~ of** *prp* por causa de

beckon ['bekən] *v/t, v/i* acenar

become [bi'kʌm] *v/i* fazer-se, tornar-se; *v/t* convir, assentar bem; ser próprio a; **~ing** conveniente; apropriado

bed [bed] *s* cama *f*, leito *m*; canteiro *m*; **go to ~** (ir) deitar-se; **~ding** roupa *f* de cama; **~room** quarto *m* (de dormir), *Braz* dormitório *m*; **~spread** colcha *f*; **~time** hora *f* de (ir) dormir

bee [biː] abelha *f*

beech [biːtʃ] faia *f*

beef [biːf] *s* carne *f* de vaca; **~steak** bife *m*, *Braz* bifesteque *m*

bee|hive ['biːhaiv] colmeia *f*,

cortiço m; ~line linha f re(c)-
ta

beer [biə] cerveja, f

beet [bi:t] beterraba f

beetle [bi:tl] escaravelho m

beetroot ['bi:tru:t] raiz f de beterraba

befall [bi'fɔ:l] v/t, v/i acontecer,
suceder

befit [bi'fit] v/t convir

before [bi'fɔ:] prp antes de; diante
de; adv antes; conj antes que;
~hand de antemão, antecipada-
mente

beg [beg] v/t, v/i pedir, suplicar;
mendigar

beggar ['begə] mendigo m

begin [bi'gin] v/t, v/i começar;
principiar; ~ner principiante
m, f; ~ning começo m; princípio m

beguile [bi'gail] v/t enganar; seduzir; divertir

behalf [bi'hɑ:f] on ~ of em
nome de, por, da parte de

behave [bi'heiv] v/i compor-
tar-se, conduzir-se; ~io(u)r
conduta f, comportamento m

behead [bi'hed] v/t degolar, decapitar

behind [bi'haind] prp atrás de,
detrás de; adv atrás, detrás; s
traseiro m, Braz bunda f

being [bi:iŋ] s ser m, ente m;
existência f; for the time ~
por agora

belated [bi'leitid] atrasado, tardio

belch [belt∫] v/t, v/i arrotar; vomitar

belfry ['belfri] campanário m

Belgi|an ['beldʒən] adj, s belga
m, f; ~um Bélgica f

belie [bi'lai] v/t desmentir

belie|f [bi'li:f] crença f; con-
vicção f; ~vable crível, verosímil; ~ve v/t, v/i acreditar,
crer; ~ver crente m, f

belittle [bi'litl] v/t minimizar,
depreciar

bell [bel] sino m; campainha f;
~boy mandarete m, paquete m

belligerent [bi'lidʒərənt] adj, s
beligerante m, f

bellow [beleu] v/i mugir; berrar; ~s s/pl fole m

belly ['beli] (pl-lies) ventre m,
barriga f

belong [bi'lɔŋ] v/i pertencer;
~ings s/pl pertences m/pl

beloved [bi'lʌvd] adj, s querido
m, amado m

below [bi'ləu] prp debaixo de; inferior; adv abaixo, por baixo

belt [belt] cinto m; faixa f; mec
correia f

bench [bent∫] banco m; tribunal
m

bend [bend] s curva f; volta f;
v/t, v/i curvar(-se), dobrar; in-
clinar(-se); on ~ed knees de
joelhos

beneath [bi'ni:θ] prp debaixo
de, sob; adv abaixo

benediction [,beni'dik∫ən] bênção f

benefactor ['benifæktə] benfeitor m

beneficial [bi'fi∫əl] benéfico,
proveitoso, útil

benefit ['benifit] s benefício m;
vantagem f

benevolent [bi'nevələnt] benévolo

benign [bi'nain] benigno

bent [bent] s propensão f, tendência f

benzene ['benzi:n] benzeno m;
~**ine** benzina f

bequeath ['bikwi:ð] v/t legar;
~**est** [-'kwest] legado m

bereave [bi'ri:v] v/t despojar,
privar; ~**ment** luto m; privação f

beret ['berei] boina f

berry ['beri] (pl -ries) bago m;
baga f

berth [bə:θ] s beliche m; mar an-
coradouro m; v/t atracar

beset [bi'set] v/t assediar, assaltar

beside [bi'said] prp ao lado de;
~**s** prp fig além de; adv além
disso

besiege [bi'si:dʒ] v/t sitiar, cercar

best [best] adj, adv o melhor; at
~ quando muito; do one's ~
fazer o melhor possível; make
the ~ of tirar o melhor partido
de; ~ man padrinho m de casamento de; ~ seller êxito m
de livraria

bestow [bi'stəu] v/t conferir,
outorgar

bet [bet] s aposta f; v/t, v/i
apostar

betray [bi'trei] v/t trair, atraiçoar; ~**al** traição f; ~**er** traidor m

betrothed [bi'trəuðd] s prometido m, noivo m

better ['betə] adj, adv melhor;

v/t melhorar; we (etc.) had ~
era melhor; **so much the** ~
tanto melhor; **get the** ~ **of** levar a melhor de

between [bi'twi:n] prp, adv entre

bevel ['bevəl] s bisel m

beverage ['bevəridʒ] bebida f

beware [bi'weə] v/t, v/i acautelar-se; ~ **of** ...! cuidado
com ...!

bewilder [bi'wildə] v/t confundir, desnortear; ~**ment** des-
norteamento m

bewitch [bi'witʃ] v/t enfeitiçar,
enguiçar

beyond [bi'jɔnd] adv além; prp
além de

bias ['baiəs] s viés m; tendência
f; preconceito m; v/t predispor

bib [bib] babador m, babete m

Bible ['baibl] Bíblia f

bibliography [,bibli'ɔgrəfi] bi-
bliografia f

bicarbonate [bai'ka:bənit] bi-
carbonato m

bicycle ['baisikl] bicicleta f

bid [bid] v/t, v/i licitar, lançar;
oferecer; mandar; s lanço m

bier [biə] ataúde m; essa f

big [big] grande; importante; to
talk ~ vangloriar-se, falar do
papo; ~ **game** caça f grossa

bigamy ['bigəmi] bigamia f

bigwig ['bigwig] magnate m, f,
Bxz mandachuva m

bike [baik] s abbr of **bicycle**

bile [bail] bílis f, fel m

bill [bil] s conta f; cartaz m; pro-
je(c)to m de lei; ~ **of exchange** letra f de câmbio; ~ **of fare**
ementa f, lista f, Braz cardápio

blemish

m; ~ **of lading** *mar* conhecimento *m* de carga
billet ['bilit] *s* mil boleto *m*; *v/t* aboletar
billiard|-cue ['biljədkju:] taco *m*, ~**s** [*z*] bilhar *m*
billion ['biljən] bilhão *m*, bilião *m*
billow ['biləu] *v/i* ondular; *s* escarcéu *m*
bind [baind] *v/t*, *v/i* atar; ligar; encadernar; obrigar(-se); ~**ing** *s* encadernação *f*; *adj* obrigatório
biography [bai'ɔgrəfi] biografia *f*
biology [bai'ɔlədʒi] biologia *f*
birch [bə:tʃ] vidoeiro *m*, bétula *f*
bird [bə:d] pássaro *m*, ave *f*. ~ **of passage** ave *f* de arribação; ~ **of prey** ave *f* de rapina; ~**'s-eye view** vista *f* geral
birth [bə:θ] nascimento *m*; **give** ~ **to** dar à luz; ~ **control** controle *m* de natalidade; ~**day** aniversário *m*, dia *m* de anos; ~**place** terra *f* natal; ~**rate** natalidade *f*
biscuit ['biskit] bolacha *f*
bishop ['biʃəp] bispo *m*
bison ['baisn] bisão, bisonte *m*
bit [bit] *s* bocado *m*; ~ **by** ~ bouco a pouco, aos poucos
bitch [bitʃ] *s* cadela *f*
bite [bait] *v/t*, *v/i* morder; *s* mordedura *f*, dentada *f*
bitter ['bitə] *adj* penetrante; amargo; ~**ness** amargura *f*, amargor *m*
bitters ['bitəz] licor *m* amargo
black [blæk] *adj*, *s* preto *m*,

negro *m*; ~**berry** amora *f* silvestre; ~**bird** melro *m*; ~**board** lousa *f*, quadro *m* negro; ~**en** *v/t*, *v/i* escurecer(-se); ~ **eye** olho *m* pisado; ~**mail** *s* chantagem *f*; ~ **market** mercado *m* negro; ~**out** obscurecimento *m*, extinção *f* de luzes; ~**smith** ferreiro *m*
bladder ['blædə] bexiga *f*
blade [bleid] lâmina *f*; folha *f* lanceolada; pá *f*
blame [bleim] *s* culpa *f*, censura *f*; *v/t* culpar, censurar; ~**less** sem culpa
bland [blænd] brando, suave
blank [blæŋk] *adj* em branco; vago; vazio; ~ **verse** verso *m* branco
blanket ['blæŋkit] *s* cobertor *m*; manta *f*
blasphemy ['blæsfimi] blasfémia *f*
blast [blɑ:st] *s* rajada *f* de vento; sopro *m*; carga *f* de explosivos; explosão *f*; *v/t* (fazer) explodir; ~ **furnace** alto-forno *m*; ~ **it!** maldito seja!; ~**off** *s* lançamento *m* (de foguetão)
blaze [bleiz] *s* chama *f*, labareda *f*; *v/t*, *v/i* chamejar; resplandecer
bleach [bli:tʃ] *v/t*, *v/i* branquear, corar, *Braz* coarar
bleak [bli:k] gelado; desabrigado; sombrio
bleat [bli:t] *v/i*, *v/t* balir; lamuriar; *s* balido *m*; lamúria *f*
bleed [bli:d] *v/t*, *v/i* sangrar, perder sangue
blemish ['blemiʃ] *v/t* danificar;

manchar; s mancha f, defeito m

blend [blend] v/t, v/i lotar; misturar(-se), combinar(-se); s mistura f

bless [bles] v/t abençoar; consagrar; ~ **me!** valha-me Deus!; ~**ed** bendito, abençoado; ~**ing** bênção f; graça f divina

blind [blaind] s toldo m, estore m; fig pretexto m; adj cego; v/t cegar; ~ **alley** beco m sem saída; ~**ness** cegueira f

blink [blink] v/t, v/i piscar, pestanejar; s piscadela f

bliss [blis] bem-aventurança f

blister ['blistə] s bolha f, empola f

blizzard [blizəd] nevasca f

bloat|ed [bləutid] inchado, cheio de si; ~**er** arenque m defumado

block [blɔk] s cepo m; bloco m; quarteirão m; v/t obstruir; bloquear; ~**ade** s bloqueio m; ~**head** cepo m; ~**letters** letra f de imprensa

blond(e) [blɔnd] adj, s loiro (-a f)

blood [blʌd] s sangue m; **in cold** ~ a sangue frio; ~**shed** matança f; ~**shot** inje(c)tado de sangue; ~**thirsty** sanguinário; ~**vessel** vaso m sanguíneo; ~**y** ensanguentado, sangrento; maldito

bloom [blu:m] s flor f; florescimento m; v/i florescer, florir

blossom ['blɔsəm] s flor f; v/i florescer, enflorar

blot [blɔt] s borrão m; ~ **out**

encobrir; exterminar; (es-)borratar; ~**ting-paper** mata-borrão m

blouse [blauz] blusa f

blow [bləu] s sopro m; golpe m; revés m; v/t, v/i soprar; ~ **one's nose** assoar-se; ~ **up** v/t, v/i explodir; ampliar; inflar; ~**pipe** maçarico m

blue [blu:] adj, s azul m; melancólico; ~**bell** bot campainha f; ~**bottle** varejeira f; ~ **print** calco m heliográfico; proje(c)to m

bluff [blʌf] s logro m, engano m, Braz blefe m; adj franco, abrupto; v/t, v/i lograr, enganar, Braz blefar

blunder ['blʌndə] s erro m crasso, deslize m; Braz gafe f; v/t, v/i cometer um lapso; tropeçar

blunt [blʌnt] adj embotado; v/t embotar

blur [blə:] s mancha f; v/t, v/i ofuscar, embaciar

blush [blʌʃ] s rubor m; v/i corar, ruborizar-se

bluster ['blʌstə] v/t, v/i esbravejar

boar [bɔ:] varrão m, cerdo m

board [bɔ:d] s tábua f, prancha f; junta f; v/t, v/i embarcar; assoalhar; hospedar; **on** ~ a bordo; ~ **and lodging** cama f e mesa f; ♀ **of Trade** Ministério m (Braz Câmara) do Comércio; ~**er** hóspede m; aluno m interno; ~**ing-card** cartão m de embarque; ~**ing-house** pensão f; ~**school** internato m

boast [bəust] v/t, v/i jactar-se;

bossy

gabar(-se); s gabarolice f, jactância f

boat [bəut] s barco m, bote m; **go ~ing** andar de barco, barque(j)ar; **~man** barqueiro m; **~-race** regata f

bob [bob] s fam xelim m; v/i bambolear-se

bobby ['bobi] fam polícia m

bodice ['bodis] corpete m

body ['bodi] (pl **-dies**) corpo m; substância f; grupo m; junta f; **~-guard** guarda-costas m

bog [bog] brejo m, paul m

boil [boil] v/t, v/i ferver; cozer; s furúnculo m; **~ over** deitar por fora; ferver em pouca água; **~ed egg** ovo m cozido; **~er** caldeira f

boisterous ['boistərəs] barulhento, turbulento

bold [bəuld] afoito

Bolshevik ['bolʃivik] adj, s bolchevique m, f

bolster ['bəulstə] s travesseiro m

bolt [bəult] s ferrolho m; parafuso m; raio m; v/t, v/i abalar, escapulir-se; aferrolhar; **~upright** direito como um fuso

bomb [bom] s bomba f; v/t bombardear; **~ard** [-'bɑːd] v/t bombardear

bombastic [bom'bæstik] bombástico

bomber ['bomə] avi bombardeiro m

bond [bond] s laço m, vínculo m; jur obrigação f; com caução f; v/t caucionar; **~age** escravidão f, servidão f; **~ed ware-**

house entreposto m alfandegário

bone [bəun] s osso m; espinha f

bonfire ['bon.faiə] fogueira f

bonnet ['bonit] touca f; boné m

bonus ['bəunəs] bónus m

bony ['bəuni] ossudo

book [buk] s livro m; mus libreto m; v/t reservar, marcar; regist(r)ar; **~binder** encadernador m; **~case** estante f; **~ing clerk** bilheteiro m; **~ing office** bilheteira f, Braz bilheteria f; **~keeper** guarda-livros m; **~keeping** contabilidade f; **~let** folheto m; **~seller** livreiro m; **~shop**, **~store** livraria f

boom [buːm] s prosperidade f

boor [buə] alarve m

boost [buːst] s incremento m; v/t levantar; fomentar

boot [buːt] s bota f; auto portabagagens m, Braz porta-mala m; **to ~** além disso; **~black** engraxador m, Braz engraxate m; **~ee** botina f; botinha f

booth [buːð] tenda f, barraca f

border ['bɔːdə] s borda f; fronteira f; v/t, v/i debruar; confinar

bor|e [bɔː] v/t, v/i perfurar; maçar, aborrecer; s maçador m; maçada f; **~edom** aborrecimento m; **~ing** maçador

borough ['bʌrə] município m

borrow ['bɔrəu] v/t, v/i pedir emprestado

bosom ['buzəm] peito m; seio m

boss [bos] s bossa f; chefe m, patrão m; v/t chefiar; **~y** mandão

botch [botʃ] *v/t* remendar, atamancar

both [bauθ] *adj, pron* os dois, as duas; ambos, ambas; **~ ... and** ... não só ... mas também

bother [boðə] *v/t, v/i* molestar; *s* moléstia

bottle [botl] *v/t* engarrafar; *s* garrafa *f*

bottom [botəm] *s* fundo *m*; **at the ~** no fundo

bough [bau] *s* ramo *m*, galho *m*

bounce [bauns] *s* salto *m*, ressalto *m*; *v/t, v/i* pular; ressaltar

bound [baund] *s* limite *m*; salto *m*; *v/t* limitar; *v/i* saltar; *adj* sujeito, obrigado, encadernado; com destino a; **~ary** [-əri] (*pl -ries*) limite *m*; fronteira *f*; **~less** ilimitado

bounty [baunti] (*pl-ties*) generosidade *f*; prêmio *m*

bouquet [bukei] *s* ramalhete *m*, *Braz* buquê *m*; aroma *m*

bourgeois [buəʒwa:] *adj, s* burguês *m*

bovine [bouvain] bovino

bow [bau] *s* vênia *f*, inclinação *f*, reverência *f*; proa *f*; *v/t, v/i* fazer uma reverência, inclinar-se, curvar-se; submeter-se; [bou] *s* arco *m*; laço *m*

bowels [bauəlz] *s/pl* intestinos *f/pl*; entranhas *f/pl*

bowl [boul] *s* tigela *f*; bola *f* de madeira; *v/t, v/i* rolar

box [boks] *s* caixa *f*; bofetada *f*; *theat* camarote *m*; *bot* buxo *m*; *v/t, v/i* encaixotar; esbofetear; boxear; **~er** pugilista *m*, *Braz*

boxador *m*; **~ing** pugilismo *m*, boxe *m*; **~-office** bilheteira *f*, *Braz* bilheteria *f*

boy [boi] rapaz *m*, moço *m*, garoto *m*, menino *m*

boycott [boikət] *v/t* boicotar

boy|friend [boifrend] namorado *m*; **~hood** meninice *f*; **~ish** pueril

bra [bra:] *abbr of* **brassière**

brace [breis] *s* par *m*, parelha *f*; gancho *m*; *v/t, v/i* atar; entesar; revigorar; **~let** bracelete *m*; **~s** *s/pl* suspensórios *m/pl*

bracket [brækit] *s* suporte *m*; grampo *m*; parêntesis *m*; colchete *m*; *v/t* emparelhar

brackish [brækiʃ] salobre

brag [bræg] *v/i* jactar-se

braid [breid] *s* galão *m*; trança *f*

brain [brein] *s* cérebro *m*; **~s** [breinz] *s/pl* miolos *m/pl*

brake [breik] *s* travão *m*, *Braz* breque *m*; *v/t, v/i* travar, *Braz* brecar

bramble [bræmbl] sarça *f*

bran [bræn] farelo *m*

branch [bra:ntʃ] *s* ramo *m*, galho *m*; *com* filial *f*, sucursal *f*; *v/i* ramificar-se; **~ line** ramal *m*

brand [brænd] *s* tição *m*; marca *f*; *v/t* marcar; estigmatizar; **~-new** [-'dnju:] novo em folha

brass [bra:s] latão *m*

brassière [bræsiɛə] sutiã *m*

brat [bræt] rapazelho *m*, fedelho *m*

brave [breiv] *adj* valente, bravo; **~ry** valentia *f*

bravo [bra:vəu] *int* bravo!

brawl [brɔːl] s rixa f, refrega f
bray [brei] v/i zurrar
brazen ['breizn] adj brônzeo; fig descarado
Brazilian [brə'ziljən] adj, s brasileiro m
breach [briːtʃ] brecha f; in-fra(c)ção f
bread [bred] pão m; ~ **and butter** fig ganha-pão m
breadth [bredθ] largura f
break [breik] s intervalo m, pausa f, recreio m; fra(c)tura f, rotura f; romper m; v/t, v/i quebrar(-se), partir(-se); interromper; ~ **away** escapar(-se); ~ **down** sucumbir; falhar; demolir; ~ **in** assaltar, arrombar; interromper; ~ **up** dissolver, dispersar(-se); **breakfast** ['brekfast] s pequeno-almoço m, *Braz* café m da manhã; v/i tomar o pequeno almoço
breast [brest] s peito m; seio m
breath [breθ] s fôlego m; hálito m; **hold one's** ~ reter o fôlego; ~**e** [briːð] v/t, v/i respirar; ~**ing** ['briːðiŋ] respiração f; ~**less** ['breθlis] esbaforido
breeches ['britʃiz] s/pl calções m/pl
breed [briːd] v/t, v/i educar, instruir; produzir; criar; s raça f; espécie f; ~**ing** criação f; educação f
breez|e [briːz] s brisa f, aragem f; ~**y** jovial, alegre
brevity ['breviti] brevidade f
brew [bruː] v/t, v/i infundir; tramar; fermentar; fazer cerveja; s infusão f; ~**er** cervejeiro m;

~**ery** (pl -ries) fábrica f de cerveja
bribe [braib] s suborno m; v/t subornar; ~**ry** suborno m
brick [brik] tijolo m; ~**layer** pedreiro m, alvenéu m; ~**work** alvenaria f
bridal ['braidl] nupcial
bride [braid] noiva f; ~**groom** noivo m; ~**smaid** dama f de honor
bridge [bridʒ] s ponte f; *mus* cavalete m; bridege m
bridle ['braidl] s freio m; v/t, v/i refrear, conter
brief [briːf] adj breve; s breve m pontifício; resumo m; *jur* causa f; v/t instruir, dar instruções a; ~**case** pasta f
brigade [bri'geid] brigada f
bright [brait] vivo; esperto; claro, brilhante; luminoso; ~**en** v/t, v/i iluminar; animar; ~**ness** brilho m, claridade f; vivacidade f
brillian|ce, ~**cy** ['briljəns] brilho m, esplendor m; ~**t** adj, s brilhante m
brim [brim] s borda f; aba f; ~**ful** cheio até à borda
brine [brain] salmoira f
bring [briŋ] v/t trazer; levar; apresentar; ~ **about** causar, provocar; ~ **forth** produzir; gerar; ~ **forward** apresentar; *com* transportar; ~ **up** educar, criar
brink [briŋk] borda f, beira f
brisk [brisk] vivo, animado
bristle ['brisl] s cerda f, pêlo m; v/i eriçar-se

British ['britiʃ] britânico

brittle ['britl] frágil, quebradiço

broach [brəutʃ] v/t espichar; encetar, abordar

broad [brɔːd] adj largo; extenso; indecente; ~ **bean** fava f; ~**cast** v/t, v/i radiodifundir; difundir; s emissão f, difusão f; ~**casting** radiodifusão f ~**en** v/t, v/i alargar; ~**minded** v/i tolerante

broil [brɔil] v/t, v/i grelhar

broke [brəuk] adj teso, Braz pronto

broker ['brəukə] corretor m

bronze [brɔnz] s bronze m

brooch [brəutʃ] broche m

brood [bruːd] s ninhada f; fig prole f; v/i chocar; cismar

brook [bruk] s regato m, riacho m

broom [bruːm] bot giesta f; [brum] vassoura f

broth [brɔθ] caldo m

brothel ['brɔθl] bordel m

brother ['brʌðə] irmão m; ~**hood** irmandade f; fraternidade f; ~**-in-law** cunhado m; ~**ly** fraternal

brow [brau] testa f; cume m; sobrancelha f

brown [braun] adj moreno; castanho; s castanho m; v/t, v/i bronzear(-se)

bruise [bruːz] v/t magoar, machucar; s contusão f, amolgadela f

brush [brʌʃ] s escova f; pincel m; v/t, v/i escovar

brussels(sprouts) ['brʌsl-'sprauts] couve-de-Bruxelas f

brutal ['bruːtl] brutal; ~**ity** [-'tæliti] brutalidade f

bubble ['bʌbl] s bolha f; v/i borbulhar

buck [bʌk] s gamo m; bode m; macho; US dólar m

bucket ['bʌkit] balde m

buckle ['bʌkl] s fivela f; v/t, v/i afivelar

bud [bʌd] s bot rebento m, botão m; v/i brotar, criar botões

budget ['bʌdʒit] s orçamento m, verba f

buffalo ['bʌfələu] búfalo m

buffet ['bufei] s bufete m; ['bʌfit] s bofetada f; aparador m; v/t esbofetear

bug [bʌg] percevejo m

bugle ['bjuːgl] clarim m

build [bild] v/t, v/i edificar, construir; ~**er** construtor m; ~**ing** s construção f; edifício m, prédio m

bulb [bʌlb] bot bolbo m; lâmpada f elé(c)trica

bulge [bʌldʒ] s bojo m; v/t, v/i fazer bojo

bulk [bʌlk] s volume m, tamanho m; massa f; carga f; a maior parte; **in** ~ a granel; ~**y** avultado

bull [bul] s zo touro m; com altista m; ~**dog** cão m de fila, buldogue m

bullet ['bulit] bala f; ~**in** boletim m

bull|fight ['bulfait] tourada f; ~**fighter** toureiro m; ~**fighting** tauromaquia f; ~**finch** pisco; ~**headed** cabeçudo

bullion ['buljən] ouro m ou prata *f* em barra

bully ['buli] (*pl*-**lies**) *s* valentão *m*, fanfarrão *m*; *v/t* intimidar, tiranizar

bumble-bee ['bʌmblbi:] abelhão *m*, zângão *m*

bump [bʌmp] *s* pancada *f*, colisão *f*; baque *m*; inchaço *m*; *v/t*, *v/i* bater contra; colidir, chocar

bun [bʌn] bolo *m* de passas

bunch [bʌntʃ] *s* molho *m*, feixe *m*; cacho *m*; rama *m*, ramalhete *m*

bundle ['bʌndl] *s* feixe *m*, trouxa *f*; *v/t* entrouxar

bungalow ['bʌŋgələu] bangaló *m*

bungle ['bʌŋgl] *v/t*, *v/i* atamancar

bunk [bʌŋk] *s* tarimba *f*

bunker ['bʌŋkə] paiol *m*, carvoeira *f*

bunny ['bʌni] (*pl*-**nies**) coelhinho *m*

buoy [bɔi] *s* bóia *f*; **~ant** flutuante; alegre

burden ['bə:dn] *s* carga *f*, peso *m*; fardo *m*; *v/t* carregar; sobrecarregar; **~some** oneroso

bureau [bjuə'rəu] (*pl*-**reaux**) escrevaninha *f*; escritório *m*; **~cracy** [bjuə'rɔkrəsi] burocracia *f*; **~cratic** [-'krætik] burocrático

burgl|ar ['bə:glə] assaltante *m*, ladrão *m*; **~ary** (*pl*-**ries**) assalto *m* no(c)turno, arrombamento *m*

burial ['beriəl] enterro *m*

burn [bə:n] *v/t*, *v/i* queimar; arder; *s* queimadura *f*; **~ing** ardente

burnish ['bə:niʃ] *v/t*, *v/i* brunir

burst [bə:st] *v/t*, *v/i* rebentar; irromper; quebrar; *s* explosão *f*, estoiro *m*; **~ into tears** desfazer-se em lágrimas; **~ out crying** desatar a chorar

bury ['beri] *v/t* enterrar

bus [bʌs] *s* autocarro *m*, *Braz* ónibus *m*

bush [buʃ] arbusto *m*; mato *m*; **~y** basto

business ['biznis] assunto *m*; ocupação *f*; dever *m*; negócio *m*, comércio *m*; **no ~ of yours** não é da tua (sua) conta; **~ hours** horas *f*/ *pl* de expediente; **~ letter** carta *f* comercial; **~-like** prático, metódico; **~ man** (*pl*-**men**) homem *m* de negócios

bust [bʌst] *s* busto *m*

bustle ['bʌstl] *s* azáfama *f*; alvoroço *m*; *v/i* mexer-se, alvoroçar-se

busy ['bizi] *adj* ocupado, atarefado

but [bʌt, bət] *adv* apenas; *prp* exce(p)to, sem; *conj* mas, porém; senão; **the last ~ one** o penúltimo

butcher ['butʃə] *s* carniceiro *m*, açougueiro *m*; **~'s shop** carniçaria *f*, talho *m*

butler ['bʌtlə] mordomo *m*

butt [bʌt] *v/t*, *v/i* marrar; *s* coronha *f*; alvo *m*

butter ['bʌtə] manteiga *f*; **~cup** ranúnculo *m*; **~fly** borboleta *f*

buttock ['bʌtək] nádega *f*; **~s** traseiro *m*

button ['bʌtn] *s* botão *m*; *v/t, v/i*
abotoar; **~hole** casa *f* de botão

buy [bai] *v/t* comprar; **~er**
comprador *m*

buzz [bʌz] *v/i* zumbir; *s* zumbido *m*

by [bai] *adv* perto, próximo; *prp*
durante; por, de; perto de; **~oneself** sozinho; **~ the way** a

propósito

bye-bye ['bai'bai] *fam* goodbye

by-election ['baii.lekʃən] eleição *f* suplementar; **~gone** passado, antigo; **~pass** desvio *m*;
~product subproduto *m*;
~stander circunstante *m, f*;
~way atalho *m*; **~word** adágio *m*, rifão *m*

C

cab [kæb] cabriolé *m*; táxi *m*; cabine *f* de maquinista

cabbage ['kæbidʒ] couve *f*;
white ~ repolho *m*

cabin ['kæbin] cabina *f*; *mar* camarote *m*; cabana *f*

cabinet ['kæbinit] armário *m*;
gabinete *m*

cable ['keibl] *v/t, v/i* telegrafar;
s cabo *m*; amarra *f*; telegrama
m; cabograma *m*

cab-rank ['kæbræŋk] praça *f*
(*Braz* ponto *m*) de táxis

cackle ['kækl] *v/i* cacarejar; *s* cacarejo *m*

cactus ['kæktəs] (*pl* **cacti** ['kæktai]) cacto *m*

cadaver [kə'deivə] cadáver *m*

café ['kæfei] café *m*, café-restaurante *m*

cage [keidʒ] *v/t* engaiolar; *s*
gaiola *f*; jaula *f*

cake [keik] *s* bolo *m*; pastel *m*;
queque *m*

calamity [kə'læmiti] calamidade *f*

calcula|te ['kælkjuleit] *v/t* calcular; **~tion** [.-'leiʃən] cálculo
m

calendar ['kælində] calendário
m

calf [kɑ:f] (*pl* **calves**) *zo* vitela *f*,
bezerro *m*; *anat* barriga *f* da
perna

call [kɔ:l] *s* chamada *f*; grito *m*;
visita *f*; *v/t, v/i* chamar(-se);
nomear; gritar; **~ at** visitar; fazer escala; **~ back** voltar a telefonar; **~ for** exigir, pedir;
~ on visitar; apelar; **~ up** telefonar; recrutar; **~box** cabina *f*
telefónica; **~er** visita *f*, visitante *m, f*

calling ['kɔ:liŋ] chamada *f*; vocação *f*

callous ['kæləs] caloso; insensível

calm [kɑ:m] *s* calma *f*, tranquilidade *f*; *adj* calmo, sereno; *v/t,
v/i* acalmar(-se), serenar

column|iate [kə'lʌmnieit] *v/t*
caluniar; **~y** ['kæləmni] calúnia *f*

cambric ['keimbrik] cambraia *f*

camel ['kæməl] camelo *m*

camera ['kæmərə] máquina *f* fotográfica; **~man** operador *m*
cinematográfico

camomile ['kæməmail] camomila f, macela f

camp [kæmp] v/i acampar; s acampamento m

campaign [kæm'pein] s campanha f

camp-bed ['kæmp'bed] cama f de campanha

camphor ['kæmfə] cânfora f

camp-stool ['kæmpstu:l] assento m dobradiço

can [kæn, kən] v/aux ser capaz de, poder; saber

can [kæn] s lata f; v/t enlatar

Canadian [kə'neidjən] adj, s canadiano m

canal [kə'næl] canal m

cancel ['kænsl] v/t, v/i cancelar; ~lation [-'leiʃən] cancelamento m

cancer ['kænsə] med cancro m; Câncer m (zodiac)

candid ['kændid] cândido, franco

candidate ['kændidit] candidato m

candied ['kændid] cristalizado, confeitado

candle ['kændl] vela f; candeia f; ~stick castiçal m

cando(u)r ['kændə] candura f, franqueza f

candy ['kændi] s cândi m; (pl -dies) US rebuçado m

cane [kein] s cana f; bengala f

canister ['kænistə] lata f, caixa f

cannon ['kænən] s canhão m; carambola f (billiards)

cannot ['kænɔt] contr de **can** and **not**

canny ['kæni] fino, astuto

canoe [kə'nu:] s canoa f

canon ['kænən] cânon(e) m

canopy ['kænəpi] (pl -pies) dossel m

cant [kænt] s hipocrisia f

canteen [kæn'ti:n] cantina f

canter ['kæntə] s meio galope m

canvas ['kænvəs] tela f; lona f

canvass ['kænvəs] v/t, v/i angariar

canyon ['kænjən] canhão m, ravina f

cap [kæp] s gorro m, barrete m, boné m

capab|ility [,keipə'biliti] (pl -ties) capacidade f; ~le [ə'keipəbl] (of capaz); hábil

capacity [kə'pæsiti] (pl -ties) capacidade f; qualidade f

cape [keip] geol cabo m; capa f

caper ['keipə] s cabriola f; bot alcaparra f; v/i cabriolar; **cut a ~** fazer das suas

capital ['kæpitl] adj capital; maiúsculo; s com capital m; capital f; arch capitel m; ~ (**letter**) (letra f) maiúscula f; int ó(p)timo; ~**ism** capitalismo m

capitulate [kə'pitjuleit] v/i capitular

capric|e [kə'pri:s] capricho m; ~**lous** [-iʃəs] caprichoso

capsize [kæp'saiz] v/t, v/i capotar

captain ['kæptin] capitão m

caption ['kæpʃən] legenda f; cabeçalho m

captious ['kæpʃəs] capcioso

captivate ['kæptiveit] v/t cativar

captive ['kæptiv] adj, s cativo m, prisioneiro m; ~**ity**

[-'tiviti] cativeiro m

capture ['kæptʃə] s captura f; v/t capturar

car [ka:] s carro m; automóvel m

caramel ['kærəmel] caramelo m

carat ['kærət] quilate m

caravan ['kærəvæn] GB reboque m, rulóte f; caravana f

carbon ['ka:bən] carbono m; ~-**paper** papel m químico

carbuncle ['ka:bʌŋkl] carbúnculo m

carburettor ['ka:bjuretə] carburador m

card [ka:d] v/t cardar; s carda f; cartão m; carta f de jogar; ~-**board** cartão m, papelão m

cardigan ['ka:digən] casaco m de lã, jaqueta f

cardinal ['ka:dinl] s cardeal m; adj principal, cardeal

care [kɛə] s cuidado m, cautela f, atenção f; inquietação f; v/i importar-se; ~ **about** fazer caso de; ~ **for** cuidar de, olhar por; importar-se com, fazer caso de, gostar de; **take** ~! tenha cuidado; **take** ~ **of** tomar conta de, tratar; **what do I** ~? que me importa?

career [kə'riə] s carreira f

care-|free ['kɛəfri:] despreocupado; ~**ful** cuidadoso; ~**less** descuidado, negligente; ~**less-ness** descuido m, negligência f

caress [kə'res] s carícia f; v/t acariciar

care-|taker ['kɛə,teikə] porteiro m; guarda m; ~**worn** consumido

cargo ['ka:gəu] (pl -**go(e)s**) carga f, frete m

caricature [,kærikə'tjuə] s caricatura f

carnal ['ka:nl] carnal

carnation [ka:'neiʃən] s bot cravo m

carnival ['ka:nivəl] carnaval m

carol ['kærəl] s cântico m de Natal

carp [ka:p] s carpa f; v/i ~ **(at)** censurar, criticar

carpenter ['ka:pintə] carpinteiro m

carpet ['ka:pit] s carpete f; alcatifa f; tapete m

carriage ['kæridʒ] carruagem f; frete m, transporte m

carrier ['kæriə] med transmissor m, portador m; carregador m

carrot ['kærət] cenoura f

carry ['kæri] v/t, v/i carregar, transportar, levar; alcançar; transmitir; trazer; ~ **away** arrebatar; ~ **on** continuar; ~ **out** levar a cabo; ~ **the day** vencer, levar a melhor

cart [ka:t] v/t acarretar; s carroça f, carreta f; ~**er** carreteiro m; ~**-horse** cavalo m de tiro

cartoon [ka:'tu:n] s caricatura f; desenhos m/pl animados

cartridge ['ka:tridʒ] cartucho m; ~**-belt** cartucheira f

carv|e [ka:v] v/t, v/i esculpir, gravar, entalhar; trinchar (meat); ~**er** entalhador m, gravador; ~**ing** gravura f; arte f de gravar; ~**ing knife** trinchante m

cascade [kæs'keid] s cascata f

case [keis] s caso m; jur causa f;

estojo *m*; in ~ no caso de; in
any ~ em todo o caso
casement ['keismənt] janela *f* de
batentes
cash [kæʃ] *s* dinheiro *m* de contado; *v/t* descontar, cobrar; ~
down pronto pagamento *m*,
pagamento *m* à vista; ~ **on de-**
livery envio *m* contra cobrança, entrega *f* contra reembolso; ~
desk caixa *f*; **~ier** [-´ʃiə] caixa
m, *f*.; **~ register** caixa *f* registra-
dora
cask [ka:sk] pipa *f*, barrica *f*;
~et guarda-jóias *m*
cassette [kə´set] cassete *f*
cast [ka:st] *v/t*, *v/i* moldar, fundir; *thea* distribuir os papéis;
atirar, lançar, arremessar; *s*
lanço *m*; tom *m*, matiz *m*; *thea*
elenco *m*; molde *m*
caste [ka:st] casta *f*
cast iron ['ka:st´aiən] ferro *m*
fundido
castle ['ka:sl] torre *f* (xadrez);
castelo *m*
castor ['ka:stə] pimenteiro *m*;
saleiro *m*
castor oil ['ka:stə oil] óleo *m* de
 rícino; **~ sugar** açúcar *m* refinado
casual ['kæʒuəl] *adj* casual,
fortuito; despreocupado; **~ty**
(*pl* -ties) *m*; sinistrado
m; *mil* baixas *s*/*pl*; perdas *s*/*pl*,
mortos e feridos *m*/*pl*
cat [kæt] gato *m*, gata *f*
cataract ['kætərækt] catarata *f*
catarrh [kə´ta:] catarro *m*
catastrophe [kə´tæstrəfi] catástrofe *f*

catch [kætʃ] *v/t*, *v/i* agarrar,
apanhar; pegar; perceber;
(a) **cold** apanhar uma constipação; **~ fire** pegar fogo; ~ **up**
alcançar; **~ing** contagioso;
~word *thea* deixa *f*; lema *m*;
~y atra(c)tivo
category ['kætigəri] (*pl* -ries)
categoria *f*
cater ['keitə] *v/i* fornecer
caterpillar ['kætəpilə] lagarta *f*
cathedral [kə´θi:drəl] sé *f*, catedral *f*
Catholic ['kæθəlik] *adj*, *s* católico *m*
cattle ['kætl] *s*/*pl* gado *m* vacum
cauliflower ['kɔliflauə] couve-
flor *f*
cause [kɔ:z] causa *f*; *v/t* causar,
ocasionar, motivar; **~less** infundado
causeway ['kɔ:zwei] calçada *f*
caution ['kɔ:ʃən] *s* admoes-
tação *f*; cautela *f*; *v/t* advertir;
admoestar; **~ous** cauto, cauteloso
cavalry ['kævəlri] cavalaria *f*
cave [keiv] *s* caverna *f*, antro *m*;
~ **in** *v/i*, *v/i* aluir, ruir
cavern ['kævən] caverna *f*
cavity ['kæviti] (*pl* -ties) cavidade *f*
caw [kɔ:] *v/i* grasnar, crocitar
cease [si:s] *v/t*, *v/i* cessar
cedar ['si:də] *bot* cedro *m*
cede [si:d] *v/t* ceder
ceiling ['si:liŋ] te(c)to *m*; máximo *m*
celebrate ['selibreit] *v/t* cele-
brar; festejar; **~ed** célebre;
~ion [-´breiʃən] celebração *f*

celebrity [si'lebriti] (pl **-ties**) celebridade f

celerity [si'leriti] celeridade f

celery [selərɪ] aipo m

celestial [si'lestʃəl] celeste, celestial

celibacy ['selibəsi] celibato m, Braz solteirismo m

cell [sel] cela f; bot célula f; elect elemento m

cellar ['selə] cave f; adega f

Celt [kelt] celta m, f; **~ic** s celta m, língua céltica; adj céltico

cement [si'ment] s cimento m; v/t cimentar (a fig)

cemetery ['semitri] (pl **-ries**) cemitério m

censor ['sensə] s censor m; v/t censurar; **~ship** censura f

censure ['senʃə] s censura f, repreensão f; v/t censurar, repreender

census ['sensəs] (pl **-suses**) censo m, recenseamento m

cent [sent] cêntimo m; **per** ~ por cento; **~enary** adj, s (pl **-ries**), US **~ennial** centenário m

centi|grade ['sentigreid] centígrado m; **~metre**, US **~ter** centímetro m; **~pede** centopeia f

central ['sentrəl] central; **~ize** v/t, v/i centralizar

centre ['sentə], US **-ter** s centro m; **~ forward** avançado-centro m, Braz centro-avante m; **~ half** médio-centro m, Braz centro-médio m

century ['sentʃuri] (pl **-ries**) século m

cereal ['siəriəl] cereal m

cerebral ['seribrəl] adj cerebral

ceremon|ial [seri'məunjəl] s, adj cerimonial m; **~ious** cerimonioso; **~y** ['-məni] (pl **-nies**) cerimónia f

certain ['sə:tn] certo; **~ty** (pl **-ties**) certeza f

certificate [sə'tifikit] s certificado m, certidão f

certify ['sə:tifai] v/t certificar, atestar

chafe [tʃeif] v/t, v/i irritar(-se)

chaff [tʃa:f] s debulho m; zombaria f; v/t zombar-se m

chaffinch ['tʃæfintʃ] tentilhão m

chain [tʃein] s cadeia f; série f; v/t encadear

chair [tʃeə] s cadeira f; **~man** presidente m, f

chalk [tʃɔ:k] s giz m

challenge ['tʃælindʒ] s desafio m; v/t desafiar

chamber ['tʃeimbə] câmara f; **~-maid** criada f de quarto, Braz arrumadeira f; **~ pot** bacio m

chameleon [kə'mi:ljən] camaleão m

champagne [ʃæm'pein] champanhe m

champion ['tʃæmpjən] s campeão m; **~ship** campeonato m

chance [tʃa:ns] s chance f; oportunidade f; probabilidade f; sorte f, acaso m; v/t, v/i acontecer, calhar; arriscar; adj casual, acidental; **by** ~ por acaso

chancellor ['tʃa:nsələ] chanceler m; ♀ **of the Exchequer** Ministro m das Finanças

chandelier [.ʃændi'liə] candelabro *m*, lustre *m*

change [tʃeindʒ] *s* mudança *f*; troco *m*; câmbio *m*; *v/t, v/i* mudar; trocar; cambiar; **for a ~** para variar; **~able** variável, instável; **~less** imutável

channel ['tʃænl] canal *m*

chant [tʃɑ:nt] *s* cântico *m*; salmodia *f*; *v/t, v/i* cantar; salmodiar

chap [tʃæp] *v/t, v/i* gretar; *s* tipo *m*, sujeito *m*, moço *m*

chapel ['tʃæpəl] capela *f*

chaplain ['tʃæplin] capelão *m*

chapter ['tʃæptə] capítulo *m*

character ['kærɪktə] *s* cará(c)ter *m*; personagem *f*; **~istic** [-'rɪstɪk] *adj* característico; *s* característica *f*

charcoal ['tʃɑ:kəul] carvão *m* de lenha; (desenho *m* a) carvão *m*

charge [tʃɑ:dʒ] *v/t, v/i* cobrar, levar; carregar; encarregar, confiar; acusar; atacar; investir; *s* carga *f*, encargo *m*; acusação *f*; investida *f*; preço *m*; **free of ~** grátis; **in ~ of** encarregado de; **in my ~** a meu cargo

charit|able ['tʃærɪtəbl] caridoso; **~y** caridade *f*

charm [tʃɑ:m] *s* encanto *m*; feitiço *m*; amuleto *m*; *v/t* encantar; enfeitiçar; **~ing** encantador

chart [tʃɑ:t] *s* carta *f* náutica; gráfico *m*, tabela *f*; *v/t* traçar

charter ['tʃɑ:tə] *s* carta *f* de privilégio; estatuto *m*; fretamento

m; *v/t* fretar

charwoman ['tʃɑ:wumən] (*pl* **-women**) mulher *f* a dias, *Braz* arrumadeira *f*

chase [tʃeis] *s* caça *f*; perseguição *f*; *v/t* caçar, perseguir, afugentar

chasm ['kæzəm] abismo *m*

chassis ['ʃæsi] chassi *m*

chast|e [tʃeist] casto, puro; **~ity** ['tʃæstiti] castidade *f*

chat [tʃæt] *s* cavaco *m*, cavaqueira *f*, *Braz* bate-papo *m*;*v/i* cavaquear; **~ter** tagarelice *f*; chilro *m*; *v/i* tagarelar; chilrear; **~terbox** tagarela *m*, *f*, fala-barato *m*

cheap [tʃi:p] *adj* barato; reles; **~en** *v/t, v/i* baratear; depreciar

cheat [tʃi:t] *s* engano *m*, fraude *f*; vigarice *f*; vigarista *m*, *f*, embusteiro *m*; *v/t, v/i* enganar, defraudar

check [tʃek] *v/t, v/i* verificar; conferir; refrear; pôr em xeque; *s* verificação *f*; obstáculo *m*; xeque *m*; quadrado *m*; **~ in** dar entrada ao hotel; **~ out** sair do hotel, deixar o hotel; **~ed** axadrezado

cheek [tʃi:k] *s* face *f*, bochecha *f*; descaro *m*; **~y** descarado, impertinente

cheer [tʃiə] *v/t, v/i* aplaudir, dar vivas; animar; *s* viva *m*; alegria *f*; ânimo *m*; **~ful** jovial, animado, alegre; **~ing** vivas *m/pl*; **~ up!** ânimo, coragem!

cheerio [tʃiəri'əu] *GB* adeus

cheese [tʃiːz] queijo *m*

chemical ['kemikəl] *adj* químico; *s* produto *m* químico

chemist ['kemist] farmacêutico
m; **~ry** química *f*; **~'s (shop)**
farmácia *f*

cheque [tʃek] cheque *m*

cherish ['tʃeriʃ] *v/t* apreciar,
estimar

cherry ['tʃeri] (*pl* **-ries**) cereja *f*

chess [tʃes] xadrez *m*;
~-board tabuleiro *m* de xadrez

chest [tʃest] peito *m*, tórax *m*;
arca *f*, baú *m*; **~ of drawers**
cómoda *f*

chestnut ['tʃesnʌt] *s* castanha *f*;
adj castanho; **~-tree** casta-
nheira *f*

chew [tʃuː] *v/t, v/i* mascar,
mastigar; **~ing gum** pastilha
elástica, goma *f* de mascar

chicken ['tʃikin] *s* frango *m*; galinha *f*; medrica(s) *m, f*; **~ pox**
['-poks] varicela *f*

chicory ['tʃikəri] chicória *f*

chief [tʃiːf] *s* chefe *m*; comandante *m*; *adj* principal

chilblain ['tʃilblein] frieira *f*

child [tʃaild] (*pl* **children**
['tʃildrən] criança *f*; filho (a) *m*
(*f*); **~-birth** parto *m*; **~hood**
infância *f*; **~ish** acriançado; infantil, pueril; **~like** infantil,
inocente

chill [tʃil] *s* calafrio *m*; resfriado
m; frieza *f*; *adj* frio, gelado; indiferente; *v/t, v/i* gelar, esfriar,
arrefecer

chime [tʃaim] *s* carrilhão *m*; *v/t,
v/i* tocar carrilhão; repicar; bater as horas

chimney ['tʃimni] chaminé *f*;
~-sweep(er) limpa-chaminés
m

chin [tʃin] queixo *m*

china ['tʃainə] louça *f*, porcelana *f*

Chinese ['tʃai'niːz] *adj, s* chinês
m

chink [tʃiŋk] frincha *f*, greta *f*,
racha *f*

chip [tʃip] *s* cavaco *m*, lasca *f*;
ficha *f*; *v/t, v/i* lascar(-se); esca-
vacar; **~s** *GB* batatas *f/pl* fritas

chirp [tʃəːp] *v/t* palrar; *v/i* gorjear, chilrear; *s* gorjeio *m*, chilro *m*

chisel ['tʃizl] *s* cinzel *m*; *v/t* cin-
zelar

chit [tʃit] fedelho *m*; pivete *m*;

chivalr|ous ['ʃivəlrəs] cavalhei-
resco; **~y** cavalheirismo *m*; cavalaria *f*

choice [tʃɔis] *s* escolha *f*; *adj*
sele(c)to, escolhido

choir ['kwaiə] coro *m*

choke [tʃəuk] *v/t, v/i* abafar, su-
focar(-se), engasgar(-se); *s auto*
borboleta *f* de ar

cholera ['kɔlərə] *med* cólera *f*

choose [tʃuːz] *v/t, v/i* optar; resolver; escolher

chop [tʃɔp] *s* costeleta *f*; *v/t, v/i*
picar; cortar; **~py** mar agitado,
encapelado

chord [kɔːd] *mus* acorde *m*; corda *f*

Christ [kraist] Cristo *m*

christen ['krisn] *v/t* ba(p)tizar

Christ|ian [-tʃən] *s adj* cristão
(*m*); **~ian name** nome *m* de
ba(p)tismo; **♀ianity** [-ti'æniti]

clap

cristianismo m; ♀ mas ['-məs]
Natal m

chron|ic ['krɔnik] crónico; ~i-
cle s crónica f; ~ological
[-nə'lɔdʒikəl] cronológico;
~ology [krɔ'nɔlədʒi] cronolo-
gia f

chuck [tʃʌk] v/t fam botar

chuckle ['tʃʌkl] s riso m abafado; v/i rir-se à socapa

chum [tʃʌm] s fam amigo m, camarada m

church ['tʃəːtʃ] s igreja f; ♀ of
England ['iŋglənd] Igreja f An-
glicana; ~yard adro m

churn [tʃəːn] s desnatadeira f,
batedeira f; v/t, v/i fazer manteiga; bater

cider ['saidə] cidra f

cigar [si'gaː] charuto m; ~et-
(te) ['sigə'ret] cigarro m;
~et(te)-case cigarreira f;
~et(te)-holder boquilha f,
Braz piteira f

cinder ['sində] escória f; brasa f;
~s cinza f

cinema ['sinəmə] cinema m

cinnamon ['sinəmən] s canela f

cipher ['saifə] cifra f, zero m

circle ['səːkl] v/t, v/i circundar;
s círculo m

circuit ['səːkit] s circuito m;
~-breaker elect interruptor m

circular ['səːkjulə] s, adj circular f

circulat|e ['səːkjuleit] v/t, v/i
(fazer) circular; ~ion [-'leiʃən]
circulação f

circum|ference [sə'kʌmfərəns]
circumferência f; ~scribe
['səːkəmskraib] circunscrever;

circum|stance ['səːkəmstəns]
circunstância f; ~stantial
[-'stænʃəl] circunstancial;
~vent [-'vent] v/t lograr; rodear

circus ['səːkəs] circo m

cistern ['sistən] cisterna f

cite [sait] v/t citar

citizen ['sitizn] cidadão m;
~ship cidadania f

city ['siti] (pl -ties) cidade f; ~
hall US câmara f municipal,
Braz prefeitura f

civic ['sivik] cívico; ~s educação
f cívica

civil ['sivl] civil; cortês; ~ian
[-'viljən] adj, s civil m; ~iza-
tion [-lai'zeiʃən] civilização f;
~ize v/t civilizar; ~ rights direitos m/pl civis; ~ servant
funcionário m público

claim [kleim] v/t, v/i exigir, reclamar, reivindicar; s recla-
mação f, reivindicação f

clairvoyance [klɛə'vɔiəns] cla-
rividência f

clamber ['klæmbə] v/i escalar

clammy ['klæmi] pegajoso

clamorous ['klæmərəs] clamo-
roso

clamo(u)r ['klæmə] s clamor m,
vozearia f; v/i clamar, gritar

clamp [klæmp] s gancho m, torno m; v/t grampar

clan [klæn] clã m, tribo f

clandestine [klæn'destin] clandestino

clang [klæŋ] s tinido m; v/t, v/i
tinir; ressoar

clap [klæp] v/t, v/i aplaudir; bater palmas

claret ['klærət] clarete *m*

clarify ['klærifai] *v/t, v/i* esclarecer(-se); clarificar

clarinet [,klæri'net] clarinete *m*

clarity ['klæriti] claridade *f*, clareza *f*

clash [klæʃ] *s* choque *m*; *fig* conflito *m*; *v/t, v/i* colidir, chocar (-se); opor-se

clasp [klɑːsp] *s* colchete *m*, fivela *f*; abraço *m*; *v/t, v/i* apertar; afivelar; abraçar

class [klɑːs] *s* classe *f*; aula *f*; *v/t* classificar

classic ['klæsik] *adj, s* clássico *m*; **~al** clássico

classification [,klæsifi'keiʃən] classificação *f*

classify ['klæsifai] *v/t* classificar

class-mate ['klɑːsmeit] condiscípulo *m*, colega *m, f*, companheiro *m*

class-room ['klɑːsrum] classe *f*, (sala *f* de) aula *f*

clause [klɔːz] cláusula *f*

claw [klɔː] *s* garra *f*; pinça *f*; *v/t* arranhar

clay [klei] argila *f*, barro *m*

clean [kliːn] *adj* limpo; puro; *v/t, v/i* limpar(-se); **~ out** limpar *(a fig)*; **~er's** tinturaria *f*, lavandaria *f*; **~liness** asseio *m*, limpeza *f*; **~ly** ['klenli] *adj* limpo, asseado; **~ up** fazer as limpezas

cleanse [klenz] *v/t* limpar, purificar

clear [kliə] *adj* claro; distinto; evidente; livre; vazio; *v/t, v/i* aclarar; esclarecer; desobstruir; saldar, liquidar; levantar (a mesa); **~ out** safar-se; **~ing** clareira *f*; **~ up** tirar a limpo; aclarar, desanuviar-se

clear-sighted ['kliə'saitid] clarividente

cleave [kliːv] *v/t* fender, rachar

clef [klef] *mus* clave *f*

cleft [kleft] racha *f*, fenda *f*

clemency ['klemənsi] clemência *f*

clench [klentʃ] *v/t* agarrar, segurar; cerrar

clergy ['klɔːdʒi]: **the ~** clero *m*; **~man** clérigo *m*

clerical ['klerikəl] clerical; de escritório

clerk [klɑːk] *s* empregado *m*; caixeiro *m*; amanuense *m, f*

clever ['klevə] esperto; destro, hábil; inteligente

click [klik] *s* estalido *m*; clique *m*; *v/t, v/i* dar estalidos; ter sucesso

client ['klaiənt] cliente *m, f*; **~èle** [kliː ɑːn'teil] clientela *f*

cliff [klif] penhasco *m*

climate ['klaimit] clima *m*

climb [klaim] *v/t, v/i* trepar, subir, escalar; *s* subida *f*; **~er** trepador *m*; alpinista *m, f*; *zo* trepadora *f*; *bot* trepadeira *f*

cling [kliŋ] *v/i* agarrar-se

clinic ['klinik] clínica *f*; **~al** clínico

clink [kliŋk] *s* tinido *m*; *v/t, v/i* tilintar, tilintar

clip [klip] *v/t* (re)cortar; tosquiar; furar (bilhetes); *s* clipe *m*, grampo *m*

cloak [kləuk] *s* capa *f*, manto *m*; *v/t* esconder; encapotar;

~-room vestiário *m*

clock [klɔk] *s* relógio *m*; **~work** mecanismo *m* de corda

clod [klɔd] torrão *m*

clog [klɔg] *s* tamanco *m*, soco *m*

close [klǝuz] *v/t, v/i* encerrar; fechar; cerrar; *s* conclusão *f*, fim *m*; [klǝus] *adj, adv* próximo, perto; fechado; estreito; íntimo, caro; abafado; de perto; **~ to** perto de; **from ~ by** de perto

closet ['klɔzit] *s US* armário *m* de parede

cloth [klɔθ] *s* pano *m*, tecido *m*

clothe [klǝuð] *v/t* vestir; **~s** *s/pl* roupa *f*, vestuário *m*; **~s-hanger** cabide *m*; **~ing** roupa *f*

cloud [klaud] *s* nuvem *f*; *v/t, v/i* nublar(-se); turvar(-se); **~less** desanuviado; **~y** nublado

clove [klǝuv] *s* cravo-da-índia *m*

clover ['klǝuvǝ] trevo *m*

clown [klaun] *s* palhaço *m*

club [klʌb] *s* clava *f*, cacete *m*; paus *m/pl*; clube *m*; **~-house** clube *m* desportivo

clue [klu:] *s* vestígio *m*, indício *m*; **~d up** bem informado

clump [klʌmp] *s* moita *f*, maciço *m*

clumsy ['klʌmzi] deselegante; desajeitado

cluster ['klʌstǝ] *s* cacho *m*; grupo *m*; *v/i* agrupar-se, apinhar-se

clutch [klʌtʃ] *s* ninhada *f*; aperto *m*; *auto* embraiagem *f*; *v/t, v/i* agarrar(-se); **~ at** fazer por agarrar

Co. [kǝu] *abbr for* **Company**

c/o [si:'ǝu] a/c *abbr for* (in) care of ao cuidado de

coach [kǝutʃ] *s* coche *m*; treinador *m*; *GB* camioneta *f*, *Braz* ónibus *m*; carruagem *f*; *v/t* preparar; treinar

coagulate [kǝu'ægjuleit] *v/t, v/i* coagular(-se)

coal [kǝul] *s* carvão *m*

coalition [,kǝuǝ'liʃǝn] coalizão *f*

coal-mine ['kǝulmain], **~-pit** hulheira *f*, mina *f* de carvão

coarse [kɔ:s] rude, grosseiro; áspero; ordinário

coast [kǝust] *s* costa *f*; **~-line** litoral *m*

coat [kǝut] *v/t* cobrir; *s* casaco *m*; camada *f*, pele *f*; **~-hanger** cabide *m*, cruzeta *f*; **~ing** camada *f*, demão *f*; cobertura *f*; **~ of arms** brasão *m*

coax [kauks] *v/t* aliciar; adular; seduzir

cobble ['kɔbl] *v/t* pavimentar com gobos; **~r** sapateiro *m*

cobweb ['kɔbweb] teia *f* de aranha

cock [kɔk] *s* galo *m*; macho *m* (de ave); válvula *f*, torneira *f*; *v/t* levantar; erguer(-se)

cockle ['kɔkl] amêijoa *f*

cockney ['kɔkni] *adj, s* londrino *m*

cock-pit ['kɔkpit] *avi* carlinga *f*, cabina *f*; **~-roach** ['-rǝutʃ] barata *f*; **~-tail** coquete(i)l *m*

coco ['kǝukǝu] cacau *m*

coco-nut ['kǝukǝnʌt] coco *m*

cocoon [kǝ'ku:n] casulo *m*

cod [kɔd] *zo* bacalhau *m*

code [kəud] *v/t* codificar; *s* código *m*

coerc|e [kəu'ə:s] *v/t* coagir; reprimir; **~ion** coerção *f*

coffee ['kɔfi] café *m*; **~-bean** grão *m* de café; **~-pot** cafeteira *f*

coffin ['kɔfin] ataúde *m*, caixão *m*

cog-wheel ['kɔgwi:l] roda *f* dentada

cohe|rence [kəu'hiərəns] coerência *f*; **~rent** coerente; **~sion** [-'hi:ʒən] coesão *f*

coil [kɔil] *s* rolo *m*; bobina *f*; serpentina *f*; *v/t, v/i* enrolar; enroscar

coin [kɔin] *s* moeda *f*; *v/t* cunhar *(a fig)*; **~age** cunhagem *f*

cold [kəuld] *adj* frio; *s* frio *m*; resfriamento *m*, constipação *f*; **be ~** ter frio; fazer frio; **~ness** frieza *f*, indiferença *f*; **~-shoulder** *v/t* desdenhar

collaborat|e [kə'læbəreit] *v/i* colaborar; **~ion** [-'reiʃən] colaboração *f*; **~or** colaborador *m*

collapse [kə'læps] *v/t, v/i* sucumbir; ter um colapso; desmoronar(-se); *s* colapso *m*; desmoronamento *m*

collapsible [kə'læpsəbl] dobradiço, desmontável

collar ['kɔlə] *s* colarinho *m*; gola *f*; coleira *f*; **~-bone** clavícula *f*

collate [kɔ'leit] *v/t* cotejar, comparar

colleague ['kɔli:g] colega *m, f*

collect [kə'lekt] *v/t, v/i* cole(c)cionar, coligir; reunir(-se); *s* cole(c)ta *f*; **~ion** cole(c)ção *f*; **~ive** *adj* cole(c)tivo; **~or** cole(c)cionador *m*; cobrador *m*; *elect* cole(c)tor *m*

college ['kɔlidʒ] colégio *m*; escola *f* superior

collide [kə'laid] *v/i* colidir

collie ['kɔli] cão *m* de pastor

collier ['kɔljə] *GB* mineiro *m*

collision [kə'liʒən] colisão *f*

colloquial [kə'ləukwiəl] familiar, coloquial

colonel ['kə:nl] coronel *m*

colonial [kə'ləunjəl] *adj* colonial; **~ism** colonialismo *m*

colon|ist ['kɔlənist] colono *m*; **~ize** *v/t* colonizar; **~y** (*pl* **-nies**) colónia *f*

colo(u)r ['kʌlə] *s* cor *f*; colorido *m*; matiz *m*; *v/t, v/i* pintar; colorir; corar, ruborizar-se; **~-blind** daltónico; **~ful** colorido; **~ing** *s* corante *m*; coloração *f*; cor *f*; **~less** incolor; descorado, semcor; **~line** *US* barreira *f* racial; **~s** *s/pl* bandeira *f*

colt [kəult] potro *m*, poldro *m*

column ['kɔləm] coluna *f*

comb [kəum] *s* pente *m*; *v/t* pentear(-se)

combat ['kɔmbæt] *s* combate *m*; *v/t, v/i* combater

combination [kɔmbi'neiʃən] combinação *f*

combine [kəm'bain] *v/t, v/i* ligar(-se), coligar-se; combinar; ['kɔmbain] *s* debulhadora *f* segadoira

come [kʌm] *v/i* vir; acontecer; vir a ser; chegar; **~ about** suceder; **~ across** deparar com; **~**

along ir; ~ **back** voltar; ~ **down** descer; ~ **for** vir buscar; ~ **in** entrar; ~ **on**! vamos!; vá lá! ~ **out** sair; ~ **up** subir; ~**-back** s regresso m

comed|ian [kə'miːdjən] comediante m; ~**y** ['kɔmidi] (pl -dies) comédia f

comfort ['kʌmfət] s conforto m; v/t confortar; ~**able** confortável, cómodo

comic ['kɔmik] adj, s cómico m; ~**s** US. ~ **strip** história f aos quadradinhos

comma ['kɔmə] vírgula f

command [kə'mɑːnd] v/t, v/i comandar; s comando m; ordem f; ~**er** comandante m; ~**ment** mandamento m

commemorat|e [kə'meməreit] v/t comemorar; ~**ion** [-'reiʃən] comemoração f

commence [kə'mens] v/t, v/i começar; ~**ment** começo m

commend [kə'mend] v/t recomendar; encomiar

comment ['kɔment] v/t, v/i fazer comentários; comentar; s, ~**ary** (pl -ries) comentário m; ~**ator** ['-eitə] comentador m; comentarista m, f

commerce ['kɔmə(ː)s] comércio m

commercial [kə'məːʃəl] comercial; ~**ize** v/t comercializar

commission [kə'miʃən] s comissão f; v/t comissionar; ~**er** comissário m

commit [kə'mit] v/t cometer; comprometer(-se); condenar; ~**ment** compromisso m; ~**tee**

comissão f, comité m

commodity [kə'mɔditi] (pl -ties) mercadoria f, produto m

common ['kɔmən] adj comum; ♀ **Market** Mercado m Comum; ~**place** adj trivial, banal; s lugar-comum; ♀ **s** s/pl the ~ a Câmara f dos Comuns; ~ **sense** senso m comum, bom senso m

Commonwealth [kɔmənwelθ] ~ **of Nations** Comunidade f das Nações Britânicas

commotion [kə'məuʃən] comoção f

communicat|e [kə'mjuːnikeit] v/t, v/i comunicar; comungar; ~**ion** comunicação f; ~**ive** comunicativo

communion [kə'mjuːnjən] comunhão f

communis|m ['kɔmjunizəm] comunismo m; ~**t** adj, s comunista m, f

community [kə'mjuːniti] (pl -ties) comunidade f

commutation [kɔmjuːteiʃən] comutação f

commute [kə'mjuːt] v/t comutar

compact ['kɔmpækt] adj compacto

companion [kəm'pænjən] companheiro m

company ['kʌmpəni] (pl -nies) companhia f

comparable ['kɔmpərəbl] comparável

compar|ative [kəm'pærətiv] adj, s comparativo m; ~**e** ['-peə] v/t comparar(-se);

~ison [-'pærisn] comparação *f*

compartment [kəm'pɑːtmənt] compartimento *m*

compass ['kʌmpəs] *s* bússola *f*; **~es** *pl* compasso *m*

compassion [kəm'pæʃən] compaixão *f*; **~ate** [-ʃənit] compassivo

compatible [kəm'pætəbl] compatível

compatriot [kəm'pætriət] compatriota *m, f*

compel [kəm'pel] *v/t* compelir

compensat|e ['kɔmpenseit] *v/t* compensar; inde(m)nizar; **~ion** [-'seiʃən] compensação *f*; inde(m)nização *f*

compete [kəm'piːt] *v/i* competir, concorrer

competen|ce ['kɔmpitəns] competência *f*; **~t** competente

competit|ion [.kɔmpi'tiʃən] competição *f*; **~or** [kəm'petitə] competidor *m*, concorrente *m, f*

compile [kəm'pail] *v/t* compilar

complacent [kəm'pleisnt] complacente

complain [kəm'plein] *v/i* queixar-se; **~t** queixa *f*

complement ['kɔmplimənt] complemento *m*; **~ary** complementar

complet|e [kəm'pliːt] *adj* completo; *v/t* completar; **~ion** acabamento *m*

complex ['kɔmpleks] *adj, s* complexo *m*; **~ion** tez *f*; compleição *f*; **~ity** complexidade *f*

compliance [kəm'plaiəns] conformidade *f*; condescendência

complicat|e ['kɔmplikeit] *v/t* complicar(-se); **~ed** complicado; **~ion** [-'keiʃən] complicação *f*

compliment ['kɔmplimənt] *s* cumprimento *m*; *v/t* cumprimentar; **~ary** obsequioso; lisonjeiro

comply [kəm'plai] *v/i*: **~ with** conformar-se com; acatar

component [kəm'pəunənt] *adj s* componente *m, f*

compos|e [kəm'pəuz] *v/t, v/i* compor; **~er** *mus* compositor *m*

composit|e ['kɔmpəzit] *adj, s* composto *m*; **~ion** [-'ziʃən] composição *f*

compos|itor [kəm'pɔzitə] tipógrafo *m*; **~ure** [-'pəuʒə] compostura *f*

compote ['kɔmpəut] compota *f*, doce *m*

compound ['kɔmpaund] *adj, s* composto *m*

comprehen|d [.kɔmpri'hend] *v/t* compreender; **~sible** compreensível; **~sion** compreensão *f*; **~sive** compreensivo

compress ['kɔmpres] *s* compressa *f*; [kəm'pres] *v/t* comprimir; **~ion** [kəm'preʃən] compressão *f*

comprise [kəm'praiz] *v/t* incluir, abranger

compromise ['kɔmprəmaiz] *s* compromisso *m*; *v/t, v/i* comprometer(-se)

compuls|ion [kəm'pʌlʃən]

compulsão *f*; ~ory compulsó-
rio

compunction [kəm'pʌŋkʃən]
compunção *f*

comput|e [kəm'pju:t] *v/t, v/i*
computar; ~er computador *m*

comrade ['kɔmrid] camarada
m, f; ~ship camaradagem *f*

conceal [kən'si:l] *v/t* esconder,
ocultar, encobrir

concede [kən'si:d] *v/t* conceder

conceit [kən'si:t] presunção *f*,
vaidade *f*; ~ed presumido, vaidoso

conceiv|able [kən'si:vəbl] con-
cebível; ~e *v/t, v/i* conceber

concentrat|e ['kɔnsəntreit] *v/t,
v/i* concentrar(-se); ~ion
[-'treiʃən] concentração *f*

conception [kən'sepʃən] concepção *f*

concern [kən'sə:n] *s* inquietação *f*; interesse *m*; empresa
f; *v/t* inquietar; interessar; tocar, concernir; ~ed preocupado; ~ing concernente, relativo
a

concert ['kɔnsət] *s* concerto *m*;
[kən'sə:t] *v/t* concertar; ~ed
combinado

concession [kən'seʃən] concessão *f*

conciliat|e [kən'silieit] *v/t* con-
ciliar; ~ion conciliação *f*

concise [kən'sais] conciso;
~ness concisão *f*

conclu|de [kən'klu:d] *v/t, v/i*
concluir; ~sion [-ʒən] conclusão *f*; ~sive conclusivo

concord ['kɔŋkɔ:d] *s* concórdia
f; *gram* concordância *f*; acordo
m

concourse ['kɔŋkɔ:s] afluência
f; confluência *f*

concrete ['kɔnkri:t] *adj* concreto; *s* betão *m*, concreto *m*

concur [kən'kə:] *v/i* coincidir;
concorrer

concussion [kən'kʌʃən] con-
cussão *f*

condemn [kən'dem] *v/t* condenar; ~ation [‚kəndem'neiʃən]
condenação *f*

condense [kən'dens] *v/t, v/i*
condensar(-se); ~er condensa-
dor *m*

condescend [‚kɔndi'send] *v/i*
condescender, dignar-se

condition [kən'diʃən] *v/t* condicionar; *s* condição *f*; ~al
condicional

condole [kən'dəul] *v/i*: ~ with
condoer-se de

condolences [kən'dəulənsiz]
s/pl condolências *f/pl*

conduct ['kɔndʌkt] *s* conduta *f*;
[kən'dʌkt] *v/t, v/i* conduzir
(-se); ~or condutor *m*; *mus* cobrador *m*; maestro *m*

cone [kəun] cone *m*

confectioner [kən'fekʃənə]
confeiteiro *m*; ~'s (shop) confeitaria *f*

confedera|cy [kən'fedərəsi]
(*pl* -cies); ~tion [kɔnfedə-
'reiʃən] confederação *f*; ~te
adj, s confederado *m*; *v/t, v/i*
confederar(-se)

confer [kən'fə:] *v/t, v/i* confe-
renciar; conferir; ~ence ['kɔn-
fərəns] conferência *f*

confess [kən'fes] *v/t, v/i* confessar(-se); ~ion confissão f; ~or confessor m

confid|ant [ˌkɔnfi'dænt] confidente m; ~e [kən'faid] v/t, v/i confiar; ~ence ['kɔnfidəns] confiança f; confidência f; ~ent confiado; confiante; ~ential [-'denʃəl] confidencial

confine [kən'fain] v/t confinar, limitar; med estar de parto; ~ment med puerpério m; reclusão f

confirm [kən'fəːm] v/t confirmar; ~ation [ˌkɔnfə'meiʃən] confirmação f; ~ed adj inveterado

confiscate ['kɔnfiskeit] v/t confiscar

conflict ['kɔnflikt] s conflito m, luta f; [kən'flikt] v/i estar em conflito

conform [kən'fɔːm] v/t, v/i conformar(-se); ~ity conformidade f

confound [kən'faund] v/t confundir; ~ you! vai (vá) para o diabo!; ~ed maldito

confront [kən'frʌnt] v/t confrontar

confus|e [kən'fjuːz] v/t confundir; ~ed confuso; ~ion [-ʒən] confusão f

confute [kən'fjuːt] v/t refutar

congestion [kən'dʒestʃən] med congestão f; congestionamento m

conglomerate [kən'glɔmərit] s, adj conglomerado m

congratulat|e [kən'grætjuleit] v/t felicitar, congratular(-se); ~ions [-'leiʃənz] s/pl parabéns m/pl

congregat|e ['kɔŋgrigeit] v/t, v/i congregar(-se); ~ion [-'geiʃən] fiéis m/pl; congregação f

congress ['kɔŋgres] congresso m

conjecture [kən'dʒektʃə] s conje(c)tura f; v/t, v/i conje(c)turar

conjugat|e ['kɔndʒugeit] v/t, v/i conjugar(-se); ~ion [kɔndʒu'geiʃən] conjugação f

conjunction [kən'dʒʌŋkʃən] conjunção f

conjunctive [kən'dʒʌŋktiv] adj, s conjuntivo m, Braz subjuntivo m

conjure ['kʌndʒə] v/t, v/i prestidigitar

conjurer ['kʌndʒərə] prestidigitador m

connect [kə'nekt] v/t, v/i ligar (-se); relacionar; fazer (um)a ligação; ~ed ligado; relacionado; ~ing rod biela f; ~ion conexão f; ligação f; relação f

connive [kə'naiv] v/i ser conivente

conquer ['kɔŋkə] v/t conquistar; ~or conquistador m

conquest ['kɔŋkwest] conquista f

conscien|ce ['kɔnʃəns] consciência f; ~tious [-ʃi'enʃəs] consciencioso

conscious ['kɔnʃəs] cônscio, consciente; ~ly conscientemente; ~ness consciência f; conhecimento m

consecrate ['kɔnsikreit] *v/t* consagrar; dedicar

consecutive [kən'sekjutiv] consecutivo, sucessivo

consent [kən'sent] *v/i* consentir; sconsentimento *m*, permissão *f*

consequen|ce ['kɔnsikwəns] consequência *f*; importância *f*; **in** sce por conseguinte; st consequente

conservation [,kɔnsə'veiʃən] conservação *f*

conserva|tism [kən'sə:və- tizəm] conservantismo *m*; stive *adj*, *s* conservador *m*; story [-tri] (*pl* -ries) *mus* conservatório *m*; estufa *f*

conserve [kən'sə:v] *v/t* conservar

consider [kən'sidə] *v/t* considerar; sable considerável; sate [-dərit] atencioso; sation consideração *f*; sing considerando que; em vista de

consign [kən'sain] *v/t* consignar; confiar; sment consignação *f*

consist [kən'sist] *v/i* consistir; sence, sency consistência *f*; sent consistente

consolation [,kɔnsə'leiʃən] consolação *f*

consol|e [kən'səul] *v/t* consolar; sing consolador

consolidat|e [kən'sɔlideit] *v/t*, *v/i* consolidar(-se); sion consolidação *f*

consonant ['kɔnsənənt] consoante *f*

consort ['kɔnsɔ:t] consorte *m*, *f*

conspicuous [kən'spikjuəs] conspícuo, notável; **be ~ by one's absence** brilhar pela ausência

conspir|acy [kən'spirəsi] (*pl* -cies) conspiração *f*; sator [-tə] conspirador *m*; se [-'speiə] *v/t*, *v/i* conspirar

constable ['kʌnstəbl] oficial *m* de polícia; condestável *m*

constancy ['kɔnstənsi] constância *f*

constant ['kɔnstənt] constante

constipation [,kɔnsti'peiʃən] prisão *f* de ventre

constituency [kən'stitjuənsi] (*pl* -cies) eleitorado *m*, círculo *m* eleitoral

constitut|e ['kɔnstitju:t] *v/t* constituir; sion [,kɔnsti'tju:- ʃən] constituição *f*; sional *adj* constitucional

constrain [kən'strein] *v/t* forçar, constranger; st constrangimento *m*

construct [kən'strʌkt] *v/t* construir; sion construção *f*; sive construtivo; sor construtor *m*

consul ['kɔnsəl] cônsul *m*; sar ['-sjulə] consular; sate ['-sjulit] consulado *m*

consult [kən'sʌlt] *v/t* consultar; sation [,kɔnsəl'teiʃən] consulta *f*; sative [kən'sʌltətiv] consultivo; sing consultor; de consulta

consum|e [kən'sju:m] *v/t* consumir; ser consumidor *m*

consummat|e [kən'sʌmit] *adj* consumado; ['kɔnsʌmeit] *v/t* consumar

consumption [kənsʌmpʃən] consumo *m*, gasto *m*

contact ['kontækt] *s* conta(c)to *m*; [kən'tækt] *v/t* conta(c)tar

contagious [kən'teidʒəs] contagioso, contagiante

contain [kən'tein] *v/t* conter (-se)

contaminat|e [kən'tæmineit] *v/t* contaminar; **~ion** [-'neiʃən] contaminação *f*

contemplat|e ['kontempleit] *v/t* contemplar; **~ion** [kontem'pleiʃən] contemplação *f*; **~ive** contemplativo

contemporary [kən'tempərəri] *adj*, *s* (*pl* **-ries**) contemporâneo *m*

contempt [kən'tempt] desprezo *m*

contend [kən'tend] *v/i*, *v/t* contender; afirmar

content ['kontent] *adj* contente; *v/t* contentar; ['kontent] *s* conteúdo *m*; assunto *m*; **~ed** contente, satisfeito; **~ion** [-'tenʃən] contenda *f*

contest ['kontest] *s* competição *f*, concurso *m*, prova *f*; [kən'test] *v/t*, *v/i* disputar; contestar

context ['kontekst] contexto *m*

continent ['kontinənt] *s* continente *m*; **~al** [-'nentl] *adj* continental

contingent [kən'tindʒənt] *adj*, *s* contingente *m*

continu|al [kən'tinjuəl] contínuo; **~ance**, **~ation** continuação *f*; **~e** [-ju:] *v/t*, *v/i* continuar; **~ity** [-'ju(:)iti] con-

tinuidade *f*; **~ous** seguido, contínuo

contort [kən'to:t] *v/t* contorcer; **~ion** contorção *f*

contraband ['kontrəbænd] *s* contrabando *m*

contraceptive [,kontrə'septiv] *adj*, *s* anticoncepcivo *m*

contract [kən'trækt] *v/t*, *v/i* contratar; contrair(-se); ['kontrækt] *s* contrato *m*; **~ion** [-'trækʃən] contra(c)ção *f*; **~or** empreiteiro *m*

contradict [,kontrə'dikt] *v/t* contradizer(-se); **~ion** contradição *f*; **~ory** contraditório

contrary ['kontrəri] *adj*, *s* (*pl* **-ries**) contrário *m*; **on the ~** pelo contrário

contrast ['kontræst] *s* contraste *m*; [kən'træst] *v/t*, *v/i* contrastar

contribut|e [kən'tribju(:)t] *v/t*, *v/i* contribuir; **~ion** [,kontri-'bju:ʃən] contribuição *f*; **~or** [kən'tribjutə] contribuinte *m*

contrite ['kontrait] contrito

contriv|ance [kən'traivəns] ideia *f*, invenção *f*; aparelho *m*, engenhoca *f*; **~e** *v/t* conseguir, arranjar

control [kən'troul] *v/t* controlar, dominar; *s* controle *m*; comando *m*

controver|sial [,kontrə'və:ʃəl] controverso; **~sy** ['kontrə'və:si] (*pl* **-sies**) controvérsia *f*

contuse [kən'tju:z] *v/t* contundir

convales|ce [,konvə'les] *v/i* convalescer; **~cence** convalescência f; **~cent** adj, s convalescente m, f

convenien|ce [kən'vi:njəns] comodidade f, conveniência f; **~t** conveniente, cómodo

convent ['kɔnvənt] convento m

convention [kən'venʃən] convenção f; **~al** convencional

converge [kən'və:dʒ] v/i convergir

convers|ant ['kɔnvə:sənt] versado; **~ation** [,kɔnvə'seiʃən] conversação f, conversa f; **~e** v/i conversar; **~ion** conversão f

convert ['kɔnvə:t] s convertido m; [kən'və:t] v/t converter; **~ible** adj conversível; s descapotável m

convey [kən'vei] v/t transportar, conduzir, levar; exprimir; **~ance** jur cedência f; **~er belt** correia f transportadora

convict ['kɔnvikt] s convicto m condenado m; [kən'vikt] v/t condenar, sentenciar

convince [kən'vins] v/t convencer

convoy ['kɔnvɔi] s comboio m; escolta f

cook [kuk] s cozinheiro m; v/t, v/i cozinhar, cozer; **~ery** culinária f; **~ie, ~y** biscoito m

cool [ku:l] adj fresco; frio, distante; v/t, v/i arrefecer, refrescar; s frescura f; calma; **~ down**, **~ off** acalmar(-se)

cooper ['ku:pə] tanoeiro m

cooperat|e [kəu'ɔpəreit] v/i cooperar; **~ion** cooperação f; **~ive** [-rətiv] s cooperativa f; adj

cooperativo

coordinate [kəu'ɔ:dnit] adj coordenado; s coordenada f

cope [kəup] v/i: **~(with)** fazer frente (a), enfrentar

copious ['kəupjəs] copioso

copper ['kɔpə] cobre m

copy ['kɔpi] v/t, v/i copiar; s (pl **-pies**) cópia f; **~ist** copista m; **~right** direitos m/pl de autor, propriedade f literária

coral ['kɔrəl] s coral m

cord [kɔ:d] s cordel m, cordão m

cordial ['kɔ:djəl] cordial

corduroy ['kɔ:dərɔi] bombazina f; **~s** pl calças f/pl de bombazina

core [kɔ:] caroço m; âmago m

cork [kɔ:k] s cortiça f; rolha f; v/t (ar)rolhar; **~-screw** saca-rolhas m

corn [kɔ:n] s calo m; cereal m; milho m; trigo m

corner ['kɔ:nə] v/t, v/i monopolizar; virar, fazer uma curva; s canto m, esquina f; **~ (kick)** (pontapé m de) canto m; Braz escanteio m

Cornish ['kɔ:niʃ] adj da Cornualha; s córnico m

coronation [,kɔrə'neiʃən] coroação f

corpor|al ['kɔ:pərəl] s mil cabo m; adj corporal, corpóreo; **~ate** ['-rit] associado, cole(c)tivo; **~ation** corporação f

corpse [kɔ:ps] cadáver m

corpulent ['kɔ:pjulənt] corpulento

correct [kə'rekt] adj corre(c)to; v/t corrigir; **~ion** corre(c)ção f

correspond [ˌkɔrisˈpɔnd] *v/i* corresponder(-se); **~ence** correspondência *f*; **~ent** *s* correspondente *m, f*; **~ing** correspondente

corridor [ˈkɔridɔː] corredor *m*

corro|de [kəˈroud] *v/t, v/i* corroer(-se); **~sion** [-ʒən] corrosão *f*

corrupt [kəˈrʌpt] *adj* corru(p)to; *v/t, v/i* corromper(-se); **~ion** corru(p)ção *f*

corset [ˈkɔːsit] espartilho *m*

cosmetic(s) [kɔzˈmetik(s)] *adj, s* cosmético *m*

cosmonaut [ˈkɔzmənɔːt] cosmonauta *m, f*

cost [kɔst] *v/i* custar; *s* custo *m*, preço *m*; **~ly** dispendioso; **~s** *jur* custas *f/pl*

costume [ˈkɔstjuːm] *s* traje *m*

cosy [ˈkəuzi] *adj* confortável, cómodo

cot [kɔt] *GB* cama *f* de grades

cottage [ˈkɔtidʒ] casa *f* de campo

cotton [ˈkɔtn] algodão *m*; **~ wool** algodão *m* em rama

couch [kautʃ] *s* divã *m*, canapé *m*

cough [kɔf] *v/i* tossir; *s* tosse *f*

council [ˈkaunsl] *s* conselho *m*; concílio *m*

counsel [ˈkaunsəl] conselho *m*

count [kaunt] *v/t, v/i* contar; *s* conde *m*; conta *f*

countenance [ˈkauntinəns] *s* semblante *m*

counter [ˈkauntə] *s* balcão *m*; ficha *f*; **~act** [-ˈrækt] *v/t* contrariar, neutralizar; **~feit** [-ˈfit] *adj* falsificado; *v/t*

falsificar; **~foil** talão *m*; **~mand** [-ˈmaːnd] *v/t* revogar; **~march** contramarcha *f*; *v/i* contramarchar; **~pane** colcha *f*, coberta *f*

countess [ˈkauntis] condessa *f*

countless [ˈkauntlis] inumerável

country [ˈkʌntri] (*pl* **-ries**) país *m*; nação *f*; campo *m*; **~man** camponês *m*; compatriota *m, f*; **~side** campo *m*, zona *f* rural

county [ˈkaunti] (*pl* **-ties**) condado *m*, comarca *f*

couple [ˈkʌpl] *s* par *m*; casal *m*; **a ~ of** *fam* alguns, uns; *v/t, v/i* copular; emparelhar

courage [ˈkʌridʒ] coragem *f*; **~ous** [kəˈreidʒəs] corajoso

courier [ˈkuriə] correio *m*, mensageiro *m*

course [kɔːs] *s* curso *m*; pista *f*, campo *m*; rumo *m*; prato *m*; **a matter of ~** uma coisa natural; **in due ~** na devida altura; **of ~** claro, com certeza; evidentemente

court [kɔːt] *s* pátio *m*; campo *m* de ténis; *jur* tribunal *m*; corte *f*; *v/t* cortejar; solicitar; **~eous** [ˈkɔːtjəs] cortês; **~esy** [ˈkɔːtisi] (*pl* **-sies**) cortesia *f*; **~yard** pátio *m*

cousin [ˈkʌzn] primo *m*, prima *f*

cove [kəuv] enseada *f*

cover [ˈkʌvə] *v/t* cobrir; *s* cobertura *f*; abrigo *m*; talher *m*; **~age** reportagem *m*; riscos *m/pl* cobertos por seguro

covert [ˈkʌvət] *adj* encoberto, oculto

covet ['kʌvit] v/t cobiçar; **~ous** cobiçoso

cow [kau] s vaca f

coward ['kauəd] cobarde m; **~ice** [-is] cobardia f

cowboy ['kaubɔi] vaqueiro m, *Braz* boiadeiro m

cower ['kauə] v/i agachar-se

cowslip ['kauslip] *bot* primavera f

coxcomb ['kɔkskəum] peralvilho m

cox(swain) ['kɔkswein] arrais m

coy [kɔi] acanhado, modesto

crab [kræb] s caranguejo m

crack [kræk] s fenda f, racha f, estalido m; v/t, v/i fender(-se); estalar; **~er** bolacha f de água e sal; estalinho m, estalo-da-china m

crackle ['krækl] v/i crepitar

cradle ['kreidl] s berço m

craft [krɑːft] s habilidade f, arte f; embarcação f; artimanha f; **~sman** artífice m, artesão; **~y** astucioso

crag [kræg] fraga f

cram [kræm] v/t, v/i abarrotar; empinar, estudar

cramp [kræmp] s caimbra f; grampo m; v/t grampar

cranberry ['krænbəri] (pl -ries) arando m, uva-do-monte f

crane [krein] s *zo* grou m; *mec* grua f, guindaste m

crank [kræŋk] *mec* manivela f; excêntrico m

crash [kræʃ] s estrondo m; choque m, colisão f, queda f; v/t, v/i estalelar-se, espatifar-se; colidir; estrondear

crass [kræs] crasso

crater ['kreitə] cratera f

crav|e [kreiv] (for) v/t suspirar (por); **~ing** s ânsia f, desejo m ardente

crawl [krɔːl] v/i rastejar; gatinhar

crayfish ['kreifiʃ] **crawfish** ['krɔ-] lagostim m

crazy ['kreizi] doido, louco

creak [kriːk] v/i chiar, ranger

cream [kriːm] s nata f (a fig); creme m; v/t bater até fazer creme; desnatar; **~y** cremoso

crease [kriːs] s ruga f, vinco m; v/t, v/i enrugar(-se); vincar

creat|e [kriˈeit] v/t criar; **~ion** criação f; **~ive** criativo, criador; **~or** criador m; **~ure** ['kriːtʃə] criatura f

credentials [kriˈdenʃəlz] s/pl credenciais m/pl

credible ['kredəbl] crível

credit ['kredit] s crédito m; honra f; v/t dar crédito a; acreditar; on **~** a crédito; **~ card** cartão m de crédito; **~or** credor m

creed [kriːd] credo m, crença f

creek [kriːk] enseada f

creep [kriːp] v/i arrastar-se, rojar-se; **~er** *bot* trepadeira f

cremate [kriˈmeit] v/t cremar, incinerar

crescent ['kresnt] s quarto crescente m; *adj* crescente

cress [kres] agrião m

crest [krest] s crista f; cimeira f; timbre m; **~fallen** abatido

crevice ['krevis] racha f, greta f

crew [kruː] s equipagem f, tripulação f

crib [krib] *s* presépio *m*; manjedoura *f*; *US* cama *f* de grades; *v/t, v/i fam* copiar, cabular, *Braz* colar

cricket ['krikit] *s* criquete *m*; *zo* grilo *m*

crime [kraim] *s* crime *m*

criminal ['kriminl] *s* criminoso *m*; *adj* criminal; criminoso

crimson ['krimzn] *adj, s* carmesim *m*

cripple ['kripl] *s* aleijado *m*, paralítico *m*, estropiado *m*; *v/t* estropiar

crisis ['kraisis] (*pl* -ses) crise *f*

crisp [krisp] *adj* tostado, estaladinho; crespo; fresco; rápido, decidido; *s* batata *f* frita

critic ['kritik] *s* crítico *m*; **~al** crítico; **~ism** ['-sizəm] crítica *f*; **~ize** [-saiz] *v/t, v/i* criticar

croak [krouk] *v/i* grasnar

crockery ['krokəri] faiança *f*, louça *f* de barro

crook [kruk] *s* gancho *m*; cajado *m*; caloteiro *m*, escroque *m*; **~ed** *adj* desonesto; curvo

crop [krop] *s* colheita *f*; chicote *m*; papo *m*; *v/t* colher ; ceifar, segar; cortar; tosquiar

cross [kros] *s* cruz *f*, *v/t, v/i* cruzar(-se); atravessar(-se); *adj* mal humorado, zangado; **~ing** cruzamento *m*; *mar* travessia *f*; **~-road(s)** encruzilhada *f*; **~word (puzzle)** palavras *f/pl* cruzadas

crouch [krautʃ] *v/i* agachar-se, acocorar-se

crow [krou] *s* corvo *m*; *v/i* cantar, cucuritar; **~-bar** alavanca

f, pé-de-cabra *m*

crowd [kraud] *v/t, v/i* agrupar (-se), apinhar(-se); *s* multidão *f*, turba *f*; **~ed** apinhado

crown [kraun] *s* coroa *f*; *v/t* coroar

crucial ['kruːʃəl] crucial

crucif|ix ['kruːsifiks] crucifixo *m*; **~ixion** [-'fikʃən] crucificação *f*; **~y** ['-fai] *v/t* crucificar

crude [kruːd] bruto; rude; grosseiro

cruel [kruəl] cruel; **~ty** (*pl* -ties) crueldade *f*

cruet ['kruːit] galheta *f*; **~-stand** galheteiro *m*

cruis|e [kruːz] *v/i* navegar; andar em cruzeiro; *s* cruzeiro *m*, travessia *f*; **~er** cruzador *m*

crumb [krʌm] migalha *f*; **~le** [-bl] *v/t, v/i* esmigalhar(-se), esfarelar(-se)

crumple ['krʌmpl] *v/t, v/i* amarrotar(-se)

crusad|e [kruː'seid] *s* cruzada *f*; **~er** cruzado *m*

crush [krʌʃ] *v/t* esmagar; moer, triturar; *s* aperto *m*, compressão *f*; aglomeração *f*

crust [krʌst] *s* crosta *f*; côdea *f*; folhado *m*

crutch [krʌtʃ] muleta *f*

cry [krai] (*pl* **cries**) *s* grito *m*; choro *m*; *v/t, v/i* gritar; chorar

crypt [kript] cripta *f*

crystal ['kristl] cristal *m*

cub [kʌb] filhote *m*, cachorro *m*

cube [kjuːb] cubo *m*

cubic ['kjuːbik] cúbico

cuckoo ['kukuː] cuco *m*

cucumber ['kjuːkʌmbə] pepino

m, cogombro *m*

cuddle ['kʌdl] *v/t, v/i* abraçar
(-se); *s* abraço *m*

cudgel ['kʌdʒəl] *s* clava *f,* bastão
m; v/t esbordoar

cue [kju:] *theat* deixa *f;* taco *m*
(de bilhar); sinal *m,* indicação *f*

cuff [kʌf] *s* punho *m* (de camisa); palmada *f; v/t* dar palmadas

culp|able ['kʌlpəbl] culpável;
~rit ['-rit] culpado *m*

cult [kʌlt] culto *m;* **~ivate** *v/t*
['-iveit] cultivar; **~ivated** culto;
cultivado; **~ivation** cultivo *m,*
cultura *f*

culture ['kʌltʃə] cultura *f*

cumbersome ['kʌmbəsəm] incómodo, enfadonho

cumulative ['kju:mjulətiv] cu-
mulativo

cunning ['kʌniŋ] *adj* astuto,
manhoso; *s* astúcia *f,* manha *f*

cup [kʌp] *s* chávena *f,* xícara *f,*
taça *f;* **~board** ['kʌbəd] guar-
da-louça *m*

cupidity [kju(:)'piditi] cupidez *f*

curable ['kjuərəbl] curável

curat|e ['kjuərit] cura *m,* pároco
m; **~or** [-'reitə] conservador *m*

curb [kə:b] *v/t* refrear

curd [kə:d] coalhada *f,* requeijão
m; **~le** ['-dl] *v/t, v/i* coalhar
(-se)

cure [kjuə] *s* cura *f; v/t, v/i* remediar; curar(-se)

curfew ['kə:fju:] recolher *m*
obrigatório

curiosity [,kjuəri'ɔsiti] curiosi-
dade *f*

curious ['kjuəriəs] curioso

curl [kə:l] *s* anel *m,* caracol *m;*
v/t, v/i encaracolar(-se)

currant ['kʌrənt] corinto *m;* groselha *f*

curren|cy ['kʌrənsi] (*pl* **-cies**)
moeda *f* corrente; circulação *f;*
aceitação *f* geral; **~t** *adj, s* corrente *f*

curry ['kʌri] (*pl* **-ries**) *s* caril *m*

curse [kə:s] *v/t* amaldiçoar; *v/i*
praguejar; *s* maldição *f;* praga *f*

curt [kə:t] abrupto, brusco

curtail [kə:'teil] *v/t* reduzir; encurtar

curtain ['kə:tn] *s* cortina *f; theat*
pano *m* de boca

curve [kə:v] *s* curva *f; v/t, v/i* cur-
var(-se), encurvar

cushion ['kuʃən] *s* almofada *f,*
coxim *m*

custard ['kʌstəd] leite-creme *m*

custody ['kʌstədi] cuidado *m;*
custódia *f*

custom ['kʌstəm] costume *m;*
~ary consuetudinário, habitual; **~er** freguês *m,* cliente *m,*
f; **~(s)house** alfândega *f;* **~s**
alfândega *f;* direitos *m/pl* alfandegários; **~s duties** direitos *m/pl* aduaneiros

cut [kʌt] *v/t, v/i* cortar; talhar; *s*
corte *m,* golpe *m;* **~away** fraque *m;* **~ down** deitar abaixo,
derrubar; reduzir; **~ in** interromper, intrometer(-se)

cutler ['kʌtlə] cuteleiro *m;* **~y**
cutelaria *f*

cutlet ['kʌtlit] costeleta *f*

cutthroat ['kʌtθrəut] *s,* degola-
dor *m,* assassino *m; adj* cruel,
sanguinário

cutting ['kʌtiŋ] *adj* cortante; mordaz; *s* recorte *m*; *bot* estaca *f*; corte *m*

cycl|e ['saikl] *v/i* andar de bicicleta; *s* ciclo *m*; bicicleta *f*; **~ic (-al)** cíclico; **~ist** ciclista *m, f*

cyclone ['saikloun] ciclone *m*

cylinder ['silində] cilindro *m*

cymbal ['simbəl] pratos *m/pl*, címbalo *m*

cynic ['sinik] *s* cínico *m*; **~al** cínico; cínico; **~ism** cinismo *m*

cypress ['saipris] cipreste *m*

czar [za:] czar *m*

Czech [tʃek] *adj, s* checo *m*, *Braz* tcheco *m*

D

don't care a ~ não faço caso; **~ation** [-'neiʃən] danação *f*, condenação *f*

damp [dæmp] *v/t, v/i* (h)umedecer; abafar; *s* (h)umidade; *adj* (h)úmido

danc|e ['da:ns] *v/t, v/i* bailar, dançar; *s* baile *m*, dança *f*; **~er** dançarino *m*, bailarino *m*; **~ing** *adj* dançante; *s* dança *f*

dandelion ['dændilaiən] *bot* dente-de-leão *m*

danger ['deindʒə] perigo *m*; **~ous** perigoso

dangle ['dæŋgl] *v/t, v/i* suspender; acenar (com)

Danish ['deiniʃ] *adj, s* dinamarquês *m*

dappled ['dæpld] malhado

dare [dɛə] *v/t, v/i* ousar, atrever-se a; desafiar; **I ~say** creio bem; sem dúvida; suponho

daring ['dɛəriŋ] *s* ousadia *f*; *adj* ousado

dark [da:k] *adj* escuro, sombrio, obscuro; *s* escuridão *f*, trevas *f/pl*; escuro *m*; **~en** *v/t, v/i* escurecer(-se); **~ness** escuridão *f*, trevas *f/pl*

darling ['da:liŋ] *adj, s* querido

dab [dæb] *s* pancadinha *f*; *v/t* esfregar, esponjar

dad(dy) ['dæd(i)] (*pl* **-dies**) papá *m*, *Braz* papai *m*; **~ longlegs** melga *f*, *Braz* pernilongo *m*

daffodil ['dæfədil] asfódelo *m*, narciso *m* amarelo

daft [da:ft] palerma, tolo

dagger ['dægə] punhal *m*

daily ['deili] *adj* quotidiano, diário; *adv* diariamente; *s* diário *m*

dainty ['deinti] *s* (*pl* **-ties**) *s* guloseima *f*; *adj* delicado, refinado; elegante

dairy ['dɛəri] (*pl* **-ries**) leitaria *f*

daisy ['deizi] (*pl* **-sies**) *bot* bonina *f*, margarida *f*

dam [dæm] *s* barragem *f*; dique *m*; *v/t* represar

damage ['dæmidʒ] *s* dano *m*, prejuízo *m*; estrago *m*, avaria *f*; *v/t* deteriorar, danificar; **~s pl** inde(m)nização *f* por perdas e danos

damask ['dæməsk] damasco *m*

damn [dæm] *v/t* condenar; amaldiçoar; *s* maldição *f*; **~ it!** maldito seja!; **I'll be damned if . . .** diabos me levem se . . .; **I**

m, amor m

darn [dɑːn] v/t cerzir; s cerzidura f

dart [dɑːt] s dardo m; flecha f; v/t, v/i lançar(-se), precipitar(-se)

dash [dæʃ] s travessia m; energia f; ímpeto m; arremetida f; arranco m; v/t, v/i arrojar; despedaçar; precipitar-se

dashboard ['dæʃbɔːd] auto painel m

dashing ['dæʃiŋ] adj impetuoso, arrojado; chibante

data ['deitə] s/pl dados m/pl

date [deit] s data f; encontro m marcado, entrevista f; bot tâmara f; v/t, v/i datar; **out of** ~ antiquado, fora de moda; **up to** ~ moderno; em dia; ~**ed** antiquado, obsoleto

daub [dɔːb] v/t (bes)untar

daughter ['dɔːtə] filha f; ~**in-law** nora f

daunt [dɔːnt] v/t intimidar; ~**less** intrépido

dawn [dɔːn] s aurora f, alvorecer m, madrugada f, amanhecer m; v/i amanhecer; despontar

day [dei] dia m; jornada f; ~ **after** ~ dia após dia; ~ **in** ~ **out** dia a dia; ~ **by** ~ dia por dia; **the** ~ **after tomorrow** depois de amanhã; **the** ~ **before yesterday** anteontem; ~**break** romper m do dia; ~**dream** s devaneio m; ~**light** luz m do dia; ~**school** externato m

daze [deiz] v/t aturdir; s aturdimento m

dazzle ['dæzl] v/t ofuscar, enca-

dear; deslumbar

deacon ['diːkən] diácono m

dead [ded] adv completamente; s: **in the** ~ **of** em pleno ...; adj profundo; sem corrente; morto, falecido, defunto; inerte; ~**en** v/t amortecer; ~**end** beco m sem saída; ~**line** prazo m marcado; ~**lock** impasse m

deaf [def] surdo; **turn a** ~ **ear** to fazer ouvidos de mercador; ~**-mute** adj, s surdo-mudo m; ~**en** v/t ensurdecer; ~**ness** surdez f

deal [diːl] s parte f, porção f, quantidade f; mão f em jogo de cartas; acordo m; **a great** ~, **a good** ~, muito; uma grande quantidade; v/t, v/i distribuir; dar cartas; ~**er** negociante m; ~ **with** tratar de; lidar com; ~**ings** s/pl negócios m/pl

dear [diə] caro, dispendioso; querido, caro; int oh ~! com a breca! ~ **me**! valha-me Deus!

death [deθ] morte f, falecimento m; ~**bed** leito m de morte; ~**rate** taxa f de mortalidade

debase [di'beis] v/t aviltar

debate [di'beit] s debate m; v/t, v/i debater

debauch [di'bɔːtʃ] v/t corromper; perverter; ~**ee** libertino m; ~**ery** libertinagem f, devassidão f

debit ['debit] s débito m; v/t debitar

debt [det] dívida f; ~**or** devedor m

decade ['dekeid] década f

decaden|ce ['dekədəns] decadência f; **~t** adj, s decadente m

decapitate [di'kæpiteit] v/t decapitar

decay [di'kei] s declínio m, decadência f; cárie f; v/t, v/i decair, declinar; apodrecer, cariar

decease [di'si:s] falecimento m; **~d** adj, s falecido m

deceit [di'si:t] engano m, fraude f, dolo m; **~tful** enganoso, falso; **~ve** [-v] v/t enganar; **~ver** enganador m

December [di'sembə] Dezembro m

decen|cy [di:snsi] decência f; **~t** decente

decept|ion [di'sepʃən] decepção f; engano m; **~ive** [-tiv] enganador, ilusório

decid|e [di'said] v/t, v/i decidir (-se); **~ed** decidido

decipher [di'saifə] v/t decifrar

decision [di'siʒən] decisão f

decisive [di'saisiv] decisivo; decidido

deck [dek] s convés m, coberta f; **~-chair** cadeira f de lona, *Braz* preguiçosa f

declaim [di'kleim] v/t, v/i declamar

declar|ation [deklə'reiʃən] declaração f; **~e** [di'kleə] v/t, v/i declarar

decline [di'klain] s declínio m; v/t, v/i declinar; decair

decompose [di:kəm'pəuz] v/t, v/i decompor(-se)

decorat|e [di'kəreit] v/t, ornamentar, decorar; **~ion** decoração f, adorno m; **~ive** ['-rətiv] decorativo; **~or** decorador m

decor|ous ['dekərəs] decoroso; **~um** [di'kɔ:rəm] decoro m, decência f

decoy [di'kɔi] v/t engodar

decrease [di:kri:s] s decrescimento m, diminuição f; [di:-'kri:s] v/t, v/i decrescer, diminuir

decree [di'kri:] s decreto m; v/t, v/i decretar

dedicat|e [dedikeit] v/t dedicar, consagrar; **~ion** [dedi'keiʃən] dedicação f; dedicatória f

deduce [di'dju:s] v/t deduzir

deduct [di'dʌkt] v/t descontar, subtrair; **~ion** dedução f; desconto m

deed [di:d] façanha f, feito m, a(c)to m; *jur* escritura f

deep [di:p] adj fundo; profundo; penetrante; grave; s pélago m; adv profundamente; **~ blue** azul vivo; **~en** v/t, v/i aprofundar(-se); **~-freeze** s congelador m; v/t congelar

deer [diə] veado m, cervo m

deface [di'feis] v/t desfigurar

defame [di'feim] v/t difamar

defeat [di'fi:t] s derrota f; v/t derrotar

defect [di'fekt] s defeito m; **~ive** defeituoso; *gram* defectivo

defence [di'fens] defesa f

defend [di'fend] v/t defender; **~ant** *jur* réu m; **~er** defensor m

defensive [di'fensiv] s defensiva f; adj defensivo

defer [di'fə:] v/t adiar, diferir; **~ to** ceder, deferir; **~ence** ['defərəns] deferência f; **~en-**

**...en∫əl] deferente

...[di'faiəns] provocação
...ssafio m; **~t** provocador, desafiante

deficien|cy [di'fi∫ənsi] (pl -cies) deficiência f; **~t** deficiente

deficit ['defisit] défice m, deficit m

defile [di'fail] v/t aviltar; [di-fail] s desfiladeiro m

define [di'fain] v/t, v/i definir; **~ite** [-'definit] definido; **~ition** [-'nifən] definição f; **~itive** [-'finitiv] definitivo

deflate [di'fleit] v/t, v/i esvaziar(-se)

deform [di'fɔːm] v/t deformar; **~ed** disforme; **~ity** deformidade f

defrost [diː'frɔst] v/t, v/i descongelar, degelar

deft [deft] hábil, destro

defy [di'fai] v/t desafiar

degenerate [di'dʒenereit] v/i degenerar(-se)

degrade [di'greid] v/t, v/i degradar(-se)

degree [di'griː] grau m

deign [dein] v/i dignar-se

deity ['diːiti] (pl -ties) divindade f

deject|ed [di'dʒektid] abatido, desanimado; **~ion** desalento m

delay [di'lei] s atraso m, demora f; v/t, v/i atrasar, (re)tardar; demorar(-se)

delegate ['deligit] s delegado m; ['deligeit] v/t delegar

deliberate [di'libərit] adj deliberado; [-'libəreit] v/t, v/i deli-

berar; **~ely** deliberadamente; **~ion** [-'rei∫ən] deliberação f

delicacy ['delikəsi] (pl -cies) delicadeza f; acepipe m, pitéu m

delicious [di'li∫əs] delicioso; saboroso

delight [di'lait] s deleite m; v/t, v/i deleitar(-se)

delineate [di'linieit] v/t delinear

delinquent [di'linkwənt] adj, s delinquente m, f

deliver [di'livə] v/t entregar; distribuir; partejar, assistir ao parto; **~er** libertador m; **~y** (pl -ries) parto m; entrega f, distribuição f

delude [di'luːd] v/t enganar

deluge ['deljuːdʒ] s dilúvio m; v/t inundar, alagar

delus|ion [di'luːʒən] ilusão f; engano m; **~ive** [-siv] ilusório

demand [di'maːnd] s demanda f; procura f; exigência f; v/t, v/i exigir, reclamar

demilitarize [diː'militəraiz] v/t desmilitarizar

demise [di'maiz] falecimento m

democracy [di'mɔkrəsi] (pl -cies) democracia f

democrat ['deməkræt] democrata m, f; **~ic** democrático

demolish [di'mɔli∫] v/t demolir

demolition [demə'li∫ən] demolição f

demon ['diːmən] demónio m

demonstrat|e [demənstreit] v/t, v/i demonstrar; manifestar; **~ion** [-'strei∫ən] demonstração f; manifestação f; **~ive** demonstrativo

demure [di'mjuə] sério, mo-

den

desto

den [den] covil *m*, antro *m*

denial [di'naiəl] desmentido *m*; negativa *f*, recusa *f*

denote [di'nəut] *v/t* denotar

denounce [di'nauns] *v/t* denunciar

dens|e [dens] compacto; obtuso; denso; espesso; **~ity** densidade *f*

dent [dent] *s* mossa *f*; *v/t*, *v/i* amolgar(-se)

dent|al [dentl] dental; **~ist** dentista *m*; **~istry** medicina *f* dentária; **~ure** ['~tʃə] dentadura *f* postiça

denude [di'nju:d] *v/t* desnudar

deny [di'nai] *v/t* negar

deodorize [di:'əudəraiz] *v/t* desodorizar

depart [di'pɑ:t] *v/i* partir, sair; **~ed** ido, passado; falecido

department [di'pɑ:tmənt] repartição *f*, departamento *m*; se(c)ção; **~ment store** armazém; **departure** [di'pɑ:tʃə] partida *f*

depend [di'pend] *v/i* depender; **~able** de confiança; **~ence** dependência *f*; **~ent** dependente

deplor|able [di'plɔ:rəbl] deplorável; **~e** *v/t* deplorar

deport [di'pɔ:t] *v/t* deportar; **~ation** deportação *f*

depos|e [di'pəuz] *v/t* depor; destituir; **~it** [~'pozit] *s* depósito *m*; *v/t* depositar; **~ition** depoimento *m*; deposição *f*

depot ['depəu] armazém *m*, depósito *m*; *US* estação *f* de caminhos de ferro, *Braz* estação ferroviária

depreciate [di'pri:ʃieit] *v/t*, *v/i* depreciar; desvalorizar(-se)

depress [di'pres] *v/t* deprimir; **~ing** deprimente; **~ion** depressão *f*

deprive [di'praiv] *v/t*: **~of** privar, despojar de

depth [depθ] profundeza *f*, profundidade *f*

deputy ['depjuti] (*pl* **-ties**) deputado *m*; delegado *m*; substituto *m*

derail [di'reil] *v/t*, *v/i* descarrilar; **~ment** descarrilamento *m*

derange [di'reindʒ] *v/t* transtornar; **~ment** loucura *f*

derision [di'riʒən] galhofa *f*, chacota *f*

derive [di'raiv] *v/t*: **~from** derivar de

descend [di'send] *v/t*, *v/i* descer; descender; **~ant** descendente *m*, *f*

descent [di'sent] descida *f*; linhagem *f*, descendência *f*

descri|be [dis'kraib] *v/t* descrever; **~ption** [~'kripʃən] descrição *f*; **~ptive** [~'kriptiv] descritivo

desegregate [di:'segrigeit] *v/t*, *v/i* abolir a segregação (de)

desert [di'zə:t] *v/t*, *v/i* desertar, abandonar; ['dezət] *s* deserto *m*; **~er** [di'zə:tə] desertor *m*

deserv|e [di'zə:v] *v/t* merecer; **~edly** merecidamente; **~ing** merecedor, digno

design [di'zain] *v/t*, *v/i* plane(j)ar; esboçar, desenhar; *s* desenho m; designio m

designat|e ['dezigneit] v/t designar; ~ion designação f

designer [di'zainə] desenhista m, f

desir|e [di'zaiə] s desejo m; v/t desejar; ~ous desejoso

desk [desk] escrivaninha f, secretária f

desolate ['desəlit] adj desolado; deserto, despovoado; ['-leit] v/t desolar; despovoar

despair [dis'pɛə] s desespero m; v/i desesperar

despatch [dis'pætʃ] s, v/t = dispatch

desperat|e ['despərit] desesperado; ~ion desespero m, desesperação f

despi|cable ['despikəbl] desprezível; ~se [dis'paiz] v/t desprezar, desdenhar

despite [dis'pait] prp a despeito de, apesar de

desponden|cy [dis'pondənsi] desânimo m, abatimento m; ~t desanimado

despot ['despot] déspota m, f; ~ic despótico; ~ism despotismo m

dessert [di'zə:t] sobremesa f

destin|ation [desti'neiʃən] destino m, destinação f; ~ed ['-tind] adj destinado; ~y destino m

destitut|e ['destitju:t] necessitado, desamparado; ~ion [desti'tju:ʃən] indigência f

destroy [dis'trɔi] v/t destruir, destroçar

destruct|ion [dis'trʌkʃən] destruição f; ~ive destrutivo

detach [di'tætʃ] v/t destacar; desligar; separar; ~able separável, destacável; ~ed adj separado; ~ment separação f; destacamento m; desapego m

detail ['di:teil] s pormenor m, detalhe m; in ~ com detalhes, pormenorizadamente

detain [di'tein] v/t deter, reter

detect [di'tekt] v/t descobrir, detectar; ~ion descoberta f; dete(c)dic f; ~ive dete(c)tive m; ~ive story conto m policial

detention [di'tenʃən] detenção f, retenção f

deter [di'tə:] v/t dissuadir

detergent [di'tə:dʒənt] s detergente f

deteriorate [di'tiəriəreit] v/t, v/i deteriorar(-se)

determin|ation [ditə:mi'neiʃən] determinação f; ~e [di'tə:min] v/t determinar; ~ed determinado

detest [di'test] v/t detestar; ~able detestável

detour ['deituə] s desvio m

detract [di'trækt] v/i: ~ from difamar; diminuir; ~or detra(c)tor m

devastat|e ['devəsteit] v/t devastar; ~ing adj devastador

develop [di'veləp] v/t, v/i revelar; desenvolver(-se); ~ment desenvolvimento m; revelação f

deviate ['di:vieit] v/i desviar-se

device [di'vais] dispositivo m; emblema m; meio m, expediente m

devil ['devl] diabo *m*, demónio *m*

devise [di'vaiz] *v/t* idear, inventar

devoid [di'vɔid] falto, desprovido

devolve [di'vɔlv] **(on)** *v/i* transferir; recair (em)

devotion [di'vəuʃən] devoção *f*

devour [di'vauə] *v/t* devorar

devout [di'vaut] devoto; sincero, ardente

dew [dju:] orvalho *m*; ~y orvalhoso, orvalhado

dexterity [deks'teriti] destreza *f*

diagnose ['daiəgnəuz] *v/t* diagnosticar

dial ['daiəl] *s* disco *m*; mostrador *m*; *v/t* marcar, ligar, *Braz* discar

dialect ['daiəlekt] diale(c)to *m*

dialog(ue) ['daiəlɔg] diálogo *m*

diamond ['daiəmənd] diamante *m*

diaper ['daiəpə] *US* fralda *f*, cueiro *m*

diaphragm ['daiəfræm] diafragma *m*

diary ['daiəri] (*pl* -ries) diário *m*

dice [dais] *v/i* jogar (os) dados; *s* dado *m*

dictat|**e** [dik'teit] *v/t*, *v/i* ditar; *s* ditame *m*; ~**ion** ditado *m*; ~**or** ditador *m*; ~**orship** ditadura *f*

dictionary ['dikʃənri] (*pl* -ries) dicionário *m*

die [dai] *s* matriz *f*; *v/i* morrer; ~ **away** des·vanecer-se; ~ **down** extinguir-se; ~-**hard** intransigente *m*

diet ['daiət] *s* dieta *f*, regime *m*

differ ['difə] *v/i* diferir, divergir; ~**ence** diferença *f*; ~**ent** diferente, distinto

difficult ['difikəlt] difícil; ~**y** (*pl* -ties) dificuldade *f*

diffident ['difidənt] tímido

diffus|**e** [di'fju:z] *v/t*, *v/i* difundir(-se); [-'fju:s] *adj* difuso; ~**ion** [-ʒən] difusão *f*

dig [dig] *v/t*, *v/i* cavar

digest [di'dʒest] *v/t*, *v/i* digerir; ~**ion** digestão *f*; ~**ive** *adj* digestivo

dignit|**ary** ['dignitəri] (*pl* -ries) dignatário *m*; ~**y** dignidade *f*

digress [dai'gres] *v/i* divagar, digressionar; ~**ion** digressão *f*

dike [daik] dique *m*, açude *m*

dilapidated [di'læpideitid] estragado, dilapidado

dilat|**e** [dai'leit] *v/t*, *v/i* dilatar (-se); ~**ion** dilatação *f*; ~**ory** ['dilətəri] lento, dilatório

diligen|**ce** [di'dildʒəns] diligência *f*; ~**t** diligente

dilute [dai'lju:t] *v/t* diluir

dim [dim] *adj* obscuro, escuro, sombrio; indistinto; *v/t*, *v/i* obscurecer, ofuscar

dimension [di'menʃən] dimensão *f*

diminish [di'miniʃ] *v/t*, *v/i* diminuir

diminution [.dimi'nju:ʃən] diminuição *f*

dimple [dimpl] covinha *f*

din [din] *s* estrondo *m*

dine [dain] *v/i* jantar; ~ **out** jantar fora

dingy ['dindʒi] manchado, sujo

dining-**car** ['dainiŋ-ka:] vagão-restaurante *m*, carruagem-restaurante *f*; **~-room** sala *f* de jantar

dinner ['dinə] jantar *m*; almoço *m*

dip [dip] *s* mergulho *m*; declive *m*; *v/t*, *v/i* baixar, mergulhar

diploma [di'pləumə] diploma *m*; **~cy** diplomacia *f*; **~t** ['dipləmæt] diplomata *m*, *f*; **~tic** [-plə'mætik] diplomático

dire ['daiə] extremo; terrível

direct [di'rekt] *adj* dire(c)to; *adv* dire(c)tamente; *v/t* dirigir en-dereçar; **~ion** dire(c)ção *f*; **~ions** intruções *f/pl*; **~or** dire(c)tor *m*; **~ory** (*pl* **-ries**) lista *f* telefónica

dirigible ['diridʒəbl] *adj*, *s* diri-gível *m*

dirt [də:t] sujidade *f*, porcaria *f*; sujeira *f*; **~y** *adj* sujo, imundo, porco; *v/t*, *v/i* sujar(-se)

disab|ility [disə'biliti] (*pl* **-ties**) incapacidade *f*; **~le** [-'eibl] *v/t* incapacitar; mutilar; **~led** *s* mutilado *m*

disadvantage [disəd'va:ntidʒ] desvantagem *f*; **~ous** [disæd-va:n'teidʒəs] desvantajoso

disagree [disə'gri:] *v/i* discor-dar; **~ment** desacordo *m*

disappear [disə'piə] *v/i* desapa-recer, sumir-se; **~ance** desapa-recimento *m*

disappoint [disə'pɔint] *v/i* desapontar; **~ment** desapon-tamento *m*

disapprov|al [disə'pru:vəl] desaprovação *f*; **~ve (of)** *v/i* de-saprovar, reprovar

disarm [dis'ɑ:m] *v/t*, *v/i* desar-mar(-se); **~ament** desarma-mento *m*

disarrange ['disə'reindʒ] *v/t* desarranjar, transtornar

disast|er [di'zɑ:stə] desastre *m*; **~rous** desastroso

disband [dis'bænd] *v/t*, *v/i* de-bandar; *mil* licenciar

disbelie|f ['disbi'li:f] increduli-dade *f*, descrença *f*; **~ve** ['-'li:v] *v/t* descrer, não acreditar

disburse [dis'bə:s] *v/t*, *v/i* de-sembolsar

disc [disk] disco *m*

discern [di'sə:n] *v/t* discernir; **~ing** *adj* discernente; **~ment** discernimento *m*

discharge [dis'tʃɑ:dʒ] *s* descar-ga *f*; despedimento *m*; desem-penho *m*; *v/t*, *v/i* desempe-nhar(-se); descarregar; despe-dir

discipl|e [di'saipl] discípulo *m*; **~ine** ['disiplin] *s* disciplina *f*; *v/t* disciplinar

disclos|e [dis'kləuz] *v/t* revelar, descobrir, desvendar; **~ure** [-ʒə] revelação *f*

discolo(u)r [dis'kʌlə] *v/t*, *v/i* descolorar(-se), desbotar(-se)

discomfort [dis'kʌmfət] des-conforto *m*, incómodo *m*

discompose [diskəm'pəuz] *v/t* descompor

disconcert [diskən'sə:t] *v/t* des-concertar; **~ing** desconcertan-te

disconnect [diskə'nekt] *v/t* des-ligar; **~ed** *adj* desconexo

disconsolate [dis'kɔnsəlit] desconsolado

discontent ['diskən'tent] s descontentamento m; **~ed** adj descontente

discontinue [diskən'tinju:] v/t, v/i descontinuar

discord ['diskɔ:d] discórdia f, discordância f; mus dissonância f; **~ant** discordante; dissonante

discount ['diskaunt] v/t descontar; s desconto m

discourage [dis'kʌridʒ] v/t desanimar, desencorajar; **~ment** desânimo m, desencorajamento m

discover [dis'kʌvə] v/t descobrir; **~er** descobridor m; **~y** (pl **-ries**) descoberta f, descobrimento m

discredit [dis'kredit] s descrédito m; v/t desacreditar; **~able** desonroso

discreet [dis'kri:t] discreto

discretion [-'kreʃən] discrição f

discriminat|e [dis'krimineit] v/i discriminar; **~ion** [-'neiʃən] discriminação f

discuss [dis'kʌs] v/t discutir; **~ion** [-'kʌʃən] discussão f

disdain [dis'dein] s desdém m; v/t desdenhar

disease [di'zi:z] doença f

disembark [disim'ba:k] v/t, v/i desembarcar

disengag|e [disin'geidʒ] v/t, v/i desengatar; desembaraçar(-se); **~ed** livre

disentangle ['disin'tæŋgl] v/t, v/i desemaranhar(-se), desenredar(-se)

disfigure [dis'figə] v/t desfigurar

disgrace [dis'greis] s vergonha f; desgraça f; v/t desonrar; **~ful** vergonhoso, desonroso

disguise [dis'gaiz] v/t disfarçar; s disfarce m

disgust [dis'gʌst] s repugnância f, aversão f; v/t repugnar; **~ing** repugnante; desgostante

dish [diʃ] s prato m

dishearten [dis'ha:tn] v/t desanimar, desalentar

dishes [diʃiz] v/pl louça f

dishevel(l)ed [di'ʃevəld] desgrenhado

dishonest [dis'ɔnist] desonesto; **~y** desonestidade f

dishono(u)r [dis'ɔnə] s desonra f; v/t desonrar; **~able** desonroso

dish-washer ['diʃ,wɔʃə] máquina f de lavar louça

disillusion [disi'lu:ʒən] v/t desiludir; s desilusão f

disinclin|ation [disinkli'neiʃən] aversão f; **~ed** [-'klaind] pouco disposto

disinfectant [disin'fektənt] s desinfe(c)tante m

disinherit ['disin'herit] v/t deserdar

disintegrate [dis'intigreit] v/t, v/i desagregar(-se), desintegrar(-se)

disinterested [dis'intristid] desinteressado

disjointed [dis'dʒɔintid] incoerente

disk [disk] US disco m

dislike [dis'laik] s aversão f, antipatia *f*; *v/t* não gostar de, antipatizar com

dislocat|e ['disləkeit] *v/t* deslocar; **~ion** deslocamento *m*

dismal ['dizməl] lúgubre

dismay [dis'mei] *s* consternação *f*; *v/t* consternar

dismember [dis'membə] *v/t* desmembrar

dismiss [dis'mis] *v/t* demitir; **~al** demissão *f*

dismount [dis'maunt] *v/t, v/i* desmontar; apear(-se)

disobedien|ce [disə'bi:djəns] desobediência *f*; **~t** desobediente

disobey [disə'bei] *v/t, v/i* desobedecer (a)

disorder [dis'ɔ:də] *s* desarranjo *m*; desordem *f*; *v/t* desordenar; desarranjar; **~ly** desordenado; turbulento

disown [dis'əun] *v/t(re)negar

disparage [dis'pæridʒ] *v/t* amesquinhar

dispar|ate ['dispərit] desigual, díspar; **~ity** [-'pæriti] disparidade *f*

dispatch [dis'pætʃ] *v/t* despachar expedir

dispel [dis'pel] *v/t* dissipar, dispersar

dispensable [dis'pensəbl] dispensável

dispense [dis'pens] *v/t* distribuir, repartir; dispensar

disperse [dis'pə:s] *v/t, v/i* dispersar(-se)

displace [dis'pleis] *v/t* deslocar; desalojar

display [dis'plei] *v/t* exibir, ex-

por, ostentar; *s* exibição *f*, exposição *f*, ostentação *f*

displeas|e [dis'pli:z] *v/t* desagradar; **~ing** desagradável; **~ure** [-'pleʒə] descontentamento *m*, desagrado *m*

dispos|al [dis'pəuzəl] disposição *f*; **~e** *v/t* dispor; **~e of** desfazer-se de; dispor de

disposition [dispə'ziʃən] disposição *f*; gênio *m*, índole *f*

disproof [dis'pru:f] refutação *f*

disproportionate [disprə'pɔ:-ʃnit] desproporcionado

disprove [dis'pru:v] *v/t* refutar

dispute [dis'pju:t] *s* disputa *f*; *v/t, v/i* disputar

disqualif|ication [dis,kwɔlifi-'keiʃən] desqualificação *f*; **~y** [-'---fai] *v/t* desqualificar, desclassificar

disquiet [dis'kwaiət] *v/t* inquietar; *s* inquietude *f*

disregard ['disri'gɑ:d] *s* descuido *m*, negligência *f*; *v/t* desdenhar; desatender, ignorar

disreput|able [dis'repjutəbl] desonroso, desacreditado; **~e** ['-ri'pju:t] descrédito *m*, má reputação *f*

disrespectful [disris'pektful] desrespeitoso, irreverente

dissatisf|action ['disætis'fæk-ʃən] descontentamento *m*; **~ied** ['-'sætisfaid] descontente

dissect [di'sekt] *v/t* dissecar; **~ion** dissecação *f*

dissension [di'senʃən] dissensão *f*

dissent [di'sent] *s* dissentimento *m*, dissidência *f*; *v/i* dissentir,

divergir; **~ing** dissidente
dissimilar ['di'similə] dissimilar; dissemelhante
dissipat|e ['disipeit] v/t, v/i dissipar(-se); **~ion** dissipação f
dissociate [di'səuʃieit] v/t dissociar
dissolut|e ['disəlu:t] dissoluto; **~ion** dissolução f
dissolve [di'zɔlv] v/t, v/i dissolver(-se)
dissua|de [di'sweid] v/t dissuadir; **~sive** dissuasivo
distance ['distəns] s distância f; **at a ~** à distância, de longe; **in the ~** ao longe
distant ['distənt] distante
distaste ['dis'teist] aversão f, desgosto m
distend [dis'tend] v/t, v/i distender(-se)
distiller [dis'tilər] destilador m; **~y** (pl **-ries**) destilaria f
distinct [dis'tiŋkt] claro, distinto; **~ion** distinção f; **~ive** distintivo
distinguish [dis'tiŋgwiʃ] v/t, v/i distinguir(-se); discernir; **~ed** adj distinto, notável
distort [dis'tɔ:t] v/t deformar, deturpar; (dis)torcer; **~ion** deformação f, distorção f
distract [dis'trækt] v/t distrair; perturbar; **~ed** adj distraído; perturbado; **~ion** distra(c)ção f; perturbação f
distress [dis'tres] s aflição f, pesar m; v/t afligir, desolar; **~ing** aflitivo
distribut|e [dis'tribju(:)t] v/t distribuir, repartir; **~ion**

[-bju:ʃən] distribuição f; **~or** distribuidor m
district ['distrikt] distrito m; comarca f
distrust [dis'trʌst] s desconfiança f; v/t desconfiar; **~ful** desconfiado
disturb [dis'tə:b] v/t perturbar, incomodar, inquietar; **~ance** perturbação f, distúrbio m
disuni|on [dis'ju:njən] desunião f; **~te** [-'nait] v/t, v/i desunir(-se)
disus|e [dis'ju:s] s desuso m; **~ed** desusado
ditch [ditʃ] s fosso m, vala f, rego m
ditty ['diti] (pl **-ties**) cançoneta f
div|e [daiv] v/i mergulhar; s mergulho m; **~er** mergulhador m
diverse [dai'və:s] diverso
diversion [dai'və:ʃən] desvio m; diversão f, divertimento m
diversity [dai'və:siti] diversidade f
divert [dai'və:t] v/t desviar; divertir
divide [di'vaid] v/t, v/i dividir(-se)
dividend ['dividend] dividendo m
divin|e [di'vain] adj divino; v/t, v/i adivinhar; **~ity** [-'viniti] divindade f; teologia f
division [di'viʒən] divisão f
divorce [di'vɔ:s] s divórcio m; v/t, v/i divorciar(-se)
dizz|iness ['dizinis] vertigem f; **~y** adj tonto, vertiginoso
do [du:] v/t, v/i fazer; executar;

cumprir; cozer, passar; bastar, ser suficiente; arranjar; ~ **away with** abolir, pôr de parte; **how ~ you ~?** como está? ~ **without** passar sem

docil|e ['dəusail] dócil; **~ity** [dəu'siliti] dǔcılıdade f

dock [dɔk] s *jur* teia f; doca f; v/t cortar, encurtar; v/t, v/i (**at**) entrar em doca; **~er** estivador m; **~yard** estaleiro m

doctor ['dɔktə] s médico m; doutor m; v/t medicar; **~ate** doutorado m

doctrine ['dɔktrin] doutrina f

document ['dɔkjumənt] s documento m; **~ary** s documentário m

dodge [dɔdʒ] v/t, v/i esquivar-se; s evasiva f, trapaça f

doe [dəu] corça f; gama f

dog [dɔg] s cão m, cachorro m; ~ **days** canícula f; **~ged** pertinaz

doings ['du(:)iŋz] s/pl feitos m/pl, acontecimentos m/pl

dole [dəul] s donativo m, doação f; **go/be on the ~** receber subsídio de desemprego; ~ **out** racionar, aquinhoar; **~ful** triste, sombrio

doll [dɔl] boneca f

dollar ['dɔlə] dólar m

dolphin ['dɔlfin] delfim m, golfinho m

dome [dəum] cúpula f

domestic [də'mestik] adj doméstico

domicile ['dɔmisail] s domicílio m

domin|ant ['dɔminənt] adj dominante; **~ate** v/t, v/i domi-

nar; **~ation** [-'neiʃən] dominação f; **~eer** [-'niə] v/i tiranizar, dominar; **~eering** dominante, tirânico

donat|e [dəu'neit] v/t, v/i doar; **~ion** doaçǎo f

done [dʌn] acabado, feito; pronto, assado, cozido

donkey ['dɔŋki] burro m

donor ['dəunə] doador m

doom [du:m] s destino m; ruína f, morte f; v/t condenar; ~-**sday** dia m do Juízo Final

door [dɔ:] porta f; **out of ~s** fora de casa, ao ar livre

door|-keeper ['dɔ:ki:pə] porteiro m; **~way** vão m, soleira f

dope [dəup] s fam estupefaciente m; v/t dopar

dormant ['dɔ:mənt] latente, ina(c)tivo

dose [dəus] s dose f; v/t dosar

dot [dɔt] s ponto m; v/t pontuar, pôr pontos em; **on the ~** em ponto, pontual

dotage ['dəutidʒ] senilidade f, segunda infância f

dote [dəut] v/t: ~ (**up)on** ser/estar doido por

double ['dʌbl] adj dobro, duplo; s sósia f; dobro m; v/t, v/i dobrar; duplicar; adv aos pares, duplicadamente; **~-decker** autocarro m de dois pisos; **~ (-bedded) room** quarto m de casal

doubt [daut] v/t duvidar; s dúvida f; **~ful** duvidoso; **~less** sem dúvida

douche [du:ʃ] chuveiro m, duche m

dough [dəu] massa f

dove [dʌv] s pombo m; ~**cot(e)**
pombal m; ~**tail** s malhete m;
v/t, v/i malhetar

down [daun] adj descendente;
desanimado; baixo; adv em
baixo, abaixo, para baixo; no
chão, por terra; prp em baixo,
por ... abaixo; ~ **payment** f,
buço m; v/t abater; pousar;
~**cast** cabisbaixo; baixo;
~**fall** queda f, ruína f;
~**hearted** abatido, desanimado; ~**hill** adv pela encosta
abaixo; em declínio; ~**pour**
aguaceiro m, carga f de água;
~**right** adv completamente;
adj direito, dire(c)to; completo;
~**stairs** adv lá em baixo; para
baixo; s rés-do-chão m; adj de
baixo; ~**stream** rio abaixo;
~**ward(s)** para baixo

dowry ['dauəri] (pl -ries) dote m

doze [dəuz] s soneca f; v/i dormitar

dozen ['dʌzn] dúzia f

drab [dræb] adj monótono

draft [drɑːft] s esboço m, rascunho m; v/t esboçar, rascunhar;
~**sman** desenhador m

drag [dræg] s draga f; v/t, v/i ar-
rastar(-se); dragar

dragon ['drægən] dragão m;
~**fly** libelinha f, libélula f

drain [drein] v/t, v/i drenar; es-
coar(-se), escorrer; s vazadouro
m, dreno m; ~**age** drenagem f,
escoamento m

drama ['drɑːmə] drama m; ~**tic**
[drəˈmætik] dramático; ~**tist**
['dræmətist] dramaturgo m

draper ['dreipə] negociante m de
panos

draught [drɑːft] = US **draft**
corrente f de ar; naut calado m;
trago m, gole m; ~**s** damas
f/pl; ~**sman** desenhador m;
~y cheio de correntes de ar

draw [drɔː] s empate m; extra(c)-
ção f; tiragem f; atra(c)ção f;
v/t, v/i atrair; empatar; levantar; puxar; tirar; extrair; estirar; traçar, desenhar; ~ **the
curtain** correr a cortina; ~
away afastar(-se); ~**back** s desvantagem f, inconveniente m;
~**bridge** ponte f levadiça

drawer [drɔːə] gaveta f

drawing [drɔːiŋ] desenho m

dread [dred] s pavor m; v/t temer, recear; ~**ful** pavoroso,
horrível

dream [driːm] v/t, v/i sonhar; s
sonho m; ~y sonhador

dreary ['driəri] aborrecido;
triste, monótono

dredge [dredʒ] v/t, v/i dragar

dregs [dregz] s/pl fezes f/pl, sedimento m; escória f, ralé f

drench [drentʃ] v/t encharcar,
ensopar

dress [dres] s vestido m; roupa f,
indumentária f, traje m; v/t,
v/i vestir(-se); ~ **circle** primeiro balcão m

dressing ['dresiŋ] curativo m;
tempero m, condimento m;
~**-gown** robe m, roupão m;
~**-table** toucador m, Braz pen-
teadeira f

dressmaker ['dresmeikə] costu-
reira f, modista f

dress rehearsal ['dres.ri'hə:səl] *theat* ensaio *m* geral

drift [drift] *s* dire(c)ção *f*, rumo *m*, tendência *f*; *v/t, v/i* ir à deriva; amontoar(-se); flutuar

drill [dril] *s* broca *f*; semeador *m*; cxereicio *m*, dril *m*; brim *m*; *v/t, v/i* brocar; perfurar; exercitar

drink [drɪŋk] *v/t, v/i* beber; *s* bebida *f*

drip [drip] *s* gotejamento *m*, gotejar *m*; goteira *f*; *v/i* gotejar, pingar; **~ping** gordura *f* de assado

driv|e [draiv] *s* passeio *m* de carro; *fig* iniciativa *f*, estrada *f*, caminho *m*; impulso *m*; *v/t, v/i* dirigir, guiar, conduzir; impelir; levar de carro; **~e at** insinuar; **~er** motorista *m*, condutor *m*, chofer *m*; **~er's licence** carta *f* de condução, *Braz* carta *f* de motorista; **~ing** condução *f*

drizzle ['drizl] *s* chuvisco *m*; *v/i* chuviscar

droll [drəul] cómico, engraçado, divertido

droop [dru:p] *v/i* inclinar-se, descair, pender

drop [drɔp] *v/t, v/i* baixar; pingar; (deixar) cair; *s* gota *f*, pingo *m*; queda *f*; baixa *f*; rebuçado *m*; **~ someone a line** escrever umas linhas a alguém

drought [draut] seca *f*

drown [draun] *v/t, v/i* afogar (-se)

drowsy ['drauzi] amodorrado, sonolento

drug [drʌg] *s* droga *f*; *v/t* drogar

(-se); **~gist** *US* droguista *m, f*, farmacêutico *m*; **~store** *US* farmácia *f*, drogaria *f*

drum [drʌm] *s* tambor *m*; *mec* cilindro *m*; *v/t, v/i* tamborilar; tocar tambor

drunk [drʌŋk] *adj, s* bêbedo *m*; **~ard** bêbedo *m*, ébrio *m*; **~enness** bebedeira *f*, embriaguez *f*

dry [drai] *adj* seco; enxuto; *v/t, v/i* secar(-se), enxugar; **~-clean** *v/t* limpar a seco; **~-cleaning** limpeza *f* a seco; **~-dock** doca *f* seca; **~ness** secura *f*, aridez *f*

dubious ['dju:bjəs] dúbio

duchess ['dʌtʃis] duquesa *f*

duck [dʌk] *s* pato *m*, pata *f*; brim *m*; *v/t, v/i* desviar(-se); esquivar(-se), abaixar(-se); **~ling** patinho *m*

ductile ['dʌktail] dúctil

due [dju:] *adj* devido; próprio, conveniente; *com* vencido; *s* devido *m*; **in ~ course/time** na devida altura, a seu tempo; **~ to** devido a

duel ['dju(:)əl] *s* duelo *m*; *v/i* (:) bater-se em duelo

duke [dju:k] duque *m*

dull [dʌl] *v/t, v/i* entorpecer, embotar; *adj* sombrio, carregado; embotado; tapado, obtuso; triste; escuro; **~ness** estupidez *f*; monotonia *f*; marasmo *m*

dumb [dʌm] mudo; **~found** *v/t* emudecer, confundir; **~ness** mudez *f*

dummy ['dʌmi] *s* (*pl* -mies) manequim *m*; pateta *m, f*; testa *f* de ferro; chupeta f

dump [dʌmp] s entulheira f, lixeira f; paiol m; v/t, v/i despejar, descarregar

dumpling ['dʌmpliŋ] pudim m

dunce [dʌns] estúpido m, ignorante m

dung [dʌŋ] bosta f; estrume m, esterco m

dungeon ['dʌndʒən] calabouço m, enxovia f

dung-hill ['dʌŋhill] monturo m

dupe [dju:p] v/t lograr, burlar; s joguete m

duplicate ['dju:plikit] v/t duplicar; s adj duplicado m

durab|**ility** [,djuərə'biliti] durabilidade f; **~le** durável

duration [djuə'reiʃən] duração f

during ['djuəriŋ] durante

dusk [dʌsk] crepúsculo m, entardecer m, anoitecer m; **~y** moreno, trigueiro; escuro, sombrio

dust [dʌst] s poeira f, pó m; v/t limpar o pó de, espanar; **~bin** caixote m do lixo; **~er** espanador m, pano m do pó; **~y** empoeirado, poeirento

Dutch [dʌtʃ] adj, s holandês m, neerlandês m

dutiable ['dju:tjəbl] sujeito a direitos alfandegários

dutiful ['dju:tiful] obediente, respeitador

duty ['dju:ti] (pl -ties) dever m; imposto m; direitos m/pl alfandegários; **be on ~** estar de serviço; **be off ~** estar de folga; **do one's ~** cumprir o seu dever; **~-free** isento de direitos

dwarf [dwɔ:f] v/t enfezar; s anão m

dwell [dwel] v/i residir; **~er** habitante m, f, residente m, f; **~ing** habitação f, residência f, domicilio m

dwindle ['dwindl] v/i definhar, diminuir

dye [dai] s tintura f, tinta; v/t, v/i tingir(-se); **~ing** tinturaria f; **~r** tintureiro m

dynam|**ic** [dai'næmik] dinâmico; **~ics** dinâmica f

dynamite ['dainəmait] dinamite f

dynamo ['dainəməu] dínamo m

dynasty ['dinəsti] (pl -ties) dinastia f

dysentery ['disntri] disenteria f

dyspepsia [dis'pepsiə] dispepsia f

E

each [i:tʃ] adj cada; pron cada um; **~ one** cada um; **~ other** mutuamente, um ao outro

eager ['i:gə] ávido, ansioso; impaciente; **~ness** avidez f, ânsia f

eagle ['i:gl] águia f; **~t** filhote m de águia, aguieta f

ear [iə] orelha f; ouvido m; bot espiga f; **~drum** tímpano m

earl [ə:l] conde m

early ['ə:li] adv cedo; adj anteci-

pado, adiantado; temporão
earn [əːn] v/t ganhar; merecer
earnest ['əːnist] s seriedade f;
adj sincero, sério
earnings ['əːniŋz] s/pl salário
m; lucro m
ear-ring ['iəriŋ] brinco m
earth [əːθ] s terra f; mundo
m; solo m; **~enware** adj
de barro; **~** f de barro;
~ly terrestre, terreno; possível; **~quake** terremoto m;
~worm minhoca f
ease [iːz] s sossego m; facilidade
f; bem-estar m; v/t, v/i aliviar,
afrouxar; facilitar; **at ~** à vontade; **stand at ~** mil descansar
easel ['iːzl] cavalete m
east [iːst] s este m, oriente m; adj
oriental, de leste; **~ward(s)** a
leste, para o leste
Easter ['iːstə] Páscoa f
eastern ['iːstən] oriental
easy ['iːzi] adj fácil; agradável;
tranquilo; **take it ~**! calma!,
não se incomode!
easy chair ['iːziˈtʃeə] poltrona f
eat [iːt] v/t, v/i comer; **~ away**
corroer; **~ up** devorar; acabar
de comer, comer tudo; **~able**
adj comestível
eatables ['iːtəblz] s/pl comestí-
veis m/pl
eating-house ['iːtiŋhaus] casa f
de pasto
eaves [iːvz] s/pl beiral m, goteira
f
ebb [eb] s baixa-mar f, vazante f;
refluxo m; v/i baixar, vazar;
~ and flow fluxo m e refluxo m
ebony ['ebəni] s ébano m; adj de
f

ébano
eccentric [ikˈsentrik] excêntrico; **~ity** [ˈtrisiti] excentricidade f
ecclesiastical [iˌkliːziˈæstikəl]
eclesiástico
echo ['ekəu] s eco m; v/t, v/i
ecoar
eclipse [iˈklips] s eclipse m; v/t
eclipsar
econom|ic [iːkəˈnɔmik] econó-
mico; **~ical** económico, poupado; **~ics** economia f
econom|ist [iˈkɔnəmist] econo-
mista m; **~ize** v/i economizar; **~y** (pl -**mies**) economia f,
frugalidade f
ecstasy ['ekstəsi] (pl -**sies**) êxtase m; arrebatamento m
eddy ['edi] (pl -**dies**) s re(de-)
moinho m; v/t redemoinhar
edge [edʒ] s borda f, margem f;
v/t aguçar; deslocar
edge|ways ['edʒweiz], **~wise** de
lado
edifice ['edifis] edifício m, prédio m
edify ['edifai] v/t edificar
edit ['edit] v/t editar; **~ion** [i-
ˈdiʃən] edição f
editor ['editə] editor m; reda(c)-
tor m; **~ial** [-'tɔːriəl] s artigo m
de fundo; adj editorial
educat|e ['edju:(ɔ)keit] v/t edu-
car, instruir; **~ion** [-'keiʃən]
educação f, instrução f
eel [iːl] enguia f
efface [iˈfeis] v/t apagar
effect [iˈfekt] v/t efetuar; s
efeito m, resultado m; **in ~**
com efeito; **~ive** efe(c)tivo

effeminate [i'femineit] efeminado

effervescent [,efə'vesnt] efervescente

efficien|cy [i'fiʃənsi] eficiência f, eficácia f; **~t** eficiente, eficaz

effort ['efət] esforço m

effus|ion [i'fjuːʒən] efusão f; **~ive** efusivo

e. g. ['iːˈdʒiː] = **exempli gratia** por exemplo

egg [eg] s ovo m; **fried** ~ ovo estrelado; **hard-boiled** ~ ovo cozido; **soft-boiled** ~ ovo meio cozido; **~plant** berinjela f; **~shell** casca f de ovo

egotism ['egəutizəm] egoísmo m

Egyptian [i'dʒipʃən] adj, s egípcio m

eider-down ['aidədaun] edredão m

eight [eit] oito; **~een** dezoito; **~h** [-θ] oitavo; **~ hundred** oitocentos; **~y** oitenta

either ['aiðə] adj, pron um ou outro; um dos dois; ambos; conj ou; também não, tão-pouco; **~ ... or** ou ... ou, quer ... quer

ejaculate [i'dʒækjuleit] v/t ejacular

eject [i(:)'dʒekt] v/t lançar, expulsar, eje(c)tar

eke [iːk] **out** v/t remediar, suprir

elaborate [i'læbərit] adj elaborado; [-bəreit] v/t elaborar

elapse [i'læps] v/i passar, decorrer

elasti|c [i'læstik] s, adj elástico

m; **~city** [-'tisiti] elasticidade f

elated [i'leitid] adj inchado, orgulhoso

elbow ['elbəu] s cotovelo m; v/t acotovelar

elder ['eldə] adj mais velho, mais idoso; s bot sabugueiro m; ancião m; primogénito m

eldest ['eldist] adj, s o mais velho

elect [i'lekt] adj eleito; escolhido; v/t eleger; **~ion** eleição f; **~or** eleitor m; **~oral** eleitoral; **~orate** eleitorado m

electri|c [i'lektrik] elé(c)trico; **~cal** elé(c)trico; **~cian** [-'triʃən] ele(c)tricista m; **~city** [-'trisiti] ele(c)tricidade f; **~fy** [-fai] v/t ele(c)trificar

electrocut|e [i'lektrəkjuːt] v/t ele(c)trocutar; **~ion** ele(c)trocução f

electron [i'lektrən] ele(c)trão m; **~ic** ele(c)trónico

elegan|ce ['eligəns] elegância f; **~t** elegante

element ['elimənt] elemento m; **~ary** [-'mentəri] elementar

elephant ['elifənt] elefante m

elevat|e ['eliveit] v/t elevar; exaltar; **~ion** elevação f; altura f; **~or** elevador m, ascensor m

eleven [i'levn] onze; **at the ~th hour** no último momento, à última hora

elf [elf] (pl elves) duende m

eligible ['elidʒəbl] elegível

eliminat|e [i'limineit] v/t eliminar; **~ion** [-'neiʃən] eliminação f

elk [elk] alce m

elm [elm] olmo m

elocution [ˌelə'kjuːʃən] elocução f

elongate ['iːlɒŋgeit] v/t, v/i alongar(-se)

elope [i'ləup] v/i fugir de casa com amante ou namorado

eloquence ['eləkwəns] eloquência f; ~t eloquente

else [els] adv mais; **anybody** ~? mais alguém?; **anything** ~? mais alguma coisa?; **nobody** ~ mais ninguém; **nothing** ~ nada mais; **or** ~ ou então, quando não; **somebody** ~ alguém mais; **what** ~? que mais? **who** ~? quem mais?

elsewhere [els'weə] noutro lugar, noutro lado

elu|de [i'luːd] v/t eludir, evitar; escapar; ~sive esquivo, elusivo

emaciate [i'meiʃieit] v/t emaciar

emancipate [i'mænsipeit] v/t emancipar

embalm [im'bɑːm] v/t embalsamar

embankment [im'bæŋkmənt] represa f

embark [im'bɑːk] v/t, v/i embarcar(-se)

embarrass [im'bærəs] v/t embaraçar; ~ing embaraçoso; ~ment embaraço m

embassy ['embəsi] (pl -sies) embaixada f

embed [im'bed] v/t embutir

embellish [im'beliʃ] v/t embelecer, enfeitar

embers ['embəz] s/pl brasas f/pl

embezzle [im'bezl] v/t desfalcar; ~ment desfalque m

embitter [im'bitə] v/t amargurar

emblem ['embləm] emblema m

embod|iment [im'bɒdimənt] incorporação f; ~y v/t incorporar; encarnar

embolden [im'bəuldən] v/t encorajar, animar

embrace [im'breis] v/t, v/i abraçar(-se); abranger; s abraço m

embroider [im'brɔidə] v/t bordar; ~y bordado m

emerald ['emərəld] s esmeralda f

emerge [i'məːdʒ] v/i emergir, aparecer; ~ency [i'məːdʒənsi] (pl -cies) emergência f

emetic [i'metik] adj emético

emigra|nt ['emigrənt] emigrante; ~te [-greit] v/i emigrar; ~tion emigração f

eminen|ce ['eminəns] eminência f; ~t eminente

emissary ['emisəri] (pl -ries) emissário m

emit [i'mit] v/t emitir

emotion [i'məuʃən] emoção f; ~al emocional

emperor ['empərə] imperador m

empha|sis ['emfəsis] ênfase f; ~size v/t dar ênfase a, acentuar; ~tic [im'fætik] enfático

empire ['empaiə] império m

employ [im'plɔi] v/t empregar; ~ee [.emplɔi'iː] empregado m; ~er patrão m, Braz empregador m; ~ment emprego m

empress ['empris] imperatriz f

emp|tiness ['emptinis] vazio m, vácuo m; **~ty** adj vazio; v/t, v/i esvaziar(-se)

enable [i'neibl] v/t habilitar, capacitar

enact [i'nækt] v/t decretar, promulgar; desempenhar

enamel [i'næməl] s esmalte m; v/t esmaltar

enamo(u)red [i'næməd] adj enamorado

encase [in'keis] v/t encaixar

enchain [in'tʃein] v/t encadear, acorrentar

enchant [in'tʃɑːnt] v/t encantar; enfeitiçar; **~ing** encantador; **~ment** feitiço m, encanto m; **~ress** feiticeira f

encircle [in'səːkl] v/t cercar, rodear

enclos|e [in'kləuz] v/t cercar, murar; juntar, incluir; **~ure** [-ʒə] cerca f; anexo m; clausura f

encore [ɔŋ'kɔː] int bis!; v/t bisar; s bis m

encounter [in'kauntə] v/t encontrar; s encontro m, recontro m

encourage [in'kʌridʒ] v/t encorajar, animar; **~ment** encorajamento m

encroach [in'krəutʃ]: **~ on** v/t invadir, usurpar; avançar

encrust [in'krʌst] v/t incrustar

encumb|er [in'kʌmbə] v/t estorvar, embaraçar; **~rance** estorvo m, empecilho m

end [end] s fim m; cabo m, extremidade f; termo m; v/t, v/i acabar, terminar, concluir; **in the**

~ afinal; no fim de contas; **no ~ of** muito; **on ~** sem fim; **put an ~ to** pôr termo a

endanger [in'deindʒə] v/t pôr em perigo, arriscar

endear [in'diə] (**to**) v/t encarecer, fazer estimar; **~ment** meiguice f, ternura f

endeavo(u)r [in'devə] s esforço m, empenho m; v/i esforçar-se, tentar

ending ['endiŋ] s fim m, conclusão f

endless ['endlis] sem fim, infinito, interminável

endorse [in'dɔːs] v/t endossar; **~ment** endosso m

endow [in'dau] v/t dotar, doar; **~ment** doação f; dote m

endur|able [in'djuərəbl] suportável, tolerável; **~ance** resistência f; **~e** v/t aguentar, suportar, tolerar

enemy ['enimi] (pl -mies) inimigo m

energ|etic [enə'dʒetik] enérgico; **~y** [-dʒi] (pl -gies) energia f

enervate ['enəːveit] v/t debilitar, enfraquecer

enfeeble [in'fiːbl] v/t enfraquecer

enfold [in'fəuld] v/t envolver, abraçar

enforce [in'fɔːs] v/t forçar, obrigar, compelir; fazer cumprir

enfranchise [in'fræntʃaiz] v/t franquear, dar o direito de votar

engage [in'geidʒ] v/t, v/i ocupar(se); engatar; contratar, empregar; **~d** ocupado; engatado; impedido; noivo; **~ment** noivado *m*;

engine ['endʒin] motor *m*; locomotiva *f*

engineer [ˌendʒi'niə] *s* engenheiro *m*; mecânico *m*; maquinista *m*; *v/t* engendrar; construir; **~ing** *s* engenharia *f*

English ['ingliʃ] *adj*, *s* inglês *m*; **~man** (*pl* **-men**) inglês *m*

engrav|e [in'greiv] *v/t* gravar; **~er** gravador *m*; **~ing** *s* gravação *f*; gravura *f*

engross [in'grəus] *v/t* absorver, ocupar; tirar pública-forma

enhance [in'hɑːns] *v/t* encarecer; realçar

enigma [i'nigmə] enigma *m*; **~tic** [ˌenig'mætik] enigmático *m*

enjoy [in'dʒɔi] *v/t* gozar (de), desfrutar, apreciar, ter prazer em; **~ oneself** divertir-se; **~able** agradável, divertido; **~ment** gozo *m*, prazer *m*

enlarge [in'lɑːdʒ] *v/t*, *v/i* aumentar; alargar(-se); dilatar; ampliar; **~ment** aumento *m*; ampliação *f*

enlighten [in'laitn] *v/t* esclarecer

enlist [in'list] *v/t*, *v/i* alistar(-se)

enliven [in'laivn] *v/t* animar

enmity ['enmiti] inimizade *f*

enorm|ity [i'nɔːmiti] enormidade *f*; **~ous** enorme

enough [i'nʌf] *adj* bastante; *adv* suficientemente; bastante

enrage [in'reidʒ] *v/t* enraivecer

enrapture [in'ræptʃə] *v/t* encantar, arrebatar

enrich [in'ritʃ] *v/t* enriquecer

enrol(l) [in'rəul] *v/t*, *v/i* alistar-se; matricular(-se); inscrever (-se)

ensign ['ensain] pavilhão *m*, bandeira *f*

enslave [in'sleiv] *v/t* escravizar

ensue [in'sjuː] *v/i* seguir(-se)

ensure [in'ʃuə] *v/t* assegurar

entangle [in'tæŋgl] *v/t* emaranhar

enter ['entə] *v/t*, *v/i* entrar (em, para); dar entrada (em)

enterprise ['entəpraiz] empresa *f*; espírito *m* empreendedor; empreendimento *m*

entertain [ˌentə'tein] *v/t*, *v/i* receber, hospedar; divertir, entreter; **~ing** *adj* divertido; **~ment** entretenimento *m*, diversão *f*; hospedagem *f*

enthusias|m [in'θjuːziæzəm] entusiasmo *m*; **~t** [-æst] entusiasta *m*, *f*; **~tic** [-'æstik] entusiástico, entusiasmado

entic|e [in'tais] *v/t* atrair, seduzir, tentar; **~ing** *adj* sedutor, tentador

entire [in'taiə] completo, inteiro

entitle [in'taitl] *v/t* intitular; dar direito a

entrails ['entreilz] *s/pl* entranhas *f/pl*, tripas *f/pl*

entrance [in'trɑːns] *v/t* extasiar, arrebatar; ['entrəns] *s* entrada *f*; admissão *f*, ingresso *m*; **~ fee** jóia *f*

entreat [in'triːt] *v/t*, *v/i* suplicar

entrust [in'trʌst] *v/t* confiar

entry ['entri] (*pl* **-ries**) entrada *f*; acesso *m*; lançamento *m*, re-

gisto *m*; inscrição *f*
enumerate [i'nju:məreit] *v/t*
enumerar
envelop [in'veləp] *v/t* envolver;
~**e** ['envələup] envelope *m*, sobrescrito *m*
envi|able ['enviəbl] invejável;
~**ous** invejoso
environment [in'vaiərənmənt]
meio *m*, ambiente *m*
envoy ['envɔi] enviado *m*
envy ['envi] *v/t* invejar; *s* inveja *f*
epidemic [epi'demik] *s* epidemia *f*; *adj* epidémico
epilepsy ['epilepsi] epilepsia *f*
episode ['episəud] episódio *m*
epitaph ['epita:f] epitáfio *m*
epoch ['i:pɔk] época *f*
equal ['i:kwəl] *adj* igual; *v/t*
igualar; *s* igual *m*, *f*, par *m*; ~
to the occasion à altura das
circunstâncias; ~**ity** [i(:)'kwɔl-
iti] igualdade *f*
equanimity [.ekwə'nimiti]
equanimidade *f*
equation [i'kweiʒən] equação *f*
equator [i'kweitə] equador *m*
equilibrium [i:kwi'libriəm]
equilíbrio *m*
equip [i'kwip] *v/t* equipar, apresta; ~**ment** equipamento *m*
equitable ['ekwitəbl] equitativo
equivalent [i'kwivələnt] *adj*, *s*
equivalente *m*
equivoca|l [i'kwivəkəl] equívoco; ~**te** [-keit] *v/i* equivocar-se
era ['iərə] era *f*
eras|e [i'reiz] *v/t* apagar, safar;
~**er** *US* borracha *f*
erect [i'rekt] *adj* levantado, ere-
(c)to; *v/t* erigir

erection [i'rekʃən] ere(c)ção *f*;
montagem *f*
ermine ['ə:min] arminho *m*
err [ə:] *v/i* errar
errand ['erənd] recado *m*, mandado *m*
erratic [i'rætik] errático; irregular
error ['erə] erro *m*
eruption [i'rʌpʃən] erupção *f*
erysipelas [.eri'sipiləs] erisipela *f*
escalator ['eskəleitə] escada *f* rolante
escape [is'keip] *v/t*, *v/i* escapar
(-se); *s* fuga *f*, evasão *f*; escape *m*
escort [esko:t] *s* escolta *f*;
[is'ko:t] *v/t* escoltar
espionage [.espiə'na:ʒ] espionagem *f*
Esquire (Esq.) [is'kwaiə] Exmo.
Sr.
essay ['esei] *s* ensaio *m*; ~**ist** ensaísta *m*
essence ['esns] essência *f*
essential [i'senʃəl] essencial
establish [is'tæbliʃ] *v/t* estabelecer; instalar; ~**ment** estabelecimento *m*; instalação *f*
estate [is'teit] bens *m/pl*, propriedade *f*; quinta *f*, fazenda *f*
esteem [is'ti:m] *s* estima *f*; *v/t* estimar
estima|ble ['estiməbl] estimável; ~**te** [-meit] *s* estimativa *f*,
avaliação *f*; *v/t* avaliar; ~**tion**
avaliação *f*
estrange [is'treindʒ] *v/t* apartar,
alienar
etch [etʃ] *v/t* gravar com água
forte

etern|al [i'tə:nl] eterno; **~ity** (pl **-ties**) eternidade f

ether ['i:θə] éter m

ethics ['eθiks] ética f

European [ˌjuərə'piən] adj, seu ropeu m

evacuate [i'vækjueit] v/t eva cuar

evade [i'veid] v/t evitar, evadir (-se)

evaporat|e [i'væpəreit] v/t, v/i evaporar(-se); **~ion** evapo ração f

evasive [i'veisiv] evasivo

eve [i:v] vigília f, véspera f; **on the ~ of** na véspera de

even ['i:vən] adj plano; regular; uniforme, par; empatado; adv mesmo, até, ainda, **be/get ~ with** estar/ficar quite com; **~ if / ~ though** mesmo que, ain da que; **~ so/then** mesmo as sim/então; **not ~** nem sequer

evening ['i:vniŋ] noitinha f, tar de f, tardinha f; **~ dress** traje m de cerimônia

event [i'vent] acontecimento m, evento m; **at all ~s** em todo o caso, seja como for

eventful [i'ventful] acidentado, cheio de acontecimentos, me morável

eventual|ity [i,ventju'æliti] (pl **-ties**) eventualidade f; **~ly** [i'ventjuəli] com o tempo, final mente

ever ['evə] sempre; já, alguma vez; **~ since** desde então; **for ~** para sempre; **for ~ and ~** para todo o sempre; **hardly ~** quase nunca

every ['evri] todo, cada; **~ now and then** de quando em quan do; **~ other day** dia sim, dia não; **~body, ~one** toda a gen te, Braz todo o mundo; todos; **~thing** tudo; **~where** por em toda a parte

eviden|ce ['evidəns] s evidência f; prova f, testemunho m; **give ~ce** dar testemunho; **~t** evi dente

evil [i:vl] adj mau, malvado; s mal m, pecado m; **~doer** mal feitor m

evince [i'vins] v/t evidenciar, de monstrar

evoke [i'vouk] v/t evocar

evolution [ˌi:və'lu:ʃən] evo lução f

ewe ['ju:] ovelha f

exact [ig'zækt] v/t exigir; extor quir; adj exa(c)to, preciso; **~i tude, ~ness** exa(c)tidão f

exaggerat|e [ig'zædʒəreit] v/t, v/i exagerar; **~ion** exagero m

exaltation [ˌegzɔ:l'teiʃən] exal tação f

examin|ation [igˌzæmi'neiʃən] exame m; examinação f; **~e** [-'zæmin] v/t examinar; **~er** examinador m

example [ig'zɑ:mpl] exemplo m; **for ~** por exemplo

exasperate [ig'zɑ:spəreit] v/t exasperar

excavate ['ekskəveit] v/t escavar

excavation [ˌekskə'veiʃən] esca vação f

exceed [ik'si:d] v/t exceder; **~ingly** excessivamente, extre mamente

excel|lence ['eksələns] excelência *f*; **♀lency** Excelência *f*; **~lent** excelente

except [ik'sept] *v/t* exce(p)tuar; *prp* exe(p)to, salvo; **~ for** se não fosse; exce(p)tuando; **~ing** *prp* exce(p)to; **~ion** exce(p)ção *f*; **~ional** excepcional

excess [ik'ses] *s* excesso *m*; **~ive** excessivo

exchange [iks'tʃeindʒ] *s* troca *f*; câmbio *m*; Bolsa *f*; central *f* telefónica; *v/t* trocar, cambiar

exchequer [iks'tʃekə] tesouro *m* público

excitable [ik'saitəbl] excitável

excite [ik'sait] *v/t* excitar; **~ment** excitação *f*

exciting [ik'saitiŋ] *adj* excitante

exclaim [iks'kleim] *v/i, v/t* exclamar

exclamation [.eksklə'meiʃən] exclamação *f*; **~ mark**, *US* **~ point** ponto *m* de exclamação

exclu|de [iks'klu:d] *v/t* excluir; **~sion** [-ʒən] exclusão *f*; **~sive** [-siv] exclusivo

excruciating [iks'kru:ʃieitiŋ] (ex)cruciante

excursion [iks'kə:ʃən] excursão *f*; **~ist** excursionista *m, f*

excusable [iks'kju:zəbl] desculpável

excuse [iks'kju:z] *v/t* desculpar; dispensar; [-'kju:s] *s* desculpa *f*; dispensa *f*, escusa *f*

execute ['eksikju:t] *v/t* executar; **~ion** [-'kju:ʃən] execução *f*; desempenho *m*; **~ioner** car-

rasco *m*, executor *m*; **~ive** [ig'zekjutiv] *adj, s* executivo *m*; **~or** testamenteiro *m*

exempl|ary [ig'zempləri] exemplar; **~ify** [-plifai] *v/t* exemplificar

exempt [ig'zempt] *v/t* isentar, dispensar; *adj* isento, livre; **~ion** isenção *f*, dispensa *f*

exercise ['eksəsaiz] *s* exercicio *m*; *v/t, v/i* exercitar(-se)

exert [ig'zə:t] *v/t* exercer; **~ oneself** esforçar-se, empenhar-se; **~ion** esforço *m*

exhalation [.eksha'leiʃən] exalação *f*

exhaust [ig'zɔ:st] *v/t* exaurir, esgotar; *s* escape *m*, descarga *f*; **~ion** [-tʃən] exaustão *f*, esgotamento *m*; **~ive** exaustivo, completo

exhibit [ig'zibit] *s* exibição *f*; *v/t, v/i* exibir, expor; **~ion** [-'biʃən] exposição *f*

exhilarate [ig'ziləreit] *v/t* alegrar, hilarizar

exhumation [.ekshju:'meiʃən] exumação *f*

exile ['eksail] *s* exílio *m*, desterro *m*; exilado *m*, desterrado *m*; *v/t* exilar, desterrar

exist [ig'zist] *v/i* existir; **~ence** existência *f*; **~ent**, **~ing** existente; a(c)tual

exit ['eksit] *s* saída *f*

exorbit|ance [ig'zɔ:bitəns] exorbitância *f*; **~ant** exorbitante

exotic [ig'zɔtik] exótico

expan|d [iks'pænd] *v/t, v/i* expandir(-se), dilatar(-se); **~sion**

expansão f; **~sive** expansivo

expect [iks'pekt] v/t esperar, aguardar; contar com; supor; **~ant** esperançoso; **~ation** [.ekspek'teiʃən] expectativa f

expedi|ency [iks'pi:djənsi] ou pediente m; **~ent** s expediente m; adj conveniente, oportuno; **~tion** [.ekspi'diʃən] expedição f

expel [iks'pel] v/t expelir, expulsar

expen|d [iks'pend] v/t despender, gastar; **~diture** [-ditʃə] gasto m, despesa f; **~se** [-s] despesa f; custo m; **~sive** dispendioso, caro

experienc|e [iks'piəriəns] s experiência f; v/t experimentar, **~ed** [-t] experimentado, experiente

experiment [iks'perimənt] s experimento m, experiência f; v/t experimentar, ensaiar

expert ['ekspə:t] adj conhecedor, perito, experto; s perito m, técnico m, especialista m, f

expiration [.ekspai'reiʃən] expiração f

expire [iks'paiə] v/i expirar; com vencer

explain [iks'plein] v/t, v/i explicar(-se)

explanat|ion [.eksplə'neiʃən] explicação f; **~ory** [iks'plæ-nətəri] explicativo

explicable ['eksplikəbl] explicável

explicit [iks'plisit] explícito; **~ness** clareza f

explode [iks'pləud] v/t, v/i

explodir

exploit [iks'plɔit] v/t explorar; ['eksplɔit] s façanha f, proeza f

explor|ation [.eksplə'reiʃən] exploração f; **~e** [iks'plɔ:] v/t explorar; **~er** explorador m

explosi|on [iks'pləuʒən] explosão f; **~ve** [-siv], s adj explosivo m

export [eks'pɔ:t] v/t exportar; s ['ekspɔ:t] exportação f; **~ation** [-'teiʃən] exportação f

expose [iks'pəuz] v/t expor

exposition [.ekspə'ziʃən] exposição f

exposure [iks'pəuʒə] exposição f, orientação f; revelação f; escândalo m

expound [iks'paund] v/t expor, explicar

express [iks'pres] v/t exprimir, expressar; mandar por expresso; adj expresso; explícito; rápido; s expresso m; **~ion** [-ʃən] expressão f; **~ive** expressivo

expropriate [eks'prəuprieit] v/t expropriar

expulsion [iks'pʌlʃən] expulsão f

exquisite ['ekskwizit] requintado, delicado, esquisito

extant [eks'tænt] existente

extend [iks'tend] v/t, v/i estender(-se)

extens|ion [iks'tenʃən] extensão f; prorrogação f; **~ive** extenso; extensivo

extent [iks'tent] extensão f, tamanho m; **to a certain ~** até certo ponto; **to a great ~** em grande parte

extenuat|e [eks'tenjueit] v/t atenuar; **~ing** adj atenuante; **~ion** atenuação f

exterior [eks'tiəriə] adj, s exterior m

exterminate [iks'tə:mineit] v/t exterminar

external [eks'tə:nl] externo; interior

extinct [iks'tiŋkt] extinto

extinguish [iks'tiŋgwiʃ] v/t extinguir; destruir; **~er** extintor m

extirpate ['ekstə:peit] v/t extirpar

extort [iks'tɔ:t] v/t **~ from** extorquir; **~ion** [-ʃən] extorsão f

extra ['ekstrə] adj extra, suplementar; adv extra(ordinariamente); s extra m; figurante, m, f

extract [iks'trækt] v/t extrair; ['ekstrækt] s extra(c)to m; essência f; **~ion** extra(c)ção f

extraneous [eks'treinjəs] extrínseco

extraordinary [iks'trɔ:dnri] extraordinário

extravagan|ce [iks'trævigəns] extravagância f; **~t** extravagante; pródigo; excessivo

extrem|e [iks'tri:m] adj, s extremo m; **~ist** extremista m, f; **~ity** [-'tremiti] (pl -ties) extremidade f; medida f extrema

extricate ['ekstrikeit] v/t desembaraçar, desenredar, livrar

exuberan|ce [ig'zju:bərəns] exuberância f; **~t** exuberante

exude [ig'zju:d] v/t, v/i transpirar; emanar

exult [ig'zʌlt] v/i exultar, triunfar; **~ation** [.egzʌl'teiʃən] exultação f

eye [ai] s olho m; v/t olhar, contemplar; **~ball** globo m ocular; **~brow** sobrancelha f; **~glass** monóculo m; **~lash** pestana f; **~let** ilhó m; **~lid** pálpebra f; **~sight** vista f; visão f; **~witness** testemunha f ocular

F

fable ['feibl] fábula f

fabric ['fæbrik] tecido m; estrutura f; **~ate** [-keit] v/t fabricar

fabulous ['fæbjuləs] fabuloso

face [feis] s face f, rosto m, cara f; v/t encarar; enfrentar; **~ to ~** cara a cara, frente a frente; **make/pull a ~** fazer caretas

facetious [fə'si:ʃəs] chistoso, faceto

facile ['fæsail] fácil; ágil

facili|tate [fə'siliteit] v/t facili-

tar

facili|ties [fə'silitiz] s/pl vantagens f/pl; **~ty** facilidade f

facing ['feisiŋ] s adorno m, revestimento m

fact [fækt] fa(c)to m; realidade f; **in ~** de fa(c)to

faction ['fækʃən] facção f

factious ['fækʃəs] faccioso

factitious [fæk'tiʃəs] factício

factor ['fæktə] fa(c)tor m

factory ['fæktəri] (pl -ries) fábrica *f*

faculty ['fækəlti] (*pl* **-ties**) faculdade *f*; aptidão *f*

fade [feid] *v/t*, *v/i* murchar; **~ away** desvanecer-se

fag [fæg] *v/i* esfalfar-se, mourejar; *s* maçada *f*; cigarro *m*

fa(g)got ['fægət] feixe *m*

fail [feil] *v/t*, *v/i* falhar; falir; faltar; fracassar; **~ an examination** reprovar num exame

failure ['feiljə] falência *f*; falha *f*; fracasso *m*

faint [feint] *adj* fraco; tímido; débil; indistinto; *s* desmaio *m*; *v/i* desmaiar

fair [fɛə] *adj* leal, honesto, justo; louro; lindo; mediano; *s* feira *f*, *adv* em cheio; com lealdade

fairly ['fɛəli] bastante; justamente

fairness ['fɛənis] honradez *f*; probidade *f*

fairy ['fɛəri] (*pl* **-ries**) fada *f*

faith [feiθ] fé *f*; **in good ~** de boa fé; **~ful** leal; fiel, crente; **~fulness** lealdade *f*, fidelidade *f*

fake [feik] *s* fraude *f*, patranha *f*, imitação *f*; *v/t* falsificar

falcon ['fɔːlkən] falcão *m*

fall [fɔːl] *s* queda *f*; baixa *f*; *US* outono *m*; *v/i* cair; baixar; diminuir; **~ down** cair no chão; **~ in love** enamorar-se, apaixonar-se; **~ flat** falhar, malograr; **~ short** faltar, ser insuficiente; **~ through** fracassar

fallac|ious [fə'leiʃəs] falaz; **~y** ['fæləsi] (*pl* **-cies**) falácia *f*; sofisma *m*

fallible ['fæləbl] falível

fallow ['fæləu] *adj*, *s* (de) pousio *m*

false [fɔːls] *adj* falso, desleal; **~ teeth** dentes *m/pl* postiços; **~hood** falsidade *f*; mentira *f*

falsify ['fɔːlsifai] *v/t* falsificar

falter ['fɔːltə] *v/t*, *v/i* vacilar; hesitar; balbuciar

fam|e [feim] fama *f*, nomeada *f*; **~ed** *adj* afamado, famoso

familiar [fə'miljə] *adj* familiar; íntimo; versado; **~ity** [ˌ-mi-li'æriti] familiaridade *f*

family ['fæmili] (*pl* **-lies**) família *f*; linhagem *f*

famine ['fæmin] fome *f*, carestia *f*

famished ['fæmiʃt] esfaimado, esfomeado, faminto

famous ['feiməs] famoso, célebre

fan [fæn] *s* leque *m*; ventilador *m*; fã *m*; *v/t* ventilar; abanar

fanatic [fə'nætik] *s*, *adj* fanático *m*; **~ism** [-sizəm] fanatismo *m*

fanciful ['fænsiful] extravagante, caprichoso

fancy ['fænsi] (*pl* **-cies**) *s* fantasia *f*; capricho *m*; inclinação *f*, afeição *f*; *v/t* imaginar, supor; gostar de, desejar; *adj* ornado, de fantasia; imaginário; invulgar; **take/catch the ~ of** atrair, captar; **~-dress** vestido *m* de fantasia

fang [fæŋ] presa *f*

fantastic [fæn'tæstik] fantástico *f*

far [fɑː] *adv* longe, distante; muito; *adj* distante, longínquo;

as/so ~ as até; tanto quanto; **by ~** de longe, decididamente; **~ and wide** por toda a parte; **how ~?** até que ponto?; **so ~** até agora, até ao presente

farce [fɑːs] s farsa f

fare [fɛə] s bilhete m, passagem f; comida f; **bill of ~** ementa f, Braz cardápio m

farewell [ˌfɛəˈwel] s adeus m, despedida f; int adeus!

far-fetched [ˈfɑːˈfetʃt] forçado; artificial; afe(c)tado

farm [fɑːm] s quinta f, herdade f, fazenda f; **~er** lavrador m, fazendeiro m; **~-house** casal m

far-off [ˌfɑːˈɒf] distante, longínquo

far-sighted [ˌfɑːˈsaitid] presbita; previdente

farther [ˈfɑːðə] adj mais distante; adv mais longe

farthest [ˈfɑːðist] adj o mais distante; adv o mais longe

fascinate [ˈfæsineit] v/t fascinar

fascinating [ˈfæsineitiŋ] adj fascinante; **~ion** [-ˈneiʃən] fascinação f

fascism [ˈfæʃizəm] fascismo m

fascist [ˈfæʃist] fascista m, f

fashion [ˈfæʃən] s moda f; v/t moldar, adaptar; **out of ~** fora da moda; **in ~** na moda; **~able** à/na moda, elegante

fast [fɑːst] v/i jejuar; s jejum m; adj rápido; adiantado; firme, fixo; adv depressa; **~ asleep** profundamente adormecido

fasten [ˈfɑːsn] v/t, v/i apertar; fixar, firmar; atar, prender

fastidious [fəsˈtidiəs] fastidioso

fastness [ˈfɑːstnis] baluarte m; firmeza f

fat [fæt] adj gordo; gorduroso; s banha f, gordura f

fatal [ˈfeitl] fatal; **~ism** fatalismo m; **~ity** [fəˈtæliti] (pl -ties) fatalidade f

fate [feit] fado m, sorte f, destino m; **~ful** fatídico

father [ˈfɑːðə] s pai m; eccl padre m; antepassado m; **~hood** paternidade f; **~-in-law** sogro m; **~ly** paternal

fathom [ˈfæðəm] s braça f; v/t sondar; compreender

fatigue [fəˈtiːg] s fadiga f

fat ness [ˈfætnis] gordura f; **~ty** s gorducho m, gordo m; adj gordurento

fatu ity [fəˈtjuːiti] fatuidade f; **~ous** fátuo

fault [fɔːlt] s falta f, culpa f; defeito m; erro m; falha f; **~less** perfeito; **~y** defeituoso

faun [fɔːn] fauno m; **~a** [ˈfɔːnə] fauna f

favo(u)r [ˈfeivə] s favor m; v/t favorecer; parecer-se com; **~able** favorável; **~ite** [-vərit] predile(c)to, favorito; **~itism** favoritismo m

fawn [fɔːn] s enho m, corça f

fear [fiə] s receio m, temor m, medo m; v/t, v/i temer; **~ful** medonho; medroso; **~less** intrépido

feast [fiːst] s festa f; banquete m; v/t, v/i festejar, banquetear

feat [fiːt] feito m, proeza f

feather [ˈfeðə] s pena f

feature ['fi:tʃə] s feição f, traço m; característica f; v/t fazer sobressair, destacar

February ['februəri] Fevereiro m

feder|al ['fedərəl] federal; **~ate** ['-reit] v/t federar; **~ation** [-'reiʃən] federação f

fee [fi:] salário m, honorários m/pl

feeble ['fi:bl] fraco, débil

feed [fi:d] v/t, v/i alimentar(-se), (dar de) comer; **~ing-bottle** biberão m, mamadeira f

feel [fi:l] v/t, v/i apalpar; sentir (-se); **~er** antena f; **~ing** s ta(c)to m; sensação f; sensibilidade f; sentimento m

feet [fi:t] pl of **foot**

feint [feint] v/i fintar

felicitations [fi,lisi'teiʃənz] s/pl felicitações f/pl

fell [fel] v/t abater, derribar; s monte m baldio, colina f baldia

fellow ['felou] s companheiro m; membro m; tipo m, sujeito m; **~-citizen** concidadão m; **~-feeling** simpatia f; **~ship** sociedade f, associação f; camaradagem f

felt [felt] s feltro m

female ['fi:meil] s fêmea f, adj feminino

feminine ['feminin] feminino

fen [fen] pântano m

fenc|e [fens] s cerca f, sebe f; v/t cercar; v/i esgrimir; **~er** esgrimador m; **~ing** ['fensiŋ] s esgrima f

fend [fend]: **~ for oneself** tratar da sua vida

fender ['fendə] guarda-fogo m; US pára-choques m

fennel ['fenl] funcho m

ferment s ['fə:ment] s fermento m; agitação f; fermentação f; [fə:'ment] v/t, v/i fermentar

fern [fə:n] feto m

ferocious [fə'rouʃəs] feroz

ferret ['ferit] s furão m

ferry ['feri] v/t transportar de barco; s (pl **-ries**) travessia f; barco m de travessia

fertil|e ['fə:tail] fértil; **~ity** ['-tiliti] fertilidade f; **~ize** ['-tilaiz] v/t fertilizar; fecundar; **~izer** adubo m, fertilizante m

fervent ['fə:vənt] fervente, ardente

fervo(u)r ['fə:və] fervor m, ardor m

festiv|al ['festəvəl] festa f, festival m; **~e** festivo; **~ity** ['-'tiviti] (pl **-ties**) festividade f

fetch [fetʃ] v/t ir buscar, trazer

fetter ['fetə] grilhão m; v/t agrilhoar

feud [fju:d] rixa f, contenda f

fever ['fi:və] febre f; **~ish** febril

few [fju:] adj, s poucos; **a ~** uns poucos, alguns

fiancé [fi'ã:nsei] noivo m; **~e** noiva f

fib [fib] s peta f

fibre ['faibə] fibra f

fickle ['fikl] inconstante; **~ness** inconstância f

fict|ion ['fikʃən] ficção f; **~itious** ['-tiʃəs] fictício

fiddle ['fidl] s violino m, rabeca f; v/i tocar violino; matar o tempo

fidelity [fi'deliti] (*pl* -**ties**) fidelidade *f*

fidgety ['fidʒiti] inquieto, nervoso

field [fi:ld] *s* campo *m*; *v/t* meter no campo; **~ event** prova *f* de atletismo de campo

fiend [fi:nd] demónio *m*; **~ish** diabólico

fierce [fiəs] feroz

fiery ['faiəri] fogoso

fif|teen ['fif'ti:n] quinze; **~th** [fifθ] quinto; **~ty** ['fifti] cinquenta

fig [fig] figo *m*

fight [fait] *s* luta *f*; peleja *f*; *v/t*, *v/i* lutar, combater; **~er** lutador *m*

figment ['figmənt] quimera *f*, ficção *f*

fig-tree ['figtri:] figueira *f*

figurative ['figjurətiv] figurativo

figure ['figə] *s* figura *f*; algarismo *m*; *v/t*, *v/i* figurar; imaginar

file [fail] *s* arquivo *m*; fila *f*; lima *f*; *v/t* arquivar; limar; *v/i* desfilar

filial ['filjəl] filial

filigree ['filigri:] filigrana *f*

fill [fil] *v/t*, *v/i* encher(-se); **~ in** preencher

fillet ['filit] *s* filete *m*

filling ['filiŋ] *s* obturação *f*; **~ station** bomba *f* / posto *m* de gasolina

film [film] *s* película *f*; filme *m*, fita *f*; *v/t*, *v/i* filmar

filter ['filtə] *s* filtro *m*; *v/t*, *v/i* filtrar(-se)

filth [filθ] porcaria *f*, imundície *f*; **~y** imundo, sujo

fin [fin] barbatana *f*

final ['fainl] *adj*, *s* final *f*; **~ly** finalmente, por fim

financ|e [fai'næns] *s* finança *f*; *v/t* financiar; **~ial** [-f-fəl] financeiro; **~ier** [-siə] financeiro *m*

finch [fintf] tentilhão *m*

find [faind] *v/t* achar, encontrar; **~ out** descobrir; **~er** achador *m*; **~ing** decisão *f*, veredicto *m*; achado *m*

fine [fain] *adj* belo, lindo; fino; *v/t* multar; *s* multa *f*; **I am ~** estou bem; **that is ~** é ó(p)timo; **~ arts** *pl* belas-artes *f/pl*

finger ['fiŋgə] *s* dedo *m*; *v/t* dedilhar; **~-board** teclado *m*; **~ing** dedilhado *m*; **~-nail** unha *f*; **~-print** impressão *f* digital; **~-stall** dedeira *f*

finish ['finif] *v/t*, *v/i* acabar, terminar; *s* fim *m*; acabamento *m*

Finnish ['finif] *adj*, *s* finlandês *m*

fir [fə:] abeto *m*; pinho *m*

fire ['faiə] *s* fogo *m*; lume *m*; incêndio *m*; *v/t*, *v/i* disparar, fazer fogo; deitar fogo a; incendiar; **on ~** em chamas, em fogo; **~-arm** arma *f* de fogo; **~-engine** furgão *m* de incêndio; **~-fly** pirilampo *m*; **~-man** bombeiro *m*; **~-works** fogos *m/pl* de artifício

firm [fə:m] *adj* firme, sólido; *s* firma *f*, casa *f* comercial

first [fə:st] *adv* em primeiro lugar; *adj* primeiro; **at ~** a princípio; **~ aid** primeiros so-

corros *m/pl*; ~ **of all** primeiro
que tudo; **at** ~ **sight** à primeira vista; ~**-born** primogénito
m; ~**-class** *adj* de primeira
classe; ~**-hand** *adj* de primeira mão; ~**-night** estreia *f*;
~**-rate** primeiro de qualidade

firth [fə:θ] braço *m* de mar,
estuário *m*

fir-tree [fə:tri:] pinheiro *m*

fish [fiʃ] *s* peixe *m*; *v/t, v/i* pescar; ~**erman** pescador *m*;
~**hook** anzol *m*

fishing [fiʃiŋ] pesca *f*; ~**boat**
barco *m* de pesca; ~**rod** cana *f*
de pesca

fissure [fiʃə] fissura *f*

fist [fist] punho *m*

fit [fit] *s* desmaio *m*, síncope *f*;
acesso *m*, ataque *m*; *adj* apto;
próprio, adequado; em boa forma; *v/t, v/i* adaptar(-se), ajustar; montar; ficar bem

fitness [fitnis] aptidão *f*, idoneidade *f*; boa condição *f* física

fitter [fitə] ajustador *m*; *mec*
montador *m*

fitting [fitiŋ] *adj* adequado,
conveniente; *s* encaixe *m*,
montagem *f*; prova *f*; ~**s** *s/pl*
instalações *f/pl*

five [faiv] cinco; ~ **hundred**
quinhentos

fix [fiks] *v/t* fixar, assentar; arranjar; consertar

fixed [fikst] fixo

fizz [fiz] *s* champanhe *m*; efervescência *f*; *v/i* efervescer

fizzle [fizl] *v/i* silvar; ~ **out** fazer fiasco, fracassar

flabbergasted [flæbəgɑːstid]

varado, estupefa(c)to

flabby [flæbi] flácido, mole

flag [flæg] *s* bandeira *f*; laje *f*,
lousa *f*; *v/i* enfraquecer

flagon [flægən] botija *f*

flake [fleik] *s* lasca *f*; floco *m*; *v/i*
lascar(-se)

flamboyant [flæmˈbɔiənt] brilhante, flamante; flamejante

flam|e [fleim] *s* chama *f*; ardor
m, paixão *f*; *v/i* chamejar;
~**ing** *adj* chamejante; ardente

flamingo [fləˈmiŋgəu] flamingo
m, *Braz* guará *m*

flank [flæŋk] *s* ilharga *f*; flanco
m; *v/t* flanquear

flannel [flænl] *s* flanela *f*

flap [flæp] *s* aba *f*; tapa *f*, palma
da *f*; *v/t, v/i* bater, esvoaçar

flare [flɛə] *s* fulgor *m*, brilho *m*;
v/i flamejar, cintilar; ~ **up** in-
flamar-se

flash [flæʃ] *s* lampejo *m*; luz
m de magnésio; clarão *m*; *v/i*
cintilar, lampejar; dardejar;
~**light** holofote *m*; lâmpada *f*
para instantâneos; lâmpada *f*
elé(c)trica; ~**y** vistoso

flask [flɑːsk] frasco *m*

flat [flæt] *adv* completamente,
francamente; *adj* chato, plano,
liso; *s* andar *m*, apartamento
m; baixio *m*; furo *m*; *mus* be-
mol *m*; **the** ~ **of the hand** a
palma da mão

flatten [flætn] *v/t, v/i* achatar

flatter [flætə] *v/t* lisonjear;
~**er** lisonjeador *m*; ~**ing** *adj*
lisonjeiro; ~**y** lisonja *f*

flavo(u)r [fleivə] *s* sabor *m*; *v/t*
condimentar

flaw [flɔ:] s falha f, defeito m;
~**less** perfeito, impecável

flax [flæks] linho m; ~**en** de linho; loiro

flay [flei] v/t esfolar

flea [fli:] pulga f

flee [fli:] v/t, v/i fugir

fleec|**e** [fli:s] s velo m, tosão m;
v/t tosquiar; depenar, despojar; ~**y** lanoso, lázudo

fleet [fli:t] s armada f, esquadra
f, frota f

fleeting ['fli:tiŋ] fugaz

Flemish ['flemiʃ] adj, s flamengo m

flesh [fleʃ] carne f; ~**y** carnudo

flexible ['fleksəbl] flexível

flick [flik] s piparote m; estalido
m; v/t chicotear

flicker ['flikə] v/i vacilar; bruxulear, tremeluzir; s centelha f;
luz f vacilante

flight [flait] voo m; fuga f; lanço
m de escadas

flimsy ['flimzi] adj débil, frágil,
inconsistente; s papel m de cópias

flinch [flintʃ] v/i vacilar, titubear

fling [fliŋ] v/t lançar, atirar, arremessar

flint [flint] pedra f de isqueiro;
pederneira f, sílex m

flip [flip] v/t, v/i sacudir; desvairar; s sacudidela f

flippant ['flipənt] irreverente

flipper ['flipə] barbatana f

flirt [flə:t] v/i namori(s)car, flertar; s namori(s)co m, flerte m

flit [flit] v/i esvoaçar; mudar de
casa

flitch [flitʃ] manta f de toucinho

float [fləut] v/t, v/i flutuar; s flutuador m; bóia f; ~**ing** adj flutuante

flock [flɔk] s bando m; manada
f; rebanho m; v/i congregar-se

flog [flɔg] v/t açoutar, fustigar,
chicotear

flood [flʌd] s inundação f; cheia
f; enchente f; v/t, v/i inundar,
alagar

floor [flɔ:] s soalho m, sobrado
m; chão m; v/t derrubar, deitar
por terra; assoalhar

florist ['flɔrist] florista m, f

flounder ['flaundə] s solha f; v/i
espojar-se, patinhar

flour ['flauə] s farinha f

flourish ['flʌriʃ] v/i florescer;
prosperar, medrar; v/t brandir

floury ['flauəri] enfarinhado; farinhento

flout [flaut] v/t escarnecer

flow [fləu] v/i fluir, correr; s fluxo m, torrente f

flower ['flauə] s flor f; ~**-bed**
canteiro m; ~**-pot** vaso m

flu [flu:] = **influenza**

fluctuate ['flʌktjueit] v/i flutuar

fluen|**cy** ['flu(:)ənsi] fluência f;
~**t** fluente

fluff [flʌf] s cotão m; penugem f,
lanugem f; ~**y** fofo, felpudo

fluid ['flu:id] s, adj fluido m

flurry ['flʌri] s (pl -ries) agitação
f; rajada f, lufada f

flush [flʌʃ] s jacto m, jorro m;
rubor m; v/t, v/i corar, enrubescer;
jorrar; adj ao mesmo nível; ~
with money cheio de dinheiro

forbidding

fluster ['flʌstə] v/t confundir, embaraçar; s confusão f

flut|e [flu:t] s flauta f; **~ed** estriado

flutter ['flʌtə] v/t, v/i esvoaçar, adejar; bater as asas; palpitar; s agitação f, alvoroço m; palpitação f

fly [flai] (pl **flies**) s mosca f; v/i voar; fugir; v/t arvorar, hastear; lançar

flying ['flaiiŋ] s aviação f; adj voador, volante; ~ **saucer** disco m voador; ~ **squad** rádio-patrulha f

foal [fəul] potro m, poldro m

foam [fəum] s espuma f; v/i espumar

focus ['fəukəs] (pl **-cuses** or **-ci** [-sai]) s foco m; v/t focar

foe [fəu] inimigo m

fog [fɔg] s nevoeiro m, cerração f; v/t, v/i enevoar(-se); velar-se; ~**gy** enevoado, nevoento

foible ['fɔibl] (ponto m) fraco m

foil [fɔil] s florete m embolado; folha f, chapa f; contraste m, realce m; v/t frustrar

fold [fəuld] s prega f, dobra f; curral m, aprisco m, v/t, v/i embrulhar; dobrar; encurralar; ~ **one's arms** cruzar os braços

folding ['fəuldiŋ] dobradiço

foliage ['fəuliidʒ] folhagem f

folk [fəuk] s povo m, gente f; **~lore** ['-lɔ:] folclore m; **~s** família f, gente f; malta f; **~song** canção f popular

follow ['fɔləu] v/t, v/i seguir (-se); perceber; **as ~s** como se

segue; **~er** adepto m; **~ing** adj seguinte; s partidários m/pl; **the ~ing** os seguintes

folly ['fɔli] (pl **-lies**) tolice f, loucura f

foment [fəu'ment] v/t fomentar

fond [fɔnd] afe(c)tuoso, terno; afeiçoado; vão; **to be ~ of** gostar de; **~le** [-l] v/t afagar, amimar

food [fu:d] alimento m, comida f; **~-stuff** géneros m/pl alimentícios

fool [fu:l] v/t; v/i disparatar, bob(e)ar; enganar; s tolo m, bobo m, pateta m; imbecil m, f; **make a ~ of oneself** fazer-se ridículo; **make a ~ of someone** fazer de alguém tolo; **play the ~** fazer de tolo, Braz fazer de bobo

foolish ['fu:liʃ] tolo, tonto

foot [fut] (pl **feet** [fi:t]) s pé m; pata f; base f; v/t pagar; **~ it** ir a pé, andar a pé; **my ~!** qual!; **on ~** a pé; **~ball** futebol m; **~fall** som m de passos; **~hold** ponto m de apoio; posição f; **~ing** situação f, pé m; **~lights** ribalta f; **~note** s nota f ao fundo da página; **~path** atalho m; **~print** pegada f; **~step** pegada f; passo m

for [fɔ:; fə] prp por; para; por causa de; durante; conj porque; pois

forbear [fɔ:'bɛə] v/i abster-se; reprimir-se; **~ance** paciência f

forbid [fə'bid] v/t proibir, impedir; **~den** adj proibido; **~ding** adj proibitivo, severo, ameaçador

force [fɔːs] *v/t* forçar, obrigar; *s* força *f*, vigor *m*; violência *f*; **in ~** em vigor, vigente; **~ful** vigoroso, enérgico

forceps [ˈfɔːseps] fórceps *m*

forcible [ˈfɔːsəbl] convincente; violento, forçado

ford [fɔːd] *s* vau *m*; *v/t* vadear; passar a vau

fore [fɔː] *adj* anterior, dianteiro; *mar* de proa; **~arm** antebraço *m*; **~bode** *v/t* pressagiar; **~boding** *s* presságio *m*, pressentimento *m*; **~cast** *s* previsão *f*; prognóstico *m*; *v/t* prever, prognosticar; **~father** antepassado *m*; **~finger** dedo *m* indicador; **~ground** primeiro plano *m*; **~head** [ˈfɔrid] testa *f*, fronte *f*

foreign [fɔrin] alheio; estranho; estrangeiro; **~er** estrangeiro *m*

fore|land [ˈfɔːlənd] cabo *m*, promontório *m*; **~lock** topete *m*; **~man** capataz *m*, mestre *m*; **~most** *adj* mais ilustre; primeiro, mais avançado; **~see** *v/t* prever; **~sight** previsão *f*

forest [fɔrist] floresta *f*, mata *f*

fore|taste [ˈfɔːteist] antegosto *m*; **~tell** [-ˈtel] predizer

forever [fəˈrevə] para sempre

forewarn [fɔˈwɔːn] *v/t* prevenir, avisar

foreword [ˈfɔːwəːd] prefácio *m*

forfeit [ˈfɔːfit] *s* multa *f*, pena *f*; *v/t* perder o direito a; **play ~s** jogar às prendas

forg|e [fɔːdʒ] *s* forja *f*; *v/t* forjar; falsificar; **~er** falsário *m*;

~ery falsificação *f*

forget [fəˈget] *v/t, v/i* esquecer, esquecer-se de; **~ful** esquecido; **~-me-not** miosótis *f*, não-me-esqueças *m*

forgive [fəˈgiv] *v/t, v/i* perdoar; **~ness** perdão *m*

forgiving [fəˈgivin] *adj* clemente, indulgente

fork [fɔːk] *s* garfo *m*; forquilha *f*; bifurcação *f*; *v/t, v/i* forcar; bifurcar(-se)

forlorn [fɔˈlɔːn] desamparado

form [fɔːm] *s* forma *f*; formulário *m*; figura *f*; classe *f*, turma *f*; *v/t, v/i* formar(-se); formular; **~al** formal; cerimonioso; **~ative** formativo

former [ˈfɔːmə] primeiro, precedente, anterior, antigo, passado; **~ly** outrora, antigamente

formidable [ˈfɔːmidəbl] formidável

formul|a [ˈfɔːmjulə] *s* fórmula *f*; **~ate** [-leit] *v/t* formular; **~ation** formulação *f*

forsake [fəˈseik] *v/t* abandonar, desertar, desamparar

fort [fɔːt] mil forte *m*

forth [fɔːθ] adiante, avante, para a frente; **and so ~** e assim por diante; **~coming** vindoiro, próximo; **~with** imediatamente

fortify [ˈfɔːtifai] *v/t* fortificar

fortnight [ˈfɔːtnait] quinzena *f*, quinze dias *m/pl*

fortress [ˈfɔːtris] fortaleza *f*

fortuitous [fɔːˈtju(ː)itəs] fortuito

fortunate [ˈfɔːtʃnit] afortunado,

venturoso, feliz; **~ly** afortunadamente, felizmente

fortune ['fɔ:tʃən] fortuna *f*; sorte *f*, sina *f*; **~teller** adivinho *m*, cartomante *m, f*

forty ['fɔ:ti] quarenta

forward ['fɔ:wəd] *s* avançado *m*; *adj* avançado; dianteiro; precoce; audaz; *adv* adiante; mais adiante; *v/t* enviar, remeter, expedir

fossil ['fɒsl] *s* fóssil *m*

foster ['fɒstə] *v/t* fomentar, alentar; alimentar, criar, nutrir; **~son** filho *m* ado(p)tivo

foul [faul] *adj* sujo, imundo, porco; fétido; infame, vil, detestável; *v/t, v/i* sujar(-se), emporcalhar; *s* violação *f*, falta *f*

found [faund] *v/t* fundar, estabelecer; fundir

foundation [faun'deiʃən] fundação *f*, estabelecimento *m*; dotação *f*; **~s** alicerces *m/pl*

founder ['faundə] *s* fundador *m*

foundry ['faundri] (*pl* **-ries**) fundição *f*

fountain ['fauntin] fonte *f*, repuxo *m*; **~-pen** caneta *f* de tinta permanente

four [fɔ:] quatro; **go on all ~s** andar de gatinhas, engatinhar; **~ hundred** quatrocentos; **~teen** catorze

fourth [fɔ:θ] quarto

fowl [faul] ave *f* de capoeira

fox [fɒks] raposa *f*; **~y** ladino, astuto

foyer ['fɔiei] *theat* salão *m*, vestíbulo *m*

fraction ['frækʃən] fra(c)ção *f*

fracture ['fræktʃə] *s* fra(c)tura *f*; *v/t, v/i* fra(c)turar(-se)

fragile ['frædʒail] frágil

fragment ['frægmənt] fragmento *m*

fragrance ['freigrəns] fragrância *f*

fragrant ['freigrənt] fragrante

frail [freil] débil, frágil, delicado; **~ty** fraqueza *f*, fragilidade *f*

frame [freim] *s* moldura *f*; caixilho *m*; estrutura *f*; *v/t* emoldurar, encaixilhar

franc [fræŋk] franco *m*

franchise ['fræntʃaiz] direito *m* de votar, sufrágio *m*

frank [fræŋk] *adj* franco; **~ness** franqueza *f*

frantic ['fræntik] frenético

fratern|al [frə'tə:nl] fraternal; **~ity** fraternidade *f*; **~ize** ['frætənaiz] *v/i* fraternizar

fraud [frɔ:d] fraude *f*; **~ulent** fraudulento

fray [frei] *s* refrega *f*; *v/t, v/i* coçar(-se), desgastar(-se)

freak [fri:k] *s* capricho *m*, veleidade *f*; fenómeno *m*

freckles ['freklz] *s/pl* sardas *f/pl*

free [fri:] *adj* livre; vago; grátis; *v/t* livrar, libertar

freedom ['fri:dəm] liberdade *f*

freemason ['fri:meisn] franco-maçom *m*, pedreiro-livre *m*

free trade ['fri:'treid] livre-câmbio *m*

freez|e [fri:z] *v/t, v/i* gelar, congelar; **~er** congelador *m*

freezing-point ['fri:ziŋpoint]

ponto *m* de congelação

freight [freit] *s mar* frete *m*, carga *f*; *v/t* fretar, carregar; **~er** carregueiro *m*

French [frent∫] *adj, s* francês *m*; **~ bean** feijão *m* verde; **~ fry** (*pl* **~ fries**) *US* batata *f* frita

frenzy ['frenzi] frenesi *m*

frequen|cy ['fri:kwensi] frequência *f*; **~t** *adj* frequente, amiudado

fresh [fre∫] fresco; novo; puro; **in the ~ air** ao ar livre; **~er** caloiro *m*; **~water** de água doce

fret [fret] *v/t, v/i* afligir(-se); **~ful** irritável, rabugento

friar ['fraiə] frade *m*

friction ['frik∫ən] atrito *m*; fricção *f*

Friday ['fraidi] sexta-feira *f*

fridge [fridʒ] *GB* = **refrigerator**

friend [frend] amigo *m*; **make ~s with** tornar-se amigo de; **~ly** amigável, amigo, amável; **~ship** amizade *f*

frigate ['frigit] fragata *f*

fright [frait] susto *m*, medo *m*; **~en** *v/t* assustar; **~ful** terrível, assustador

frigid ['fridʒid] frígido, gélido

frill [fril] folho *m*

fringe [frindʒ] *s* franja *f*, orla *f*; *v/t* orlar

frisky ['friski] vivo, brincalhão; fogoso

fritter ['fritə] *s* frito *m*; **~ away** desperdiçar

frivol|ity [fri'vɔliti] frivolidade *f*; **~ous** ['-vələs] frívolo

frizz|le ['frizl] *v/t* frisar; **~(l)y** frisado, encaracolado

frock-coat [frɔk'kəut] sobrecasaca *f*

frog [frɔg] rã *f*

frolic ['frɔlik] *s* brincadeira *f*, travessura *f*; **~some** brincalhão, travesso

from [frɔm, frəm] de; desde; da parte de; **~ memory** de memória; **~ . . . to de . . . a**

frond [frɔnd] fronde *f*

front [frʌnt] *s* frente *f*; fachada *f*; *adj* anterior, da frente, dianteiro

frontier ['frʌntjə] fronteira *f*

frontispiece ['frʌntispi:s] frontispício *m*

frost [frɔst] *s* geada *f*; *v/t, v/i* gelar, cobrir de geada; foscar; polvilhar; **~y** gelado, glacial

froth [frɔθ] *s* espuma *f*, escuma *f*

frown [fraun] *s* franzimento *m* de sobrancelhas; *v/i* franzir as sobrancelhas; **~ on** desaprovar

frugal ['fru:gəl] frugal; **~ity** [-'gæliti] frugalidade *f*

fruit [fru:t] *s* fruto *m*; fruta *f*; **~erer** fruteiro *m*; **~ful** frutífero; **~s** *pl* frutos *m*/*pl*

frustrat|e [frʌs'treit] *v/t* frustrar; **~ion** frustração *f*

fry [frai] *v/t* frigir, fritar; **~ing-pan** frigideira *f*, sertã *f*

fuel ['fjuəl] *s* combustível *m*

fugitive ['fju:dʒitiv] *s* fugitivo *m*; *adj* passageiro

fulfil(l) [ful'fil] *v/t* cumprir; **~ment** cumprimento *m*, execução *f*

full [ful] *adj* cheio; repleto; completo; pleno; *adv* completamente; em cheio; *s* totalidade *f*; plenitude *f*; ~ **well** muito bem; **in** ~ por extenso; na totalidade, completamente; ~ **length** de corpo inteiro, tamanho natural; ~ **moon** lua *f* cheia

ful(l)ness ['fulnis] abundância *f*, plenitude *f*

full stop ['fulstɔp] ponto *m* final; ~**time** tempo *m* integral/completo; ~ *adv* completamente; na íntegra

fumble ['fʌmbl] *v/t*, *v/i* ta(c)tear, apalpar, remexer

fume [fju:m] *v/t* fumegar; encolerizar-se; ~**s** *s/pl* vapores *m/pl*, gás *m*, fumo *m*

fun [fʌn] graça *f*, divertimento *m*, diversão *f*; **for** ~ por brincadeira; **have** ~ divertir-se; **make** ~ **of** fazer troça/pouco de

function ['fʌŋkʃən] *s* função *f*; *v/i* funcionar; ~**al** funcional

fund [fʌnd] *s* reserva *f*, fundo *m*; ~**s** fundos *m/pl*

funeral ['fju:nərəl] *s* funeral *m*; *adj* fúnebre

funicular [fju'nikjulə] funicular *m*

funnel ['fʌnl] funil *m*; tubo *m*; *naut* chaminé *f*

funny ['fʌni] invulgar, estranho; divertido, engraçado, cómico

fur [fə:] *s* pele *f*; pêlo *m*

furious ['fjuəriəs] furioso

furl [fə:l] *v/t*, *v/i* dobrar(-se), enrolar(-se); desfraldar

furlough ['fə:ləu] licença *f*, baixa *f* militar

furnace ['fə:nis] fornalha *f*

furnish ['fə:niʃ] *v/t* mobilar; fornecer

furniture ['fə:nitʃə] móveis *m/pl*, mobília *f*, mobiliário *m*

furrier ['fʌriə] peleiro *m*

furrow ['fʌrəu] *s* sulco *m*, rego *m*; *v/t* sulcar

further ['fə:ðə] *adj* mais distante; suplementar, adicional; *adv* mais longe; além disso; mais; mais adiante; *v/t* favorecer; ~**more** [fə:ðə'mɔː] demais, além disso; ~**most** ['fə:ðəməust] o mais distante, o mais afastado

furthest ['fə:ðist] *adj* extremo; o mais distante

furtive ['fə:tiv] furtivo

fury ['fjuəri] (*pl* -**ries**) fúria *f*

fuse [fju:z] *s* fusível *m*; *v/t*, *v/i* fundir(-se)

fuselage ['fju:zila:ʒ] fuselagem *f*

fusion ['fju:ʒən] fusão *f*

fuss [fʌs] *v/i* espalhafatar, atarantar-se; *s* espalhafato *m*, estardalhaço *m*, barulho *m*; ~**y** niquento

fustian ['fʌstiən] fustão *m*

fusty ['fʌsti] bafiento, mofento

futile ['fju:tail] fútil

future ['fju:tʃə] *s* futuro *m*, porvir *m*; *adj* futuro; vindoiro

G

gab [gæb] tagarelice f; **have the gift of the ~** ter boa lábia
gable ['geibl] empena f
gag [gæg] s mordaça f; v/t amordaçar
gage [geidʒ] s penhor m
gaiety ['geiəti] alegria f
gaily ['geili] alegremente
gain [gein] s ganho m, lucro m; v/t, v/i ganhar; adiantar-se
gait [geit] andar m
gaiter ['geitə] polaina f
gale [geil] ventania f
gall [gɔ:l] s fel m; amargura f, amargor m; v/t ferir, vexar
gallant ['gælənt] adj galante; valente
gall-bladder ['gɔ:lblædə] vesícula f biliar
gallery ['gæləri] (pl -ries) galeria f
galley ['gæli] galera f; galé f
gallon ['gælən] galão m
gallop ['gæləp] s galope m; v/i galopar
gallows ['gæləuz] forca f
galosh [gə'lɔʃ] galocha f
gambl|e ['gæmbl] v/t, v/i jogar a dinheiro; ~er jogador m de azar
gambol ['gæmbəl] v/i cabriolar
game [geim] s jogo m; caça f; partida f; adj corajoso, valente
gander ['gændə] ganso m
gang [gæŋ] bando m; malta f; grupo m; quadrilha f; ~ster ['-stə] gatuno m, pistoleiro m; ~way passagem f; prancha f

gaol [dʒeil] s GB cadeia f, prisão f; ~er carcereiro m
gap [gæp] abertura f, fenda f; vazio m, lacuna f; intervalo m
gape [geip] v/i embasbacar
garage ['gærɑ:dʒ] s garagem f
garbage ['gɑ:bidʒ] US lixo m
garden ['gɑ:dn] s jardim m; horta f
gargle ['gɑ:gl] v/i gargarejar
garland ['gɑ:lənd] grinalda f
garlic ['gɑ:lik] alho m
garment ['gɑ:mənt] artigo m de vestuário, peça f de roupa
garnet ['gɑ:nit] min granate m, granada f
garnish ['gɑ:niʃ] v/t guarnecer
garret ['gærət] sótão m
garrison ['gærisn] guarnição f
garter ['gɑ:tə] liga f; jarreteira f
gas [gæs] s gás m; cavaco m, conversa f fiada; US gasolina f; v/t, v/i gasear; tagarelar
gash [gæʃ] s incisão f; v/t acutilar
gas|light ['gæslait] lâmpada f a gás; ~mask máscara f antigás
gasoline ['gæsəli:n] US gasolina f
gasp [gɑ:sp] v/i arfar, arquejar; s arfada f
gas|-stove ['gæsstəuv] fogão m a gás; ~works fábrica f de gás
gate [geit] portão m, entrada f; cancela f, porta f
gather ['gæðə] v/t, v/i juntar (-se), reunir(-se); ~ing reunião f, assembleia f

gaudy ['gɔːdi] *adj* berrante, garrido

ga(u)ge [geidʒ] *v/t* medir, calibrar, aferir; *s* medida *f*, padrão *m*

gaunt [gɔːnt] magro, descarnado; desolado

gauze [gɔːz] gaze *f*

gay [geɪ] alegre

gaze [geɪz] *s* olhar *m* fixo; *v/i:* ~ **at** contemplar, fitar

gear [giə] *v/t, v/i* engrenar; *s auto* engrenagem *f*; equipamento *m*; ~**box** caixa *f* de velocidades, *Braz* caixa *f* de câmbio; ~ **lever**, *US* ~ **shift** alavanca *f* de velocidades, *Braz* alavanca *f* de câmbio

geld [geld] *v/t* capar, castrar

gem [dʒem] gema *f*, jóia *f*

gender ['dʒendə] *gram* género *m*

general ['dʒenərəl] *adj* geral; *s* general *m*; **in** ~ em geral; ~**ity** generalidade *f*; ~**ize** *v/t, v/i* generalizar; ~**ly** geralmente, em geral

generation [dʒenə'reiʃən] geração *f*

generosity [dʒenə'rositi] generosidade *f*

generous ['dʒenərəs] generoso

genial ['dʒiːnjəl] ameno; afável

genius ['dʒiːnjəs] (*pl* -**ses**) génio *m*

gentian ['dʒenʃiən] genciana *f*

gentle ['dʒentl] suave, brando, dócil; ligeiro; ~**folk** gente *f* da alta; ~**man** (*pl* -**men**) cavalheiro *m*; ~ **sex** sexo *m* fraco

gentry ['dʒentri] pequena nobreza *f*

genuine ['dʒenjuin] genuíno

geography [dʒi'ɔgrəfi] geografia *f*

geology [dʒi'ɔlədʒi] geologia *f*

geometry [dʒi'ɔmitri] geometria *f*

germ [dʒəːm] germe *m*

German ['dʒəːmən] *adj, s* alemão *m*

germinate ['dʒəːmineit] *v/t, v/i* germinar

gerund ['dʒerənd] gerúndio *m*

gesticulate [dʒes'tikjuleit] *v/i* gesticular

gesture ['dʒestʃə] gesto *m*

get [get] *v/t, v/i* obter, ganhar, adquirir, conseguir; tornar-se, fazer-se; ~ **about** viajar; andar; espalhar-se; ~ **along** ir-se embora; avançar, progredir; ~ **along with** dar-se com; ~ **away** escapar-se; fugir; ~ **back** regressar, voltar; ~ **down** descer; engolir; apontar; ir-se abaixo; ~ **in** chegar; entrar; ~ **off** descer, sair; partir; ~ **on** entrar, subir; continuar; montar; progredir; ~ **out** sair, ir-se embora; publicar; ~ **over** restabelecer-se; dominar, superar; ~ **up** levantar-se

get-up ['getʌp] *s* arranjo *m*, traje *m*

ghastly ['gɑːstli] lívido; horrível

gherkin ['gəːkin] pepino *m* pequeno

ghost [goust] *s* fantasma *m*, espe(c)tro *m*; ~**ly** espe(c)tral

giant ['dʒaiənt] gigante *m*

giblets ['dʒiblits] *s/pl* miudezas *f/pl*, miúdos *m/pl*

giddy ['gidi] tonto, estonteado

gift [gift] dom *m*; oferta *f*, dádiva *f*; **~ed** dotado

gigantic [dʒai'gæntik] gigantesco

giggle ['gigl] *s* risadinha *f*; *v/i* dar risadinhas

gild [gild] *v/t* dourar

gimlet ['gimlit] verruma *f*

gin [dʒin] gim *m*; genebra *f*

ginger ['dʒindʒə] *adj.* ruivo; *s* gengibre *m*; **~bread** pão *m* de gengibre

gipsy ['dʒipsi] (*pl -sies*) cigano *m*

giraffe [dʒi'rɑːf] girafa *f*

gird [gəːd] *v/t* cingir; **~le** ['-dl] *s* cinta *f*

girl [gəːl] rapariga *f*, moça *f*, menina *f*; **~ish** de rapariga, de moça, de menina

girth [gəːθ] volume *m*, espessura *f*; cilha *f*

give [giv] *s* elasticidade *f*; *v/t*, *v/i* dar; entregar; fornecer; ceder; **~ away** distribuir; revelar; **~ back** devolver, restituir; **~ in** ceder; entregar; **~ up** abandonar; desistir de; **~ oneself up** entregar-se, render-se

given [givn] *adj* dado; fixado

glaci|al ['gleisjəl] glacial; **~er** ['glæsjə] geleira *f*, glaciar *m*

glad [glæd] satisfeito, contente, alegre; **~ly** de boa vontade; **~ness** alegria *f*, prazer *m*

glamo(u)r ['glæmə] encanto *m*, fascinação *f*

glance [glɑːns] *s* relance *m*, vista *f* de olhos; *v/t* **~ at** dar uma vista de olhos a; **at a ~** à primeira vista

gland [glænd] glândula *f*

glar|e [glɛə] *s* clarão *m*; olhar *m* furioso; *v/t*, *v/i* deslumbrar, ofuscar; lançar olhares furiosos; **~ing** deslumbrante, brilhante; evidente; penetrante

glass [glɑːs] vidro *m*; copo *m*; espelho *m*; **~es** *pl* óculos *m/pl*; **~y** vidrado, vítreo

glaz|e [gleiz] *s* verniz *m*; *v/t* envidraçar; envernizar; **~ier** ['-zjə] vidraceiro *m*

gleam [gliːm] *s* raio *m*, vislumbre *m*; fulgor *m*, clarão *m*; *v/i* fulgurar, brilhar, cintilar

glean [gliːn] *v/t*, *v/i* respigar

glee [gliː] júbilo *m*; **~ful** jubiloso

glen [glen] vale *m* estreito

glide [glaid] *v/i* deslizar; planar

glider ['glaidə] planador *m*

glimmer ['glimə] *s* vislumbre *m*; *s* luz *f* fraca; *v/i* bruxulear, tremeluzir

glimpse [glimps] *s* vislumbre *m*; *v/t* vislumbrar, entrever

glint [glint] *v/i* reluzir

glisten ['glisn] *v/i* brilhar

glitter ['glitə] *v/i* luzir, resplandecer, cintilar; *s* brilho *m*, resplendor *m*; **~ing** resplandecente

globe [gləub] globo *m*

gloom [gluːm] escuridão *f*, trevas *f/pl*; *fig* melancolia *f*; **~y** escuro, sombrio; melancólico

glorious ['glɔːriəs] glorioso; esplêndido

glory ['glɔːri] *s* glória *f*; resplendor *m*

gloss [glɔs] *s* brilho *m*, lustre *m*;

glosa *f*, comentário *m*; **~ary** ['-əri] glossário *m*; **~y** lustroso *m*

glove [glʌv] luva *f*

glow [gləu] *v/i* arder, reluzir; *s* clarão *m*; ardor *m*; **~-worm** pirilampo *m*

glue [gluː] *s* grude *m*, cola *f*; *v/t* grudar, colar

glut [glʌt] *s* excesso *m*, superabundância *f*; **~ton** glutão *m*

gnarled [nɑːld] nodoso

gnash [næʃ]*v/t*ranger; **~ one's teeth** ranger os dentes

gnat [næt] mosquito *m*

gnaw [nɔː] *v/t*, *v/i* (co)roer

go [gəu] *v/i* andar, marchar; funcionar; ir dar, ir ter; **~ ahead** avançar; começar; **~ away** ir se embora; **~ by** passar; seguir, guiar-se; **~ by the name of** dar pelo nome de; ser conhecido pelo nome de; **~ in** entrar; **~ in for** dedicar-se; participar; **~ off** sair-se; explodir; **~ on** continuar; acontecer; **~ up** subir; **~ with** condizer com; **~ without** passar sem

goad [gəud] *s* aguilhão *m*; *v/t* aguilhoar

goal [gəul] obje(c)tivo *m*, meta *f*, fim *m*; ponto *m*, golo *m*; **~keeper** guarda-redes *m*, *Braz* goleiro *m*

goat [gəut] cabra *f*

go-between 'gəubi.twiːn] *s* intermediário *m*

goblet ['goblit] taça *f*, cálice *m*

goblin ['goblin] duende *m*

God [god] Deus *m*; **thank ~** graças a Deus

god|child ['godtʃaild] afilhado *m*; afilhada *f*; **~dess** deusa *f*; **~father** padrinho *m*; **~less** ímpio; ateu; **~mother** madrinha *f*

goggle ['gogl] *v/i* arregalar os olhos; **~s** ['-lz] *s/pl* óculos *m/pl* de prote(c)ção

going ['gouiŋ] *s* ida *f*; **~s-on** ocorrências *f/pl*

goitre ['goitə] papeira *f*

gold [gould] ouro *m*; **~-dust** ouro *m* em pó; **~en** de ouro, dourado; **~smith** ourives *m*

golf [golf] *s* golfe *m*; **~-course, ~-links** campo *m* de golfe

good [gud] *s* bem *m*; *adj* bom; **a ~ deal** muito; **~ afternoon!** boa tarde; **~-bye** *int* adeus; **~-for-nothing** inútil; **♀ Friday** Sexta-Feira *f* Santa; **~-looking** bonito, formoso; **~-natured** de bom génio; **~ness** bondade *f*; **my ~ness!** meu Deus!

goods [gudz] *s/pl* bens *m/pl*, mercadorias *f/pl*; **~ train** comboio *m* de mercadorias

goodwill ['gud'wil] boa vontade *f*

goose [guːs] *s* (*pl* geese [giːs]) gansa *f*; **~berry** ['guzbəri] groselha *f* verde

gorge [goːdʒ] *s* barranco *m*; *v/t* **~ on** empanturrar-se

gorgeous ['goːdʒəs] magnífico, esplêndido

gosh! [goʃ] caramba!

Gospel ['gospəl] Evangelho *m*

gossip ['gosip] *s* mexerico *m*, tagarelice *f*; tagarela *m*, *f*; *v/i* tagarelar

gourd [guəd] cabaça f

gout [gaut] gota f; **~y** gotoso

govern ['gʌvən] v/t, v/i gram reger; governar; **~ing** adj dire(c)tivo, administrativo; **~ment** governo m; **~or** governador m

gown [gaun] toga f; bata f; vestido m comprido; batina f

grab [græb] v/t apanhar, agarrar

grace [greis] graça f; favor m; **~ful** gracioso

gracious ['greiʃəs] cortês, amável; benévolo, benigno

grad|e [greid] s grau m; v/t graduar, classificar; **~ient** ['-jənt] declive m, rampa f; **~ual** ['grædʒuəl] gradual; **~uate** ['grædʒueit] v/i graduar-se, formar-se; ['grædʒuət] s graduado m

graft [grɑ:ft] s enxerto m; negociata f; v/t enxertar

grain [grein] grão m; fibra f; veio m; cereais m/pl

grammar ['græmə] gramática f; **~-school** liceu m; escola f secundária

gram(me) [græm] grama m

grand [grænd] adj grandioso, sublime; **~daughter** ['græn.dɔ:tə] neta f; **~eur** ['-dʒə] grandeza f; **~father** avô m; **~mother** avó f; **~son** neto m

grange [greindʒ] granja f

granite ['grænit] granito m

granny ['græni] (pl -nies) vovó f

grant [grɑ:nt] s concessão f, doação f; subvenção f; bolsa f, sub-

sídio m; v/t conceder, outorgar; **take for ~ed** tomar por certo

granul|ar ['grænjulə] granular; **~e** grânulo m

grape [greip] uva f; **~-fruit** toronja f

graphic ['græfik] gráfico

grapple [græpl] v/i: **~ with** lutar com; agarrar(-se) a

grasp [grɑ:sp] v/t agarrar, empunhar; compreender; s aperto m; compreensão f

grass [grɑ:s] s relva f; erva f, grama f; **~hopper** gafanhoto m

grate [greit] v/t raspar; ralar; s grade f, grelha f

grateful ['greitful] grato, agradecido

grater ['greitə] ralador m

gratify ['grætifai] v/t gratificar

gratitude ['grætitju:d] gratidão f, reconhecimento m

gratuit|ous [grə'tju(:)itəs] gratuito; **~y** (pl -ties) gorjeta f

grave [greiv] s sepultura f, tumba f; adj grave, sério

gravel ['grævəl] s saibro m, cascalho m

gravestone ['greivstəun] campa f, lápide f

graveyard ['greivjɑ:d] cemitério m

gravitation [grævi'teiʃən] gravitação f

gravity ['græviti] gravidade f

gravy ['greivi] molho m; **~-boat** molheira f

graze [greiz] v/t, v/i roçar; pastar

greas|e [gri:s] s gordura f; [-:z]

v/t untar; **~y** ['-zi] gorduroso

great [greit] *adj* grande; célebre; ó(p)timo, excelente; **a ~ deal (of)** muito; **a ~ while** muito tempo; **a ~ many** muitos; **~ grandfather** bisavô *m*; **~-grandson** bisneto *m*; **~ness** grandeza *f*

greed [gri:d] avidez *f*; glutonaria *f*; **~y** ávido, voraz

Greek [gri:k] *adj, s* grego *m*

green [gri:n] *adj* verde; **~ery** verdura *f*, verdor *m*; **~grocer** fruteiro *m*, hortaliceiro *m*, *Braz* quitandeiro *m*; **~house** estufa *f*; **~ish** esverdeado; **~s** *s/pl* verduras *f/pl*, hortaliça *f*

greet [gri:t] *v/t* cumprimentar, saudar; **~ing** saudação *f*, cumprimento *m*

grey [grei] *adj* cinzento; **~hound** galgo *m*

gridiron ['grid.aiən] grelha *f*

grief [gri:f] dor *f*, pesar *m*

grievance ['gri:vəns] agravo *m*, queixa *f*

grieve [gri:v] *v/t, v/i* afligir(-se); lamentar(-se)

grievous ['gri:vəs] penoso, grave, severo

grill [gril] *s* grelha *f*; *v/t, v/i* grelhar, assar na grelha

grim [grim] torvo, sinistro

grimace [gri'meis] *s* careta *f*

grin [grin] *s* sorriso *m* largo, arreganho *m*; *v/i* sorrir

grind [graind] *v/t* moer; esmagar; triturar; **~er** mó *m*; moleiro *m*; dente *m* molar

grip [grip] *s* aperto *m*; *v/t, v/i* agarrar, prender; apertar

grisly ['grizli] macabro, horrível

groan [grəun] *v/i* gemer; *s* gemido *m*

grocer ['grəusə] merceeiro *m*; **~y** mercearia *f*

grog [grɔg] grogue *m*

groggy ['grɔgi] cambaleante

groin [grɔin] virilha *f*

groom [grum] *s* moço *m* de estrebaria; noivo *m*; *v/t*: **~ horses** tratar de cavalos

groove [gru:v] *s* ranhura *f*

grope [grəup] *v/t, v/i* ta(c)tear; procurar às apalpadelas

gross [grəus] *s* grosa *f*; *adj* grosseiro; *com* bruto

grotto ['grɔtəu] gruta *f*

ground [graund] *s* chão *m*; solo *m*, terreno *m*; terra *f*; motivo *m*, base *f*; fundo *m*; *v/t, v/i* encalhar; fundar, estabelecer; **~-floor** rés-do-chão *m*; **~s** *s/pl* borra *f*; razão *f*, motivo *m*

group [gru:p] *s* grupo *m*; *v/t, v/i* agrupar(-se)

grouse [graus] *v/i* queixar-se, resmungar

grove [grəuv] arvoredo *m*

grow [grəu] *v/t, v/i* crescer; aumentar; tornar-se, ficar; criar, cultivar

growl [graul] *v/i* rosnar; *s* rosnadela *f*

grown-up ['grəunʌp] *adj, s* adulto *m*

growth [grəuθ] crescimento *m*, aumento *m*

grudge [grʌdʒ] *s* rancor *m*; *v/t* dar de má vontade; invejar

gruel [gruəl] papa *f*

gruff [grʌf] rude, brusco

grumble ['grʌmbl] *v/i* resmungar; roncar; *s* resmungadela *f*

grunt [grʌnt] *v/i* grunhir; *s* grunhido *m*

guarantee [ˌgærən'ti:] *s* garantia *f*; caução *f*; *v/t* garantir; caucionar

guard [gɑːd] *v/t* guardar; *s* guarda *f*; sentinela *f*; condutor *m*, Braz guarda-trem *m*; ~**ed** *adj* cauto, cauteloso

guardian ['gɑːdjən] tutor *m*; guardião *m*

guess [ges] *s* suposição *f*, conje(c)tura *f*, *v/t*, *v/i* adivinhar; supor

guest [gest] *s* hóspede *m*, convidado *m*

guidance ['gaidəns] orientação *f*; governo *m*, dire(c)ção *f*

guide [gaid] *v/t* guiar; *s* guia *m*; ~**book** guia *f*, roteiro *m*

guild [gild] corporação *f*, grémio *m*

guileless [ges] ['gaillis] inocente, ingénuo

guilt [gilt] culpa *f*; ~**less** inocente; ~**y** culpável; culpado

guinea pig ['ginipig] porquinho-da-Índia *m*

guise [gaiz] aparência *f*

guitar [gi'taː] guitarra *f*; viola *f*, violão *m*

gulf [gʌlf] *mar* golfo *m*; abismo *m*

gull [gʌl] *s* gaivota *f*

gulp [gʌlp] *s* gole *m*, trago *m*; *v/t* tragar, engolir

gum [gʌm] *s* goma *f*; gengiva *f*; *v/t* engomar, colar

gumption ['gʌmpʃən] bom senso *m*; iniciativa *f*

gun [gʌn] espingarda *f*; canhão *m*; ~**man** salteador *m* armado; ~**ner** artilheiro *m*; ~**powder** pólvora *f*; ~**smith** espingardeiro *m*

gurgle ['gəːgl] *v/i* gorgolejar, gorgolhar

gush [gʌʃ] *v/i* jorrar, brotar; *s* jorro *m*, borbotão *m*; ~**ing** *adj* efusivo

gust [gʌst] pé *m* de vento, rajada *f*

gut [gʌt] *s* intestino *m*, tripa *f*; *v/t* desventrar, estripar; ~**s** *s/pl* *fig* coragem *f*, valentia *f*

gutter ['gʌtə] *s* goteira *f*; sarjeta *f*

guy [gai] *s* sujeito *m*, gajo *m*; espantalho *m*

gymnasium [dʒim'neizjəm] ginásio *m*; ~**t** [-'næst] ginasta *m*, *f*; ~**tics** ['næstiks] ginástica *f*

gynaecologist [ˌgaini'kɔlədʒist] ginecologista *m*, *f*

gyrate [ˌdʒaiə'reit] *v/i* girar

H

haberdasher ['hæbədæʃə] capelista *m*, Braz armarinheiro *m*

habit ['hæbit] hábito *m*, costume *m*

habit|able ['hæbitəbl] habitável; ~**at** ['-æt] habitat *m*

habit|ual [hə'bitjuəl] habitual; ~**ué** [hə'bitjuei] frequentador *m*

hack [hæk] *v/t*, *v/i* cortar, des-

pedaçar; s cavalo m de aluguel;
sendeiro m, pileca f; mercenário m; escritor m mau

hackneyed ['hæknid] adj corri-
queiro, banal

haddock ['hædək] eglefim m

haggard ['hægəd] macilento, pálido

hail [heil] s saraiva f; v/i sarai-
var; v/t aclamar, saudar; chamar

hair [hɛə] cabelo m; pêlo m;
~-**cut** corte m de cabelo;
~-**do** penteado m; ~**dresser**
cabeleireiro m; ~**pin** gancho
m; ~-**raising** arrepiante; ~**y**
peludo, cabeludo

half [hɑ:f] (pl **halves** [hɑ:vz]) s
metade f, meio m; parte f, tem-
po m; adj meio; semi ...; adv
meio; ~-**breed** adj. s mestiço
m; ~-**time** meio tempo m;
~-**way** adj, adv a meio caminho, a meia distância; ~-**wit**
parvo m, idiota m, f

halibut ['hælibət] hipoglosso m

hall [hɔ:l] residência f; salão m;
entrada f, vestíbulo m; refeitório m

hallo [hə'ləu] int olá; alô

hallow ['hæləu] v/t santificar,
consagrar

halo ['heiləu] halo m; auréola f

halt [hɔ:lt] s parada f, paragem f;
v/t, v/i fazer alto, parar, deter
(-se)

halve [hɑ:v] v/t dividir ao meio

ham [hæm] s presunto m

hamlet ['hæmlit] lugarejo m, al-
deola f

hammer ['hæmə] s martelo m;

v/t, v/i martelar

hammock ['hæmək] rede f,
maca f

hamper ['hæmpə] s canastra f;
v/t embaraçar, estorvar

hand [hænd] v/t passar, dar, entregar; s mão f; ponteiro m; at
~ à mão, perto; **at second** ~
em segunda mão; **get the upper** ~ levar vantagem; **give/
lend a** ~ to dar uma ajuda; ~
in glove unha e carne; ~ **in** ~
de mãos dadas; **on the other**
~ por outro lado

hand|bag ['hændbæg] carteira f,
bolsa f, mala f; ~-**ball** (h)ande-
bol m; ~**cuffs** s/pl algemas
f/pl; ~**ful** punhado m, mão-
-cheia f

handicap ['hændikæp] s desvantagem f

handicraft ['hændikrɑ:ft] habilidade f manual, mão-de-obra f

handkerchief ['hæŋkətʃif]
lenço m

handle ['hændl] s cabo m, punho m; v/t tratar; manejar, ma-
nusear; ~-**bars** s/pl guiador
m, guidão m

hand|made ['hænd'meid] adj
feito à mão, manufa(c)turado
handrail ['hændreil] corrimão
m

handsome ['hænsəm] belo, formoso

handwriting ['hænd.raitiŋ] caligrafia f, letra f

handy ['hændi] hábil; jeitoso; à
mão

hang [hæŋ] v/t pendurar, suspender; pender

hang [hæŋ] v/t enforcar

hangar ['hæŋə] hangar m

hangman ['hæŋmən] (pl -men) carrasco m, algoz m

hangover ['hæŋ͵əuvə] s ressaca f, resto m

hanky ['hæŋki] = **handker-chief**

haphazard ['hæp'hæzəd] adj casual, acidental

happen ['hæpən] v/i acontecer, suceder, ocorrer; **~ing** s acontecimento m, sucesso m

happ|ily ['hæpili] felizmente; **~iness** felicidade f; **~y** feliz

harangue [hə'ræŋ] s arenga f; v/t arengar

harass ['hærəs] v/t acossar

harbo(u)r ['ha:bə] s porto m; fig asilo m; v/t abrigar, acolher; acalentar

hard [ha:d] adv demasiado, muito; adj duro; rude; difícil; **~en** v/t, v/i endurecer; **~-hearted** austero, inflexível; **~iness** robustez f; intrepidez f; **~ labour** trabalhos m/pl forçados; **~ly** mal, apenas; **~ness** dureza f; rigor m; **~ship** miséria f, privação; **~ware** quinquilharia f; ferragens f/pl; **~y** robusto; intrépido

hare [heə] s lebre f; **~-brained** insensato, cabeça-no-ar; **~lip** lábio m leporino

harm [ha:m] s mal m, dano m, prejuízo m; v/t danificar; fazer mal a; **~ful** nocivo; **~less** inofensivo, inocente

harmony ['ha:məni] harmonia f

harness ['ha:nis] s arnês m, arreios m/pl; v/t ajaezar, arrear

harp [ha:p] harpa f; **~ist** harpista m, f

harpoon [ha:'pu:n] s arpão m; v/t arpoar

harrow ['hærəu] s grade f, trilho m; v/t gradar; atormentar

harsh [ha:ʃ] áspero, severo

hart [ha:t] veado m

harvest ['ha:vist] v/t colher, ceifar; s ceifa f, colheita f; **~er** ceifeiro m; segadora f

hash [hæʃ] s picado m; v/t picar

hash(ish) ['hæʃ(i:ʃ)] haxixe m

hast|**e** [heist] pressa f; **~en** [-sn] v/t, v/i apressar(-se), aviar-se; **~y** apressado, precipitado

hat [hæt] chapéu m

hatch [hætʃ] s ninhada f; v/t, v/i incubar, chocar; tramar

hatchet ['hætʃit] machadinha f

hate [heit] v/t odiar, detestar; s ódio m; **~ful** odioso, detestável

hatred ['heitrid] ódio m

haught|**iness** ['hɔ:tinis] altivez f; **~y** altivo, altaneiro

haunch [hɔ:ntʃ] anca f; quadril m

haunt [hɔ:nt] s refúgio m, retiro m; v/t frequentar, visitar; assombrar, infestar; obcecar; **~ing** adj obsidiante, fixo

have [hæv, həv] v/t ter; receber, obter; tomar, comer; **~ to** ter de, ter que; **I** etc. **had better** era melhor que; **~ (some-thing) done** mandar fazer (alguma coisa); **~ it** insistir;

~ **on** trazer

haven ['heivn] abrigo m, refúgio m

havoc ['hævək] estrago m, destruição f; **play ~ with/among** causar grandes estragos em

hawk [hɔːk] s falcão m

hawthorn ['hɔːθɔːn] espinheiro-alvar m

hay [hei] feno m; ~ **fever** febre f dos fenos; ~**stack** meda f de feno

hazard ['hæzəd] s risco m, perigo m; v/t aventurar, arriscar; ~**ous** arriscado, perigoso

haze [heiz] s cerração f

hazel ['heizl] s avelaneira f; ~**-nut** avelã f

hazy ['heizi] enevoado; confuso, vago

he [hi:, hi] pron ele; s macho m; ~ **who** aquele que

head [hed] s cabeça f; cabeceira f; cabeçalho; dire(c)tor m, chefe m; v/t encabeçar, dirigir; cabecear; ~**s or tails?** cara ou coroa?

head|ache ['hedeik] dor f de cabeça; ~**ing** s cabeçalho m; ~**lamp**, ~**light** auto farol m; ~**line** s título m; ~**long** adv precipitadamente; adj impetuoso, precipitado; ~**master** dire(c)tor m, reitor m; ~**quarters** quartel-general m; ~**strong** cabeçudo; ~**way** progresso m

heal [hi:l] v/t, v/i curar, sarar, cicatrizar; ~**ing** s cura f

health [helθ] saúde f; ~**y** saudável, sadio, são

heap [hi:p] s montão m; v/t amontoar

hear [hiə] v/t, v/i ouvir; ouvir dizer; ~ **of** ouvir falar de; ~ **en**, ouvinte, m, f; ~**ing** s audição f; audiência f; interrogatório m

hearsay ['hiəsei] boato m

hearse [hə:s] carro m fúnebre

heart [hɑ:t] coração m; âmago m; coragem f; copas f; **at** ~ no fundo, no íntimo; **by** ~ de cor; ~**breaking** dilacerante; ~**en** v/t animar, encorajar

hearth [hɑ:θ] lar m; lareira f

heart|less ['hɑ:tlis] cruel, desapiedado; ~**-to-** ~ adj franco, sincero; ~**y** cordial

heat [hi:t] s calor m; ardor m; v/t, v/i aquecer(-se); ~**er** aquecedor m

heath [hi:θ] charneca f

heathen ['hi:ðən] pagão m

heather ['heðə] urze f

heating ['hi:tiŋ] s aquecimento m

heave [hi:v] v/t, v/i elevar(-se), levantar; alçar, içar; lançar, arremessar; s lançamento m, arremesso m

heaven ['hevn] céu m; **good** ~**s!** céus!; ~**ly** celeste, celestial

heav|iness ['hevinis] pesadume f; entorpecimento m; abatimento m; ~**y** adj pesado; forte

Hebrew ['hi:bru:] adj, s hebreu m

hectic ['hektik] agitado, turbulento; héctico

hedge [hedʒ] s sebe f, cerca f; v/t, v/i vedar, cercar de sebes; ladear, fugir à pergunta hedgehog ['hedʒhɔg] ouriço (-cacheiro) m

heed [hi:d] s atenção f, tento m; v/t prestar atenção a; ~less imprudente

heel [hi:l] s calcanhar m, talão m; tacão m, salto m

heifer ['hefə] vitela f

height [hait] altura f; altitude f; cúmulo m, auge m; ~en v/t, v/i aumentar, intensificar

heir [ɛə] herdeiro m; ~ess herdeira f

helicopter ['helikɔptə] helicóptero m

helium ['hi:ljəm] hélio m

hell [hel] s inferno m; ~ish infernal

hello ['hə'ləu] = hallo

helm [helm] mar temão m, barra f do leme

helmet ['helmit] elmo m, capacete m

help [help] s ajuda f, auxílio m; v/t, v/i ajudar; socorrer; servir; int socorro! I can't ~ não posso deixar de, não posso evitar; it can't be ~ed não há remédio; ~er ajudante m, auxiliar m; ~ful serviçal; útil, proveitoso; ~ing s porção f, dose f; ~less desamparado

hem [hem] s bainha f

hemisphere ['hemisfiə] hemisfério m

hemlock ['hemlɔk] cicuta f

hemp [hemp] cânhamo m

hen [hen] galinha f

hence [hens] porr isso, portanto; ~forth, ~forward daqui em diante

hen-house ['henhaus] galinheiro m

her [hə:, hə] obj pron a; ela; lhe; poss seu, dela

herald ['herəld] s arauto m, heraldo m; ~ic [he'rældik] heráldico; ~ry ['herəldri] heráldica f

herb [hə:b] erva f; ~aceous [-'bei∫əs] herbáceo; ~al herbóreo; ~ivorous [-'bivərəs] herbívoro

herd [hə:d] s rebanho m, manada f

here [hiə] adv aqui, cá; ~ and there cá e lá, aqui e acolá; ~'s to . . .! à saúde de . . .!

hereditary [hi'reditəri] hereditário; ~y hereditariedade f

heresy ['herəsi] (pl -sies) heresia f; ~tic herege m, f; ~tical [hi'retikəl] herético

hermit ['hə:mit] ermitão m, eremita m, f

hero ['hiərəu] herói m; ~ic [hi'rəuik] heróico; ~ine ['herəuin] heroína f; ~ism ['herəuizəm] heroísmo m

heron ['herən] garça f

herring ['heriŋ] arenque m

hers [hə:z] o seu, a sua, os seus, as suas; dela

herself [hə:'self] se; ela mesma; si; si mesma; si própria

hesitate ['heziteit] v/i hesitar; ~ion [-'tei∫ən] hesitação f

hew [hju:] v/t, v/i abater, cortar; talhar

hey [hei] eh!; eia! ena!

heyday ['heidei] auge m, apogeu m

hi [hai] olá!

hoard

hibernate ['haibəneit] *v/i* hibernar

hiccup ['hikʌp] *s* soluço *m*; *v/i* estar com soluços

hide [haid] *v/t, v/i* esconder (-se); *s* pele *f* couro *m*

hideous ['hidiəs] horrível, hediondo

hiding ['haidiŋ] *s* sova *f*, surra *f*

hi-fi ['hai'fai] *adj, s* (de) alta fidelidade *f*

high [hai] *adj* alto; elevado; eminente; superior; ~brow intelectual *m*; sabichão *m* de alta categoria; ~**class** de primeira qualidade; de alta categoria; ~**fidelity = hi-fi** de alta qualidade; ~**handed** despótico, arbitrário; ~ **life** via *f* da alta sociedade; ~**ly** altamente; sumamente; ~**minded** magnânimo, de ideias largas; ~**ness** altura *f*, elevação *f*; ♀ **ness** Alteza *f*; ~ **road** estrada *f* nacional; ~ **school** *US* escola *f* secundária; ~ **season** plena estação *f*; ~**way** *US* estrada *f* nacional, *Braz* rodovia *f*

hijack ['haidʒæk] *v/t* assaltar; sequestrar

hike [haik] *v/i* andar a pé, caminhar

hilarious [hi'lɛəriəs] alegre; ~**ty** [-'læriti] hilaridade *f*

hill [hil] colina *f*, outeiro *m*; ~**side** encosta *f*, ladeira *f*; ~**y** montanhoso

hilt [hilt] cabo *m*; copos *m/pl*, punho *m*

him [him, im] o; ele, a ele; lhe

himself [him'self] se; ele mesmo; si; si próprio

hind [haind] *s* corça *f*; *adj* posterior, traseiro

hinder ['hində] *v/t* impedir, embaraçar, estorvar

hindrance ['hindrəns] impedimento *m*, empecilho *m*, estorvo *m*

hinge [hindʒ] *s* gonzo *m*, charneira *f*

hint [hint] *s* sugestão *f*, indício *m*, lamiré *m*; *v/t, v/i* insinuar, sugerir

hip [hip] *s* anca *f*, quadril *m*; *bot* fruto *m* da rosa brava

hire [haiə] *s* aluguer *m*, aluguel *m*; salário *m*; *v/t* alugar; ~**purchase** compra *f* a prestações

his [hiz, iz] (o) seu, (a) sua, (os) seus, (as) suas; dele

hiss [his] *s* assobio *m*, silvo *m*; *v/i* assobiar; ~ **at** apupar

historian [his'tɔːriən] historiador *m*; ~**ic(al)** [-'tɔrik(əl)] histórico; ~**y** [-'təri] (*pl* -ries) história *f*

hit [hit] *s* golpe *m*, pancada *f*; acerto *m*; sucesso *m*, êxito *m*; sensação *f*; *v/t* golpear, bater; acertar; ~ **the mark** acertar no alvo; ~ **the nail on the head** acertar em cheio, dar no vinte

hitch [hitʃ] *s* puxão *m*; nó *m*, volta *f* de cabo; dificuldade *f*; encrenca *f*; *v/t* prender, amarrar; ~**hike** *v/i* andar à boleia, *Braz* viajar de carona

hive [haiv] *s* colmeia *f*, cortiço *m*

hoard [hɔːd] *s* tesouro *m*; reserva *f*; *v/t* amealhar, armazenar

hoarfrost ['hɔː'frɒst] geada *f*

hoarse [hɔːs] rouco; **~ness** rouquidão *f*

hoax [həuks] *s* engano *m*, logro *m*; *v/t* enganar, lograr

hobble ['hɒbl] *v/i* coxear, manquejar

hobby ['hɒbi] (*pl* -**bies**) passatempo *m*

hock [hɒk] *s* vinho *m* do Reno

hockey ['hɒki] hóquei *m*

hog [hɒg] *s* porco *m*

hoist [hɔist] *v/t* içar; guindar

hold [həuld] *v/t*, *v/i* possuir; conter, levar; manter; julgar, considerar; pegar, agarrar, segurar; *s* pega *f*, apoio *m*; domínio *m*, influência *f*; porão *m*; **~ on** aguentar; continuar, persistir; **~ up** exibir, mostrar; manter-se; fazer parar; demorar; **catch/lay ~ of** agarrar, deitar a mão a; **~er** possuidor *m*, detentor *m*; **~ing** *s* propriedade *f*; arrendamento *m*

hole [həul] *s* buraco *m*

holiday ['hɒlədi] *s* (dia *m*) feriado *m*; férias *f/pl*; **~-maker** veraneante *m*, *f*, Braz veranista *m*, *f*

hollow ['hɒləu] *adj* oco, côncavo; *s* vale *m*; cavidade *f*; recôncavo *m*; *v/t* cavar, escavar

holly ['hɒli] azevinho *m*, Braz azevim *m*

holy ['həuli] *adj* santo, sagrado; ♀ **Ghost** Espírito *m* Santo; ♀ **Land** Terra *f* Santa; **~ water** água *f* benta

homage ['hɒmidʒ] homenagem

f, respeito *m*; **do ~, pay ~** prestar homenagem

home [həum] *s* lar *m*, casa *f* paterna; residência *f*, domicílio *m*; asilo *m*, albergue *m*; terra *f* natal; *adv* para casa; *adj* doméstico; nativo, nacional; **at ~** em casa; **~land** pátria *f*; **~ly** simples, caseiro; ♀ **Office** Ministério *m* do Interior; **~ rule** autonomia *f*; **~sick** nostálgico, saudoso do lar ou da pátria; **~sickness** nostalgia *f*, saudade *f*; **~ truth** verdade *f* nua e crua; **~work** trabalhos *m/pl* de/para casa, deveres *m/pl* da escola

honest ['ɒnist] honesto, probo; **~y** honestidade *f*, probidade *f*

honey ['hʌni] mel *m*; US querido, amor; **~comb** favo *m* de mel; **~moon** *s* lua *f* de mel; **~suckle** madressilva *f*

honorary ['ɒnərəri] honorário

hono(u)r ['ɒnə] ♀ honradez *f*, honra *f*; *v/t* honrar; **~able** honroso, honrado

hood [hud] capuz *m*, touca *f*; capelo *m*; *auto* capota *f*

hoodwink ['hudwiŋk] *v/t* lograr, enganar

hoof [huːf] casco *m*

hook [huk] *s* gancho *m*, colchete *m*; anzol *m*; *v/t* enganchar

hoop [huːp] *s* aro *m*, argola *f*

hoover ['huːvə] *s* = **vacuum cleaner**

hop [hɒp] *s* salto *m*, pulo *m*; baile *m*; *bot* lúpulo *m*; *v/i* saltar ao pé coxinho, saltitar, pular

hope [həup] *v/i* esperar, ter esperança; *s* esperança *f*; **~ful** *adj* esperançoso; **~less** desesperado, desesperançado

horde [hɔːd] horda *f*

horizon [hə'raizn] horizonte *m*; **~tal** [,hɔri'zɔntl] horizontal

horn [hɔːn] chifre *m*, corno *m*; *mus* corneta *f*; buzina *f*; **~et** ['it] vespão *m*; **~y** caloso

horrible ['hɔrəbl] horrível

horrid ['hɔrid] hórrido, horrendo

horrify ['hɔrifai] *v/t* horrorizar

horror ['hɔrə] horror *m*

horse [hɔːs] cavalo *m*; cavalete *m*; **on ~back** a cavalo; **~hair** crina *f*; **~man** (*pl* **-men**) cavaleiro *m*; **~manship** equitação *f*; **~power** cavalo-vapor *m*; **~racing** corrida *f* de cavalos; **~shoe** ferradura *f*

hose [həuz] *s* meias *f/pl*; peúgas *f/pl*; mangueira *f*; *v/t* regar com mangueira

hosier ['həuʒə] camiseiro *m*, negociante *m* de meias e roupa interior de homem

hospitable ['hɔspitəbl] hospitaleiro

hospital ['hɔspitl] hospital *m*

hospitality [,hɔspi'tæliti] hospitalidade *f*

host [həust] *s* anfitrião *m*, hospedeiro *m*; *eccl* hóstia *f*; multidão *f*

hostage ['hɔstidʒ] refém *m*

hostel ['hɔstel] albergue *m*, lar *m*

hostess ['həustis] anfitriã *f*, hospedeira *f*, dona *f* de casa

hostil|e ['hɔstail] hostil; **~ity** [hɔs'tiliti] hostilidade *f*

hot [hɔt] quente; caloroso; cálido; picante; **~ dog** cachorro-quente *m*

hotel [həu'tel] hotel *m*

hound [haund] *s* podengo *m*, cão *m* de caça

hour ['auə] hora *f*; **~glass** ampulheta *f*; **~ly** de hora em hora

house [haus] *s* casa *f*; câmara *f*; ♀ Câmara *f* dos Comuns; ♀ **of Commons** Câmara *f* dos Comuns; ♀ **of Lords** Câmara *f* dos Lordes; ♀ **s of Parliament** Casas *f/pl* do Parlamento; **~hold** família *f*; governo *m* da casa, *Braz* negócios *m/pl* domésticos; **~keeper** governanta *f*; **~maid** criada *f*; **~wife** (*pl* **wives**) dona *f* de casa; **~work** trabalho *m* doméstico

housing ['hauziŋ] *s* alojamento *m*, habitação *f*

hovel ['hɔvəl] cabana *f*, choupana *f*

hover ['hɔvə] *v/i* pairar

how [hau] *adv* quanto; como; quão; que; **~ are you?** como está?, como vai?; **~ come?** como se explica?; **~ do you do?** muito prazer!; **~ far?** até onde?; **~ long?** quanto tempo?; **~ many?** quantos?; **~ever** *adv* de qualquer modo, seja como for; *conj* todavia, porém, contudo; **~ever much** por muito que

howl [haul] *v/i* uivar; *s* uivo *m*

hubbub ['hʌbʌb] alarido *m*

huddle ['hʌdl] *v/t*, *v/i* juntar (-se), amontoar(-se)

hue [hjuː] matiz *m*, tonalidade *f*

hug [hʌg] *v/t* abraçar; *s* abraço *m*

huge [hju:dʒ] imenso, enorme, colossal

hull [hʌl] *s* casco *m*

hullo ['hʌ'ləu] = **hello**

hum [hʌm] *v/t, v/i* zumbir; trautear, cantarolar; *s* zumbido *m*

human ['hju:mən] humano; ~e [-'mein] humano, humanitário; ~itarian [-ˌmæni'tɛəriən] *adj, s* humanitário *m*; ~ity [-'mæniti] humanidade *f*

humble ['hʌmbl] *adj* humilde

humbug ['hʌmbʌg] *s* mistificação *f*, embuste *m*

humdrum ['hʌmdrʌm] monótono, banal

humid ['hju:mid] (h)úmido

humidity [hju:'miditi] (h)umidade *f*

humili|ate [hju:'milieit] *v/t* humilhar; ~ation [-'eiʃən] humilhação *f*; ~ty [-'militi] humildade *f*

humorist ['hju:mərist] humorista *n, f*

humorous ['hju:mərəs] divertido, engraçado

humo(u)r ['hju:mə] *s* humor *m*; *v/t* comprazer

hump [hʌmp] *s* corcova *f*, giba *f*, corcunda *f*, bossa *f*

hunch [hʌntʃ] *s* palpite *m*, pressentimento

hunchback ['hʌntʃbæk] corcunda *m, f*, corcovado *m*

hundred ['hʌndrəd] cento; cem; centena *f*

Hungarian [hʌŋ'gɛəriən] *s, adj*

húngaro *m*

hunger ['hʌŋgə] *s* fome *f*

hungry ['hʌŋgri] esfomeado, esfaimado, faminto

hunt [hʌnt] *v/t, v/i* caçar; *s* caça *f*; caçada *f*; ~er caçador *m*; ~ing *s* caça *f*

hurdle ['hə:dl] barreira *f*

hurl [hə:l] *v/t* arremessar, arrojar, lançar

hurray! [hu'rei] hurra! viva!

hurricane ['hʌrikən] furacão *m*

hurry ['hʌri] *v/t, v/i* aviar-se, apressar(-se), despachar-se; *s* pressa *f*; **in a** ~ com pressa; ~ **up** aviar-se, acelerar

hurt [hə:t] *v/t, v/i* doer, magoar; ferir

husband ['hʌzbənd] *s* marido *m*, esposo *m*

hush [hʌʃ] *s* silêncio *m*, quietude *f*; *v/t, v/i* aquietar, fazer calar; *int* silêncio!; ~ **up** abafar, encobrir; ~**-money** suborno *m*, peita *f*

husk [hʌsk] *s* casca *f*, folhelho *m*

husky ['hʌski] *adj* rouco, áspero

hustle ['hʌsl] *s* a(c)tividade *f*; *v/t, v/i* despachar, empurrar

hut [hʌt] cabana *f*; barraca *f*

hydro|carbon ['haidrə'ka:bən] hidrocarboneto *m*; ~**gen** [-dʒən] hidrogénio *m*; ~**phobia** hidrofobia *f*; ~**plane** hidroplano *m*, hidrodeslizador *m*

hyena [hai'i:nə] hiena *f*

hygien|e ['haidʒi:n] higiene *f*; ~**ic** [-'dʒi:nik] higiénico

hymn [him] hino *m*

hyphen ['haifən] hífen *m*, traço *m* de união

hypno|sis [hip'nəusis] hipnose *f*; **~tic** [hip'nɒtik] hipnótico; **~tism** ['hipnətizəm] hipnotismo *m*; **~tist** ['hipnətist] hipnotista *m, f*; **~tize** ['hipnətaiz] *v/t* hipnotizar

hypo|chondria [,haipə'kɒndriə] hipocondria *f*; **~chondriac** [-riæk] *s, adj* hipocondríaco *m*;

~crisy [hi'pɒkrəsi] hipocrisia *f*; **~crite** ['hipəkrit] *s* hipócrita *m, f*

hypothetical [,haipə'θetikəl] hipotético

hyster|ia [his'tiəriə] histeria *f*; **~ical** [-'terikəl] histérico; **~ics** [-'teriks] ataques *m/pl* histéricos

I

I [ai] eu
Iberian [ai'biəriən] *adj* ibérico
ice [ais] *s* gelo *m*; **~berg** iceberg *m*; **~cream** sorvete *m*, gelado *m*
Icelandic [ais'lændik] *adj* islandês
icicle ['aisikl] sincelo *m*
icy ['aisi] gelado, álgido
idea [ai'diə] ideia *f*
ideal [ai'diəl] *adj, s* ideal *m*; **~ism** idealismo *m*; **~ist** idealista *m, f*
identi|cal [ai'dentikəl] idêntico; **~fication** [-,fi'keiʃən] identificação *f*; **~fy** [-fai] *v/t* identificar; **~ty** [-ti] (*pl* **-ties**) identidade *f*; **~ty card** bilhete *m* de identidade
idiom ['idiəm] idiotismo *m*, idioma *m*
idiot ['idiət] idiota *m, f*; **~ic** [-'ɔtik] idiota
idle [aidl] *adj* preguiçoso; ocioso, desocupado; vão; **~ness** preguiça *f*; ócio *m*
idol [aidl] ídolo *m*; **~atry** [-'dɒlətri] idolatria *f*; **~ize** ['-dəlaiz] *v/t* idolatrar

idyl(l) ['idil] idílio *m*; **~ic** idílico
i. e. [ai'i:] = that is (to say) isto é
if [if] *conj* se
ignit|e [ig'nait] *v/t, v/i* inflamar(-se), acender; **~ion** [-'niʃən] ignição *f*
ignoble [ig'nəubəl] ignóbil
ignor|ance ['ignərəns] ignorância *f*; **~ant** ignorante; **~e** [-'nɔ:] *v/t* não fazer caso de, ignorar
ill [il] *s* mal *m*; *adj* doente; mau; *adv* mal; **~advised** imprudente; **~bred** malcriado, mal-educado
illegal [i'li:gəl] ilegal
illegible [i'ledʒəbl] ilegível
illegitimate [,ili'dʒitimit] ilegítimo
ill-fated ['il'feitid] malaventurado
illicit [i'lisit] ilícito
illiterate [i'litərət] *adj, s* iletrado *m*, analfabeto *m*
ill-|natured ['il'neitʃəd] maldoso, malvado; **~ness** doença *f*; **~timed** inoportuno; **~treat** *v/t* maltratar

illuminat|e [i'lju:mineit] *v/t* iluminar; **~ion** [-'neiʃən] iluminação *f*

illus|ion [i'lu:ʒən] ilusão *f*; **~ive** [-siv] ilusório

illustrat|e [iləstreit] *v/t* ilustrar; **~ion** [----] ilustração *f*

illustrious [i'lʌstriəs] ilustre

image ['imidʒ] imagem *f*

imagin|able [i'mædʒinəbl] imaginável; **~ary** imaginário; **~ation** imaginação *f*; **~e** [-in] *v/t* imaginar

imita|te ['imiteit] *v/t* imitar; **~tion** [-'teiʃən] imitação *f*; **~tor** imitador *m*

immature [,imə'tjuə] imaturo

immeasurable [i'meʒərəbl] imensurável

immediate [i'mi:djət] imediato

immerse [i'mə:s] *v/t* imergir

immigrat|e ['imigreit] *v/i* imigrar; **~ion** [-'greiʃən] imigração *f*

immoderate [i'mɔdərit] imoderado, desmedido

immodest [i'mɔdist] imodesto

immoral [i'mɔrəl] imoral

immortal [i'mɔ:tl] imortal

immovable [i'mu:vəbl] imóvel

immune [i'mju:n] imune, imunizado, isento

imp [imp] diabrete *m*

impact ['impækt] impacto *m*

impair [im'pɛə] *v/t* enfraquecer, prejudicar

impalpable [im'pælpəbl] impalpável

impart [im'pa:t] *v/t* participar, comunicar

impartial [im'pa:ʃəl] impar-cial

impass|able [im'pɑ:səbl] intransitável; **~ive** [-'pæsiv] impassivo

impatien|ce [im'peiʃəns] impaciência *f*; **~t** impaciente

impediment [im pedimənt] impedimento *m*, obstáculo *m*

impel [im'pel] *v/t* impelir

impending [im'pendiŋ] ameaçador, iminente

impenetrable [im'penitrəbl] impenetrável

imperative [im'perətiv] *s, adj* imperativo *m*

imperceptible [,impə'septəbl] imperceptível

imperfect [im'pə:fikt] *s, adj* imperfeito *m*

imperial [im'piəriəl] imperial

imperil [im'peril] *v/t* pôr em perigo

imperishable [im'periʃəbl] imperecível

impersonal [im'pə:snl] impessoal

impersonate [im'pə:səneit] *v/t* personificar; representar

impertinen|ce [im'pə:tinəns] impertinência *f*; **~t** impertinente

impervious [im'pə:vjəs] impermeável

impetu|ous [im'petjuəs] impetuoso; **~s** [-'pitəs] ímpeto *m*

impish ['impiʃ] traquinas, travesso

implacable [im'plækəbl] implacável

implant [im'plɑ:nt] *v/t* implantar

implement ['implimənt] s implemento m, apetrecho m

implicat|e ['implikeit] (in) v/t implicar (em); **~ion** [-'keiʃən] implicação f

implicit [im'plisit] implícito

implore [im'plɔ:] v/t implorar

imply [im'plai] v/t implicar

impolite [impə'lait] descortês; **~ness** descortesia f

import [im'pɔ:t] importância f, importância f; com importação f; [im'pɔ:t] v/t importar

importan|ce [im'pɔ:təns] importância f; **~t** importante

importation [impɔ:'teiʃən] importação f

importunate [im'pɔ:tjunit] importuno

impos|e [im'pəuz] v/t impor; **~e (up)on** incomodar, molestar; **~ing** imponente

impossib|ility [im.pɔsə'biliti] impossibilidade f; **~le** [-'pɔsəbl] impossível

impostor [im'pɔstə] impostor m

impotent ['impətənt] impotente

impoverish [im'pɔvəriʃ] v/t empobrecer

impracticable [im'præktikəbl] impraticável

impress [im'pres] v/t imprimir; impressionar; **~ion** impressão f; **~ionable** impressionável; **~ive** impressionante, impressivo

imprint [im'print] v/t imprimir; ['imprint] s impressão f

imprison [im'prizn] v/t aprisionar; **~ment** aprisionamento m, prisão f

improbab|ility [im.prɔbə'biliti] (pl **-ties**) improbabilidade f; **~le** [-'prɔbəbl] improvável

improper [im'prɔpə] impróprio, inconveniente

improve [im'pru:v] v/t, v/i melhorar, aperfeiçoar(-se); progredir; **~ment** melhoramento m, aperfeiçoamento m, progresso m

improvise ['imprəvaiz] v/t, v/i improvisar

impruden|ce [im'pru:dəns] imprudência f; **~t** imprudente

impud|ence ['impjudəns] impudência f; **~ent** impudente

impulse ['impʌls] impulso m

impulsive [im'pʌlsiv] impulsivo

impure [im'pjuə] impuro

imput|ation [impju'teiʃən] imputação f; **~e** [-'pju:t] **~ to** imputar a

in [in] prp em; dentro de; adv dentro, em casa; **~ the afternoon** à tarde; **day ~ day out** dia após dia

inability [.inə'biliti] incapacidade f

inaccurate [in'ækjurit] inexa(c)to, incorre(c)to, erróneo

inaction [in'ækʃən] ina(c)ção f

inadequate [in'ædikwit] inadequado

inadmissible [.inəd'misəbl] inadmissível

inadvertent [.inəd'və:tənt] inadvertido

inanimate [in'ænimit] inanimado

inapplicable [in'æplikəbl]

inaplicável

inapt [in'æpt] inapto

inarticulate [.inɑ:'tikjulit] inarticulado

inasmuch as [inəz'mʌtʃ əz] visto que, porquanto

inattentive [.inə'tentiv] desatento

inaudible [in'ɔ:dəbl] inaudível

inaugurate [i'nɔ:gjureit] v/t inaugurar

inborn ['in'bɔ:n] inato

incalculable [in'kælkjuləbl] incalculável

incandescent ['inkæn'desnt] incandescente

incapable [in'keipəbl] incapaz

incapaci|tate [.inkə'pæsiteit] v/t incapacitar; **~ty** incapacidade f

incautious [in'kɔ:ʃəs] incauto

incense ['insens] s incenso m; [in'sens] v/t irritar

incentive [in'sentiv] incentivo m

incessant [in'sesnt] incessante

inch [intʃ] s polegada f; **~ by ~** palmo a palmo

incident ['insidənt] s incidente m; **~al** [.-'dentəl] adj incidental, casual; **~ally** a propósito

incineration [in.sinə'reiʃən] incineração f

incis|e [in'saiz] v/t incisar; **~ion** [in'siʒən] incisão f; **~ive** incisivo; **~or** incisivo m

incite [in'sait] v/t incitar

inclination [.inkli'neiʃən] inclinação f

incline [in'klain] s declive m, vertente f; v/t v/i inclinar(-se)

include [in'klu:d] v/t incluir

inclusive [in'klu:siv] inclusivo

incoherent [.inkou'hiərənt] incoerente

incombustible [.inkəm'bʌstəbl] incombustível

income [in'kʌm] rendimento m, renda f; **~tax** imposto m de rendimento

incomparable [in'kɔmpərəbl] incomparável

incompatible [.inkəm'pætəbl] incompatível

incompetent [in'kɔmpitənt] incompetente

incomplete [.inkəm'pli:t] incompleto

incomprehensible [inkɔmpri-'hensəbl] incompreensível

inconceivable [.inkən'si:vəbl] inconcebível

incongruous [in'kɔŋgruəs] incongruente

inconsidera|ble [.inkən'sidərəbl] insignificante; **~te** [.-'rit] inconsiderado

inconsistent [.inkən'sistənt] inconsistente; incompatível

inconsolable [.inkən'səuləbl] inconsolável

inconstant [in'kɔnstənt] inconstante

inconvenien|ce [.inkən'vi:njəns] s inconveniência f; inconveniente m; **~t** incómodo, inconveniente

incorporat|e [in'kɔ:pəreit] v/t, v/i incorporar(-se); **~ed** incorporado, associado

incorrect [.inkə'rekt] incorre(c)to

incorrigible [in'kɔridʒəbl] in-

corrigível
incorruptible [,inkə'rʌptəbl] incorru(p)tível
increase [in'kri:s] s aumento m; [in'kri:s] v/t, v/i aumentar
increasingly [in'kri:siŋli] cada vez mais
incredible [in'kredəbl] incrível
incredulous [in'kredjuləs] incrédulo
incriminate [in'krimineit] v/t incriminar
incur [in'kə:] v/t incorrer em
incurable [in'kjuərəbl] incurável
indebted [in'detid] individado; obrigado, grato
indecen|cy [in'di:snsi] s indecência f; ~t indecente
indecision [,indi'siʒən] indecisão f
indeed [in'di:d] com efeito, deveras, de fa(c)to, na verdade
indefatigable [,indi'fætigəbl] infatigável
indefensible [,indi'fensəbl] indefensável
indefinite [in'definit] indefinido
indelicate [in'delikit] indelicado
indemni|fy [in'demnifai] v/t inde(m)nizar; ~ty (pl -ties) inde(m)nização f; inde(m)nidade f
indent [in'dent] v/t recortar, dentear; ~ure [-'dentʃə] s contrato m
independen|ce [,indi'pendəns] independência f; ~t adj independente

indescribable [,indis'kraibəbl] indescritível
indestructible [,indis'trʌktəbl] indestrutível
indeterminate [,indi'tə:minit] indeterminado
index ['indeks] (pl -dexes, -dices) ['indisi:z] índice m, indice m; ~ finger dedo m indicador
Indian ['indiən] adj, s índio m; indiano m; ~ corn milho m; ~ summer verão m de S. Martinho
india-rubber [indjə'rʌbə] borracha f; cauchu m
indicat|e ['indikeit] v/t indicar; ~ion indicação f; ~ive [-'dikətiv] adj, s indicativo m
indict [in'dait] v/t acusar; ~ment acusação f
indifferen|ce [in'difrəns] indiferença f; ~t indiferente; medíocre
indigest|ible [,indi'dʒestəbl] indigesto; ~ion [-tʃən] indigestão f
indign|ant [in'dignənt] indignado; ~ation [-'neiʃən] indignação f; ~ity indignidade f
indirect [,indi'rekt] indire(c)to
indiscreet [,indis'kri:t] indiscreto
indiscretion [,indis'kreʃən] indiscreção f
indiscriminate [,indis'kriminit] indiscriminado
indispensable [,indis'pensəbl] indispensável
indispos|ed [,indis'pəuzd] indisposto; ~ition indisposição f
indisputable ['indis'pju:təbl]

indisputável

indistinct [,indis'tiŋkt] indistinto

indistinguishable [,indis'tiŋgwiʃəbl] indistinguível

individual [,indi'vidjuəl] *s* indivíduo *m*; *adj* individual

indolen|ce ['indələns] indolência *f*; ~**t** indolente

indoor ['indɔ:] interior; caseiro; ~**s** dentro, em casa

induce [in'dju:s] *v/t* induzir

induction [in'dʌkʃən] indução *f*

indulge [in'dʌldʒ] *v/t, v/i* saciar, satisfazer; ~ **in** entregar-se a; ~**nce** [-dʒəns] indulgência *f*; ~**nt** [-dʒənt] indulgente

industri|al [in'dʌstriəl] industrial; ~**alist** industrial *m, f*; ~**alize** *v/t, v/i* industrializar; ~**ous** industrioso

industry ['indəstri] (*pl* -**ries**) indústria *f*

ineffective [,ini'fektiv] ineficaz

inept [i'nept] inepto

inequality [,ini'kwɔliti] (*pl* -**ties**) desigualdade *f*

inequitable [in'ekwitəbl] injusto

inert [i'nə:t] inerte; ~**ia** [-ʃjə] inércia *f*

inestimable [in'estiməbl] inestimável

inevitable [in'evitəbl] inevitável

inexcusable [,iniks'kju:zəbl] indesculpável, imperdoável

inexhaustible [,inig'zɔ:stəbl] inexaurível, inesgotável

inexorable [in'eksərəbl] inexorável

inexpensive [,iniks'pensiv] barato

inexperienced [,iniks'piəriənst] inexperiente

inexplicable [in'eksplikəbl] inexplicável

inexpressible [,iniks'presəbl] inexprimível

inextinguishable [,iniks'tiŋgwiʃəbl] inextinguível

infallible [in'fæləbl] infalível

infam|ous ['infəməs] infame; ~**y** infamia *f*

infancy ['infənsi] infância *f*

infant ['infənt] infante *m*, criança *f*; ~**ile** [-tail] infantil

infantry ['infəntri] infantaria *f*

infatuated [in'fætjueitid] *adj* apaixonado

infect [in'fekt] *v/t* infe(c)tar; ~**ion** [-kʃən] infecção *f*; ~**ious** infeccioso

infer [in'fə:] *v/t* deduzir, inferir; ~**ence** ['infərəns] inferência *f*, dedução *f*

inferior [in'fiəriə] inferior; ~**ity** [infiəri'ɔriti] inferioridade *f*

infernal [in'fə:nl] infernal

infest [in'fest] *v/t* infestar

infidelity [,infi'deliti] (*pl* -**ties**) infidelidade *f*

infinit|e ['infinit] infinito; ~**ive** [-'finitiv] *adj, s* infinitivo *m*; ~**y** infinidade *f*; infinito *m*

infirm [in'fə:m] enfermo; débil, fraco; ~**ary** (*pl* -**ries**) enfermaria *f*; ~**ity** (*pl* -**ties**) enfermidade *f*

inflame [in'fleim] *v/t* inflamar

inflamm|able [in'flæməbl] inflamável; ~**ation** [-flə'mei-

ʃən] inflamação f
inflat|e [in'fleit] v/t inflar;
~**ion** inflação f
inflexibility [in.fleksə'biliti] inflexibilidade f
inflict [in'flikt] v/t infligir
influen|ce ['influəns] s influência f; v/t influir em, influenciar; ~**tial** [-'enʃəl] influente
influenza [.influ'enzə] gripe f, influenza f
inform [in'fɔːm] v/t informar;
~ **against** denunciar
informal [in'fɔːml] sem cerimônia
inform|ation [infə'meiʃən] informação f, informações f/pl;
~**ed** adj informado, inteirado;
~**er** delator m, informante m, f
infringe [in'frindʒ] v/t infringir
infuriate [in'fjuərieit] v/t enfurecer
infus|e [in'fjuːz] v/t, v/i infundir; ~**ion** [-ʒən] infusão f
ingen|ious [in'dʒiːnjəs] engenhoso; ~**uity** [-'njuːiti] engenho m, habilidade f; ~**uous** [-'dʒenjuəs] ingênuo
ingratitude [in'grætitjuːd] ingratidão f
ingredient [in'griːdjənt] ingrediente m
inhabit [in'hæbit] v/t habitar;
~**able** habitável; ~**ant** habitante m
inhale [in'heil] v/t, v/i inalar
inherent [in'hiərənt] inerente
inherit [in'herit] v/t, v/i herdar;
~**ance** herança f
inhibit [in'hibit] v/t inibir;
~**ion** [-'biʃən] inibição f

inhospitable [in'hɔspitəbl]
inóspito; inospitaleiro
inhuman [in'hjuːmən] inumano, desumano
initial [i'niʃəl] adj, s inicial f
initiate [i'niʃieit] v/t iniciar
initiative [i'niʃiətiv] iniciativa f
inject [in'dʒekt] v/t inje(c)tar;
~**ion** inje(c)ção f
injur|e [in'dʒə] v/t prejudicar;
injuriar; ferir, lesar; ~**ious**
[-'dʒuəriəs] prejudicial, nocivo;
~**y** (pl -ries) injúria f; lesão f;
dano m, prejuízo m
injustice [in'dʒʌstis] injustiça f
ink [iŋk] tinta f
inkling ['iŋkliŋ] menor ideia f
inland [in'lənd] adj (do) interior; interno, nacional
inlay [in'lei] v/t embutir
inlet [inlet] enseada f, angra f
inmate [inmeit] ocupante m, f,
residente m
inmost [inməust] íntimo, recôndito
inn [in] estalagem f
innate [i'neit] inato
inner [inə] interior; oculto
innkeeper [in.kiːpə] estalajadeiro m
innocen|ce ['inəsəns] inocência f;
~**t** adj inocente
innovation [.inə'veiʃən] inovação f
innumerable [i'njuːmərəbl]
inumerável
inoculate [i'nɔkjuleit] v/t inocular
inoffensive [.inə'fensiv] inofensivo
inopportune   [in'ɔpətjuːn]

inoportuno

inquest ['inkwest] investigação *f* judicial

inquietude [in'kwaiitju:d] inquietação *f*

inquir|e [in'kwaiə] *v/t*, *v/i* inquirir, perguntar; **~e into** indagar, pesquisar; **~y** (*pl* **-ries**) inquérito *m*, pesquisa *f*

inquisitive [in'kwizitiv] curioso, inquiridor

inroad ['inraud] incursão *f*

insan|e [in'sein] demente, louco; **~ity** [-'sæniti] loucura *f*, demência *f*

inscribe [in'skraib] *v/t* inscrever

inscription [in'skripʃən] inscrição *f*

insect ['insekt] inse(c)to *m*; **~icide** [-'sektisaid] inse(c)ticida *m*

insecure [.insi'kjuə] inseguro

insensible [in'sensəbl] imperceptível

inseparable [in'sepərəbl] inseparável

insert [in'sə:t] *v/t* introduzir, inserir

inside [in'said] *adj*, *s* interior *m*; *adv* dentro; *prp* dentro de; **~ out** do avesso, às avessas

insight [insait] penetração *f*; compreensão *f*

insignificant [.insig'nifikənt] insignificante

insincere [.insin'siə] insincero

insinuate [in'sinjueit] *v/t* insinuar

insipid [in'sipid] insípido

insist [in'sist] (**on**) *v/i* insistir (**em**); **~ence** insistência *f*

insolen|ce ['insələns] insolência *f*; **~t** insolente

insoluble [in'sɔljubl] insolúvel

insolvent [in'sɔlvənt] insolvente

insomnia [in'sɔmniə] insónia *f*

insomuch as [.insəu'mʌtʃ əz] a tal ponto que

inspect [in'spekt] *v/t* inspe(c)cionar; revistar; **~ion** [-ʃən] inspe(c)ção *f*; revista *f*; **~or** revisor *m*; inspe(c)tor *m*

inspiration [.inspə'reiʃən] inspiração *f*

inspire [in'spaiə] *v/t* inspirar

install [in'stɔ:l] *v/t* instalar; **~ation** [-stə'leiʃən] instalação *f*

insta(l)lment [in'stɔ:lmənt] prestação *f*; episódio *m*

instance ['instəns] *s* instância *f*; exemplo *m*, caso *m*; **for ~** por exemplo

instant ['instənt] *s* instante *m*; *adj* imediato; instantâneo; **~aneous** [-'teinjəs] instantâneo

instead [in'sted] *adv* em vez disso; **~ of** em vez de, em lugar de

instep ['instep] peito *m* do pé

instigate ['instigeit] *v/t* instigar

instinct ['instiŋkt] *s* instinto *m*; **~ive** [-'stiŋktiv] instintivo

institut|e [in'institju:t] *s* instituto *m*; *v/t* instituir, estabelecer; **~ion** [-'tju:ʃən] instituição *f*

instruct [in'strʌkt] *v/t* instruir, ensinar; **~ion** instrução *f*; **~ive** instrutivo; **~or** instrutor *m*

instrument ['instrumənt] instrumento *m*

insubordinate [.insə'bɔ:dənit] insubordinado

insufferable [inˈsʌfərəbl] insuportável

insufficient [ˌinsəˈfiʃənt] insuficiente

insular [ˈinsjulə] insular

insulat|e [ˈinsjuleit] v/t isolar; ~**or** isolador m

insult [inˈsʌlt] v/t insultar; [ˈinsʌlt] s insulto m

insuperable [inˈsju:pərəbl] insuperável

insupportable [ˌinsəˈpɔ:təbl] insuportável

insur|ance [inˈʃuərəns] seguro m; ~**ance company** companhia f de seguros; ~**ance policy** apólice f de seguro; ~**e** v/t segurar

insurgent [inˈsə:dʒənt] adj insurgente

insurmountable [ˌinsəˈmauntəbl] insuperável

insurrection [ˌinsəˈrekʃən] insurreição f

intact [inˈtækt] inta(c)to

integrate [ˈintəgreit] v/t, v/i integrar(-se)

integration [ˌintiˈgreiʃən] integração f

integrity [inˈtegriti] integridade f

intellect [ˈintilekt] intelecto m; ~**ual** [ˌ-ˈlektjuəl] adj, s intelectual m, f

intellig|ence [inˈtelidʒəns] inteligência f; ~**ent** inteligente; ~**ible** inteligível

intemperate [inˈtempərit] intemperado, desenfreado

intend [inˈtend] v/t tencionar; ~**ed** s prometido m, futuro m

inten|se [inˈtens] intenso; ~**sity** intensidade f; ~**sive** intensivo

intent [inˈtent] s intento m; adj atento; ~**ion** intenção f

interact [ˌintərˈækt] v/i intera(c)tuar-se

intercede [ˌintəˈsi:d] v/i interceder

intercept [ˌintəˈsept] v/t interceptar

intercession [ˌintəˈseʃən] intercessão f

interchange [ˈintəˈtʃeindʒ] s intercâmbio m; [ˌintəˈtʃeindʒ] v/t trocar, (inter)cambiar; ~**able** permutável

intercourse [ˈintəkɔ:s] trato m, relações f/pl; relações f/pl sexuais

interdict [ˌintəˈdikt] v/t interdizer, interditar

interest [ˈintrist] s interesse m; juro(s) m (pl); v/t interessar; ~**ed** adj interessado; ~**ing** interessante

interfer|e [ˌintəˈfiə] v/i interferir; intrometer-se; ~**ence** interferência f

interior [inˈtiəriə] adj, s interior m

interlude [ˈintə(ː)luːd] interlúdio m; intervalo m; entremez m

intermedia|ry [ˌintəˈmi:djəri] adj, s (pl -**ries**) intermediário m; ~**te** m intermédio

interminable [inˈtə:minəbl] interminável

intermingle [ˌintəˈmiŋgl] v/t, v/i misturar(-se), entremear

intermittent [ˌintəˈmitənt] in-

termitente
intern [in'tə:n] *v/t* internar, encarcerar
internal [in'tə:nl] interno, interior, intestino
international [.intə'næ∫ənl] *adj* internacional
interpose [.intə'pəuz] *v/t, v/i* interpor(-se); intervir
interpret [in'tə:prit] *v/t* interpretar; **~ation** [-'tei∫ən] interpretação *f*; **~er** intérprete *m, f*
interrogate [in'terəgeit] *v/t* interrogar
interrogat|ion [in.terə'gei∫ən] interrogação *f*; **~ive** [-'tɔ-rə-gətiv] *adj* interrogativo; **~or** [in'terəgeitə] interrogador *m*
interrupt [.intə'rʌpt] *v/t, v/i* interromper; atalhar; **~ion** interrupção *f*
interval ['intəvəl] intervalo *m*
interven|e [.intə'vi:n] *v/i* intervir; **~tion** [-'ven∫ən] intervenção *f*
interview ['intəvju:] *s* entrevista *f*; *v/t* entrevistar
intestine [in'testin] intestino *m*
intima|cy ['intiməsi] intimidade *f*; **~te** [-'mit] *adj* íntimo; ['-meit] dar a entender, insinuar
intimidate [in'timideit] *v/t* intimidar
into ['intu, 'intə] em; para, para dentro de
intoler|able [in'tɔlərəbl] intolerável; **~ant** intolerante
intoxicate [in'tɔksikeit] *v/t* embriagar; intoxicar
intractable [in'træktəbl] intratável

intrepid [in'trepid] intrépido
intricate ['intrikit] intrincado
intrigue [in'tri:g] *s* enredo *m*, intriga *f*; *v/t, v/i* intrigar
introduc|e [.intrə'dju:s] *v/t* apresentar; **~e into** introduzir; **~tion** [-'dʌk∫ən] apresentação *f*; introdução *f*; **~tory** introdutório
introvert ['intrəuvə:t] introvertido *m*
intru|de [in'tru:d] *v/t, v/i* introduzir(-se), intrometer(-se); **~der** intruso *m*; **~sion** [-ʒən] intrusão *f*
intuition [.intju'i∫ən] intuição *f*
invad|e [in'veid] *v/t* invadir; **~er** invasor *m*
invalid [in'vælid] *adj* nulo, inválido; ['invəli:d] *s* inválido *m*
invaluable [in'væljuəbl] inestimável
invariable [in'vεəriəbl] invariável
invasion [in'veiʒən] invasão *f*
invective [in'vektiv] invectiva *f*
invent [in'vent] *v/t* inventar; **~ion** invento *m*, invenção *f*; **~ive** inventivo; **~or** inventor *m, f*
inventory [in'ventri] (*pl* **-ries**) inventário *m*
inverse [in'və:s] *adj, s* inverso *m*
invert [in'və:t] *v/t* inverter; **~ed commas** *pl* aspas *f/pl*
invest [in'vest] *v/t, v/i* investir
investigate [in'vestigeit] *v/t, v/i* investigar, indagar
investigation [in.vesti'gei∫ən] investigação *f*, inquérito *m*
investment [in'vestmənt] in-

vestimento *m*

invigorate [in'vigəreit] *v/t* revigorar

invincible [in'vinsəbl] invencível

invisible [in'vizəbl] invisível

invit|**ation** [.invi'teiʃən] convite *m*; **~e** [-'vait] *v/t* convidar; **~ing** [-'vaitiŋ] *adj* convidativo

invoice ['invɔis] *s* fa(c)tura *f*

invoke [in'vəuk] *v/t* invocar

involuntary [in'vɔləntəri] involuntário

involve [in'vɔlv] *v/t* envolver, implicar; **~d** *adj* envolvido, implicado; complicado

invulnerable [in'vʌlnərəbl] invulnerável

inward ['inwəd] *adj* interior; íntimo; **~s** para dentro

iodin(e) ['aiədi:n] iodo *m*

Irish ['aiəriʃ] *adj, s* irlandês *m*; **~man** (*pl* -**men**) irlandês *m*

irksome ['ə:ksəm] fastidioso, cansativo

iron ['aiən] *s* ferro *m*; *adj* de ferro; férreo; *v/t, v/i* passar a ferro

ironic(al) [ai'rɔnik(əl)] irónico

irony ['aiərəni] ironia *f*

irradiate [i'reidieit] *v/t* irradiar

irrational [i'ræʃənl] irracional

irrefutable [i'refjutəbl] irrefutável, incontestável

irregular [i'regjulə] irregular

irrelevant [i'relivənt] irrelevante

irreparable [i'repərəbl] irreparável

irreproachable [.iri'prəutʃəbl] irrepreensível

irresistible [.iri'zistəbl] irresistível

irresolute [i'rezəlu:t] irresoluto

irresponsible [.iris'pɔnsəbl] irresponsável

irretrievable [.iri'tri:vəbl] irrecuperável, irreparável

irreverent [i'revərənt] irreverente

irrevocable [i'revəkəbl] irrevocável, irreparável

irrigat|**e** ['irigeit] *v/t* irrigar; **~ion** [-'geiʃən] irrigação

irrita|**ble** ['iritəbl] irritável, irascível; **~nt** irritante; **~te** [-teit] *v/t* irritar; **~tion** [-'teiʃən] irritação *f*

is [iz, əz] *3rd sg pres of* **be** é; está; fica

island ['ailənd] ilha *f*; **~er** ilhéu *m*, insulano *m*

isolat|**e** ['aisəleit] *v/t* isolar; **~ion** [-'leiʃən] isolação *f*

issue ['iʃu:] *v/t* distribuir; publicar; emitir; *s* distribuição *f*; tiragem *f*, edição *f*; **~ from** provir, brotar

isthmus ['isməs] istmo *m*

it [it] *pron* ele, ela, o, a, isto, isso; **that's ~** é tudo; isso, assim

Italian [i'tæljən] *adj, s* italiano *m*

itch [itʃ] *s* prurido *m*, comichão *f*; desejo *m*, ânsia *f*; *v/i* prurir; ter comichão

item ['aitəm] *s* item *m*, rubrica *f*; *adv* item, também

itinerary [ai'tinərəri] (*pl* -**ries**) itinerário *m*

its [its] *poss pron* seu, sua, seus,

suas; dele, dela
itself [it'self] *pron* se; ele mesmo,
ela mesmo; **by ~** sozinho; **in**

~ em si mesmo
ivory ['aivəri] marfim *m*
ivy ['aivi] hera *f*

J

jabber ['dʒæbə] *v/i* papaguear,
palrar; *s* tagarelice *f*
jack [dʒæk] *s mec* macaco *m*; ♀
of all trades pau *m* para toda
obra; *v/t* **~ up** levantar com
macaco
jackal ['dʒækɔ:l] chacal *m*
jackdaw ['dʒækdɔ:] gralha *f*
jacket ['dʒækit] casaco *m* curto;
jaqueta *f*
jad|e [dʒeid] jade *f*; rocim *m*;
~ed estafado
jagged ['dʒægid] *adj* entalhado,
denteado
jaguar ['dʒægjuə] jaguar *m*
jail [dʒeil] *s* cadeia *f*, prisão *f*;
~er carcereiro *m*
jam [dʒæm] *s* compota *f*; engarrafamento *m*, congestionamen-
to *m*; aperto *m*; *v/t*, *v/i* empurrar; interferir com; entalar; esmagar, comprimir, apertar
janitor ['dʒænitə] *US* porteiro *m*
January ['dʒænjuəri] Janeiro *m*
Japanese [.dʒæpə'ni:z] *adj*, *s* japonês *(m)*
jar [dʒɑ:] *s* frasco *m*; pote *m*, jarro *m*, cântaro *m*; vibração *f*,
choque *m*, sacudidela *f*; *v/t* sacudir, chocar; *v/i* vibrar, ranger
jargon ['dʒɑ:gən] jargão *m*, calão *m*, gíria *f*
jasmin(e) ['dʒæsmin] jasmim *m*
jaundice ['dʒɔ:ndis] icterícia *f*

jaunt [dʒɔ:nt] *s* passeata *f*, volta
f; **~y** animado, airoso
javelin ['dʒævlin] dardo *m*
jaw [dʒɔ:] *s* maxila *f*, maxilar *m*;
queixada *f*; **~s** garras *f/pl*
jay [dʒei] gaio *m*
jealous ['dʒeləs] cioso, zeloso;
ciumento; **~y** ciúme *m*
jeer [dʒiə] *s* escárnio *m*; *v/i*, *v/t*
escarnecer
jelly ['dʒeli] geleia *f*; **~fish** me-
dusa *f*, alforreca *f*
jeopard|ize ['dʒepədaiz] *v/t* ar-
riscar, comprometer; **~y** perigo *m*, risco *m*
jerk [dʒə:k] *s* sacudidela *f*; *v/t*
sacudir; **~y** espasmódico
jersey ['dʒə:zi] jérsei *m*
jest [dʒest] *s* gracejo *m*; *v/i* gracejar
jet [dʒet] *s* jacto *m*; avião *m* a ja-
(c)to; *min* azeviche *m*
jettison ['dʒetisn] *v/t* alijar
jetty ['dʒeti] *(pl* **-ties)** molhe *m*,
quebra-mar *m*
Jew [dʒu:] judeu *m*
jewel ['dʒu:əl] jóia *f*; **~(l)er** joalheiro *m*; **~(le)ry** joalharia *f*,
jóias *f/pl*
Jewish ['dʒu:iʃ] judeu, judaico
jingle ['dʒiŋgl] *s* tinido *m*; *v/t*,
v/i tinir
job [dʒɔb] trabalho *m*; emprego
m; tarefa *f*; **out of a ~** desempregado

jockey ['dʒɔki] s jóquei m

jocular ['dʒɔkjulə] jovial

jog [dʒɔg] v/t, v/i sacudir, empurrar

join [dʒɔin] v/t, v/i juntar(-se) (a), unir(-se) (a)

joiner ['dʒɔinə] marceneiro m

joint [dʒɔint] s junção f; juntura f, junta f; articulação f; quarto m de carne; adj comum; unido; ~ **account** conta f comum; ~ **-stock company** sociedade f anónima

joke [dʒəuk] s piada f, brincadeira f, gracejo m; v/i gracejar, brincar, galhofar; **no** ~ é (a) sério, não é brincadeira

joker ['dʒəukə] brincalhão m

jolly ['dʒɔli] adj afável, alegre; adv muito; v/t animar

jolt [dʒəult] s solavanco m, sacudidela f; v/t, v/i ir aos solavancos; sacudir

jostle ['dʒɔsl] v/t, v/i acotovelar (-se)

jot [dʒɔt] s ponta f, mínimo m; v/t ~ **down** anotar, apontar

journal ['dʒə:nl] jornal m; diário m; periódico m; ~**ism** ['-izəm] jornalismo m; ~**ist** jornalista m, f

journey ['dʒə:ni] s viagem f; v/i viajar

jovial ['dʒəuvjəl] jovial

joy [dʒɔi] alegria f; ~**ful** alegre

jubilation [dʒu:bi'leiʃən] júbilo m; ~**ee** ['dʒu:bili:] jubileu m

judge [dʒʌdʒ] s juiz m; v/t, v/i julgar

judg(e)ment ['dʒʌdʒmənt] julgamento m; juízo m; sentença f

judic|ial ['dʒu(:)'diʃəl] judicial; ~**iary** adj judiciário; ~**ious** judicioso

judo ['dʒu:dəu] judo m, jiu-jitsu m

jug [dʒʌg] s cântaro m, jarro m, Braz moringa f

juggl|e ['dʒʌgl] v/t, v/i fazer prestidigitação; ~**er** prestidigitador m; ~**ery** prestidigitação f

juic|e [dʒu:s] s sumo m, suco m; ~**y** suculento, sumarento

July [dʒu'lai] Julho m

jumble ['dʒʌmbl] v/t, v/i misturar, confundir; s salgalhada f, trapalhada f

jump [dʒʌmp] s salto m; pulo m; v/t, v/i saltar, pular, galgar

junct|ion ['dʒʌŋkʃən] junção f, entroncamento m; ~**ure** ['-tʃə] conjuntura f

June [dʒu:n] Junho m

jungle ['dʒʌŋgl] selva f

junior ['dʒu:niə] adj, s júnior m

junk [dʒʌŋk] s sucata f; refugo m

juror ['dʒuərə] jurado m

jury ['dʒuəri] (pl -ries) júri m

just [dʒʌst] adj justo; adv meramente, só; justamente; há pouco; agora mesmo; **have** ~ ... acabar de ...; ~ **now** agora mesmo

justice ['dʒʌstis] justiça f

justify ['dʒʌstifai] v/t justificar

jut out [dʒʌt] v/i salientar-se, proje(c)tar-se

juvenile ['dʒu:vinail] juvenil m

juxtapos|e ['dʒʌkstəpəuz] v/t justapor; ~**ition** [-pə'ziʃən] justaposição f

K

kangaroo [.kæŋɡə'ru:] canguru m

keel [ki:l] s quilha f

keen [ki:n] adj afiado, agudo, penetrante; veemente, ardente, entusiasta; astuto; be ~ on gostar muito de; ~ness agudeza f; entusiasmo m

keep [ki:p] v/t, v/i continuar, ficar; guardar; dirigir, manejar; cumprir; deter, demorar; manter, conservar(-se); ~ back reter; ~ from impedir, impossibilitar; ~ off manter(-se) afastado, afastar(-se); ~ on continuar; seguir; ~ out excluir, afastar; ~ to seguir; ficar; restringir-se, limitar-se; ~ up manter(-se); ~ up with acompanhar, não ficar atrás

keeper [ki:pə] guardião m; guarda m; ~ing guarda f; conservação f; in safe ~ing a salvo; ~sake recordação f, lembrança f

kennel [kenl] canil m

kerchief ['kə:tʃif] lenço m de cabeça

kernel ['kə:nl] miolo m; cerne m; núcleo m

kettle ['ketl] chaleira f; ~-drum timbale m

key [ki:] s chave f; tecla f; mus clave f; ~hole buraco m de fechadura; ~note s nota f tónica; ~stone chave f de abóbada

kick [kik] s pontapé m; chuto m, chute m; coice m; estímulo m, energia f; v/t, v/i dar pontapés (a/em); escoucear; chutar; ~ the bucket esticar o pernil; ~-off s pontapé m de saída; ~ out pôr na rua

kid [kid] s cabrito m; criança f, miúdo m, garoto m; pele f de cabrito, pelica f; v/t, v/i brincar, caçoar, pegar com alguém; ~ gloves luvas f/pl de pelica

kidnap ['kidnæp] v/t raptar, sequestrar; ~per raptor m

kidney ['kidni] rim m; ~ bean feijão m

kill [kil] v/t, v/i matar; ~er s assassino m; ~ing adj assassino, mortal; cansativo, exaustivo

kiln [kiln] forno m, fornalha f

kilo ['ki:ləu] quilo m

kilogram(me) ['kiləɡræm] quilograma m

kilometre ['kiləˌmi:tə] quilómetro m

kilt [kilt] saiote m escocês

kin [kin] parentes m/pl

kind [kaind] adj bondoso, amável; s espécie f, género m qualidade f; ~ of bastante; como que

kindle ['kindl] v/t, v/i acender (-se)

kindly ['kaindli] adj bondoso, amável; adv amavelmente; ~ness bondade f, amabilidade f

kindred ['kindrid] s parentela f, família f; adj aparentado; congénere

king [kiŋ] rei *m*; **~dom** ['-dəm] reino *m*; **~ly** real

kink [kiŋk] retorcimento *m*; *fig* mania *f*

kinship ['kinʃip] parentesco *m*

kiosk [ki'ɔsk] quiosque *m*

kipper ['kipə] arenque *m* salgado defumado

kiss [kis] *s* beijo *m*; *v/t* beijar

kit [kit] indumentária *f*, equipamento *m*

kitchen ['kitʃin] cozinha *f*; **~ette** [kitʃi'net] conzinha *f* pequena

kite [kait] milhafre *m*; papagaio *m* de papel

kitten ['kitn] gatinho *m*, bichano *m*

kleptomaniac [.kleptəu'meiniæk] cleptomaníaco *m*

knack [næk] jeito *m*, habilidade *f*

knave [neiv] valete *m*

knead [ni:d] *v/t*, *v/i* amassar; massajar

knee [ni:] *s* joelho *m*; **~cap** *s* joelheira *f*; rótula *f*; **~l** [ni:l] *v/i* ajoelhar(-se)

knell [nel] dobre *m* a finados

knickers ['nikəz] *s/pl* cuecas *f/pl*

knick-knack ['niknæk] bugiganga *f*

knife [naif] *s* (*pl* knives [-vz]) faca *f*; navalha *f*; *v/t* apunhalar, esfaquear

knight [nait] *s* cavaleiro *m*; cavalo *m* (*chess*); *v/t* armar cavaleiro

knit [nit] *v/t*, *v/i* tricotar; **~ting** *s* tricô *m*

knob [nɔb] protuberância *f*; puxador *m*; castão *m*; maçaneta *f*

knock [nɔk] *s* pancada *f*; golpe *m*; *v/t*, *v/i* bater; golpear; **~ down** *v/t* atropelar, abater, derrubar; **~er** bater *m*, aldraba *f*; **~ out** *v/t* pôr fora de combate; **~out** *s* nocaute *m*, fora *m* de combate

knoll [nəul] outeiro *m*, morro *m*

knot [nɔt] *s* nó *m*; laço *m*, vínculo *m*; grupo *m*; *v/t*, *v/i* dar um nó, laçar; **~ty** nodoso; *fig* emaranhado

know [nəu] *v/t*, *v/i* saber; conhecer; **you ~** sabe; **~ about** saber, estar informado; **~-how** perícia *f*, técnica *f*; **~ing** *adj* conhecedor, entendido; **there's no ~ing** não há meio de saber; **~ingly** ciente-mente; intencionalmente; **~ledge** ['nɔlidʒ] saber *m*; conhecimento *m*, conhecimentos *m/pl*; **to one's ~ledge** que se saiba

known [nəun] *adj* conhecido; **make it ~ that** dar a conhecer que

knuckle ['nʌkl] *s* nó *m* do dedo; *v/i* **~ under** submeter-se

L

label ['leibl] *s* etiqueta *f*, rótulo *m*; *v/t* pôr etiqueta em, rotular; classificar

laboratory [lə'bɔrətəri] (*pl*

-ries) laboratório *m*

laborious [ləˈbɔːriəs] laborioso; árduo

labo(u)r ['leibə] *s* trabalho *m*, lida *f*, labor *m*, faina *f*; dores *f/pl* de parto; *v/i* trabalhar, esforçar-se, afanar-se; estar em trabalho de parto; **~er** operário *m*, trabalhador *m*, jornaleiro *m*; ♀ **Party** Partido *m* Trabalhista

lace [leis] *s* renda *f*; galão *m*; atacador *m*; *v/t* apertar, atar

lack [læk] *s* falta *f*, míngua *f*; *v/t* carecer de, faltar; **for ~ of** por falta de, à míngua de

lacking ['lækiŋ] *adj* falto, deficiente; **be ~ in** ter falta de

laconic [ləˈkɔnik] lacónico

lacquer ['lækə] *s* laca *f*

lad [læd] rapaz *m*, moço *m*, garoto *m*

ladder ['lædə] *s* escadote *m*; escada *f* de mão; malha *f* caída

laden [leidn] *adj* carregado

Ladies ['leidiz] Senhoras *f/pl*

ladle ['leidl] *s* concha *f*, caço *m*

lady ['leidi] (*pl* **-dies**) senhora *f*; dama *f*; **~ of the house** dona *f* da casa; **~bird** joaninha *f*; **~killer** conquistador *m*, galanteador *m*; **~like** senhoril, elegante

lag [læg] *v/i* ficar atrás, demorar-se

lager ['lɑːgə] cerveja *f* de reserva

lagoon [ləˈguːn] laguna *f*

lair [lɛə] covil *m*, toca *f*

lake [leik] lago *m*

lamb [læm] *s* anho *m*, cordeiro *m*

lame [leim] *adj* coxo, manco; fraco, pouco convincente; *v/t* aleijar, estropiar

lament [ləˈment] *s* lamento *m*; *v/t*, *v/i* lamentar(-se); **~able** ['læməntəbl] lamentável; **~ation** [ˌlæmənˈteiʃən] lamentação *f*

lamp [læmp] candeeiro *m*; lâmpada *f*; lampião *m*; **~post** poste *m* de iluminação

lamprey ['læmpri] lampreia *f*

lamp-shade ['læmpʃeid] abajur(r) *m*, quebra-luz *m*

lance [lɑːns] *s* lança *f*; *v/t* lancetar; **~t** ['-sit] lanceta *f*

land [lænd] *s* terra *f*; solo *m*; país *m*; *v/t*, *v/i* desembarcar; *avi* aterrar; **~ing** desembarque *m*; *avi* aterragem *f*; *arch* patamar *m*; **~lady** senhoria *f*, proprietária *f*; estalajadeira *f*; **~lord** senhorio *m*, proprietário *m*; estalajadeiro *m*; **~mark** marco *m*, limite *m*, baliza *f*; **~scape** *s* paisagem *f*; **~slide** desmoronamento *m*

lane [lein] beco *m*; azinhaga *f*

language ['læŋgwidʒ] língua *f*, idioma *m*; linguagem *f*

languid ['læŋgwid] lânguido

languish ['læŋgwiʃ] *v/i* e(n)languescer, languir

lank [læŋk] corredio; magro, esgrouviado; **~y** esgalgado

lantern ['læntən] lanterna *f*

lap [læp] *s* colo *m*; regaço *m*; *v/t* sorver, lamber

lapel [ləˈpel] lapela *f*

lapse [læps] *s* lapso *m*; *v/i* decorrer; decair; cair em erro; cadu-

lax

car, prescrever

lard [lɑːk] s banha f, toucinho m; v/t untar; lardear; ~er despensa f

large [lɑːdʒ] grande; vasto, amplo; extenso, largo; volumoso, espaçoso; abundante, copioso; **at** ~ em liberdade, à solta; ~**ly** largamente, grandemente; em grande parte

lark [lɑːk] s cotovia f, calhandra f; brincadeira, partida f

larynx ['lærɪŋks] laringe f

lash [læʃ] s látego m, açoite m, chicote m; chicotada f; v/t, v/i açoitar; espicaçar

lass [læs] rapariga f, moça f, garota f

last [lɑːst] adv da última vez; em último lugar, por/no fim; s forma f, molde m; v/i durar; adj ~ por fim; ~, **but not least** o último, mas não o menos importante; ~ **but one** penúltimo; **the** ~ **straw** a última gota; ~ **week** a semana passada; **the** ~ **word** a última palavra; o último grito

lasting ['lɑːstiŋ] adj duradouro

lastly ['lɑːstli] finalmente, por fim

latch [lætʃ] s aldrava f, trinco m, fecho m; ~**key** chave f de trinco

late [leit] adv tarde; adj último, recente; atrasado; defunto; tarde; tardio; **be** ~ chegar tarde; ~**ly** ultimamente, recentemente, há pouco; ~**r on** mais tarde; **at the** ~**st** o mais tardar

lathe [leið] torno m

lather ['lɑːðə] s espuma f de sabão; v/t ensaboar

Latin ['lætin] s latim m; adj latino

latitude ['lætitjuːd] latitude f

latter ['lætə] este último; ~**ly** ultimamente, há pouco

lattice ['lætis] gelosia f, rótula f

laudable ['lɔːdəbl] louvável

laugh [lɑːf] s riso m; gargalhada f; risota f; v/i rir(-se); ~ **at** rir-se de; ~**able** risível, ridículo; divertido; **burst out** ~**ing** desatar a rir

laughter ['lɑːftə] risada f, riso m; gargalhada f

launch [lɔːntʃ] s lancha f, chalupa f; v/t lançar à agua; lançar, arremessar; encetar

laundry ['lɔːndri] (pl -dries) lavandaria f

laurel ['lɔrəl] loureiro m, louro m

lava ['lɑːvə] lava f

lavatory ['lævətəri] (pl -ries) retrete f; instalações f/pl sanitárias, privada f

lavender ['lævində] s alfazema f

lavish ['læviʃ] adj generoso, pródigo; v/t ~ **on** prodigalizar

law [lɔː] lei f; direito m; **go to** ~ litigar, demandar, recorrer à justiça; ~**breaker** transgressor m da lei; ~**court** tribunal m; ~**ful** legal, legítimo

lawn [lɔːn] relvado m

lawsuit ['lɔːsjuːt] processo m

lawyer ['lɔːjə] advogado m, jurisconsulto m

lax [læks] negligente; lasso, frouxo, solto; **~ative** ['-ətiv] s laxante m; adj laxativo

lay [lei] v/t pôr, meter, colocar; **~ aside** pôr de lado; **~ down** pôr, depor, assentar; **~ out** v/t planear, fazer o proje(c)to de; expor, estender; gastar, desembolsar; **~ the table** pôr a mesa; **~ up** guardar, armazenar; ficar de cama, guardar o leito

layer ['leiə] s camada f; poedeira f

layman ['leimən] leigo m

layout ['leiaut] s plano m, planta f, esquema f

laz|iness ['leizinis] preguiça f; **~y** preguiçoso, indolente

lead [led] s chumbo m

lead [li:d] s primazia f, dianteira f; elect cabo m condutor; papel m principal; mão f; trela f; v/t, v/i conduzir, dirigir, guiar; levar (a); jogar de mão, ser mão; **take the ~** tomar a iniciativa, tomar a dianteira, assumir o comando

leaden ['ledn] de chumbo; pesado, plúmbeo

lead|er ['li:də] chefe m, f; artigo m de fundo; **~ing** adj principal, primeiro; **~ing article** artigo m de fundo

leaf [li:f] s (pl **leaves** [-vz]) folha f; **~let** folheto m; panfleto m

league [li:g] s liga f; v/t, v/i coligar(-se)

leak [li:k] s fenda f, abertura f; fuga f, escape m; v/t, v/i fazer água, meter água; verter, pingar; **~ out** tornar-se público,

transpirar; **~age** fuga f; derrame m; divulgação f

lean [li:n] adj magro; v/t, v/i apoiar(-se), encostar(-se), inclinar(-se); **~ (up)on** depender, apoiar-se; **~ out of** debruçar-se em; **~ing** s inclinação f, propensão f

leap [li:p] s salto m, pulo m; v/t, v/i saltar, pular; **~-year** ano m bissexto

learn [lə:n] v/t, v/i aprender; saber, ser informado

learned ['lə:nid] adj douto, erudito

learn|er ['lə:nə] aprendiz m, aluno m; **~ing** s erudição f, saber m

lease [li:s] s arrendamento m; v/t arrendar

least [li:st] adv o menos; adj o menor; o menos; o mínimo; **at ~** pelo menos; **not in the ~** de maneira nenhuma

leather ['leðə] s couro m, coiro m, pele f, cabedal m; adj de coiro; **~y** semelhante ao coiro; rijo

leave [li:v] s licença f, permissão f, despedida f; v/t, v/i deixar; partir, ir-se embora, part; **take ~ (of)** despedir-se (de); partir (de); **~ behind** deixar ficar; **~ off** deixar de

lectur|e ['lektʃə] s prele(c)ção f, conferência f, repreensão f; v/t, v/i **~e** dar cursos; dar uma conferência; repreender; **~er** lente m, f, leitor m; conferencista m, f

ledge [ledʒ] borda f; saliência f

ledger ['lɛdʒə] livro-mestre, m; livro-razão m

leech [li:tʃ] sanguessuga f

leek [li:k] alho-porro m

leer [liə] (at) v/i olhar de soslaio (para)

left [left] s esquerda f; adj esquerdo; **to the** ~ à esquerda; ~**-handed** canhoto

left-luggage office ['left 'lʌgidʒ 'ɔfis] depósito m de volumes/bagagens

leg [leg] s perna f; pé m; pata f; **pull someone's** ~ entrar com alguém, fazer alguém de tolo

legacy ['legəsi] (pl **-cies**) legado m

legal ['li:gəl] legal; ~**ize** v/t legalizar

legation [li'geiʃən] legação f

legend ['ledʒənd] lenda f; ~**ary** lendário

legible ['ledʒəbl] legível

legion ['li:dʒən] legião f

legislation [.ledʒis'leiʃən] legislação f

legislator ['ledʒisleitə] legislador m

legitimate [li'dʒitimit] adj legitimo

leisure ['leʒə] lazer m, vagar m; **at** ~ à vontade, com vagar; ~ desocupado; ~**ly** adj vagaroso

lemon ['lemən] limão m; ~**ade** [.-'neid] limonada f; ~**squash** limonada f; ~**-tree** limoeiro m

lend [lend] v/t emprestar; ~ **a hand** dar uma ajuda

length [leŋθ] comprimento m; duração f; **at** ~ afinal, por fim; pormenorizadamente, de-

talhadamente; ~**en** v/t, v/i alongar, estender, prolongar; ~**y** longo, prolongado

lenient ['li:njənt] suave, compassivo

lens [lenz] lente f

Lent [lent] s quaresma f

lentil ['lentil] lentilha f

leopard ['lepəd] leopardo m

leper ['lepə] leproso m

leprosy ['leprəsi] lepra f

less [les] adj menor; menos; adv menos; ~ **and** ~ cada vez menos

less|en ['lesn] v/t, v/i diminuir; ~**er** adj menor, mais pequeno

lesson ['lesn] lição f; aula f

lest [lest] para que não; com medo de que

let [let] v/t deixar, permitir; alugar; ~ **alone** quanto mais; sem falar de; ~ **alone** deixar em paz; ~ **be** deixar à vontade, não interferir; ~ **down** baixar; soltar; desiludir, abandonar; ~ **go** (of) largar; ~ **in** admitir; ~ **off** descarregar, disparar; perdoar; ~ **on** revelar, divulgar; ~ **out** deixar escapar; deixar sair; alugar; alargar; ~ **us/** ~**'s go** vamos

letter ['letə] s carta f; by ~ por carta; por escrito; **to the** ~ à letra, à risca; ~**-box** marco m do correio; caixa f do correio; ~**head** cabeçalho m; ~**s** s/pl (as) letras f/pl

lettuce ['letis] alface f

level ['levl] s nível m; v/t, v/i nivelar; adj horizontal, plano, liso, raso; ~ **crossing** passagem *f* de nível

lever ['li:və] *s* alavanca *f*

levy ['levi] *v/t* arrecadar; recrutar; *s* (*pl* -**vies**) arrecadação *f*; recrutamento *m*

liab|ility [.laiə'biliti] (*pl* -**ties**) responsabilidade *f*; *pl com* passivo *m*; **~le** [-bl] responsável; **~le to** sujeito a; propenso a; **~le to duty** sujeito a direitos alfandegários

liar ['laiə] mentiroso *m*, aldrabão *m*

libel ['laibəl] *s* libelo *m*; difamação *f*

liberal ['libərəl] *adj* liberal; generoso; **~ism** liberalismo *m*

liberate ['libəreit] (**from**) *v/t* libertar (de); livrar (de)

liberty ['libəti] liberdade *f*; **at ~** livre, desocupado; em liberdade

librarian [lai'brɛəriən] bibliotecário *m*

library ['laibrəri] (*pl* -**ries**) biblioteca *f*

licence ['laisəns] *s* licença *f*; permissão *f*

license ['laisəns] *s v/t* permitir; autorizar

lick [lik] *s* lambidela *f*, lambedura *f*; *v/t* lamber

lid [lid] tampa *f*; pálpebra *f*

lie [lai] *s* mentira *f*; *v/i* mentir

lie [lai] *v/i* jazer; estar deitado; estar situado, situar-se; existir, encontrar-se; conservar-se, permanecer; **~ down** deitar-se, descansar; submeter-se, tolerar; **~ in** deixar-se ficar na cama

lieutenant [lef'tenənt, *US* lu:-] tenente *m*

life [laif] (*pl* **lives** [laivz]) vida *f*; **~ assurance** seguro *m* de vida; **~belt** cinto *m* de salvação; **~boat** barco *m* de salvavidas; **~guard** salva-vidas *m*; guarda *m* pessoal; **~jacket** colete *m* de salvação; **~less** morto, inanimado; **~long** vitalício, perpétuo; **~time** existência *f*, vida *f*

lift [lift] *s* boleia *f*, *Braz* corona *f*; elevador *m*, ascensor *m*; *v/t*, *v/i* levantar(-se), erguer(-se); *v/i* roubar

ligature ['ligətʃuə] ligadura *f*

light [lait] *s* luz *f*; lume *m*; claridade *f*, clarão *m*; *fig* ponto *m* de vista; *v/t*, *v/i* iluminar(-se); acender(-se); alumiar(-se); *adj* leve, ligeiro; claro; **~en** *v/t*, *v/i* aclarar(-se); relampejar; aliviar, aligeirar; **~er** isqueiro *m*; **~-headed** delirante, estouvado, decabeça-no-ar; **~-hearted** alegre; **~house** farol *m*; **~ing** *s* iluminação *f*; **~ness** ligeireza *f*

lightning ['laitniŋ] relâmpago *m*; **~-conductor** pára-raios *m*

like [laik] *prp* como; *s* igual *m*; semelhante *m*; *v/t* gostar de; querer; *adj* semelhante, igual, parecido; **how do you ~ ...?** que tal the parece ...?; **feel ~** ter vontade de, estar/sentir-se disposto a; **look ~** parecer, estar com cara/aspecto de; **~lihood** ['-lihud] verosimilhança *f*; probabilidade *f*; **~ly**

adj verosímil, provável; **~ness** semelhança *f*; **~wise** outrossim, do mesmo modo

liking ['laikiŋ] *s* gosto *m*, inclinação *f*; predile(c)ção *f*

lilac ['lailək] *s bot* lilás *m*

lily ['lili] (*pl* **-lies**) lírio *m*

limb [lim] membro *m*

lime [laim] *s cal f*; tília *f*; **~-juice** sumo *m* de lima; **~light** ribalta *f*

limit ['limit] *s* limite *m*; *v/t* limitar; **~ation** [-'teiʃən] limitação *f*; **~less** sem limites, ilimitado

limp [limp] *v/i* coxear, manquejar; *s* coxeadura *f*; *adj* débil, mole

limy ['laimi] calcáreo; viscoso

line [lain] *s* linha *f*; fila *f*, fileira *f*; ruga *f*, vinco *m*; *v/t* alinhar (-se); riscar, traçar linhas (em); forrar

lineage ['liniidʒ] linhagem *f*

linen ['linin] *s* linho *m*; roupa *f* branca

liner ['lainə] vapor *m* de carreira, paquete *m*; transatlântico *m*

linesman ['lainzmən] (*pl* **-men**) juiz *m* de linha

linger ['liŋgə] *v/i* demorar-se, tardar, hesitar; definhar-se, arrastar-se

lining ['lainiŋ] *s* forro *m*

link [liŋk] *s* elo *m*; enlace *m*; *v/t*, *v/i* ligar, unir(-se)

links [liŋks] *s/pl* dunas *f/pl*; campo *m* de golfe

lion ['laiən] leão *m*; **~ess** leoa *f*

lip [lip] beiço *m*, lábio *m*; **~stick** batom *m*, bâton *m*

liquefy ['likwifai] *v/t*, *v/i* liquefazer(-se)

liqueur [li'kjuə] licor *m*

liquid ['likwid] *s*, *adj* líquido *m*; **~ate** *v/t* liquidar; **~ation** [-'deiʃən] liquidação *f*

liquor ['likə] bebida *f* alcoólica; **~ice** [-ris] regoliz *m*, alcaçuz *m*

lisp [lisp] *v/t*, *v/i* ciciar; *s* cício *m*

list [list] *s* lista *f*, rol *m*; *mar* inclinação *f*; *v/t* registar; *v/i* marinclinar-se

listen ['lisn] (to) *v/i* escutar; **~er** ouvinte *m*, *f*; **~ in** ouvir rádio; pôr-se à escuta

literal ['litərəl] *adj* literal; **~ly** ao pé da letra

literary ['litərəri] literário

literature ['litərətʃə] literatura *f*

litre ['li:tə] litro *m*

litter ['litə] *s* lixo *m*; liteira *f*; ninhada *f*; **~ bin** cesto *m* dos papéis

little ['litl] *s* pouco *m*; *adv* pouco; *adj* pequeno; **a ~ (bit)** um bocado, um pouco; **~ by ~** aos poucos; **~ finger** mindinho *m*

live [laiv] *adj* vivo; carregado; dire(c)to; [liv] *v/t*, *v/i* viver; morar; **~ on** alimentar-se de, sustentar-se de

livelihood ['laivlihud] sustento *m*, subsistência *f*

lively ['laivli] animado, vivo, vivaz

liver ['livə] fígado *m*

livery ['livəri] *s* libré *f*

live-stock ['laivstɔk] gado *m*

livid ['livid] lívido; zangadíssimo

living ['liviŋ] *adj* vivo; *s* subsistência *f*; vida *f*; **~-room** sala *f* de estar

lizard ['lizəd] lagarto m

load [ləud] s carga f; fardo m; v/t carregar

loaf [ləuf] s (pl loaves [-vz]) s pão m; v/i mandriar, preguiçar

loam [ləum] marga f

loan [ləun] s empréstimo m; v/t emprestar

loath [ləuθ] relutante; ~e [ləuð] v/t detestar; ~some ['-ðsəm] repugnante

lobby ['lobi] s (pl -bies) vestíbulo m; grupo m de representantes; v/t, v/i influenciar, intrigar

lobe [ləub] lóbulo m, lobo m

lobster ['lobstə] lagosta f

local ['ləukəl] adj local; s habitante m, f local; taberna f (local); ~ity [-'kæliti] (pl -ties) localidade f; ~ize v/t localizar

locate [ləu'keit] v/t localizar, situar; instalar, estabelecer

lock [lok] s fechadura f; anel m de cabelo; eclusa f, comporta f; v/t trancar, travar; fechar à chave; ~et medalhão m; ~jaw tétano m

locomotive ['ləukə.məutiv] s locomotiva f

locust ['ləukəst] gafanhoto m

lodg|e [lodʒ] v/t, v/i alojar(-se), hospedar(-se); ~er hóspede m, f, inquilino m; ~ing s alojamento m; ~ings s/pl aposentos m/pl

loft [loft] s sótão m; palheiro m; ~y elevado; altivo

log [log] s toro m, cepo m; diário de bordo

logic ['lodʒik] lógica f; ~al lógico

loin [loin] lombo m

loiter ['loitə] v/i demorar-se, tardar; vadiar

lonely ['ləunli] solitário

long [loŋ] adv muito (tempo); adj comprido, longo, extenso; largo, muito; v/i desejar, ansiar; **as/so ~ as** enquanto; desde que; **before ~** em breve; **for ~** por muito tempo; **in the ~ run** com o tempo, no fim de tudo; **no/any ~er** já não, não ... mais; ~ **for** ansiar, suspirar por; **so ~** até à vista; até logo; ~**ing** s anelo m, anseio m; ~**i-tude** ['londʒitju:d] longitude f

look [luk] s olhar m, olhadela f; aspecto m, ar m, aparência f; v/i ~ olhar; parecer; ~ **after** cuidar de; tomar conta de; ~ **at** olhar para; considerar, examinar; ~ **for** buscar, procurar; ~ **forward to** estar ansioso por; ~ **in** dar uma saltada a; ver televisão; ~ **into** examinar, investigar; ~ **out** v/i ter cuidado, acautelar-se; ~ **up** procurar, consultar

looker-on ['lukər'on] espectador m

look-out ['luk'aut] s vigilância f, atalaia f

loom [lu:m] s tear m; v/i assomar, levantar-se

loop [lu:p] volta f, curva f; presilha f; ~**-hole** seteira f; fig evasiva f

loos|e [lu:s] adj frouxo; móvel; solto; v/t afrouxar; soltar; desatar; ~**en** ['-ən] v/t, v/i soltar (-se); desapertar

loot [lu:t] s pilhagem f, saque m

lord [lɔ:d] s lorde m, senhor m

Lord [lɔ:d] s Senhor m, Deus m; *int* meu Deus!; **~ Mayor** prefeito m, Lorde-maior m; ♀ ly senhoril

lorry ['lɔri] (*pl* **-ries**) camião m, *Braz* caminhão m

lose [lu:z] v/t, v/i perder

loss [lɔs] perda f

lot [lɔt] lote m; sorte f; fortuna f; quota-parte f; **a ~ of** muito

lotion ['ləuʃən] loção f

lottery ['lɔtəri] (*pl* **-ries**) lotaria f

loud [laud] *adj* alto, forte, ruidoso; vistoso, berrante; **~speaker** alto-falante m

lounge [laundʒ] s salão m; v/i recostar-se

louse [laus] s (*pl* **lice** [lais]) piolho m

lovable ['lʌvəbl] amável

love [lʌv] v/t, v/i amar, querer, adorar; s amor m; **in ~ with** enamorado de; **~ affair** ['lʌvə] aventura f amorosa, caso m de amor; **~ly** *adj* belo, lindo; **~r** amante m, f

loving ['lʌvɪŋ] *adj* afe(c)tuoso, terno, amoroso

low [ləu] *adj* baixo; profundo; fraco; vulgar; **~er** *adj* inferior; v/t, v/i abaixar; diminuir, reduzir; humilhar

low|-necked ['ləu'nekt] decotado; **~-spirited** desanimado; **~ water** vazante f

loyal ['lɔiəl] leal, fiel; **~ty** lealdade f, fidelidade f

lozenge ['lɔzindʒ] losango m; pastilha f

lubricate ['lu:brikeit] v/t lubrificar

lucid ['lu:sid] lúcido

luck [lʌk] fortuna f, sorte f; **be in ~** estar com sorte; **worse ~** tanto pior, infelizmente; **~ily** felizmente; **~y** afortunado, ditoso; propício

lucrative ['lu:krətiv] lucrativo

ludicrous ['lu:dikrəs] ridículo; lúdico

luggage ['lʌgidʒ] bagagem f; **~-rack** rede f

lukewarm ['lu:kwɔ:m] tépido, morno; indiferente

lull [lʌl] s calmaria f; v/t, v/i embalar; acalentar

lullaby ['lʌləbai] (*pl* **-bies**) canção f de embalar/de ninar

lumber ['lʌmbə] s trastes m/pl velhos; v/i arrastar-se pesadamente

luminous ['lu:minəs] luminoso

lump [lʌmp] s pedaço m, massa f, bloco m; **~ of sugar** torrão m de açúcar; **~ in the throat** nó m na garganta

lunatic ['lu:nətik] *adj* lunático

lunch [lʌntʃ] s almoço m; v/i almoçar; dar de almoçar (a)

lung [lʌŋ] pulmão m

lurch [lə:tʃ] v/i andar aos bordos; guinar; s guinada f

lure [ljuə] s engodo m; v/t tentar, engodar, aliciar

lurk [lə:k] v/i esconder-se; emboscar-se

luscious ['lʌʃəs] delicioso, saboroso

lust [lʌst] s luxúria f; **~ful** luxurioso

lustre ['lʌstə] brilho *m*, resplendor *m*

lute [l(j)uːt] *s* alaúde *m*

luxurious [lʌg'zjuəriəs] luxuoso; **~y** ['lʌkʃəri] (*pl* **-ries**) luxo *m*

lye [lai] lixívia *f*

lynch [lintʃ] *v/t* linchar

lynx [liŋks] lince *m*

lyric ['lirik] *adj* lírico; *s* poema *m* lírico; **~al** lírico; **~s** *s/pl mus* letra *f*

M

macaroni [‚mækə'rəuni] macarrão *m*

macaroon [‚mækə'ruːn] bolo *m* de amêndoa

machine [mə'ʃiːn] *s* máquina *f*; **~gun** metralhadora *f*; **~ry** maquinaria *f*; mecanismo *m*, maquinismo *m*

mackerel ['mækrəl] cavala *f*

mackintosh ['mækintɔʃ] impermeável *m*

mad [mæd] louco, doido; **like ~** furiosamente; intensamente

madam ['mædəm] (minha) senhora *f*

madden ['mædn] *v/t* enlouquecer; irritar

made [meid] *adj* feito, fabricado

madman ['mædmən] louco *m*

madness ['mædnis] loucura *f*, demência *f*

magazine [‚mægə'ziːn] revista *f*, magazine *m*; carretel *m*

maggot ['mægət] gusano *m*, verme *m*

magic ['mædʒik] *s* magia *f*; *adj* mágico; **~al** mágico; **~ian** [mə'dʒiʃən] mágico *m*

magistrate ['mædʒistreit] magistrado *m*

magnanimous [mæg'næniməs]

magnânimo

magnet ['mægnit] magnete *m*, iman *m*, Braz imã *m*; **~ize** *v/t* imanizar, magnetizar

magnificent [mæg'nifisnt] magnífico

magnify ['mægnifai] *v/t* aumentar; exagerar

magnitude ['mægnitjuːd] magnitude *f*

magpie ['mægpai] pega *f*

mahogany [mə'hɔgəni] mogno *m*

maid [meid] criada *f*; **~en** *adj* primeiro, inaugural; virgem; solteira; **~servant** criada *f*

mail [meil] *s* correio *m*; correspondência *f*; *v/t* deitar ao correio; **~-bag** saco *m* do correio; **~-box** caixa *f* do correio; marco *m* do correio

maim [meim] *v/t* estropiar, mutilar

main [mein] *adj* principal, maior; *s* tubo *m* principal; **~land** terra *f* firme, continente *m*; **~ly** mormente, principalmente, sobretudo

maintain [mein'tein] *v/t* manter; sustentar; defender, afirmar

maintenance ['meintənəns] manutenção *f*

maize [meiz] milho *m*

majestic [mə'dʒestik] majestoso; ~ty ['mædʒisti] (*pl* -**ties**) majestade *f*

major ['meidʒə] *adj* maior, principal; *s* major *m*; ~**ity** [mə-'dʒɔriti] *s* (*pl* -**ties**) maioria *f*

make [meik] *s* marca *f*; fabrico *m*; *v/t* fazer; ganhar; fabricar; ~ **believe** fingir; ~ **haste** aviar-se, apressar-se; ~ **it** conseguir; ~ **love** fazer amor; ~ **money** ganhar dinheiro; ~ **out** decifrar; ~ **sure** of assegurar-se de, certificar-se; ~**believe** *s* simulacro *m*; *adj* fictício; ~ **up** *v/t*, *v/i* fazer as pazes; pintar(-se), maquilhar(-se); completar

maker ['meikə] fabricante *m*

makeshift ['meik∫ift] *s* substituto *m*; *adj* provisório

make-up ['meikʌp] *s* maquil(h)agem *f*; caracterização *f*; composição *f*

male [meil] *adj* másculo; masculino; macho

malice ['mælis] malícia *f*; ~**afore-thought** *jur* premeditação *f*; ~**ious** [mə'li∫əs] malicioso

malignant [mə'lignənt] maligno

mallet ['mælit] malho *m*, maço *m*

malt [mɔ:lt] *s* malte *m*

mammal ['mæməl] mamífero *m*

mammy ['mæmi] (*pl* -**mies**)

mamã(e); *US* aia *f* preta

man [mæn] *s* (*pl* **men** [men]) homem *m*; varão *m*; *v/t* tripular; guarnecer; equipar; ~ **and wife** marido *m* e mulher *f*; to a ~ todos, sem exce(p)ção, unanimemente

manage ['mænidʒ] *v/t*, *v/i* administrar, gerir; conseguir, lograr; ~**ement** gerência *f*, administração *f*; ~**er** gerente *m*

mane [mein] crina *f*

manganese ['mæŋgə'ni:z] manganês *m*

manger ['meindʒə] manjedoura *f*

mangle ['mæŋgl] *s* calandra *f*; *v/t* calandrar; mutilar

mango ['mæŋgəu] manga *f*

manhood ['mænhud] virilidade *f*; idade *f* viril

mania ['meinjə] mania *f*

manifest ['mænifest] *adj* manifesto; *v/t* manifestar

manifold ['mænifəuld] *adj* múltiplo

manipulate [mə'nipjuleit] *v/t* manipular

mankind [mæn'kaind] humanidade *f*

manly ['mænli] viril; varonil

manner ['mænə] maneira *f*, modo *m*; ~**ism** maneirismo *m*; ~**s** maneiras *f/pl*, modos *m/pl*

manor ['mænə] solar *m*

manpower ['mæn.pauə] mão-de-obra *f*

mansion ['mæn∫ən] palacete *m*

manslaughter ['mæn.slɔ:tə] homicídio *m* involuntário

mantelpiece ['mæntlpi:s] prateleira *f* da lareira

manual ['mænjuəl] *s, adj* manual *m*

manufactur|e [,mænju'fæktʃə] *s* fabricação *f*; *v/t* fabricar; **~er** fabricante *m, f*

manure [mə'njuə] *s* estrume *m*, adubo *m*; *v/t* estrumar

manuscript ['mænjuskript] manuscrito *m*

many ['meni] muitos, muitas

map [mæp] *s* mapa *m*; planta *f*; *v/t* traçar um mapa

maple ['meipl] *bot* bordo *m*

marauder [mə'rɔ:də] *s* saqueador *m*

marble ['mɑ:bl] mármore *m*

March [mɑ:tʃ] Março *m*

march [mɑ:tʃ] *s* marcha *f*; *v/i* marchar

mare [mɛə] égua *f*

margarine [,mɑ:dʒə'ri:n] margarina *f*

margin ['mɑ:dʒin] margem *f*

marigold ['mærigəuld] malmequer *m*

marine [mə'ri:n] *adj* marítimo; marinho; *s* marinha *f*; fuzileiro *m* naval

mark [mɑ:k] *s* marca *f*; sinal *m*; nota *f*, ponto *m*; *v/t* marcar; assinalar; classificar; **~ed** *adj* marcado; marcante

market ['mɑ:kit] *s* mercado *m*; *v/t, v/i* pôr à venda; ir às compras; **~ing** *s* compra *f* e venda *f*; **~place** praça *f*, mercado *m*

marmalade ['mɑ:məleid] compota *f*/doce *m* de laranja

maroon [mə'ru:n] *v/t* abando-nar; *adj* castanho-avermelhado

marqu|ess, ~is ['mɑ:kwis] marquês *m*

marriage ['mæridʒ] casamento *m*

married ['mærid] *adj* casado

marry ['mæri] *v/t, v/i* casar(-se)

marsh [mɑ:ʃ] pântano *m*

marshal ['mɑ:ʃəl] *s* marechal *m*

marshy ['mɑ:ʃi] pantanoso

marten ['mɑ:tin] marta *f*

martial ['mɑ:ʃəl] marcial

martyr ['mɑ:tə] *s* mártir *m, f*; **~dom** martírio *m*

marvel ['mɑ:vəl] *s* maravilha *f*; *v/i* **~** at estranhar, admirar-se; **~(l)ous** maravilhoso

marzipan [,mɑ:zi'pæn] maçapão *m*

mascara [mæs'kɑ:rə] rimel *m*

mascot ['mæskət] mascote *f*

masculine ['mæskjulin] *adj, s* masculino *m*

mash [mæʃ] *v/t* esmagar, triturar; **~ed potatoes** puré *m* de batata

mask [mɑ:sk] *s* máscara *f*; *v/t* mascarar; disfarçar; **~ed ball** baile *m* de máscaras

mason ['meisn] pedreiro *m*; mação *m*; **~ry** alvenaria *f*; maçonaria *f*

mass [mæs] *s* massa *f*; *eccl* missa *f*

massacre ['mæsəkə] *s* massacre *m*

mass|age ['mæsɑ:ʒ] *v/t* massajar, dar massagens a; *s* massagem *f*; **~eur** [mæ'sə:] massagista *m, f*

massive ['mæsiv] maciço

mast [mɑ:st] mastro *m*

master ['mɑ:stə] *s* mestre *m*; dono *m*, senhor *m*, amo *m*; patrão; *v/t* dominar; **~ly** magistral; **~piece** obra-prima *f*; **~y** mestria *f*; domínio *m*

mat [mæt] *s* tapete *m*; esteira *f*, capacho *m*

match [mætʃ] *s* fósforo *m*; desafio *m*, partida *f*; igual *m*; *v/t*, *v/i* igualar(-se); condizer; competir; **~box** caixa *f* de fósforos; **~less** incomparável, sem igual

mate [meit] *s* camarada *m, f,* companheiro *m*; *v/t, v/i* acasalar(-se)

material [mə'tiəriəl] *adj* material; *s* fazenda *f*, tecido *m*; matéria *f*; material *m*; **~ist** *adj, s* materialista *m, f;* **~ize** *v/t, v/i* materializar(-se)

maternal [mə'tə:nl] maternal

mathematics [,mæθi'mætiks] matemática *f*

matrimony ['mætriməni] matrimónio *m*

matron ['meitrən] enfermeira-chefe *f*

matter ['mætə] *s* matéria *f*; caso *m*, assunto *m*; *v/i* importar; **what's the ~?** o que há?, que aconteceu?; o que é isso?; o que tem?; **a ~ of** uma questão de; **as a ~ of fact** na realidade, de fa(c)to; **~-of-fact** realista, terra-a-terra

mattress ['mætris] colchão *m*

matur|e [mə'tjuə] *adj* maduro; *v/t, v/i* amadurecer; **~ity** maturidade *f*, madureza *f*

maximum ['mæksiməm] *adj, s* máximo *m*

May [mei] Maio *m*

may [mei] *v/aux* poder, ser possível; ter licença

maybe ['meibi:] talvez, acaso, quiçá

mayor [mɛə] presidente *m* da câmara, prefeito *m*

maze [meiz] labirinto *m*

me [mi:,mi] me; mim

meadow ['medəu] prado *m*

meagre ['mi:gə] magro, macilento; escasso; insuficiente

meal [mi:l] refeição *f*; farinha *f*; **~time** horas *f/pl* da refeição

mean [mi:n] *v/t* significar, querer dizer; pensar, propor-se; *adj.* mau, mesquinho, ruim; vil, baixo; médio; *s* média *f*; meio *m*, meio termo *m*

meander [mi'ændə] *v/i* colear, serpentear

meaning ['mi:nin] *s* significado *m*, significação *f*; sentido *m*

means [mi:nz] *s* meio *m*; recursos *m/pl*; **by all ~** certamente, sem dúvida; **by no ~** de modo nenhum; **by ~ of** por meio de

mean|time ['mi:n'taim], **~while** entretanto, no entanto

measles ['mi:zlz] sarampo *m*

measure ['meʒə] *s* medida *f*; **made to ~** feito à medida; *v/t, v/i* medir; **~d** *adj* comedido, ponderado; **~ment** medição *f*

meat [mi:t] carne *f*; **~ ball** almôndega *f*

mechanic [mi'kænik] mecânico *m*; **~al** mecânico; maquinal; **~ally** maquinalmente; **~s**

mecânica f

mechanism ['mekənizəm] mecanismo m

medal ['medl] medalha f

meddle ['medl] v/i meter-se, intrometer-se

mediat|e ['mi:dieit] v/i servir de intermediário / medianeiro, mediar; **~ion** [-'eiʃən] mediação f; **~or** mediador m

medica|l ['medisinl] adj médico; medicinal; **~ment** [me'dikəmənt] medicamento m

medicin|al [me'disinl] medicinal; **~e** [-sin] medicamento m, remédio m; medicina f

medieval [.medi'i:vəl] medieval

mediocr|e ['mi:diəukə] mediocre; **~ity** [-'ɔkriti] mediocridade f

medit|ate ['mediteit] v/i meditar; **~ion** [-'teiʃən] meditação f; **~ive** [-'tətiv] meditativo

Mediterranean [.meditə'reinjən] adj mediterrâneo

medium ['mi:djəm] s médio m; adj mediano, médio

medley ['medli] mistura f; miscelânea f; mixórdia f

meek [mi:k] manso, humilde, meigo

meet [mi:t] v/t, v/i encontrar (-se); travar conhecimento, conhecer(-se); satisfazer; reunir-se; s reunião f; **make ends ~** equilibrar receitas e despesas; **~ with** topar com, encontrar; US reunir-se com; **~ing** reunião f; encontro m

melancholy ['melənkəli] s melancolia f; adj melancólico

mellow ['meləu] adj maduro; suave, brando

melody ['melədi] (pl-dies) melodia f

melt [melt] v/t, v/i derreter(-se), fundir(-se)

member ['membə] membro m

memoirs ['memwɑ:z] memórias f/pl

memorial [mi'mɔ:riəl] adj comemorativo; s monumento m comemorativo

memory ['meməri] (pl-ries) memória f; recordação f, lembrança f

menace ['menəs] s ameaça f

mend [mend] v/t, v/i reparar; remendar, consertar

mental ['mentl] mental; **~ity** [-'tæliti] mentalidade f

mention ['menʃən] s alusão f, menção f; v/t fazer menção de, mencionar

menu ['menju:] ementa f, Braz cardápio m

mercenary ['mə:sinəri] adj mercenário

merchant ['mə:tʃənt] comerciante m, f, negociante m, f

merci|ful ['mə:siful] clemente, misericordioso; **~less** cruel, desalmado

mercury ['mə:kjuri] mercúrio m, azougue m

mercy ['mə:si] (pl-cies) misericórdia f; **at the ~ of** à mercê de

mere [miə] adj simples, mero

merg|e [mə:dʒ] v/t, v/i fundir (-se), unir(-se); **~er** com fusão f

meridian [mə'ridiən] meridiano

merit ['merit] s mérito m; v/t merecer

mer|maid ['mə:meid] sereia f; **~man** tritão m

merry ['meri] jovial, divertido, alegre; **make ~** divertir-se; ♀ **Christmas!** Boas Festas! Feliz Natal!; **~-go-round** carrocel m

mesh [meʃ] s malha f

mess [mes] s messe f; apuros m/pl, dificuldades f/pl; confusão f; desordem f, porcaria f, trapalhada f

message ['mesidʒ] mensagem f

messenger ['mesindʒə] mensageiro m

metal ['metl] s metal m; **~lic** [mi'tælik] metálico

method ['meθəd] método m; **~ical** [mi'θɔdikəl] metódico

metre ['mi:tə] metro m

metropolitan [.metrə'pɔlitən] adj metropolitano

mew [mju:] v/i miar; s miadela f, miado m

miaow [mi(:)'au] v/i miar; s miau m

mice [mais] pl of mouse

microphone ['maikrəfəun] microfone m

midday ['middei] meio-dia m

middle [midl] s meio m; adj do meio, médio, mediano; **in the ~** of no meio de; **~ age** idade f madura; **~-aged** de meia idade; ♀ **Ages** s/pl Idade f Média

middling ['midliŋ] adj médio;

meão; mediocre

midget ['midʒit] anão m

midnight ['midnait] meia-noite f

midshipman ['midʃipmən] aspirante m de marinha

midsummer ['mid.samə] solstício m do verão, pleno verão m; ♀ **Day** dia m de São João

midway ['mid'wei] adv a meio do caminho

midwife ['midwaif] (pl-wives) ['-waivz] parteira f

might [mait] s poder m, força f, pujança f; **~y** adv extremamente, muito

migraine [mi:'grein] enxaqueca f

mild [maild] adj brando; manso, suave, meigo

mildew ['mildju:] s míldio m; bolor m, mofo m

mile [mail] milha f; **~stone** marco m miliário, pedra f miliária

military ['militəri] adj militar

militia [mi'liʃə] milícia f

milk [milk] s leite m; v/t, v/i ordenhar; **~man** leiteiro m; **~-shake** batido m de leite; **~y** leitoso; ♀y **Way** Via f Láctea

mill [mil] v/t moer; esfarelar; s moinho m; fábrica f; **~er** moleiro m

millet ['milit] painço m

milliner ['milinə] chapeleira f

million ['miljən] s milhão m; **~aire** [.-'nɛə] milionário m

milt [milt] láctea f

mimic ['mimik] adj mímico; v/t

imitar, remedar

mince [mins] *s* carne *f* picada; *v/t* picar; **~meat** US picado *m* de carne; recheio *m* de fruta; **~ pie** pastel *m* de recheio de frutas

mind [maind] *s* mente *f*; espírito *m*; *v/t*, *v/i* cuidar de, olhar por; importar-se; ocupar-se; prestar atenção a, notar; **call/ bring to ~** trazer à memória; **change one's ~** mudar de opinião; **make up one's ~** decidir-se, tomar uma resolução; **never ~** mão faz mal, não importa; **to one's ~** na sua opinião, a seu ver; **would you ~ ...?** importa(va)-se de ...?; **~ed** *adj* disposto, inclinado

mine [main] *pron* (o) meu, (a) minha, (os) meus, (as) minhas; *s* mina *f*; *v/t*, *v/i* minar; minerar

miner ['mainǝ] mineiro *m*

mineral ['minǝrǝl] *adj*, *s* mineral *m*

mingle ['miŋgl] *v/t* mesclar, misturar

mining ['mainiŋ] *s* exploração *f* de minas

minister ['ministǝ] *s* ministro *m*; **~ial** [-'tiǝriǝl] ministerial

ministry ['ministri] (*pl* -ries) ministério *m*; sacerdócio *m*

mink [miŋk] (pele *f* de) marta *f*

minor ['mainǝ] *adj* menor; secundário; *s* menor *m*, *f*; **~ity** [-'nɔriti] (*pl* -ties) minoria; menoridade *f*

minster ['minstǝ] basílica *f*, sé *f*

minstrel ['minstrǝl] menestrel

m; jogral *m*

mint [mint] *s* bot hortelã *f*, menta *f*; casa *f* da moeda; *v/t* cunhar.

mint sauce molho *m* de hortelã

minus ['mainǝs] *prp* menos; *adj* negativo

minute [minit] *s* minuto *m*; minuta *f*, nota *f*; [mai'nju:t] *adj* minucioso; minúsculo, diminuto; **~s** *s/pl* a(c)tas *f/pl*

mirac|le ['mirǝkl] milagre *m*; **~ulous** [-'rækjulǝs] milagroso

mirage ['mira:3] miragem *f*

mirror ['mirǝ] *s* espelho *m*; *v/t* espelhar

misapprehension ['mis,æpri-'henʃǝn] mal-entendido *m*, equívoco *m*

misbehavio(u)r ['misbi'heivjǝ] má conduta *f*, mau comportamento *m*

miscalculation ['mis,kælkju-'leiʃǝn] erro *m* de cálculo

miscarriage ['mis'kærid3] aborto *m*; *p* aborto

miscellaneous [,misi'leinjǝs] variado, vário, misto

mischief [mistʃif] mal *m*, dano *m*; travessura *f*, diabrura *f*

mischievous [mistʃivǝs] travesso, brincalhão

misdemeano(u)r [,misdi-'mi:nǝ] delito *m*

miser ['maizǝ] sovina *m*, *f*, avaro *m*

miserable ['mizǝrǝbl] desgraçado, infeliz; miserável

misery ['mizǝri] miséria *f*, desgraça *f*

misfortune ['mis'fɔːtʃən] infortúnio *m*, desventura *f*

misgiving ['mis'givin] apreensão *m*, receio *m*

misgovern ['mis'gʌvən] *v/t* governar mal, desgovernar

misguided [-] *adj* extraviado, desencaminhado

mishap ['mishæp] azar *m*, revés *m*, contratempo *m*

misinterpret ['misin'təːprit] *v/t* interpretar mal

misjudge ['mis'dʒʌdʒ] *v/t* julgar mal, fazer mau juízo de

mislay [mis'lei] *v/t* perder, extraviar

mislead [mis'liːd] *v/t* enganar, desencaminhar

misprint ['mis'print] *s* erro *m* tipográfico

misrule ['mis'ruːl] *s* má administração *f*

miss [mis] *s* menina *f*; moça *f*; senhora *f*; *Braz* senhorita *f*

miss [mis] *v/t*, *v/i* falhar, errar; perder; faltar a; sentir a falta de; *s* falhanço *m*, falha *f*

misshapen ['mis'ʃeipən] disforme

missile ['misail] projé(c)til *m*

missing ['misiŋ] *adj* perdido; extraviado; ausente

mission ['miʃən] missão *f*; **~ary** [-'nəri] (*pl*-ries) missionário *m*

mist [mist] *s* névoa *f*, neblina *f*

mistake [mis'teik] *s* erro *m*; equívoco *m*; *v/t* enganar-se, equivocar-se; confundir; **by ~** por engano; **~n** [-'teikən] enganado, equivocado; errado, errôneo

mister ['mistə] senhor *m*

mistletoe ['mislitəu] visco *m*

mistress ['mistris] dona *f*, senhora *f*; professora *f*; amante *f*

mistrust ['mis'trʌst] *v/t* desconfiar de; *s* desconfiança *f*

misty ['misti] nebuloso, enevoado

misunderstand ['misʌndə'stænd] *v/t* entender mal, compreender mal; **~ing** *s* mal-entendido *m*, equívoco *m*; desinteligência *f*

misuse ['mis'juːz] *v/t* abusar de; maltratar; [-'juːs] *s* abuso *m*; mau trato *m*

mite [mait] criancinha *f*; migalha *f*

mitigate ['mitigeit] *v/t* mitigar

mitten ['mitn] mitene *f*

mix [miks] *v/t*, *v/i* mesclar, misturar(-se); imiscuir-se; **~ed** *adj* misto; misturado; **~ up** confundir, atrapalhar; **~ed in** metido em, implicado em; confuso; **~er** batedeira *f*; **~ture** [-tʃə] mistura *f*, mescla *f*

moan [məun] *v/i* gemer; *s* gemido *m*

mob [mɔb] *s* multidão *f*, populaça *f*, turba *f*, gentalha *f*

mobil|**e** ['məubail] *adj* móvel; **~ity** [-'biliti] mobilidade *f*

mock [mɔk] *adj* simulado, falso; *v/t* mofar de, zombar de; **~ery** zombaria *f*

mode [məud] modo *m*; moda *f*

model ['mɔdl] *s* modelo *m*; *v/t* modelar; *adj* modelar

moderat|**e** ['mɔdərit] *adj* mode-

rado; v/t, v/i moderar; **~ion**
[-'reiʃən] moderação f

modern ['mɔdən] adj moderno;
~ize v/t, v/i modernizar(-se)

modest ['mɔdist] modesto; **~y**
modéstia f

modify ['mɔdifai] v/t modificar

Mohammedan [məu'hæmidən] adj, s maometano m

moist [mɔist] (h)úmido; **~en**
['-sn] v/t (h)umedecer;
~ure ['-tʃə] (h)umidade f

molar ['məulær] adj molar

mole [məul] lunar m; zo toupeira f; mar molhe m

molecule ['mɔlikju:l] molécula f

molest [məu'lest] v/t molestar;
~ation [-'teiʃən] molestação f

moment ['məumənt] momento
m; at the **~** de/neste momento; **~ary** momentâneo

monarch ['mɔnək] monarca m;
~y monarquia f

monastery ['mɔnəstəri] (pl -ries) mosteiro m

Monday ['mʌndi] segunda-feira f

money ['mʌni] dinheiro m; **~ed**
abastado; **~lender** prestamista m, f; **~ order** vale m postal

mongrel ['mʌŋgrəl] adj mestiço, híbrido

monk [mʌŋk] monge m

monkey ['mʌŋki] s macaco m

mono|gram ['mɔnəgræm] monograma m; **~log(ue)** ['-lɔg]
monólogo m; **~mania** [-nəu'meinjə] monomania f; **~poly**
[mə'nɔpəli] monopólio m;
~tonous [mə'nɔtənəs] monó-

tono; **~tony** [mə'nɔtni] monotonia f

monster ['mɔnstə] monstro m

monstrous ['mɔnstrəs] monstruoso

month [mʌnθ] mês m; **~ly** adj
mensal; adv mensalmente

monument ['mɔnjumənt] monumento m; **~al** ['-mentl] monumental

moo [mu:] v/t mugir

mood [mu:d] disposição f, humor m; modo m; **~y** mal-humorado

moon [mu:n] s lua f; **~light** s
luar m; **~shine** devaneio m,
disparate m, Braz bobagem f

moor [muə] s charneca f; v/t
amarrar, atracar

Moor [muə] mouro m; **~ish** mourisco, mouro

mop [mɔp] s esfregão m; v/t esfregar

moral ['mɔrəl] adj, s moral f; **~e**
[mɔ'rɑ:l] moral m; **~ity**
[mə'ræliti] moralidade f; **~s**
moral f, ética f

morass [mə'ræs] pântano m

morbid ['mɔ:bid] mórbido

more [mɔ:] adj, adv mais; **~**
and ~ cada vez mais; **~ or**
less mais ou menos; **the ~ ...,**
the ~ quanto mais ..., (tanto)
mais; **~over** além do mais,
além disso

morgue [mɔ:g] morgue f

morning ['mɔ:niŋ] manhã f; **to-**
morrow ~ amanhã de manhã

morose [mə'rəus] taciturno, sorumbático

morphine ['mɔ:fi:n] morfina f

morsel ['mɔ:səl] bocado *m*, bocadinho *m*

mortal ['mɔ:tl] *s, adj* mortal *m*; **~ity** [-'tæliti] mortalidade *f*

mortar ['mɔ:tə] *s* argamassa *f*; mil morteiro *m*; almofariz *m*

mortgage ['mɔ:gidʒ] *s* hipoteca *f*; *v/t* hipotecar

mortify ['mɔ:tifai] *v/t* mortificar

mortuary ['mɔ:tjuəri] (*pl* -ries) necrotério *m*

mosaic [mə'zeiik] *s* mosaico *m*

Moslem ['mɔzləm] *adj, s* muçulmano *m*

mosque [mɔsk] mesquita *f*

mosquito [mə'ski:təu] (*pl* -toes) mosquito *m*

moss [mɔs] musgo *m*; **~y** musgoso

most [məust] *s* o máximo; *adj* o(s) mais; a maior parte de; *adv* o mais; muito, sumamente; at (the) ~ quando muito; for the ~ part na grande maioria; na sua maior parte; make the ~ of tirar o melhor partido/proveito de; **~ly** principalmente; na maior parte das vezes

moth [mɔθ] traça *f*; **~-eaten** roído pela traça

mother ['mʌðə] *s* mãe *f*; **~country** pátria *f*; **~-in-law** sogra *f*; **~ly** maternal; *s* **~ of pearl** madrepérola *f*, nácar *m*; **~ tongue** língua/materna

motion ['məuʃən] *v/t, v/i* acenar, gesticular; fazer sinal (para); *s* movimento *m*; moção *f*, proposta *f*; **~less** imóvel

motivate ['məutiveit] *v/t* motivar; **~tion** [-'veiʃən] motivação *f*

motive ['məutiv] *s* motivo *m*; *adj* motor, motriz

motley ['mɔtli] *adj* variegado

motor ['məutə] *s* motor *m*; **~boat** gasolina; *m*, lancha *f*; **~-car** carro *m*, automóvel *m*; **~cycle** motocicleta *f*; **~ist** motorista *m, f*, automobilista *m, f*; **~way** GB auto-estrada *f*

mottled ['mɔtld] *adj* mosqueado, sarapintado

motto ['mɔtəu] moto *m*, divisa *f*

mo(u)ld [məuld] *s* molde *m*; forma *f*; bolor *m*, mofo *m*; *v/t* moldar; **~y** bolorento

mount [maunt] *v/t, v/i* montar, subir

mountain ['mauntin] montanha *f*, serra *f*; **~eer** [-'niə] alpinista *m, f*; **~eering** alpinismo *m*; **~ous** montanhoso

mourn [mɔ:n] *v/t, v/i* lamentar (-se), carpir(-se), deplorar, estar de luto; **~ful** triste, choroso; **~ing** luto *m*

mouse [maus] (*pl*-mice [mais]) rato *m*, Braz camundongo *m*; **~-trap** ratoeira *f*

m(o)ustache [məs'tɑ:] ʃ bigode *m*

mouth [mauθ] *s* boca *f*; foz *f*; *v/t, v/i* declamar; **shut your ~!** cale a boca; **~ful** trago *m*, bocado *m*; **~piece** bocal *m*; porta-voz *m*

movable ['mu:vəbl] móvel, movediço

move [mu:v] *v/t, v/i* mover(-se),

avançar; mudar de casa; mexer-se; comover; s jogada f, lance m; movimento m; mudança f

movement ['mu:vmənt] movimento m

movies ['mu:viz] s/pl fam cinema m

moving ['mu:viŋ] adj comovente; movediço

mow [mau] v/t segar, ceifar

Mr. ['mistə] abbr of mister

Mrs. ['misiz] senhora f

much [mʌtʃ] adj muito; adv muito; **as ~ as** tanto como; **how ~?** quanto? **so ~** tanto; **so ~ the better** tanto melhor; **so ~ the worse** tanto pior; **too ~** demais, muito, demasiado; **very ~** muitíssimo

mud [mʌd] lama f, lodo m; **~dy** lamacento, lodoso; **~guard** auto guarda-lamas m

muff [mʌf] s regalo m

muffle ['mʌfl] v/t abafar; embuçar; tapar

mug [mʌg] s caneca f; simplório m; fuça f; v/t assaltar; **~ up** decorar, empinar, picar; **~gy** abafado, mormacento

mulberry ['mʌlbəri] (pl -ries) amora f; **~ tree** amoreira f

mule [mju:l] mula f

mull [mʌl] v/t: **~ wine** preparar vinho quente

multi|ple ['mʌltipl] adj múltiplice, múltiplo; s múltiplo m; **~plication** [-,pli'keiʃən] multiplicação f; **~ply** [-plai] v/t, v/i multiplicar(-se)

multitude ['mʌltitju:d] multi-

dão f

mumble ['mʌmbl] v/t, v/i murmurar, falar entre dentes

mummy ['mʌmi] (pl -mies) mamã f, Braz mamãe f; múmia f

mumps [mʌmps] papeira f, Braz caxumba f

munch [mʌntʃ] v/t mastigar

municipal [mju:(')nisipəl] municipal

murder ['mə:də] s assassínio m; v/t assassinar; **~er** assassino m; **~ous** assassino

murmur ['mə:mə] s murmúrio m; v/t, v/i murmurar

musc|le ['mʌsl] músculo m; **~ular** ['mʌskjulə] musculoso; muscular

muse [mju:z] v/i meditar, cismar

museum [mju:(')ziəm] museu m

mushroom ['mʌʃrum] cogumelo m

music ['mju:zik] música f; **~al** adj musical; **~ian** [-'ziʃən] músico m

musk [mʌsk] almíscar m

musket ['mʌskit] mosquete m; **~eer** [-'tiə] mosqueteiro m

Muslim ['mʌzlim] adj, s muçulmano m

muslin ['mʌzlin] musselina f

mussel ['mʌsl] mexilhão m

must [mʌst] v/aux dever, ter que, ter de; s mosto m; obrigação f, dever m, necessidade f

mustard ['mʌstəd] mostarda f

muster ['mʌstə] s chamada f; v/t reunir; fazer a chamada de

musty ['mʌsti] bafiento, mofoso

mutable ['mju:təbl] mudável; **~tion** [-'teiʃən] mutação *f*

mute [mju:t] *adj, s* mudo *m*

mutilat|e ['mju:tileit] *v/t* mutilar; **~ion** [-'leiʃən] mutilação *f*

mutin|eer [,mju:ti'niə] amotinador *m*; **~ous** amotinado, sedicioso; **~y** *s* (*pl* **-nies**) motim *m*

mutter ['mʌtə] *v/t, v/i* resmungar

mutton ['mʌtn] carne *f* de carneiro

mutual ['mju:tjuəl] mutual,

mútuo, recíproco

muzzle ['mʌzl] *s* focinho *m*; açaime *m*, focinheira *f*; *v/t* açaimar

my [mai] *adj* meu(s), minha(s); *int* caramba!; **~ dear** meu caro

myrtle ['mə:tl] mirto *m*

myself [mai'self] eu mesmo; mim mesmo; me; **(all) by ~** sozinho

myster|ious [mis'tiəriəs] misterioso; **~y** ['-təri] (*pl* **-ries**) mistério *m*

mystify ['mistifai] *v/t* mistificar

myth [miθ] mito *m*

N

nag [næg] *s* rocim *m*; *v/t, v/i* chatear, aborrecer

nail [neil] *s* unha *f*; prego *m*; *v/t* cravar, pregar

naïve [na:'i:v] ingénuo

naked ['neikid] nu, despido; **~ eye** olho *m* nu; **~ truth** verdade *f* nua e crua; **~ness** nudez *f*

name [neim] *s* nome *m*; nomeada *f*; *v/t* denominar; dar nome a; designar, nomear; **by ~** de/pelo nome; **~ly** a saber; **~sake** homónimo *m*, Braz xará *m*, *f*

nap [næp] *v/i* dormitar, Braz cochilar; *s* sesta *f*, soneca *f*, Braz cochilo *m*; **have a ~** fazer sesta, dormitar; **be caught ~ping** ser apanhado desprevenido

nape [neip] nuca *f*

napkin ['næpkin] guardanapo

m; **~ ring** argola *f* de guardanapo

nappy ['næpi] (*pl* **-pies**) fralda *f*, cueiro *m*

narcissus [na:'sisəs] narciso *m*

narcotic [na:'kɔtik] *adj, s* narcótico *m*

narrat|e [næ'reit] *v/t* narrar; **~ion** narração *f*; **~ive** ['-rətiv] *s* narrativa *f*; **~or** narrador *m*

narrow ['nærəu] *adj* estreito; apertado; restrito, limitado; *v/t, v/i* estreitar(-se); limitar, restringir; **~-minded** tacanho; **~ness** estreiteza *f*; **~s** *s/pl* estreitamento *m*, estreito *m*

nasty ['na:sti] desagradável; nojento; sério, grave; grosseiro, repugnante

nation ['neiʃən] nação *f*

national ['næʃənl] *adj* nacional; **~ism** nacionalismo *m*; **~ist** *adj, s* nacionalista *m, f*; **~ity**

[-'næliti] (pl **-ties**) nacionalidade f; **~ize** v/t nacionalizar

native ['neitiv] adj natural; nativo; s indígena m, f

natural ['nætʃrəl] adj natural; **~ist** naturalista m, f; **~ize** v/t naturalizar

nature ['neitʃə] natureza f

naughty ['nɔːti] traquinas, mau, travesso

nausea ['nɔːsjə] náusea f, enjoo m; **~te** ['-sieit] v/t nausear

nautical ['nɔːtikəl] náutico

naval ['neivəl] naval

nave [neiv] arch nave f

navel ['neivəl] umbigo m

navig|able ['nævigəbl] navegável; **~ate** ['-geit] v/t, v/i navegar; **~ation** ['-geiʃən] navegação f; náutica f; **~ator** ['-geitə] navegador m

navy ['neivi] (pl **-vies**) marinha f; **~ blue** s azul-marinho m

nay [nei] s voto m negativo

near [niə] adj próximo; adv perto; prp perto de; **~by** adv pertinho; adj próximo; **~ly** quase; **~ness** proximidade f

neat [niːt] limpo, asseado; elegante, claro; porreiro; puro, não diluído

nebulous ['nebjuləs] nebuloso

necessaries ['nesisəriz] s/pl necessário m

necessary ['nesisəri] necessário, preciso, essencial

necessit|ate [ni'sesiteit] v/t necessitar; **~y** (pl **-ties**) necessidade f

neck [nek] s pescoço m; gargalo m; **~ or nothing** tudo ou nada; **~lace** ['-lis] colar m

need [niːd] v/t precisar (de), necessitar (de); s necessidade f, falta f

needle ['niːdl] 'niːdl] s agulha f; **~ in a haystack** agulha f em palheiro

need|less ['niːdlis] desnecessário; **~y** indigente

negation [ni'geiʃən] negação f

negative ['negətiv] adj negativo; s negativa f; negativo m

neglect [ni'glekt] v/t negligenciar, descuidar; s descuido m; **~ful** descuidado

negligen|ce ['neglidʒəns] negligência f; **~t** negligente

negotia|ble [ni'gouʃjəbl] negociável; **~te** ['-ʃieit] v/t, v/i negociar

negress ['niːgris] negra f

negro ['niːgrou] negro m

neigh [nei] v/i rinchar, relinchar

neighbo(u)r ['neibə] s vizinho m; **~hood** vizinhança f; **~ing** vizinho

neither ['naiðə] conj nem; adv também não, tão-pouco; adj nenhum, nem um nem outro; **~...nor** nem ... nem

nephew ['nevju:] sobrinho m

nerv|e [nəːv] s nervo m; **~ous** nervoso

nest [nest] s ninho m

nestle ['nesl] v/t, v/i aninhar (-se), aconchegar-se

net [net] s rede f; v/t apanhar à rede, pescar; adj líquido, livre

nettle ['netl] s urtiga f; v/t irritar, picar

network ['netwəːk] rede f

neutral ['nju:trəl] *adj* neutro, neutral; **~ity** [-'træliti] neutralidade *f*

never ['nevə] nunca, jamais; **~theless** contudo, todavia

new [nju:] novo; **~-born** recém--nascido; **~-comer** recém-chegado *m*; **~ly** recentemente; novamente; **~ly wed s** recém--casado *m*

news [nju:z] *s/pl* notícias *f/pl*; **~paper** jornal *m*

newt [nju:t] tritão *m*

New Year's Day dia *m* de Ano Novo

next [nekst] *adj* próximo; seguinte; *adv* depois, em seguida; (the) **~ day** o dia seguinte; **~ door** *adv* do lado; **~ to** *prp* a seguir a; junto a; *adv* quase

nib [nib] bico *m*, aparo *f*

nibble ['nibl] *v/t, v/i* mordiscar

nice [nais] bom; gentil; bonito; fino, su(b)til

nick [nik] *s* corte *m*, entalhe *m*; **in the ~ of time** a tempo, no momento oportuno

nickel ['nikl] *s* níquel *m*; moeda *f* de 5 cêntimos

nickname ['nikneim] *s* alcunha *f*

niece [ni:s] sobrinha *f*

niggardly ['nigədli] mesquinho

night [nait] noite *f*; **at ~** à de noite; **~-club** cabaré *m*; **~-dress, ~-gown** camisa *f* de dormir, *Braz* camisola *f*

nightingale ['aitiŋgeil] rouxinol *m*

nightly ['naitli] *adj* no(c)turno

nightmare ['naitmɛə] pesadelo *m*

nil [nil] nada *m*, zero *m*

nimble ['nimbl] ágil

nine [nain] nove

nine|teen ['nain'ti:n] dezanove; **~ty** noventa

ninth [nainθ] nono

nip [nip] *s* beliscão *m*; dentada *f*; *v/t, v/i* abocanhar; beliscar

nipple ['nipl] mamilo *m*; bico *m*, chupeta *f*

nitre ['naitə] nitro *m*, salitre *m*

nitrogen ['naitrədʒən] nitrogénio *m*, azoto *m*

no [nəu] *adv* não; *adj* nenhum a; **~ longer, ~ more** já não, não … mais

nobility [nəu'biliti] nobreza *f*

noble ['nəubl] *adj s* nobre *m*

nobody ['nəubədi] *pron* ninguém; *s* zé-ninguém *m*, joão--ninguém *m*

nod [nɔd] *v/t, v/i* acenar com a cabeça, inclinar a cabeça; cabecear; *s* aceno *m*

nois|e [nɔiz] ruído *m*, barulho *m*; **~eless** [-lis] silencioso; **~y** ruidoso, barulhento

nominal ['nɔminl] nominal

nominat|e ['nɔmineit] *v/t* nomear, designar; **~ion** [-'nei-ʃən] nomeação *f*; **~ive** ['-nətiv] *adj, s* nominativo *s*

nonchalant ['nɔnʃələnt] indiferente, despreocupado

nondescript ['nɔndiskript] indefinível

none [nʌn] *pron* nenhum a; *adv* de modo algum; **~ the less** nem por isso, não obstante

nonentity [nɔ'nentiti] (*pl* **-ties**)

nulidade f

nonplus ['nɔn'plʌs] v/t confundir

nonsens|e ['nɔnsəns] disparate m, asneira f, Braz bobagem f; ~ical absurdo

non-stop ['nɔn'stɔp] dire(c)to, sem escala; ininterrupto

noodles ['nu:dlz] s/pl massa f

noon [nu:n] meio-dia m

no one ninguém

noose [nu:s] nó m, laço m

nor [nɔ:] nem

norm [nɔ:m] norma f

normal ['nɔ:məl] normal

north [nɔ:θ] s norte m; ~east s nordeste m; ~ern ['-ðən] setentrional, do norte; ~west s noroeste m

nose [nəuz] s nariz m

nostril ['nɔstril] narina f

nosy ['nəuzi] curioso, indiscreto

not [nɔt] não; ~ a nem um/-a; ~ at all de maneira nenhuma

notary ['nəutəri] (pl -ries) notário m

notch [nɔtʃ] s entalhe m, encaixe m; v/t entalhar

note [nəut] v/t notar, tomar nota de; s nota f; apontamento m; bilhete m; **take ~ of** prestar atenção a, tomar nota de; ~-book agenda f; caderno m de apontamentos; ['nəutid] adj notável; ~paper papel m de carta; ~worthy notável, digno de nota

nothing ['nʌθiŋ] pron, s nada m; **for ~** de graça, grátis; para nada; ~ ... **but** apenas, só; ~ **doing!** nada feito!

notice ['nəutis] v/t, v/i reparar em, notar; s nota f; aviso m; ~ **to quit** aviso m de despejo; ~able perceptível; notável

notion ['nəuʃən] noção f

notorious [nəu'tɔ:riəs] notório

notwithstanding [,nɔtwiθ-'stændiŋ] prp não obstante

nought [nɔ:t] zero m

noun [naun] substantivo m

nourish ['nʌriʃ] v/t nutrir, alimentar; ~ing nutritivo; ~ment alimentação f; alimento m

novel ['nɔvəl] s novela f, romance m; adj novo, original; ~ty (pl -ties) novidade f; inovação f

November [nəu'vembə] Novembro m

now [nau] adv agora; já; s agora m; int ora! qual!; **just ~** há pouco, agora mesmo; ~ **and then/again** de vez em quando; ~adays ['-ədeiz] hoje em dia

nowhere ['nəuwεə] em parte alguma

noxious ['nɔkʃəs] nocivo

nuclear ['nju:kliə] nuclear

nude [nju:d] adj, s nu m

nudge [nʌdʒ] s cotovelada f, Braz cutucada f; v/t acotovelar, Braz cutucar

nudism ['nju:dizm] nudismo m

nugget ['nʌgit] pepita f

nuisance ['nju:səns] maçada f, incómodo m, aborrecimento m

null [nʌl] nulo; ~ **and void** sem efeito/validade

numb [nʌm] *adj* entorpecido
number ['nʌmbə] *s* número *m*; *v/t* numerar, contar; ~ **plate** placa *f* de matrícula
numerous ['nju:mərəs] numeroso
nun [nʌn] monja *f*, freira *f*
nunnery ['nʌnəri] (*pl* -ries) convento *m*
nurse [nə:s] *s* ama *f*; enfermeira *f*; *v/t*, *v/i* amamentar; mamar; tratar de; ~**ry** infantário *m*,

Braz berçário *m*; ~**ry rhyme** rima *f* infantil; ~ **school** jardim-escola *m* de infância *m*
nut [nʌt] *s* noz *f*; *mec* porca *f*; ~**cracker** quebra-nozes *m*
nutri|ment ['nju:trimənt] alimento *m*; ~**tion** [-'triʃən] nutrição *f*
nuts [nʌts] *adj* doido, louco; ~ **about/over** louco por
nylon ['nailən] náilon *m*; ~**s** *s/pl* meias *f/pl* de náilon

O

oak [əuk] carvalho *m*
oar [ɔ:] remo *m*, ~**sman** remador *m*
oasis [əu'eisis] (*pl* -ses [-si:z]) oásis *m*
oath [əuθ] juramento *m*; **take an** ~ prestar juramento
oats [əuts] *s/pl* aveia *f*
obedien|ce [ə'bi:djəns] obediência *f*; ~**t** obediente
obey [ə'bei] *v/t*, *v/i* obedecer
obituary [ə'bitjuəri] (*pl* -ries) *s* necrologia *f*; *adj* obituário
object ['ɔbdʒikt] *s* obje(c)to *m*; fim *m*, obje(c)tivo *m*; *gram* complemento *m*; [əb'dʒekt] *v/t*, *v/i* ~ **(to)** opor-se (a); obje(c)tar; ~**ion** [əb'dʒekʃən] obje(c)ção *f*; ~**ionable** [-ʃnəbl] censurável; ~**ive** [əb'dʒektiv] *adj*, *s* obje(c)tivo *m*
obligat|ion [ˌɔbli'geiʃən] obrigação *f*; ~**ory** [ə'bligətəri] obrigatório
oblig|e [ə'blaidʒ] *v/t* obrigar, forçar; **much ~ed** muito obri-

gado; ~**ing** *adj* serviçal, prestável
oblique [ə'bli:k] *adj* oblíquo
obliterate [ə'blitəreit] *v/t* obliterar
obli|vion [ə'bliviən] olvívio *m*, esquecimento *m*; ~**ous** esquecido; distraído
obnoxious [əb'nɔkʃəs] ofensivo, odioso
obscene [ɔb'si:n] obsceno
obscur|e [əb'skjuə] *adj* obscuro; *v/t* obscurecer; ~**ity** (*pl* -ties) obscuridade *f*
observ|able [əb'zə:vəbl] observável; ~**ant** observador; ~**a-tion** [-'veiʃən] observação *f*; ~**tory** [-təri] (*pl* -ries) observatório *m*
observ|e [əb'zə:v] *v/t* observar; ~**er** [-və] observador *m*
obsess [əb'ses] *v/t* atormentar; ~**ion** obsessão *f*
obsolete ['ɔbsəli:t] obsoleto
obstacle ['ɔbstəkl] obstáculo *m*
obstina|cy ['ɔbstinəsi] obstina-

ção *f*; **~te** ['-nit] obstinado

obstruct [əb'strʌkt] *v/t* obstruir; tapar; **~ion** obstrução *f*; **~ive** obstrutivo

obtain [əb'tein] *v/t* obter; **~able** conseguível

obtrusive [əb'truːsiv] intruso; importuno

obviate ['ɔbvieit] *v/t* obviar, evitar

obvious ['ɔbviəs] óbvio

occasion [ə'keiʒən] *s* ocasião *f*; caso *m*, assunto *m*; *v/t* ocasionar; **~al** casual, ocasional, fortuito

occult [ə'kʌlt] oculto; encoberto

occupant ['ɔkjupənt] ocupante *m*, *f*; **~y** [-pai] *v/t* ocupar; **be ~ied in doing** estar ocupado a fazer

occur [ə'kəː] *v/i* ocorrer, acontecer, suceder; **~ to** ocorrer, vir à ideia; **~rence** [ə'kʌrəns] ocorrência *f*, acontecimento *m*

ocean ['əuʃən] oceano *m*

o'clock [ə'klɔk] horas *f/pl*: **at three ~** às três horas

October [ɔk'təubə] Outubro *m*

oculist ['ɔkjulist] oculista *m*, *f*, oftalmologista *m*, *f*

odd [ɔd] impar, desirmanado; estranho; **~s** *s/pl* diferença *f*; vantagem *f* **at ~s** with de ponta; **~s and ends** bugigangas *f/pl*

odious ['əudjəs] odioso, detestável

odo(u)r ['əudə] odor *m*; aroma *m*; **in bad ~ with** em desfavor; **~less** inodoro

of [ɔv, əv] de; **all ~ a sudden** de repente; **all ~ us** todos nós; **~ late** ultimamente

off [ɔf] *prp* de; fora de; longe de; *adv* embora; afastado; distante; *adj* desligado; anulado, cancelado; livre; **be ~!** fora daqui! vai-te embora!; **better ~** melhor servido; **well ~** em boa situação financeira

offence [ə'fens] ofensa *f*; delito *m*

offend [ə'fend] *v/t* ofender; *v/i* transgredir; **~er** transgressor *m*, delinquente *m*, *f*

offensive [ə'fensiv] *adj* ofensivo; *s* ofensiva *f*

offer ['ɔfə] *v/t*, *v/i* oferecer(-se); apresentar; sacrificar; **~** oferecimento *m*, oferta *f*; **~ing** s oferta *f*; oferenda *f*

offhand [ɔf'hænd] *adv* de improviso, de pronto; *adj* improvisado; brusco

office ['ɔfis] emprego *m*; cargo *m*; ministério *m*; escritório *m*; oficina *f*; **~er** oficial *m*; funcionário *m*; polícia *m*

official [ə'fiʃəl] *adj* oficial

officious [ə'fiʃəs] intrometido

offside ['ɔf'said] *adj* fora-de-jogo

offspring ['ɔfspriŋ] prole *f*, descendência *f*

often ['ɔːfn] amiúde, muitas vezes

oil [ɔil] s óleo *m*; azeite *m*; petróleo *m*; **~cloth** oleado *m*, encerado *m*; **~-painting** pintura *f* a óleo; **~well** poço *m* de petróleo; **~y** oleoso; gorduroso

ointment ['ɔintmənt] unguento *m* pomada *f*

okay, OK [əuˈkei] *adv* está bem; em ordem; *adj* corre(c)to, exa(c)to

old [əuld] velho, antigo, idoso; **how ~ are you?** quantos anos tem/tens?; **~ age** velhice *f*; **~ age pension** subsídio *m* da velhice; **~-fashioned** *adj* antiquado, fora de moda; **~-timer** veterano *m*

olive [ˈɔliv] azeitona *f*

Olympic games [əˈlimpik geimz] jogos *s/pl* Olímpicos

omelet(te) [ˈɔmlit] omelete *f*, omeleta *f*

omen [ˈəumən] agoiro *m*, presságio *m*

ominous [ˈɔminəs] ominoso, agoireiro

omission [əuˈmiʃən] omissão *f*

omit [əuˈmit] *v/t* omitir

on [ɔn] *adj* aceso, ligado; *prp* em, sobre, em cima de; *adv* em cima; em diante; para a frente; **and so ~** e assim por diante, etc.; **~ and ~** sem cessar

once [wʌns] *conj* uma vez que; *s* uma vez, ocasião *f*; *adv* uma vez; outrora; **all at ~** de repente; **at ~** em seguida, imediatamente; **~ more** mais uma vez; **~ upon a time there was ...** era uma vez ...

one [wʌn] *pron* um; se, alguém, a gente, uma pessoa; *adj* um, uma; um único, um só; **~ by ~** um a um; **~ another** uns aos outros

oneself [wʌnˈself] se; si, si mesmo, si próprio

one-way [ˈwʌnwei] de uma só mão, de sentido único

onion [ˈʌnjən] cebola *f*

onlooker [ˈɔnlukə] espectador *m*

only [ˈəunli] *adj* único, só; *adv* somente, só, unicamente; *conj* mas, porém

onset [ˈɔnset] investida *f*, arremetida *f*

onto [ˈɔntu, -tə] para, para cima de

onward [ˈɔwəd] para a frente, para diante; **~s** em, diante

ooze [u:z] *v/t, v/i* emanar

opal [ˈəupəl] ópala *f*

opaque [əuˈpeik] opaco

open [ˈəupən] *adj* aberto; *s* ar livre *m*; *v/t, v/i* inaugurar; abrir (-se); começar; **~ing** *adj* inicial; *s* abertura *f*; começo *m*; inauguração *f*; **~ing night** estreia *f*

opera [ˈɔpərə] ópera *f*; **~-glasses** *s/pl* binóculo *m*; **~-house** teatro *m*, ópera *f*

operat|e [ˈɔpəreit] *v/t, v/i* operar; funcionar, trabalhar; **~ion** [-ˈreiʃən] funcionamento *m*; a(c)ção *f*, manobras *f/pl*; operação *f*; **~or** telegrafista *m, f*; operário *m*, mecânico *m*

opinion [əˈpinjən] opinião *f*

opponent [əˈpəunənt] adversário *m*

opportunity [ɔpəˈtjuːniti] (*pl* **-ties**) oportunidade *f*

oppose [əˈpəuz] *v/t* opor-se a

opposit|e [ˈɔpəzit] *adj* oposto; contrário; *s* contrário *m*; *prp* em frente de, defronte; **~ion** [-ˈziʃən] oposição *f*

oppress [ə'pres] v/t oprimir;
afligir; **~ion** [ə'preʃən] opressão f; **~ive** opressivo; **~or** opressor m

optic|ian [ɔp'tiʃən] ó(p)tico m,
oculista m, f; **~s** ó(p)tica f

optimism ['ɔptimizəm] o(p)timismo m

option ['ɔpʃən] opção f; **~al** facultativo

opulent ['ɔpjulənt] opulento

or [ɔ:] ou; quer; seja; **either ...
~** ou...ou; **~ else** senão

orange ['ɔrindʒ] s laranja f; adj
cor-de-laranja; **~ade** [-eid]
laranjada f

orator ['ɔrətə] orador m

orbit ['ɔ:bit] s órbita f

orchard ['ɔ:tʃəd] pomar m

orchestra ['ɔ:kistrə] orquestra f

ordain [ɔ:'dein] v/t ordenar

ordeal [ɔ:'di:l] provação f, prova f

order ['ɔ:də] v/t, v/i ordenar;
encomendar, mandar vir; receitar; s ordem f; regra f; mandado m; **in ~ to** para; **out of
~** avariado, estragado; **~ly** adj
ordenado; s plantão m, ordenança f

ordinance ['ɔ:dinəns] decreto m

ordinary ['ɔ:dnri] ordinário

ore [ɔ:] minério m

organ ['ɔ:gən] órgão m; **~ic**
[-gænik] orgânico; **~ization**
[-ai'zeiʃən] organização f; **~ize**
v/t, v/i organizar(-se); **~izer**
organizador m

orient|al [ɔ:ri'entl] oriental;
~ate [-'teit] v/t, v/i orientar
(-se)

origin ['ɔridʒin] origem f

origin|al [ə'ridʒənl] adj, s original m; **~ality** [-'næliti] originalidade f; **~ate** [-eit] v/t, v/i originar(-se)

ornament ['ɔ:nəmənt] s ornamento m; v/t ornamentar

ornate [ɔ:'neit] ornamentado

orphan ['ɔ:fən] s órfão m; **~age**
orfanato m

oscillate ['ɔsileit] v/i oscilar

ostentatious [.ɔsten'teiʃəs]
pomposo, ostentoso

ostrich ['ɔstritʃ] avestruz m

other ['ʌðə] outro; diferente;
each ~ um ao outro; **every
~ day** dia sim, dia não; **~ than** a
não ser; **~wise** doutra maneira, aliás, caso contrário

ought [ɔ:t] v/aux dever; **you ~
to** devias

ounce [auns] onça f

our [auə] nosso(s), nossa(s); **~s**
o(s) nosso(s), a(s) nossa(s);
~selves nós mesmos

oust [aust] v/t desapossar,
desalojar

out [aut] adv, prp fora; adj
ausente, fora de casa; **~ of
breath** sem fôlego; **~ with it!**
desembucha!; **~ you go!** fora!; **~ of** fora de; para fora
de; de

out|balance [aut'bæləns] v/t
exceder; **~bid** v/t cobrir o
lanço de; **~break** erupção f;
~burst explosão f; acesso m;
~cast s proscrito m; **~cry** clamor m; **~do** v/t exceder;
~door exterior; **~doors** adv
ao ar livre, fora de casa

outer ['autə] exterior

out|fit ['autfit] s equipamento m; vestuário m; **~grow** v/t crescer mais que; passar a idade de; não caber em

outing ['autiŋ] s excursão f, passeio m

out|last [aut'lɑːst] v/t durar mais que, sobreviver a; **~lay** s gastos m/pl, despesas f/pl; **~let** saída f; escoadouro m; **~line** s/t delinear, esboçar; s contorno m; **~number** v/t exceder em número; **~of-date** antiquado; **~patient** doente m externo; **~put** produção f

outrage ['autreidʒ] s ultraje m afronta f; v/t ultrajar; **~ous** ultrajante

out|right ['autrait] adj absoluto, total, completo; [-'rait] adv completamente; num instante; sem rodeios, francamente; **~run** v/t deixar atrás, passar, alcançar; **~shine** v/t eclipsar; **~side** s exterior m; adv fora, lá fora; prp fora de; **~sider** forasteiro m, intruso m; **~skirts** s/pl arrabaldes m/pl, cercanias f/pl; **~spoken** franco; **~standing** saliente, proeminente; pendente, a cobrar; **~ward** adj exterior, externo; **~ward(s)** adv para fora; **~weigh** v/t prevalecer sobre; pesar mais que; **~wit** v/t exceder em astúcia

oven ['ʌvn] forno m

over ['əuvə] adj acabado; passado; adv acima, por cima, em cima; prp sobre; por cima de;

através de; acerca de; **(all)** ~ **again** outra vez; ~! fim!; ~ **and** ~ repetidas vezes; ~ **there** lá, acolá; para lá; **~act** v/t, v/i exagerar; **~alls** s/pl fato m de macaco, Braz macacão m; **~balance** v/t, v/i perder o equilíbrio; **~board** ao mar; **~burden** v/t sobrecarregar; **~coat** sobretudo m; **~come** v/t, v/i vencer, superar; **~crowded** apinhado; abarrotado; **~do** v/t exagerar; **~done** el passado demais; **~due** atrasado; com vencido; **~flow** s transbordamento m, v/t, v/i transbordar; **~grown** coberto; **~head** adv ao alto, adj suspenso, aéreo; geral; **~heads** s/pl despesas f/pl gerais; **~hear** v/t ouvir por acaso; **~look** v/t dominar; omitir; **~night** adv de noite; de um dia para outro; **~power** v/t subjugar, superar; **~seas** adj ultramarino; **~see** v/t, v/i vigiar, fiscalizar; **~seer** inspe(c)tor m, superintendente m; **~shoe** galocha f; **~shoot** v/t, v/i ir além de, ultrapassar; **~sight** inadvertência f; **~sleep** v/i dormir demais; **~take** v/t, v/i ultrapassar, alcançar; **~tax** v/t sobrecarregar de impostos; **~throw** v/t derrubar; subverter; **~time** s horas f/pl extraordinárias; **~turn** v/t, v/i derrubar, entornar; emborcar; **~weening** pretensioso, arrogante; **~weight** s excesso m de peso;

~whelm v/t acabrunhar; **~work** s excesso m de trabalho
owe [əu] v/t dever
owing ['əuiŋ] adj devido; **~** to devido a, por causa de
owl [aul] s mocho m, coruja f
own [əun] adj próprio; v/t, v/i

possuir; admitir; **~** up confessar; **~er** proprietário m, dono m; **~ership** propriedade f
ox [ɔks] s (pl oxen ['-ən]) boi m
oxygen ['ɔksidʒən] oxigênio m
oyster ['ɔistə] ostra f
ozone ['əuzəun] ozone m, ozônio m

P

pace [peis] v/t, v/i andar a passo; s passo m; passada f; **keep ~ with** acompanhar, manter-se no mesmo andamento
pacific [pə'sifik] pacífico
pacifist ['pæsifist] pacifista m, f
pacify ['pæsifai] v/t pacificar; acalmar
pack [pæk] s fardo m; pacote m; embrulho m; baralho m; matilha f; súcia f; v/t, v/i empacotar; enfardar, enfardelar; arrumar, fazer as malas; **~ off** despachar; **~age** s embrulho m, pacote m; **~et** [-it] maço m; pacote m; mar paquete m; **~ing** s acondicionamento m
pact [pækt] pacto m
pad [pæd] s caneleira f; almofada f; bloco m; v/t forrar, acolchoar
paddle ['pædl] s remo m; pá f; v/t, v/i remar; chapinhar, patinhar
paddock ['pædək] recinto m, cercado m
padlock ['pædlɔk] s cadeado m; v/t, v/i fechar a cadeado
pagan ['peigən] adj, s pagão m; **~ism** paganismo m

page [peidʒ] s página f; paquete m, moço m de recados; v/t paginar; chamar em voz alta
pageant ['pædʒənt] cortejo m, desfile m
pail [peil] balde m
pain [pein] s dor f, sofrimento m; v/t angustiar; entristecer; **~ful** doloroso; **~less** sem dor; **~staking** cuidadoso
paint [peint] s pintura f; tinta f; v/t, v/i pintar; **~er** pintor m; **~ing** s quadro m; pintura f
pair [pɛə] s par m; casal m; parelha f; v/t, v/i emparelhar(-se); acasalar(-se); **in ~s** aos pares; **~ of scales** balança f
pajamas [pə'dʒɑːməz] s/pl US pijama m
pal [pæl] amigo m, camarada m, Braz capanga m
palace ['pælis] palácio m
palat|able ['pælətəbl] saboroso; **~al** adj palatal
palate ['pælit] paladar m
pale [peil] adj pálido; v/i empalidecer; **~ness** palidez f
palette ['pælit] paleta f
paling ['peiliŋ] s cerca f, paliçada f

palliative ['pæliətiv] *adj* paliativo

pallid ['pælid] pálido; **~or** palidez *f*, palor *f*

palm [pɑːm] *s* palma *f*; **~-tree** palmeira *f*

palpable ['pælpəbl] palpável

paltry ['pɔːltri] insignificante, miserável

pan [pæn] *s* panela *f*; **~cake** *s* panqueca *f*

pane [pein] vidraça *f*

panel ['pænl] *s* painel *m*; caixilho *m*, almofada *f*; lista *f* de jurados, júri *m*

pang [pæŋ] angústia *f*, ânsia *f*

panic ['pænik] *s* pânico *m*; *v/t, v/i* aterrorizar(-se), encher(-se) de pânico

pansy ['pænzi] (*pl* **-sies**) amor-perfeito *m*

pant [pænt] *v/i* arfar, arquejar

panties ['pæntiz] *s/pl* cuecas *f/pl*, calcinhas *f/pl*

pantry ['pæntri] (*pl* **-ries**) despensa *f*, copa *f*

pants [pænts] *s/pl* ceroulas *f/pl*; calças *f/pl*; cuecas *f/pl*

pap [pæp] papa *f*, mingau *m*; teta *f*

papa [pə'pɑː] papá *m*, Braz papai *m*

paper ['peipə] *s* papel *m*; jornal *m*; prova *f*, exercício *m* escrito; dissertação *f*; *v/t* forrar de papel; **~back** brochura *f*, **~-money** papel-moeda *m*; **~s** *s/pl* documentos *m/pl*

parachute ['pærəʃuːt] *s* pára-quedas *m*

parade [pə'reid] *s* parada *f*, revista *f*; *v/t, v/i* alardear; passar revista (a); desfilar

paradise ['pærədais] paraíso *m*

paragraph ['pærəgrɑːf] *s* parágrafo *m*

parallel ['pærələl] *adj* paralelo; *s* paralela *f*

paralyse ['pærəlaiz] *v/t* paralisar; **~sis** [pə'rælisis] paralisia *f*; **~tic** [-'litik] *adj, s* paralítico *m*

paramount ['pærəmaunt] superior, supremo

parcel [pɑːsl] *s* pacote *m*, embrulho *m*; parcela *f*, lote *m*; *v/t* **~ up** empacotar

parch [pɑːtʃ] *v/t, v/i* tostar; torrar; ressecar

parchment ['pɑːtʃmənt] pergaminho *m*

pardon ['pɑːdn] *s* perdão *m*; *v/t* perdoar, desculpar; **I beg your ~,** **~ me** desculpe(-me); **~?** como (disse)?; **~able** perdoável

pare [peə] *v/t* aparar, cortar

parent ['peərənt] pai *m*, mãe *f*; **~age** origem *f*; paternidade *f*; **~al** paternal, maternal; dos pais; **~s** *s/pl* pais *m/pl*

parings ['peəriŋz] *s/pl* aparas *f/pl*, restos *m/pl*

parish ['pæriʃ] paróquia *f*, freguesia *f*

parity ['pæriti] paridade *f*, igualdade *f*

park [pɑːk] *s* parque *m*; *v/t, v/i* estacionar; **~ing** *s* estacionamento *m*; **~ing lot** US parque *m* de estacionamento

parliament ['pɑːləmənt] parlamento *m*; **~ary** ['-mentəri] parlamentar

parquet ['pɑːkei] parquete *m*

parrot ['pærət] papagaio *m*

parsley ['pɑːsli] salsa *f*

parsnip ['pɑːsnip] pastinaca *f*

parson ['pɑːsn] cura *m*, pároco *m*

part [pɑːt] *s* parte *f*; *theat* papel *m*; *v/t, v/i* repartir, dividir; separar-se; partir; **for my ~** quanto a mim, cá por mim, eu cá; **for the most ~** na maioria dos casos, geralmente; **play a ~** representar, fingir

partial ['pɑːʃəl] parcial; **~ity** [-ʃi'æliti] parcialidade *f*

participate [pɑː'tisipeit] *v/i* participar

particle ['pɑːtikl] partícula *f*

particular [pə'tikjulə] *s* pormenor *m*, particularidade *f*; *adj* particular, singular; especial; **~ity** [-'læriti] particularidade *f*; **~ize** *v/t, v/i* particularizar; **~ly** particularmente; especialmente

parting ['pɑːtiŋ] *s* separação *f*; despedida *f*; risca *f* de cabelo; *adj* de despedida

partisan [,pɑːti'zæn] partidário *m*

partition [pɑː'tiʃən] *s* divisão *f*, partição *f*; tabique *m*; *v/t* dividir, repartir

partly ['pɑːtli] em parte, parcialmente

partner ['pɑːtnə] *s* sócio *m*; parceiro *m*; companheiro *m*; **be ~s with** ser parceiro de; **~ship** sociedade *f*, associação *f*

partridge ['pɑːtridʒ] perdiz *f*

part-time ['pɑːt'taim] *adj* de meio dia, de meio tempo

party ['pɑːti] (*pl* **-ties**) partido *m*; reunião *f*, festa *f*; grupo *m*

pass [pɑːs] *s* passagem *f*; passe *m*; desfiladeiro *m*; *v/t, v/i* passar (**through** por); **~ away** morrer; **~ by** passar por; ignorar; **~ on** prosseguir; passar adiante; morrer; **~ out** desmaiar

pass|able ['pɑːsəbl] passável; transitável; aceitável; navegável; **~age** ['pæsidʒ] passagem *f*; corredor *m*; viagem *f*, travessia *f*

passenger ['pæsindʒə] passageiro *m*

passer-by ['pɑːsə'bai] (*pl* **passers-by**) transeunte *m*

passing ['pɑːsiŋ] *s* passagem; *adj* passageiro; passante

passion ['pæʃən] paixão *f*; cólera *f*; **~ate** ['-it] apaixonado; ardente

passive ['pæsiv] *adj* passivo; *s* passiva *f*

pass|key ['pɑːskiː] chave *f* mestra; **~port** passaporte *m*; **~word** santo-e-senha *m*, palavra *f* de passe

past [pɑːst] *s* passado *m*; *adj* passado; decorrido, último; *prp* depois de; além de; fora de; **half ~ two** duas e meia

paste [peist] *s* pasta *f*, massa *f*; grude *m*, cola *f*; *v/t* colar, pegar

pastime ['pɑːstaim] passatempo *m*

pastry ['peistri] (*pl* **-ries**) massas

f/pl, folhados *m/pl*, pastelaria *f*; **~-cook** pasteleiro *m*

pasture ['pɑ:stʃə] *s* pasto *m*, pastagem *f*; *v/t* pastar, apascentar

pat [pæt] *s* palmadinha *f*; afago *m*; *v/t* afagar; dar palmadas a; *adj* oportuno

patch [pætʃ] *s* remendo *m*; *v/t* remendar

patent ['peitənt] *s* patente *f*; *v/t* patentear; obter uma patente para; *adj* manifesto, patente

patern|al [pə'tə:nl] paternal; **~ity** paternidade *f*

path [pɑ:θ] caminho *m*, senda *f*, vereda *f*

patien|ce ['peiʃəns] paciência *f*; **~t** *adj*, *s* paciente *m*, *f*

patriotic [ˌpætri'ɔtik] patriótico

patrol [pə'trəul] *s* patrulha *f*; *v/t* patrulhar

patron ['peitrən] patrono *m*, prote(c)tor *m*; **~age** ['pætrənidʒ] patrocínio *m*; patronato *m*

pattern ['pætən] *s* modelo *m*; amostra *f*; padrão *m*; desenho *m*; *v/t* modelar

paunch [pɔ:ntʃ] pança *f*

pause [pɔ:z] *s* pausa *f*; *v/i* fazer pausa

pave [peiv] *v/t* pavimentar, calcetar; **~ment** passeio *m*; pavimento *m*

paw [pɔ:] *s* pata *f*

pawn [pɔ:n] *s* peão *m* de xadrez; penhor *m*; *v/t* empenhar; **~broker** penhorista *m*, *f*; **~shop** casa *f* de penhores

pay [pei] *v/t*, *v/i* render, dar lucro; pagar; *s* paga *f*, salário *m*,

soldo *m*; **~ attention** prestar atenção; **~ back** restituir, devolver; **~ off** liquidar; dar resultado; **~ one's respects** apresentar seus respeitos; **~ a visit** fazer uma visita; **~able** pagável; **~ment** pagamento *m*

pea [pi:] ervilha *f*

peace [pi:s] paz *f*; tranquilidade *f*; **~ful** pacífico; tranquilo; **~maker** pacificador *m*

peach [pi:tʃ] *s* pêssego *m*

pea|cock ['pi:kɔk] pavão *m*; **~hen** pavoa *f*

peak [pi:k] *s* pico *m*, cume, cimo *m*; **~ed** *adj* macilento, doentio; pontiagudo, pontudo; **~ hours** *f/pl* horas *f/pl* de ponta

peal [pi:l] *s* repique *m* de sinos; *v/i* repicar

peanut ['pi:nʌt] amendoim *m*

pear [pɛə] pêra *f*

pearl [pə:l] *s* pérola *f*

peasant ['pezənt] camponês *m*, lavrador *m*

peat [pi:t] turfa *f*

pebble ['pebl] seixo *m*, calhau *m*

peck [pek] *s* bicada *f*; *v/i* debicar; bicar, dar bicadas a; picar

peculiar [pi'kju:ljə] peculiar; singular; **~ity** [-li'æriti] peculiaridade *f*; singularidade *f*

pedal ['pedl] *s* pedal *m*; *v/t*, *v/i* pedalar

pedestal ['pedistl] pedestal *m*, peanha *f*

pedestrian [pi'destriən] *s* peão *m*; *adj* pedestre; prosaico, vulgar; **~ crossing** passagem *f* para peões; **~ precinct** zona *f* para peões

pedigree ['pedigri:] genealogia *f*, linhagem *f*

pedlar, *US* **pedler** ['pedlə] bufarinheiro *m*, *Braz* mascate *m*

peel [pi:l] *s* casca *f*, pele *f*; *v/t*, *v/i* descascar, pelar

peep [pi:p] *s* espiadela *f*, espreitadela *f*; *v/i* espiar, espreitar

peer [piə] *s* par *m*, nobre *m*; igual *m*, *f*; *v/i* espreitar, olhar; **~age** pariato *m*; **~less** incomparável, sem par

peevish ['pi:viʃ] impertinente, rabugento

peg [peg] *s* cavilha *f*; grampo *m*, mola *f*; pretexto *m*

pelican ['pelikən] pelicano *m*

pelt [pelt] *s* pele *f*, couro *m*; *v/t*, *v/i* encher, crivar; bater, malhar; cair; apedrejar, lapidar

pen [pen] *s* caneta *f*; pena *f*

penal ['pi:nl] penal; **~ servitude** trabalhos *m/pl* forçados; **~ty** ['penlti] (*pl* -**ties**) penalidade *f*

penance ['penəns] penitência *f*

pence [pens] *pl* of **penny**

pencil ['pensl] *s* lápis *m*

pend|ant ['pendənt] pendente *m*; **~ing** *adj* pendente; *prp* até

pendulum ['pendjuləm] pêndulo *m*

penetra|te ['penitreit] *v/t*, *v/i* penetrar; **~tion** [-'treiʃən] penetração *f*

penguin ['pengwin] pinguim *m*

peninsula [pi'ninsjulə] península *f*; **~r** peninsular

peniten|ce ['penitəns] penitência *f*; **~t** *adj*, *s* penitente *m*, *f*

pennant ['penənt] flâmula *f*, galhardete *m*

penniless ['penilis] sem vintém

penny ['peni] (*pl* **pennies** *or* **pence**) péni *m*; **a pretty ~** uma soma considerável; **~ royal** poejo *m*; **turn an honest ~** ganhar dinheiro honestamente

pension ['penʃən] *s* pensão *f*; **~ off** aposentar, reformar

pensive ['pensiv] pensativo

penthouse ['penthaus] apartamento *m* acima do telhado

people ['pi:pl] *s* povo *m*; pessoas *f/pl*, gente *f*; vulgo *m*; *v/t* povoar

pepper ['pepə] *s* pimenta *f*; **~mint** hortelã-pimenta *f*; **~ pot** pimenteiro *m*

per [pə:] por

perambulator ['præmbjuleitə] carrinho *m* de criança

perceive [pə'si:v] *v/t* perceber, compreender; notar, ver

percentage [pə'sentidʒ] percentagem *f*

perception [pə'sepʃən] percepção *f*

perch [pə:tʃ] *s* zo perca *f*; poleiro *m*; vara *f*; *v/t*, *v/i* empoleirar (-se)

peremptory [pə'remptəri] peremptório

perfect ['pə:fikt] *adj* perfeito; [pə'fekt] *v/t* aperfeiçoar; **~ion** [pə'fekʃən] perfeição *f*

perforate ['pə:fəreit] *v/t*, *v/i* perfurar

perform [pə'fɔ:m] *v/t*, *v/i* representar; executar; **~ance** representação f; execução f

perfume [pəˈfjuːm] s perfume m; [pəˈfjuːm] v/t perfumar

perhaps [pəˈhæps] talvez, quiçá

peril [ˈperil] perigo m; **~ous** perigoso

perimeter [pəˈrimitə] perímetro m

period [ˈpiəriəd] s período m; época f; termo m; gram ponto m; **~ic** [-ˈɔdik] periódico; **~ical** [-ˈɔdikəl] s revista f

perish [ˈperiʃ] v/t, v/i perecer; **~able** perecível

perjury [ˈpəːdʒəri] perjúrio m

perm [pəːm] s permanente f; v/t fazer uma permanente a

permanen|ce [ˈpəːmənəns] permanência f; **~t** permanente

permission [pəˈmiʃən] permissão f, licença f

permit [ˈpəːmit] v/t, v/i permitir; [ˈpəːmit] s permissão f, licença f

pernicious [pəːˈniʃəs] pernicioso

perpendicular [ˌpəːpənˈdikjulə] adj, s perpendicular f

perpetual [pəˈpetjuəl] perpétuo; **~te** [-eit] v/t perpetuar

perplex [pəˈpleks] v/t embaraçar; confundir; deixar perplexo; **~ed** adj perplexo; **~ity** (pl -ties) perplexidade f

persecut|e [ˈpəːsikjuːt] v/t perseguir; **~ion** [-ˈkjuːʃən] perseguição f; **~or** perseguidor m

persever|ance [ˌpəːsiˈviərəns] perseverança f; **~e** v/i perseverar

Persian [ˈpəːʃən] adj, s persa m,

f

persist [pəˈsist] v/i persistir; **~ence** persistência f; **~ent** persistente

person [ˈpəːsn] pessoa f; **~age** personagem f; **~al** pessoal; **~ality** [-səˈnæliti] (pl -ties) personalidade f

personify [pəˈsɔnifai] v/t personificar

personnel [ˌpəːsəˈnel] pessoal m

perspective [pəˈspektiv] perspectiva f

perspicacious [ˌpəːspiˈkeiʃəs] perspicaz

perspir|ation [ˌpəːspəˈreiʃən] suor m, transpiração f; **~e** [pəˈspaiə] v/i suar, transpirar

persua|de [pəˈsweid] v/t persuadir; **~sion** [-ʒən] persuasão f; **~sive** [-siv] persuasivo

pert [pəːt] espevitado, vivo; impertinente

peruse [pəˈruːz] v/t ler atentamente

Peruvian [pəˈruːvjən] adj, s peruano (m)

pervade [pəˈveid] v/t penetrar, impregnar

perverse [pəˈvəːs] perverso

pervert [ˈpəːvəːt] s invertido m; [pəˈvəːt] v/t perverter

pessimis|m [ˈpesimizəm] pessimismo m; **~t** pessimista m, f; **~tic** [-ˈmistik] pessimista

pest [pest] peste f

pester [ˈpestə] v/t, v/i maçar, ralar, incomodar

pet [pet] s animal m de estimação; favorito m; v/t acariciar, afagar, animar

petal ['petl] pétala f

petition [pi'tiʃən] s petição f; súplica f; requerimento m; v/t, v/i peticionar, requerer; suplicar

petrify ['petrifai] v/t, v/i petrificar(-se)

petrol ['petrəl] gasolina f; **~eum** [pi'trəuljəm] petróleo m

petticoat ['petikəut] combinação f; saiote m

petty ['peti] trivial; mesquinho

petulan|ce ['petjuləns] petulância f; **~t** petulante

petunia [pi'tju:njə] petúnia f

pew [pju:] banco m de igreja

pewter ['pju:tə] peltre m, liga f de estanho

phantom ['fæntəm] fantasma m

phase [feiz] s fase f

pheasant ['feznt] faisão m

phenomen|al [fi'nɔminl] fenomenal; **~on** (pl **-ena**) fenómeno m

philanthrop|ist [fi'lænθrəpist] filantropo m; **~y** filantropia f

philosoph|er [fi'lɔsəfə] filósofo m; **~y** filosofia f

phone [fəun] s telefone m; v/t, v/i telefonar

phonograph ['fəunəgra:f] US = **record player**

photograph ['fəutəgra:f] v/t fotografar; s fotografia f; **~er** [fə'tɔgrəfə] fotógrafo m; **~ic** [-'græfik] fotográfico; **~y** [fə'tɔgrəfi] fotografia f

phrase [freiz] mus frase f; expressão f; locução f; **~ology** [-zi'ɔlədʒi] fraseologia f

phrenetic [fri'netik] frenético

physic|al ['fizikəl] físico; **~ian** [-'ziʃən] médico m; **~ist** ['-sist] físico m; **~s** física f

piano [pi'ænəu] s piano m

pick [pik] v/t apanhar; colher; escolher, eleger; palitar; s picareta f, picão m; escolha f; escol m; palito m; **~ up** v/t, v/i captar, sintonizar; apanhar; recolher; recuperar

picket ['pikit] s estaca f; mil piquete m; v/t, v/i cercar de estacas; estacionar piquetes

pickle ['pikl] s salmoura f; escabeche m; conservas f/pl de vinagre; fig apuro m; v/t salgar; pôr em salmoura

pick|pocket ['pik.pokit] carterista m, f, Braz batedor m de carteiras; **~up** s captador m sonoro

picnic ['piknik] s piquenique m

pictorial [pik'tɔ:riəl] adj ilustrado

picture ['piktʃə] s quadro m; pintura f; gravura f; ilustração f, imagem f; retrato m; filme m, fita f; v/t imaginar; retratar, pintar; **~s** s/pl cinema m

picturesque [.piktʃə'resk] pitoresco

pie [pai] pastel m, empada f

piece [pi:s] s bocado m, pedaço m; retalho m; peça f

pier [piə] quebra-mar m, molhe m

pierc|e [piəs] v/t, v/i penetrar, furar; **~ing** adj cortante; penetrante

piety ['paiəti] piedade f

pig [pig] porco m

plain

pigeon ['pidʒin] pombo *m*; **~-hole** *s* buraco *m* de pombal

pigmy ['pigmi] pigmeu *m*

pigsty ['pigstai] pocilga *f*, chiqueiro *m*

pike [paik] *s* zo lúcio *m*

pilchard [pilt∫əd] sardinha *f*

pile [pail] *s* montão *m*, pilha *f*; *v/t* empilhar

pilfer ['pilfə] *v/t, v/i* furtar, surripiar; **~er** ratoneiro, larápio *m*

pilgrim ['pilgrim] peregrino *m*; **~age** peregrinação *f*

pill [pil] pílula *f*, comprimido *m*

pillage ['pilidʒ] *s* pilhagem *f*; *v/t* saquear

pillar ['pilə] pilar *m*; **~-box** marco *m* postal

pillory ['piləri] (*pl* -ries) *s* pelourinho *m*; *v/t* expor

pillow ['pilou] *s* travesseiro *m*; almofada *f*; **~-case** fronha *f*

pilot ['pailət] *s* piloto *m*; *v/t* pilotar

pimp [pimp] *s* alcoviteiro *m*

pimple ['pimpl] borbulha *f*

pin [pin] *s* alfinete *m*; cavilha *f*; *v/t* pregar; prender; imobilizar

pincers ['pinsəz] *s/pl* turquês *m*, *Braz* torquês *f*; zo pinça *f*, tenaz *f*

pinch [pint∫] *v/t, v/i* beliscar; *s* beliscão *m*; pitada *f*

pine [pain] *s* pinheiro *m*; pinho *m*; *v/i* definhar-se; ansiar

pine|apple ['painæpl] ananás *m*; **~-cone** pinha *f*

ping-pong ['piŋpɔŋ] pingue-pongue *m*

pink [piŋk] *adj* cor-de-rosa; *s* cravo *m*

pinnacle ['pinəkl] pináculo *m*

pint [paint] pinta *f*, quartilho *m*

pioneer [.paiə'niə] *s* pioneiro *m*

pious ['paiəs] pio, piedoso

pipe [paip] *s* cachimbo *m*; cano *m*, tubo *m*; **~line** oleoduto *m*

pirate ['paiərit] *s* pirata *m*

pistol ['pistl] pistola *f*

pit [pit] *s* fosso *m*, buraco *m*, cova *f*; mina *f*

pitch [pit∫] *s* piche *m*, breu *m*, resina *f*; tom *m*; grau *m*; *v/t, v/i* armar, montar; arrojar, lançar, arremessar; **~er** jarro *m*, cântaro *m*, bilha *f*; arrojador *m*; **~fork** *s* forquilha *f*, forcado *m*

piteous ['pitiəs] lastimoso

pitfall ['pitfɔ:l] cilada *f*, armadilha *f*; rasteira *f*, dificuldade *f*

pith [piθ] seiva *f*; medula *f*; *fig* âmago *m*

pitiless ['pitilis] desapiedado

pity ['piti] *s* compaixão *f*, piedade *f*; *v/t* condoer-se de, compadecer-se de; **what a ~!** que pena!

placard ['plæka:d] *s* cartaz *m*

place [pleis] *s* lugar *m*, sítio *m*; *v/t* pôr, meter, colocar; **in ~ of** em lugar/vez de; **take ~** ter lugar, realizar-se

placid ['plæsid] plácido

plague [pleig] *s* peste *f*, praga *f*; *v/t* atormentar, afligir

plaice [pleis] solha *f*, solho *m*

plaid [plæd] manta *f* escocesa em xadrez

plain [plein] *adj* claro, evidente; *adj* simples, franco, sincero; *s* planície *f*; **in ~ clothes** à paisana

plaint [pleint] queixa *f*

plait [plæt] *s* trança *f*; *v/t* entrançar

plan [plæn] *s* plano *m*, projec(c)to *m*; planta *f*; *v/t*, *v/i* planear; proje(c)tar

plane [plein] *s* plano *m*; plaina *f*; aeroplano *m*, avião *m*; *v/t*, *v/i* planar; aplainar

planet ['plænit] planeta *m*

plank [plæŋk] *s* prancha *f*

plant [plɑ:nt] *s bot* planta *f*; *mec* instalação *f*; *v/t* plantar, semear; **~ation** [-'teiʃən] plantação *f*; **~er** plantador *m*

plaster ['plɑ:stə] *s* emplastro *m*; **~ of Paris** gesso-de-Paris *m*

plastic ['plæstik] *s* plástico *m*

plate [pleit] *s* prato *m*; chapa *f*, folha *f*, lâmina *f*; baixela *f* de prata *f*; *v/t* chapear; blindar

plateau ['plætəu] planalto *m*

platform ['plætfɔ:m] linha *f*, cais *m*; plataforma *f*; estrado *m*, tribuna *f*

platinum ['plætinəm] platina *f*

play [plei] *v/t*, *v/i* brincar; jogar; *theat* representar, desempenhar; tocar; *s* brincadeira *f*; jogo *m*; recreio *m*; *theat* peça *f* teatral; **~bill** programa *m*; **~boy** estroina *m*, farrista *m*; **~er** jogador *m*; **~ful** brincalhão; **~goer** frequentador *m* de teatros; **~ground** pátio *m* de recreio; **~wright** dramaturgo *m*

plea [pli:] alegação *f*, pretexto *m*; *jur* contestação *f*; rogo *m*, súplica *f*

plead [pli:d] *v/t*, *v/i* rogar, suplicar; *jur* pleitear; **~ guilty** confessar-se culpado

pleasant ['pleznt] agradável, prazenteiro, ameno

pleas|e [pli:z] *int* faz favor; *v/t*, *v/i* agradar, deleitar, contentar; **if you ~e** faça favor; **~ed** *adj* satisfeito; **~ing** *adj* agradável; **~ure** ['pleʒə] prazer *m*

pleat [pli:t] *s* prega *f*, dobra *f*

pledge [pledʒ] *s* penhor *m*, fiança *f*; garantia *f*; promessa *f*; *v/t* empenhar

plentiful ['plentiful] abundante, copioso

plenty ['plenti] *adv* bastante; *adj* abundante; *s* abundância *f*, plenitude *f*; **~ of** ... muito ...

pliable ['plaiəbl] flexível

pliers ['plaiəz] *s/pl* alicate *m*

plight [plait] *s* apuro *m*, aperto *m*; condição *f*

plot [plot] *s* enredo *m*, trama *f*; lote *m*, parcela *f* de terreno; *v/t*, *v/i* tramar, urdir; conspirar

plough [plau] *s* arado *m*, charrua *f*; *v/t*, *v/i* lavrar; **~man** lavrador *m*; **~share** relha *f*

pluck [plʌk] *v/t*, *v/i* dedilhar; arrancar; depenar; *s* coragem *f*

plug [plʌg] *s* ficha *f*, tomada *f*; batoque *m*, bujão *m*, bucha *f*; *v/t* tapar, rolhar; obturar; **~ in** ligar

plum [plʌm] ameixa *f*

plumb [plʌm] *s* sonda *f*, prumo *m*; *adj* a prumo; *v/t* sondar; **~er** canalizador *m*; picheleiro *m*

plume [plu:m] *s* pluma *f*; pena-

pool

cho *m*

plump [plʌmp] *s* baque *m*; *adj* roliço, rechonchudo

plum pudding [.plʌm'pudiŋ] pudim *m* de Natal; **~-tree** ameixeira *f*

plunder [plʌndə] *v/t, v/i* saquear, pilhar; *s* pilhagem *f*, saque *m*

plunge [plʌndʒ] *v/t, v/i* mergulhar; precipitar(-se), lançar (-se); *s* mergulho *m*

plural [pluərəl] *adj, s* plural *m*

plus [plʌs] *prp* mais

plush [plʌʃ] *s* pelúcia *f*

ply [plai] *v/t* fazer carreira

pneumatic [nju(:)'mætik] pneumático

pneumonia [nju(:)'məunjə] pneumonia *f*

poach [pəutʃ] *v/t, v/i* caçar ilegalmente, pescar ilicitamente; escalfar; **~er** ladrão *m* de caça

pocket ['pɔkit] *s* algibeira *f*, bolso *m*; *v/t* embolsar, meter ao bolso

pod [pɔd] *s* vagem *f*

poem ['pəuim] poema *m*

poet ['pəuit] poeta *m*; **~ic** [-'etik] poético; **~ry** poesia *f*

point [pɔint] *s* ponto *m*; ponta *f*; questão *f*, assunto *m*; **~ of view** ponto de vista; *v/t, v/i* apontar; afiar; indicar; **come/get to the ~** vir ao caso

pointer ['pɔintə] indicador *m*; ponteiro *m*; perdigueiro *m*

pointsman ['pɔintsmən] agulheiro *m*, guarda-agulhas *m*

poise [pɔiz] *s* equilíbrio *m*; porte *m*; *v/t* equilibrar

poison ['pɔizn] *s* peçonha *f*; veneno *m*; *v/t* envenenar; intoxicar; **~ous** venenoso

poker ['pəukə] póquer *m*; atiçador *m*

polar ['pəulə] polar

pole [pəul] *s* vara *f*, pau *m*, varapau *m*; estaca *f*; pólo *m*; ♀ *s adj* polaco *m*, *Braz* polonês *m*

police [pə'li:s] polícia *f*; **~man** polícia *m*, *Braz* policial *m*; **~-station** esquadra *f* de polícia, *Braz* delegacia *f* de polícia; **~woman** mulher-polícia *f*

policy ['pɔlisi] (*pl* **-cies**) política *f*; apólice *f*

polish ['pɔliʃ] *v/t* polir; *s* lustro *m*; verniz *m*; graxa *f*

Polish ['pəuliʃ] *adj, s* polaco *m*

polite [pə'lait] cortês; **~ness** cortesia *f*

politic|**al** [pə'litikəl] político; **~ian** [.pɔli'tiʃən] político *m*; **~s** ['pɔlitiks] política *f*

poll [pəul] *s* votação *f*; lista *f* eleitoral; escrutínio *m*; **~ tax** capitação *f*

pollu|**te** [pə'lu:t] *v/t* poluir; **~tion** poluição *f*

polo ['pəuləu] pólo *m*

pomp [pɔmp] pompa *f*

pond [pɔnd] tanque *m*, charco *m*

ponder ['pɔndə] *v/t, v/i* (**on**, **over**) ponderar, meditar; **~ous** pesado, ponderoso

pontoon [pɔn'tu:n] pontão *m*; **~-bridge** ponte *f* de barcas

pony ['pəuni] (*pl* **-nies**) pónei *m*, garrano *m*

poodle ['pu:dl] cão *m* de água

pool [pu:l] *s* poça *f*, charco *m*;

tanque m; v/t partilhar

poor [puə] pobre; **~ health** má saúde f; **~ly** adv pobremente; **~ness** pobreza f

pop [pɔp] s estalo m, estoiro m; gasosa f; v/t, v/i estoirar; estalar; dar uma saltada

popcorn ['pɔpkɔ:n] pipocas f/pl

pope [pəup] papa m

poplar ['pɔplə] choupo m, álamo m

poppy ['pɔpi] (pl -pies) papoula f

popul|ar ['pɔpjulə] popular; **~arity** [-'læriti] popularidade f; **~arize** ['-raiz] v/t popularizar

popul|ate ['pɔpjuleit] v/t povoar; **~ation** [-'lei∫ən] população f; **~ous** populoso

porcelain ['pɔ:səlin] porcelana f

porch [pɔ:t∫] pórtico m; alpendre m

pore [pɔ:] s poro m; v/i **~ over** estudar com atenção

pork [pɔ:k] carne f de porco

porous ['pɔ:rəs] poroso

porpoise ['pɔ:pəs] toninha f, porco-marinho m

porridge ['pɔridʒ] papa f de aveia, Braz mingau m de aveia

port [pɔ:t] porto m

portable ['pɔ:təbl] portátil

portal ['pɔ:tl] portal m

porter ['pɔ:tə] bagageiro m; carregador m; porteiro m

portfolio [pɔ:t'fəuljəu] pasta f

porthole ['pɔ:thəul] mar vigia f, portinhola f

portion ['pɔ:∫ən] s porção f

portly ['pɔ:tli] corpulento

portrait ['pɔ:trit] retrato m

portray [pɔ:'trei] v/t retratar

Portuguese [,pɔ:tju'gi:z] adj, s português m

pose [pəuz] s pose f; v/t, v/i posar; pôr

position [pə'zi∫ən] s posição f; v/t colocar

positive ['pɔzitiv] adj positivo

possess [pə'zes] v/t possuir; **~ed** adj possesso; **~ion** posse f; possessão f

possib|ility [,pɔsə'biliti] (pl -ties) possibilidade f; **~le** ['-bl] adj, s possível m; **~ly** possivelmente; talvez

post [pəust] s poste m; emprego m; correio m; posto m; v/t deitar ao correio; postar, estacionar; afrancar; **~age** franquia f, porte m; **~age stamp** selo m postal; **~al** postal; **~box** apartado m, caixa f postal; **~card** bilhete m postal

poster ['pəustə] cartaz m

posterity [pɔs'teriti] posteridade f

post|man ['pəustmən] carteiro m; **~mark** s carimbo m postal; v/t carimbar

post| office ['pəust.ɔfis] correio m; **~-paid** franco de porte

postpone [pəust'pəun] v/t adiar; pospor; **~ment** adiamento m

postscript ['pəusskript] pós-escrito m

posture ['pɔst∫ə] s postura f, atitude f

post-war ['pəust'wɔ:] do após-guerra

pot [pɔt] s pote m; panela f

potato [pə'teitəu] batata *f*

potency ['pəutənsi] potência *f*

potent ['pəutənt] potente; poderoso; **~ate** [-eit] potentado *m*; **~ial** [nə'tenʃəl] *adj* spotencial *m*

potter ['pɔtə] *s* oleiro *m*; **~y** (*pl* -ries) olaria *f*

pouch [pautʃ] saco *m*, bolsa *f*; cartucheira *f*; papo *m*

poultice ['pəultis] cataplasma *m*

poultry ['pəultri] criação *f*, aves *f/pl* domésticas

pounce [pauns] *v/i*: **~ on** lançar-se sobre

pound [paund] *s* libra *f*; *v/t, v/i* martelar; bater, esmagar

pour [pɔː] *v/t, v/i* verter, derramar(-se); deitar; precipitar(-se), lançar(-se); jorrar; chover a potes

pout [paut] *v/t, v/i* amuar, fazer beiço

poverty ['pɔvəti] pobreza *f*

powder ['paudə] *s* pó *m*; pólvora *f*; *v/t* polvilhar; empoar

power ['pauə] *s* poder *m*; potência *f*; **~ful** poderoso, potente

practic|able ['præktikəbl] praticável; **~al** *adj* prático; **~e** ['-tis] clientela *f*; prática *f*; ensaio *m*; clínica *f*; treino *m*

practise ['præktis] *v/t* praticar; treinar(-se); exercitar; **~ed** *adj* experiente, experimentado

practitioner [præk'tiʃnə] profissional *m*; *med* facultativo *m*

prairie ['prɛəri] pradaria *f*

praise [preiz] *v/t* louvar, elogiar; *s* louvor *m*, elogio *m*; **~worthy** louvável

pram [præm] carrinho *m* de criança

prance ['pɔutənsi] potência *f*

prank [præŋk] partida *f*, travessura *f*

prawn [prɔːn] *s* gamba *f*, *Braz* pitu *m*

pray [prei] *v/t, v/i* rezar; **~er** [prɛə] oração *f*, reza *f*; **~er-book** livro *m* de orações

preach [priːtʃ] *v/t, v/i* pregar

precarious [pri'kɛəriəs] precário

preced|e [pri'siːd] *v/t, v/i* preceder; **~ence** ['presidəns] precedência *f*; **~ent** ['presidənt] precedente *m*; **~ing** [-'siːdiŋ] *adj* precedente

precept ['priːsept] preceito *m*

precinct [pri'siŋkt] recinto *m*; **~s** *s/pl* imediações *f/pl*

precious ['preʃəs] *adj* precioso

precipice ['presipis] precipício *m*

precipi|tate [pri'sipiteit] *v/t, v/i* precipitar(-se); [-tit] *adj* precipitado; **~tous** escarpado, íngreme

precis|e [pri'sais] preciso, exa(c)to; **~ion** [-'siʒən] precisão *f*, exa(c)tidão *f*

precursor [pri'kɔːsə] precursor *m*

predecessor ['priːdisesə] antecessor *m*, predecessor *m*

predestination [pri(ː)desti'neiʃən] predestinação *f*

predict [pri'dikt] *v/t* predizer, prognosticar

predominant [pri'dɔminənt] predominante

prefabricate [priː'fæbrikeit] *v/t*

prefabricar

preface ['prefis] *s* prefácio *m*; *v/t* prefaciar

prefer [pri'fə:] *v/t* preferir; **~able** [prefərəbl] preferível; **~ence** [prefərəns] preferência *f*; **~ential** [.prefə'renʃəl] preferencial; **~ment** promoção *f*

prefix ['pri:fiks] *s* prefixo *m*

pregnant ['pregnənt] pregnante; grávida

prejudice ['predʒudis] *s* preconceito *m*; *v/t* predispor

prelate ['prelit] prelado *m*

preliminar|ies [pri'liminəriz] *s/pl* preliminares *m/pl*; **~y** *adj* preliminar

prelude ['prelju:d] prelúdio *m*

premature [.premə'tjuə] prematuro

premeditate [pri:'mediteit] *v/t* premeditar

premier ['premiə] *s* primeiro ministro *m*

premise ['premis] *s* premissa *f*; **~s** *s/pl* propriedade *f*

premium ['pri:mjəm] prémio *m*

preoccup|ied [pri:'ɔkjupaid] *adj* preocupado, absorto; **~y** *v/t* preocupar

prepare [pri'pɛə] *v/t*, *v/i* preparar(-se)

prepay [pri:'pei] *v/t* pagar adiantado

preposition [.prepə'ziʃən] preposição *f*

prepossessing [.pri:pə'zesiŋ] *adj* atraente

preposterous [pri'pɔstərəs] absurdo, despropositado

prerogative [pri'rɔgətiv] prerro-

gativa *f*

prescribe [pris'kraib] *v/t*, *v/i med* receitar; prescrever

prescription [pris'kripʃən] prescrição *f*; *med* receita *f*

presence ['prezns] presença *f*; **~ of mind** presença *f* de espírito

present [preznt] *adj*, *s* presente *m*; [pri'zent] *v/t* apresentar; oferecer; **at** **~** presentemente, de momento; **for the ~** por agora, por enquanto; **~ly** daqui a pouco; *US* presentemente

preserve [pri'zə:v] *v/t* conservar; preservar; *s* conserva *f*, compota *f*; tapada *f*, coutada *f*

presid|e [pri'zaid] *v/i* presidir; **~ent** ['prezidənt] presidente *m*; **~ential** [.prezi'denʃəl] presidencial

press [pres] *v/t*, *v/i* carregar em; apressar(-se); comprimir, apertar; prensar, espremer; estreitar, abraçar; *s* prensa *f*; imprensa *f*; lagar *m*; prelo *m*; **~ing** urgente; **~ure** [-fə] *s* pressão *f*

prestige [pres'ti:ʒ] prestígio *m*

presume [pri'zju:m] *v/t*, *v/i* presumir, supor

presumpt|ion [pri'zʌmpʃən] presunção *f*; **~uous** presunçoso, presumido

pretence [pri'tens] pretensão *f*; pretexto *m*

preten|d [pri'tend] *v/t*, *v/i* simular, fingir; pretender; pretextar; **~tious** [-ʃəs] pretensioso

pretext ['pri:tekst] pretexto *m*

pretty ['priti] *adj* bonito, lindo; *adv* bastante

prevail [pri'veil] *v/i* prevalecer;

~ on convencer
prevent [pri'vent] *v/t* impedir; evitar; **~ from** impedir de; **~ion** [-ʃən] prevenção *f*; impedimento *m*; **~ive** preventivo
previous ['priːvjəs] anterior, prévio
pre-war ['priːwɔː] *de* antes da guerra
prey [prei] *s* presa *f*; **of ~** de rapina
price [prais] *s* preço *m*; *v/t* apreçar; **~less** inestimável
prick [prik] *s* picada *f*, picadura *f*; *v/t, v/i* picar; **~ up one's ears** apurar o ouvido
pride [praid] *s* orgulho *m*
priest [priːst] padre *m*, sacerdote *m*; **~hood** sacerdócio *m*
prim [prim] afe(c)tado; empertigado
primary ['praiməri] *adj* primário
prime [praim] *s, adj* primeiro, sumo; **~ minister** primeiro-ministro *m*; **~number** número *m* primo
primer ['praimə] cartilha *f*, manual *m*
primitive [primitiv] *adj, s* primitivo *m*
primrose ['primrəuz] prímula *f*, primavera *f*
prince [prins] príncipe *m*
princess [prin'ses] princesa *f*
principal ['prinsəpəl] *adj* principal; *s* dire(c)tor *m*, reitor *m*; *com* capital *m*
principle ['prinsəpl] princípio *m*; **in ~** em princípio; **on ~** por princípio

print [print] *s* impressão *f*; estampa *f*, gravura *f*; tipografia *f*; *v/t* imprimir; estampar; **out of ~** esgotado; **~ed matter** impressos *m/pl*; **~er** impressor *m*; tipógrafo *m*; **~ing** *s* imprensa *f*; impressão *m*; tiragem *f*
prior ['praiə] *adj* anterior, precedente, prévio; **~ to** antes de; **~ity** [-'ɔriti] *(pl* **-ties)** prioridade *f*
prison ['prizn] cadeia *f*, prisão *f*; **~er** prisioneiro *m*
privacy ['privəsi] isolamento *m*, retiro *m*; intimidade *f*; segredo *m*, reserva *f*
private ['praivit] *adj* privado; particular
privation [prai'veiʃən] privação *f*
privileg|e ['priviliʤ] privilégio *m*; **~ed** privilegiado
prize [praiz] *s* prémio *m*; *v/t* estimar
probab|le ['prɔbəbl] *adj* provável; **~ly** provavelmente
probation [prə'beiʃən] *jur* liberdade *f* condicional; estágio *m*
problem ['prɔbləm] problema *m*
proceed [prə'siːd] *v/i* proceder; prosseguir; **~ings** *s/pl* a(c)ta *f*, minuta *f*; procedimento *m*; processo *m*; debate *m*; **~s** ['prəusiːdz] *s/pl* produto *m*, rendimento *m*
process ['prəuses] *s* processo *m*, método *m*
procession [prə'seʃən] procis-

são f
proclaim [prə'kleim] v/t proclamar
proclamation [.prɔklə'meiʃən] proclamação f
procure [prə'kjuə] v/t obter; alcovitar
prodigious [prə'didʒəs] prodigioso
produce [prə'djuːs] v/t, v/i exibir, apresentar; pôr em cena; produzir; ['prɔdjuːs] s produto m; **~r** produtor m
product ['prɔdʌkt] produto m; **~ion** [prə'dʌkʃən] produção f; **~ive** [prə'dʌktiv] produtivo
profess [prə'fes] v/t professar; **~ion** profissão f; **~ional** adj profissional
professor [prə'fesə] catedrático m; **~ship** cátedra f
proficien|cy [prə'fiʃənsi] proficiência f; **~t** proficiente
profile ['prəufail] s perfil m
profit ['prɔfit] s lucro m; proveito m; **~ by/from** v/t tirar proveito de; **~able** proveitoso; **~eer** [-'tiə] aproveitador m, explorador m
profound [prə'faund] profundo
profundity [prə'fʌnditi] (pl **-ties**) profundeza f, profundidade f
profuse [prə'fjuːs] profuso, abundante
progenitor [prəu'dʒenitə] progenitor m
prognosis [prɔg'nəusis] prognóstico m
program(me) ['prəugræm] s programa m

progress ['prəugres] s progresso m; [prəu'gres] v/i progredir; **~ion** [prəu'greʃən] progressão f; **~ive** [prəu'gresiv] adj progressivo; s progressista m, f
prohibit [prə'hibit] v/t proibir; **~ion** [.prəui'biʃən] proibição f; **~ive** [-'hibitiv] proibitivo; **~ory** proibitório
project ['prɔdʒekt] s proje(c)to m; [prə'dʒekt] v/t, v/i proje(c)tar; **~ile** [-tail] projé(c)til; **~ion** [prə'dʒekʃən] proje(c)ção f; **~or** proje(c)tor m
prolog(ue) ['prəulɔg] prólogo m
prolong [prə'lɔŋ] v/t prolongar
prominent ['prɔminənt] proeminente; eminente
promis|e ['prɔmis] v/t, v/i prometer; s promessa f; **~ing** prometedor; **~sory** [-'səri] promissório
promontory ['prɔməntri] (pl **-ries**) promontório m
promot|e [prə'məut] v/t promover; **~ion** promoção f
prompt [prɔmpt] adj pronto, expedito; pontual; v/t, v/i incitar, instigar; servir de ponto a; **~er** thea ponto m
prone [prəun] propenso
prong [prɔŋ] s dente m de garfo; ponta f
pronoun ['prəunaun] pronome m
pronounc|e [prə'nauns] v/t pronunciar; declarar; **~ed** adj acentuado, marcado; vincado; nítido
pronunciation [prə.nʌnsi'eiʃən] pronúncia f

provoke

proof [pru:f] *s* prova *f*; *adj*: ... ~ à prova de; *v/t* impermeabilizar

prop [prɔp] *s* amparo *m*; estaca *f*, esteio *m*; *v/t* sustentar; apoiar

propaga|te ['prɔpəgeit] *v/t, v/i* propagar(-se); ~**tion** [-'geiʃən] propagação *f*

propel [prə'pel] *v/t* impelir, propulsar; ~**ler** propulsor *m*; hélice *f*

proper ['prɔpə] próprio, conveniente, decente; oportuno, apropriado; ~**ty** (*pl* **-ties**) propriedade *f*; bens *m/pl*

prophe|cy ['prɔfisi] (*pl* **-cies**) profecia *f*, vaticínio *m*; ~**sy** ['-sai] *v/t, v/i* profetizar; ~**t** profeta *m*; ~**tic** [prə'fetik] profético

propitious [prə'piʃəs] propício

proportion [prə'pɔ:ʃən] *s* porção *f*; ~**al** proporcional

propos|al [prə'pəuzəl] proposta *f*; ~**e** *v/t* propor; ~**er** proponente *m*; ~**ition** [prɔpə'ziʃən] proposição *f*

propriet|or [prə'praiətə] proprietário *m*; ~**y** decência *f*, conveniência *f*

pros|aic [prəu'zeiik] prosaico; ~**e** [prəuz] prosa *f*

prosecut|e [prɔsikju:t] *v/t, v/i jur* processar; ~**ion** acusação *f*; ~**or** demandante *m, f*; promotor *m* da acusação

prospect [prɔspekt] *s* perspectiva *f*, expectativa *f*; [prɔs'pekt] *v/t, v/i* explorar; ~**or** [-'spektə] prospe(c)tor *m, Braz* garimpeiro *m*

prosper ['prɔspə] *v/i* prosperar; ~**ity** [-'periti] prosperidade *f*; ~**ous** próspero

prostitution [.prɔsti'tju:ʃən] prostituição *f*

prostrate [prɔs'treit] *v/t* prostrar; ['-] *adj* prosternado; prostrado

protect [prə'tekt] *v/t* proteger; ~**ion** prote(c)ção *f*; ~**ive** prote(c)tivo; ~**or** prote(c)tor *m*

protest [prə'test] *v/t, v/i* protestar; ['prautest] *s* protesto *m*

Protestant ['prɔtistənt] *s* protestante *m, f*; ♀ **ism** protestantismo *m*

protract [prə'trækt] *v/t* prolongar, protelar; ~**or** transferidor *m*

protrude [prə'tru:d] *v/t, v/i* ressaltar, sobressair

proud [praud] *adj* orgulhoso

prove [pru:v] *v/t* provar, demonstrar

proverb ['prɔvəb] provérbio *m*

provid|e [prə'vaid] *v/t* prover, abastecer; ~**ed (that)** contanto que, desde que

providen|ce ['prɔvidəns] providência *f*; ~**t** previdente; prudente

provinc|e ['prɔvins] província *f*; ~**ial** [prə'vinʃəl] *s* provinciano *m*; *adj* provincial

provision [prə'viʒən] *s* provisão *f*, abastecimento *m*; cláusula *f*, estipulação *f*; ~**al** provisório

provoca|tion [prɔvə'keiʃən] provocação *f*; ~**tive** [prə'vɔkətiv] provocativo

provoke [prə'vəuk] *v/t* provocar

prowl [praul] v/t, v/i rondar

proxy ['proksi] (pl -xies) procuração f; procurador m

prude [pru:d] pudico, afe(c)tado

pruden|ce ['pru:dəns] prudência f; ~t prudente

prune [pru:n] s ameixa f seca; v/t podar, desbastar

Prussian ['prʌʃən] adj, s prussiano m

psalm [sɑ:m] salmo m; ~ist salmista m

psychia|trist [sai'kaiətrist] psiquiatra m, f; ~try psiquiatria f

psycholog|ical [saikə'lɔdʒikəl] psicológico; ~ist [-'kɔlədʒist] psicólogo m; ~y [-'kɔlədʒi] psicologia f

pub [pʌb] cervejaria f, taberna f

puberty ['pju:bəti] puberdade f

public ['pʌblik] adj, s público m; ~ation [-'keiʃən] publicação f; ~ house taberna f, cervejaria f; ~ity [-'lisiti] publicidade f; ~ize [-'saiz] v/t propalar, divulgar; ~ school GB colégio m, internato m; US escola f pública

publish ['pʌbliʃ] v/t, v/i publicar, editar; ~er editor m

pucker ['pʌkə] v/t, v/i enrugar, franzir

pudding ['pudiŋ] pudim m

puddle ['pʌdl] s poça f, charco m

puff [pʌf] s baforada f, sopro m; v/t, v/i soprar; ofegar, arfar

pull [pul] s arranco m, puxão m; v/t puxar; arrancar; ~ down demolir

pullet ['pulit] frango m

pulley ['puli] roldana f

pullover ['pul.əuvə] pulóver m, camisola f

pulp [pʌlp] s polpa f

pulpit ['pulpit] púlpito m

puls|ate [pʌl'seit] v/i pulsar; ~ation [-'seiʃən] pulsação f; ~e s pulso m

pumice(-stone) ['pʌmis(staun)] pedra-pomes f

pump [pʌmp] s bomba f; v/t dar à bomba

pumpkin ['pʌmpkin] abóbora f

pun [pʌn] s trocadilho m, calembur m

punch [pʌntʃ] s soco m, murro m; ponche m; perfurador m, punção m; v/t, v/i perfurar; esmurrar

punctual ['pʌŋktjuəl] pontual; ~ity [-'æliti] pontualidade f

punctuation [pʌŋktju'eiʃən] pontuação f

puncture ['pʌŋktʃə] s furo m; v/t, v/i furar

punish ['pʌniʃ] v/t punir, castigar; ~able punível; ~ment castigo m

puny ['pju:ni] débil, fraco; insignificante

pupil ['pju:pl] anat pupila f; aluno m, pupilo m

puppet ['pʌpit] marionete f, fantoche m

puppy ['pʌpi] cachorrinho m

purchase ['pə:tʃəs] v/t comprar; s compra f

pure [pjuə] puro

puri|fy ['pjuərifai] v/t purificar; ~tan adj, s puritano m; ~ty pureza f

purple ['pə:pl] s púrpura f; adj

purpúreo, purpurino
purpose ['pə:pəs] s propósito m, tenção f; **on ~ de** propósito
purr [pə:] s ronrom m; v/i ronronar
purs|**e** |pə:s] s porta-moedas m, bolsa f; **~er** mar comissário m de bordo
pursu|**e** [pə'sju:] v/t perseguir; **~er** perseguidor m; **~it** [-'sju:t] perseguição f; a(c)tividade f, ocupação f
purvey [pə:'vei] v/t prover, abastecer
pus [pʌs] med pus m
push [puʃ] v/t, v/i empurrar; s impulso m; empurrão m; **get the ~** ser posto na rua; **~ up** forçar a alta; fazer subir
pussy ['pusi] (pl-**sies**) bichano m
put [put] v/t, v/i pôr, botar, colocar, meter; **~ down** reprimir; pousar; **~ off** adiar; **~ on** calçar; vestir; **~ out** apagar; **~ up with** aguentar, suportar, tolerar
putr|**efy** ['pju:trifai] v/t, v/i putrefazer, apodrecer
putrid ['pju:trid] pútrido
putty ['pʌti] poteia f
puzzl|**e** ['pʌzl] s quebra-cabeça m, s enigma m; embaraço m, perplexidade f; v/t, v/i embaraçar, confundir; **crossword ~** palavras f/pl cruzadas
pygmy ['pigmi] (pl-**mies**) pigmeu m
pyjamas [pə'dʒa:məz] s/pl pijama m
pyramid ['pirəmid] pirâmide f
pyre ['paiə] pira f funerária
python ['paiθən] pitão m

Q

quack [kwæk] v/i grasnar; s grasnido m; charlatão m; **~ery** charlatanismo m
quadrangle ['kwɔdræŋgl] quadrângulo m; pátio m
quadrant ['kwɔdrənt] quadrante m
quadruped ['kwɔdruped] s, adj quadrúpede m
quadruple ['kwɔdrupl] adj, s quádruplo m
quagmire ['kwægmaiə] tremedal m, pântano m
quail [kweil] s codorniz f
quaint [kweint] estranho, pitoresco
quake [kweik] s tremor m de terra; v/i tremer
quali|**fication** [,kwɔlifi'keiʃən] aptidão f, capacidade f; qualificação f; **~fied** ['-faid] adj qualificado, habilitado; **~fy** ['-fai] v/t, v/i habilitar(-se); qualificar; **~ty** (pl-**ties**) qualidade f
qualm [kwɔ:m] escrúpulo m; receio m
quandary ['kwɔndəri] (pl-**ries**) dilema m
quantity ['kwɔntiti] (pl-**ties**) quantidade f
quarantine ['kwɔrənti:n] s quarentena f
quarrel ['kwɔrəl] s disputa f, altercação f; v/i disputar, discu-

tir, brigar; **~some** brigão

quarry ['kwɔri] s (pl **-ries**) pedreira f; v/t, v/i extrair de pedreira

quarter ['kwɔːtə] s quarto m, quarta parte f; trimestre m; quarteirão m, bairro m; v/t esquartejar; aquartelar; **~ly** adj trimestral; s publicação f trimestral; **~s** pl alojamento m; **from all ~s** de todas as direc(c)ões

quartet(te) [kwɔː'tet] quarteto m

quartz [kwɔːts] quartzo m

quash [kwɔʃ] v/t suprimir, anular

quaver ['kweivə] v/i tremer, tremular; s mus colcheia f

quay [kiː] cais m

queen [kwiːn] s rainha f

queer [kwiə] adj estranho, singular, curioso

quench [kwentʃ] v/t apagar; mitigar, matar

querulous ['kwerʊləs] queixoso

query ['kwiəri] s (pl **-ries**) pergunta f; v/t inquirir, perguntar; duvidar de

question ['kwestʃən] s pergunta f; questão f; problema m; v/t interrogar; duvidar de; **ask a ~** fazer uma pergunta; **in ~** em questão; **out of the ~** fora de questão; impossível; **~able** contestável; **~mark** ponto m de interrogação

questionnaire [,kwestiə'neə] questionário m

queue [kjuː] s fila f, bicha f; v/i fazer bicha

quibble ['kwibl] s argúcia f; v/i sofismar

quick [kwik] adv depressa; adj rápido; pronto; s âmago m; sabugo m, medula f; **~en** v/t acelerar; **~lime** cal f viva; **~ly** depressa; **~ness** rapidez f; **~sand** areia f movediça; **~witted** perspicaz, esperto

quiet ['kwaiət] adj calmo, sossegado, adj tranquilo; s tranquilidade f; calma f; **~(en)** v/t, v/i acalmar, aquietar; **~ude** quietação f; quietude f

quill [kwil] pena f; tubo m de pena

quilt [kwilt] colcha f

quince [kwins] marmelo m

quinsy ['kwinzi] angina f

quire ['kwaiə] mão f de papel

quit [kwit] adj quite, livre; v/t, v/i deixar, abandonar; **notice to ~** aviso m de despejo

quite [kwait] completamente, totalmente; bastante; muito; **~ a/an** ... realmente um/uma ...; **~ (so)** exa(c)tamente

quiver ['kwivə] v/i tremer, vibrar; s tremor m; aljava f

quiz [kwiz] v/t interrogar; s interrogatório m; **~zical** motejador, zombador

quoit [kɔit] malha f, conca f

quota ['kwəutə] quota f

quotation [kwəu'teiʃən] citação f; com cotação f; **~marks** aspas f/pl

quote [kwəut] v/t, v/i citar; com cotizar

quotient ['kwəuʃənt] quociente m

R

rabbi ['ræbai] rabino *m*

rabbit ['ræbit] *s* coelho *m*

rabble ['ræbl] turba *f*; ralé *f*, populaça *f*

rabid ['ræbid] rábido; furioso *f*

rabies ['reibi:z] raiva *f*

race [reis] *s* raça *f*; carreira *f*, corrida *f*; corrente *f* de água; competição *f*; *v/t, v/i* correr; fazer uma corrida; competir; **~-course** hipódromo *m*; **~-track** pista *f* de corridas

racial ['reiʃəl] racial; **~ism** racismo *m*

racism [reisizəm] *US* racismo *m*

rack [ræk] *s* grade *f*; cabide *m*; prateleira *f*, rede *f*; *mec* cremalheira *f*; *v/t* torturar; **~ one's brains** quebrar a cabeça

racket ['rækit] barafunda *f*, barulho *m*; raqueta *f*

racy [reisi] vigoroso

radar ['reidə] radar *m*

radiant ['reidjənt] radiante

radiate ['reidieit] *v/t* irradiar; iluminar; *v/i* enfurecer-se, encolerizar-se; **~ion** [-'eiʃən] irradiação *f*; **~or** radiador *m*

radical ['rædikəl] radical

radio [reidiəu] *s* rádio *f*; **~ (set)** (aparelho *m* de) rádio *m*

radio-active [reidiəu'æktiv] radio(c)tivo; **~graphy** [-'ɔgrəfi] radiografia *f*

radish ['rædiʃ] rabanete *m*

radius ['reidiəs] *(pl* **-dii** [-diai]) raio *m*; *anat* rádio *m*

raffle ['ræfl] *s* rifa *f*, sorteio *m*

raft [rɑːft] *s* jangada *f*, balsa *f*

rafter ['rɑːftə] barrote *m*, viga *f*

rag [ræg] *s* farrapo *m*, trapo *m*

rage [reidʒ] *s* raiva *f*, furor *m*, fúria *f*; *v/i* enfurecer-se, encolerizar-se; **(all) the ~** à moda

ragged ['rægid] *adj* esfarrapado

raid [reid] *s* ataque *m*, incursão *f*; *v/t, v/i* atacar, invadir

rail [reil] *s* carril *m*; corrimão *m*, balaustrada *f*; *v/i* **~ (at)** injuriar, invectivar; **by ~** por caminho de ferro; **~ing** *s* grade *f*; **~way** caminho *m* de ferro, *Braz* estrada *f* de ferro

rain [rein] *s* chuva *f*; *v/i* chover; **~ cats and dogs** chover a cântaros; **~bow** [-bəu] arco-íris *m*; **~coat** impermeável *m*; **~drop** pingo *m* de chuva; **~y** chuvoso

raise [reiz] *v/t* levantar, erguer; elevar, aumentar; provocar; cultivar, produzir; criar

raisin [reizn] passa *f*, uva *f* seca

rake [reik] *s* ancinho *m*; *v/t, v/i* limpar com o ancinho; revolver

rally ['ræli] *v/t, v/i* reunir(-se); reanimar(-se); *s* *(pl* **-lies**) rali *m*; reunião *f*

ram [ræm] *s* carneiro *m*; *v/t* calcar; abalroar, chocar

ramble ['ræmbl] *s* excursão *f*, passeio *m*; *v/i* vaguear, deambular; divagar

ramify ['ræmifai] *v/t, v/i* ramificar(-se)

ramp [ræmp] rampa f

ranch [rɑːntʃ,ræntʃ] rancho m, fazenda f; **~er** rancheiro m

rancid ['rænsid] rançoso

ranco(u)r ['ræŋkə] rancor m

random ['rændəm] adj casual, fortuito; **at ~** à toa, ao acaso

range [reindʒ] s cordilheira f; extensão f, alcance m; classe f, ordem f; série f, gama f, escala f; v/t, v/i percorrer; arranjar, alinhar; estender-se, ir

rank [ræŋk] s posto m; linha f, fileira f; classe f, ordem f; adj luxuriante, viçoso; rançoso; v/t, v/i ordenar, classificar

ransack ['rænsæk] v/t saquear, pilhar

ransom ['rænsəm] s resgate m; v/t resgatar

rap [ræp] s pancada f; v/t bater

rapac|ious [rə'peiʃəs] rapace; **~ity** [-'pæsiti] rapacidade f

rape [reip] s estupro m, violação f; v/t violar

rapid ['ræpid] adj, s rápido m; **~ity** [rə'piditi] rapidez f

rapt [ræpt] arrebatado, extasiado; **~ure** [-tʃə] arrebatamento m, êxtase m; **~urous** [-tʃərəs] extático

rar|e [rɛə] raro; mal passado, meio cru; **~efy** ['-rifai] v/t rarefazer

rarity ['rɛəriti] (pl -ties) raridade f

rascal ['rɑːskəl] maroto m, velhaco m

rash [ræʃ] adj temerário; precipitado, imprudente; s erupção f

rasher ['ræʃə] tira f de toucinho

rasp [rɑːsp] s grosa f, lima f grossa; v/t grosar

raspberry ['rɑːzbəri] (pl -ries) framboesa f

rat [ræt] s ratazana f

rate [reit] s velocidade f, marcha f; preço m, valor m; taxa f; tarifa f; v/t, v/i estimar, avaliar; **at any ~** em todo o caso; **at this/that ~** nesse caso, desta forma; **~ of exchange** taxa f de câmbio

rather ['rɑːðə] adv antes; um tanto

ratio ['reiʃiəu] razão f, proporção f

ration ['ræʃən] s ração f; v/t racionar

rational ['ræʃənl] racional; **~ism** ['ræʃnəlizəm] racionalismo m

rattle ['rætl] s matraca f, cegarrega f; guizo m; v/t, v/i matraquear, chocalhar; agitar(-se)

rattlesnake ['rætlsneik] cobra f cascável

ravage ['rævidʒ] v/t devastar; **~s** [-iz] s/pl estragos m/pl

rave [reiv] v/i delirar

raven ['reivn] corvo m

ravine [rə'viːn] barranco m, ravina f

raw [rɔː] adj cru; bruto; inexperiente; **~ material** matéria-prima f

ray [rei] raio m; zo (ar)raia f

razor ['reizə] navalha f; máquina f de barbear

reach [riːtʃ] v/t, v/i alcançar; chegar a; entregar, passar; s alcance m; **out of ~** fora do alcance

react [ri'ækt] v/i reagir; **~ion** rea(c)ção f; **~ionary** [-ʃnəri] adj, s (pl -ries) rea(c)cionário m, **~or** rea(c)tor m

read [ri:d] v/t ler; estudar; **~able** legível; fácil de ler; **~er** leitor m

readi|ly ['redili] prontamente; de boa vontade; **~ness** prontidão f, presteza f; boa vontade f

reading ['ri:diŋ] s leitura f

readjust [ri:ə'dʒʌst] v/t, v/i reajustar

ready ['redi] adj pronto, preparado; **~made** já feito, pronto a vestir

real [riəl] adj real, verdadeiro; genuíno, autêntico; **~ism** realismo m; **~ist** realista, m, f; **~istic** realista; **~ity** [ri'æliti] (pl -ties) realidade f

reali|zation [,riəlai'zeiʃən] realização f; compreensão f; **~ze** ['-laiz] v/t realizar; fazer ideia, dar-se conta de

really ['riəli] realmente, na verdade, deveras

reanimate [ri:'ænimeit] v/t reanimar

reap [ri:p] v/t, v/i ceifar, segar; **~er** segadora f mecânica

reappear [ri:ə'piə] v/i reaparecer

rear [riə] s traseiro m; retaguarda f; v/t, v/i criar; empinar-se

rearrange [ri:ə'reindʒ] v/t arranjar de novo

reason ['ri:zn] s razão f, motivo m; v/t, v/i raciocinar; persuadir; debater; **~ with** discutir

without rhyme or ~ sem tom nem som; **~able** razoável; **~ing** s raciocínio m

reassure [,ri:ə'ʃuə] v/t tranquilizar

rebel ['rebl] s, adj rebelde m, f; [ri'bel] v/i rebelar-se, revoltar-se; **~lion** [ri'beljən] rebelião f, sublevação f; **~lious** [ri'beljəs] rebelde

rebound [ri'baund] v/i ressaltar; s ressalto m

rebuff [ri'bʌf] s recusa f; v/t repelir

rebuild [ri:'bild] v/t reconstruir

rebuke [ri'bju:k] v/t repreender, admoestar; s repreensão f, censura f

recall [ri'kɔ:l] v/t recordar; revogar; s revocação f; **beyond/past ~** irrevogável; esquecido

recapitulate [,ri:kə'pitjuleit] v/t, v/i recapitular

recast [ri:'kɑ:st] v/t refundir

recede [ri'si:d] v/i retirar-se; recuar

receipt [ri'si:t] s recibo m; recepção f; **acknowledge ~ of** acusar a recepção de

receiv|e [ri'si:v] v/t receber; **~er** receptor m; auscultador m, Braz fone m

recent [ri:sənt] recente; **~ly** recentemente

reception [ri'sepʃən] recepção f; acolhimento m

recess [ri'ses] s férias f/pl; nicho m; suspensão f; **~ion** [-'seʃən] depressão f, baixa f de produção

recipe ['resipi] receita f

reciprocal [ri'siprəkəl] recíproco

recital [ri'saitl] recital *m*, récita *f*

recite [ri'sait] *v/t, v/i* recitar

reckless ['reklis] estouvado, temerário

reckon ['rekən] *v/t, v/i* calcular, contar; considerar, julgar; **~ing** *s* cálculo *m*; **day of ~ing** dia *m* do ajuste de contas

reclaim [ri'kleim] *v/t* reclamar, reivindicar; reformar; recuperar, conquistar

recline [ri'klain] *v/t, v/i* reclinar(-se), recostar(-se)

recognition [.rekəg'niʃən] reconhecimento *m*

recognize ['rekəgnaiz] *v/t* reconhecer

recoil [ri'koil] *v/i* recuar

recollect [.rekə'lekt] *v/t* recordar, lembrar-se de

recommend [.rekə'mend] *v/t* recomendar; **~ation** [-'deiʃən] recomendação *f*

recompense ['rekəmpens] *s* recompensa *f*; *v/t* recompensar

reconcile ['rekənsail] *v/t* reconciliar, conciliar

reconsider ['ri:kən'sidə] *v/t, v/i* reconsiderar

reconstruct ['ri:kəns'trʌkt] *v/t* reconstruir; **~ion** reconstrução *f*

record [ri'kɔ:d] *v/t* registr(r)ar; gravar; ['rekɔ:d] *s* recorde *m*; disco *m*; regist(r)o *m*; **off the ~** confidencial; **on ~** registado; **~er** registr(r)ador *m*; *mus* flautim *m*; **~ing** *s* gravação *f*; **~ player** gira-discos *m*

recourse [ri'kɔ:s] recurso *m*

recover [ri'kʌvə] *v/t, v/i* recuperar, recobrar; restabelecer-se; **~y** recuperação *f*; restabelecimento *m*

recreation [.rekri'eiʃən] recreio *m*

recruit [ri'kru:t] *s* recruta *m*

rectangle ['rek.tæŋgl] re(c)tângulo *m*

rectify ['rektifai] *v/t* re(c)tificar

rector ['rektə] reitor *m*; *eccl* cura *m*; **~y** presbitério *m*

recur [ri'kə:] *v/i* repetir-se; **~ to** ocorrer; recorrer a; **~rence** [-'kʌrəns] repetição *f*

red [red] *adj* vermelho, encarnado; **~ wine** vinho *m* tinto

redd|en ['redn] *v/t, v/i* avermelhar; corar, ruborizar-se; **~ish** avermelhado

redeem [ri'di:m] *v/t* remir, redimir; *com* amortizar; **2 er** Redentor *m*

redemption [ri'dempʃən] redenção *f*; *com* amortização *f*

redness ['rednis] vermelhidão *f*

redouble [ri'dʌbl] *v/t, v/i* redobrar

reduce [ri'dju:s] *v/t* reduzir, diminuir, rebaixar

reduction [ri'dʌkʃən] redução *f*; *com* rebaixa *f*

redundant [ri'dʌndənt] redundante

re-echo [ri(:)'ekəu] *v/t* ressoar

reed [ri:d] cana *f*, caniço *m*; flauta *f* de cana

reef [ri:f] *s* recife *m*; *v/t* rizar

reek [ri:k] *v/i* fumegar; **~ of** cheirar a, feder a

reel [ri:l] s carretel m, bobina f;
dança f escocesa; v/t bobinar,
dobar; v/i cambalear

reentry [ri:'entri] (pl -ries) reen-
trada f

refer [ri'fə:]: **~to** v/t referir-se
a; recorrer a

referee [ˌrefə'ri:] s árbitro m;
v/t, v/i arbitrar

reference ['refrəns] referência f;
recomendação f; consulta f; **~
book** livro m de consulta

refill [ˌri:'fil] v/t encher de
novo; ['ri:fil] s recarga f

refine [ri'fain] v/t refinar; **~ry**
refinaria f

reflect [ri'flekt] v/t, v/i re-
tle(c)tir; **~ion** [-ʃən] reflexão f

reflex ['ri:fleks] reflexo m

reform [ri'fɔ:m] v/t, v/i corri-
gir(-se), melhorar(-se); reformar; s reforma f; ♀ **ation** [ˌre-
fə'meiʃən] Reforma f

refrain [ri'frein] s refrão m,
estribilho m; v/i refrear-se, abster-se

refresh [ri'freʃ] v/t refrescar;
~ing adj refrescante; **~ment**
refresco m

refrigera|te [ri'fridʒəreit] v/t re-
frigerar; **~tion** [-'reiʃən] refri-
geração f; **~tor** refrigerador
m, frigorífico m, geladeira f

refuel [ˌri:'fjuəl] v/t, v/i re-
abastecer(-se) de combustível

refuge ['refju:dʒ] refúgio m; **~e**
[-'dʒi] refugiado m

refund [ri'fʌnd] v/t reembolsar

refusal [ri'fju:zəl] recusa f

refuse [ri'fju:z] v/t, v/i recusar;
rejeitar; ['refju:s] s lixo m, en-

tulho m

regain [ri'gein] v/t recuperar; recobrar; readquirir

regal ['ri:gəl] real, régio

regard [ri'gɑ:d] s consideração f,
respeito m, v/t considerar;
respeitar, acatar; **with ~ to** a
respeito de, quanto a; **~s** s/pl
cumprimentos m/pl, sauda-
ções f/pl; **with kind ~s** com
os melhores cumprimentos

regency ['ri:dʒənsi] regência f

regent ['ri:dʒənt] s regente m, f

regiment ['redʒimənt] s regi-
mento m

region ['ri:dʒən] região f

register ['redʒistə] s regist(r)o m;
v/t, v/i regist(r)ar; inscrever
(-se), matricular(-se)

registrar [ˌredʒis'trɑ:] regist(r)a-
dor m, arquivista f

registry ['redʒistri] (pl -tries)
arquivo m, cartório m

regret [ri'gret] s pena f, pesar m;
v/t lamentar; **~s** s/pl descul-
pas f/pl; **~table** lamentável

regular ['regjulə] adj regular;
~ity [-'læriti] regularidade f;
~ize v/t regularizar; **~ly** re-
gularmente

regulat|e ['regjuleit] v/t regular;
acertar; **~ion** [-'leiʃən] regulamento m; regulação f

rehears|al [ri'hə:səl] s ensaio m;
~e v/t, v/i ensaiar

reign [rein] s reinado m; v/i
reinar

reimburse [ˌri:im'bə:s] v/t
reembolsar

rein [rein] rédea f

reindeer ['reindiə] rena f, rangifer m

reinforce [.ri:in'fɔ:s] v/t reforçar; ~ment reforço m

reiterate [ri:'itəreit] v/t reiterar

reject [ri'dʒekt] v/t rejeitar;
~ion [-ʃən] rejeição f

rejoice [ri'dʒɔis] v/i regozijar-
-se; ~ing s regozijo m

rejoin [ri:'dʒɔin] v/t reunir;
~der réplica f

rejuvenate [ri'dʒu:vineit] v/t,
v/i rejuvenescer

rekindle ['ri:'kindl] v/t, v/i re-
acender(-se)

relapse [ri'læps] v/i recair, rein-
cidir; s med recaída f, recidiva f

relate [ri'leit] v/t relatar, relacionar

relation [ri'leiʃən] relato m; relação f; parente m

relative ['relətiv] adj relativo; s
parente m

relax [ri'læks] v/t, v/i relaxar,
afrouxar; descansar, repousar;
~ation [.ri:læk'seiʃən] relaxa-
mento m; afrouxamento m;
descanso m

relay [ri'lei] s posta f, muda f;
substituição f; v/t substituir;
retransmitir; ~ race corrida f
de estafetas, Braz corrida f de
revezamento

release [ri'li:s] v/t soltar, des-
prender; s soltura f

relegate ['religeit] v/t relegar

relent [ri'lent] v/i abrandar-se;
ceder; ~less implacável

relevant ['relivant] relevante;
pertinente

reliable [ri'laiəbl] resistente;
seguro, de confiança

reliance [ri'laiəns] confiança f

relic ['relik] relíquia f

relief [ri'li:f] alívio m; auxílio m,
socorro m; relevo m; revezamento m

relieve [ri'li:v] v/t aliviar; socorrer; render

religion [ri'lidʒən] religião f;
~ous adj, s religioso m

relinquish [ri'liŋkwiʃ] v/t abandonar

relish ['reliʃ] v/t saborear; s
gosto m; sabor m; tempero m

reluctant [ri'lʌktənt] relutante

rely [ri'lai] on v/i confiar em,
contar com

remain [ri'mein] v/i ficar, permanecer; ~der s restante m,
resto m; ~s restos m/pl

remark [ri'mɑ:k] v/t observar; s
observação f; ~able notável

remedy ['remidi] s (pl -dies)
remédio m; v/t remediar

remember [ri'membə] v/t lembrar-se de; ter presente; ~ran-
ce lembrança f, recordação f

remind [ri'maind] v/t (fazer)
lembrar; ~ of fazer lembrar;
~er advertência f

remit [ri'mit] v/t, v/i remeter,
enviar; remitir, perdoar;
~tance remessa f de dinheiro

remnant ['remnənt] resto m

remodel [ri:'mɔdl] v/t remode-
lar

remonstrate ['remənstreit]
(with) v/i protestar

remorse [ri'mɔ:s] remorso m;
~less sem remorso; desapiedado

remote [ri'məut] remoto

removal [ri'mu:vəl] mudança *f*; ~ **van** camioneta *f* de mudanças

remove [ri'mu:v] *v/t* remover, afastar

render ['rendə] *v/t* tornar; executar, representar; ~**ing** *s* versão *f*; interpretação *f*

renew [ri'nju:] *v/t* renovar

renounce [ri'nauns] *v/t* renunciar a

renovate ['renəveit] *v/t* renovar

renown [ri'naun] renome *m*, fama *f*; ~**ed** famoso

rent [rent] *s* rasgão *m*, fenda *f*; renda *f*, aluguer *m*; *v/t* alugar

reopen [ri:'əupən] *v/t*, *v/i* reabrir

repair [ri'pɛə] *s* reparação *f*, conserto *m*; *v/t*, *v/i* reparar, consertar

reparation [,repə'reiʃən] reparação *f*

repartee [,repɑ:'ti:] réplica *f*

repay [ri:'pei] *v/t* pagar; compensar; reembolsar; ~**ment** reembolso *m*

repeat [ri'pi:t] *v/t* repetir; ~**ed-ly** repetidas vezes

repel [ri'pel] *v/t* repelir

repent [ri'pent] *v/t* ~ **of** *v/i* arrepender-se de; ~**ance** *s* arrependimento *m*

repetition [,repi'tiʃən] repetição *f*

replace [ri'pleis] *v/t* substituir; repor; ~**ment** substituição *f*

replenish [ri'pleniʃ] *v/t* reabastecer

reply [ri'plai] *v/t*, *v/i* responder; *s* resposta *f*

report [ri'pɔ:t] *v/t*, *v/i* relatar; fazer a reportagem de; contar; denunciar; comparecer; *s* relatório *m*; reportagem *f*; ~**er** repórter *m*, *f*

repose [ri'pəuz] *s* repouso *m*, descanso *m*; *v/t*, *v/i* repousar, descansar

reprehensible [,repri'hensəbl] repreensível

represent [,repri'zent] *v/t* representar; ~**ative** *adj* representativo; *s* representante *m*, *f*

repress [ri'pres] *v/t* reprimir; ~**ion** repressão *f*

reprieve [ri'pri:v] *s* suspensão *f* de pena; *v/t* suspender a pena de morte de ...

reprimand ['reprimɑ:nd] *v/t* repreender, admoestar; *s* repreensão *f*, reprimenda *f*

reprint ['ri:'print] *v/t*, *v/i* reimprimir; *s* reimpressão *f*

reproach [ri'prəutʃ] *v/t* exprobrar, censurar, repreender; *s* censura *f*, increpação *f*

reproduce [ri'prə'dju:s] *v/t* reproduzir(-se)

reproduction [,ri:prə'dʌkʃən] reprodução *f*

reproof [ri'pru:f] *s* reprovação *f*, increpação *f*

reprove [ri'pru:v] *v/t* reprovar, censurar

reptile ['reptail] réptil *m*

republic [ri'pʌblik] república *f*; ~**an** *adj*, *s* republicano *m*

repugnance [ri'pʌgnəns] repugnância *f*; ~**t** repugnante

repulse [ri'pʌls] *v/t* repelir; *s* repulsa *f*, recusa *f*; revés *m*; ~**ion**

[-ʃən] repulsa *f*; repulsão *f*; **~ive** repelente

reput|able ['repjutəbl] honroso, honrado; **~ation** [-'teiʃən] reputação *f*

repute [ri'pju:t] fama *f*, reputação *f*; **of bad/evil ~** de má fama *f*; **~d to be ...** ter fama de ser ...

request [ri'kwest] *s* petição *f*, pedido *m*; *v/t* rogar, pedir

require [ri'kwaiə] *v/t* requerer, necessitar, exigir

requisite ['rekwizit] *s* requisito *m*; *adj* necessário, preciso, requerido

requite [ri'kwait] *v/t* retribuir

rescue ['reskju:] *v/t* salvar; *s* salvamento *m*, salvação *f*

research [ri'sə:tʃ] *s* investigação *f*, pesquisa *f*; *v/t*, *v/i* investigar

resembl|ance [ri'zembləns] semelhança *f*, parecença *f*; **~e** *v/t* parecer-se com, assemelhar-se a

resent [ri'zent] *v/t* ressentir(-se de); **~ful** ressentido; **~ment** ressentimento *m*

reservation [.rezə'veiʃən] reservação *f*, reserva *f*

reserv|e [ri'zə:v] *v/t* reservar; **~ed** *adj* reservado; retraído

reservoir ['rezəvwa:] reservatório *m*; depósito *m*

resid|e [ri'zaid] *v/i* residir; **~ence** ['rezidəns] residência *f*; **~ent** ['rezidənt] *s*, *adj* residente *m*, *f*

resign [ri'zain] *v/t*, *v/i* demitir-se; **~ation** [.rezig'neiʃən] demissão *f*; **~ed** *adj* resignado

resist [ri'zist] *v/t*, *v/i* resistir (a); **~ance** resistência *f*; **~ant** resistente

resolut|e ['rezəlu:t] resoluto; **~ion** [.-'lu:ʃən] resolução *f*, decisão *f*

resolve [ri'zolv] *v/t* resolver

resort [ri'zo:t] *s* estância *f*; lugar *m*; recurso *m*; **in the last ~** em último recurso; **~ to** *v/t* recorrer a

resound [ri'zaund] *v/i* ressoar, retumbar

resource [ri'so:s] recurso *m*; **~ful** expedito; **~s** *s/pl* recursos *m/pl*

respect [ris'pekt] *v/t* respeitar; *s* respeito *m*; **with ~ to** com respeito a; **out of ~ for** em atenção a; **~able** respeitável; **~ful** respeitoso

respective [ris'pektiv] respectivo

respite ['respait] pausa *f*, folga *f*, descanso *m*

resplendent [ris'plendənt] resplandecente

respond [ris'pond] *v/i* responder; **~ to** reagir a

responsi|bility [ris.ponsə'biliti] (*pl* **-ties**) responsabilidade *f*; **~ble** [-'ponsəbl] (**for**) responsável (por); **~ve** [-'ponsiv] sensível

rest [rest] *v/i* descansar; *s* descanso *m*; resto *m*

restaurant ['restərənt] restaurante *m*

rest|ful ['restful] repousado, sossegado; **~less** inquieto, desassossegado

restor|ation [,restə'reiʃən] restauração f; restituição f; **~e** [ri-'stɔ:] v/t restaurar; restabelecer; restituir

restrain [ris'trein] restauro m; v/t refrear, reprimir, conter; **~t** constrangimento m

restrict [ris'trikt] v/t restringir; **~ion** restrição f

result [ri'zʌlt] s resultado m; v/i resultar; **~ant** resultante

resume [ri'zju:m] v/t, v/i retomar; reatar, recomeçar

resurrection [,rezə'rekʃən] ressurreição f

retail [ri:teil] s com retalho m, Braz varejo m; v/t vender a retalho

retain [ri'tein] v/t reter, guardar, conservar; **~er** pagamento m adiantado

retaliate [ri'tælieit] v/i retaliar, revidar

retir|e [ri'taiə] v/t, v/i retirar (-se); reformar-se; **~ed** adj reformado; retirado, afastado; **~ement** reforma f

retort [ri'tɔ:t] v/t, v/i retorquir, replicar; s réplica f; chem retorta f

retouch [ri:'tʌtʃ] v/t retocar

retrace [ri'treis] v/t rememorar, referir; **~ one's steps** retroceder

retract [ri'trækt] v/t, v/i recolher; retra(c)tar(-se)

retreat [ri'tri:t] v/i retirar-se; bater em retirada; s retirada f

retribution [,retri'bju:ʃən] justo castigo m

retrieve [ri'tri:v] v/t recuperar, recobrar

retrospect ['retrəspekt] retrospecto m

return [ri'tə:n] v/t, v/i devolver, restituir; voltar, regressar; s volta f, regresso m, devolução f, restituição f; **by ~** na volta do correio; **in ~ (for)** em paga de; em troca de; **~ ticket** bilhete m de ida e volta; **many happy ~s (of the day)!** muitos parabéns! felicitações cordiais!

reunion [ri:'ju:njən] reunião f

revaluation [ri:,vælju:'eiʃən] nova avaliação f

reveal [ri'vi:l] v/t revelar, desvendar, descobrir

revelry ['revəlri] (pl **-ries**) festança f, folia f

revenge [ri'vendʒ] s desforra f; vingança f; v/t vingar; **~ful** vingativo

revenue ['revinju:] rendimento m, receita f

revere [ri'viə] v/t venerar

reverse [ri'və:s] v/t, v/i fazer marcha-atrás; inverter; s reverso m, contrário m; inverso m; revés m, contratempo m; **~ gear** engrenagem f de inversão de marcha

review [ri'vju:] s revista f; crítica f; v/t rever; passar revista a; criticar

revis|e [ri'vaiz] v/t, v/i rever, reler; **~ion** [-'viʒən] revisão f

reviv|al [ri'vaivəl] renascimento m; **~e** v/t reanimar; restabelecer; voltar a si

revoke [ri'vəuk] v/t revogar

revolt [ri'vəult] s revolta f; v/t,

v/i repugnar; revoltar(-se)

revolution [ˌrevəˈluːʃən] revolução *f*; **~ary** [-ʃnəri] *adj, s* revolucionário *m*; **~ize** [-ʃnaiz] *v/t* revolucionar

revolve [riˈvɒlv] *v/t, v/i* rodar, girar; voltear, revolver

revolver [riˈvɒlvə] revólver *m*

revolving [riˈvɒlviŋ] *adj* giratório, rotativo

revulsion [riˈvʌlʃən] aversão *f*

reward [riˈwɔːd] *s* recompensa *f*; *v/t* recompensar

rheumatism [ˈruːmətizəm] reumatismo *m*

rhubarb [ˈruːbɑːb] ruibarbo *m*

rhyme [raim] *s* rima *f*; *v/t, v/i* rimar

rhythm [ˈriðəm] ritmo *m*; **~ic** rítmico

rib [rib] *s* costela *f*

ribbon [ˈribən] fita *f*

rice [rais] arroz *m*

rich [ritʃ] rico; substancial; **the ~os** ricos; **~ly** ricamente; **~ness** riqueza *f*

ricket|s [ˈrikits] *s/pl* raquitismo *m*; **~y** instável, frágil, vacilante

rid [rid] **of** *v/t* desembaraçar de, livrar de; **get ~ of** desembaraçar-se de, livrar-se de

riddle [ˈridl] *s* enigma *m*, adivinha *f*; crivo *m*, joeira *f*

rid|e [raid] *v/t, v/i* cavalgar, montar; ir, andar; *s* passeio *m*; **~er** cavaleiro *m*; amazona *f*

ridge [ridʒ] *s* cume *m*, espinhaço *m*

ridicul|e [ˈridikjuːl] *s* ridículo *m*; *v/t* ridicularizar; **~ous**

[-ˈdikjuləs] ridículo

riding [ˈraidiŋ] *s* equitação *f*

rifle [ˈraifl] *s* carabina *f*, espingarda *f*; *v/t* pilhar

rigging [ˈrigiŋ] *naut* cordame *m*

right [rait] *adj* direito; correc(t)o, justo; verdadeiro; *adv* justamente, bem; *s* direito *m*; justiça *f*; direita *f*; bem *m*; *v/t* endireitar; **all ~** está bem; **be ~** ter razão; **(quite) ~ in the head** em seu juízo; **~ you are!**, **~ oh!** certo!, perfeitamente, pois sim; **~ away**, **~** imediatamente; **~ful** legítimo; **~ly** convenientemente; justamente; **~s** *s/pl* direitos *m/pl*

rigid [ˈridʒid] rígido; **~ity** [-ˈdʒiditi] rigidez *f*

rigo|rous [ˈrigərəs] rigoroso; **~(u)r** rigor *m*

rim [rim] *s* borda *f*; *auto* aro *m*

rind [raind] casca *f*

ring [riŋ] *s* anel *m*; argola *f*; círculo *m*; aro *m*; ringue *m*; arena *f*; toque *m* de campainha; *v/t, v/i* tocar; repicar; tinir; soar; telefonar; **~ up** telefonar

rink [riŋk] ringue *m*, pista *f* de patinagem

rinse [rins] *v/t* enxaguar

riot [ˈraiət] *v/i* amotinar-se; *s* tumulto *m*, motim *m*; **~er** amotinador *m*; **~ous** sedicioso; desenfreado

rip [rip] *v/t, v/i* rasgar(-se); *s* rasgão *m*

rip|e [raip] maduro; **~en** *v/t, v/i* amadurecer

ripple [ˈripl] *s* ondulação *f*, enca-

peladura *f*; *v/t, v/i* encapelar-
-se; murmurar

rise [raiz] *v/i* levantar-se, erguer-
se; surgir; elevar-se; sublevar-
se; aumentar; nascer; subir; *s*
aumento *m*; elevação *f*; subida
f; rampa *f*; origem *f*

rising ['raizin] *s* sublevação *f*;
prp cerca de

risk [risk] *s* risco *m*; *v/t* arriscar;
run a ~ correr um risco; **~y**
arriscado

ritual ['ritjuəl] *adj, s* ritual *m*

rival [raivəl] *adj, s* rival *m, f*;
~ry rivalidade *f*

river ['rivə] *s* rio *m*; **~side** *s* margem *f* do rio; *adj* ribeirinho,
marginal

rivet ['rivit] *s* rebite *m*; *v/t* rebi-
tar

roach [rəutʃ] *zo* leucisco *m*; barata *f*

road [rəud] *s* estrada *f*; **on the
~** de viagem, de passagem;
~side *s* beira *f* da estrada;
~way pista *f* de rodagem

roam [rəum] *v/t, v/i* vaguear,
deambular

roar [rɔ:] *v/i* rugir; *s* rugido *m*

roast [rəust] *s* assado *m*, carne *f*
assada; *v/t, v/i* torrar; assar;
~beef rosbife *m*

rob [rɔb] *v/t* roubar; **~ber** ladrão *m*; **~bery** (*pl* -ries) roubo
m

robe [rəub] *s* veste *f*; manto *m*;
túnica *f*

robot ['rəubɔt] autómato *m*, ro-
bote *m*

robust [rə'bʌst] robusto

rock [rɔk] *s* rocha *f*, rochedo *m*;

roca *f*; *v/t, v/i* embalar, acalentar; balançar-se

rocket ['rɔkit] *s* foguete *m*

rocking-chair ['rɔkiŋtʃeə] cadeira *f* de balanço/baloiço

rocky ['rɔki] rochoso

rod [rɔd] vara *f*, varapau *m*

rodent ['rəudənt] roedor *m*

roe [rəu] ova *f* de peixe; **~-deer**
corça *f*

rogue [rəug] *s* velhaco *m*; **~ery**
velhacaria *f*

role [rəul] papel *m*

roll [rəul] *s* rolo *m*; pãozinho *m*;
rol *m*, lista *f*; *v/t, v/i* rodar; rolar; enrolar; **~ up** arregaçar;
enrolar(-se); chegar, aparecer;
~er rolo *m*; cilindro *m*; **~er
skate** *s* patim *m* de rodas;
~ing *adj* ondulado; rolante;
~ing-pin rolo *m* da massa

Roman ['rəumən] *adj, s* romano
m; ♀ **~ce** [rə'mæns] *s* romance
m; *adj* românico

romantic [rə'mæntik] *adj, s* romântico *m*; **~ism** [-sizəm] romantismo *m*

romp [rɔmp] *s* jogo *m* barulhento; *v/i* brincar doidamente

roof [ru:f] *s* telhado *m*

rook [ruk] *s* gralha *f*; torre *f*
(*chess*); *v/t* trapacear

room [rum] *s* quarto *m*, sala *f*; lugar *m*, espaço *m*; **~y** espaçoso

roost [ru:st] *s* poleiro *m*; *v/i*
empoleirar-se; **~er** galo *m*

root [ru:t] *s* raiz *f*; *v/t, v/i* criar
raízes, enraizar; **~ out** erradi-
car, exterminar; achar; **~ed**
adj arraigado; enraizado; espe-
cado

rope [rəup] *s* corda *f*; cabo *m*; fio *m*; *v/t* amarrar com corda

rosary ['rəuzəri] (*pl* **-ries**) rosário *m*

ros|e [rəuz] *s* rosa *f*; **~ebud** botão *m* de rosa; **~emary** rosmarinho *m*; **~y** róseo, rosado

rot [rɔt] *v/t*, *v/i* apodrecer; *s* podridão *f*, putrefa(c)ção *f*

rotary ['rəutəri] *adj* rotativo, giratório

rotate [rəu'teit] *v/t*, *v/i* girar, rodar

rotten ['rɔtn] *adj* podre; corru(p)to; choco; mau, ruim

rouge [ru:ʒ] *s* ruge *m*

rough [rʌf] *adj* rude, grosseiro; áspero; agitado, bravo; borrascoso, tempestuoso; duro, brutal; aproximado, geral; tosco; *v/t* **~ it** passar trabalhos; **~ly** aproximadamente; bruscamente

round [raund] *adj* redondo; arredondado; *s* circuito *m*; rodela *f*, fatia *f*, rodada *f*; ronda *f*; prp ao redor de, em torno de; *adv* à roda; *v/t*, *v/i* arredondar(-se); dobrar; **~about** *s* carrocel *m*; *adj* vago, indire(c)to; **~ish** arredondado; **~ness** redondeza *f*; **~shouldered** curvado; **~trip** *s* viagem *f* de ida e volta; curva *f*, volta *f*, giro *m*

rouse [rauz] *v/t* despertar; animar, sacudir

route [ru:t] *s* rota *f*, rumo *m*; caminho *m*

routine [ru:'ti:n] *s* rotina *f*; *adj* rotineiro

rove [rəuv] *v/t*, *v/i* vaguear

row [rəu] *v/t*, *v/i* remar; *s* fileira *f*, fila *f*

row [rau] *s* barulho *m*; rixa *f*; *v/i* brigar, disputar-se

rowdy ['raudi] *adj* barulhento, turbulento

royal ['rɔiəl] *adj* real, régio; **~ist** *adj*, *s* realista *m*, *f*, monárquico *m*; **~ty** (*pl* **-ties**) realeza *f*; direitos *m/pl* de autor

rub [rʌb] *v/t*, *v/i* esfregar; **~ber** ['-ə] borracha *f*; galocha *f*

rubbish ['rʌbiʃ] *s* entulho *m*, lixo *m*; disparate *m*, *Braz* bobagem *f*

rubble ['rʌbl] *s* cascalho *m*

ruby ['ru:bi] rubi(m) *m*

rucksack ['rʌksæk] mochila *f*

rudder ['rʌdə] *s* leme *m*

ruddy ['rʌdi] *adj* corado, rosado

rude [ru:d] *adj* rude, grosseiro; descortês, malcriado

ruffle ['rʌfl] *v/t*, *v/i* encrespar; irritar(-se); eriçar

rug [rʌg] *s* manta *f* de viagem; tapete *m*

rugby ['rʌgbi] râguebi *m*

rugged ['rʌgid] *adj* duro, austero

ruin [ruin] *s* ruína *f*; *v/t* arruinar; **~ous** ruinoso

rule [ru:l] *s* regra *f*; governo *m*, mando *m*; régua *f*; *v/t*, *v/i* decidir, decretar; reger, governar; **~ out** excluir; **~r** ['-ə] governante *m*; régua *f*

rum [rʌm] rum *m*

Rumanian [ru(:)'meinjən] *adj*, *s* romeno *m*

rumble ['rʌmbl] *s* rumor *m*, ruído *m*; estrondo *m*; *v/i* retumbar; estrondear

ruminate ['ru:mineit] v/i ruminar; magicar, meditar

rumo(u)r ['ru:mə] boato m

rump [rʌmp] alcatra f

rumple ['rʌmpl] v/t amarrotar; desgrenhar

run [rʌn] s corrida f; marcha f; percurso m; traje(c)to m; série f, sequência f; v/t, v/i dirigir, administrar; correr; circular; andar, funcionar; fazer carreira; **in the long ~** com o decorrer do tempo; **~ after** correr atrás de; andar atrás de; **~-away** adj, s fugitivo m; **~ away** fugir; **~ back** voltar, retroceder; **~ into** espetar; esbarrar(-se) com; **~ on** continuar; **~ out** esgotar-se; **~ out of** esgotar, não ter mais; **~ to** chegar, montar a; **~ up** v/t hastear; acumular; **~ner** corredor m; **~ning** s corrida f; adj corrente; consecutivo; contínuo

runway ['rʌnwei] pista f de descolagem

rupture ['rʌptʃə] s rompimento m, ruptura f; hérnia f; v/t, v/i romper(-se)

rurál [ruərəl] rural

rush [rʌʃ] s investida f, acometida f; pressa f; torrente f; tropel m; bot junco m; v/t, v/i precipitar(-se); investir, acometer; apressar-se, lançar-se; **~-hour** hora f de ponta

Russian ['rʌʃən] adj, s russo m

rust [rʌst] s ferrugem f; v/t, v/i enferrujar(-se)

rustic ['rʌstik] adj rústico; s camponês m

rustle ['rʌsl] s sussurro m; v/t, v/i farfalhar, sussurrar

rusty ['rʌsti] ferrugento, enferrujado

rut [rʌt] s sulco m, trilho m

ruthless ['ru:θlis] desapiedado, implacável, cruel; **~ness** crueldade f, implacabilidade f

rye [rai] centeio m

S

sable ['seibl] szibelina f; pele f de marta-zibelina

sabotage ['sæbəta:ʒ] s sabotagem f; v/t sabotar

sabre ['seibə] s sabre m

sack [sæk] s saco m, saca f; saque m; v/t saquear; demitir; **get the ~** ser despedido, ser posto na rua; **give the ~** despedir, pôr na rua; **hit the ~** ir deitar-se

sacrament ['sækrəmənt] sacramento m

sacred ['seikrid] sagrado

sacri|fice ['sækrifais] v/t, v/i sacrificar; s sacrifício m; **~le-gious** [-'lidʒəs] sacrílego; **~sty** [-sti] (pl **-ties**) sacristia f

sad [sæd] triste; **~den** v/t, v/i entristecer(-se)

saddl|e ['sædl] s sela f; selim m; v/t selar; **~er** seleiro m

sadness ['sædnis] tristeza f

safe [seif] s cofre m; adj salvo; seguro; ~ **and sound** são e salvo; ~ **conduct** salvo-conduto *m*; ~**guard** *s* salvaguarda *f*; *v/t* proteger, salvaguardar

safety ['seifti] segurança *f*; ~ **belt** cinto *m* de segurança; ~**pin** alfinete *m* de segurança; ~ **razor** gilete *f*; ~**valve** válvula *f* de segurança

saffron ['sæfrən] açafrão *m*

sag [sæg] *v/i* vergar, ceder; baixar

sagacity [sə'gæsiti] sagacidade *f*

sage [seidʒ] *s* sábio *m*; *bot* salva *f*

sago ['seigəu] sagu *m*

sail [seil] *v/t, v/i* navegar; velejar; *s* vela *f*; veleiro *m*; **set** ~ fazer-se à vela; ~**ing** *s* navegação *f*; ~**ing-boat** barco *m* à vela, veleiro *m*; ~**or** marinheiro *m*

saint [seint] santo *m*

sake [seik]: **for the** ~ **of** por causa de, por amor de; **for my** ~ por mim; **for God's** ~ por amor de Deus; **for the** ~ **of appearances** para salvar as aparências

salad ['sæləd] salada *f*; ~ **dressing** tempero *m* para salada

salary ['sæləri] (*pl* -**ies**) ordenado *m*

sale [seil] venda *f*; leilão *m*; saldo *m*, liquidação *f*; **on** ~ à venda; ~**able** vendável, vendível

sales|man ['seilzmən] (*pl* -**men**) caixeiro *m*, vendedor *m*; ~**woman** vendedora *f*

salient ['seiljənt] *adj* saliente

saliva [sə'laivə] saliva *f*

sallow ['sæləu] *adj* pálido, amarelado

sally ['sæli] (*pl* -**lies**) *mil* saída *f*; dito *m* espirituoso

salmon ['sæmən] salmão *m*

saloon [sə'lu:n] salão *m*; bar *m*

salt [sɔ:lt] *s* sal *m*; *v/t* salgar

saltpetre ['sɔ:ltpi:tə] salitre *m*

salty ['sɔ:lti] salgado

salu|tary ['sæljutəri] salutar; ~**tation** [-'teiʃən] saudação *f*; ~**te** [sə'lu:t] *v/t* saudar; *s* saudação *f*; salva *f*

salvage ['sælvidʒ] *s* salvados *m/pl*; salvamento *m*; *v/t* salvar

salvation [sæl'veiʃən] salvação *f*

salve [sa:v] *s* unguento *m*, pomada *f*, emplastro *m*

same [seim] *adj* mesmo, idêntico, igual; *pron* o mesmo; **all the** ~ do mesmo modo; **all the** ~ ainda assim, apesar disso; ~ **to you!** igualmente!

sample ['sa:mpl] *s* amostra *f*; *v/t* provar

sanatorium [.sænə'tɔ:riəm] sanatório *m*

sanctify ['sæŋktifai] *v/t* santificar

sanction ['sæŋkʃən] [-ʃən] *s* sanção *f*; aprovação *f*; *v/t* sancionar

sanct|ity ['sæŋktiti] (*pl* -**ties**) santidade *f*; ~**uary** [-tjuəri] (*pl* -**ries**) santuário *m*

sand [sænd] *s* areia *f*

sandal ['sændl] sandália *f*

sand|bank ['sændbæŋk] banco *m* de areia; ~**paper** *v/t* lixar; *s* lixa *f*

sandwich ['sænwidʒ] *s* anduíche *f*, sande *f*

sandy ['sændi] arenoso

sane [sein] são, sensato
sanit|ary ['sænitəri] sanitário; higiénico; **~ary towel/napkin** penso m higiénico; **~ation** [-'teiʃən] saneamento m; **~y** razão f
Santa Claus [sæntə 'klɔːz] Pai Natal m, Braz Papai m Noel
sap [sæp] s seiva f
sapper ['sæpə] sapador m
sapphire ['sæfaiə] safira f
sarcas|m ['sɑːkæzəm] sarcasmo m; **~tic** [-'kæstik] sarcástico
sardine [sɑː'diːn] sardinha f
sardonic [sɑː'dɒnik] sardónico
sash [sæʃ] cinto m, faixa f; caixilho m
Satan ['seitən] Satanás m; ♀ ic [sə'tænik] satânico
satchel ['sætʃəl] sacola f, pasta f
satellite ['sætəlait] satélite m
sat|iate ['seiʃieit] v/t saciar; **~iety** [sə'taiəti] saciedade f
satin ['sætin] cetim m
satis|faction [sætis'fækʃən] satisfação f; **~factory** satisfatório; **~fy** ['sætisfai] v/t, v/i satisfazer
Saturday ['sætədi] sábado m
sauc|e [sɔːs] s molho m; **~epan** caçarola f; **~er** pires m
saucy ['sɔːsi] impertinente, atrevido
saunter ['sɔːntə] v/i vaguear, saracotear; s passeio m
sausage ['sɒsidʒ] salsicha f
savage ['sævidʒ] adj, s selvagem m, f; **~ry** selvajaria f
save [seiv] v/t salvar; poupar, economizar; prp salvo, exce(p)to

savings ['seiviŋz] s/pl economias f/pl; **~-bank** caixa f económica
savio(u)r ['seivjə] salvador m
savo(u)r ['seivə] s sabor; v/t saborear; v/i ... saborear; s petisco m
savoy [sə'vɔi] sabóia f
saw [sɔː] s serra f; v/t, v/i serrar; **~dust** serradura f; **~yer** serrador m
Saxon ['sæksn] adj, s saxão m
saxophone ['sæksəfəun] saxofone m
say [sei] v/t, v/i dizer; **that is to ~** quer dizer; **you don't ~ (so)!** não me diga!; **you said it** assim o diz, tu o dizes; **~ing** s dito m; ritão m
scab [skæb] s escara f, crosta f
scabbard ['skæbəd] bainha f
scaffold ['skæfəld] cadafalso m, patíbulo m; andaime m; **~ing** andaime m
scald [skɔːld] v/t, v/i escaldar
scale [skeil] s escala f; escama f; balança f; v/t escalar, trepar por
scalp [skælp] s escalpo m; couro m cabeludo; v/t escalpar
scalpel ['skælpəl] escalpelo m
scan [skæn] v/t esquadrinhar; escandir
scandal ['skændl] escândalo m; maledicência f; **~ize** v/t escandalizar; **~ous** escandaloso
Scandinavian [skændi'neivjən] adj, s escandinavo m
scant [skænt] adj escasso
scanty ['skænti] exíguo
scapegoat ['skeipgəut] bode m

expiatório

scar [skɑ:] s cicatriz f; v/t, v/i cicatrizar

scarce [skɛəs] adj raro, escasso; **~ely** apenas, mal; **~ity** escassez f

scare [skɛə] v/t, v/i assustar (-se), espantar, amedrontar; **~ away** afugentar; **~crow** [-krəu] espantalho m

scarf [skɑ:f] cachecol m; lenço m de pescoço

scarlet ['skɑ:lit] s, adj escarlate m

scatter ['skætə] v/t, v/i espalhar; dispersar-se

scavenge ['skævindʒ] v/t, v/i vascular

scene [si:n] cena f; espe(c)táculo m; cenário m; vista f

scenery ['si:nəri] cenário m; panorama m

scent [sent] s cheiro m, aroma m, perfume m; faro m; pista f, rasto m; v/t cheirar; farejar; perfumar

sceptical ['skeptikəl] céptico

schedule ['ʃedju:l] s horário m, plano m; v/t marcar

scheme [ski:m] s esquema m, proje(c)to m, plano m

scholar ['skɔlə] erudito m; sábio m; bolseiro m, bolsista m, f; **~ly** erudito; **~ship** erudição f; bolsa f de estudos

school [sku:l] v/t treinar, adestrar; disciplinar; s escola f; colégio m; **~boy** aluno m; **~fellow** condiscípulo m; **~girl** aluna f; **~ing** s instrução f; educação f; **~mate** companheiro

m de escola

schooner ['sku:nə] escuna f

sciatica [saɪ'ætɪkə] ciática f

scien|ce ['saiəns] ciência f; **~tific** [-'tifik] científico; **~tist** ['-tist] cientista m, f

scissors ['sizəz] s/pl tesoura f

scoff [skɔf] v/i caçoar, zombar; s zombaria f

scold [skəuld] v/t, v/i ralhar, repreender

scoop [sku:p] s colherão m; alcatruz m; v/t vazar, despejar; escavar

scooter ['sku:tə] trotinete f, Braz patinete m; motoreta f

scope [skəup] alcance m, extensão f; espaço m; esfera f, campo m; **give ~ to** dar largas a

scorch [skɔ:tʃ] v/t, v/i queimar, chamuscar; s queimadura f

score [skɔ:] s contagem f, marcação f; vintena f; mus partitura f; v/t riscar, cortar; marcar; mus orquestrar

scorn [skɔ:n] s desprezo m, desdém m; v/t desprezar, desdenhar; **~ful** desdenhoso

Scotch [skɔtʃ] adj escocês; s uísque m

scot-free ['skɔt'fri:] impune

Scottish ['skɔtiʃ] escocês

scoundrel ['skaundrəl] velhaco m, patife m

scour ['skauə] v/t esfregar, arear; **~ for** percorrer

scourge [skə:dʒ] s açoute m; v/t açoutar

scout [skaut] v/t, v/i espiar, patrulhar; sentinela f avançada; escuteiro m, Braz escoteiro m

scowl [skaul] v/i franzir a testa, fazer carranca; s carranca f

scraggy ['skrægi] escanifrado, macilento

scramble ['skræmbl] s escalada f; luta f, disputa f; v/t, v/i trepar; disputar, lutar; **~d eggs** ovos m/pl mexidos

scrap [skræp] s pedaço m, fragmento m

scrape [skreip] v/t raspar; s raspadela f; aperto m, dificuldade f; **~e together/up** juntar, poupar; v/t raspador m

scratch [skrætʃ] v/t, v/i arranhar(-se); coçar; esgaravatar; s arranhão m, arranhadura f

scrawl [skrɔ:l] s rabisco m, gatafunho m; v/t, v/i rabiscar, garatujar

scream [skri:m] v/t, v/i, gritar; s grito m

screech [skri:tʃ] s guincho m; v/t, v/i guinchar; chiar

screen [skri:n] s tela f, écran m; biombo m; guarda-fogo m; v/t proteger, abrigar; abrigar; encobrir; proje(c)tar, exibir

screw [skru:] s parafuso m; naut hélice f; v/t aparafusar; **~driver** chave f de parafuso

scribble ['skribl] v/t, v/i escrevinhar, rabiscar; s rabisco m, garatuja f

script [skript] s escrita f, texto m, manuscrito m

Scripture ['skriptʃə] escritura f sagrada

scrub [skrʌb] v/t, v/i esfregar; s mato m; **~bing-brush** escova f de esfrega

scruffy ['skrʌfi] desmazelado, sujo

scruple ['skru:pl] s escrúpulo m; **~ulous** [-pjuləs] escrupuloso

scrutin|eer [skru:ti'niə] escrutinador m; **~ize** [-naiz] v/t escrutar, esquadrinhar; escrutinar; **~y** (pl -nies) exame m; escrutínio m

scuffle ['skʌfl] s rixa f, bulha f, tumulto m

scull [skʌl] s remo m; v/i remar

sculpt|or ['skʌlptə] escultor m; **~ure** [-tʃə] s escultura f; v/t, v/i esculpir

scum [skʌm] escuma f

scurf [skə:f] caspa f

scurry ['skʌri] v/i escapulir-se; apressar-se

scurvy ['skə:vi] s med escorbuto m; adj vil, ruim, desprezível

scuttle ['skʌtl] s balde m; v/t meter a pique; v/i escapar, fugir

scythe [saið] s gadanha f, segadeira f

sea [si:] mar m; **at ~** no mar, no mar alto; desnorteado, confuso; **~board** litoral m; **~food** mariscos m/pl; **~gull** gaivota f

seal [si:l] s selo m, sinete m, carimbo m; zo foca f; v/t selar; lacrar

sea|level ['si:'levl] nível m do mar

seam [si:m] s costura f

seaman ['si:mən] (pl -men [-men]) marinheiro m

search [sə:tʃ] v/t, v/i investigar;

buscar, procurar; *s* procura *f*, busca *f*, pesquisa *f*; **in ~ of** em busca de, à procura de; **~ing** *adj* penetrante; **~light** holofote *m*

sea|shell ['si:ʃel] concha *f*; **~ -shore** costa *f*, beira-mar *f*

seasick [si:sik] enjoado

seaside ['si:said] praia *f*, beira-mar *f*; **~ resort** estância *f* balnear

season ['si:zn] *s* estação *f*; temporada *f*; tempo *m*; ocasião *f*; *v/t* temperar, condimentar; **in ~** na época; **out of ~** fora de estação, fora da época; **~ing** *s* tempero *m*, condimento *m*; **~ ticket** bilhete *m* de assinatura

seat [si:t] *s* assento *m*; fundilhos *m/pl*; sede *f*; lugar *m*; *v/t* sentar; ter lugares para; **have/ take a ~** sentar-se; **~ belt** cinto *m* de segurança

seaweed ['si:wi:d] alga *f* marinha

seclu|ded [si'klu:did] *adj* retirado; **~sion** [-ʒən] retiro *m*; separação *f*

second ['sekənd] *s* segundo *m*; padrinho *m*; *adj* segundo; **on ~ thoughts** pensando melhor; *v/t* secundar, apoiar; **~ary** secundário *f*; **~ class** *s* segunda classe *f*; **~hand** *adj* em/de segunda mão

secrecy ['si:krisi] segredo *m*, sigilo *m*

secret ['si:krit] *s* segredo *m*; *adj* secreto; **in ~** em segredo; **~ariat** [.sekrə'teəriət] secretariado *m*; **~ary** ['sekrətri] (*pl*

-ries) secretário *m*, secretária *f*

secretion [si'kri:ʃən] secreção *f*

secretive ['si:kritiv] reservado, calado

sect [sekt] seita *f*; **~arian** [-'teəriən] *adj*, *s* sectário *m*

section ['sekʃən] *s* se(c)ção *f*

sector ['sektə] se(c)tor *m*

secular ['sekjulə] secular, profano; **~ize** [-'raiz] *v/t* secularizar

secure [si'kjuə] *adj* seguro; certo; firme; *v/t* assegurar; pôr no seguro; prender, amarrar

security [si'kjuəriti] (*pl* **-ties**) segurança *f*; garantia *f*, penhor *m*, fiança *f*; *pl* títulos *m/pl*, valores *m/pl*

sedate [si'deit] *adj* sereno, calmo, sossegado; **~ive** ['sedətiv] *s*, *adj* sedativo *m*, calmante *m*

sedentary ['sedntəri] sedentário

sediment ['sedimənt] sedimento *m*

seduc|e [si'dju:s] *v/t* seduzir; **~er** sedutor *m*; **~tion** [-'dʌkʃən] sedução *f*; **~tive** [-'dʌktiv] sedutor

see [si:] *s* sé *f*, sede *f* pontifical; *v/t*, *v/i* ver; acompanhar; compreender; **~ you later!** até à vista! **let me ~** deixe-me ver; you **~** como vê; **~ about** tratar de; **~ off** *v/t* ir despedir-se de, ir dizer adeus a

seed [si:d] *s* semente *f*

seeing [si:iŋ] *conj* (**that**) visto (que)

seek [si:k] *v/t* procurar, buscar

seem [si:m] *v/i* parecer; **~ing** *adj* aparente; **~ly** decente, decoroso

shilling [ˈʃiliŋ] xelim *m*

shin [ʃin] *s* canela *f* da perna

shine [ʃain] *v/i* brilhar; *v/t* dar lustre a; *s* brilho *m*

shingle [ˈʃiŋgl] *v/t* cobrir com ripas; *s* ripa *f*; seixo *m*

shiny [ˈʃaini] lustroso; brilhante, cintilante

ship [ʃip] *s* navio *m*, embarcação *f*, barco *m*; **~ment** embarque *m*; carregamento *m*; **~ping** *s* navegação *f*; marinha *f* mercante; **~wreck** *s* naufrágio *m*; *v/t* naufragar; **~yard** estaleiro *m*

shirk [ʃə:k] *v/t*, *v/i* fugir (a), esquivar-se (a)

shirt [ʃə:t] camisa *f*; **in one's ~sleeves** em mangas de camisa

shiver [ˈʃivə] *v/i* tiritar; *s* calafrio *m*, arrepio *m*

shoal [ʃəul] cardume *m*; baixio *m*

shock [ʃɔk] choque *m*, encontrão *m*; *v/t*, *v/i* chocar(-se); dar choque (a); assustar(-se); **~absorber** *auto* amortecedor *m*; **~ing** *adj* chocante; péssimo

shoe [ʃu:] *s* sapato *m*; *v/t* calçar; ferrar; **~black** engraxador *m*, *Braz* engraxate *m*; **~horn** calçadeira *f*; **~lace** atacador *m*; **~maker** sapateiro *m*; **~shop** sapataria *f*

shoot [ʃu:t] *v/t*, *v/i* matar a tiro, caçar; filmar; tirar um instantâneo (de); fuzilar; disparar, atirar, fazer fogo; chutar

shooting [ˈʃu:tiŋ] *s* caça *f*; tiros *m/pl*, tiroteio *m*; **~ star** estrela *f* cadente

shop [ʃɔp] *s* loja *f*; armazém *m*; *v/i* ir às compras, fazer compras; **~assistant** empregado *m*, vendedor *m*; **~keeper** lojista *m*, *f*; **~lifter** ladrão *m* de lojas

shopping [ˈʃɔpiŋ] *s* compras *f/pl*; **go ~** ir às compras; **~ centre** centro *m* comercial

shop-|steward [ˈʃɔp,stjuəd] representante *m*, *f* sindicalista; **~window** montra *f*

shore [ʃɔ:] *s* praia *f*; costa *f*; **on ~** em terra

short [ʃɔ:t] *adv* de repente; bruscamente; *adj* curto, breve; **in ~** em suma, em resumo; **~age** falta *f*; **~ circuit** *s* curto-circuito *m*; **~coming** defeito *m*, falta *f*; **~ cut** atalho *m*; **~en** *v/t*, *v/i* encurtar; **~hand** taquigrafia *f*, estenografia *f*; **~ly** brevemente, em breve; **~s** *s/pl* calções *m/pl* **~sighted** míope

shot [ʃɔt] *s* tiro *m*; bom atirador *m*; inje(c)ção *f*; tentativa *f*; foto *f*, instantâneo *m*; remate *m*, pontapé *m*

should [ʃəd, ʃud] *v/aux* I **~ like** queria, gostaria

shoulder [ˈʃəuldə] *s* ombro *m*; espádua *f*; *v/t* empurrar com os ombros; pôr ao ombro; arcar com, assumir; **~blade** omoplata *f*

shout [ʃaut] *s* grito *m*; *v/t*, *v/i* gritar; **~ing** *s* gritaria *f*

shove [ʃʌv] *v/t*, *v/i* empurrar; *s* empurrão *m*

shovel [ˈʃʌvl] *s* pá *f*

shifty

you a chair? quer que lhe vá buscar uma cadeira?

shallow [ˈʃæləu] adj raso; baixo, pouco profundo; fig superficial, trivial

sham [ʃæm] s impostura f; adj falso, fingido, postiço

shambles [ˈʃæmblz] s campo m de batalha; matadouro m; barafunda f

shame [ʃeim] s vergonha f; **what a ~!** que pena!; **~ful** vergonhoso; **~less** impúdico, imodesto, desavergonhado

shampoo [ʃæmˈpuː] s champô m, Braz xampu m

shape [ʃeip] s forma f, figura f, contorno m; v/t formar, dar forma a

share [ʃɛə] s parte f, porção f; com a(c)ção f; relha f; v/t, v/i repartir, distribuir; participar de, compartilhar

shark [ʃɑːk] zo tubarão m

sharp [ʃɑːp] adj agudo; aguçado, afiado; penetrante; astuto; acre; mordaz; picante; nítido, distinto; brusco; adv em ponto; **~en** v/t, v/i afiar, aguçar; **~ener** afia-lápis m, afiador m; **~ness** agudeza f; perspicácia f; mordacidade f

shatter [ˈʃætə] v/t, v/i estilhaçar; esmigalhar; despedaçar (-se)

shav|e [ʃeiv] v/t, v/i fazer a barba; barbear(-se); **~ing-brush** pincel m de barba; **~ing-cream** creme m para a barba; **~ing-stick** sabão m de barba

shawl [ʃɔːl] xa(i)le m

she [ʃiː, ʃi] pron ela; s fêmea f; menina f

sheaf [ʃiːf] (pl sheaves) [ʃiːvz] molho m, feixe m

shear [ʃiə] v/t tosquiar; **~s** [-z] s/pl tesoura f grande

sheath [ʃiːθ] bainha f, estojo m; **~e** [-ð] v/t embainhar

shed [ʃed] v/t, v/i deixar cair, largar, mudar; derramar; s alpendre m, barracão m

sheep [ʃiːp] ovelha f, carneiro m; **~fold** aprisco m, ovil m; **~ish** acanhado

sheer [ʃiə] adj fino; simples, puro; escarpado, íngreme

sheet [ʃiːt] folha f; lâmina f; lençol m

shelf [ʃelf] (pl shelves) [ʃelvz] prateleira f; estante f

shell [ʃel] s casca f; concha f; mil bomba f, granada f; v/t, v/i descascar; bombardear

shellfish [ˈʃel.fiʃ] marisco m

shelter [ˈʃeltə] s abrigo m; amparo m; asilo m, refúgio m; v/t, v/i abrigar(-se), resguardar, amparar

shepherd [ˈʃepəd] s pastor m

sherbet [ˈʃəːbət] sorvete m

sheriff [ˈʃerif] xerife m

sherry [ˈʃeri] xerez m, vinho m de Xerez

shield [ʃiːld] s escudo m; v/t amparar, proteger

shift [ʃift] s mudança f, desvio m; turno m; ardil m; v/t, v/i mudar; empurrar; mover(-se); **~ for oneself** governar a sua vida sozinho; **~y** ardiloso, astuto

seesaw ['si:sɔ:] *s* arre-burrinho *m*, *Braz* gangorra *f*

seethe [si:ð] *v/i* ferver; fervilhar

segregat|**e** ['segrigeit] *v/t*, *v/i* segregar; **~ed** *adj* segregado, separado

seiz|**e** [si:z] *v/t* agarrar; apreender; **~ure** [-ʒə] apreensão *f*; *med* ataque *m*

seldom ['seldəm] raras vezes, raramente

select [si'lekt] *v/t* escolher; *adj* sele(c)to, escolhido; **~ion** [-'lekʃən] sele(c)ção *f*, escolha *f*

self [self] *s* (*pl* **-selves** [selvz]) ego *m*, eu *m*; pessoa *f*; *pron* mesmo, próprio

self|-command ['selfkə'ma:nd] autodomínio *m*; **~-confident** seguro de si; **~-control** autodomínio *m*; **~-denial** abnegação *f*; **~-government** autonomia *f*; **~-importance** presunção *f*

selfish ['selfiʃ] egoísta; **~ness** egoísmo *m*

self|-made ['self'meid] feito por si; **~-possession** sangue-frio *m*; **~-respect** respeito *m* próprio, dignidade *f*; **~-sacrifice** abnegação *f*; **~-sufficient** auto-suficiente; **~-willed** teimoso, voluntarioso

sell [sel] *v/t*, *v/i* vender(-se); **~ off** liquidar; **~ out** esgotar; liquidar; **~er** vendedor *m*

semblance ['sembləns] aparência *f*, semelhança *f*

semicolon ['semi'kəulən] ponto *m* e vírgula *f*

seminary ['seminəri] (*pl* **-ries**)

seminário *m*

semolina [.semə'li:nə] sémola *f*

senat|**e** ['senit] senado *m*; **~or** ['-ətə] senador *m*

send [send] *v/t*, *v/i* enviar, mandar; transmitir, emitir

sender ['sendə] remetente *m*, *f*

senile ['si:nail] senil; **~ity** [si'niliti] senilidade *f*

senior ['si:njə] *adj* sénior, mais velho; mais antigo; **~ity** [.ni'oriti] antiguidade *f*

sensation [sen'seiʃən] sensação *f*; **~al** sensacional

sense [sens] *s* sentido *m*; juízo *m*, senso *m*; sentimento *m*; *v/t* perceber; pressentir, sentir; **~less** insensato; sem sentidos, desmaiado

sensib|**ility** [.sensi'biliti] sensibilidade *f*; **~le** ['-əbl] sensato

sens|**itive** ['sensitiv] sensível; sensitivo, impressionável; **~ual** ['-sjuəl] sensual

sentence ['sentəns] *s* frase *f*; sentença *f*, julgamento *m*

sentiment ['sentimənt] sentimento *m*; **~al** ['-mentl] sentimental

sentry ['sentri] (*pl* **-ries**) sentinela *f*; **~ box** guarita *f*

separat|**e** ['sepəreit] *v/t*, *v/i* separar(-se); ['sepərit] *adj* separado; **~ion** [-'reiʃən] separação *f*

September [sep'tembə] Setembro *m*

septic ['septik] séptico

sequel ['si:kwəl] consequência *f*

sequence ['si:kwens] sequência *f*, série *f*, sucessão *f*

serene [si'ri:n] sereno

sergeant ['sɑːdʒənt] sargento *m*

seri|al ['siəriəl] *adj* serial, em série; *s* folhetim *m*; **~es** ['-riːz] série *f*

serious ['siəriəs] serio; **~ly** *a* sério; **~ness** gravidade *f*

sermon ['səːmən] sermão *m*

serpent ['səːpənt] serpente *f*

serum ['siərəm] soro *m*

servant ['səːvənt] criado *m*

serve [səːv] *v/t, v/i* servir

service ['səːvis] *s* serviço *m*; **~able** útil

serviette [ˌsəːvi'et] *s* guardanapo *m*

servile ['səːvail] servil

session ['seʃən] sessão *f*

set [set] *s* jogo *m*, cole(c)ção *f*; série *f*; aparelho *m*; círculo *m*; grupo *m*; cenário *m*; *v/t, v/i* colocar, pôr, meter; solidificar-se; pôr-se; acertar, regular; *adj* marcado, fixo; decidido, determinado; prescrito; **~ fire to** deitar fogo a; **~ the table** pôr a mesa; **~ down** pousar; anotar, pôr por escrito; deixar; **~ off** abalar, partir; realçar; **~back** *s* revés *m*, contratempo *m*

settee [se'tiː] sofá *m*

setting ['setiŋ] *s* fundo *m*, cenário *m*; pôr *m*, ocaso *m*; engaste *m*; montagem *f*

settle ['setl] *v/t, v/i* colocar, fixar(-se); liquidar, pagar; ajustar; pousar; fixar residência; estabelecer-se; **~ment** estabelecimento *m*; povoado *m*; **~r** colono *m*

seven ['sevn] sete; **~ hundred** setecentos; **~teen** dezassete;

~th ['-θ] sétimo; **~ty** setenta

sever [sevə] *v/t, v/i* separar, cortar

several ['sevərəl] *adj, pron* vários

sever|e [si'viə] severo; **~ity** ['-'veriti] severidade *f*

sew [sou] *v/t, v/i* coser, costurar

sewer ['sjuːə] cano *m* de esgoto

sewing ['souiŋ] *s* costura *f*; **~-machine** máquina *f* de costura

sex [seks] sexo *m*

sexton ['sekstən] sacristão *m*

sexual ['seksjuəl] sexual

shabby ['ʃæbi] coçado; mal vestido; mesquinho

shade [ʃeid] *s* sombra *f*; matiz *m*; *v/t* sombrear; matizar; **in the ~** à sombra

shadow ['ʃædou] *s* sombra *f*; *v/t* sombrear; seguir, perseguir; **in, under the ~** of à sombra de; **~y** sombrio, tenebroso; vago

shady ['ʃeidi] sombrio, sombreado, umbroso; *fig* suspeito

shaft [ʃɑːft] *s* haste *f*; fuste *m*; eixo *m*, veio *m*; raio *m*, feixe *m*

shaggy ['ʃægi] hirsuto; cabeludo

shake [ʃeik] *v/t, v/i* abanar; abalar, tremer; sacudir, agitar; apertar; *s* abalo *m*, estremecimento *m*; sacudidela *f*; vibração *f*; aperto *m*; batido *m*; **~ hands (with someone)** apertar a(s) mão(s) (a alguém); **~ one's head** abanar a cabeça

shaky ['ʃeiki] trémulo, vacilante

shall [ʃæl, ʃəl] *v/aux* dever, ter de; **~ we go?** vamos?; **~ I get**

you a chair? quer que lhe vá buscar uma cadeira?

shallow ['ʃæləu] *adj* raso; baixo, pouco profundo; *fig* superficial, trivial

sham [ʃæm] *s* impostura *f*; *adj* falso, fingido, postiço

shambles ['ʃæmblz] *s* campo *m* de batalha; matadouro *m*; barafunda *f*

shame [ʃeim] *s* vergonha *f*; **what a ~!** que pena!; **~ful** vergonhoso; **~less** impúdico, imodesto, desavergonhado

shampoo [ʃæm'pu:] *s* champô *m*, *Braz* xampu *m*

shape [ʃeip] *s* forma *f*, figura *f*, contorno *m*; *v/t* formar, dar forma a

share [ʃɛə] *s* parte *f*, porção *f*; *com* a(c)ção *f*; relha *f*; *v/t*, *v/i* repartir, distribuir; participar de, compartilhar

shark [ʃɑːk] *zo* tubarão *m*

sharp [ʃɑːp] *adj* agudo; aguçado, afiado; penetrante; astuto; acre; mordaz; picante; nítido, distinto; brusco; *adv* em ponto; **~en** *v/t*, *v/i* afiar, aguçar; **~ener** afia-lápis *m*, afiador *m*; **~ness** agudeza *f*; perspicácia *f*; mordacidade *f*

shatter ['ʃætə] *v/t*, *v/i* estilhaçar; esmigalhar; despedaçar (-se)

shav|e [ʃeiv] *v/t*, *v/i* fazer a barba; barbear(-se); **~ing-brush** pincel *m* de barba; **~ing-cream** creme *m* para a barba; **~ing-stick** sabão *m* de barba

shawl [ʃɔːl] xa(i)le *m*

she [ʃiː, ʃi] *pron* ela; *s* fêmea *f*; menina *f*

sheaf [ʃiːf] (*pl* **sheaves** [ʃiːvz]) molho *m*, feixe *m*

shear [ʃiə] *v/t* tosquiar; **~s** [-z] *s/pl* tesoura *f* grande

sheath [ʃiːθ] bainha *f*, estojo *m*; **~e** [-ð] *v/t* embainhar

shed [ʃed] *v/t*, *v/i* deixar cair, largar, mudar; derramar; *s* alpendre *m*, barracão *m*

sheep [ʃiːp] ovelha *f*, carneiro *m*; **~fold** aprisco *m*, ovil *m*; **~ish** acanhado

sheer [ʃiə] *adj* fino; simples; puro; escarpado, íngreme

sheet [ʃiːt] folha *f*; lâmina *f*; lençol *m*

shelf [ʃelf] (*pl* **shelves** [ʃelvz]) prateleira *f*; estante *f*

shell [ʃel] *s* casca *f*; concha *f*; *mil* bomba *f*, granada *f*; *v/t*, *v/i* descascar; bombardear

shellfish ['ʃel.fiʃ] marisco *m*

shelter ['ʃeltə] *s* abrigo *m*; amparo *m*; asilo *m*, refúgio *m*; *v/t*, *v/i* abrigar(-se), resguardar, amparar

shepherd ['ʃepəd] *s* pastor *m*

sherbet ['ʃɜːbət] sorvete *m*

sheriff ['ʃerif] xerife *m*

sherry ['ʃeri] xerez *m*, vinho *m* de Xerez

shield [ʃiːld] *s* escudo *m*; *v/t* amparar, proteger

shift [ʃift] *s* mudança *f*, desvio *m*; turno *m*; ardil *m*; *v/t*, *v/i* mudar; empurrar; mover(-se); **~ for oneself** governar a sua vida sozinho; **~y** ardiloso, astuto shilling [ˈʃiliŋ] xelim *m*

shin [ʃin] *s* canela *f* da perna

shine [ʃain] *v/i* brilhar; *v/t* dar lustre a; *s* brilho *m*

shingle [ˈʃiŋgl] *v/t* cobrir com ripas; *s* ripa *f*; seixo *m*

shiny [ˈʃaini] lustroso; brilhante, cintilante

ship [ʃip] *s* navio *m*, embarcação *f*, barco *m*; ~ment embarque *m*; carregamento *m*; ~ping *s* navegação *f*; marinha *f* mercante; ~wreck *s* naufrágio *m*; *v/t* naufragar; ~yard estaleiro *m*

shirk [ʃəːk] *v/t, v/i* fugir (a), esquivar-se (a)

shirt [ʃəːt] camisa *f*; in one's ~-sleeves em mangas de camisa

shiver [ˈʃivə] *v/i* tiritar; *s* calafrio *m*, arrepio *m*

shoal [ʃəul] cardume *m*; baixio *m*

shock [ʃɔk] *s* choque *m*, encontrão *m*; *v/t, v/i* chocar(-se); dar choque (a); assustar(-se); ~-absorber *auto* amortecedor *m*; ~ing *adj* chocante; péssimo

shoe [ʃuː] *s* sapato *m*; *v/t* calçar; ferrar; ~black engraxador *m*, *Braz* engraxate *m*; ~horn calçadeira *f*; ~-lace atacador *m*; ~maker sapateiro *m*; ~-shop sapataria *f*

shoot [ʃuːt] *v/t, v/i* matar a tiro, caçar; filmar; tirar um instantâneo (de); fuzilar; disparar, atirar, fazer fogo; chutar

shooting [ˈʃuːtiŋ] *s* caça *f*; tiros *m/pl*, tiroteio *m*; ~ star estrela *f* cadente

shop [ʃɔp] *s* loja *f*; armazém *m*; *v/i* ir às compras, fazer compras; ~-assistant empregado *m*, vendedor *m*; ~-keeper lojista *m, f*; ~-lifter ladrão *m* de lojas

shopping [ˈʃɔpiŋ] *s* compras *f/pl*; go ~ ir às compras; ~ centre centro *m* comercial

shop-steward [ˈʃɔpˌstjuəd] representante *m, f* sindicalista *f*; ~-window montra *f*

shore [ʃɔː] *s* praia *f*; costa *f*; on ~ em terra

short [ʃɔːt] *adv* de repente; bruscamente; *adj* curto, breve; in ~ em suma, em resumo; ~age falta *f*; ~ circuit *s* curto-circuito *m*; ~coming defeito *m*, falta *f*; ~cut atalho *m*; ~en *v/t, v/i* encurtar; ~hand taquigrafia *f*, estenografia *f*; ~ly brevemente, em breve; ~s *s/pl* calções *m/pl* ~-sighted míope

shot [ʃɔt] *s* tiro *m*; bom atirador *m*; inje(c)ção *f*; tentativa *f*; foto *f*, instantâneo *m*; remate *m*, pontapé *m*

should [ʃəd, ʃud] *v/aux* 1 ~ like queria, gostaria

shoulder [ˈʃəuldə] *s* ombro *m*; espádua *f*; *v/t* empurrar com os ombros; pôr ao ombro; arcar com, assumir; ~-blade omoplata *f*

shout [ʃaut] *s* grito *m*; *v/t, v/i* gritar; ~ing *s* gritaria *f*

shove [ʃʌv] *v/t, v/i* empurrar; *s* empurrão *m*

shovel [ˈʃʌvl] *s* pá *f*

cunhada f

sit [sit] *v/t, v/i* sentar(-se); estar sentado; pousar, empoleirar-se; ficar/estar situado; reunir-se em sessão; posar; chocar; **~ up** *v/t, v/i* ficar até tarde, deitar-se tarde; endireitar-se

site [sait] *s* local *m*, sítio *m*; terreno *m*

sitting ['sitiŋ] *adj* sentado; *s* sessão *f*; **~-room** sala *f* de estar

situat|ed ['sitjueitid] *adj* situado, sito, colocado; **~ion** situação *f*

six [siks] seis; **~ hundred** seiscentos; **~teen** [-'ti:n] dezasseis; **~th** [-θ] sexto; **~ty** sessenta

size [saiz] *s* tamanho *m*; medida *f*, número *m*

sizzle ['sizl] *v/i* chiar

skate [skeit] *s* patim *m*; *zo* arraia *f*; *v/i* patinar; andar de patins

skating-rink ['skeitiŋriŋk] recinto *m* de patinagem

skeleton ['skelitn] esqueleto *m*

sketch [sketʃ] *s* esboço *m*, bosquejo *m*; *v/t, v/i* esboçar, bosquejar

ski [ski:] *s* esqui *m*; *v/i* esquiar, andar de esqui

skid [skid] *v/i* derrapar; *s* derrapagem *f*

skil(l)ful ['skilful] destro, hábil

skill [skil] perícia *f*, destreza *f*, habilidade *f*; **~ed** *adj* perito, especializado

skim [skim] *v/t* roçar; escumar; desnatar; tirar a nata ao

skin [skin] *s* pele *f*; casca *f*; *v/t* esfolar; descascar; **~-deep** superficial; **~flint** sovina *m, f*;

~ny magro, descarnado

skip [skip] *v/t, v/i* saltar, pular; omitir; *s* salto *m*, pulo *m*

skirmish ['skə:miʃ] *s* escaramuça *f*; *v/i* escaramuçar

skirt [skə:t] *s* saia *f*; *v/t* costear, marginar

skittles ['skitlz] *s* jogo *m* da bola aos pinos, *Braz* jogo *m* de boliche

skull [skʌl] crânio *m*

sky [skai] *s* (*pl* **skies**) céu *m*; **~-blue** azul-celeste; **~lark** *s* cotovia *f*; **~light** clarabóia *f*; **~scraper** arranha-céus *m*

slab [slæb] chapa *f*, laje *f*, tábua *f*, prancha *f*

slack [slæk] *v/i* mandriar; *adj* frouxo, lasso, bambo; negligente; **~en** *v/t, v/i* afrouxar; relaxar; diminuir; **~s** *s/pl* calças *f/pl*

slag [slæg] escória *f*

slake [sleik] *v/t* mitigar, satisfazer

slam [slæm] *v/t, v/i* bater, fechar com violência; *s* pancada *f*, batimento *m*; capote *m*

slander ['slɑ:ndə] *v/t* difamar, caluniar; *s* calúnia *f*, difamação *f*

slang [slæŋ] *s* calão *m*, gíria *f*

slant [slɑ:nt] *s* inclinação *f*; *v/t, v/i* inclinar(-se)

slap [slæp] *s* palmada *f*, bofetada *f*; *v/t* esbofetear

slash [slæʃ] *s* cutilada *f*; *v/t, v/i* acutilar, retalhar

slate [sleit] *s* lousa *f*; ardósia *f*; telha *f*; *v/t* censurar

slaughter ['slɔ:tə] *s* matança *f*,

carnificina f; v/t matar, massacrar; abater; **~-house** matadoiro m, açougue m

slave [sleiv] s escravo m; **~ry** escravidão f

Slavic ['slævik] adj eslavo

sled(ge) [sled(ʒ)] s trenó m; v/i andar de trenó

sleek [sli:k] adj liso, macio

sleep [sli:p] s sono m; v/i dormir; **go to ~** adormecer; **~ing-bag** saco m de dormir; **~less** sem dormir; **~-walker** sonâmbulo m; **~y** sonolento, amodorrado, com sono

sleet [sli:t] s pedrisco m

sleeve [sli:v] manga f; **laugh up one's ~** rir-se à socapa

sleigh [slei] s trenó m de cavalo

slender ['slendə] franzino, esbelto, fino

slice [slais] s fatia f; v/t cortar em fatias

slick [slik] adj escorregadio; manhoso

slide [slaid] v/t, v/i resvalar, deslizar, escorregar; esguerrar-se; s diapositivo m; resvaladouro m

sliding ['slaidiŋ] adj corrediço, corredio

slight [slait] adj leve, ligeiro; pequeno, curto; fraco; s afronta f; v/t desprezar, desdenhar; **~ly** levemente

slim [slim] adj diminuto; franzino, esbelto; v/i emagrecer

slim|e [slaim] limo m; **~y** limoso

sling [sliŋ] s funda f; tiracolo m; v/t suspender; arrojar, atirar, arremessar

slip [slip] s escorregadela f; combinação f; deslize m, lapso m; tira f de papel; v/i escorregar, resvalar; escapulir-se; enfiar

slipper ['slipə] chinelo m, chinela f

slippery ['slipəri] escorregadio

slit [slit] s fenda f; v/t fender

slobber ['slɔbə] s baba f; v/t, v/i babar(-se)

sloe [sləu] abrunho m

slogan ['sləugən] divisa f, lema m

slope [sləup] s inclinação f; s ladeira f, rampa f, declive m; v/i inclinar-se; **~ off** escapulir-se

sloppy ['slɔpi] desmazelado; piegas, lamecha

slot [slɔt] s ranhura f

sloth [sləuθ] zo preguiça f

slot-machine ['slɔtmə,ʃi:n] automático m

slouch [slautʃ] v/i andar curvado

slough [slau] s lamaçal m

slovenly ['slʌvnli] desleixado

slow [sləu] adj lento, vagaroso; atrasado; v/t, v/i abrandar, afrouxar a velocidade **~ly** devagar, vagarosamente; **~ness** lentidão f

slug [slʌg] s zo lesma f

sluice [slu:s] s comporta f

slum [slʌm] s bairro m da lata, Braz favela f

slur [slə:] mancha f, desdoiro m; v/t arrastar, engolir (as palavras); mus modular

slush [slʌʃ] lama f; neve f lamacenta

sly [slai] astuto; dissimulado,

snarl

manhoso

smack [smæk] *s* estalo *m*; pancada *f*, palmada *f*; sabor *m*, gosto *m*; beijoca *f*; *v/t* espancar; estalar

small [smɔ:l] *adj* pequeno; miúdo, ténue, exíguo; **~ change** troco *m* miúdo; **~ hours** altas horas *f/pl* da noite; **~ness** pequenez *f*

smallpox ['smɔ:lpɔks] varíola *f*

smalls [smɔ:lz] *s/pl* roupa *f* miúda

small talk [smɔ:l 'tɔ:k] conversa *f* banal

smart [smɑ:t] *adj* vivo, hábil, engenhoso; elegante; inteligente; *v/i* picar; doer; **~ness** elegância *f*

smash [smæʃ] *v/t*, *v/i* esmagar (-se); quebrar, espatifar; *s* colisão *f*, acidente *m*; **~ing** *adj* formidável, bestial

smear [smiə] *v/t*, *v/i* cobrir, untar; caluniar; *s* mancha *f*, nódoa *f*; difamação *f*

smell [smel] *s* odor *m*, cheiro *m*, aroma *m*; olfa(c)to *m*; *v/t*, *v/i* cheirar

smelt [smelt] *v/t* fundir

smil|e [smail] *v/t*, *v/i* sorrir; *s* sorriso *m*; **~ing** *adj* sorridente, risonho

smirk [smə:k] *s* sorriso *m* afe(c)tado; *v/i* sorrir afe(c)tadamente

smith [smiθ] forjador *m*; **~y** ['-ði] forja *f*

smitten ['smitn] enamorado, apaixonado

smog [smɔg] nevoeiro *m* de fumos

smoke [smouk] *s* fumo *m*; fumaça *f*; *v/t*, *v/i* fumar; fumegar; **~less** sem fumo, sem fumaça

smok|er ['smoukə] fumador *m*, fumista *m*, *f*; **~ing** *s* fumar *m*; **no ~ing** é proibido fumar; **~y** fumegante, fumarento

smooth [smu:ð] *adj* macio; liso, plano

smother ['smʌðə] *v/t*, *v/i* abafar, sufocar

smou(l)der ['smouldə] *v/i* arder sem chama; estar latente

smudge [smʌdʒ] *s* mancha *f*, nódoa *f*; borrão *m*; *v/t* manchar; borrar

smuggl|e ['smʌgl] *v/t* passar em contrabando; fazer contrabando; **~er** contrabandista *m*, *f*; **~ing** *s* contrabando *m*

smut [smʌt] *s* farrusca *f*, mascarra *f*; obscenidade *f*; **~ty** sujo, tisnado; obsceno

snack [snæk] *s* refeição *f* ligeira

snag [snæg] *s* empecilho *m*, obstáculo *m*

snail [sneil] caracol *m*; **at a ~'s pace** como um caracol

snake [sneik] *s* cobra *f*

snap [snæp] *s* estalo *m*, estalido *m*; *v/t*, *v/i* abocanhar; tirar um instantâneo (de); romper, quebrar; (fazer) estalar; **~pish** resmungão; **~shot** instantâneo *m*

snare [snɛə] *s* laço *m*, armadilha *f*; cilada *f*

snarl [snɑ:l] *v/t*, *v/i* rosnar; resmungar; *s* rosnadura *f*

snatch [snætʃ] *s* bocado *m*; *v/t*, *v/i* arrebatar

sneak [sni:k] *s* delator *m*

sneaker ['sni:kə] alpergatas *f/pl*; sapatos *m/pl* de ginástica

sneer [sniə] *v/i* mofar, zombar; *s* riso *m* zombador

sneeze [sni:z] *v/i* espirrar; *s* espirro *m*

sniff [snif] *s* fungadel(a) *f*; *v/i* farejar; cheirar; fungar; ~ **at** torcer o nariz, desdenhar

snip [snip] *v/t*, *v/i* cortar; *s* tesourada *f*

snipe [snaip] *s* narceja *f*

snob [snɔb] snobe *m*, *Braz* esnobe *m*

snoop [snu:p] *v/i* meter o nariz em, bisbilhotar

snooze [snu:z] *s* soneca *f*; *v/i* dormitar

snore [snɔ:] *v/i* ressonar, roncar; *s* ronco *m*

snort [snɔ:t] *v/i* bufar

snout [snaut] focinho *m*

snow [snəu] *s* neve *f*; *v/i* nevar; ~**-storm** nevasca *f*; ~**y** nevoso

snub [snʌb] *v/t* desprezar, ignorar; *s* desdenho *m*; ~**-nosed** de nariz chato

snuff [snʌf] *s* rapé *m*

snug [snʌg] *adj* aconchegado, agasalhado; cómodo, confortável

so [səu] *adv* assim; portanto, por isso; tão; tanto; *conj* para que; de maneira que; ~ **as to** de maneira a; ~ **long!** adeus! , até logo!; ~ **then** com que então; ~ **much** tanto; **and** ~

on e assim por diante; **I hope** ~ espero que sim; **I think** ~ creio que sim

soak [səuk] *v/t*, *v/i* embeber (-se), ensopar(-se), encharcar (-se)

soap [səup] *s* sabão *m*; sabonete *m*; *v/t* ensaboar

soar [sɔ:] *v/i* elevar-se, remontar-se

sob [sɔb] *s* soluço *m*; *v/i* soluçar

sober ['səubə] *adj* sóbrio; *v/t*, *v/i* moderar; ~ **up** desembriagar-se

sobriety [səu'braiəti] sobriedade *f*

so-called ['səu'kɔ:ld] assim chamado

soccer ['sɔkə] futebol *m*

sociable ['səuʃəbl] sociável

social ['səuʃəl] social; ~**ist** *adj*, *s* socialista *m*, *f*; ~**ize** *v/t* socializar

society [sə'saiəti] (*pl* -ties) sociedade *f*

sociology [.səusi'ɔlədʒi] sociologia *f*

sock [sɔk] *s* soquete *m*, meia *f*, peúga *f*

socket ['sɔkit] encaixe *m*; órbita *f*; alvéolo *m*; *elect* tomada *f*

sod [sɔd] *s* céspede *m*, torrão *m*

soda ['səudə] soda *f*

sodden ['sɔdn] ensopado, encharcado

sofa ['səufə] sofá *m*

soft [sɔft] mole, macio, tenro; brando, suave; flexível; ~**en** ['sɔfn] *v/t*, *v/i* amaciar, amolecer; enternecer; suavizar; ~**ness** maciez *f*, doçura *f*; suavidade f

soil [sɔil] s solo m, terra f; v/t, v/i sujar, manchar

solace ['sɔləs] s consolação f

solder ['sɔldə] v/t soldar

soldier ['səuldʒə] s soldado m

sole [səul] adj só, único; s sola f; planta f do pé; zo linguado m

solemn ['sɔləm] solene; **~ity** [sə'lemniti] (pl **-ties**) solenidade f

solicit [sə'lisit] v/t, v/i pedir, solicitar; **~or** procurador m

solicit|ous [sə'lisitəs] solícito; ansioso; **~ude** [-tju:d] ansiedade f

solid ['sɔlid] sólido

solidarity [sɔli'dæriti] solidariedade f

solidity [sə'liditi] solidez f

solitary ['sɔlitəri] adj solitário

solitude ['sɔlitju:d] solidão f

solo ['səuləu] s mus solo m

sol|uble ['sɔljubl] solúvel; **~ution** [sə'luʃən] solução f

solve [sɔlv] v/t resolver

solvent ['sɔlvənt] adj solvente

sombre ['sɔmbə] sombrio

some [sʌm] adj um pouco de; um, uma; certo, certa; algun(s), alguma(s), uns, umas; pron algum(s), alguma(s); um pouco, certa quantidade; adv um tanto; **~body**, **~one** alguém; **~how** de algum modo

somersault ['sʌməsɔ:lt] s cambalhota f; salto m mortal

some|thing ['sʌmθiŋ] adv algo, um tanto; pron alguma coisa; qualquer coisa; **~time** adv algum dia; outrora, antigamente;

~times às/por vezes; **~what** um tanto, algo; **~where** nalgum sítio, algures

somnambul|ism [sɔm'næmbjulizəm] sonambulismo m; **~ist** ɒonâmbulo m

son [sʌn] filho m

song [sɔŋ] canção f

son-in-law ['sʌninlɔ:] genro m

sonorous [sə'nɔ:rəs] sonoro

soon [su:n] em breve; **the ~er the better** quanto mais depressa melhor; **no ~er ... than** mal; **~er or later** mais cedo ou maistarde

soot [sut] s fuligem f

soothe [su:ð] v/t acalmar; aliviar

sophisticated [sə'fistikeitid] adj sofisticado

sorcer|er ['sɔ:sərə] feiticeiro m; **~ess** feiticeira f; **~y** feitiçaria f

sordid ['sɔ:did] sórdido; **~ness** sordidez f

sore [sɔ:] adj inflamado; dorido; magoado; s úlcera f, chaga f

sorrow ['sɔrəu] s pesar m, tristeza f, dor f; **~ful** pesaroso, triste

sorry ['sɔri] adj triste, desconsolado; **~!** desculpe!, sinto muito; **be/feel ~ for** ter/sentir pena de

sort [sɔ:t] s género m, espécie f; v/t classificar; selec(c)ionar; separar

sot [sɔt] bêbedo m

soul [səul] s alma f; **~ful** sentimental

sound [saund] adj são, sadio; bom, sólido; profundo; s som

m; v/t, v/i tocar; sondar; med
auscultar; soar, ressoar
soup [su:p] sopa f
sour ['sauə] adj azedo; v/t, v/i
azedar
source [sɔ:s] fonte f, origem f,
manancial m
souse [saus] v/t pôr de escabeche; ensopar, empapar
south [sauθ] s sul m; adv ao sul;
adj do sul, meridional;
~ward(s) [-wəd(s)] adv para o
sul
souther|ly ['sʌðəli] meridional; **~n** meridional, do sul
south-west [sauθ'west] s sudoeste m
souvenir ['su:vəniə] lembrança f
sovereign ['sɔvrin] adj, s soberano m; **~ty** [-'rənti] soberania f
Soviet ['səuviət] adj soviético
sow [sau] s porca f; [səu] v/t, v/i
semear
spa [spɑ:] estância f termal
space [speis] s espaço m; v/t espaçar; **~ship** nave f espacial
spacious ['speiʃəs] espaçoso
spade [speid] s pá f; espadas f/pl
span [spæn] s período m, espaço
m; envergadura f; palmo m;
v/t atravessar; abarcar, cobrir
spangle ['spæŋgl] s lentejoula f
Spaniard ['spænjəd] espanhol
m
spaniel ['spænjəl] sabujo m
Spanish ['spæniʃ] adj, s espanhol m
spank [spæŋk] v/t espancar
spanner ['spænə] chave f de
parafusos
spare [spɛə] v/t dispensar, pas-

sar sem; poupar; dispor de; adj
magro; de sobra, sobresselente,
de reserva; sóbrio, frugal, disponível
spark [spɑ:k] s centelha f, fagulha f, faísca f, chispa f; **~ing-plug** auto vela f de ignição;
~le [-l] v/i cintilar, faíscar
sparrow ['spærəu] pardal m
sparse [spɑ:s] escasso; ralo; raro
spasm ['spæzəm] espasmo m
spatter ['spætə] v/t salpicar; s
salpico m
speak [spi:k] v/t, v/i falar; **so to
~** por assim dizer; **~ one's
mind** falar com franqueza; **~
for** falar por; **~ out** falar abertamente; **~ up** falar alto; **~er** orador m; presidente m
spear [spiə] s lança f
special ['speʃəl] adj especial;
~ist especialista m, f; **~(i)ty**
[-ʃi'æliti] (pl -ties) especialidade f; **~ize** v/i especializar-se
species ['spi:ʃi:z] espécie f
specific [spi'sifik] adj específico
specify ['spesifai] v/t especificar
specimen ['spesimin] exemplar
m, espécime f
speck [spek] ponto m; mancha f;
partícula f; **~le** pinta f, salpico
m
spectac|le ['spektəkl] espe(c)táculo m; **~les** s/pl óculos m/pl;
~ular [-'tækjulə] adj espe(c)tacular
spectator [spek'teitə] espectador m
speculate ['spekjuleit] v/t, v/i
especular
speculation [spekju'leiʃən] es-

peculação f

speech [spiːtʃ] maneira f de falar; palavra f, fala f; discurso m; ~less sem fala

speed [spiːd] s velocidade f, rapidez f; v/i seguir a grande velocidade; acelerar; ~ limit limite m de velocidade; ~ometer [-'dɔmitə] conta-quilómetros m, velocímetro m; ~y veloz, rápido

spell [spel] v/t, v/i soletrar; escrever; s encanto m, feitiço m; ~bound encantado, fascinado; ~ing s ortografia f

spend [spend] v/t, v/i passar, despender, gastar; consumir; ~thrift esbanjador m, perdulário m, pródigo m

spent [spent] adj gasto; esgotado, estafado

sperm [spaːm] esperma m

sphere [sfiə] esfera f

spice [spais] s especiaria f

spick and span [ˌspikənˈspæn] novo em folha, flamante

spicy ['spaisi] condimentado; apimentado

spider ['spaidə] aranha f

spike [spaik] s espigão m; ponta f; cavilha f

spill [spil] v/t, v/i derramar, entornar; s queda f

spin [spin] v/t, v/i tecer, fiar; rodar, girar; s giro m, volta f

spinach ['spinidʒ] espinafre m

spinal ['spainl] espinhal

spindle ['spindl] fuso m

spine [spain] espinha f dorsal

spinning-wheel ['spiniŋwiːl] roda f de fiar

spinster ['spinstə] solteirona f

spiral ['spaiərəl] adj (em) espiral; s espiral f

spire [spaiə] flecha f, agulha f

spirit ['spirit] s espírito m; ânimo m; energia f; ~ed adj animado, vivaz; fogoso, brioso; ~less sem ânimo, sem vigor; ~ual [-'tjuəl] adj espiritual; ~ualism [ˈspiritjuəlizəm] espiritismo m; ~ualist espírita m, f

spit [spit] s cuspe m; espeto m; v/t, v/i espetar; cuspir

spite [spait] s rancor m, despeito m; **in** ~ **of** apesar de, a despeito de; ~ful vingativo, malévolo

spittle ['spitl] escarro m

splash [splæʃ] v/t, v/i patinhar, chapinhar; salpicar; s salpico m; chape m

spleen [spliːn] baço m; mau humor m

splend|id ['splendid] esplêndido; ~o(u)r esplendor m

splint [splint] tala f

splinter ['splintə] s lasca f, estilhaço m; v/t, v/i estilhaçar(-se)

split [split] v/t, v/i separar-se; fender; s fenda f, greta f

spoil [spoil] v/t, v/i estragar (-se), (a)mimar; ~t **child** mimalho m; ~s s/pl emolumentos m/pl

spoke [spəuk] s raio m

spokesman ['spəuksmən] (pl -men ['-men]) porta-voz m, f, representante m, f

sponge [spʌndʒ] s esponja f; v/t lavar com esponja

sponsor ['spɔnsə] s patrocinador

m; fiador *m*; padrinho *m*; *v/t* promover, patrocinar

spontaneous [spɔn'teinjəs] espontâneo

spook [spu:k] *s* fantasma *m*

spool [spu:l] bobina *f*; carretel *m*; rolo *m*

spoon [spu:n] *s* colher *f*; **~ful** colherada *f*

sporadic [spə'rædik] esporádico

sport [spɔ:t] *s* desporto *m*, *Braz* esporte *m*; *v/t* ostentar; **~ing** *adj* desportivo, *Braz* esportivo; **~ive** brincalhão; **~sman** desportista *m*, *Braz* esportista *m*

spot [spɔt] *s* sítio *m*, lugar *m*; ponto *m*; mancha *f*, nódoa *f*; *v/t*, *v/i* manchar(-se); enodoar, sujar; notar, reconhecer; **~light** *s* holofote *m*; publicidade *f*

spout [spaut] *s* jacto *m*, jorro *m*, goteira *f*; bico *m*; *v/t*, *v/i* jorrar; declamar

sprain [sprein] *v/t* torcer; *s* torcedura *f*, entorse *f*

sprat [spræt] espadilha *f*

sprawl [sprɔ:l] *v/i* estender-se; estatelar-se

spray [sprei] *s* borrifo *m*; espuma *f*; pulverizador *m*, vaporizador *m*; *v/t* borrifar; pulverizar

spread [spred] *v/t*, *v/i* espalhar (-se); abrir; estender(-se); propagar(-se); *s* extensão *f*; envergadura *f*

sprig [sprig] vergôntea *f*, raminho *m*

sprightly ['spraitli] esperto, vivo, alegre

spring [spriŋ] *s* primavera *f*; mola *f*; pulo *m*, salto *m*; fonte *f*; *v/i* pular, saltar, galgar; **~-board** trampolim *m*

sprinkle ['spriŋkl] *v/t*, *v/i* chuvisco *m*; *v/t*, *v/i* chuviscar; aspergir, borrifar

sprint [sprint] *v/i* correr a toda a velocidade

sprout [spraut] *s* renovo *m*, grelo *m*; couve-de-bruxelas *f*; *v/t*, *v/i* grelar, brotar

spruce [spru:s] *adj* elegante, janota

spur [spə:] *s* espora *f*; *v/t* esporear

spurt [spə:t] *v/i* esguichar; *s* esguicho *m*; arranco *m*; esforço *m*

spy [spai] *s* (*pl* spies) espia *m*, *f*, espião *m*; *v/i* espiar; espreitar; descortinar, notar

squabble ['skwɔbl] *s* briga *f*, rixa *f*; *v/i* brigar, bulhar

squadron ['skwɔdrən] esquadrão *m*; *naut* esquadra *f*

squalid ['skwɔlid] esquálido, sujo

squall [skwɔ:l] *s* berro *m*; ventania *f*, pé *m* de vento

squalor ['skwɔlə] sordidez *f*

squander ['skwɔndə] *v/t* esbanjar, malgastar

square [skweə] *s* quadrado *m*; praça *f*; *adj* quadrado; *v/t* quadrar, esquadr(i)ar; ajustar

squash [skwɔʃ] *s* suco *m*, sumo *m*; *v/t*, *v/i* espremer, esmagar; achatar

squat [skwɔt] *v/i* agachar-se, acocorar-se; *adj* atarracado squeak [skwi:k] s chiadeira f; grito m, chio m; v/i chiar, ranger

squeal [skwi:l] v/i guinchar; s guincho m

squeamish [ˈskwl:mlʃ] melindroso

squeeze [skwi:z] v/t, v/i comprimir; espremer; apertar; s apertão m

squid [skwid] lula f, calamar m

squint [skwint] s estrabismo m; v/i piscar os olhos

squire [ˈskwaiə] s escudeiro m

squirm [skwə:m] v/i contorcer-se

squirrel [ˈskwirəl] esquilo m

squirt [skwə:t] v/t, v/i esguichar; s esguicho m

stab [stæb] v/t, v/i apunhalar; s punhalada f

stabil|ity [stəˈbiliti] estabilidade f; ~ize [ˈsteibilaiz] v/t, v/i estabilizar

stable [ˈsteibl] s estrebaria f, cavalariça f; adj estável

stack [stæk] s montão m; pilha f; v/t amontoar; empilhar

stadium [ˈsteidiəm] estádio m

staff [sta:f] s mil estado-maior m; corpo m docente; pessoal m; bordão m; bastão m; vara f; mus pauta f

stag [stæg] veado m, cervo m

stage [steidʒ] s thea palco m; fase f; etapa f; v/t encenar, pôr em cena; organizar, preparar; representar; ~-coach diligência f

stagger [ˈstægə] v/i titubear, cambalear; alternar; s cambaleio m

stagna|nt [ˈstægnənt] estagnante; ~te [-ˈneit] v/i estagnar-se

staid [steid] grave, sério

stain [stein] s mancha f, nódoa f; v/t, v/i manchar; tingir, pintar; ~ed glass vitral m; ~less inoxidável

stair [steə] degrau m; ~case escadaria f; ~s s/pl escada f

stake [steik] s estaca f, poste m; pelourinho m; aposta f; v/t marcar com estacas; apostar, arriscar; at ~ em jogo, em risco

stale [steil] rançoso; seco, duro; velho, antiquado

stalk [stɔ:k] s haste f, talo m; pé m

stall [stɔ:l] s presebe m; tenda f, barraca f; thea poltrona f; v/t, v/i parar, deixar de trabalhar

stallion [ˈstæljən] garanhão m

stalwart [ˈstɔ:lwət] adj resoluto, decidido

stammer [ˈstæmə] v/t, v/i gaguejar; tartamudear; s gaguez f

stamp [stæmp] selo m; estampilha f; cunho m; carimbo m; v/t, v/i selar, pôr selo em; estampar, imprimir; carimbar; bater com os pés

stanch [stɑ:ntʃ] v/t estancar

stand [stænd] v/t, v/i estar de/ em pé; estar, estar situado; levantar-se, erguer-se, pôr(-se) de/em pé; colocar; aguentar, suportar; ficar; ~ by v/t, v/i manter(-se) dar apoio a; estar de lado; ~ for significar, representar; permitir, tolerar; ~ up *v/t* resistir; *s* resistência *f*, defesa *f*; posição *f*, opinião *f*; estante *f*; praça *f* de táxis; tribuna *f*; bancada *f*; sítio *m*, posto *m*; tenda *f*, barraca *f*

standard ['stændəd] *s* padrão *m*; nível *m*; critério *m*, medida *f*; norma *f*, estandarte *m*, bandeira *f*; *adj* normal, clássico, oficial; **~ize** *v/t* estandardizar

standby ['stændbai] *s* reserva *f*

standing ['stændiŋ] *adj* permanente; em pé; *s* posição *f*, reputação *f*; **of ten years' ~** com dez anos de exercício; **of long ~** de longa data

stand|offish ['stænd'ɔ:fiʃ] retraído, reservado; **~point** ponto *m* de vista; **~still** paragem *f*; imobilização *f*

star [sta:] *s* estrela *f*; astro *m*; *v/t, v/i* marcar com asteriscos; representar

starboard ['sta:bəd] estibordo *m*

starch [sta:tʃ] *s* amido *m*; goma *f*; fécula *f*; *v/t* engomar

stare [stɛə] *s* olhar *m* fixo; *v/i* fitar, olhar fixamente

stark [sta:k] *adj* completo, total; rígido

starling ['sta:liŋ] estorninho *m*

start [sta:t] *v/t, v/i* começar, principiar; estremecer; partir, iniciar viagem; *s* partida *f*; início *m*, começo *m*, princípio *m*; estremecimento *m*

startl|e ['sta:tl] *v/t* assustar, alarmar; **~ing** *adj* alarmante

starvation [sta:'veiʃən] fome *f*; inanição *f*

starve [sta:v] *v/t, v/i* passar fome; morrer de fome

state [steit] *s* estado *m*, condição *f*; estado *m*, nação *f*; pompa *f*; *v/t* declarar, expor; *jur* depor, asseverar

stately ['steitli] augusto, majestoso

statement ['steitmənt] declaração *f*; relatório *m*; *com* balanço *m*

statesman ['steitsmən] estadista *m*, homem *m* de estado

static ['stætik] *adj* estático

station ['steiʃən] *s* estação *f*; *v/t* estacionar, postar; **~ary** estacionário, fixo

station|er ['steiʃnər] dono *m* de papelaria; **~ery** ['steiʃnri] artigos *m/pl* de escritório

statistic|al [stə'tistikəl] estatístico; **~s** estatística *f*

statue ['stætju:] estátua *f*

statute ['stætju:t] estatuto *m*

sta(u)nch [sta:ntʃ (stɔ:ntʃ)] *v/t* estancar; *adj* dedicado, leal

stay [stei] *s naut* estai *m*; estada *f*, estadia *f*; *v/t* ficar, permanecer, demorar-se

stead|fast ['stedfəst] constante, firme; **~y** *adj* firme; seguro, estável

steak [steik] bife *m*

steal [sti:l] *v/t, v/i* roubar, furtar

stealth [stelθ] recato *m*; **by ~** às furtadelas, às escondidas; **~y** furtivo, clandestino

steam [sti:m] *s* vapor *m*; *v/t, v/i* fumegar; cozinhar a vapor; deitar vapor; **~er** (navio *m* a) vapor *m*

steel [sti:l] *s* aço *m*; *v/t* acerar, revestir de aço; fortalecer-se, endurecer

steep [sti:p] *adj* escarpado, íngreme; exorbitante, excessivo

steeple ['sti:pl] torre *f*, campanário *m*

steeplechase ['sti:pltʃeis] corrida *f* de obstáculos

steer [stiə] *s* novilho *m*; *v/t*, *v/i* conduzir, dirigir, guiar; **~ing-wheel** volante *m*

stem [stem] *s* haste *f*, talo *m*; *v/t* represar; deter, conter

stench [stentʃ] fedor *m*

step [step] *s* passo *m*, passada *f*; degrau *m*; medida *f*; *v/i* dar um passo, andar, caminhar

step|daughter ['step.dɔːtə] en teada *f*; **~father** padrasto *m*

step-ladder ['step.lædə] escadote *m*

stepmother ['step.mʌðə] madrasta *f*

stepping-stone 'steping stəun] alpondra *f*, passadeira *f*

stepson ['stepsʌn] enteado *m*

stereo ['stiəriəu] *adj* estereofónico

sterile ['sterail] estéril; **~ity** [-'riliti] esterilidade *f*; **~ize** ['sterilaiz] *v/t* esterilizar

sterling ['stəːliŋ] *adj* esterlino; puro, nobre, verdadeiro

stern [stəːn] *adj* severo, austero; *s* popa *f*

stew [stjuː] *s* guisado *m*, estufado *m*; *v/t*, *v/i* guisar, estufar

steward ['stjuəd] *s* despenseiro *m*; administrador *m*; criado *m* de bordo; hospedeiro *m* de bor-

do, aeromoço *m*; **~ess** hospedeira *f* de bordo, aeromoça *f*

stick [stik] *s* pau *m*, vara *f*; bengala *f*; *v/t*, *v/i* espetar; colar; encravar; cravar; afixar; atolar-se; deter-se; aderir; **~er** etiqueta *f* aderente; **~ to** manter-se fiel a; **~y** pegajoso, viscoso; desagradável, difícil

stiff [stif] *adj* rígido, teso; formal; **~en** *v/t*, *v/i* endurecer (-se); entesar(-se); **~ness** rigidez *f*, dureza *f*

stifle ['staifl] *v/t*, *v/i* sufocar; extinguir, suprimir; abafar

stigma ['stigmə] estigma *m*

still [stil] *adj* imóvel; calmo; sereno, tranquilo; *s* tranquilidade *f*, silêncio *m*; alambique *m*; *adv* ainda; todavia, contudo; *v/t* acalmar, sossegar; **~ life** natureza *f* morta; **~ness** calma *f*, silêncio *m*

stilt [stilt] anda *f*; **~ed** afe(c)tado, pomposo

stimulate ['stimjuleit] *v/t* estimular

sting [stiŋ] *v/t*, *v/i* arder, doer; picar, dar ferroadas em; *s* picada *f*, ferroada *f*

stingy ['stindʒi] avaro, avarento, mesquinho

stink [stiŋk] *s* fedor *m*; *v/i* feder, tresandar

stint [stint] *s* tarefa *f*

stipulate ['stipjuleit] *v/t* estipular

stir [stəː] *v/t*, *v/i* excitar, instigar; agitar, sacudir; bater, mexer; mover(-se); bulir; *s* rebuliço *m*; excitação *f*; agitação *f*, comoção f; **~ring** adj excitante; arrebatador; emocionante

stirrup ['stirəp] estribo m

stitch [stit∫] s ponto m; med pontada f; v/t, v/i coser, dar pontos (a)

stock [stɔk] s estoque m, sortido m; linhagem f, estirpe f; caldo m; com a(c)ções f/pl; sortimento m; gado m; tronco m, cepo m; v/t fornecer, prover; sortir; acumular; **out of** ~ esgotado; **~ade** [-'keid] estacada f; **~broker** corretor m; ~ **exchange** bolsa f de valores

stocking ['stɔkiŋ] s meia f

stock|-jobber ['stɔk.dʒɔbə] agiota m

stock-taking ['stɔk.teikiŋ] inventário m

stocky ['stɔki] atarracado

stodgy ['stɔdʒi] indigesto; maçador, monótono

stoic ['stəuik] adj, s estóico m

stoke [stəuk] v/t atiçar

stole [stəul] s estola f

stolid ['stɔlid] estólido, impassível

stomach ['stʌmək] s estômago m

stone [stəun] s pedra f; gema f, pedra f preciosa; caroço m; med cálculo m; 14 arráteis; v/t apedrejar; lapidar; descaroçar

stony ['stəuni] pedregoso; duro, cruel

stool [stu:l] tamborete m, escabelo m, mocho m

stoop [stu:p] v/t, v/i inclinar-se, abaixar-se

stop [stɔp] v/t, v/i obstruir, tapar; parar, deter(-se); s paragem f, Braz parada f; ponto m; **~per** tampão m, rolha f, bucha f

storage ['stɔ:ridʒ] armazenagem f

store [stɔ:] v/t armazenar, acumular; s abundância f; armazém m; depósito m; **~house** mina f, tesouro m; armazém m; **~keeper** lojista m; **~-room** despensa f

stor(e)y ['stɔ:ri] andar m, pavimento m

stork [stɔ:k] cegonha f

storm [stɔ:m] s tempestade f, tormenta f; borrasca f; v/t, v/i vociferar; assaltar, atacar; **~y** tempestuoso; violento

story ['stɔ:ri] (pl -ries) história f, conto m; **~book** livro m de histórias

stout [staut] adj corpulento; firme, sólido; intrépido; s cerveja f preta forte

stove [stəuv] s fogão m; estufa f

stow [stəu] v/t guardar, arrumar; **~away** s passageiro m clandestino

straddle ['strædl] v/t, v/i escarranchar-se, escanchar-se; escarrapachar

straight [streit] adv à direita, em linha re(c)ta; dire(c)tamente, imediatamente; sem rodeios; adj re(c)to; dire(c)to; honesto; em ordem; ~ **away** imediatamente, já; sem ni endireitar; arrumar; pôr em ordem; **~forward** [-'fɔ:wəd] franco; claro

strain [strein] v/t, v/i forçar; torcer; estender; coar; esforçar--se; **~er** coador m

strait [streit] estreito m

strand [strænd] s fio m, fibra f; v/t encalhar; perder-se; **~ed** adj abandonado, perdido

strang|e [streindʒ] estranho; **~er** desconhecido m, forasteiro m

strangle [ˈstræŋgl] v/t estrangular

strap [stræp] s correia f, tira f; alça f; v/t segurar com correia; amarrar; açoitar com uma correia; **~ping** adj robusto, forte, rijo

stratagem [ˈstrætidʒəm] estratagema m

strateg|ic [strəˈtiːdʒik] estratégico; **~ist** [ˈstrætidʒist] estrategista m; **~y** [ˈstrætidʒi] estratégia f

straw [strɔː] palha f

strawberry [ˈstrɔːbəri] (pl -ries) morango m

stray [strei] v/i extraviar-se, perder-se; divagar; adj extraviado, desgarrado; s pessoa f ou animal m desgarrado

streak [striːk] s listra f, risco m; v/t, v/i correr; listrar, riscar; **~y** listrado

stream [striːm] s corrente f; torrente f; riacho m, regato m; fluxo m, jacto m; v/i correr, fluir; afluir; jorrar, brotar

street [striːt] rua f; **~car** US (carro m) elé(c)trico m, Braz bonde m

strength [streŋθ] força f; vigor

m, energia f; **~en** v/t, v/i fortificar(-se); fortalecer(-se)

strenuous [ˈstrenjuəs] enérgico; intenso, agitado

stress [stres] s ênfase f; acento tónico; pressão f, tensão f; v/t acentuar; realçar, frisar

stretch [stretʃ] v/t, v/i esticar (-se), estirar(-se); estender(-se); espreguiçar-se; s estiramento m; extensão f; trecho m; elasticidade f; período m, espaço m; re(c)ta f de chegada

stretcher [ˈstretʃə] maca f

strew [struː] v/t espalhar, espargir

stricken [ˈstrikən] adj ferido; atacado, acometido

strict [strikt] estrito, rigoroso; severo

stride [straid] v/i andar a passos largos; s passo m largo, passada f

strife [straif] contenda f

strik|e [straik] v/t, v/i dar na vista, chamar a atenção; ocorrer; golpear, bater; tocar; fazer greve; s greve f; **~er** grevista m, f

striking [ˈstraikiŋ] adj notável, impressionante

string [striŋ] s cordão m, cordel m, fio m, barbante m; mus corda f; réstia f; chorrilho m

stringy [ˈstriŋi] fibroso

strip [strip] s faixa f, tira f; v/t, v/i despojar; despir(-se)

stripe [straip] risca f, listra f

strive [straiv] v/i esforçar-se

stroke [strəuk] s golpe m, pancada f; rasgo m; braçada f; remada *f*; afago *m*; *v/t* acariciar, afagar

stroll [strəul] *s* volta *f*, passeio *m*; *v/i* passear, dar uma volta

strong [strɔŋ] forte, poderoso, vigoroso; ~**hold** forte *m*, fortaleza *f*; cidadela *f*

structure ['strʌktʃə] *s* estrutura *f*

struggle ['strʌgl] *s* luta *f*; *v/i* lutar

strut [strʌt] *v/i* pavonear-se, empertigar-se

stub [stʌb] *s* ponta *f*, coto *m*; talão *m*, canhoto *m*

stubble ['stʌbl] restolho *m*; barba *f* hirsuta

stubborn ['stʌbən] teimoso, obstinado, cabeçudo

stuck-up ['stʌk'ʌp] *adj* presumido, vaidoso

stud [stʌd] *s* botão *m* de camisa; coudelaria *f*; tacha *f*; *v/t* tachonar

student ['stju:dənt] estudante *m*, *f*

studied ['stʌdid] *adj* estudado, premeditado

studio ['stju:diəu] estúdio *m*

studious ['stju:djəs] estudioso

study ['stʌdi] *v/t*, *v/i* estudar; *s* (*pl* -**dies**) gabinete *m*; escritório *m*; estudo *m*

stuff [stʌf] *v/t*, *v/i* empanturrar-se; rechear; encher, atulhar; *s* matéria *f*, material *m*; fazenda *f*

stuffing ['stʌfiŋ] *s* recheio *m*

stuffy ['stʌfi] abafado; enfadonho

stumble ['stʌmbl] *v/i* tropeçar

stump [stʌmp] toco *m*, cepo *m*; coto *m*

stun [stʌn] *v/t* aturdir, atordoar; ~**ning** *adj* formidável, esplêndido

stunt [stʌnt] *s* proeza *f*, façanha *f*

stupefy ['stju:pifai] *v/t* embasbacar

stupendous [stju(:)'pendəs] estupendo

stupid ['stju:pid] palerma, estúpido; ~**ity** [-'piditi] estupidez *f*

stupor ['stju:pə] estupor *m*

sturdy ['stə:di] robusto, vigoroso

sturgeon ['stə:dʒən] esturjão *m*

stutter ['stʌtə] *v/i* gaguejar; *s* gaguez *f*

sty [stai] (*pl* **sties**) pocilga *f*, chiqueiro *m*

style [stail] *s* estilo *m*; elegância *f*; ~**ish** elegante, à moda

suave [swɑ:v] suave

subdue [səb'dju:] *v/t* subjugar, submeter; suavizar

subject ['sʌbdʒikt] *s* assunto *m*; sujeito *m*; sú(b)dito *m*; matéria *f*; *adj* sujeito; propenso; dominado; ~ **to** ['sʌbdʒikt tə] *prp* conforme, dependente; [səb'dʒekt] *v/t* sujeitar; ~**ion** [səb'dʒekʃən] sujeição *f*; ~**ive** [səb'dʒektiv] subje(c)tivo

subjugate ['sʌbdʒugeit] *v/t* subjugar

subjunctive [səb'dʒʌŋktiv] *s* conjuntivo *m*, subjuntivo

sublet ['sʌb'let] *v/t*, *v/i* subalugar, sublocar

sublime [sə'blaim] sublime

submarine [‚sʌbmə'ri:n] *adj*, *s* submarino *m*

submerge [səb'mə:dʒ] v/t, v/i submergir(-se)

submission [səb'miʃən] submissão f

submit [səb'mit] v/t, v/i submeter(-se)

subordinate [sə'bɔ:dnit] adj, s subordinado m; v/t subordinar

subscrib|e [səb'skraib] v/t, v/i subscrever; assinar; **~er** assinante m, f; subscritor m

subscription [səb'skripʃən] subscrição f; assinatura f

subsequent ['sʌbsikwənt] subsequente

subsid|e [səb'said] v/i acalmar, assentar; aluir, abater-se; **~ence** derrocada f, aluimento m

subsid|iary [səb'sidiəri] adj subsidiário; **~ize** ['sʌbsidaiz] v/t subsidiar; **~y** (pl **-dies**) subsídio m

subsist [səb'sist] v/i subsistir, sustentar-se

substan|ce ['sʌbstəns] substância f; **~tial** [səb'stænʃəl] substancial

substitut|e ['sʌbstitju:t] v/t substituir; s substituto m; **~ion** [-'tju:ʃən] substituição f

subterranean [sʌbtə'reinjən] subterrâneo

subtle ['sʌtl] su(b)til

subtract [səb'trækt] v/t subtrair; **~ion** subtra(c)ção f

suburb ['sʌbə:b] subúrbio m; **~an** [sə'bə:bən] suburbano

subway ['sʌbwei] passagem f subterrânea; US metropolitano m

succeed [sək'si:d] v/t, v/i ter

êxito; suceder a

success [sək'ses] sucesso m, êxito m; **~ful** feliz, próspero; **~ion** sucessão f, série f; **~ive** sucessivo; **~or** sucessor m

succinct [sək'siŋkt] sucinto

succulent ['sʌkjulənt] adj suculento

succumb [sə'kʌm] v/i sucumbir

such [sʌtʃ] tal; assim; **~ a** tal, semelhante; **~ as** tal como

suck [sʌk] v/t, v/i chuchar; mamar; chupar; sugar; **~le** v/t amamentar, dar de mamar

sudden ['sʌdn] repentino, súbito; brusco; **all of a ~** de repente/súbito

sue [sju:] v/t processar

suède [sweid] camurça f

suet ['sjuit] sebo m

suffer ['sʌfə] v/t, v/i sofrer, padecer; aguentar; **~er** sofredor m, vítima f; **~ing** s sofrimento m

suffice [sə'fais] v/i bastar

sufficien|cy [sə'fiʃənsi] suficiência f; **~t** suficiente

suffix ['sʌfiks] sufixo m

suffocat|e ['sʌfəkeit] v/t, v/i sufocar(-se); **~ion** [-'keiʃən] sufocação f

suffrage ['sʌfridʒ] sufrágio m

sugar ['ʃugə] açúcar m; v/t açucarar; **~-beet** beterraba f; **~-cane** cana-de-açúcar f; **~y** açucarado

suggest [sə'dʒest] v/t sugerir; **~ion** sugestão f; **~ive** sugestivo

suicide ['sjuisaid] suicídio m; suicida m, f; **commit ~** suicidar-se

suit [sju:t] s fato m, Braz terno m; fato m de saia e casaco; naipe m; jur pleito m; v/t, v/i convir; adaptar, ajustar; assentar, ficar bem

suitable ['sju:təbl] conveniente, apto, próprio, idóneo

suitcase ['sju:tkeis] mala f

suite [swi:t] apartamento m; jogo m de móveis

suitor ['sju:tə] litigante m, f

sulk [sʌlk] v/i amuar

sulky ['sʌlki] adj amuado

sullen ['sʌlən] carrancudo, rabugento; sombrio

sulphur ['sʌlfə] enxofre m

sultry [ˌsʌltri] abafadiço, abrasador

sum [sʌm] soma f, total m; **in ~** em suma

summarize ['sʌməraiz] v/t resumir

summary ['sʌməri] s (pl -ries) resumo m, sumário m

summer ['sʌmə] verão m, estio m; ~ **time** hora f de verão

summit ['sʌmit] cimo m, cume m

summon ['sʌmən] v/t convocar; jur notificar; ~s ['-z] s notificação f

sumptuous ['sʌmptjuəs] sumptuoso, Braz suntuoso

sun [sʌn] s sol m; v/t apanhar sol; ~**bathe** v/i tomar banhos de sol; ~**blind** toldo m; veneziana f; ~**burnt** queimado, bronzeado; **☉day** domingo m

sundry ['sʌndri] diversos

sun-flower ['sʌn.flauə] girassol m

sunken ['sʌŋkən] adj submerso; encovado, fundo; cavado

sunny ['sʌni] soalheiro; radiante

sun|rise ['sʌnraiz] nascer m do sol; ~**set** pôr m do sol; ~**shade** guarda-sol m; ~**shine** luz m do sol, sol m; ~**stroke** insolação f

superb [sju(:)'pə:b] magnífico, soberbo

super|ficial [sju:pə'fiʃəl] superficial; ~**fine** superfino; ~**fluity** superfluidade f; ~**fluous** supérfluo; ~**human** sobre-humano; ~**impose** v/t sobrepor; ~**intendent** superintendente m

superior [sju:'piəriə] adj superior; ~**ity** [-'ɔriti] superioridade f

superlative [sju:'pə:lətiv] adj, s superlativo m

super|man ['sju:pəmæn] super-homem m; ~**natural** sobrenatural; ~**numerary** adj supranumerário; ~**sede** v/t substituir; ~**stition** superstição f; ~**stitious** supersticioso; ~**vise** v/t, v/i vigiar, fiscalizar; ~**visor** fiscal m

supper ['sʌpə] jantar m, ceia f; **have ~** jantar, cear

supple ['sʌpl] flexível

supplement ['sʌplimənt] s suplemento m; ~**ary** ['-'mentəri] suplementar

supplier [sə'plaiə] fornecedor m

supply [sə'plai] v/t fornecer, prover, abastecer; suprir; s provisão f, fornecimento m, abastecimento *m*

support [sə'pɔːt] *s* sustento *m*, manutenção *f*; apoio *m*; *v/t* sustentar, manter; apoiar

suppos|e [sə'pəuz] *v/t* supor; julgar, crer; *conj* se, caso; que tal se; **~ed** *adj* suposto; pretenso; **~edly** supostamente, provàvelmente

supposing [sə'pəuziŋ] *conj* se, caso, suponhamos

supposition [ˌsʌpə'ziʃən] suposição *f*; hipótese *f*, conje(c)tura *f*

suppress [sə'pres] *v/t* suprimir

supreme [sju(:)'priːm] supremo

sure [ʃuə] *adj* seguro, certo; *adv* claro, sem dúvida; **make ~ of/that** verificar, assegurar-se; **for ~** de certeza; **~enough** de fa(c)to; **~ly** com certeza; com segurança; **~ty** caução *f*; fiador *m*

surf [səːf] *s* ressaca *f*

surface ['səːfis] *s* superfície *f*

surg|eon ['səːdʒən] cirurgião *m*; **~ery** consultório *m*; cirurgia *f*; **~ical** cirúrgico

surly ['səːli] carrancudo, rabugento

surmise [sə:'maiz] *v/t*, *v/i* supor, suspeitar; ['--] *s* suposição *f*, suspeita *f*

surmount [sə:'maunt] *v/t* superar

surname ['səːneim] apelido *m*

surpass [sə:'pɑːs] *v/t* sobrepujar, exceder

surpris|e [sə'praiz] *v/t* surpreender; *s* surpresa *f*; **~ing** *adj* surpreendente

surrender [sə'rendə] *v/t*, *v/i* render(-se), entregar(-se); capitular; *s* rendição *f*, capitulação *f*

surreptitious [ˌsʌrəp'tiʃəs] sub-reptício

surround [sə'raund] *v/t* circundar, rodear, cercar; **~ings** *s/pl* ambiente *m*, meio *m*

survey [sə'vei] *v/t* estudar, examinar; medir; ['sə:'vei] *s* estudo *m*, inspe(c)ção *f*

survival [sə'vaivəl] sobrevivência *f*

surviv|e [sə'vaiv] *v/t*, *v/i* sobreviver (a); **~or** sobrevivente *m*, *f*

susceptible [sə'septəbl] susce(p)tível; sensível

suspect [səs'pekt] *v/t* suspeitar; ['sʌspekt] *s*, *adj* suspeito *m*

suspend [səs'pend] *v/t* suspender

suspense [səs'pens] expe(c)tativa *f*, incerteza *f*, ansiedade *f*

suspension [səs'penʃən] suspensão *f*; **~bridge** ponte *f* pênsil

suspic|ion [səs'piʃən] suspeita *f*; **~ious** suspeitoso; suspeito

sustain [səs'tein] *v/t* sustentar, suster, manter; suportar, sofrer

sustenance ['sʌstinəns] subsistência *f*, alimento *m*

swagger ['swægə] *v/i* pavonear-se; bazofiar; *s* pavonada *f*

swallow ['swɔləu] *v/t* tragar, engolir

swallow ['swɔləu] *s* zo andorinha *f*; trago *m*

swamp [swɔmp] *s* brejo *m*, pântano *m*, paúl *m*

swan [swɔn] s cisne m

swarm [swɔːm] s enxame m; v/i enxamear; fervilhar, pulular

swarthy ['swɔːði] moreno, trigueiro

sway [swei] s balanço m; v/t, v/i balançar(-se)

swear [swɛə] v/t, v/i jurar; blasfemar, praguejar

sweat [swet] s suor m; v/i suar

sweater ['swetə] suéter m

Swed|e [swiːd] sueco m; ~**ish** adj, s sueco m

sweep [swiːp] v/t varrer, vasculhar; s extensão f; curva f; gesto m; limpa-chaminés m; varredela f; ~**ing** adj extenso, vasto

sweepings [swiːpiŋz] s/pl lixo m

sweet [swiːt] adj doce; suave; encantador, gentil; s rebuçado m; doce m, guloseima f; ~**en** v/t, v/i adoçar(-se); açucarar; ~**heart** querido m, querida f; ~**ness** doçura f; suavidade f; encanto m

swell [swel] adj porreiro, formidável; v/t, v/i inchar(-se); intumescer, distender; ~**ing** s inchação f, intumescência f

swelter ['sweltə] v/i abafar

swerve [swəːv] v/t, v/i guinar, desviar(-se); s desvio m, guinada f

swift [swift] adj veloz, rápido

swim [swim] v/t, v/i nadar; ~ **across** atravessar a nado; ~**mer** nadador m; ~**ming** s natação f; ~**ming-pool** piscina f

swindl|e ['swindl] v/t lograr, calotear; ~**er** caloteiro m

swine [swain] suíno m

swing [swiŋ] v/t, v/i balançar-se, baloiçar(-se); s baloiço m; balanço m

swirl [swəːl] s turbilhão m, torvelinho m, redemoinho m; v/i redemoinhar

Swiss [swis] adj, s suíço m

switch [switʃ] s chibata f; interruptor m, comutador m; v/t açoutar; comutar; ~ **off** desligar; ~ **on** ligar; ~**board** quadro m de distribuição

swollen ['swəulən] adj inchado

swoop [swuːp] s batida f, investida f; v/i precipitar-se, picar

sword [sɔːd] espada f

syllable ['siləbl] sílabo f m

symbol ['simbəl] símbolo m

symbolic [sim'bɔlik] simbólico

symmetry ['simitri] simetria f

sympath|etic [ˌsimpə'θetik] simpatizante; ~**ize** [-aiz] v/i simpatizar; ~**y** [-θi] simpatia f; compaixão f; compreensão f; solidariedade f

symphony ['simfəni] (pl -**nies**) sinfonia f

symptom ['simptəm] sintoma m

synchronize ['siŋkrənaiz] v/t, v/i sincronizar

syndicate ['sindikit] s sindicato m

synonym ['sinənim] sinónimo m; ~**ous** [-'nɔniməs] sinónimo

syringe ['sirindʒ] v/t seringa f

syrup ['sirəp] xarope m, calda f

system ['sistim] sistema m; ~**atic** [-'mætik] sistemático; ~**atize** [-ətaiz] v/t sistematizar, reduzir a sistema

T

tab [tæb] presilha *f*; alça *f*, aselha *f*

table ['teibl] *s* mesa *f*; **~-cloth** toalha *f* de mesa; **~-spoon** colher *f*

tablet ['tæblit] comprimido *m*; tablete *f*, barra *f*

tacit ['tæsit] tácito; **~urn** [-ə:n] taciturno

tack [tæk] *s* brocha *f*, tacha *f*; *naut* bordada *f*; *v/t, v/i* alinhavar; pregar com tachas; *naut* bordejar, virar de bordo

tackle ['tækl] *s* equipamento *m*, aparelhagem *f*; *naut* cordoalha *f*; intercepção *f*; *v/t, v/i* atacar, enfrentar; interceptar, derrubar

tact [tækt] ta(c)to *m*, discernimento *m*, jeito *m*, diplomacia *f*; **~ful** com/de ta(c)to, diplomático; **~ile** [-ail] tá(c)til; **~less** sem ta(c)to

taffeta ['tæfitə] tafetá *m*

tag [tæg] *s* etiqueta *f*; agulheta *f*; estribilho *m*; *v/t* etiquetar

tail [teil] *s* cauda *f*, rabo *m*; **~coat** fraque *m*; **~light** farol *m* da retaguarda

tailor ['teilə] *s* alfaiate *m*; **well ~ed** bem cortado; **~-made** feito á/sob medida; **~'s (shop)** alfaiataria *f*

taint [teint] *s* mácula *f*, mancha *f*; *v/t* macular, manchar; corromper; poluir

take [teik] *v/t* tomar; pegar em; receber; levar; conduzir, guiar;

tirar; alugar; **~ a chance** arriscar a sorte, aproveitar a oportunidade; **~ to one's heels/legs** dar ás canelas; **~ aback** tomar de surpresa; **~ in** alojar; encurtar; **~ off** despir, tirar; levantar voo, descolar; **~off** *s* descolagem *f*; caricatura *f*; **~ on** empregar; aceitar; **~ out** arrancar; levar a sair, convidar; **~ over** tomar posse de; **~ to** passar a gostar de; simpatizar com; entregar-se a; **~ up** dedicar-se a; ocupar; seguir

taking ['teikin] *adj* atraente

tale [teil] conto *m*, história *f*

talent ['tælənt] talento *m*; **~ed** talentoso

talisman ['telizmən] talismã *m*

talk [tɔ:k] *s* conversa *f*; palestra *f*; discurso *m*; fala *f*; *v/t, v/i* falar, conversar; tagarelar; **~a-tive** ['-ətiv] loquaz, falador; **~er** conversador *m*

tall [tɔ:l] alto

tallow ['tælou] sebo *m*

tally ['tæli] *v/t, v/i* condizer, corresponder (a)

tame [teim] *adj* manso, domesticado; *v/t* domesticar, amansar, domar

tamper ['tæmpə]: **~ with** mexer em; manipular

tan [tæn] *v/t, v/i* bronzear(-se); curtir; *s* cor *f* bronzeada, tom *m* queimado

tangerine [.tændʒə'ri:n] tangerina *f*

tangible ['tændʒəbl] tangível, palpável

tangle ['tæŋgl] s nó m, emaranhamento m; v/t, v/i emaranhar(-se)

tank [tæŋk] reservatório m, cisterna f; tanque m

tankard ['tæŋkəd] caneca f; pichel m

tanner ['tænə] curtidor m; ~y curtume m

tantalize ['tæntəlaiz] v/t tantalizar

tantamount ['tæntəmaunt] igual, equivalente

tap [tæp] s pancadinha f, golpe m leve; torneira f; v/t, v/i bater ao de leve

tape [teip] s fita f, banda f

taper ['teipə] s círio m; pavio m; v/t, v/i afilar(-se), terminar-se em ponta

tape-recorder ['teipri.kɔːdə] gravador m; ~-recording gravação f

tapestry ['tæpistri] (pl -ries) tapeçaria f

tapeworm ['teipwə:m] bicha f solitária

tar [tɑː] s alcatrão m; v/t alcatroar

tare [tɛə] com tara f

target ['tɑːgit] alvo m

tariff ['tærif] tarifa f

tarmac ['tɑːmæk] s pista f macadamizada

tarnish ['tɑːniʃ] v/t, v/i empanar(-se), deslustrar

tart [tɑːt] adj acre, ácido, azedo; mordaz; s torta f, pastel m

Tartar ['tɑːtə] tártaro m

task [tɑːsk] tarefa f

tassel ['tæsəl] borla f

taste [teist] s gosto m; sabor; v/t provar, saborear; ~eful gostoso; com bom gosto; ~eless sem gosto, insípido; de mau gosto; ~y saboroso

ta-ta ['tæ'tɑː] adeusinho

tatter ['tætə] trapo m, farrapo m, andrajo m; ~ed esfarrapado

tattle ['tætl] s tagarelice f; v/i tagarelar

tattoo [tə'tuː] s tatuagem f; mil toque m de recolher; v/t tatuar

taunt [tɔːnt] s insulto m; troça f; v/t escarnecer, mofar(-se) de

tax [tæks] s taxa f, imposto m; encargo m; esforço m; v/t sobrecarregar, pôr à prova; lançar impostos sobre

taxi ['tæksi] s táxi m; v/t, v/i deslizar, rolar; ~meter taximetro m; ~-rank/ ~-stand praça f de táxis, Braz ponto m de estacionamento de táxis

taxpayer ['tæks.peiə] contribuinte m, f

tea [tiː] chá m

teach [tiːtʃ] v/t, v/i ensinar, instruir; ~er professor m; ~ing s ensinamento m; ensino m, instrução f

tea-cosy ['tiː.kəuzi] abafador m; ~cup chávena f

team [tiːm] equipa f, equipe f

teapot ['tiːpɔt] bule m

tear [tɛə] s rasgão m; v/t rasgar

tear [tiə] s lágrima f; ~ful lacrimoso

tease [tiːz] v/t, v/i gozar com, entrar com, arreliar, Braz cacetear

tea-spoon ['ti:spu:n] colher *f* de chá

teat [ti:t] teta *f*

techni|cal ['teknikəl] técnico; **~cian** ['nifən] técnico *m*; **~que** ['ni:k] técnica *f*

tedious ['ti:djəs] fastidioso, maçador

teem [ti:m] *v/i* chover a potes; **~ with rain** chover a cântaros

teenager ['ti:neidʒə] jovem *m*, *f* adolescente

teens [ti:nz] *s/pl* idade *f* de 13 a 19 anos; **he's still in his ~** ainda não chegou aos vinte anos

teeth [ti:θ] *pl* of **tooth**; **~e** [-ð] *v/i* criar dentes, começar a ter dentes

teetota(l)ler ['ti:'təutlə] abstémio *m*

tele|gram ['teligræm] telegrama *m*; **~graph** ['-gra:f] *s* telégrafo *m*; *v/t*, *v/i* telegrafar; **~graphic** [-'græfik] telegráfico; **~pathy** ['lepəθi] telepatia *f*; **~phone** *s* telefone *m*; *v/t*, *v/i* telefonar; **~phone booth** cabine *f* telefónica; **~phone directory** lista *f* telefónica; **~phone exchange** central *f* telefónica; **~phonist** [-'lefənist] telefonista *m*, *f*; **~phony** [ti'lefəni] telefonia *f*; **~scope** ['-skəup] telescópio *m*; **~scopic** [-'skɔpik] telescópico; **~vision** ['-viʒən] televisão *f*

tell [tel] *v/t*, *v/i* contar, relatar; dizer, informar; **~ lies** dizer

mentiras; **~ the truth** dizer a verdade; **~er** pagador *m*, caixa *m*; escrutinador *m*; **~ing** *adj* eficaz; notável; **~tale** *adj* traiçoeiro; *s* mexeriqueiro *m*

temper ['tempə] *s* génio *m*, humor *m*; índole *f*; mau gênio *m*, mau humor; têmpera *f*; *v/t* temperar; **lose one's ~** perder a calma; **~ament** temperamento *m*; **~amental** caprichoso; **~ance** temperança *f*; **~ate** ['-rit] temperado; moderado, sóbrio; **~ature** ['-ritʃə] temperatura *f*

tempest ['tempist] tempestade *f*

temple ['templ] templo *m*; *anat* fonte *f*

temporary ['tempərəri] temporário

tempt [tempt] *v/t* tentar, induzir; **~ation** [-'teiʃən] tentação *f*; **~er** sedutor *m*; **~ing** *adj* tentador; **~ress** sedutora *f*

ten [ten] dez

ten|able ['tenəbl] sustentável, defensável; **~acious** [ti'neiʃəs] tenaz; **~acity** [ti'næsiti] tenacidade *f*; **~ant** ['tenənt] *s* inquilino *m*, locatário *m*

tend [tend] *v/t* guardar, velar; *v/i* tender; **~ency** (*pl* **-cies**) tendência *f*

tender ['tendə] *s* tênder *m*; encarregado *m*; oferta *f*, proposta *f*; *adj* tenro; brando; delicado; **~ness** delicadeza *f*; ternura *f*; brandura *f*

tendon ['tendən] tendão *m*

tenement ['tenimənt] habitação *f*, casa *f*

tennis ['tenis] ténis *m*

tenor ['tenə] *mus* tenor *m*; teor *m*

tens|e [tens] *s* tempo *m*; *adj* tenso; teso, esticado; **~ion** ['tenʃən] tensão *f*

tent [tent] tenda *f*

tentacle ['tentəkl] tentáculo *m*

tenth [tenθ] décimo

tenuous ['tenjuəs] ténue

tepid ['tepid] tépido

term [təːm] *s* termo *m*; prazo *m*; período *m*; *v/t* nomear, chamar

terminal ['təːminl] *adj* terminal; *s* término *m*; estação *f* terminal

termin|ate ['təːmineit] *v/t* terminar; **~ation** [-'neiʃən] terminação *f*

terminology [təːmi'nɔlədʒi] terminologia *f*

terminus ['təːminəs] estação *f* terminal, término *m*

terrace ['terəs] *s* terraço *m*; socalco *m*

terrestrial [ti'restriəl] terrestre

terrible ['terəbl] terrível

terrific [tə'rifik] estupendo

terrify ['terifai] *v/t* assustar, aterrorizar

territory ['teritəri] (*pl* -ries) território *m*

terror ['terə] terror *m*; **~ism** terrorismo *m*; **~ist** *adj*, *s* terrorista *m*, *f*; **~ize** *v/t* aterrorizar

terse [təːs] conciso

test [test] *s* prova *f*; ensaio *m*; teste *m*; análise *f*, exame *m*; *v/t* pôr à prova; examinar

testament ['testəmənt] testamento *m*

testify ['testifai] *v/t*, *v/i* atestar, testemunhar; depor

testimon|ial [.testi'məunjəl] atestado *m*, certificado *m*; **~y** ['-əni] testemunho *m*, depoimento *m*

text [tekst] texto *m*; **~ile** [-ail] *s* tecido *m*; *adj* têxtil; **~ual** ['-tjuəl] textual

texture ['tekstʃə] (con)textura *f*

than [ðæn, ðən] *conj* que, do que

thank [θæŋk] *v/t* agradecer; **~ you** obrigado; **~ heaven!** graças aos céus! **~ful** agradecido, grato; **~less** ingrato, desagradecido; **~s** *s/pl* agradecimentos *m/pl*

thanksgiving ['θæŋks.giviŋ] a(c)ção *f* de graças

that [ðæt] (*pl* **those** [ðəuz]) *adj*, *pron* aquele, aquela, esse, essa, *pron* aquilo; isso; que, o qual; *conj* que

thatch [θætʃ] *s* colmo *m*

thaw [θɔː] *s* degelo *m*; *v/t*, *v/i* degelar, descongelar

the [ðiː, ðə] *art* o, a, os, as; *adv* **~ ...** quanto ..., tanto

theatre [θ'iətə] teatro *m*; **~ical** [θi'ætrikəl] teatral

theft [θeft] roubo *m*

their [ðɛə, ðɛr] seu, sua, seus, suas; deles, delas; **~s** [-z] o seu, a sua, os seus, as suas; o deles, o delas

them [ðem, ðəm] os, as; eles, elas; lhes

theme [θiːm] tema *m*, assunto *m*; *mus* motivo *m*

thrash

themselves [ðəm'selvz] *pron/pl* se; eles mesmos, elas mesmas, a si mesmos, a si mesmas

then [ðen] *adv* então; ora; depois; *adj* de então

thenceforth ['ðens'fɔːθ] desde então

theologi|an [θiə'ləudʒjən] teólogo *m*; ~gy [θi'ɔlədʒi] teologia *f*

theorem ['θiərəm] teorema *m*

theoretical [θiə'retikəl] teórico

theory ['θiəri] (*pl* -ries) teoria *f*

there [ðeə] *adv* ali, acolá, lá, aí; *int* ora toma!, então!; ~ **you are!** ora aí está

there|about(s) [ðeərəbauts] nas cercanias; por aí, mais ou menos; ~**fore** portanto, por isso, por conseguinte; ~**upon** nisso; por isso

therm|al ['θəːməl] *adj* termal, térmico; ~**ometer** [-'mɔmitə] termómetro *m*

these [ðiːz] *pl* estes, estas

thesis ['θiːsis] (*pl* -ses [-siːz]) tese *f*

they [ðei] eles, elas

thick [θik] *adj* espesso, denso; grosso; cerrado; ~**en** *v/t, v/i* engrossar, tornar(-se) espesso; complicar-se; ~**ness** espessura *f*; densidade *f*; grossura *f*

thief [θiːf] (*pl* thieves [θiːvz]) gatuno *m*, ladrão *m*

thieve [θiːv] *v/t, v/i* roubar, furtar

thigh [θai] coxa *f*

thimble ['θimbl] dedal *m*

thin [θin] *adj* delgado, fino, ténue; magro, franzino; ralo; escasso; *v/t, v/i* adelgaçar, afi-

nar; rarefazer

thing [θiŋ] coisa *f*

think [θiŋk] *v/t, v/i* pensar; crer, julgar; meditar; ~ **of** pensar em; achar; ~ **over** repensar, pensar bem; ~**er** pensador *m*; ~**ing** *s* pensamento *m*; opinião *f*; *adj* pensante; refle(c)tido

third [θəːd] *adj* terceiro; *s* terço *m*

thirst [θəːst] *s* sede *f*; ~**y** sedento, sequioso

thir|teen ['θəː'tiːn] *adj* treze; ~**ty** *adj* trinta

this [ðis] (*pl* these [ðiːz]) *pron* este, esta; isto; *pron* este, esta; *adv* assim (tão)

thistle ['θisl] cardo *m*

thorn [θɔːn] espinho *m*

thorough ['θʌrə] esmerado; inteiro, completo, cabal; ~**bred** ['-bred] *s* puro-sangue *m*; ~**fare** passagem *f*; via *f* pública; ~**ly** inteiramente, por completo; ~**ness** esmero *m*

those [ðəuz] *pl* of **that** esses, essas; aqueles, aquelas

though [ðəu] *conj* ainda que, posto que, embora; *adv* contudo; **as** ~ como se

thought [θɔːt] *s* pensamento *m*; ~**ful** atento, cuidadoso; pensativo; ~**less** desatento, irrefle(c)tido

thousand ['θauzənd] *adj* mil; milhar; ~**th** [-tθ] milésimo

thraldom ['θrɔːldəm] escravidão *f*

thrash [θræʃ] *v/t* bater, sovar, espancar

thread [θred] *s* flo *m*, linha *f*; *v/t* enfiar

threat [θret] ameaça *f*; **~en** *v/t* ameaçar

three [θri:] *adj* três; **~ hundred** trezentos

thresh [θreʃ] *v/t*, *v/i* malhar, debulhar; **~ing-floor** eira *f*; **~ing-machine** debulhadora *f*

threshold [ˈθreʃhəuld] limiar *m*, soleira *f*

thrifty [ˈθrifti] económico, poupado

thrill [θril] *s* emoção *f* viva, estremecimento *m*; *v/t* emocionar; estremecer; **~er** romance *m* policial; **~ing** *adj* emocionante

thriv|e [θraiv] *v/i* medrar, prosperar; **~ing** *adj* próspero, florescente

throat [θrəut] garganta *f*

throb [θrɔb] *v/i* latejar, palpitar

throne [θrəun] trono *m*

throng [θrɔŋ] *s* multidão *f*, tropel *m*; *v/t* apinhar(-se), acorrer

through [θru:] *prp* por; através de; durante; por intermédio de; *adv* completamente; totalmente; de um lado a outro; do princípio ao fim; *adj* dire(c)to; completo, terminado; **~out** *prp* durante todo; por todo; *adv* por/em toda a parte; completamente

throw [θrəu] *v/t*, *v/i* deitar; lançar, atirar, arremessar; *s* lanço *m*, arremesso *m*; **~ away** deitar fora, jogar fora; **~ out** rejeitar; **~ up** abandonar, renunciar a; vomitar

thrush [θrʌʃ] tordo *m*

thrust [θrʌst] *s* empurrão *m*; investida *f*; *v/t* empurrar, impelir

thud [θʌd] *s* baque *m*

thumb [θʌm] *s* polegar *m*; *v/t* folhear

thump [θʌmp] *s* pancada *f*, soco *m*; baque *m*; *v/t*, *v/i* martelar, bater em; esmurrar, dar socos a

thunder [ˈθʌndə] strovão *m*; *v/i* trovejar; **~bolt** raio *m*; **~storm** trovoada *f*; **~struck** estupefa(c)to, assombrado

Thursday [ˈθə:zdi] quinta-feira *f*

thus [ðʌs] assim

thwart [θwɔ:t] *v/t* frustrar; *s* banco *m* de remador

tick [tik] *v/t*, *v/i* fazer tiquetaque; marcar, pôr visto em; *s* sinal *m* de visto; tiquetaque *m*

ticket [ˈtikit] *s* bilhete *m*; etiqueta *f*, rótulo *m*; *US* lista *f* de chapa; **~-collector** revisor *m*

tickl|e [ˈtikl] *v/t* fazer cócegas a; **~ish** coceguento; delicado, melindroso

tide [taid] maré *f*

tidy [ˈtaidi] *adj* asseado, arrumado; *v/t* assear, arrumar

tie [tai] *s* gravata *f*; empate *m*; *v/t*, *v/i* empatar; dar nó/laço (a); atar, ligar; amarrar, *naut* atracar

tier [tiə] camada *f*; bancada *f*; fileira *f*, fila *f*

tiger [ˈtaigə] tigre *m*

tight [tait] *adj* apertado; teso, entesado; *adv* firmemente; bem; **~en** *v/t*, *v/i* apertar; entesar

tights [taits] *s/pl* calças *f/pl* justas

tigress ['taigris] tigre *m* fêmea

tile [tail] *s* telha *f*; ladrilho *m*; azulejo *m*; *v/t* ladrilhar; telhar; cobrir com azulejos

till [til] *prp* até que; *s* gaveta *f* da caixa; *v/t* lavrar, cultivar; **~age** lavoura *f*; **~er** lavrador *m*; *naut* cana *f* do leme

tilt [tilt] *v/t*, *v/i* inclinar(-se), virar(-se)

timber ['timbə] *s* madeira *f*

time [taim] *s* tempo *m*; hora *f*, ocasião *f*; hora *f*; horas *f/pl*; época *f*; estação *f*; *mus* compasso *m*; *v/t* marcar o tempo; cronometrar; estar marcado; regular, acertar; **at** ~ às vezes; **from ~ to ~** de vez em quando; **in a tempo** a compasso; **in no ~** num instante; **on ~** a horas, pontualmente

time|less ['taimlis] sem fim; eterno; intemporal; **~ly** oportuno; **~s** *prp* vezes; **~-table** *s* horário *m*

tim|id ['timid] tímido, **~idity** [-'miditi] timidez *f*; **~orous** ['-ərəs] medroso, timorato, temeroso

tin [tin] *s* estanho *m*; lata *f*; *v/t* conservar em latas, enlatar

tincture ['tiŋktʃə] tintura *f*

tinfoil ['tin'fɔil] folha *f* de estanho

tinge [tindʒ] *v/t* tingir; *s* matiz *m*

tingl|e ['tiŋgl] *v/i* formigar; **~ing** formigueiro *m*

tinkle ['tiŋkl] *v/t*, *v/i* tinir, tilintar; *s* tinido *m*

tin-opener ['tinəup:nə] abre-latas *m*

tint [tint] *s* cor *m*, tom *m*, tinta *f*; *v/t* pintar (o cabelo)

tiny [taini] minúsculo; **~ tot** pequenino *m*, criancinha *f*

tip [tip] *s* ponta *f*, extremidade *f*; gorjeta *f*, palpite *m*; conselho *m*; sugestão *f*; *v/t*, *v/i* dar palpite, sugerir; inclinar(-se); tombar, virar(-se); tocar levemente em; dar gorjeta (a)

tipsy ['tipsi] tocado, alegre

tiptoe ['tiptəu] *v/i* andar em bicos de pés; **on ~** na ponta dos pés

tire ['taiə] *v/t*, *v/i* cansar(-se); **~ out** estafar; **~d** *adj* cansado, fatigado; **~less** incansável, infatigável; **~some** enfadonho, maçador, *Braz* macante

tissue ['tisju:, 'tiʃu:] tecido *m*; lenço *m* de papel; **~-paper** papel *m* de seda

tit [tit] *zo* chapim *m*; *anat* teta *f*

titbit ['titbit] pitéu *m*, gulodice *f*

title ['taitl] título *m*

to [tu:, tu, tə] *prp* até; a, para; com; de; *adv* a si; **it's 5 minutes ~** 4 são 4 menos 5

toad [təud] sapo *m*

to and fro ['tu ən' frəu] *adj* de vaivém; *s* vaivém *m*; **~ ~ ~** *adv* de um lado para o outro

toast [təust] *s* torrada *f*; brinde *m*, saúde *f*; *v/t* torrar, tostar; beber à saúde de, brindar a; **~er** torradeira *f*

tobacco [tə'bækəu] tabaco *m*

toboggan [tə'bɔgən] *s* tobogã *m*

today [tə'dei] *adv* hoje

toe [təu] *s* dedo *m* de pé

toffee ['tɔfi] caramelo *m*, *Braz*

bala f de leite, tofé m

together [təˈgeðə] juntos, juntas

toil [tɔil] s lida f, faina f; v/i lidar, moirejar

toilet [ˈtɔilit] casa f de banho, *Braz* privada f; retrete f, *Braz* bacia f sanitária; **~-paper** papel m higiénico; **~ soap** sabonete m

token [ˈtəukən] sinal m, marca f, recordação f

tolera|ble [ˈtɔlərəbəl] tolerável; **~nce** tolerância f; **~nt** tolerante

tolerate [ˈtɔləreit] v/t tolerar

toll [təul] s peagem f, portagem f, *Braz* pedágio m; v/t, v/i tocar, dobrar; **~-gate** barreira f onde se paga portagem

tomato [təˈmɑːtəu] tomate m

tomb [tuːm] túmulo m, sepulcro m

tom-cat [ˈtɔmkæt] gato m

tomorrow [təˈmɔrəu] adv amanhã f; **~ week** de amanhã a oito dias

ton [tʌn] tonelada f

tone [təun] s tom m; som m; timbre m

tongs [tɔŋz] s/pl pinça f, tenaz f

tongue [tʌŋ] língua f; **hold one's ~** calar a boca; **~-tied** calado; **~-twister** trava-línguas m

tonight [təˈnait] adv hoje à noite, esta noite

tonsil [ˈtɔnsl] amígdala f; **~litis** [-iˈlaitis] amigdalite f

too [tuː] demasiado, demais; também

tool [tuːl] s instrumento m, fer-

ramenta f

tooth [tuːθ] (pl teeth [tiːθ]) dente m; **~ and nail** com unhas e dentes; **~ache** dor f de dentes; **~-brush** escova f de dentes; **~-paste** pasta f dentifrica

top [tɔp] s cimo m, cume m, topo m; copa f, pitorra f, pião m; tampo m; adj superior; primeiro, principal; v/t cobrir, coroar; chegar ao topo; sobrepujar, exceder; **at ~ speed** a toda a velocidade; **from ~ to bottom** de alto a baixo; **on ~ of** ainda por cima

topic [ˈtɔpik] tópico m; **~al** a(c)tual

top|mast [ˈtɔpmɑːst, -məst] mastaréu m; **~sail** gávea f

topsyturvy [ˈtɔpsiˈtəːvi] adv às avessas, de pernas para o ar

torch [tɔːtʃ] tocha f, archote m, facho m; lâmpada f eléctrica, *Braz* farolete m

torment [ˈtɔːment] s tormento m; [-ˈment] v/t atormentar

tornado [tɔːˈneidəu] tornado m

torpedo [tɔːˈpiːdəu] s torpedo m; v/t torpedear; **~-boat** torpedeiro m

torp|id [ˈtɔːpid] entorpecido; **~or** torpor m

torrent [ˈtɔrənt] torrente f, caudal m; **~ial** [-ˈrenʃəl] torrencial

tortoise [ˈtɔːtəs] tartaruga f

torture [ˈtɔːtʃə] s tortura f; v/t torturar

toss [tɔs] s sacudid(el)a f, abanadela f; meneio m; arremesso m; v/t, v/i atirar ao ar; sacudir, abanar; arrojar, lançar

total ['təutl] *s, adj* total *m; v/t* totalizar; montar a; **~itarian** [-tæli'teəriən] totalitário; **~ity** [-'tæliti] totalidade *f*

totem ['təutəm] totem *m*

totter ['tɔtə] *v/i* titubear, cambalear

touch [tʌtʃ] *s* ta(c)to *m;* toque *m,* apalpadela *f;* conta(c)to *m,* ligação *f,* relação *f;* retoque *m; v/t, v/i* tocar, apalpar; chegar a; comover; **~ up** retocar; **~y** irascível; melindroso

tough [tʌf] *adj* rijo, forte, duro; penoso, difícil; **~en** *v/t, v/i* endurecer, enrijecer; **~ness** dureza *f,* rijeza *f*

tour [tuə] *s* volta *f;* viagem *f;* giro *m; v/t* viajar por, percorrer; **~ism** turismo *m;* **~ist** turista *m, f;* **~istic** [-'ristik] turístico

tow [təu] *v/t* rebocar; *s* estopa *f;* reboque *m;* **in ~** a reboque

toward(s) [tə'wɔ:d(z)] para; para com

towel ['tauəl] *s* toalha *f*

tower ['tauə] *s* torre *f; v/i* erguer-se, elevar-se; estar sobranceiro

town [taun] cidade *f;* centro *m,* baixa *f;* **~ hall** câmara *f* municipal, prefeitura *f*

toy [tɔi] *s* brinquedo *m*

trace [treis] *s* traço *m;* rasto *m,* pista *f; v/t* seguir a pista de, descobrir; traçar, delinear

track [træk] *s* rasto *m,* vestígio *m;* trilho *m;* pista *f;* caminho *m; v/t* seguir a pista de

tract [trækt] extensão *f;* opúsculo *m;* **~ion** [-'kʃən] tra(c)ção *f;* **~or** tra(c)tor *m*

trade [treid] *s* comércio *m,* negócio *m,* tráfico *m; v/t, v/i* negociar, comerciar; **~mark** marca *f* registada; **~ union** sindicato *m*

tradition [trə'diʃən] tradição *f;* **~al** tradicional

traffic ['træfik] *s* tráfego *m,* trânsito *m;* tráfico *m;* **~ in** *v/t* traficar; **~light/signal** semáforo *m,* sinal *m* luminoso

tragedy ['trædʒidi] *(pl* **-dies)** tragédia *f*

tragic ['trædʒik] trágico

trail [treil] *s* vereda *f,* picada *f;* pista *f,* rasto *m,* pegada *f; v/t, v/i* seguir a pista de; arrastar (-se)

train [trein] *s* comboio *m, Braz* trem *m;* comitiva *f,* séquito *m;* série *f; v/t, v/i* preparar(-se), formar(-se), estudar; treinar; exercitar

trainer ['treinə] instrutor *m;* treinador *m;* domador *m;* **~ing** *s* instrução *f,* educação *f;* ensino *m;* treino *m*

trait [treit] feição *f,* traço *m*

traitor ['treitə] traidor *m*

trajectory [trə'dʒektəri] *(pl* **-ries)** traje(c)tória *f*

tram(-car) ['træm(ka:)] (carro *m*) eléctrico *m, Braz* bonde *m*

tramp [træmp] *s* vagabundo *m,* vadio *m;* tropel *m,* tropeada *f;* caminhada *f; v/t, v/i* pisar; palmilhar

trample ['træmpl] *v/t, v/i* esmagar, pisar, calcar

trance [trɑ:ns] transe *m,* êxtase *m*

tranquil ['træŋkwil] tranquilo;
~(l)ity [-'kwiliti] tranquilidade
f; ~(l)ize v/t tranquilizar-se

transact [træn'zækt] v/t executar, levar a cabo; ~ion [-'zæk-
ʃən] transa(c)ção f

transatlantic [trænzət'læntik]
transatlântico

transcend [træn'send] v/t trans-
cender; ultrapassar, exceder

transcribe [træns'kraib] v/t
transcrever

transfer [træns'fə:] v/t, v/i
transferir; trasladar; ~able
[-'fə:rəbl] transferível; ~ence
transferência f

trans|figure [træns'figə] v/t
transfigurar; ~form v/t trans-
formar; ~formation transformação f; ~fusion [-'fju:ʒn]
transfusão f

transgress [træns'gres] v/t
transgredir; ~ion [-'greʃən]
transgressão f, violação f

transient ['trænziənt] adj transitório, passageiro

transistor [træn'zistə] transistor
m

transitive ['trænsitiv] adj transitivo

translat|able [træns'leitəbl] tra-
duzível; ~e (into) v/t, v/i tra-
duzir (para); ~ion tradução f;
~or tradutor m

transmission [trænz'miʃən]
transmissão f

transmit [trænz'mit] v/t transmitir

transmute [trænz'mju:t] v/t
transmutar

transparent [træn'speərənt]

transparente

transpire [træns'paiə] v/t, v/i
transpirar; tornar-se conhecido

transplant [træns'pla:nt] v/t
transplantar

transport [træns'pɔ:t] v/t transportar; [-] s transporte m

transpose [træns'pəuz] v/t
transpor; mus transportar

trap [træp] s armadilha f; cilada
f; v/t apanhar no laço

trapeze [trə'pi:z] trapézio m

trash [træʃ] refugo m; bagatela
f; lixo m

travel ['trævl] s viagem f; v/i viajar; ~ agency/bureau agên-
cia f de viagens; ~(l)er viajan-
te m, f; caixeiro m viajante; ~|
(l)er's cheque cheque m de
viagem

traverse ['trævə(:)s] v/t atravessar, cruzar

travesty ['trævisti] (pl -ties) pa-
ródia f

trawler ['trɔ:lə] barco m de arrasto, traineira f

tray [trei] tabuleiro m, bandeja f

treacher|ous ['tretʃərəs] trai-
çoeiro; ~y perfídia f, traição f

treacle ['tri:kl] melaço m

tread [tred] v/t pisar, calcar; seguir, trilhar; s piso m; passo m

treadle ['tredl] s pedal m

treason ['tri:zn] traição f

treasur|e ['treʒə] s tesouro m;
v/t entesourar; prezar; ~er te-
soureiro m; ~y tesouraria f

treat [tri:t] s regalo m, festim m;
v/t tratar; regalar

treatise ['tri:tiz] tratado m, dissertação f

treatment ['tri:tmənt] tratamento *m*

treaty ['tri:ti] (*pl* **-ties**) tratado *m*

treble ['trebl] *v/t, v/i* triplicar (-se); *s* mustiple *f*; *adj* triplo

tree [tri:] *s* árvore *f*

trefoil ['trefɔil] trevo *m*

tremble ['trembl] *v/i* tremer

tremendous [tri'mendəs] tremendo; estupendo

trem|or [tremə] tremura *f*; tremor *m*; **~ulous** [-juləs] trémulo

trench [trentʃ] *s* mil trincheira *f*; fosso *m*, vala *f*

trend [trend] *s* inclinação *f*, tendência *f*

trespass ['trespəs] *v/i* entrar ilegalmente; **~er** intruso *m*

trestle ['tresl] cavalete *m*

trial ['traiəl] prova *f*, ensaio *m*; *jur* processo *m*, julgamento *m*; tentativa *f*; **on** ~ à prova

triang|le ['traiæŋgl] triângulo *m*; **~ular** [-'æŋgjulə] triangular

tribe [traib] tribo *f*

tribunal [trai'bju:nl] tribunal *m*

tribut|ary ['tribjutəri] *s* (*pl* **-ries**) tributário *m*; afluente *m*; **~e** [-u:t] tributo *m*; homenagem *f*

trick [trik] *s* artifício *m*, artimanha *f*; partida *f*; fraude *f*, embuste *m*; ardil *m*; truque *m*; *v/t* enganar, iludir, lograr; **~ery** velhacaria *f*, trapaça *f*

trickle ['trikl] *v/i* gotejar, escorrer; *s* fio *m* de água

tricky ['triki] astucioso; complicado, intricado

trifle ['traifl] ninharia *f*, bagatela *f*; **a** ~ um pouco, um tudo nada

trifling ['traiflin] *adj* trivial, insignificante

trigger ['trigə] *s* gatilho *m*

trill [tril] *s* trilo *m*, trinado *m*; *v/t, v/i* trinar

trim [trim] *s* condição *f*, estado *m*; *v/t* adaptar, ajustar; enfeitar; aparar; *adj* garboso, catita

trimming ['trimin] *s* enfeite *m*, guarnição *f*

Trinity ['triniti] Trindade *f*

trinket ['trinkit] berloque *m*

trip [trip] *s* viagem *f*, excursão *f*, passeio *m*; *v/t, v/i* (fazer) tropeçar

tripe [traip] tripas *f/pl*

triple ['tripl] *adj* triplo, tríplice

tripod ['traipod] tripé *m*

trite [trait] banal, comum

triumph ['traiəmf] *s* triunfo *m*; *v/i* triunfar; **~al** [-'ʌmfəl] triunfal; **~ant** [-'ʌmfənt] triunfante

trolley ['troli] trólei *m*; *US* carro *m* eléctrico, *Braz* bonde *m*

troop [tru:p] *s* grupo *m*, bando *m*; tropa *f*

trophy ['troufi] (*pl* **-phies**) troféu *m*

tropic|al ['tropikəl] tropical; **~s** *s/pl* trópicos *m/pl*

trot [trot] *s* trote *m*; *v/t, v/i* trotar

trouble ['trʌbl] *s* incómodo *m*; moléstia *f*, inconveniente *m*; trabalho *m*; preocupação *f*, arrelia *f*; dificuldade *f*, dissabor *m*; *v/t, v/i* preocupar-se; afligir, molestar, incomodar(-se); ~ **some** enfadonho

trough [trɔf] gamela f

trousers ['trauzəz] s/pl calças f/pl

trout [traut] truta f

trowel ['trauəl] trolha f

truant ['tru:ənt] gazeteiro m; **play ~** fazer gazeta

truce [tru:s] trégua f

truck [tʌk] camião m, *Braz* caminhão m

trudge [trʌdʒ] v/i arrastar-se, andar a custo

true [tru:] adj verdadeiro; justo; seguro, certo; genuíno

truffle ['trʌfl] túbera f, trufa f

truism ['tru:izəm] truísmo m

truly ['tru:li] verdadeiramente; sinceramente; realmente, na verdade

trump [trʌmp] s trunfo m; v/t trunfar

trumpet ['trʌmpit] s trombeta f; **~er** trombeteiro m

truncheon ['trʌntʃən] casse-tête m, cacete m

trunk [trʌŋk] tromba f; tronco m; torso m; baú m

trunk call ['trʌŋkkɔ:l] chamada f interurbana

truss [trʌs] s med funda f; v/t atar

trust [trʌst] s confiança f; fé f; crédito m; depósito m; v/t fiar-se em, confiar em

trustee [trʌs'ti:] depositário m, consignatário m

trustworthy ['trʌst.wə:ði] digno de confiança

truth [tru:θ] verdade f; **~ful** verídico; sincero

try [trai] v/t, v/i experimentar, provar, tentar; pôr à prova; julgar; s tentativa f; **~ on** provar

tub [tʌb] tina f

tube [tju:b] tubo m, cano m; bisnaga f; *GB* metro m, *Braz* trem m subterrâneo

tuberculosis [tju(:)bə:kju'ləusis] tuberculose f

tuck [tʌk] s dobra f, prega f; v/t meter, esconder; **~ in** cobrir, agasalhar

Tuesday ['tju:zdi] terça-feira f

tuft [tʌft] tufo m

tug [tʌg] s arranco m, puxão m; v/t, v/i arrastar; puxar; **~boat** rebocador m

tulip ['tju:lip] tulipa f

tumble ['tʌmbl] v/i cair, rolar; tombar; dar um trambolhão; dar cambalhotas; s queda f; tombo m

tumbler ['tʌmblə] copo m; acrobata m

tummy ['tʌmi] estômago m; barriga f

tumo(u)r ['tju:mə] tumor m

tumult ['tju:mʌlt] tumulto m; **~uous** [-'mʌltjuəs] tumultuoso

tune [tju:n] s toada f; v/t afinar; **out of ~** desafinado

tunic ['tju:nik] túnica f

tunnel ['tʌnl] s túnel m

turban ['tə:bən] turbante m

turbid ['tə:bid] turvo

turbine ['tə:bin] turbina f

turbot ['tə:bət] rodovalho m

turbulence ['tə:bjuləns] turbulência f; **~turbulent** turbulento

tureen [tə'ri:n] terrina f, sopeira f

turf [tə:f] *s* relvado *m*

Turk [tə:k] turco *m*

turkey ['tə:ki] peru *m*

Turkish ['tə:kiʃ] *adj, s* turco *m*

turmoil ['tə:mɔil] barafunda *f*, atrapalhação *f*

turn [tə:n] *s* volta *f*; vez *f*; turno *m*; curva *f*; mudança *f*, transformação; *v/t, v/i* transformar(-se), virar, revirar, torcer, converter, mudar; voltar(-se); **~ away** recusar ver; mandar embora; **~ back** voltar; **~ down** baixar; rejeitar; **~ in** ir deitar-se; apresentar, entregar

turn | off *v/t, v/i* fechar; desligar, apagar; **~ on** abrir; ligar; depender de; **~ out** expulsar; vir a ser, tornar-se; confirmar-se, verificar-se; a, voltar-se para; **~ up** aparecer, suceder

turncoat ['tə:nkəut] vira-casaca *m*

turning ['tə:niŋ] *s* curva *f*, esquina *f*

turnip ['tə:nip] nabo *m*

turtle ['tə:tl] tartaruga *f*; **~-dove** rola *f*

tusk [tʌsk] presa *f*

tutor ['tju:tə] *s* tutor *m*; preceptor *m*

twang [twæŋ] *v/t, v/i* vibrar; *s* som *m* agudo; som *m* fanhoso

tweezers ['twi:zəz] *s/pl* pinça *f*

twelfth [twelfθ] *adj* décimo segundo; duodécimo

twelve [twelv] *adj* doze

twent|ieth ['twentiiθ] *adj* vigésimo

twenty ['twenti] vinte

twice [twais] duas vezes

twig [twig] *s* rebento *m*, broto *m*

twilight ['twailait] crepúsculo *m*

twill [twil] tecido *m* com velos em diagonal

twin [twin] *s* gêmeo *m*

twine [twain] *s* guita *f*, cordel *m*, retrós *m*; *v/t* enlaçar; torcer

twinkle ['twiŋkl] *s* centelha *f*, vislumbre *m*; *v/i* cintilar; piscar

twirl [twə:l] *v/t, v/i* girar, voltear; torcer, enrolar

twist [twist] *v/t, v/i* torcer(-se), retorcer

twitch [twitʃ] *s* contra(c)ção *f*; espasmo *m*; *v/t, v/i* contorcer (-se); contrair-se

twitter ['twitə] *s* gorjeio *m*; *v/i* trinar, gorjear, chilrear

two [tu:] *adj* dois, duas; **put ~ and ~ together** tirar as suas conclusões

type [taip] *s* tipo *m*; *v/t, v/i* escrever à máquina

typewriter ['taipraitə] máquina *f* de escrever

typhoon [tai'fu:n] tufão *m*

typical ['tipikəl] típico

typist ['taipist] dactilógrafo *m*

typography [tai'pɔgrəfi] tipografia *f*

tyran|ny ['tirəni] (*pl* **-nies**) tirania *f*; **~t** ['taiərənt] tirano *m*

tyre [taiə] pneumático *m*, pneu *m*

tyro ['taiərəu] novato *m*, noviço *m*

U

udder ['ʌdə] úbere *m*

ugly ['ʌgli] feio

ulcer ['ʌlsə] úlcera *f*

ulterior [ʌl'tiəriə] ulterior

ultimate ['ʌltimit] último, final

umbrella [ʌm'brelə] guarda-
-chuva *m*, chapéu-de-chuva *m*;
guarda-sol *m*

umpire ['ʌmpaiə] *s* árbitro *m*;
v/t, v/i arbitrar

unabashed [ʌnə'bæʃt] impassível; descarado

unabated [ʌnə'beitid] sem diminuição, constante

unable ['ʌn'eibl] incapaz; im-
possibilitado; **be ~** não poder

unabridged [ʌnə'bridʒd] integral, completo

unacceptable ['ʌnək'septəbl]
inaceitável

unaccustomed [ʌnə'kʌstəmd]
não usual; não habituado;
desacostumado

unadvised [ʌnəd'vaizd] inconsiderado, irrefle(c)tido

unaffected [ʌnə'fektid] desa-
fe(c)tado, sincero, natural

unalterable [ʌn'ɔ:ltərəbl] inal-
terável

unanimity [ˌju:nə'nimiti] unanimidade *f*

unanswerable [ʌn'ɑ:nsərəbl]
incontestável, irrespondível

unapproachable [ˌʌnə'prəu-
tʃəbl] inabordável

unarmed [ʌn'ɑ:md] desarma-
do, inerme

unasked [ʌn'ɑ:skt] espontâneo;
não solicitado

unassuming ['ʌnə'sju:miŋ] des-
pretensioso, modesto

unavailing ['ʌnə'veiliŋ] vão;
ineficaz

unawares [ʌnə'wɛəz] inespera-
damente; de surpresa

unbar ['ʌn'bɑ:] *v/t* destrancar

unbearable [ʌn'bɛərəbl] intolerável, insuportável

unbelievable [ʌnbi'li:vəbl] incrível

unbelieving [ʌnbi'li:viŋ] incrédulo, descrente

unbind [ʌn'baind] *v/t* desatar

unborn [ʌn'bɔ:n] por nascer

unbounded [ʌn'baundid] ilimitado, infinito; imenso

unburden [ʌn'bə:dn] *v/t* descarregar; desabafar; aliviar

unbuttoned [ʌn'bʌtnd] desabo-
toado

uncanny [ʌn'kæni] estranho, esquisito

uncertain [ʌn'sə:tn] incerto, duvidoso; indeciso, irresoluto; variável; **~ty** incerteza *f*

unchecked [ʌn'tʃekt] desenfreado; não controlado

uncle ['ʌŋkl] tio *m*

uncomfortable [ʌn'kʌmfətəbl]
desconfortável, incómodo;
desagradável; constrangido

uncommitted ['ʌnkə'mitid] não
comprometido; sem compro-
missos

unconcerned ['ʌnkən'sə:nd] indiferente, despreocupado

unconscious [ʌnˈkɔnʃəs] *adj, s* inconsciente *m, f*; **~ness** *s* inconsciência *f*

unconsidered [ˈʌnkənˈsidəd] lrreflc(e)tido, inconsiderado

uncouple [ˈʌnˈkʌpl] *v/t* desengatar; soltar

uncouth [ʌnˈkuːθ] grosseiro, rude

uncover [ʌnˈkʌvə] descobrir

uncritical [ˈʌnˈkritikəl] não crítico

uncut [ˈʌnˈkʌt] sem cortes, completo; não talhado; não cortado

undaunted [ʌnˈdɔːntid] intrépido, denodado

undeceive [ˈʌndiˈsiːv] *v/t* desenganar, desiludir

undecided [ˈʌndiˈsaidid] indeciso

undeniable [ˈʌndiˈnaiəbl] inegável

under [ˈʌndə] *prp* debaixo de, sob; abaixo de; com menos de; por baixo de; inferior a; *adv* debaixo, em baixo; por baixo; **~age** menor; **~clothing** roupa *f* de baixo, roupa *f* interior; **~current** subcorrente *f*; tendência *f* oculta; **~done** mal passado; **~estimate** *v/t* subestimar; **~go** *v/t* sofrer, passar por; **~ground** *s* metropolitano *m*; *adj* subterrâneo; **~hand** clandestino; **~line** *v/t* sublinhar; **~ling** subalterno *m*; **~mine** *v/t* minar, solapar; **~neath** *prp* debaixo de, por baixo de; *adv* debaixo, em baixo, por baixo; **~pants** *s/pl* cuecas *f/pl*, ceroulas *f/pl*;

~stand *v/t, v/i* entender, compreender, perceber; **~standing** *s* compreensão *f*; entendimento *m*; **~statement** atenuação *f*, afirmação *f* atenuada; **~take** *v/t* empreender; tomar a seu cargo, encarregar-se de; comprometer-se a; **~taker** agente *m* funerário; **~taking** *s* empresa *f*

under|wear [ˈʌndəwɛə] roupa *f* interior; **~weight** *adj* com peso a menos

undesirable [ˈʌndiˈzaiərəbl] *adj* indesejável

undeveloped [ˈʌndiˈveləpt] não desenvolvido

undies [ˈʌndiːz] *s/pl* roupa *f* interior de senhora

undo [ʌnˈduː] *v/t* desfazer; desatar

undoubted [ʌnˈdautid] indubitável

undress [ʌnˈdres] *v/t, v/i* despir(-se)

undue [ʌnˈdjuː] indevido; excessivo

undulat|e [ˈʌndjuleit] *v/i* ondular, ondear; **~ion** ondulação *f*

unearthly [ʌnˈəːθli] sobrenatural

uneas|iness [ʌnˈiːzinis] inquietude *f*; **~y** inquieto

uneducated [ˈʌnˈedʒukeitid] ignorante, inculto

unemploy|ed [ˈʌnimˈplɔid] desempregado; **~ment** desemprego *m*, falta *f* de trabalho

unequal [ʌnˈiːkwəl] desigual; **be ~ to the task** não estar à altura da tarefa; **~(l)ed** sem igual, inigualável

unequivocal ['ʌni'kwivəkəl] inequívoco

uneven ['ʌn'iːvən] irregular; desigual; ímpar; acidentado

unexampled [ˌʌnig'zɑːmpld] sem igual, sem exemplo

unexpected [ˌʌniks'pektid] inesperado, imprevisto

unfailing [ʌn'feiliŋ] infalível; incansável

unfair ['ʌn'fɛə] injusto; desleal; parcial

unfaltering [ʌn'fɔːltəriŋ] inabalável; firme

unfavo(u)rable [ʌn'feivərəbl] desfavorável, adverso

unfit [ʌn'fit] adj inadequado, impróprio; incapacitado

unfold [ʌn'fəuld] v/t desdobrar

unforeseen ['ʌnfɔː'siːn] imprevisto

unforgettable ['ʌnfə'getəbl] inesquecível

unfortunate [ʌn'fɔːtʃnit] adj infeliz, desgraçado; **~ly** infelizmente

unfriendly [ʌn'frendli] hostil

unfurnished [ʌn'fɔːniʃt] desmobilado

ungainly [ʌn'geinli] sem graça, tosco, desajeitado

ungodly [ʌn'gɔdli] ímpio; malvado, terrível

ungracious [ʌn'greiʃəs] indelicado, rude

ungrateful [ʌn'greitful] ingrato

unguarded [ʌn'gɑːdid] incauto, descuidado

unhapp|iness [ʌn'hæpinis] in-

felicidade f; **~y** triste; infeliz

unhealthy [ʌn'helθi] insalubre; doentio

unheard [ʌn'hɔːd] não ouvido; **~of** inaudito

unhook [ʌn'huk] v/t desenganchar; desacolchetar

unhoped for [ʌn'həuptfɔː] inesperado

uniform ['juːnifɔːm] s, adj uniforme m; **~ity** uniformidade f

unify ['juːnifai] v/t unificar

unilateral [juːni'lætərəl] unilateral

uninhabitable [ˌʌnin'hæbitəbl] inabitável

uninterrupted ['ʌnintə'rʌptid] ininterrupto

union ['juːnjən] sindicato m; união f

unit ['juːnit] unidade f; **~e** [-'nait] v/t, v/i unir(-se); **~y** ['juːniti] (pl -ties) unidade f

univers|al [juːni'vɔːsəl] universal; **~e** ['-vɔːs] universo m; **~ity** [-'vɔːsiti] (pl -ties) universidade f

unjust [ʌn'dʒʌst] injusto

unkempt [ʌn'kempt] despenteado, desgrenhado

unkind [ʌn'kaind] indelicado, grosseiro; cruel

unknow|ing [ʌn'nəuiŋ] desconhecedor, sem o saber; **~n** adj desconhecido

unlawful [ʌn'lɔːful] ilícito

unless [ən'les] a menos que, a não ser que, senão

unlike [ʌn'laik] adj diferente, distinto; **~lihood** inverosimilitude f, inverosimilhança f;

~ly inverosímil, pouco provável

unlimited [ʌn'limitid] ilimitado

unload [ʌn'ləud] *v/t, v/i* descarregar

unlock ['ʌn'lɔk] *v/t* abrir com chave

unloosen [ʌn'lu:sən] *v/t* despertar

unlucky [ʌn'lʌki] desventurado, infeliz

unmannerly [ʌn'mænəli] descortês, malcriado

unmarried ['ʌn'mærid] solteiro

unmask ['ʌn'ma:sk] *v/t* desmascarar

unmatched ['ʌn'mætʃt] incomparável, sem par

unmentionable [ʌn'menʃnəbl] não mencionável

unmindful [ʌn'maindful] descuidado

unmistakable ['ʌnmis'teikəbl] evidente, manifesto; inequívoco

unmoved [ʌn'mu:vd] impassível, insensível; firme

unnatural [ʌn'nætʃrəl] desnatural; desnaturado

unnecessary [ʌn'nesisəri] desnecessário

unnerve ['ʌn'nə:v] *v/t* desalentar

unnoticed ['ʌn'nəutist] despercebido

unobserved ['ʌnəb'zə:vd] despercebido, inobservado

unobtrusive ['ʌnəb'tru:siv] comedido, discreto

unpack ['ʌn'pæk] *v/t, v/i* desfazer as malas; desembrulhar

unparalleled [ʌn'pærəleld] sem paralelo

unpleasant [ʌn'pleznt] desagradável

unpopular ['ʌn'pɔpjulə] impopular

unpractised [ʌn'præktist] inexperiente, sem prática

unprejudiced [ʌn'predʒudist] imparcial

unprincipled [ʌn'prinsəpld] sem princípios

unprovoked ['ʌnprə'vəukt] não provocado

unpublished ['ʌn'pʌbliʃt] inédito

unquestionable [ʌn'kwestʃənəbl] inquestionável, incontestável

unravel [ʌn'rævəl] *v/t, v/i* deslindar(-se); desemaranhar(-se)

unreasonable [ʌn'ri:znəbl] pouco razoável; desarrazoado; **~ing** irracional, cego

unrelenting [ʌnri'lentiŋ] inexorável

unrest ['ʌn'rest] inquietação *f*, agitação *f*

unrestrained ['ʌnri'streind] desenfreado

unriva(l)led [ʌn'raivəld] incomparável, sem rival

unroll ['ʌn'rəul] *v/t, v/i* desenrolar(-se)

unruffled ['ʌn'rʌfld] sereno, tranquilo, calmo

unruly [ʌn'ru:li] rebelde, indisciplinado

unsaid ['ʌn'sed] *adj* não dito, não proferido

unscathed [ʌn'skeiðd] incólume, ileso

unscrupulous [ʌnˈskruːpjuləs] pouco escrupuloso; sem escrúpulos

unseemly [ʌnˈsiːmli] inconveniente, impróprio

unseen [ˈʌnˈsiːn] *adj* despercebido

unserviceable [ʌnˈsəːvisəbl] imprestável

unsettle [ˈʌnˈsetl] *v/t* perturbar; desarranjar, transtornar; **~d** *adj* variável, instável, incerto

unsightly [ʌnˈsaitli] feio

unskilled [ˈʌnˈskild] não especializado

unso|ciable [ʌnˈsəuʃəbl] insociável; **~cial** insocial

unsound [ˈʌnˈsaund] infundado, errôneo; instável; defeituoso; doentio

unspeakable [ʌnˈspiːkəbl] indizível

unstable [ˈʌnˈsteibl] instável

unsteady [ˈʌnˈstedi] inconstante; vacilante

unstudied [ˈʌnˈstʌdid] natural

unsuitable [ˈʌnˈsjuːtəbl] impróprio, inconveniente

untangle [ˈʌnˈtæŋgl] *v/t* desembaraçar, des(e)maranhar

unthankful [ˈʌnˈθæŋkful] ingrato, mal-agradecido

unthink|able [ʌnˈθiŋkəbl] inconcebível, impensável; **~ing** irrefle(c)tido

unthought-of [ʌnˈθɔːt-ɔv] inesperado, imprevisto

untidy [ʌnˈtaidi] desordenado

untie [ˈʌnˈtai] *v/t* desatar

until [ənˈtil] *prp* até; *conj* até que

untimely [ʌnˈtaimli] inoportuno; prematuro

untiring [ʌnˈtaiəriŋ] incansável, infatigável

untold [ˈʌnˈtəuld] incalculável, incontável; não contado, por contar

untruth [ˈʌnˈtruːθ] falsidade *f*

unusual [ʌnˈjuːʒuəl] invulgar, insólito

unutterable [ʌnˈʌtərəbl] completo, chapado; indizível, inexprimível

unveil [ʌnˈveil] *v/t* descobrir, desvendar

unwarranted [ʌnˈwɔrəntid] injustificado

unwell [ʌnˈwel] indisposto

unwholesome [ˈʌnˈhəulsəm] insalubre

unwilling [ʌnˈwiliŋ] de má vontade, pouco disposto

unwind [ʌnˈwaind] *v/t, v/i* desenrolar(-se)

unwise [ʌnˈwaiz] desajuizado, insensato

unwitting [ʌnˈwitiŋ] involuntário; inconsciente

unwonted [ʌnˈwəuntid] inusitado

unworthy [ʌnˈwəːði] indigno

unwrap [ˈʌnˈræp] *v/t* desembrulhar

unwritten [ˈʌnˈritn] não escrito, oral, verbal, tradicional

up [ʌp] *adj* ascendente; levantado; *adv* acima, para cima; em pé; *prp* por ... acima; **be ~** acontecer, haver; **what's ~?** que foi? que há?; **~ and down** para cima e para baixo; **~**

there lá em cima

upbringing ['ʌpbriŋiŋ] s educação f, formação f

upcountry ['ʌp'kʌntri] adj interior

uphill ['ʌp'hil] adj fig difícil, árduo; ascendente; adv para cima; colina acima

uphold [ʌp'həuld] v/t sustentar, manter

upholster|er ['ʌp'həulstərə] estofador m; **~y** tapeçaria f

upon [ə'pɔn] em, sobre

upper ['ʌpə] adj superior; **~most** o mais alto

upright ['ʌprait] adj vertical, direito; em/de pé; justo, íntegro, honesto; adv direito

uprising [ʌp'raiziŋ] sublevação f

uproar ['ʌprɔ:] algazarra f, tumulto m, barulho m

upset ['ʌpset] s transtorno m; [-'set] v/t derrubar, derramar; transtornar, perturbar; adj perturbado, transtornado; preocupado; desarranjado

upside down ['ʌpsaid'daun] de pernas para o ar

upstairs [ʌp'stɛəz] adv lá em cima

upstart ['ʌpstɑ:t] novo-rico m, filho m da sorte

upstream ['ʌp'stri:m] adj, adv rio acima

up to ['ʌp tu] até; à altura, bastante bom, bem; **be ~ someone** caber a alguém; **by ~ get ~ ~ do s. th.** estar a fazer a/c. **~ ~ date** moderno, em dia

upward(s) ['ʌpwəd(z)] adv para cima

urban ['ə:bən] urbano; **~e** [-'bein] cortês

urchin ['ə:tʃin] gaiato m, brejeiro m, garoto m, Braz moleque m

urg|e [ə:dʒ] s impulso m, desejo m, ânsia f; v/t incitar; insistir em; urgir, instar; **~ency** urgência f; **~ent** urgente

urin|ate ['juərineit] v/i urinar; **~e** urina f

urn [ə:n] urna f

us [ʌs, əs, s] nós, nos

usage ['ju:zidʒ] emprego m, uso m, prática f

use [ju:s] s uso m; [ju:z] v/t usar, empregar, fazer uso de; **~d** [ju:zd] usado; **~d** [ju:st]: **~d to** habituado a, acostumado a; **~ful** útil; **~fulness** utilidade f; **~less** inútil; **~lessness** inutilidade f

usher ['ʌʃə] v/t introduzir, anunciar; **~ette** [-'ret] arrumadora f, indicadora f

usual ['ju:ʒuəl] costumado, usual, habitual; **as ~** como de costume

usurer ['ju:ʒərə] usurário m

usurp [ju:'zə:p] v/t usurpar; **~er** usurpador m

usury ['ju:ʒuri] usura f

utensil [ju:'tensl] utensílio m

utility [ju:'tiliti] (pl -ties) utilidade f; benefício m; serviço m público

utilize ['ju:tilaiz] v/t utilizar

utmost ['ʌtməust] adj máximo, extremo; **do one's ~** fazer todo o possível

utopia [juːˈtoupjə] utopia *f*; **~n** utópico

utter [ˈʌtə] *adj* completo, total;

v/t proferir, pronunciar; soltar; passar; **~ance** articulação *f*, expressão *f*; **~most** extremo

uvula [ˈjuːvjulə] úvula *f*

V

vacan|cy [ˈveikənsi] (*pl*-cies) vaga *f*, vacatura *f*, vacância *f*; **~t** vago, livre, desocupado; vazio

vacate [vəˈkeit] *v/t* evacuar, deixar

vacation [vəˈkeiʃən] *s* férias *f/pl*

vaccinate [ˈvæksineit] *v/t* vacinar

vacillat|e [ˈvæsileit] *v/i* vacilar; **~ion** [-ˈleiʃən] vacilação *f*

vacuum [ˈvækjuəm] *s* vácuo *m*, vazio *m*; **~-cleaner** aspirador *m*

vagabond [ˈvægəbɔnd] vagabundo *m*

vagary [ˈveigəri] (*pl*-ries) capricho *m*, veneta *f*

vague [veig] vago, impreciso

vain [vein] vão; vaidoso, **in ~** em vão

valet [ˈvælit] *s* criado *m* de quarto

valid [ˈvælid] válido, **~ity** [vəˈliditi] validade *f*

valley [ˈvæli] vale *m*

valuable [ˈvæljuəbl] valioso, de valor, precioso; **~s** [-z] *s/pl* obje(c)tos *m/pl* de valor

value [ˈvælju] *s* valor *m*; *v/t* avaliar; **~less** sem valor; **~er** [-juə] avaliador *m*

valve [vælv] válvula *f*

van [væn] furgoneta *f*; vagão *m*;

furgão *m*

vane [vein] cata-vento *m*, grimpa *f*

vanilla [vəˈnilə] baunilha *f*

vanish [ˈvæniʃ] *v/i* desaparecer, desvanecer-se; dissipar-se

vanity [ˈvæniti] (*pl*-ties) vaidade *f*

vaporize [ˈveipəraiz] *v/t*, *v/i* vaporizar(-se)

vapo(u)r [ˈveipə] vapor *m*

vari|able [ˈveəriəbl] *adj* variável; **~ance** desacordo *m*, desavença *f*; **at ~ance with** em desacordo com; **~ant** *s* variante *f*; **~ation** [-ˈeiʃən] variação *f*

variety [vəˈraiəti] (*pl*-ties) variedade *f*

various [ˈveəriəs] vários, diversos

varnish [ˈvɑːniʃ] *s* verniz *m*; *v/t* envernizar

vary [ˈveəri] *v/t* *v/i* variar

vase [vɑːz] vaso *m*

vast [vɑːst] vasto, imenso; **~ness** vastidão *f*, imensidade *f*

vat [væt] tonel *m*, tina *f*

vault [vɔːlt] *s* abóbada *f*; salto *m* à vara; *v/t*, *v/i* saltar à vara

veal [viːl] (carne *f* de) vitela *f*

vegeta|ble [ˈvedʒitəbl] *adj* vegetal; *s* legume *m*, hortaliça *f*; **~rian** [-ˈteriən] vegetariano;

~te ['-teit] v/i vegetar; **~tion** [-'teiʃən] vegetação f

vehement ['viːimənt] veemente

vehicle ['viːikl] veículo m

veil [veil] s véu m; v/t velar

vein [vein] veia f; veio m

velocity [vi'lositi] velocidade f

velvet ['velvit] veludo m; **~een** belbutina f; **~y** aveludado

vend [vend] v/t vender; **~ing-machine** distribuidor m automático; **~or** vendedor m

venerable ['venərəbəl] venerável

venerate ['venəreit] v/t venerar

venereal [vi'niəriəl] venéreo

Venetian [vi'niːʃən] veneziano; **♀ blind** veneziana f, persiana f

vengeance ['vendʒəns] vingança f

venison ['venzn] carne f de veado

venom ['venəm] veneno m; **~ous** venenoso

vent [vent] s respiradouro m; v/t desafogar, desabafar

ventilat|e ['ventileit] v/t ventilar; **~ion** [-'leiʃən] ventilação f; **~or** ventilador m

ventriloquist [ven'trilǝkwist] ventríloquo m

venture ['ventʃə] s especulação f; v/t, v/i aventurar(-se), arriscar(-se)

veranda(h) [və'rændə] varanda f

verb [vəːb] verbo m

verbal ['vəːbəl] adj verbal; literal

verbose [vəː'bəus] prolixo, verboso

verge [vəːdʒ] s borda f, beira f; **on the ~ of** à beira de, prestes a

verify ['verifai] v/t verificar

veritable ['veritəbl] verdadeiro

vermicelli [vəːmi'seli] aletria f

vermin ['vəːmin] vérmina f

verm(o)uth ['vəːməθ] vermute m

versatil|e ['vəːsətail] versátil; **~ity** versatilidade f

vers|e [vəːs] verso m; estrofe f; **~ify** [-sifai] v/t versificar; **~ion** [-ʃən] versão f

vertical ['vəːtikəl] adj vertical

vertigo ['vəːtigəu] vertigem f

very ['veri] adv muito; adj mesmo; **~ good** muito bom; muito bem; **~ well** muito bem; **the ~ idea** mas que ideia

vessel ['vesl] vaso m, recipiente m; navio m

vest [vest] s US colete m; GB camisola f interior

vestibule ['vestibjuːl] vestíbulo m

vestige ['vestidʒ] vestígio m

vestry ['vestri] (pl-tries) sacristia f

vet [vet] s veterinário m

veteran ['vetərən] adj, s veterano m

veterinary ['vetərinəri] veterinário

veto ['viːtəu] s veto m; v/t vetar

vex [veks] v/t vexar; molestar; **~ation** [-k'seiʃən] contrariedade f; vexame m; **~atious** [-k'seifəs] vexatório; molesto

via ['vaiə] via, por (via de)

viable ['vaiəbl] viável

viaduct ['vaiədʌkt] viaduto *m*

vibrat|e [vai'breit] *v/t, v/i* vibrar; **~ion** vibração *f*

vicar ['vikə] vigário *m*; cura *m*; **~age** vicariato *m*

vice [vais] *s* vício *m*

vice versa ['vaisi'və:sə] vice--versa

vicinity [vi'siniti] (*pl* **-ties**) vizinhança *f*

vicious ['viʃəs] mau, malvado

vicissitude [vi'sisitju:d] vicissitude *f*

victim ['viktim] vítima *f*; **~ize** *v/t* vitimar

victorious [vik'tɔ:riəs] vitorioso; **~y** ['-təri] (*pl* **-ries**) vitória *f*

vie [vai] *v/i* rivalizar, competir

view [vju:] *s* vista *f*; *v/t* ver, observar; considerar, ponderar; **in ~** em vista; **in ~ of** devido a, em vista de; **on ~** em exposição; **~er** telespectador *m*

vigil ['vidʒil] vigília *f*; **~ance** vigilância *f*; **~ant** vigilante

vigorous ['vigərəs] vigoroso

vigo(u)r ['vigə] vigor *m*

vil|e [vail] vil; abje(c)to; **~ify** ['vilifai] *v/t* vilipendiar, aviltar

villa ['vilə] vila *f*, vivenda *f*

villag|e ['vilidʒ] aldeia *f*, povoação *f*; **~er** aldeão *m*

villain ['vilən] celerado *m*, vilão *m*

vindic|ate ['vindikeit] *v/t* vindicar, justificar; **~ation** ['-keiʃən] vindicação *f*, justificação *f*; **~tive** vingativo

vine [vain] vinha *f*, videira *f*

vinegar ['vinigə] vinagre *m*

vint|age ['vintidʒ] *s* vindima *f*; **~ner** ['-nə] negociante *m* de vinhos, vinhateiro *m*

viola [vi'əulə] viola *f*

violat|e ['vaiəleit] *v/t* violar; **~ion** ['-leiʃən] violação *f*

violen|ce ['vaiələns] violência *f*; **~t** violento

violet ['vaiəlit] *adj, s* violeta *f*

viol|in [vaiə'lin] violino *m*; **~inist** violinista *m, f*; **~oncello** ['-lənˈtʃeləu] violoncelo *m*

viper ['vaipə] víbora *f*

virgin ['və:dʒin] virgem *f*; **~al** virginal; **~ity** ['-dʒiniti] virgindade *f*

viril|e ['virail] viril; **~ity** ['-riliti] virilidade *f*

virtu|al ['və:tjuəl] virtual; **~e** ['-tju:] virtude *f*; **~osity** ['-ɔsiti] virtuosidade *f*; **~oso** ['-əuzəu] virtuoso *m*; **~ous** ['-tjuəs] virtuoso

virulen|ce ['viruləns] virulência *f*; **~t** virulento

virus ['vaiərəs] vírus *m*

visa ['vi:zə] *s* visto *m*

viscount ['vaikaunt] visconde *m*; **~ess** viscondessa *f*

viscous ['viskəs] viscoso

visib|ility [,vizi'biliti] visibilidade *f*; **~le** ['vizibl] visível

vision ['viʒən] visão *f*; **~ary** *adj, s* visionário *m*

visit ['vizit] *s* visita *f*; *v/t, v/i* visitar; **~or** visita *f*, visitante *m, f*

visor ['vaizə] viseira *f*

vista ['vistə] perspectiva *f*

visual ['vizjuəl] visual; **~ize** *v/t* imaginar, visualizar

vital ['vaitl] vital; **~ity** ['-'tæliti]

vitalidade *f*; **~ize** *v/t* vitalizar
vitamin(e) ['vitəmin] vitamina *f*

vitriol ['vitriəl] acrimónia *f*; vitríolo *m*; **~ic** [-'ɔlik] vitriólico; cáustico, acerbo

vituperation [vi.tju:pə'reiʃən] vituperação *f*, vitupério *m*

vivaci|ous [vi'veiʃəs] vivaz, vivo, animado; **~ty** [-'væsiti] vivacidade *f*

vivid ['vivid] vívido, brilhante, intenso; **~ness** vivacidade *f*

vixen ['viksn] raposa *f* fêmea; megera *f*

voc|abulary [və'kæbjuləri] (*pl* **-ries**) vocabulário *m*; **~al** ['vəukəl] *adj* vocal; **~alist** ['vəukəlist] vocalista *m, f*

vocation [vəu'keiʃən] vocação *f*

vociferous [vəu'sifərəs] vociferante

vogue [vəug] voga *f*, moda *f*

voice [vɔis] *s* voz *f*; *v/t* exprimir, formular; sonorizar

void [vɔid] *adj* vazio; sem efeito, nulo; *s* vazio *m*, vácuo *m*; *v/t* invalidar, anular

volatile ['vɔlətail] volátil

volcan|ic [vɔl'kænik] vulcânico; **~o** [-'keinəu] (*pl* **-noes**) vulcão *m*

volley ['vɔli] *s* descarga *f*, salva *f*; **~-ball** vol(e)ibol *m*

volt [vəult] vóltio *m*; **~age** voltagem *f*

voluble ['vɔljubl] volúvel

volum|e ['vɔljum] volume *m*; **~inous** [və'lju:minəs] volum(in)oso

volunt|ary ['vɔləntəri] *adj* voluntário; **~eer** [-'tiə] *s* voluntário *m*; *v/i* oferecer(-se); apresentar-se como voluntário

voluptuous [və'lʌptjuəs] voluptuoso

vomit ['vɔmit] *s* vómito *m*; *v/t*, *v/i* vomitar

voraci|ous [və'reiʃəs] voraz; **~ity** [-'ræsiti] voracidade *f*

vot|e [vəut] *s* voto *m*; *v/i* votar; **~er** votante *m, f*, eleitor *m*

vouch ['vautʃ]: **~ for** *v/i* garantir, responder por; **~er** senha *f*, talão *m*; vale *m*; **~safe** *v/t* conceder

vow [vau] *s* voto *m*; *v/t* fazer voto, jurar; consagrar

vowel ['vauəl] vogal *f*

voyag|e ['vɔidʒ] *s* viagem *f* por mar; **~er** viajante *m, f*, navegante *f*

vulgar ['vʌlgə] grosseiro; vulgar; **~ity** [-'gæriti] grosseria *f*, grosseirismo *m*

vulnerable ['vʌlnərəbl] vulnerável

vulture ['vʌltʃə] abutre *m*

W

wad [wɔd] *s* maço *m*; chumaço *m*; bucha *f*

waddle ['wɔdl] *v/i* bambolear (-se), gingar

wad|e [weid] *v/i* patinhar; vadear, passar a vau; **~ers** *s/pl* botas *f/pl* altas e impermeáveis

wafer ['weifə] *eccl* hóstia *f*; bolacha *f*; obreia *f*

wag [wæg] *s* folgazão *m*, gracejador *m*; *v/t*, *v/i* abanar, agitar, sacudir

wage [weidʒ] salário *m*; *v/t* empreender, empenhar-se em; **~earner** assalariado *m*; **~r** *s* aposta *f*; *v/t*, *v/i* apostar; **~s** *s/pl* salário *m*

waggish [wægiʃ] pilhérico, folgazão, gracejador

waggle [wægl] *v/t*, *v/i* menear (-se), abanar

wa(g)gon [wægən] carroça *f*; vagão *m*; **~er** carreteiro *m*, carroceiro *m*

wagtail [wægteil] alvéloa *f*

wail [weil] *s* lamentação *f*; vagido *m*; *v/i* lamentar-se; choramingar

wainscot [weinskət] lambril *m*

waist [weist] cintura *f*, cinta *f*; **~coat** colete *m*

wait [weit] *s* espera *f*; *v/t*, *v/i* esperar, aguardar; ficar; **~ at table** servir à mesa; **~er** criado *m* de mesa

waiting-room [weitiŋ-ru:m] sala *f* de espera

waitress [weitris] criada *f* de mesa, *Braz* garçonete *f*

wake [weik] *v/t*, *v/i* despertar, acordar; *s* esteira *f*, sulco *m*; vigília *f*, velório *m*; **~ful** acordado, desperto; insone; vigilante

walk [wɔːk] *s* passeio *m*, volta *f*; alameda *f*; andar *m*; caminhada *f*; *v/t*, *v/i* andar, caminhar, passear, ir a pé; **~er** caminhante *m*, *f*

walkie-talkie [wɔːkiˈtɔːki]

transmissor-receptor *m* portátil

walking [wɔːkiŋ] *adj* ambulante; a pé; para andar; **~-stick** bengala *f*, bastão *m*

wall [wɔːl] *s* muro *m*; muralha *f*; parede *f*; *v/t* murar; emparedar; entaipar

wallet [wɔlit] carteira *f* de bolso

wallow [wɔləu] *v/i* chafurdar; espojar-se

walnut [wɔːlnət] noz *f*

walrus [wɔːlrəs] morsa *f*

waltz [wɔːls] *s* valsa *f*; *v/i* valsar

wand [wɔnd] vara *f*, varinha *f*

wander [wɔndə] *v/i* vaguear, errar, vadiar; delirar; divagar, desviar-se de; **~er** viandante *m*, *f*, viajante *m*, *f*; **~ing** *adj* errante; nómada

want [wɔnt] *v/t* querer, desejar; precisar (de), necessitar (de); *s* carência *f*, falta *f*, necessidade *f*; **~ing** *adj* falho (de), falto (de); *prp* sem

war [wɔː] *s* guerra *f*

warble [wɔːbl] *v/i* gorjear, trinar; *s* gorjeio *m*, trinado *m*

ward [wɔːd] *s* pupilo *m*, tutelado *m*; enfermaria *f*; quarteirão *m*, bairro *m*; **~en** guarda *m*; dire(c)tor *m*, administrador *m*; **~er** carcereiro *m*

wardrobe [wɔːdrəub] guarda-roupa *m*

warehouse [wεəhaus] armazém *m*

warlike [wɔːlaik] bélico, belicoso, marcial

warm [wɔːm] *s* quente *m*, aquecimento *m*; *adj* quente; caloroso; ardente; *v/t*, *v/i* aquecer

(-se), esquentar

warmth [wɔːmθ] *adj* calor *m*

warn [wɔːn] *v/t, v/i* prevenir; avisar

warning ['wɔːniŋ] *s* aviso *m*, advertência *f*

warp [wɔːp] *v/t, v/i* empenar

warrant ['wɔrənt] *v/t* justificar; garantir; **~y** (*pl* -ties) garantia *f*

warren ['wɔrən] lura *f*, coelheira *f*

warrior ['wɔriə] guerreiro *m*

wart [wɔːt] verruga *f*

wary ['wɛəri] cauteloso, circunspecto, prudente

was [wɔz,wəz] 1. a 3. *sg past of* be

wash [wɔʃ] *s* lavagem *f*; *v/t, v/i* lavar(-se); **~out** *s* fiasco *m*; **~ up** lavar a louça; lançar à praia; **~able** lavável; **~basin** lavatório *m*; **~erwoman** lavadeira *f*; **~house** lavadouro *m*; **~ing** *s* roupa *f* lavada/suja; **~ing-machine** máquina *f* de lavar roupa; **~ing-up** *s* lavagem *f* da louça; **~y** débil, fraco

wasp [wɔsp] vespa *f*

waste [weist] *adj* inculto; vago; pérdido; inútil; *s* desperdício *m*; estrago *m*, desgaste *m*; perda *f*; *v/t, v/i* gastar; desperdiçar, estragar, esbanjar; perder; **~ away** definhar-se; **~ful** esbanjador; **~paper basket** cesto *m* dos papéis

watch [wɔtʃ] *v/t, v/i* observar, olhar; ver, assistir a; vigiar; *s* relógio *m*; vigilância *f*; vigia *f*, guarda *f*; ronda *f*; **~ for** espe-

rar por; **~ out** ter cuidado, estar alerta; **~ful** vigilante; **~fulness** vigilância *f*; **~maker** relojoeiro *m*

water ['wɔːtə] *s* água *f*; *v/t, v/i* molhar; banhar; regar; aguar; **~ down** aguar, diluir; atenuar; **~colo(u)r** aguarela *f*; **~cress** ['-krɛs] agrião *m*

water|fall ['wɔːtəfɔːl] cascata *f*, catarata *f*, queda *f* de água; **~ing can** regador *m*; **~level** nível *m* de água; **~line** linha *f* de flutuação; **~mill** moinho *m* de água, azenha *f*; **~power** força *f* hidráulica; **~proof** *adj*, *s* impermeável *m*; **~shed** linha *f* divisória das águas; **~tight** estanque; inequívoco; **~works** obras *f/pl* hidráulicas

watery ['wɔːtəri] aguado, aquoso; (h)úmido; encharcado

watt [wɔt] vátio *m*

wattle [wɔtl] *s* caniçada *f*

wave [weiv] *s* vaga *f*, onda *f*, aceno *m*, gesto *m*; *v/t, v/i* ondear; agitar; ondular; acenar; tremular

waver ['weivə] *v/i* hesitar, vacilar

wax [wæks] *s* cera *f*; *v/t* encerar; **~en** de cera

way [wei] *s* caminho *m*; modo *m*, maneira *f*, meio *m*; **by the ~** a propósito; **by ~ of** por via de; para servir de; **in a ~** de certo modo; **in no ~** de nenhum modo; **on the ~ (to)** a caminho de; **this ~** por aqui; **that ~** por ali; **give ~** ceder; desmoronar-se; **make ~** abrir caminho; ~**lay** v/t armar ciladas a; ~**ward** caprichoso, cabeçudo

we [wiː, wi] nós

weak [wiːk] fraco; débil; deficiente; ~**en** v/t, v/i enfraquecer; ~**ness** fraqueza f, debilidade f; fraco m

wealth [welθ] riqueza f; abundância f; ~**y** rico, abastado

wean [wiːn] v/t desmamar

weapon ['wepən] arma f

wear [weə] s uso m; desgaste m; vestuário m; v/t, v/i usar, vestir, trazer; desgastar, gastar (-se), consumir-se; ~ **out** gastar-se; esgotar-se, estafar-se; ~ **and tear** desgaste m; ~ **away** desgastar; ~**ing** adj cansativo, fatigante

wear|isome ['wiərisəm] cansativo, enfadonho, maçador; ~**y** adj exausto, estafado; estafante

weasel ['wiːzl] s doninha f

weather ['weðə] s tempo m atmosférico; v/t resistir a, aguentar; ~**forecast** boletim m meteorológico

weav|e [wiːv] v/t, v/i tramar, urdir; tecer; ~**er** tecelão m

web [web] teia f

wedding ['wediŋ] s casamento m; ~**ring** aliança f

wedge [wedʒ] s cunha f; v/t rachar com cunha

wedlock ['wedlɔk] casamento m, matrimónio m

Wednesday ['wenzdi] quarta-feira f

wee [wiː] adj diminuto, minúsculo; v/i fazer chichi

weed [wiːd] serva f daninha; v/t, v/i arrancar as ervas daninhas, sachar; ~**y** débil

week [wiːk] semana f; **last** ~ a semana passada; **next** ~ na próxima semana; ~**day** dia m útil; ~**end** s fim m de semana; ~**ly** s semanário m; adj semanal

weep [wiːp] v/t, v/i chorar; ~**ing willow** chorão m

weigh [wei] v/t pesar; ~ **anchor** zarpar, levantar âncora

weight [weit] s peso m; ~**y** pesado; grave, importante

weir [wiə] represa f, açude m

weird [wiəd] esquisito, estranho; misterioso, fantástico

welcome ['welkəm] adj bem-vindo; s boas-vindas f/pl; v/t dar as boas-vindas a; receber, acolher

weld [weld] v/t, v/i soldar; caldear

welfare ['welfeə] bem-estar m

well [wel] s poço m; v/i manar, brotar; adj bom, bem, de/com saúde; adv bem; int ora, bem; **as ~ as** assim como; ~**-being** bem-estar m; ~**-bred** bem-criado, bem-educado; ~**-done** bem passado; ~**-known** bem conhecido; ~**-meaning** bem-intencionado

Welsh [welʃ] adj galês

went [went] past of **go**

were [wəː, wə] past pl of **be**

west [west] s oeste m, ocidente m; ~**ern** ocidental, do oeste

wet [wet] adj molhado; (h)úmido; chuvoso; v/t molhar; (h)umedecer

whale [weil] baleia *f*; **~r** pescador *m* de baleias; baleiro *m*

wharf [wɔːf] cais *m*, desembarcadouro *m*

what [wot] *pron* que, o que; qual; quê; *adj* que; **~ (...) for?** para quê? **~ if ...?** que tal se ...? e se ...?; **~ the ...?** mas que ...?; **~ever, ~soever** *pron*, *adj* qualquer que; tudo o que, tanto quanto; seja o que for; qualquer que seja

wheat [wiːt] trigo *m*

wheel [wiːl] *s* roda *f*; *v*/*t*, *v*/*i* voltar-se; rolar, fazer rodar; **~barrow** carrinho *m* de mão

whelp [welp] *s* cachorrinho *m*

when [wen] *adv*, *pron* quando; *conj* quando, no tempo que

whenever [wen'evə] *adv*, *conj* sempre que

where [wɛə] *adv* onde; aonde; **~abouts** *s* paradeiro *m*; *adv* onde, em que lugar; **~as** [wɛər'æz] porquanto, ao passo que; **~upon** ao que, depois do que

wherever [wɛə'revə] *adv*, *conj* onde quer que (seja); para onde quer que

wherry ['weri] (*pl* **-ries**) bote *m*

whet [wet] *v*/*t* estimular; afiar

whether ['weðə] se; quer, ou

whey [wei] soro *m* do leite

which [witʃ] *pron* que, o qual, o que; qual, qual?; **~ever** [-tʃ'evə] qualquer que; seja qual for

whiff [wif] *s* baforada *f*

while [wail] *conj* enquanto; ao passo que; *s* pouco *m*, espaço *m* de tempo; **a ~** um pouco; **once in a ~** de vez em quando; **~ away** *v*/*t* passar, matar

whilst [wailst] ao passo que

whim [wim] capricho *m*, veneta *f*

whimper ['wimpə] *v*/*i* choramingar

whimsical [wimzikəl] caprichoso

whimsy ['wimzi] extravagância *f*

whine [wain] *s* ganido *m*; *v*/*i* lamuriar, choramingar; ganir

whinny ['wini] *v*/*i* relinchar

whip [wip] *s* chicote *m*; *v*/*t* chicotear; bater; **~ping** açoite *m*, surra *f*

whirl [wəːl] *s* rodopio *m*; *s* turbilhão *m*; *v*/*t* turbilhonar; rodopiar; **~pool** remoinho *m*; **~wind** turbilhão *m*

whir(r) [wəː] *v*/*i* zunir, zumbir; *s* zumbido *m*

whisk [wisk] *v*/*t* sacudir; bater; *s* batedor *m*; sacudidela *f*

whiskers ['wiskəz] *s*/*pl* suíças *f*/*pl*

whisk(e)y [wiski] uísque *m*

whisper ['wispə] *v*/*t*, *v*/*i* cochichar; *s* cochicho *m*

whistle ['wisl] *v*/*t*, *v*/*i* assobiar, apitar; silvar; *s* assobio *m*, silvo *m*; apito *m*

white [wait] *adj*, *s* branco *m*; **~n** *v*/*t*, *v*/*i* branquear, embranquecer; **~ness** brancura *f*; **~wash** *s* cal *f*; *v*/*t* caiar

whitlow [witləu] panarício *m*

Whitsun(tide) ['witsən(taid)] Pentecostes *m*

whittle ['witl] v/t aparar, cortar, talhar

whiz(z) [wiz] v/i zunir; silvar

who [hu:,hu] quem; que; o que, o qual; **~ever** quem quer que seja

whole [həul] adj todo; inteiro; integral; inta(c)to; completo; total; s todo m; total m, totalidade f; **~sale** adj, adv em massa; com por atacado; **~some** são, sadio, salutar

whom [hu:m] pron quem; que; o que, o qual

whoop [hu:p] s vaia f, grito m, apupo m; v/i vaiar, gritar, apupar; **~ing-cough** coqueluche f

whose [hu:z] pron cujo; de quem, do qual

why [wai] adv porquê?; porque ...?; por que; int quê!; ora! bem!

wick [wik] mecha f, pavio m

wicked ['wikid] mau, ruim, malvado

wicker ['wikə] vime m

wicket ['wikit] postigo m, portinhola f

wide [waid] adj largo, amplo, grande, vasto, imenso; **~ly** amplamente; **~n** v/t, v/i alargar (-se), estender(-se); dilatar(-se); **~spread** muito divulgado, muito comum

widow ['widəu] viúva f; **~er** viúvo m; **~hood** viuvez f

width [widθ] largura f

wield [wi:ld] v/t manejar

wife [waif] (pl wives [-vz]) mulher f, esposa f

wig [wig] peruca f, cabeleira f postiça

wild [waild] adj selvagem; feroz, bravo, bravio; silvestre; deserto, inculto; **~ boar** javali m; **~erness** ['wildənis] lugar m selvagem; ermo m; **~ly** descontroladamente

wil(l)ful ['wilful] voluntarioso; intencional

will [wil] s vontade f; testamento m; v/t legar, testar; v/aux desejar; querer; at **~** à vontade; where there's a **~**, there's a way querer é poder; **~ing** disposto, pronto; voluntário; **~ingly** de boa vontade

willow ['wiləu] salgueiro m

wilt [wilt] v/t, v/i murchar

wily ['waili] ardiloso, manhoso, astucioso

win [win] s vitória f; v/t, v/i ganhar, vencer

wince [wins] v/i estremecer; s estremecimento m

wind [wind] s vento m; flatulência f; fôlego m; get **~ of** ouvir dizer

wind [waind] v/t enrolar(-se); serpentear; dar corda a; içar, levantar; s rotação f, volta f; **~ing** ['waindiŋ] adj sinuoso, tortuoso; s volta f, dobra f; sinuosidade f; elect enrolamento m

windlass ['windləs] molinete m, bolinete m

windmill ['win,mil] moinho m de vento

window ['windəu] janela f; **~pane** vidraça f, vidro m; **~sill** peitoril m

windpipe ['windpaip] traqueia f

wind-screen ['windskri:n] pára-

-brisas *m*; ~ **wiper** limpa-pára-
-brisas *m*

windy ['windi] ventoso

wine [wain] *s* vinho *m*

wing [wiŋ] *s* asa *f*; ala *f*, flanco *m*;
~ed *adj* alado

wink [wiŋk] *s* piscadela *f*, pesta-
nejo *m*; *v/t, v/i* piscar, pestanejar

winner ['winə] vencedor *m*

winning ['winiŋ] *adj* cativante

winnings ['winiŋz] *s/pl* ganhos
m/pl, lucros *m/pl*

winsome ['winsəm] agradável,
encantador

win|ter ['wintə] *s* inverno *m*; *v/i*
passar o inverno; ~**try** ['-tri] in-
vernal, invernoso

wipe [waip] *s* limpadela *f*; esfre-
gadela *f*; *v/t* limpar; enxugar;
esfregar; ~ **off** saldar, pagar;
~ **up** limpar

wire ['waiə] *s* fio *m*; arame *m*;
US telegrama *m*; *v/t* pôr instalação elé(c)trica em; telegrafar

wireless ['waiəlis] *adj* sem fio(s)

wiry ['waiəri] magro

wisdom ['wizdəm] sabedoria *f*,
sagacidade *f*

wise [waiz] *adj* sábio, sagaz

wish [wiʃ] *s* desejo *m*; vontade *f*;
anelo *m*; *v/t, v/i* desejar, ane-
lar, querer, ter vontade de

wistful ['wistful] ansioso, ane-
lante; saudoso

wit [wit] *s* espírito *m*; graça *f*, fi-
nura *f*; engenho *m*

witch [witʃ] feiticeira *f*, bruxa *f*

with [wið] com

withdraw [wið'drɔ:] *v/t, v/i* reti-
rar(-se); ~**al** retirada *f*

wither ['wiðə] *v/t, v/i* murchar,
secar

withhold [wið'həuld] *v/t* reter,
deter; impedir; negar, recusar

within [wi'ðin] *prp* dentro de; no
espaço de

without [wi'ðaut] *prp* sem

withstand [wið'stænd] *v/t* resistir a

witness ['witnis] *v/t* testemunhar; presenciar, assistir a; *s*
testemunha *f*; **bear** ~ **to** testi-
ficar, testemunhar

witty [witi] espirituoso, engraçado

wizard ['wizəd] feiticeiro *m*

woe [wəu] dor *f*; desgraça *f*, calamidade *f*; ~**ful** triste; lamentável

wolf [wulf] *s* (*pl* **wolves** [-vz])
lobo *m*; *v/t* devorar

woman ['wumən] (*pl* **women**
['wimin]) mulher *f*; ~**ly** feminino

womb [wu:m] útero *m*, matriz *f*;
ventre *m*; *fig* entranhas *f/pl*

wonder ['wʌndə] *s* admiração *f*;
assombro *m*, espanto *m*; prodígio *m*, maravilha *f*; *v/i* espan-
tar-se, maravilhar-se; estranhar; perguntar a si mesmo;
querer saber; ~**ful** maravilhoso

wont [wəunt] *s* costume *m*

woo [wu:] *v/t* granjear, conquistar

wood [wud] *s* bosque *m*, mata *f*;
mato *m*; madeira *f*; lenha *f*; *adj*
de madeira; ~**en** de madeira;
~**pecker** pica-pau *m*; ~**work**
carpintaria *f*; madeira *f* traba-

lhada

wool [wul] lã f; ~(l)en de lã; ~ly s malha f de lã; adj confuso, vago; lanoso

word [wə:d] s palavra f; termo m, vocábulo m; letra f, texto m; v/t exprimir; redigir; ~ing s reda(c)ção f, fraseologia f; ~y verboso

work [wə:k] s obra f; trabalho m; emprego m; v/t, v/i trabalhar; andar, funcionar; manobrar, operar; explorar; lavrar, talhar; ~able realizável; manejável, manobrável; ~day dia m útil; ~er operário m trabalhador m; ~ing adj trabalhador; de trabalho; admissível; ~man trabalhador m, operário m; artífice m; ~manship artesanato m; mão-de-obra f; ~s s fábrica f; mecanismo m; ~shop oficina f

world [wə:ld] mundo m; ~liness mundanidade f; ~ly mundano; ~-power potência f mundial; ~-wide adj mundial

worm [wə:m] s verme m, bicho m; lombriga f

worn-out [wɔːnˈaut] adj gasto, usado; coçado; alquebrado; fatigado

worried [wʌrid] adj preocupado, inquieto

worry [wʌri] s (pl -ries) preocupação f, ânsia f, ansiedade f; v/t, v/i ralar, atormentar; preocupar(-se), arreliar-se

wors [we|əs] adv, adj pior; ~en v/t, v/i piorar

worship [ˈwəːʃip] v/t adorar, venerar; s adoração f, veneração f

worst [wəːst] adj péssimo; o pior; adv da pior maneira, pior

worsted [ˈwustid] fio m de lã

worth [wəːθ] s valor m; adj que vale a pena; merecedor, digno; **be** ~ valer, merecer; ~less sem valor; ~while que vale a pena; ~y [-ði] adj digno, merecedor

wound [wuːnd] s ferida f, ferimento m, chaga f; v/t ferir

wrangle [ˈræŋgl] s disputa f; v/i disputar

wrap [ræp] v/t envolver, embrulhar; ~per invólucro m

wreath [riːθ] grinalda f, coroa f; ~e [-ð] v/t engrinaldar; cingir

wreck [rek] s mar naufrágio m; ruína f, destruição f; v/t arruinar, destruir; naufragar

wren [ren] carriça f

wrench [rentʃ] s torcedura f; arranco m, puxão m; chave f inglesa; v/t arrancar; deslocar, torcer

wrest [rest] v/t arrebatar, arrancar; desvirtuar, distorcer

wrestle [resl] v/i lutar; ~r lutador m

wretch [retʃ] infeliz m, f, desgraçado m; patife m

wretched [ˈretʃid] infeliz, desgraçado, miserável; ~ness miséria f

wriggle [ˈrigl] v/i torcer-se, menear-se

wring [riŋ] v/t torcer, retorcer

wrinkle [ˈriŋkl] s ruga f; v/t, v/i

enrugar(-se)

wrist [rist] pulso *m*, munheca *f*

writ [rit] *s* mandado *m*; escritura *f*

write [rait] *v/t, v/i* escrever; **~down** anotar, pôr por escrito; **~ off** eliminar, anular; **~ out** redigir; preencher, passar

writer ['raitə] escritor *m*

writhe [raið] *v/i* contorcer-se

writing ['raitiŋ] *s* escrita *f*; caligrafia *f*, letra *f*; **in ~** por escrito; **~desk** escrivaninha *f*, se-

cretária *f*; **~-paper** papel *m* de carta; **~s** *s/pl* escrito *m*, obra *f*

wrong [rɔŋ] *adj* falso, errado, erróneo, incorre(c)to; enganado; **~ side** avesso *m*; *s* injúria *f*; agravo *m*; dano *m*; injustiça *f*; mal *m*; *adv* mal, erradamente; *v/t* afrontar, ofender, injuriar; **be ~** não ter razão; **~doing** má (a)c(ç)ão *f*; **~ful** injusto; ilegal

wry [rai] forçado; de esguelha

X

X-mas ['krisməs] = **Christmas**

X-ray ['eks'rei] *s* raio *m* X; *v/t* radiografar, examinar ao

raio X

xylophone ['zailəfəun] xilofone *m*

Y

yacht [jɔt] iate *m*; **~ing** *s* navegação *f* em iate

yak [jæk] *s* iaque *m*

yam [jæm] inhame *m*

Yank(ee) ['jæŋk(i)] ianque *m, f*, americano *m* do norte

yap [jæp] *v/i* latir

yard [jɑ:d] jarda *f*; pátio *m*; **~-arm** ponta *f* da verga, lais *m*

yarn [jɑ:n] *s* fio *m*; patranha *f*

yawn [jɔ:n] *v/i* bocejar; *s* bocejo *m*

yeah [je:jæ] sim

year [jiə] ano *m*; **~ly** *adv* anualmente; *adj* anual

yearn [jə:n] *v/i* suspirar, ansiar

yearning ['jə:niŋ] *s* ânsia *f*; saudade *f*

years [jiəz] *s/pl* idade *f*, anos

m/pl

yeast [ji:st] fermento *m*; levedura *f*

yell [jel] *s* berro *m*, grito *m*; *v/i* berrar, gritar; vociferar

yellow ['jeləu] *adj, s* amarelo *m*; *v/t, v/i* amarelecer

yelp [jelp] *s* ganido *m*; *v/i* ganir

yes [jes] *adv* sim

yesterday ['jestədi] *adv* ontem

yet [jet] *conj* mas, contudo; *adv* ainda; já

yew [ju:] teixo *m*

yield [ji:ld] *s* produção *f*; rendimento *m*; *v/t, v/i* produzir, render; ceder; **~ing** *adj* submisso, fraco; moldável

yogh(o)urt ['jəugə:t] iogurte *m*

yoke [jəuk] *s* canga *f*, jugo *m*; *v/t*

jungir; emparelhar

yokel ['jəukəl] saloio m, labrego m, Braz caipira m

yolk [jəuk] gema f de ovo

yon(der) ['jɔn(də)] acolá

you [ju:, ju, jə] tu; vós; você; o senhor; te, vos; o, a; lhe, lhes; ti; se, a gente

young [jʌŋ] adj jovem, novo; s/pl jovens m/pl; cria f; ~er mais novo; ~ster ['-stə] menino m, jovem m

your [jɔ:] teu(s), tua(s); seu(s), sua(s); vosso(s), vossa(s); do(s) senhor(es), da(s) senhora(s)

yours [jɔ:z] o(s) teu(s), a(s) tua(s); seu(s), sua(s); vosso(s), vossa(s); do(s) senhor(es), da(s) senhora(s), de você(s); ~ truly atenciosamente, respeitosamente

yourself [jə'self] (pl -selves ['selvz]) te, se; a ti/si mesmo; você mesmo, o senhor mesmo, tu próprio; (all) by ~ sòzinho, sem ajuda

youth [ju:θ] mocidade f, juventude f; moço m, jovem m; ~ful jovem, juvenil; ~ hostel albergue m da juventude

Z

zeal [zi:l] zelo m; ~ot ['zelət] fanático m; ~ous ['zeləs] zeloso m

zebra ['zi:brə] zebra f; ~ crossing passadeira f para peões

zenith ['zeniθ] zénite m; apogeu m, auge m

zeppelin ['zepəlin] zepelim m

zero ['ziərəu] zero m

zest [zest] ardor m, gosto m

zigzag ['zigzæg] s ziguezague m; v/i ziguezaguear

zinc [ziŋk] zinco m

Zionism ['zaiənizəm] sionismo m

zip [zip] s, **zip-fastener** fecho m de correr; silvo m; fig vitalidade f, energia f

zither ['ziðə] cítara f

zodiac ['zəudiæk] zodíaco m

zone [zəun] s zona f

zoo [zu:] jardim m zoológico

zoolog|ical [zəuə'lɔdʒikəl] zoológico; ~ist [-'ɔlədʒist] zoólogo m; ~y [-'ɔlədʒi] zoologia f

zoom [zu:m] s subida f vertical; ~ lens obje(c)tiva f de foco variável

Zulu ['zu:lu:] adj zulo

a *art* f the; *pers pron* her, it; *dem pron* that, the one, her; *prp* to, at, in, on, by; ~ **custo** with difficulty; ~ **direito** straight on; ~ **pé** on foot; ~ **que horas?** at what time?

à *contr of prp* a *and art* f a; ~ **esquerda** on the left; ~s **escuras** in the dark; ~ **meia-noite** at midnight; ~ **pressa** in haste

aba f brim; edge; tail

abacate *m* avocado (pear)

abacaxi *m* ananas; *Braz* mess

abad|e *m* abbot; ~**essa** f abbess; ~**ia** f abbey

abafado *adj* sultry

abafar *v/t, v/i* choke; suffocate; smother

abaixar *v/t* lower; humble

abaixo down, below, under

abalar *v/t, v/i* affect; go off; shock; shake

abalo *m* shock; disturbance

abalro|amento *m* collision; ~**ar** *v/t* collide

abanar *v/t* fan; shake; winnow

abandon|ar *v/t* abandon; ~**o** *m* abandonment; desertion

abarrotar *v/t* fill (up), glut

abast|ado rich, well off; ~**ança** f wealth, easy circumstances

abastecer *v/t* supply, provide

abastecimento *m* supply; refuel(l)ing

abat|er *v/t, v/i* abate; decrease;

cast down; fell; ~**ido** down cast, dejected; faint; ~**imento** *m* allowance, discount; dejection

abdica|ção f abdication, renunciation; ~**r** *v/t, v/i* abdicate

abdómen *m* abdomen

abeirar *v/r* approach

abelha f bee

abençoar *v/t* bless

aberta f opening, gap

abert|o *adj* open; ~**ura** f opening; aperture; *mus* overture

abeto *m* fir

abismo *m* abyss

abje(c)ção f abjection

abje(c)to *adj* abject, base

abjudicar *v/t* oust, dispossess

abjurar *v/t* abjure

abnega|ção f abnegation; ~**r** *v/t* abnegate, renounce

abóbada f vault

abóbora f pumpkin

aboli|ção f abolition; ~**ir** *v/t* abolish

abominar *v/t* abominate, detest, abhor

abominável abominable

abon|ar *v/t* answer for; guarantee; ~**o** *m* warranty; ~**o de família** family allowance

abordar *v/t* board; accost; ~ **um assunto** broach a subject

aborrec|er *v/t, v/r* bore; weary; disgust; displease; ~**ido** weari-

some; bored; weary; **~imento**
m bore(dom); nuisance; weariness

abort|ar v/i abort, miscarry;
fail; **~o** m abortion

abotoar v/t button (up), fasten

abraç|ar v/t embrace; **~o** m
embrace, hug

abrandar v/t, v/i soften; relent;
appease; slacken

abranger v/t include, comprise

abras|ador burning, scorching;
~ar v/t burn, scorch

abre-latas m tin/can opener

abrevi|ação f abridg(e)ment;
~ar v/t abbreviate; abridge;
~atura f abbreviation

abrig|ar v/t, v/r shelter, protect; **~o** m shelter, protection,
cover; **ao ~o de** under (the)
cover of; **~o antiaéreo** air-
raid shelter

Abril m April; **1° de ~** All
Fool's Day

abrir v/t, v/i, v/r open; unfold;
unfasten; **~ os olhos a alguém** open someone's eyes; **~-se com alguém** unbosom
oneself to someone

abrunho m sloe

absolut|amente absolutely,
quite; **~o** adj absolute

absolv|er v/t absolve; **~ição** f
absolution

absor|ção f absorption; **~to**
absorbed; **~ver** v/t, v/i/r absorb

abstenção f abstention

abster v/t, v/r **(de)** abstain
(from)

abstinência f abstinence

abstra|(c)ção f abstraction;

~(c)to adj abstract; absent-
minded; **~ir** v/t abstract, separate; **~ir-se** v/r collect one's
thoughts

absurdo m absurdity; adj
absurd

abund|ância f abundance;
~ante abundant; **~ar (em)**
v/i abound (in)

abusar (de) v/t, v/i abuse, misuse

abuso m abuse, misuse

abutre m vulture

acabado adj finished; worn-out,
old; perfect, faultless

acabar v/t, v/i finish, end, conclude; complete; **~ de ...**
have just ...

acabrunhado downcast

acabrunhar v/t deject, distress

acácia f acacia

academia f academy

açaime m muzzle

acalentar v/t lull, rock

acalmar v/t, v/i calm

acamar v/t lay, dispose in layers

açambarc|ador m monopolizer; **~ar** v/t monopolize

acampamento m camp

acampar v/i camp

acanhado bashful, shy, timid;
narrow, close

acanhar v/t, v/r intimidate;
narrow, make tight

acariciar v/t fondle, caress,
stroke

acaso m chance, hazard; **ao ~**
at random; **por ~** by chance

acatar v/t respect, revere, venerate

acautel|ado cautious, wary;

~ar *v/t, v/r* beware of; caution, warn; be on one's guard

a(c)ção *f* action, deed; **com stock**, share

a(c)cionista *m, f* shareholder

aceder *v/i* accede, comply

aceitação *f* acceptance

aceitar *v/t* accept

aceler|ador *m* accelerator; **~ar** *v/t* accelerate

acenar *v/t* nod; beckon; **~ com a mão** wave one's hand

acend|edor *m* lighter; **~er** *v/t* light, kindle; switch on

aceno *m* nod; wave

acent|o *m* accent; **~uação** *f* accentuation; **~uar** *v/t* accentuate

acepção *f* meaning, sense

acepipe *m* dainty, titbit; **~s** *m/pl* hors d'oeuvre

acerbo tart, bitter; harsh

acerca de about, with regard to

acercar-se de *v/r* approach

acertar *v/t* set right; hit the mark; guess right; adjust; **~ em cheio** hit the nail on the head

aceso lighted, lit, on; excited, hot

acessível accessible

acesso *m* access; fit, attack

acessório *m* accessory, appendage; *adj* accessory

achado *m* find, discovery; **não se dar por ~** pretend to ignore

achaque *m* ailment; defect

achar *v/t* find, hit on; think; **~-se** be; find oneself

achatar *v/t* flatten, squash

acident|ado *adj* uneven; **~al**

accidental; **~e** *m* accident

acidez *f* acidity

ácido *adj* acid, sour, tart; *m* acid

acima above; up; **~ de** above; beyond; over; **~ de tudo** above all; **pela rua ~** up the street

acinte *m* spite, malice

aclam|ação *f* acclamation; **~ar** *v/t* acclaim

aclarar *v/t, v/i* clear up; make clear, clarify

aclima(ta)r *v/t, v/r* acclimatize

aço *m* steel

acobardar *v/t, v/r* discourage, intimidate

acocorar-se *v/r* squat; crouch

açodar *v/t* incite; hurry

acolá there; **~ adiante** over there

acolchoar *v/t* wad, quilt

acolh|er *v/t, v/r* welcome; shelter; take refuge; **~ida** *f*, **~imento** *m* reception, welcome; shelter

acometer *v/t* attack, assault, assail

acomodar *v/t, v/r* accommodate; fit, suit; arrange

acompanh|amento *m* accompaniment; **~ar** *v/t* accompany; keep company

acondicionamento *m* packing

acondicionar *v/t* condition; pack, box

aconselhar *v/t, v/r* advise; **~-se com o travesseiro** sleep on a thing/question

acontec|er *v/i* happen; **~imento** *m* happening, event

açor *m* goshawk

açorda *f* bread panada

acordar *v/t, v/i* awake, wake(n)

acordo *m* agreement; **de ~!** it's agreed!; **de ~ com** in accordance with; **chegar a (um) ~** come to terms

acorrer *v/i* run to help

acossar *v/t* harass

acostar *v/t, v/i* run ashore; join; **~-se** lean on/against

acostumar (a) *v/t, v/r* accustom; get used (to), get accustomed (to)

acotovelar *v/t* elbow, jostle

açougue *m* slaughterhouse, abattoir

acre *adj* acrid, tart; mordant

acredit|ado accredited; credible; **~ar** *v/t* believe; accredit

acrescentar *v/t* add

acrescer *v/t, v/i* grow, increase

acréscimo *m* addition, increase

acroba|cia *f* acrobatics; **~ta** *m, f* acrobat

a(c)ta *f* record; **~s** *f/pl* minutes *s/pl*

a(c)tiv|ar *v/t* activate; **~idade** *f* activity; **~o** *adj* active

a(c)to *m* act, deed, action

a(c)t|or *m* actor; **~riz** *f* actress

a(c)tual present, current; **~idade** *f* (the) present moment; **~idades** *f/pl* news

a(c)tuar *v/t* actuate; act

açúcar *m* sugar

açúcar|ar *v/t* sugar, sweeten; **~eiro** sugar-basin

açude *m* dam, sluice, weir

acudir *v/i* run to help

acuidade *f* acuity, sharpness

açular *v/t* incite, set on

acumular *v/i, v/r* accumulate

acus|ação *f* accusation; **~ado** *m* accused; **~ar** *v/t* accuse; **a recepção de** acknowledge the receipt of

acústica *f* acoustics

adágio *m* adage; adagio

adapt|ação *f* adaptation; **~ar** *v/t* adapt; **~ável** adaptable

adega *f* (wine) cellar

adej|ar *v/i* flutter; **~o** *m* flutter

adelgaçar *v/t* make thin, make slender

adentro indoors; inward(s)

adepto *m* adept

adequado adequate, suitable

adereç|ar *v/t* adorn, attire; **~o** *m* attire, finery

ader|ência *f* adherence; **~ente** *adj, m, f* adherent; **~ir** *v/i* adhere

aderno *m bot* privet

ades|ão *f* adhesion; **~ivo** *adj* adhesive; *m* sticking-plaster

adestrar *v/t* instruct, train

adeus *int, s* good-bye; **~inho!** cheerio! bye-bye!

adiamento *m* postponement

adiantado *adj* fast; advanced

adiant|amento *m* progress, improvement; advance; advancement; **~ar** *v/t* advance; put on/forward; **isso não adianta** that is no good

adiante *adv* forward(s), onward(s); **int** go on!

adiar *v/t* postpone; put off

adi|ção *f* addition; supplement; appendix; **~cionar** *v/t* add up, tot up

adido *m* attaché

aditamento m addition, supplement

adivinh|a f riddle, puzzle; **~ar** v/t guess; **~o** m fortune-teller

adjac|ência f contiguity; **~ente** adjacent

adje(c)tivo m adjective

adjudic|ação f adjudication; **~ar** v/t adjudicate

adjunto m adjunct; assistant

adjurar v/t adjure

administr|ação f administration; **~ar** v/t administer

admir|ação f admiration; surprise; **~ar** v/t, v/r admire; wonder; **não admira** no wonder

admirável admirable

admiss|ão f admission; **~ível** admissible

admitir v/t admit; concede

adoçar v/t sweeten; assuage, soften

adocicado sweetish

adoçicar v/t sweeten

adoecer v/i become ill, fall sick

adoentado seedy, unwell

adoentar v/t make ill, sicken

adolescência f adolescence

adolescente adj, m, f adolescent

ado(p)|ção f adoption; **~tar** v/t adopt

ador|ação f adoration; worship; **~ar** v/t adore; worship

adormecer v/t, v/i put to sleep; fall asleep

adormecido asleep, sleeping

adornar v/t adorn

adquirir v/t acquire

adro m churchyard

adstringente adj, s m astringent

aduana f custom-house

adub|ar v/t fertilize; **~o** m manure, fertilizer

adula|ção f adulation; **~dor** m flatterer; **~r** v/t flatter

adulter|ador m adulterer; **~ar** v/t adulterate

adultério m adultery

adulto adj, m adult; grown-up

adunco hooked, crooked

advent|ício adj adventitious; **~o** m advent; eccl Advent

advérbio m adverb

advers|ão f opposition; **~ário** m adversary; **~idade** f adversity; **~o** adverse

advert|ência f warning, remark; **~imento** m warning; **~ir** v/t warn

advogado m lawyer, advocate

advogar v/t advocate

aéreo aerial

aerodinâmica f aerodynamics

aeródromo m aerodrome

aeromoça f stewardess

aeronáutica f aeronautics

aeronave f airship

aeroplano m aeroplane, airplane

aeroporto m airport

afã m anxiety; eagerness

afabilidade f affability

afadigar v/t, v/r fatigue, tire

afag|ar v/t caress, stroke, pat, fondle; **~o** m caress, pat

afamado renowned

afanar v/i, v/r toil, labour

afastado remote, distant

afast|amento m remoteness;

removal; separation; **~ar** v/t remove, separate

afável affable

afazer v/t, v/r accustom; **~es** m/pl business, affairs

afe(c)t|ação f affectation; affectedness; **~ado** affected; conceited; **~ar** v/t, v/r affect; pretend; **~o** m affection; **~uoso** affectionate

afeição f affection

aferir v/t check; gauge

aferrolhar v/t bolt, lock

afiançar v/t guarantee

afiar v/t sharpen

afigurar v/t, v/r shape; imagine

afilhado m godson

afim adj akin; m relative

afinação f refining; tuning

afinal after all; at last; finally

afinar v/t, v/i get angry; refine; tune

afirm|ação f affirmation; **~ar** v/t, v/i affirm, aver

afivelar v/t buckle

afixar v/t affix, stick

afli|ção f affliction; grief; **~gir** v/t, v/r afflict; grieve; **não se aflija!** don't worry!

afluência f affluence; crowd, concourse

afluente adj affluent; abundant

afluir v/i flow; abound

afogar v/t, v/r choke, stifle; drown

afoit|ado bold; **~ar** v/t encourage; **~eza** f boldness

afora adv, prp except; save; excluding

afortunado fortunate

afreguesado frequented

africano African

afronta f insult, affront

afrontar v/t insult, affront

afrouxar v/t slacken, loosen

afugentar v/t put to flight, scare away

afundar v/t, v/r sink; deepen

agachar-se v/r squat; crouch; cower

agarrar v/t, v/r clasp, grip; grasp; seize

agasalh|ar v/t, v/r wrap up; lodge, shelter; **~o** m shelter, lodging; warm clothes

agência f agency; bureau; office; **~ de informações** information bureau; **~ de viagens** travel agency/bureau; **~ funerária** funeral parlo(u)r

agenda f notebook

agente m agent; **~ marítimo** shipping agent; **~ provocador** agent provocateur

ágil agile

agilidade f agility

agir v/i act

agita|ção f agitation; **~do** excited, agitated; rough; restless; **~r** v/t, v/r shake; agitate

aglomer|ação f agglomeration; **~r** v/t agglomerate

agoni|a f agony; **~ado** seasick, sick; **~ar** v/t, v/r nauseate, sicken; afflict; **~zar** v/t, v/i agonize; be in agony

agora now

Agosto m August

agour|ar v/t forebode, augur; **~o** m augury, omen

agraciar v/t invest with, award

agradar v/t, v/r like; please

agradável pleasant

agradec|er v/t, v/i thank; **~ido** grateful; **~imento** m thanks

agrado m pleasure, liking; satisfaction

agravamento m aggravation

agrav|ar v/t, v/r insult; aggravate; **~o** m offence, injury

agre|dir v/t attack; **~ssão** f aggression; **~ssivo** aggressive; **~ssor** m aggressor

agreste rural; rustic

agrião m water-cress

agrícola adj agricultural

agricultor m agricultur(al)ist, farmer

agricultura f agriculture

agrupamento m grouping; group

agrupar v/t group

água f water; **~ mineral** mineral water

aguaceiro m shower

água-de-colónia f (eau de) cologne

aguardar v/t wait for, await

aguardente f brandy, aqua vitae

aguarela f water-colo(u)r

aguçar v/t sharpen

agud|eza f sharpness; acuity; **~o** sharp; acute

aguentar v/t suffer, bear; endure

águia f eagle

aguilhão m goad

agulha f needle

ai m groan, moan; int ah!; **num ~** instantly

aí there; **~ tens!** there you are!

ainda still; yet; even; **~ bem** fortunately; **~ assim** nevertheless; even so; **~ não** not yet; **~ por cima** into the bargain; **~ que** although; even if

aipo m celery

ajeitar v/t, v/i adapt; arrange

ajoelhar v/t, v/i kneel (down)

ajud|a f aid, help; **~ar** v/t aid, help, assist

ajuizado sensible

ajuizar v/t judge; estimate

ajunt|amento m assembly; **~ar** v/t assemble; add

ajustar v/t adjust; agree on, settle; **~ contas com** get even with

ajuste m agreement, settlement

ala f wing

alagar v/t, v/r overflow; inundate

alameda f alley, lane

álamo m poplar

alargar v/t, v/i, v/r enlarge (on); spread out; widen

alarido m outcry

alarm|ante alarming; **~ar** v/t, v/r frighten; alarm; **~e** m alarm

alastrar v/i spread

alavanca f lever; crowbar

albatroz m albatross

alberg|ar v/t lodge; harbo(u)r; **~ue** m shelter, refuge; **~ue m da juventude** youth hostel

alcachofra f artichoke

alcançar v/t, v/i obtain; attain; reach

alcance m reach; range; **ao ~ da mão** within reach

alcaparra *f* caper
alçar *v/t* raise
alcatifa *f* carpet
alcatrão *m* tar
álcool *m* alcohol
alcoolismo *m* alcoholism
alcunha *f* nickname
aldeão *m* villager
aldeia *f* village
aldrabão *m* liar, fibber
alecrim *m* rosemary
alegar *v/t* allege
alegoria *f* allegory
alegr|ar *v/t, v/r* cheer up; gladden; ~e joyful, glad, gay; tipsy; ~ia *f* joy, gladness
aleij|ado *adj* crippled; *m* cripple; ~ão *m* deformity; ~ar *v/t* cripple; hurt
além *adv* beyond; (over) there; ~ disso besides
alemão *adj, m* German
além-mar *adv* overseas
alentado courageous; vigorous
alento *m* breath; courage; vigo(u)r; dar ~ a encourage
alerta *m* alert
aletria *f* vermicelli
alface *f* lettuce
alfaiate *m* tailor
alfândega *f* customs; custom-house
alfazema *f* lavender
alfinete *m* pin
algarismo *m* figure, cypher
algazarra *f* uproar, hubbub
algemas *f/pl* handcuffs
algibeira *f* pocket; **andar de mãos nas ~s** idle (away)
álgido chilly, cold
algo *adv* rather, somewhat; *pron*

something
algodão *m* cotton; ~ **em rama** cotton wool
algoz *m* hangman
alguém somebody, someone; anyone, anybody
algum, ~**a** some; any; ~ **tanto** somewhat; ~ **dia** one day
alguns, algumas some; any; a few
algures somewhere
alheio belonging to another; alien
alho *m* garlic
ali there
alia|do *m* ally; *adj* allied; ~r *v/t, v/r* unite; ally; ~nça *f* alliance
aliás *adv* besides; by the way; otherwise
alibi *m* alibi
alicate *m* pliers
alicerce *m* foundations
aliciar *v/t* allure
aliena|ção *f* alienation; ~do *adj* alienated
alienar *v/t* alienate
aligeirar *v/t* lighten; hasten, speed up
aliment|ação *f* nourishment; ~ar *v/t* feed; *adj* nourishing
alimento *m* food
alindar *v/t* embellish
alínea *f* paragraph
alinh|ar *v/t* align; ~o *m* neatness
alisar *v/t* smooth
alistar *v/t, v/r* enlist
aliviar *v/t, v/i* lighten; alleviate; relieve
alívio *m* relief; alleviation

alma *f* soul
almejar *v/t* covet, long for
almirante *m* admiral
almoçar *v/t*, *v/i* have lunch, lunch
almoço *m* lunch
almofada *f* cushion; pillow
almôndega *f* meat ball
alocução *f* address
alojamento *m* lodging
alojar *v/t* lodge; billet
alongar *v/t* prolong, lengthen
alperc(h)e *m* apricot
alpinismo *m* mountaineering
alta *f* com rise, boom; discharge
altaneiro arrogant, haughty
altar *m* altar; **~-mor** *m* high altar
altear *v/t*, *v/i* raise; rise
alteração *f* alteration, change
alterar *v/t* alter, change
alternar *v/t* alternate
alternativa *f* alternative
altiv|ez *f* haughtiness; pride; **~o** haughty; proud
alto *int* stop!, halt!; *adv* loudly; *m* height; summit; *adj* high, tall; loud; **alta noite** in the dead of the night; **em voz alta** aloud; **por ~** superficially
alto-falante *m* loudspeaker
altruísmo *m* altruism
altura *f* height; altitude; occasion, time; **à ~ da situação** equal to the occasion
aludir *v/i* allude to, hint at
alug|ar *v/t* hire; let; rent; **~uer** *m* hire; rent
aluir *v/t*, *v/i* shake; crumble
alumiar *v/t* illuminate
alumínio *m* aluminium

aluno *m* pupil
alusão *f* allusion
alva *f* dawn
alvejar *v/t* aim at
alvíssaras *f/pl* reward
alvitr|ar *v/t* suggest, propose; **~e** *m* suggestion
alvo *adj* white; *m* target; aim, intent
alvorada *f* dawn
alvoroço, alvoroto *m* excitement; agitation; tumult
ama *f* governess, mistress; nurse
amabilidade *f* kindness
amada *f* darling
amador *m* amateur
amadurecer *v/t*, *v/i* ripen; mature
âmago *m* heart, core
amainar *v/i* abate
amaldiçoar *v/t* curse
amálgama *m* amalgam
amamentar *v/t* suckle
amanhã *adv* tomorrow
amanhecer *v/i* dawn; *m* daybreak
amanho *m* cultivation, tillage
amansar *v/t* tame; mitigate
amante *m*, *f* lover
amar *v/t*, *v/i* love
amarar *v/i* avi land on water
amarel|ado yellowish; **~ecer** *v/t*, *v/i* yellow; **~o** *adj*, *m* yellow
amarfanhar *v/t* wrinkle; ill-treat
amarg|ar *v/t*, *v/i* taste bitter; make bitter; **~o** *adj* bitter; **~ura** *f* bitterness; **~urar** *v/t* embitter
amarr|a *f* hawser; **~ar** *v/t*

make fast, moor; fasten, tie

amarrotar v/t crumple

amassar v/t knead

amável kind

âmbar m amber

ambição f ambition

ambici|onar v/t hanker after; **~oso** ambitious

ambiente adj surrounding; m surroundings; atmosphere; environment

ambíguo ambiguous

âmbito m ambit; scope

amb|os, ~as both

ambulância f ambulance

ameaça f threat; **~dor** threatening; **~r** v/t, v/i threaten

amealhar v/t save

amedrontar v/t, v/i frighten

ameia f battlement

amêijoa f cockle

ameix|a f plum; **~(o)eira, ~-(o)eira** f plum-tree

amêndoa f almond

amendo|eira f almond-tree; **~im** m ground-nut, peanut

ameno pleasant

americano adj, m American

amesquinhar v/t, v/r belittle, disparage

amestrar v/t train, break in

amical amicable

amig|a f (girl) friend; **~ável** friendly, amicable; **~o** m friend; adj fond of; **~o-da--onça** m, **~** de Peniche fair--weather friend; **ter cara de poucos ~os** have an un-friendly look; **tornar-se ~o de** make friends with

amimar v/t pet, spoil

amiúde often

amizade f friendship

a(m)nistia f amnesty

amo m master

amolar v/t, v/i, v/r brood over; grind; harass; Braz annoy, bother

amolecer v/t, v/i soften; mollify

amolgar v/t squash, crush

amontoar v/t heap up

amor m love

amora f mulberry

amordaçar v/t gag

amorfo amorphous

amornar v/t warm; make luke-warm

amoroso adj loving; lovable, sweet

amor-perfeito m pansy

amortecedor m shock-absorber; damper

amortecer v/t, v/i damp; absorb; deaden; weaken

amortiz|ação f amortization; **~ar** v/t amortize

amostra f sample

amotinar v/t, v/r mutiny

ampar|ar v/t support; prop; protect; **~o** m shelter; protection

ampli|ação f enlargement; **~ar** v/t amplify, enlarge

amplific|ador m amplifier; **~ar** v/t amplify

amplitude f amplitude

amplo ample, spacious

ampola f blister

amuar v/i, v/r sulk

amurada f naut rail

anais m/pl annals

analisar v/t analyse
análise f analysis
analogia f analogy
análogo analogous
ananás m pineapple
anão m dwarf
anca f haunch, hip
anchova f anchovy
ancião m old man
ancinho m rake
âncora f anchor
ancorar v/t, v/i anchor
andaime m scaffold(ing)
andamento m course, proceeding; *mus* measure
andar v/t, v/i go; walk; m stor(e)y, floor; gait
andas f/pl stilts
andebol m handball
andorinha f zo swallow
andrajo m rag; ~**so** ragged
anedota f anecdote
anel m ring; curl
anel|ar v/t long for; ~**o** m desire, longing
anemia f an(a)emia
anémico an(a)emic
anestesia f an(a)esthesia
anestésico m an(a)esthetic
anex|ação f annexation; ~**ar** v/t annex; ~**o** adj included; m annex(e)
angariar v/t canvass; obtain
angular angular
ângulo m angle; corner
angústia f anguish
anho m lamb
animação f animation
animal m, adj animal
animar v/t, v/r cheer up; animate

ânimo m courage; mind; int come on!; cheer up!
aninhar v/t, v/r nestle; snuggle
aniquilamento m annihilation
aniquilar v/t annihilate
aniversário m anniversary; ~ **natalício** birthday
anjo m angel
ano m year; ~ **bissexto** leap year; **quando fazes** ~**s?** when is your birthday?; **ter dez** ~**s** be ten years old
anoitecer v/i grow dark; m nightfall; **ao** ~ at nightfall
anomalia f anomaly
anónim|o anonymous
anormal abnormal
anot|ação f annotation; ~**ar** v/t annotate
ânsia f anxiety
ansi|ar v/t, v/i yearn for, crave; ~**edade** f anguish; ~**oso** anxious; **estar** ~**oso por** be eager for
antagonista m antagonist
ante prp before
antebraço m forearm
antecâmara f antechamber, anteroom
anteced|ente m, adj antecedent; ~**er** v/t, v/i precede
antecessor m predecessor
antecipar v/t, v/r anticipate
antemão: de ~ beforehand
antena f antenna; aerial
anteontem the day before yesterday
antepassado m ancestor, forefather
anterior previous
antes before; rather; ~ **de** be-

fore; **~ de mais nada** first of all; **~ que** before

antever v/t foresee

anti|aéreo anti-aircraft; **~ciclone** m anticyclone

antídoto m antidote

antigamente formerly

antig|o adj ancient, old; antique; **~uidade** f antiquity

antílope m antelope

anti|patia f antipathy; **~pático** antipathetic; disagreeable

antiquado antiquated, outmoded

antítese f antithesis

antro m cave, den

anual yearly, annual

anuir v/i assent, accede

anular v/t annul, cancel

anunciar v/t advertise; announce

anúncio m advertisement; **pôr um ~** advertise

anzol m fish-hook

ao to the; in the; at the; by the; **~ pé** near by; **~ pé de** close to

aonde where ... to, where; **~ vais?** where are you going?

apagar v/t extinguish; put out; switch off

apaixon|ado passionate; **~ar** v/t, v/r fall in love; impassion

apalpa|dela f grope; **às ~delas** groping(ly); **~r** v/t feel, fumble; grope; **~r (o) terreno** spy out the land

apanhar v/t, v/i pick; be beaten; grasp; catch; seize; gather; get

aparador m sideboard

aparar v/t pare, clip; parry

aparato m pomp

aparec|er v/i appear; **~imento** m appearance

aparelh|ar v/t prepare; rig; **~o** m set; apparatus; mar rigging

aparência f appearance, aspect

aparent|ar v/t feign, pretend; **~e** apparent

aparição f apparition

aparo m nib

aparta|do m post-box; adj separated, secluded; **~mento** m apartment; separate

aparte m aside

à parte apart

apatia f apathy

apático apathetic

apátrida adj stateless

apavorar v/t terrify

apaziguar v/t pacify

apear-se v/r get off; alight; dismount

apegar-se a v/r cling to; be attached to

apego m attachment to

apel|ação f appeal; **~ar** v/i appeal

apelido m surname

apenas adv hardly, scarcely; only

apêndice m appendix

apendicite f appendicitis

apenso m appendage; adj joined, added

aperceber v/t, v/r become aware of; perceive; distinguish

aperfeiçoamento m improvement

aperfeiçoar v/t perfect; improve

aperitivo *m* aperitif

apert|ão *m* squeeze; **~ar** *v/t, v/i* press; pinch; tie; tighten; squeeze; **~ar a mão** shake hands; **~o** *m* pressure; distress, scrape

apesar de in spite of; **~ ~ tudo** for all that

apetecer *v/t* feel like

apetite *m* appetite

apetitoso appetizing

apimentado peppery, spicy

apinhar *v/t* heap up; crowd

apit|ar *v/i* whistle; **~o** *m* whistle

aplacar *v/t, v/i* appease

aplanar *v/t* level

aplaudir *v/t, v/i* clap, applaud

aplauso *m* applause

aplica|ção *f* application; **~do** industrious; **~r** *v/t, v/i* apply

apoderar-se *v/r* seize, take hold of

apodo *m* scoff; taunt

apodrecer *v/i* rot

apogeu *m* apogee

apoia|do *adj* supported; *int* hear! hear!

apoi|ar *v/t* support, prop up; **~o** *m* support, prop

apólice *f* policy; **~ de seguro** insurance policy

apologia *f* apology, defence

apont|amento *m* note, annotation; **~ar** *v/t* note down; take aim at; point at

apoplexia *f* apoplexy

apoquent|ado upset; **~ar** *v/t* worry, bother

aportar *v/i* call at a port

após *prp* after; behind; **~-guer-** ra *m* post-war time

aposent|ação *f* retirement; **~ar** *v/t* lodge; retire, pension off; **~o** *m* apartment; room

apost|a *f* bet, wager; **~ar** *v/t* bet, wager

aprazar *v/t* appoint, fix

aprazível pleasant, agreeable

apre! by jingo!

apreci|ação *f* appreciation; **~ar** *v/t* appreciate; **~ável** appreciable

apreço *m* estimate; esteem

apreensivo apprehensive

aprend|er *v/t, v/i* learn; **~iz** *m* apprentice; **~izagem** *f* apprenticeship

apresent|ação *f* introduction; **~ar** *v/t, v/r* present; introduce

apressado hasty, hurried

apressar *v/t, v/r* hasten; make haste, hurry up

apresto *m* preparation

aprisionar *v/t* imprison

aprofundar *v/t* deepen

aprontar *v/t* prepare, get ready

a-propósito *adv* to the purpose; by the way

apropria|ção *f* appropriation; **~do** appropriate; **~r** *v/t, v/i* appropriate

aprovação *f* approval; approbation

aprovar *v/t* approve; pass

aproveitar *v/t, v/i, v/r* avail of; profit by

aprovisionar *v/t* equip; victual

aproxima|ção *f* approximation; approach; **~damente** approximately; **~do** approximate; **~r** *v/t, v/r* approxi-

mate; come near to; approach
aptidão f aptitude
apto apt, fit
apunhalar v/t stab
apupar v/t hiss at; hoot at
apurar v/t purify; verify
apuro m refinement; hardship;
 estar em ~s be hard up; **ver-
 -se em ~s** be in a tight corner
aquário m aquarium
aquec|edor m heater; **~er** v/t,
 v/i warm, heat; **~imento** m
 central central heating
aquel|e, ~a that
àquele to that (one)
aquém adv below; on this side;
 estar ~ de not to come up to;
 ~ e além here and there
aqui adv here
aquietar v/t quiet(en)
aquilo that
ar m air; look; **ao ~ livre** in the
 open air, outdoors; **dar-se ~es
 de** put on airs, give oneself airs
árabe m Arab; Arabic; adj Ara-
 bian; Arabic
arado m plough
arame m wire; **~ farpado**
 barbed wire; **ir aos ~s** see red
aranha f spider; **andar às ~s**
 be irresolute; **tirar as teias de
 ~** blow away the cobwebs
arar v/t plough
arbitrar v/t arbitrate; referee
arbitrário arbitrary
arbítrio m will, judg(e)ment
árbitro m referee, umpire
arbusto m bush
arca f chest, coffer; ark
arcebispo m archbishop
archote m torch

arco m bow; arc; arch
ardente ardent
arder v/i burn
ardil m stratagem, trick; **~oso**
 subtle, crafty
ardina m news-boy, US paper-
 -boy
ardor m ardo(u)r
ardósia f slate
árduo arduous; steep; hard
área f area
areal m sands
areia f sand
arejado airy
arejar v/t, v/i take the air, get
 some fresh air; air, ventilate
arenoso sandy
arenque m herring
aresta f edge
arfar v/i pant
argila f clay
argola f ring
argúcia f subtlety
arguir v/t, v/i reprove; argue
argument|ar v/i argue; **~o** m
 argument; summary
arguto shrewd
ária f aria
aridez f aridity, dryness
árido arid, dry
arisco adj sandy; surly; coy
aritmética f arithmetic
arma f weapon
armada f fleet
armadilha f snare, trap
armador m shipowner
arm|amento m armament;
 ~ar v/t, v/i, v/r plot; lay; arm
armário m cupboard
armazém m store; warehouse
armistício m armistice

aro *m* ring, hoop

aroma *m* aroma, scent

aromático aromatic

arquear *v/t* arch, curve

arquejar *v/i* pant; gasp

arquite(c)t|o *m* architect; **~ura** *f* architecture

arquivo *m* archives

arrabalde *m* suburb, environs

arraia *f zo* skate

arraial *m* encampment; festival; *Braz* hamlet

arrais *m* skipper; coxswain

arranc|ar *v/t* start; pull, tug; draw out; **~o** *m* tug; jolt; jerk

arranha-céu *m* skyscraper

arranhar *v/t* scratch; scrape

arranjar *v/t, v/r* manage; get; tidy; arrange; fix; **ele que se arranje** let that be his problem

arranque *m auto* starter

arrasar *v/t, v/r* raze, level, demolish; overflow

arrastar *v/t, v/r* drag, haul; crawl, creep; **~ a asa** court

arre! gee up!

arrebatar *v/t* snatch

arredar *v/t* remove, set aside; **não ~ pé** stay put

arredondar *v/t* round (off)

arredores *m/pl* surroundings, environs; outskirts

arrefec|er *v/i* cool; **~imento** *m* cooling

arreig|ado deep-seated; **~ar** *v/i* take root

arreliar *v/t, v/r* tease, vex; worry

arrematar *v/t* auction

arremessar *v/t* throw, dump

arremeter *v/i* attack

arrend|amento *m* hire; lease; **~ar** *v/t* hire; let; lease; rent

arrepend|er-se *v/r* repent; **~imento** *m* repentance

arrepi|ar *v/t, v/r* shudder; **~ar caminho** retrace one's steps; **~o** *m* shudder

arribação *f* arrival; **de ~** of passage

arriscar *v/t, v/r* risk, hazard

arrogância *f* arrogance

arrogante arrogant

arroj|ado bold, daring; **~ar** *v/t* cast; **~o** *m* boldness; effrontery

arrombar *v/t* stave in; force open

arrot|ar *v/i* belch; **~o** *m* belch

arroz *m* rice

arruinar *v/t* ruin

arrum|ação *f* arrangement; stowage; **~ar** *v/t* stow; tidy; arrange

arte *f* art

artéria *f* artery

artesanato *m* workmanship

articula|ção *f* articulation; **~do** articulate; articulated

artífice *m* artisan

artificial artificial

artifício *m* artifice; trick

artigo *m* article

artista *m, f* artist

árvore *f* tree; mast

as *pl* of **a**

ás *m* ace

asa *f* wing

ascen|der *v/i* ascend; **~sor** *m* lift, elevator

asfixiar *v/t* asphyxiate, suffocate

asilo *m* asylum

asma *f* asthma

asneira *f* nonsense

asno *m* ass

aspe(c)to *m* aspect; appearance

aspereza *f* harshness; bleakness

áspero harsh; bleak

aspirador *m* vacuum cleaner, hoover

aspirar *v/t*, *v/i* aspirate; draw in; ~ a aspire to

assado *m* roast, roasted meat

assalt|ar *v/t* assault; ~o *m* assault

assar *v/t* roast

assassin|ar *v/t* murder; assassinate; ~o *m* murderer; assassin

assassínio *m* murder; assassination

asseado neat, tidy; clean

assegurar *v/t*, *v/i* ensure; make sure of; assure

asseio *m* neatness, tidiness; cleanliness

assembleia *f* assembly

assemelhar *v/r* resemble

assent|ar *v/t* place, settle; write down; ~o *m* seat

asseverar *v/t* maintain, asseverate

assiduidade *f* assidy

assíduo assiduous

assim so, thus; ~ que as soon as

assimilar *v/t* assimilate

assin|ar *v/t*, *v/i* subscribe; sign; ~ante *m*, *f* subscriber; ~atura *f* signature; subscription

assist|ência *f* assistance; presence; ~ente *m*, *f* assistant; bystander; ~ir *v/t*, *v/i* be present at; attend

assoar *v/t*, *v/r* blow one's nose

assobi|ar *v/t*, *v/i* whistle; ~o *m* whistle, hiss

associ|ação *f* association; ~ar *v/t*, *v/r* associate

assombr|ar *v/t*, *v/i*, *v/r* shadow; astonish; ~o *m* astonishment; awe

assumir *v/t* assume, take upon oneself

assunto *m* subject, topic, matter, case

assustar *v/t*, *v/r* frighten

astro *m* star

astúcia *f* astuteness, cunning

atacador *m* shoe-lace

atacar *v/t* attack

atado *adj* timid

atalh|ar *v/t*, *v/i* intercept; cut across; interrupt; ~o *m* short cut

ataque *m* attack

atar *v/t* tie, fasten

até *prp* till; until; up to; *adv* even; ~ à vista see you later; ~ onde? how far?; ~ que until

atemorizar *v/t*, *v/r* frighten, horrify

aten|ção *f* attention; regard; ~cioso kind, polite; ~der *v/t* attend, pay attention

atentado *m* attempt, assault

atento attentive

atenu|ante attenuating; ~ar *v/t* attenuate

aterra|gem *f* avi landing; ~r *v/t*, *v/i* terrify; *avi* land

atest|ado *m* certificate; ~ar *v/t* attest, certify

ateu *m* atheist

atilho m band, tie, string

atingir v/t attain; **~ a maioridade** come of age

atirar v/t, v/r cast, throw; **~se a alguém** throw oneself at someone

atitude f attitude

atleta m, f athlete

átomo m atom

atónito astounded, astonished

atormentar v/t torment

atracar v/i moor

atra(c)ção f attraction

atraente attractive

atraiçoar v/t betray

atrair v/t attract

atrapalhar v/t, v/r muddle; confuse

atrás behind, back; **~ de** after; behind

atras|ado backward; late, delayed; slow; **~ar** v/t, v/r put back; delay, retard; get in arrears; **~o** m delay

através de across; through

atravessar v/t cross; pass through

atrever-se v/r dare; **~ido** bold, daring

atribuir v/t attribute to, ascribe to

atrito m attrition; friction; **~s** m/pl difficulties

atrocidade f atrocity

atropelar v/t run over

atroz atrocious

atum m tunny, tuna

audácia f audacity

audaz audacious

audi|ção f audition; **~ência** f audience; **~tório** m audito-

rium; audience

audível audible

auge m height, climax

aula f class-room; lesson

aument|ar v/t, v/i increase; grow; **~o** m increase

aurora f dawn

auscultador m receiver

ausência f absence

ausent|ar-se v/r absent oneself; **~e** adj absent

auster|idade f austerity; **~o** austere

australiano adj, s Australian

austríaco adj, s Austrian

autenticidade f authenticity

autêntico authentic

autocarro m bus

auto-estrada f motorway, US highway

autógrafo m autograph

automático automatic

autómato m automaton

autom|obilismo m motoring; **~obilista** m motorist; **~óvel** m car; **~óvel de praça** taxi

autor m author; **~idade** f authority; **~ização** f authorization; **~izar** v/t authorize

auxiliar v/t help

auxílio m help

avalancha f avalanche

avaliar v/t appraise, evaluate

avançar v/t, v/i advance

avante adv forward(s); onward(s)

avar|ento avaricious, miserly; **~eza** f avarice

avaria f damage; breakdown

ave f bird; **~ de arribação** bird of passage; **~s de capoeira**

poultry
aveia f oats
avelã f hazel-nut, filbert
avença f agreement
avenida f avenue
avental m apron
aventura f adventure; love affair
averigu|ação f inquiry, investigation; **~ar** v/t ascertain, find out
avermelhado reddish
avessas f/pl opposite; **às ~** inside out; upside down
avesso m reverse, back
avestruz m ostrich
avia|ção f aviation; **~dor** m flier
avião m (aero)plane, US airplane
aviar-se v/r hasten, hurry up
avidez f avidity, eagerness
ávido avid; greedy; eager

aviltar v/t vilify; degrade
avis|ado sensible, circumspect; **~ar** v/t inform; advise; warn; **~o** m warning; notice
avistar v/t catch sight of, glimpse
avô m grandfather
avó f grandmother
à vontade adv at ease
avós m/pl grandparents; forefathers
avulso single
avultar v/t augment, enlarge
azáfama f hurry, bustle
azar m bad luck; **jogo** m **de ~** game of chance
azedo adj sour, tart
azeit|e m olive oil; **~ona** f olive
azia f heartburn
aziago unlucky, ill-fated
azo m occasion, motive, pretext
azul blue
azulejo m tile

B

bacalhau m cod(-fish)
bacana Braz splendid, posh
baci|a f basin; **~o** m chamberpot
baço adj tarnished; dull, dim; m spleen
badal|ada f clang of a bell; **~ar** v/t, v/i clang; gossip, chatter; **~o** m clapper
badejo m haddock
bafo m breath; protection
baga f berry
bagaceira f brandy
bagaço m husk; money

bagageiro m porter
bagagem f luggage, US baggage
bagatela f bagatelle, trifle
bago m grape; berry; cash, dough
baía f bay
bail|ar v/t, v/i dance; **~arina** f ballerina; **~arino** m male ballet-dancer; **~e** m dance, ball
bainha f hem
bairro m district, ward, quarter; **~ da lata** slum; **~ económico** housing estate
baixa f decrease, fall

baixa-mar f low tide, ebb

baixar v/t, v/i lower, bring down; let down

baixela f table-ware

baixeza f vileness

baixio m sandbank, shoal

baixo adj low; vile; short; adv in a low voice

bala f bullet

balanç|a f scales, balance; **~ar** v/t, v/i balance; swing; rock; **~o** m com balance

balão m balloon

balaustrada f balustrade

balbuciar v/t, v/i stammer, stutter

balbúrdia f confusion, disorder; tumult

balcão m counter

baldado void, frustrated, ineffectual

balde m bucket

baldear v/t transfuse, decant; transship

baleia f whale

balela f false report, lie, fib

baliza f seamark; landmark; buoy; beacon; goal post

balouç|ar v/t swing, rock; **~o** m swing

baluarte m bulwark

bambo slack, loose

bambolear v/i, v/r swagger

banana f banana

banc|a f stake, pool; stand, stall; **~ada** f row of benches or seats

bancarrota f bankruptcy

banco m bench, form; com bank

banda f side; mus band

bandeira f flag, banner

bandeja f tray

bandido m bandit

bando m band, flock; gang; faction

bandolim m mandolin

banha f lard, fat

banh|ar v/t, v/r bath; bathe; **~eira** f bath(-tub); **~eiro** m beach attendant; **~ista** m, f bather; **~o** m bath; **~os** m/pl banns of marriage

banir v/t banish; outlaw

banqueiro m banker

banquete m banquet

banzé m row, brawl

ba(p)t|ismo m baptism; **~izar** v/t baptize

baque m fall; thud; throb; Braz instant

barafunda f tumult, confusion, bustle

baralh|ar v/t shuffle; **~o** m pack of cards

barão m baron

barata f cockroach

barato cheap

barba f beard; **nas ~s de alguém** to someone's face; **fazer a ~** shave

barbaridade f barbarity

bárbaro m barbarian; adj barbarous, barbaric

barbatana f fin

barbear v/t, v/r shave

barbearia f barber's shop

barbeiro m barber

barbo m zo barbel

barc|a f bark; ferry-boat; **~aça** f barge

barco m boat; ship; **~ de arrasto** trawler; **~ a motor** mo-

torboat; ~ **a remos** rowing-
-boat; ~ **à vela** sailing-boat
barda f hedge; fence; **em** ~ in
plenty, a lot of
barómetro m barometer
baronesa f baroness
barqueiro m boatman, ferry-
man
barra f bar; crow-bar
barraca f hut; tent; stall
barragem f dam
barranco m ravine
barrar v/t bar, impede; spread
barreira f barrier; toll-gate; clay
pit
barrento clayey
barrete m cap, beret
barrica f cask
barrig|a f belly; ~**a da perna**
calf of the leg; ~**udo** pot-
-bellied
barril m barrel
barro m clay
barulhento noisy
barulho m noise, din
base f base; ~**ar (em)** v/t, v/r
base, found (on, upon)
básico basic
basta! int enough!
bastante adj enough, sufficient;
adv quite
bastão m staff, stick
bastar v/i be enough
basto adj thick; numerous
bata f gown
batalh|a f battle; ~**ar** v/i fight,
struggle
batata f potato; ~**s** f/pl **fritas**
chips, US French fries
bate|deira f (elé(c)trica) mix-
er; ~**dor** m whisk

batel m skiff
bate-papo m chat
bater v/t, v/i beat, strike;
knock; ~ **palmas** clap one's
hands
bateria f battery; ~ **de cozin-**
ha kitchen utensils
batida f tracking, drive; reprimand; Braz shake
batido m (de leite) (milk)
shake
batom m lipstick
batota f fraud, cheating
batuta f conductor's baton
baú m trunk, chest
baunilha f vanilla
bávaro m, adj Bavarian
bazófia f boast; swagger
bazofiar v/i boast; swagger
beat|ificar v/t beatify; ~**o** adj
blessed; bigoted
bebedeira f drunkenness
bêbedo adj drunk(en); s
drunk(ard)
bebedouro m water-trough
beb|er v/t, v/i drink; ~**ida** f
drink, beverage
beco m alley; ~ **sem saída** fig
deadlock
beiço m lip
beij|ar v/t kiss; ~**o** m kiss
beira f edge, brink
beira-mar f seaside, sea-shore;
à ~ by the sea
belas-artes f/pl fine arts
beldade f beauty
beleza f beauty
belga m, f, adj Belgian
beliche m berth; bunk
bélico warlike
beligerante belligerent

beliscar v/t pinch, nip

belo adj fine, fair, beautiful

bem s good; darling; adv right, very, well; int well; **se ~ que** although; **levar a ~** take in good part

bem-estar m well-being, welfare

bem-querer m affection

bem-vindo welcome

bem-visto beloved

bênção f blessing

bendizer v/t bless; praise

benefic|ência f beneficence; **~iar** v/t benefit

benefício m benefit

benéfico beneficial

benevolência f benevolence

benévolo benevolent

benfeitor m benefactor

bengal|a f walking-stick; **~eiro** m hat and umbrella stand

benigno benign

benquisto beloved

bens m/pl estate, property

benzer v/t bless, hallow

berbigão m cockle

berço m cradle

beringela f aubergine, egg-plant

berma f roadside

berrante glaring

berr|ar v/t, v/i bellow; cry, shout; bawl; **~eiro** m bawling; **~o** m bellow; scream

besta f beast; blockhead

bestial bestial

besuntar v/t besmear, daub

beterraba f beetroot

bétula f birch

betume m bitumen

bexig|a f bladder; **~as** f/pl smallpox; **~as doidas** chicken-pox

bezerro m calf

biberão m feeding bottle

Bíblia f Bible

bibliotec|a f library; **~ário** m librarian

bicha f leech; queue; **~ solitária** tapeworm

bichano m pussy-cat

bicho m worm; animal; fig ugly person; **ter ~s carpinteiros** be fidgety

bicicleta f bicycle, bike

bico m beak, bill; nib; **~-de-obra** m knotty problem

bicudo adj difficult; beaked; pointed

bidé m bidet

bienal biennial

bife m (beef)steak; fig Englishman

bifurc|ação f bifurcation; **~ar** v/t, v/r bifurcate

bigamia f bigamy

bigode m moustache

bigorna f anvil

bilhar m billiards

bilhet|e m ticket; **~e de ida** single ticket; **~e de ida e volta** return ticket; **~eira** f booking-office; box-office

bilião m billion

bilingue bilingual

bílis f bile

bilro m bobbin

binóculo m binoculars; opera-glasses; field-glasses

biografia f biography

biógrafo m biographer

biologia f biology

biólogo *m* biologist
biombo *m* screen
biqueira *f* toecap; gutter, spout
birr|a *f* whim; peevishness;
  ~ento obstinate; peevish
bis *adv* twice; *int* encore!
bisavô *m* great-grandfather
bisbilhotar *v/i* tittle-tattle
biscoito *m* biscuit; bun; cookie
bisnaga *f* tube
bispo *m* bishop; **ter ~** be burnt
bitola *f* gauge, standard; pattern; *bcap*
bizarr|ia *f* elegance; ostentation; **~o** elegant; ostentatious
blasfemar *v/t*, *v/i* blaspheme
blasfémia *f* blasphemy
blindado armo(u)red
bloco *m* block; bloc; writing-pad
bloqu|ear *v/t* blockade, block;
  ~eio *m* blockade
blusa *f* blouse
boa *adj* good; **é ~!** amazing!
  really!; **metido em ~s** in a
  tight spot, in a real fix
Boas-festas *f/pl* Christmas
  wishes
boas-vindas *f/pl* welcome
boato *m* rumo(u)r, hearsay
bobagem *f* nonsense
bobina *f* coil
bobo *m* buffoon; jester
boca *f* mouth; **à ~ cheia** frankly, openly
bocado *m* bit, piece; short
  while; **há ~** recently, a short
  time ago
bocej|ar *v/i* yawn; **~o** *m* yawn
bochecha *f* cheek
boda *f* wedding breakfast; **~s**

f/pl **de prata** silver wedding
bode *m* (billy-)goat; **~ expiatório** scapegoat
bofetada *f* slap, cuff
boi *m* ox
bóia *f* buoy; **~ de salvação** life
  buoy
boiar *v/i* float
boina *f* beret
bola *f* ball
bolacha *f* biscuit; slap
bolbo *m* *bot* bulb
boleia *f* lift
boletim *m* bulletin; **~ meteorológico** weather-forecast
bolha *f* bubble; blister; **ter ~**
  be dotty/cracked
bolo *m* cake; state
bolor *m* mo(u)ld; **~ento**
  mo(u)ldy
bolota *f* acorn
bolsa *f* purse; *com* stock exchange; scholarship, grant
bolseiro *m* scholar
bolso *m* pocket
bom *adj* good; kind
bomb|a *f* bomb; pump; **~a de
  gasolina** petrol pump; filling/
  gas station; **~ardear** *v/t*
  bomb(ard); **~ardeio** *m* bombardment; **~eiro** *m* fireman
bombom *m* sweet, bonbon
bombordo *m* port
bonança *f* calm; prosperity
bondade *f* goodness, kindness,
  bounty
bonde *m* *Braz* tram
bondoso kind-hearted
boné *m* cap
boneca *f* doll
bonito *adj* pretty, fine

boquiaberto gaping

boquilha *f* cigarette holder

borboleta *f* butterfly

borborinho *m* murmur, rumble

borbulh|a *f* pimple; bud; bubble; **~ar** *v/i* gush; bubble

borda *f* bank; brink; brim; border

bordado *m* embroidery

bordão *m* staff

bordo *m* tack; **a ~** on board

borla *f* tassel; doctoral cap; **de ~ gratis**, free

borracha *f* india-rubber; eraser, rubber

borr|ão *m* blot; rough draft; **~ar** *v/t* blot, stain

borrasca *f* storm, squall

borrifar *v/t* sprinkle; damp

bosque *m* wood, forest

bota *f* boot

botânica *f* botany

botão *m* button; bud; knob

botar *v/t* put, cast, throw; pour out

bote *m* boat

botequim *m* coffee-house; bar

botija *f* flagon

boxe *m* boxing

bracelete *m* bracelet

braço *m* arm; worker, hand; **de ~ dado** arm in arm

brad|ar *v/t, v/i* bawl; **~o** *m* bawl, roar

bram|ido *m* bellow; **~ir** *v/i* bellow; bluster

branc|o *adj* white; blank; **~ura** *f* whiteness

brandir *v/t* brandish

brand|o soft, gentle; bland;

~ura *f* softness, gentleness

branquear *v/t, v/i* whiten

bras|a *f* live coal; ember; **estar em ~a** be on tenterhooks; **~eiro** *m* brazier

brasileiro *m, adj* Brazilian

brav|io *adj* wild; savage; **~o** *int* bravo!; *adj* brave; wild; rugged; **~ura** *f* bravery

breca *f* cramp; **com a ~!** damn it!

brecar *v/t Braz* brake

brecha *f* breach

breque *m Braz* brake

breu *m* pitch; tar

brev|e *adj* short, brief; *adv* soon; **em ~** soon, shortly; **~idade** *f* brevity

brida *f* bridle; **a toda a ~** at full gallop; at full speed

briga *f* strife

brigad|a *f* brigade; **~eiro** *m* brigadier

brigar *v/i* fight; quarrel

brilh|ante *s* brilliant; bright, shining; **~ar** *v/i* shine; **~o** *m* shine, brilliance

brinca|deira *f* fun, joke; **~lhão** *m* wag, joker

brincar *v/i* play; joke

brinco *m* ear-ring

brind|ar *v/t, v/i* offer, present; drink a toast; **~e** *m* present; toast

brinquedo *m* toy; plaything

brio *m* hono(u)r; mettle; **~so** proud

brisa *f* breeze

britânico British

broa *f* maize bread; **~ de mel** gingerbread

broca *f* drill
broche *m* brooch
bronco coarse; stupid; dull
bronquite *f* bronchitis
bronz|e *m* bronze; **~ear** *v/t, v/r* tan; bronze
brotar *v/t, v/i* spring, well; produce; bud; sprout
broxa *f* paint-brush
brum|a *f* fog; **~oso** foggy
brusco rough; brusque
brut|al brutal; **~alidade** *f* brutality; **~o** *adj* raw, coarse; *m* brute, beast
brux|a *f* witch; **~aria** *f* witchcraft
bucha *f* wad; bung; mouthful
buço *m* down
búfalo *m* buffalo
bufar *v/i* puff, blow
bufete *m* buffet
bugigangas *f/pl* knick-knack

bule *m* teapot
bulh|a *f* noise, din; disorder; **~ar** *v/i* squabble
bulício *m* bustle
bulir *v/t, v/i* move, stir
buraco *m* hole
burg|uês *m* bourgeois; **~uesia** *f* bourgeoisie
burl|a *f* fraud, trick; **~ar** *v/t* dupe, trick; **~esco** *adj* burlesque
burr|ice *f* stupidity, blunder; **~o** *m* ass, donkey; blockhead; *adj* stupid, obstinate
busc|a *f* search; **~ar** *v/t* look for
bússola *f* compass
busto *m* bust
buxo *m* box(-tree)
buzina *f* auto horn
buzinar *v/i* hoot
búzio *m zo* whelk, conch

C

cá *adv* here
cabaça *f* gourd
cabal just, complete, exact
cabana *f* hut
cabeça *f* head
cabeceira *f* upper end; head of a bed
cabeço *m* top, summit; hillock
cabeçudo headstrong
cabedal *m* leather; capital; means; stock
cabel|eira *f* head of hair; wig; **~eireiro** *m* hairdresser; **~o** *m* hair
caber *v/i* fit; have room for;

concern; **não ~ em si de contente** be overjoyed
cabide *m* coat-hanger
cabidela *f* stewed giblets
cabimento *m* reason
cabisbaixo downcast, dejected
cabo *m* end; cape, headland; handle; cable; *mil* corporal
caboclo *Braz m* mestizo, half-breed; *adj* copper-coloured; sunburnt
cabra *f* goat; nannygoat
caç|a *f* chase; hunting; hunt; game; **~ador** *m* huntsman; **~ar** *v/t*, hunt; chase

cacarejar v/i cluck, cackle
caçarola f saucepan, casserole
cacatua f cockatoo
cacau m cacao; cocoa
cachaça f rum
cachecol m scarf
cachimbo m pipe
cacho m bunch, cluster
cachopa f lass, girl
cachopo m lad, urchin
cachorro m pup; whelp; cub; **~ quente** hot dog
caco m potsherd
caçoila f stew-pan
cacto m cactus
cada each; every; **~ vez que** whenever
cadafalso m scaffold
cadastr|ado m known criminal; **~o** m cadastre; census; criminal record
cadáver m corpse, cadaver
cadeado m padlock
cadeia f chain; prison
cadeira f chair; **~ de braços** arm-chair
cadela f bitch
cadência f cadence, rhythm
cadern|eta f notebook; register; passbook, bank-book; **~o** m exercise-book
caduc|ar v/i become decrepit; lapse, become invalid; **~o** decrepit
caf|é m coffee; café; **~ com leite** white coffee; **~eteira** f coffee-pot
cágado m tortoise
caiar v/t whitewash
cãibra f cramp
cair v/i fall, tumble, drop

cais m (pl **cais**) quay
caix|a f box; **~a económica** savings bank; **~ão** m chest; coffin
caixote m case; **~do lixo** dustbin, US garbage can
cal f lime; whitewash
calafrio m shiver, chill
calamidade f calamity
calar v/t, v/r silence; hush up; omit; be silent; **~ a boca, ~ o bico** shut up, shut one's mouth
calç|ada f roadway, street; causeway; **~adeira** f shoehorn; **~ado** m footwear
calcanhar m heel
calcar v/t tread, trample
calçar v/t put on
calças f/pl trousers
calcetar v/t pave
calcular v/t calculate
cálculo m calculation; calculus
calda f syrup
caldas f/pl spa
caldeira f kettle; boiler
caldeirada f fish stew
caldo m broth; **~ verde** cabbage soup
calendário m calendar
calhar v/i happen; suit; **se ~** probably
calibre m caliber
cálice m wine-glass
cálido hot; sanguine
caligrafia f calligraphy
calm|a f calm; heat; **~a!** take it easy!; **~o** calm
calo m callus; corn
calor m heat, warmth; **~ífero** m heater; **~oso** hot, warm
caloteiro m swindler

caluda! silence!, quiet!

calúnia f calumny, slander

caluniar v/t calumniate, slander

calv|a f baldness; **~o** adj bald; bare

cama f bed; **~ de casal** double bed

camada f layer; stratum

câmara f chamber; **~ municipal** town/city hall

camarada m comrade

camarão m prawn

camarote m thea box; cabin

cambalear v/i totter, stagger

cambiar v/t exchange

câmbio m exchange; rate of exchange

camelo m camel

camião, camnhão m lorry

caminh|ar v/t, v/i walk, go; **~o** m path, road, way; **~o de ferro** railway, US railroad

camioneta f bus, coach

camisa f shirt; **~ de dormir** night-dress, US night-gown

camisola f pullover; **~ interior** vest, US undershirt

camomila f camomile

campa f grave(stone)

campainha f bell

campanário m steeple, belfry

campanha f campaign

campe|ão m champion; **~onato** m championship

campin|a f plain; **~o** m countryman; herdsman

campo m field; country; court, ground

camponês m peasant

camurça f chamois

cana f cane; reed

canal m canal; channel; **~izar** v/t canalize

canário m canary

canastra f basket

cancela f gate; wicket

cancelar v/t cancel

canceroso adj cancerous

cancro m med cancer

candeeiro m lamp

candelabro m chandelier

caneca f mug; tankard

canela f cinnamon; shin; shuttle

caneta f pen; **~ de tinta permanente** fountain-pen

cânhamo m hemp

canhão m cannon

canhoto adj left-handed

canil m kennel

canivete m penknife

canja f chicken broth; cinch

cano m pipe, tube

canoa f canoe

cansa|ço m weariness; **~do** weary, tired; **~r** v/t, v/i, v/r weary, tire; get tired

cantar v/t, v/i sing

cântaro m pitcher, jug

canteiro m flower-bed

cantiga f song

cantina f canteen

canto m singing; corner

cantor m singer

canudo m pipe, tube

cão m dog; **~ de água** poodle

capa f cloak, cape; cover, wrapper

capacete m helmet

capacho m mat

capacidade f capacity; capability

capar v/t geld, castrate

capaz capable, able; fit

capel|a f chapel; **~ão** m chaplain

capim m grass

capital m, f, adj capital

capitalista adj, m, f capitalist

capitão m captain

capitular v/i capitulate

capítulo m chapter

capoeira f hen-coop

capota f bonnet, US hood

capotar v/i capsize

capote m cloak

caprichar em v/i take pride in

capricho m whim, caprice; **~so** painstaking; capricious

cápsula f capsule

capt|ar v/t captivate; **~ura** f capture; **~urar** v/t capture

cara f face; look, appearance

carabina f rifle; carbine

caracol m snail

cará(c)ter m character

cara(c)terísti|ca f characteristic; **~co** adj characteristic

cara(c)terizar v/t characterize

caramelo m caramel, toffee

caranguejo m crab

carapau m horse mackerel

carbúnculo m carbuncle

carburador m carburet(t)or

cárcere m prison

carcunda f hump

cardápio Braz m menu

cardeal m, adj cardinal

cardo m thistle

cardume m shoal

careca f baldness; adj bald

carecer v/i want, need; lack

carestia f dearness; scarcity

careta f grimace

carga f load, burden; cargo

cargo m post, position

cargueiro m freighter

carícia f caress

carid|ade f charity; **~oso** charitable

carimb|ar v/t stamp; **~o** m rubber stamp

carinh|o m affection; **~oso** affectionate

carioca m weak coffee; Braz m, f native of Rio de Janeiro

carnal adj carnal

carnaval m carnival

carne f flesh; meat; **~** assada roasted meat; **~ de carneiro** mutton; **~ de porco** pork; **~ de vaca** beef; **~ de vitela** veal

carneiro m sheep, ram

carn|iceiro m butcher; **~ívoro** carnivorous; **~udo** fleshy; meaty

caro adj dear; expensive

caroço m stone

carona f Braz lift, ride

carpa f carp

carpete f carpet

carpinteiro m carpenter

carranc|a f frown; grimace; **~udo** sullen, surly

carrasco m hangman; executioner

carreg|ador m porter; **~ar** v/t, v/i weigh, rest on; load; charge

carreira f race; career

carriça f wren

carril m rail

carro m (motor-car); **~ elé(c)-**

trico tram, US streetcar
carroça f cart
carrocel m roundabout, merry-
-go-round, US carousel
carruagem f carriage; ~cama
f sleeping-car; ~restaurante
f dining-restaurant car
carta f letter; map; (playing-)-
card; ~ de condução, Braz ~
de motorista driving licence,
US driver's license
cartão m card, cardboard; ~ de
visita visiting-card
cartaz m bill, poster, placard
carteira f wallet; desk; brief-
-case
carteirista m pickpocket
carteiro m postman
cartório m notary's office; file,
archive
carvalho m oak
carvão m coal
casa f house; home; buttonhole;
room; firm; square; ~ de câmbio money-changer's
casac|a f dress-coat; ~o m coat,
jacket
cas|ado married; ~al m mar-
ried couple; farm-house; ~a-
mento m wedding, marriage;
~ar v/t, v/i, v/r marry, get
married
casca f bark; shell; peel; skin;
husk; pod; rind
cascata f waterfall; cascade
casco m skull; hoof; cask; hull
caserna f barracks
caso m case; accident; event;
matter
caspa f dandruff, scurf
casta f lineage; breed; caste

castanh|a f chestnut; ~eiro m
chestnut-tree
castanho adj brown
castelo m castle; fazer ~s no
ar build castles in the air/in
Spain
castiçal m candlestick
castiço pure, genuine; pure-
-bred
castidade f chastity
castig|ar v/t punish; ~o m
punishment
casto chaste
castor m beaver
castrar v/t castrate
casual casual, accidental; ~i-
dade f chance
catálogo m catalogue
catarata f waterfall; med cataract
catástrofe f catastrophe
cata-vento m weather vane
cátedra f university chair
catedral f cathedral
catedrático m professor
categoria f category
categórico categorical
cativ|ante captivating; ~ar v/t
captivate; ~eiro m captivity;
~o m captive
católico Catholic
catorze fourteen
caução f bail; guarantee; surety
caucho, cauchu m caoutchouc,
rubber
cauda f tail
caudal m torrent; ~oso torren-
tial
caudilho m leader
caule m stem, stalk
caus|a f cause; origin; jur case;

por ~ de because of; ~ar *v/t* cause

cáustico caustic

cautel|a *f* care, caution; ~oso cautious

cava *f* armhole

cavaco *m* chat; dar o ~ por be very fond of; não dar ~ say nothing

cavala *f* mackerel

caval|ariça *f* stable; ~eiro *m* horseman; knight; ~ete *m* easel; trestle; ~gar *v/t*, *v/i* ride

cavalheiro *m* gentleman

cavalo *m* horse

cavar *v/t*, *v/i* dig

caverna *f* cave, cavern

cavidade *f* cavity

cear *v/t*, *v/i* dine; have supper

cebola *f* onion

ceder *v/i* yield, give in; cede

cedo *adv* early; soon; mais ~ ou mais tarde sooner or later

cedro *m* cedar

cédula *f* certificate; note

ceg|ar *v/t*, *v/i* blind; ~o blind; ~ueira *f* blindness

ceia *f* supper

celebr|ação *f* celebration; ~ar *v/t* celebrate

célebre famous

celebridade *f* celebrity

celeiro *m* granary, barn

celest|e, ~ial heavenly, celestial

celibat|ário *m* bachelor; ~o *m* celibacy

célula *f* cell

cem hundred

cemitério *m* cemetery

cen|a *f* scene; ~ário *m* scenery

cenoura *f* carrot

censo *m* census

cens|or *m* censor; ~ura *f* censorship; ~urar *v/t* censor; censure

centeio *m* rye

centelha *f* spark

centen|a *f* hundred; ~ário *m* centenary

centésimo hundredth

centímetro *m* centimeter

cento *m* hundred

central *adj* central; *f* station; ~al elé(c)trica power station/plant; ~al telefónica telephone exchange; ~o *m* centre, *US* center

cepa *f* vine

cepo *m* stump; block; log

cé(p)tico sceptical

cera *f* wax

cerâmica *f* ceramics

cerca *f* fence; hedge; *adv* near; about; *prep* ~ de near; nearly

cerc|adura *f* border; ~anias *f/pl* surroundings, environs; ~ar *v/t*, *v/r* enclose; surround; besiege

cerco *m* siege; circle

cereal *m* cereal

cerebral cerebral

cérebro *m* brain

cerej|a *f* cherry; ~eira *f* cherry-tree

cerimónia *f* ceremony

ceroulas *f/pl* underpants

cerrar *v/t*, *v/r* close in; shut, close; lock

cert|eiro sure; well-aimed; ~eza *f* certainty

certidão *f* certificate

certific|ado *m* certificate; ~ar *v/t, v/r* assure; certify; make sure of

certo *adj* certain; exact

cervej|a *f* beer; ~aria *f* pub; brewery; ~eiro *m* brewer

cervo *m* stag

cessar *v/t, v/i* cease; sem ~ incessantly

cesta *f* wicker basket

cesto *m* basket; ~ de papéis waste-paper basket

céu *m* sky; heaven

cevada *f* barley

chá *m* tea; tea party

chácara *f Braz* farm; country house

chacota *f* scorn; derision

chafariz *m* public fountain

chaga *f* wound; sore

chaleira *f* kettle

chama *f* flame

cham|ada *f* call; roll-call; ~ar *v/t, v/i, v/r* call; name; como se ~a? what is your name?

chaminé *f* chimney; funnel

champanhe *m* champagne

chamuscar *v/t* singe

chantag|em *f* blackmail; fazer ~em blackmail; ~ista *m, f* blackmailer

chão *m* ground; floor; *adj* smooth; level; plain

chapa *f* plate, sheet

chapéu *m* hat

charada *f* charade

charco *m* puddle, pool

charcutaria *f* delicatessen shop

charlatão *m* charlatan

charneca *f* heath

charrua *f* plough

charuto *m* cigar

chatear *v/t* annoy, bore

chato *adj* dull; annoying; flat

chave *f* key

chávena *f* cup

chef|e *m* chief; leader; ~iar *v/t* lead

cheg|ada *f* arrival; ~ar *v/i, v/r* approach; arrive

cheia *f* high water; flood; ~o *adj* full; em ~o completely

cheir|ar *v/t, v/i* smell; ~o *m* smell

cheque *m* cheque, *US* check

cherne *m* turbot

chiar *v/i* creak; squeak; chirp

chibata *f* switch, rod

chicana *f* chicanery

chicória *f* chicory

chicot|ada *f* lash; ~e *m* whip; ~ear *v/t* whip

chifre *m* horn; antler

chilr|(e)ar *v/i* twitter; ~(ei)o *m* twittering

chinela *f, ~o *m* slipper

chinês *adj, m* Chinese

chiqueiro *m* pigsty, *US* pigpen

chispa *f* spark; ~r *v/i* spark

chocalh|ar *v/i* jingle; ~o *m* cow-bell

chocar *v/t, v/i* shock; incubate; brood; collide

choco *m* cuttle-fish; *adj* broody; addled

chocolate *m* chocolate

chofre *m* blow; de ~ suddenly unexpectedly

choque *m* shock; collision

chorão *m bot* weeping willow; cry-baby

chorar *v/i* weep, cry

choro *m* weeping, tears

choupana *f* hut

choupo *m* poplar

chouriço *m* pork sausage

chover *v/i* rain; ~ **a cântaros** rain cats and dogs

chuchar *v/t* suck

chulo *adj* coarse; vulgar

chumb|ar *v/t* plug with lead; fail; ~**o** *m* lead

chupar *v/t* suck

churrasco *m* barbecue

chuv|a *f* rain; ~**iscar** *v/i* drizzle; ~**isco** *m* drizzle; ~**oso** rainy

cicatriz *f* scar; ~**ar** *v/t*, *v/i* scar

ciclista *m* cyclist

ciclo *m* cycle

ciclone *m* cyclone

cidad|ão *m* citizen; ~**e** *f* city; town

cidra *f* cider

ciência *f* science

cient|ífico scientific; ~**ista** *m*, *f* scientist

cifr|a *f* cypher; ~**ão** *m* sign for dollar or escudo ($)

cigano *m* gipsy, *US* gypsy

cigarr|eira *f* cigarette-case; ~**o** *m* cigarette

cilada *f* ambush; trap

cilindro *m* cylinder

cima *f* top; **em** ~ on; ~ **para** ~ upward(s); **por** ~ above, over

ciment|ar *v/t* cement; *fig* strengthen; ~**o** *m* cement, concrete

cimo *m* summit

cinco five

cinema *m* cinema, pictures, *US* movies

cingir *v/t*, *v/r* restrict oneself; surround

cínico cynical

cinquenta fifty

cint|a *f* sash; ~**o** *m* belt; ~**ura** *f* waist

cinz|a *f* ash; ~**eiro** *m* ash-tray

cinzel *m* chisel; ~**ar** *v/t* carve, chisel

cinzento grey

cioso jealous; envious

cipreste *m* cypress

circo *m* circus

circuito *m* circuit

circul|ação *f* circulation; ~**ar** *v/t*, *v/i* circulate; *adj* circular; *f* circular

círculo *m* circle

circundar *v/t* surround

circunferência *f* circumference

circunscrição *f* circumscription

circunstância *f* circumstance

cirurgi|a *f* surgery; ~**ão** *m* surgeon

cismar *v/t*, *v/i* rack one's brains, brood over

cisne *m* swan

cit|ação *f* citation, quotation; ~**ar** *v/t* cite, quote

cítara *f* zither

ciúme *m* jealousy; envy

ciumento jealous; envious

cívico civic

civil *adj* civil; ~**idade** *f* civility; ~**ização** *f* civilization; ~**izar** *v/t* civilize

clam|ar *v/t*, *v/i* shout; clamo(u)r; ~**or** *m* clamo(u)r

clandestino clandestine
clara f (de ovo) white (of egg)
clarabóia f skylight
clarão m gleam; flash
clar|ear v/t, v/i clear (up); ~eira f clearing; glade; ~idade f
brightness; clarity; ~o adj
clear; evident
class|e f class; ~ificação f classification; ~ificar v/t classify
claustro m cloister
cláusula f clause
clavícula f clavicle
clem|ência f clemency; ~ente
merciful
clerical clerical
clérigo m clergyman
clero m clergy
client|e m, f patient; customer;
client; ~ela f clientele
clima m climate
clínica f clinic; practice
clínico adj clinical
coabitar v/t, v/i cohabit, live
together
coa(c)ção f coercion
coagir v/t coerce, force
coar v/t strain, filter
cobard|e m, f coward; adj cowardly; ~ia f cowardice
cobert|a f cover; quilt; naut
deck; ~o adj covered; ~or m
blanket; ~ura f covering
cobiç|a f covetousness; ~ar v/t
desire
cobra f snake
cobr|ador m collector; ~ar v/t
collect; regain
cobre m copper
cobrir v/t cover
coçar v/t scratch

cócegas f/pl tickles
coche m coach
cochichar v/t, v/i whisper
coco m coco-nut
côdea f crust
código m code
codorniz f quail
coeducação f co-education
coeficiente m coefficient
coelh|eira f burrow, warren;
~o m rabbit
coerente coherent
coexistir v/i coexist
cofre m coffer, chest, safe
cogitar v/t, v/i think, cogitate
cognome m cognomen
cogumelo m mushroom
coibir v/t curb, repress
coincid|ência f coincidence;
~ir v/i coincide
coisa f thing; matter
coitado int poor fellow/thing;
adj poor, unfortunate
coito m coitus, intercourse
cola f gum, glue; crib
colabor|ação f collaboration;
~ador m collaborator; ~ar
v/i collaborate
colar m necklace; v/t glue,
stick; ~inho m collar
colcha f quilt, counterpane
colchão m mattress
colear v/i meander
cole(c)|ção f collection; ~cionador m collector; ~cionar
v/t collect
cole(c)tividade f collectivity
colega m, f colleague
colégio m college, school
cólera f anger; cholera
colérico choleric

colete *m* waistcoat, *US* vest

colheita *f* harvest, crop

colher *v/t* pick, gather

colher *f* spoon

colidir *v/i* collide

coligação *f* coalition

coligir *v/t* collect, gather

colina *f* hill

colisão *f* collision

colmeia *f* beehive

colmo *m* thatch

colo *m* neck; lap; **ao ~** in one's arms; on one's lap

coloc|ação *f* job; placing; **~ar** *v/t, v/r* get a job; put, place, set

colónia *f* colony; **~ de férias** summer camp

coloni|al colonial; **~zação** *f* colonization; **~zar** *v/t* colonize

colono *m* settler; colonist

colóquio *m* colloquy

color|ido *m* colo(u)ring; **~ir** *v/t* colo(u)r

coluna *f* column

com with

comand|ante *m* commandant; commander; **~ar** *v/t* command; **~o** *m* command

comarca *f* district, region

combat|e *m* combat; **~er** *v/t, v/i* combat, fight

combin|ação *f* combination; slip, petticoat; **~ar** *v/t, v/i, v/r* settle, fix; match; combine; agree

comboio *m* train; convoy; **~dire(c)to** through train; **~expresso** express (train)

combust|ão *f* combustion; **~ível** *m* fuel; *adj* combustible

começ|ar *v/t, v/i* begin, start; **~o** *m* start, beginning

comédia *f* comedy; play

comemor|ação *f* commemoration; **~ar** *v/t* commemorate

coment|ar *v/t* comment (on); **~ário** *m* commentary

comer *v/t, v/i* eat

comerci|al commercial; **~ante** *m, f* merchant; **~ar** *v/i* trade, do business

comércio *m* trade, commerce

comestív|eis *m/pl* eatables; **~el** eatable

cometer *v/t* commit

comichão *f* itch

comício *m* meeting, assembly

cómico comic(al), funny

comida *f* food; meal

comigo with me

cominho *m* cumin

comiss|ão *f* commission; committee; **~ária** *f Braz* stewardess; **~ário** *m* commissioner; **~ário de polícia** chief constable

como *conj* as; like; *int* what!, why!; *adv* how

comoção *f* commotion; emotion

cómoda *f* chest of drawers

comodidade *f* convenience; comfort

cómodo *adj* comfortable

como|vente moving, touching; **~ver** *v/t, v/i* move, touch

compadecer-se de *v/r* sympathize with

compaixão *f* pity, compassion

companheiro *m* companion

companhia *f* company

compar|ação f comparison; ~ar v/t compare; ~ativo adj, m comparative; ~ável comparable

comparecer v/i appear

comparti|lhar v/t share (in); ~mento m compartment

compasso m beat; rhythm; compasses

compat|ibilidade f compatibility; ~ível compatible

compatriota m, f compatriot, countryman, countrywoman

compêndio m compendium

compens|ação f compensation; ~ar v/t compensate

compet|ência f competence; competition; ~ente competent; suitable; ~ição f competition

competidor m competitor

competir v/i compete, vie; be incumbent on

compil|ação f compilation; ~ar v/t compile

compleição f physical constitution

complement|ar adj complementary; ~o m complement

complet|ar v/t complete, finish; ~o adj complete

complic|ação f complication; ~ado complicated; ~ar v/t complicate

componente m component

compor v/t, v/r compose (oneself)

comportamento m behavio(u)r

comportar v/r behave

composi|ção f arrangement; composition; ~tor m composer; compositor

compostura f composure

compota f jam; ~ de laranja marmalade

compr|a f purchase; ir às ~as go shopping; ~ador m buyer, purchaser; ~ar v/t buy, purchase

compreen|der v/t understand, realize; ~são f understanding, comprehension; ~sível understandable, comprehensible; ~sivo comprehensive, comprehending

compri|do adj long; ~mento m length

comprim|ido m tablet, pill; ~ir v/t (com)press

comprometer v/t, v/r compromise; commit oneself

compromisso m compromise

comprovar v/t confirm; verify; prove

compungido contrite

comput|ador m computer; ~ar v/t compute

comum adj common; general, ordinary

comuna f community

comunhão f communion

comunic|ação f communication; ~ado m communiqué; ~ar v/t communicate; ~ativo communicative

comunidade f community

comun|ismo m communism; ~ista m, f, adj communist

comut|ador m switch; ~ar v/t commute

côncavo *adj* concave
conceber *v/t, v/i* conceive (of)
conceder *v/t* allow, grant, concede
conceito *m* concept; opinion
concelho *m* municipality
concentrar *v/t, v/r* concentrate
concepção *f* conception
concertar *v/t, v/i* settle; adjust
concertina *f* concertina
concerto *m* concert
concessão *f* concession
concha *f* shell, conch
conciliar *v/t* conciliate; reconcile; win
conciso *adj* concise
conclu|ir *v/t, v/i, v/r* conclude; infer; ~são *f* conclusión; inference
concordar *v/t, v/i* agree
concórdia *f* concord, harmony
concorr|ência *f* throng; competition; ~ente *m, f* competitor; ~er *v/i* gather; compete
concretizar *v/t* make concrete
concreto *adj* concrete
concurso *m* competition
cond|ão *m* prerogative, privilege; ~e *m* count; earl
condecor|ação *f* decoration, medal; ~ar *v/t* decorate, invest
conden|ação *f* condemnation; ~ar *v/t* condemn
condens|ação *f* condensation; ~ar *v/t* condense
condescend|ência *f* compliance; ~ente condescending; ~er *v/i* condescend, comply
condessa *f* countess

condição *f* condition
condicional *adj* conditional
condicionar *v/t* condition
condigno condign, merited
condimento *m* spice
condiscípulo *m* schoolfellow
condizer *v/i* tally, match; suit
condolência *f* condolence
condução *f* conduction; transport
conduta *f* conduct; conduit
condutor *m* driver; conductor
conduzir *v/t, v/i, v/r* conduct; lead; drive
confeccionar *v/t* make
confederação *f* confederation
confeitaria *f* confectioner's
confer|ência *f* lecture; conference; ~enciar *v/i* confer, consult together; ~encista *m, f* lecturer; ~ir *v/t* check; confer, bestow
confessar *v/t* confess
confi|ança *f* confidence; ~ar *v/t, v/i* trust, confide; entrust
confidente *m, f* confidant(e)
confinar *v/t, v/i* confine; border
confins *m/pl* confines
confirm|ação *f* comfirmation; ~ar *v/t* confirm
confisc|ação *f* confiscation; ~ar *v/t* confiscate
confissão *f* confession
conflito *m* conflict
confluir *v/i* join, flow
conform|ar *v/t, v/i, v/r* conform; harmonize; resign oneself to; ~e *conj* as, according to; *adv* in agreement; (é) ~! it depends; ~idade *f* conformity

confortar v/t comfort

confortável comfortable

conforto m comfort

confrontar v/t confront

confundir v/t confuse

confus|ão f confusion; **~o** confused; embarrassed

congelar v/t freeze; congeal

congénere identical

congénito congenital

congestão f congestion

congestionar v/t, v/r congest

congratular v/t, v/r congratulate

congress|ista m, f Congresswoman, Congressman; **~o** m congress

conhec|edor m connoisseur; expert; **~er** v/t, v/i, v/r know; get to know; be acquainted with; **~ido** adj known; m acquaintance; **~imento** m acquaintance; knowledge; **~imentos** m/pl knowledge

conje(c)tur|a f conjecture; **~ar** v/t, v/i conjecture

conjugar v/t conjugate

cônjuge m spouse

conjunção f conjunction

conjunto m assemblage; whole; entirety

conjur|ação f conspiracy; **~ado** m conspirator; **~ar** v/i conspire

con(n)osco with us

conquanto although

conquist|a f conquest; **~ar** v/t conquer

consagr|ação f consecration; **~ar** v/t consecrate

consci|ência f conscience; consciousness; **~encioso** conscientious

consciente conscious

consecutivo consecutive

conseguinte consequent; **por ~** in consequence

conseguir v/t get, obtain; succeed in, manage

conselheiro m counsel(l)or, adviser

conselho m counsel, advice

consent|imento m consent; **~ir** v/t, v/i consent (to)

consequência f consequence

conserva f preserves; mixed pickles; **~ção** f preservation; **~dor** adj, m conservative; **~r** v/t, v/r conserve; preserve; keep

consider|ação f consideration; **~ar** v/t, v/r consider; **~ável** considerable

consigo pron with him(self)/ her(self)/itself; with themselves; with you

consist|ência f consistency; **~ente** consistent

consistir em v/i consist in, of

consoada f Christmas eve dinner

consoante f, adj consonant; prp according to

consol|ação f consolation; **~ar** v/t, v/r solace, console

consolid|ação f consolidation; **~ar** v/t consolidate

consolo m consolation

consórcio m partnership

consorte m, f consort

conspir|ação f conspiracy; **~ador** m conspirator; **~ar** v/i conspire, plot

constância f constancy

constante constant

constar v/i be known, be reported; **~ de** consist of

constern|ação f consternation; **~ar** v/t, v/i dismay

constip|ação f cold; **~ado** having a cold; **~ar-se** v/r catch cold

constitucional adj constitutional

constituição f constitution

constituinte adj constituent

constituir v/t constitute

constru|ção f construction; **~ir** v/t construct; **~tor** m constructor

cônsul m consul

consulado m consulate

consult|a f consultation; **~ar** v/t consult; **~ório** m consulting room

consum|idor m consumer; **~ir** v/t consume

consumo m consumption

conta f account; bill

contabil|idade f book-keeping; **~ista** m, f book-keeper; accountant

contactar v/t, v/i contact

conta(c)to m contact

contado counted; told, narrated

cont|agiar v/t infect; **~ágio** m contagion; **~agioso** contagious

contanto que provided that

conta-quilómetros m speedometer

contar v/t, v/i tell; count; relate; **~ com** rely on

contempl|ação f contemplation; **~ar** v/t contemplate

contemporâneo m, adj contemporary

contenda f strife, quarrel

content|amento m contentment; **~ar** v/t, v/r satisfy, content; **~e** content(ed), happy

conter v/t, v/r contain

contest|ar v/t, v/i dispute; contest; **~ável** contestable

conteúdo m contents

contigo with you

continência f continence

continente m continent

continu|ação f continuation; **~ar** v/t, v/i go on, continue; **~idade** f continuity

contínuo adj continuous, continual; m care-taker, US janitor

conto m tale; thousand escudos/cruzeiros

contornar v/t outline; go round

contorno m outline; contour

contra prp against

contraband|ista m, f smuggler; **~o** m contraband

contra(c)ção f contraction

contraceptivo m contraceptive

contradição f contradiction

contradizer v/t, v/i, v/r contradict

contrair v/t contract

contramestre m foreman

contrapartida f counterpart

contrapeso m counterpoise

contrapor v/t oppose

contrari|ar v/t, v/r thwart; annoy; **~edade** f contrariety; worry

contrário adj contrary, oppo-

site
contraste *m* contrast
contrat|ar *v/t* contract; **~o** *m* contract
contraveneno *m* antidote
contribu|ição *f* contribution; **~inte** *m, f* taxpayer; **~ir** *v/i* contribute
contrição *f* contrition
contristar *v/t* sadden
contrito contrite
controle *m* control
controvérsia *f* controversy
contudo *conj* nevertheless
contusão *f* bruise, contusion
convalesc|ença *f* convalescence; **~er** *v/i* convalesce
convenção *f* convention; agreement
convencer *v/t, v/r* convince
convencion|al *adj* conventional; **~ar** *v/t* stipulate
conveni|ência *f* convenience; propriety; **~ente** convenient; proper
convénio *m* pact, covenant
convento *m* convent
converg|ência *f* convergence; **~ir** *v/i* converge
convers|a *f* talk, chat; **~ação** *f* conversation; **~ar** *v/t* converse
conversão *f* conversion
converter *v/t* convert
convés *m* deck
convic|ção *f* conviction; **~to** *adj* convinced
convid|ado *m* guest; **~ar** *v/t* invite
convincente convincing
convir *v/i* suit, be proper; befit

convite *m* invitation
conviver *v/i* be on familiar terms
convívio *m* banquet; conviviality
convoc|ação *f* convocation; **~ar** *v/t* convoke
convulsão *f* convulsion
cooper|ação *f* co-operation; **~ar** *v/i* co-operate; **~ativa** *f* co-operative society; **~ativo** co-operative
coorden|ação *f* co-ordination; **~ar** *v/t* co-ordinate
copa *f* treetop; crown; pantry; **~s** *f/pl* hearts
cópia *f* copy
copiar *v/t* copy
copioso copious
copista *m* copyist
copo *m* glass
coqueiro *m* coconut tree
cor *f* colo(u)r
cor: de ~ by heart
coração *m* heart
corado red, ruddy
coragem *f* courage
corajoso courageous
coral *m* coral
corante *m* colo(u)ring
corar *v/i* blush
corça *f* doe, hind
corcovar *v/i* stoop; curve
corcunda *m, f* hunchback
cord|a *f* rope; string; **~ão** *m* cord; twine; cordon
cordeiro *m* lamb
cordel *m* string
cordial *adj* hearty, cordial
cordoeiro *m* rope-maker
córneo horny, corneous

cornet|a f cornet; bugle; **~eiro** m bugler

corno m horn

coro m chorus; choir

coro|a f crown; **~ação** f coronation; **~ar** v/t crown

ooronel m colonel

coronha f butt end

corpo m body; mil corps

corporação f corporation

corpóreo corporeal

corpulento corpulent

corre(c)ção f correction

corredor m passage, corridor

correia f strap; belt

correio m post, US mail; post office; **~ aéreo** airmail; **na volta do ~** by return of post

correlação f correlation

corrente adj, f current; **~ alterna** alternating current; **~ contínua** direct current

correr v/t, v/i run; flow; draw; examine

correspond|ência f correspondence; **~ente** m, f, adj correspondent; **~er** v/i correspond

corretor m broker

corrida f race, run; **~ de touros** bullfight

corrigir v/t correct

corrimão m handrail

corroer v/t corrode

corromper v/t corrupt

corrosão f corrosion

corru(p)ção f corruption

cort|ar v/t, v/i, v/r cut; **~e m** cut, gash

corte f court; **~jar** v/t court;

cortejo m procession; cortège;

retinue

cortês polite, courteous

cortesia f courtesy

cortiça f cork

cortina f curtain

cortinado m curtain

coruja f owl

coruscar v/i flash, glitter

corvo m raven

coser v/t, v/i sew

cosmético adj, m cosmetic

costa f coast; shore; **~s** f/pl back

costela f rib

costeleta f cutlet, chop

costumar v/t, v/i use (to)

costume m custom; **como de ~** as usual

costur|a f sewing; seam; **~eira** f seamstress

cota f quota

coto m stump

cotovelo m elbow

cotovia f lark

couro m leather

couve f cabbage; **~-de-Bruxelas** Brussels (sprout); **~-flor** f cauliflower; **~ galega** kale; **~ lombarda** white cabbage

cova f cave

covil m den

coxa f thigh

coxear v/i limp

coxo adj lame

cozer v/t cook; boil; bake

cozido m **(à portuguesa)** Portuguese stew

cozinh|a f kitchen; cooking; **~ar** v/t, v/i cook; **~eiro** m cook

cravar v/t nail; stare

cravinho m clove
cravo m nail; bot carnation; ~-da-india, ~-de-cabecinha clove
creditar v/t credit
crédito m credit
credor m creditor
creme m cream; custard
cren|ça f belief; ~te m, f believer
crepúsculo m twilight, dusk
crer v/t, v/i suppose; believe
crescer v/i grow
criação f creation
criada f maid, servant
criado m waiter; servant
criança f child
criar v/t create; rear
criatura f creature
crim|e m crime; ~inoso m, adj criminal
crise f crisis
cristandade f Christendom
crist|ão m, adj Christian; ~ianismo** m Christianity
critica f cirticism
criticar v/t criticize
critico m critic; adj critical
crivar v/t riddle; sift
crivo m sieve; riddle
crocodilo m crocodile
croquete m croquette
cru raw; rough; coarse
cruel cruel; ~dade** f cruelty
cruz f cross
cruzar v/t cross
cubo m cube
cuco m cuckoo
cuecas f/pl (under)pants, briefs, panties
cuidado m care; ~so careful

cuidar (de) v/t care for, tend
cujo whose; of which
culp|a f blame; guilt; fault; ~ado** adj guilty; ~ar** v/t blame
cultivar v/t cultivate, till
cultivo m cultivation, tillage
culto adj cultivated, cultured; m cult
cultura f culture; cultivation
cume m summit
cumpriment|ar v/t greet; compliment; ~o** m geeting; fulfil(l)ment; ~os** m/pl kind regards, greetings; best wishes
cumprir v/t, v/i, v/r accomplish, fulfil(l), carry out; ~ a palavra** keep one's word
cúmulo m height, acme
cunha f wedge
cunha|da f sister-in-law; ~do** m brother-in-law
cunho m stamp, impress
cúpula f dome
cura m parish priest; f cure, healing
curandeiro m quack
curar v/t, v/i, v/r cure, heal
curios|idade f curiosity; ~o** curious
curral m corral, pen
curso m course
curtir v/t tan; soak
curt|o short; ~o-circuito** m short circuit
curv|a f bend, curve; ~ar** v/t, v/i curve, bend; ~o** curved, bent
cusp|ir v/i spit; ~o** m spittle
cust|ar v/t, v/i cost; be difficult; ~ear** v/t defray; ~o** m cost(s),

expense; **a** ~o with difficulty
custódia f custody
custoso costly, expensive

cutelaria f cutlery
cutel|eiro m cutler; ~o m chopper; cutlass
cútis f skin

D

da contr of **de** and **a**
da(c)til|ógrafa f typist; ~o-grafar v/t, v/i type
dado m dice; ~s m/pl data
daí from there, thence; therefore; ~ **em diante** from then on; **e** ~? and what then?
dama f lady; queen; ~s f/pl draughts
damasco m apricot; damask
danar v/t, v/i irritate, get angry
danç|a f dance; ~ar v/t, v/i dance
danificar v/t damage, spoil
dano m hurt, injury; damage
dantes before, formerly
dar v/t, v/i, v/r give; beat; ~ **com** meet, come across; ~-se **bem com** get on well with; ~ **às de vila-diogo** take to one's heels; ~ **um passeio** take a walk
dardo m dart
dat|a f date; ~ar (de) v/t, v/i date (from)
de of; from; by; on; in
debaixo underneath; ~ **de** under
debalde in vain
deband|ada f dispersing; stampede; ~ar v/t, v/i disband
debat|e m debate; ~er v/t debate
débil weak

debilidade f debility, weakness
debitar v/t, v/r debit
débito m debit
debruar v/t hem, border
debruçar-se v/r lean out
debulh|a f threshing; ~adora f threshing-machine; ~ar v/t thresh; ~ar-se em lágrimas dissolve into tears
década f decade
decadência f decadence
decair v/i fall, decay
decapitar v/t behead
dec|ência f decency; ~ente decent
decepar v/t mutilate, mangle
decepção f disappointment
decepcionar v/t disappoint
decidido resolute
decidir v/t, v/i, v/r decide
decifrar v/t decipher
décimo m, adj tenth
decis|ão f decision; ~ivo decisive
declam|ação f declamation; ~ar v/t, v/i declaim
declar|ação f declaration; ~ar v/t, v/r declare
declin|ação f declination; declension; ~ar v/t, v/i decline
declínio m decline
decompo|r v/t, v/r decompose; ~sição f decomposition
decor|ação f decoration; ~ar

v/t. decorate; learn by heart
decor|o *m* decorum; **~oso** *adj* decorous
decorrer *v/i* pass away, elapse; occur
decote *m* low neckline
decrépito decrepit
decrescer *v/i* decrease
decret|ar *v/t* decree; **~o** *m* decree
decurso *m* lapse, course
ded|ada *f* finger-print; **~al** *m* thimble
dedic|ação *f* dedication, devotion; **~ar** *v/t, v/r* dedicate, devote
dedo *m* finger; **~ do pé** toe
dedu|ção *f* deduction; **~zir** *v/t* deduct; deduce
defectivo defective
defeit|o *m* defect, fault; **~uoso** *adj* defective, faulty
defen|der *v/t, v/r* defend; **~sável** defensible; **~siva** *f* defensive; **~sor** *m* defender
deferência *f* deference
defer|imento *m* granting; compliance; **~ir** *v/t, v/i* yield, concede, grant; defer
defes|a *f* defence; **~as** *f/pl* tusks; **~o** *m* closed season; *adj* prohibited
defici|ência *f* deficiency; **~ente** deficient
definhar *v/t, v/i, v/r* wilt; pine; languish
defin|ição *f* definition; **~ido** *adj* defined, definite; **~ir** *v/t* define; **~itivo** definitive
deflagr|ação *f* deflagration; **~ar** *v/i* deflagrate

deform|ação *f* deformation; **~ar** *v/t* deform
deformidade *f* deformity
defraud|ação *f* defrauding; **~ar** *v/t* defraud, cheat
defrontar *v/t* face
defronte opposite, facing; **~ de** in front of
defumar *v/t* smoke
defunto *adj* defunct, deceased
degelar *v/t* thaw
degelo *m* thaw
degener|ação *f* degeneration; **~ar** *v/i* degenerate
degrad|ação *f* degradation; **~ar** *v/t* degrade
degrau *m* step, stair; rung
degredar *v/t* deport, exile
degredo *m* deportation
deitado *m* lying down
deitar *v/t, v/i, v/r* lay; cast; throw; pour; go to bed, lie down
deixar *v/t, v/i, v/r* quit; let; leave; **~ de** give up; **~ cair** drop; **não poder ~ de** can't help it
dele *contr of* **de + ele** his
deleg|ação *f* delegation; **~ado** *m* delegate; **~ar** *v/t* delegate
deleit|ar *v/t, v/r* delight; **~e** *m* delight; **~oso** delightful
delgado *adj* thin, slender
deliberar *v/t, v/i* deliberate
delicad|eza *f* delicacy, gentleness; **~o** delicate
delícia *f* delight
delici|ar *v/t, v/r* delight; **~oso** delicious; delightful
delinear *v/t* delineate
delinquente *m* delinquent

delir|ante delirious, raving; **~ar** v/i be delirious, rave

delirio m delirium

delito m crime, offense

demais adv besides; adj too much, too; **o ~** m the rest; **~ a mais** furthermore

demanda f lawsuit; plea; quest; **em ~ de** in search of

demasi|a f excess; **~ado** adv too; adj excessive

demência f madness, insanity

demente adj mad, insane

demissão f dismissal; resignation

demitir v/t, v/r dismiss; resign

democra|cia f democracy; **~ta** m, f democrat

demolir v/t demolish

demónio m demon, devil

demonstr|ação f demonstration; **~ar** v/t demonstrate; **~ativo** demonstrative; **~ável** demonstrable

demor|a f delay; **~ar** v/t, v/r be long; delay

demover v/t dissuade

denodado bold

denodo m boldness

denomin|ação f denomination; **~ar** v/t, v/r denominate, name

denotar v/t denote

dens|idade f density; **~o** dense

dent|ada f bite; **~ado** indented, jagged; **~adura** f set of teeth; **~adura postiça** false teeth; **~al** adj dental; **~e** m tooth; **~ifrício** m dentifrice; **~ista** m, f dentist

dentro inside, within; **~ de** in, within; **~ em breve** soon, shortly

denúncia f denunciation; publication of banns

denunci|ante m, f denunciator; **~ar** v/t denounce

deparar v/t, v/r reveal; come across; present

departamento m department

depenar v/t deplume, pluck

depend|ência f dependence; outbuilding; **~ente** dependent; **~er de** v/i depend on

depilar v/t depilate

deplorar v/t deplore

deplorável deplorable

depoimento m deposition, evidence

depois afterwards; then; **~ de** after; **~ de amanhã** the day after tomorrow; **e ~?** what of it?; **~ que** after; since

depor v/t, v/i put aside; depose

deportar v/t deport

deposição f deposition

depositar v/t deposite

depósito m deposit

depravar v/t deprave

depreci|ação f depreciation; **~ar** v/t depreciate

depreender v/t perceive

depressa quickly, fast

depressão f depression

deprimir v/t depress

depurar v/t purify

deputado m deputy; member of parliament

deriv|ação f derivation; **~ar** v/t, v/i, v/r derive from

derradeiro last

derramar v/t scatter, spread;

spill; shed

derrapar v/i skid, sideslip

derreter v/t, v/r melt

derroc|ada f collapse; **~ar** v/t knock down; demolish

derrot|a f rout, defeat; **~ar** v/t rout, defeat

desabafar v/t, v/i uncover, relieve; open one's heart

desab|amento m crumbling; **~ar** v/i crumble

desabitado uninhabited

desabituar v/t wean from, cure of a habit

desabotoar v/t, v/r unbutton

desabrido sharp; rough; peevish

desabrigado unsheltered; exposed, open

desabrochar v/i bloom, blossom

desaf|iar v/t defy, challenge; **~io** m challenge; contest; match

desafog|ar v/t, v/i unburden; ease; **~o** m ease, comfort

desagrad|ar v/t displease; **~ável** disagreeable; **~o** m displeasure

desaguar v/i flow

desaire m setback; awkwardness

desajeitado clumsy, awkward

desalent|ar v/t, v/i, v/r discourage; **~o** m dejection, dismay

desalinho m slovenliness; disorder

desalojar v/t dislodge

desampar|ado abandoned, forsaken; **~ar** v/t forsake, abandon; **~o** m abandonment

desanim|ado discouraged; **~ar** v/t, v/i discourage

desânimo m discouragement

desaparec|er v/i disappear; **~ido** adj missing; **~imento** m disappearance

desapertar v/t loosen, slacken

desaprovar v/t disapprove

desarmar v/t disarm

desarmonia f disharmony

desarranj|ar v/t disarrange; **~o** m disorder

desarrumar v/t disarrange

desassossega|r v/t disquiet, disturb; **~o** m uneasiness

desastr|ado unlucky; awkward; **~e** m disaster

desastroso disastrous

desatar v/t, v/i untie, unfasten; **~ a chorar** burst out crying; **~ a rir** burst out laughing

desatento heedless

desavergonhado shameless

desavindo at variance

desbarat|ar v/t destroy; defeat; **~o** m havoc; defeat; **ao ~o** at a sacrifice, dirt-cheap

desbotar v/t, v/i fade

descabido improper

descair v/i decay; droop

descalçar v/t, v/r take off

descalço barefoot

descans|ado rested; tranquil, easy; **~ar** v/t, v/i rest; **~o** m rest; repose

descar|ado cheeky, impudent; **~amento** m effrontery

descarg|a f unloading; discharge; volley; **~o** m acquittal

descarregar v/t, v/i relieve;

unload; discharge

descarril|amento m derailment; **~ar** v/t, v/i derail

descascar v/t peel, shell

descend|ência f progeny, offspring; **~ente** m, f descendant; adj descending

descender v/i descend from

descer v/t, v/i descend; get/go down

desclassificar v/t disqualify

descob|erta f discovery; **~rimento** m discovery; **~rir** v/t, v/i, v/r uncover; discover

descol|agem f avi take-off; **~ar** v/i take off

descomp|or v/t disarrange; **~ostura** f rebuke

desconcertado disconcerted, upset

desconfi|ado distrustful; **~ança** f distrust; **~ar** v/t, v/i distrust; suspect

descongelar v/t thaw

desconhecido adj unknown

descont|ar v/t discount; **~o** m discount

descorado colo(u)rless; pale

descoser v/t unsew, unstitch

descrédito m discredit

descren|ça f disbelief; **~te** m, f unbeliever

descrever v/t describe

descrição f description

descritivo descriptive

descuid|ado careless; negligent; **~ar** v/t, v/r disregard, neglect; **~o** m oversight, neglect

desculp|a f excuse; **~ar** v/t, v/r apologize, excuse; **~e!** sorry!,

excuse me

descurar v/t neglect

desde since; from; **~ que** since; as soon as; provided

desdém m disdain

desdenh|ar v/t, v/i disdain; **~oso** disdainful

desdita f misfortune

desdizer v/t contradict

desdobr|amento m unfolding; **~ar** v/t unfold; duplicate

desej|ar v/t desire; wish; **~ável** desirable; **~o** m desire; wish; **~oso** desirous

desembaraç|ar v/t, v/r rid; disentangle; disembarrass; **~o** m ease

desembarcar v/t, v/i disembark, land

desembarque m disembarking, landing

desemboc|adura f mouth; **~ar** v/i flow out

desembols|ar v/t disburse, spend; **~o** m disbursement, outlay

desembrulhar v/t unwrap; unravel

desempacotar v/t unpack

desempat|ar v/t decide, resolve; **~e** m decision

desempenh|ar v/t redeem from pawn; perform; **~ar um papel** play a part; **~o** m discharge; performance

desempregado unemployed

desemprego m unemployment

desencadear v/t, v/r break, burst; unchain

desencalhar v/t refloat

desencaminhar v/t lead astray;

mislead

desencontr|ado disagreeing, opposite; **~ar** v/t, v/r fail to meet; disagree

desencorajar v/t discourage

desencostar v/t straighten up, not to lean

desenferrujar, v/t clean the rust off; **~ a língua** find one's tongue

desenfre|ado unbridled; **~ar** v/t, v/r unbridle

desengan|ar v/t, v/r undeceive; **~o** m undeceiving

desengatar v/t unhook

desengonç|ado unhinged; ungainly; **~ar** v/t, v/r totter; unhinge

desenh|ador m draughtsman; designer; **~ar** v/t, v/i draw; design; **~o** m drawing; design

desenlace m dénouement

desenredar v/t unravel

desenrolar v/t, v/r unfold; spread; unroll

desenterrar v/t dig up

desentupir v/t unstop

desenvolt|o nimble; **~ura** f nimbleness

desenvolv|er v/t, v/r develop; **~imento** m development

desenxabido insipid; silly

desequilibrar v/t, v/r unbalance; throw off balance

desequilibrio m imbalance

deser|ção f desertion; **~tar** v/t, v/i desert; **~to** m desert; adj deserted

desesperado adj desperate

desesperar v/i despair

desespero m despair

desfalcar v/t embezzle

desfalec|er v/t faint; **~imento** m faintness

desfalque m embezzlement

desfavorável unfavo(u)rable

desfazer v/t undo, unmake; annul; **~se em lágrimas** burst into tears

desfech|ar v/t, v/i fire; end; burst; hurl; **~o** m outcome, upshot

desfeita f insult

desfigurar v/t disfigure

desfiladeiro m gorge, defile

desfil|ar v/i file past; **~e** m march-past

desforr|a f revenge; **~ar-se** v/r be/get even with, revenge

desfrutar v/t enjoy

desgarr|ado astray; **~ar** v/i, v/r go astray

desgastar v/t wear away

desgost|ar v/t, v/i dislike; displease; **~o** m sorrow, trouble

desgovernado wasteful

desgraç|a f mishap, misfortune; **~ado** unfortunate

desgrenhado dishevelled

design|ação f designation; **~ar** v/t designate, appoint

desígnio m design, purpose

desigual unequal; **~dade** f inequality

desilu|dir v/t disillusion; **~são** f disillusion(ment)

desimpedir v/t disencumber; clear away

desinfe(c)tar v/t disinfect

desinteligência f misunderstanding

desinteress|ado disinterested;

uninterested; **~ar-se** v/r lose interest

desinteresse m disinterestedness

desist|ência f desistance; **~ir** v/i desist, give up

desleal disloyal

desleix|ado slovenly, negligent; **~ar** v/t, v/r neglect; become negligent; **~o** m slovenliness, negligence

desligar v/t untie, unfasten; switch off; ring off

desliz|ar v/i slip, slide; **~e** m faux pas

desloc|ação f dislocation; **~ar** v/t dislocate

deslumbrar v/t dazzle

desmai|ado fainted; pale; **~ar** v/i faint

desmanchar v/t, v/r disarrange; undo

desmascarar v/t, v/r unmask

desmazelado slovenly

desmazelo m slovenliness

desmedido excessive

desment|ido m denial; **~ir** v/t belie; deny

desmesurado excessive, enormous

desmont|ar v/t, v/i, v/r dismantle, take to pieces; dismount; **~ável** collapsible

desmoraliz|ação f demoralization; **~ar** v/t demoralize

desmoron|amento m collapse, cave-in; **~ar** v/i, v/r demolish; cave in

desnatado skimmed

desnaturado unnatural

desnecessário unnecessary

desnivelado uneven

desnorte|ado bewildered; **~ar** v/t put off course; bewilder

desnudar v/t strip, denude

desobed|ecer v/t disobey, **~iência** f disobedience; **~iente** disobedient

desobstruir v/t disencumber; clear of obstructions

desocup|ação f leisure; **~ado** idle; vacant, unoccupied; **~ar** v/t vacate; evacuate

desol|ação f desolation; **~ado** desolate; **~ar** v/t desolate; lay waste

desonestidade f dishonesty

desonesto dishonest

desonrar v/t dishono(u)r

desord|eiro adj, s rowdy; **~em** f rowdiness; disorder; **~enado** disordered; disorderly

desorganiz|ação f disorganization; **~ar** v/t disorganize

desorient|ação f disorientation; bewilderment; **~ar** v/t, v/r mislead; lead astray; bewilder

despach|ar v/t, v/i, v/r make haste; expedite; dispatch; **~o** m dispatch

despedaçar v/t smash to pieces, shatter

desped|ida f leave taking, good-bye; **~ir** v/t, v/r say good-bye, take leave; dismiss

despegar v/t detach

despeito m spite; **a ~ de** in spite of

despejar v/t empty; pour out

despenh|adeiro m precipice; **~ar** v/r crash

despensa f pantry, larder

despercebido unnoticed

desperd|içar v/t waste, squander; **~ício** m waste; **~ícios** m/pl refuse, waste products

despert|ador m alarm-clock; **~ar** v/t, v/i wake (up), awake(n); **~o** awake

despesa f expense

desp|ido naked; bare; **~ir** v/t, v/r take off; undress

despistar v/t mislead; throw off the track

despojo m loot, spoils, booty

despontar v/i break

desport|ista f, m sportswoman, sportsman; **~ivo** sports, sporting; **~o** m sport

despovoar v/t depopulate

despregar v/t draw out; unfurl; **~ os olhos de** take one's eyes off

desprend|er v/t, v/r loose, unfasten; **~imento** m loosening; indifference

despreocupação f carelessness

despreocupado care-free, unconcerned

desprevenido unwary; unprovided

desprez|ar v/t despise; disregard; **~ível** despicable

desprezo m scorn, contempt

desproporcionado disproportionate

despropositado ill-timed; absurd

despropósito m nonsense, absurdity

desregr|ado unruly; **~amento** m unruliness

desrespeito m disrespect

destacar v/t, v/r detach; project, surpass

destapar v/t uncover; take the top off ...

destemido fearless, bold

destemperado uncontrolled

desterrar v/t banish, exile

desterro m banishment, exile

destilar v/t distil

destin|ar v/t, v/r determine; destine; **~atário** m addressee

destino m destiny; destination

destitu|ição f dismissal; **~ir** v/t deprive of; dismiss, discharge

desto|ante discordant; out-of-key; **~ar** v/i jar

destreza f skill, dexterity

destrinçar v/t specify, particularize

destro dext(e)rous, skil(l)ful

destroçar v/t destroy; ruin; shatter

destroço m destruction, havoc; **~s** m/pl wreck(age)

destru|ição f destruction; **~ir** v/t destroy

desumano inhuman

desun|ião f disunion; **~ir** v/t disunite, separate

desuso m disuse

desvair|ado adj bewildered; **~ar** v/t, v/i, v/r distract, mislead, bewilder

desvalorização f devaluation

desvalorizar v/t devalue

desvanec|er v/t, v/r fade, vanish; dissipate; **~imento** m disappearance

desvant|agem f disadvantage;

~**ajoso** disadvantageous
desvão m loft, attic
desvario m extravagance
desvelar v/t, v/r unveil, reveal; be zealous; keep awake
desvendar v/t unveil, disclose
desventur|a f misfortune; ~**ado** unfortunate
desvi|ar v/t, v/r divert; deviate; embezzle; lead astray; ~**o** m deviation; diversion; detour
detalh|ar v/t describe minutely; ~**e** m detail
detenção f detention
deter v/t, v/r detain; stop
detergente m detergent
deterior|ação f deterioration; ~**ar** v/t deteriorate
determin|ação f determination; ~**ar** v/t, v/r decide, determine
detest|ar v/t detest; ~**ável** detestable
detido hindered, detained
detonação f detonation
detrás behind
deturpar v/t alter, disfigure
Deus m God; ♀a f goddess
devagar adv slowly
devan|ear v/t, v/i muse, daydream; ~**eio** m fancy, daydream
devass|idão f debauchery; ~**o** adj debauched
devast|ação f devastation; ~**ar** v/t lay waste, devastate
devedor m debtor
dever v/t owe; ought; must; m duty
deveras truly, indeed
devido adj due; proper; ~ **a** owing to

devoção f devotion
devolução f devolution
devolver v/t give back, return
devorar v/t devour
devotar v/t devote to
dez ten
dezanove nineteen
dezasseis sixteen
dezassete seventeen
Dezembro m December
dezoito eighteen
dia m day; ~ **a ~** day by day; ~ **de anos** birthday; ~ **feriado** holiday; ~ **útil** working day, workday; ~ **sim, ~ não** every other day
diabo m devil
diáfano diaphanous
diale(c)to m dialect
diálogo m dialog(ue)
diamante m diamond
diâmetro m diameter
diante in front; ~ **de** in front of, before; **em** ~ henceforth, hereafter
dianteira f front, vanguard
diapositivo m slide
diária f daily expense; daily charge
diário adj daily; m daily newspaper; diary
dicionário m dictionary
dieta f diet
difam|ação f defamation; ~**ante** defamatory; ~**ar** v/t defame
diferenç|a f difference; ~**ar** v/t distinguish, differentiate
diferente different

diferir *v/t, v/i* differ; defer
difícil difficult
dificuldade *f* difficulty
dificultar *v/t* make difficult
difundir *v/t, v/r* diffuse
difusão *f* diffusion
digerir *v/t, v/i* digest
digestão *f* digestion
dignar-se *v/r* deign
dignidade *f* dignity
digno worthy
digressão *f* digression
dilacerar *v/t* dilacerate
dilat|ação *f* dilation; **~ar** *v/t, v/r* dilate
diligência *f* diligence
diligenciar *v/i* exert oneself, do one's best
diligente diligent
diluir *v/t* dilute
dilúvio *m* deluge
dimensão *f* dimension
diminu|ição *f* diminution; **~ir** *v/t, v/i* diminish
diminutivo *m* diminutive
diminuto tiny, minute
dinamarquês *m* Dane; *adj* Danish
dinamite *f* dynamite
dinheirão *m* large sum of money
dinheiro *m* money
diploma *m* diploma
diplom|acia *f* diplomacy; **~ata** *m, f* diplomat; **~ático** diplomatic
dique *m* dike
dire(c)|ção *f* direction; administration; steering; **~tivo** directive; **~to** direct; **~tor** *m* director

direita *f* right hand; **à ~** on/to the right; **às ~s** as it should be, upright
direito *m* law; right duty, tax; *adj* straight; right
dirig|ente *m* manager, director; **~ir** *v/t, v/r* address; run, manage; conduct; make for; direct
discar *v/t, v/i* dial
discern|imento *m* discernment; **~ir** *v/t* discern
disciplin|a *f* discipline; subject; **~ar** *v/t* discipline; *adj* disciplinary
discípulo *m* disciple
disco *m* disc; record
discorrer *v/i* ponder; talk
discrepância *f* discrepancy
discreto discreet
discrição *f* discretion; **à ~** at will, at one's discretion
discurs|ar (sobre) *v/i* discourse (up)on; **~o** *m* discourse
discussão *f* discussion
discutir *v/t, v/i* discuss
disfarç|ado disguised, in disguise; **~ar** *v/t* disguise
disfarce *m* disguise
disforme deformed
disparar *v/t* shoot, fire
disparatado foolish, silly
disparat|ar *v/i* blunder; talk nonsense; **~e** *m* nonsense, rubbish
dispendioso expensive, costly, dear

dispens|a f exemption; **~ar** v/t exempt, excuse

dispensário m dispensary

dispensável dispensable

dispersar v/t, v/i disperse

disponibilidade f availability

disponível available

dispor v/t, v/i, v/r count on; settle, decide; dispose; arrange; prepare; m disposal; **ao seu ~** at your disposal

disposi|ção f disposition; **~tivo** m contrivance, device, gear

disposto adj disposed, inclined; **bem ~** feeling fine, in good fettle; **mal ~** indisposed; in a mood

disput|a f dispute; **~ar** v/t dispute; **~ável** disputable

dissabor m annoyance, nuisance

dissecar v/t dissect

disseminar v/t disseminate

dissert|ação f dissertation; **~ar sobre** v/i discourse on

dissid|ência f dissidence; **~ente** adj, m, f dissident

dissimul|ação f dissimulation; **~ar** v/t, v/i disguise; dissemble

dissipar v/t dissipate

dissolu|ção f dissolution; **~to** dissolute

dissol|úvel dissoluble; **~vente** m, f dissolvent; **~ver** v/t, v/r dissolve

dissonância f dissonance

dissuadir v/t dissuade

distância f distance

distanciar v/t, v/r move away; (out)distance

distante distant, far-off

distar v/i be distant

distensão f distension

distinção f distinction

distinguir v/t, v/r distinguish

distintivo m badge, adj distinctive

distinto distinct

distra(c)ção f distraction

distraído distracted, absent-minded

distrair v/t, v/r amuse, entertain; distract

distribu|ição f distribution; **~ir** v/t distribute; **~tivo** distributive

distrito m district

distúrbio m disorder, row, riot, disturbance

dita f good luck

ditado m dictation; proverb, saying

ditad|or m dictator; **~ura** f dictatorship

ditame m dictate

ditar v/t dictate

ditoso fortunate

diurno adj daily

divã m divan

divag|ação f divagation, digression; **~ar** v/i digress

diversão f diversion; pastime

diverso diverse; **~s** various, several

divert|ido amusing; **~imento** m amusement; entertainment; **~ir** v/t, v/r divert; amuse; enjoy oneself

dívida f debt

dividir v/t divide

divin|dade f divinity; **~o** adj divine

divisa f emblem, motto, device; exchange rate

divisão f division; room

divisar v/t discern, descry

divórcio m divorce

divulg|ação f divulgence; **~ar** v/t divulge; spread

dizer v/t, v/i, v/r say, tell, speak; **~ respeito a** concern; **a bem ~** properly speaking; **por assim ~** so to speak

do contr of **de** and **o**

dó m pity, compassion

doação f donation

doar v/t donate

dobra f fold, tuck

dobradiça f hinge

dobrar v/t, v/i fold; double; bend, yield

dobre adj double; m knell

dobro m double

doca f dock

doçaria f confectioner's (shop); sweets

doce m sweet; adj sweet; mild, gentle

dócil docile

documento m document

doçura f sweetness

doen|ça f diseasc, sickness, illness; **~te** m, f patient; adj sick, ill; **~tio** sickly

doer v/i ache, hurt

doid|ice f foolishness, madness; **~o** adj silly, mad

dois m two

doloroso painful; sorrowful; grievous

dom m gift; endowment

dom|ador m tamer; **~ar** v/t tame

doméstico domestic

dom-fafe m zo bullfinch

domicílio m domicile

domin|ação f domination; **~ante** adj dominant; **~ar** v/t, v/i control; overlook; dominate

domingo m Sunday

domínio m dominion; domain; control

dona f Mrs; owner; **~ de casa** housewife

donaire m grace, charm

donativo m donation, gift

donde from where

dono m master, owner, proprietor; **~ de casa** master of the house; **~ da taverna** innkeeper

dor f pain; grief

dormente adj asleep, numb

dorm|ida f night's lodging; **~ir** v/t, v/i sleep; **~itório** m dormitory; Braz bedroom

dorso m back

dos|ar v/t dose; **~e** f dose

dot|ação f endowment, foundation; **~ar** v/t endow; **~e** m dowry

dourar v/t gild

dout|o learned; **~or** m doctor

doutrin|a f doctrine; **~ação** f indoctrination; **~ar** v/t indoctrinate

doze twelve

dragão m dragon; mil dragoon

dragar v/t dredge

dram|a m drama, play; **~ático** dramatic; **~atizar** v/t dramatize; **~aturgo** m dramatist, playwright

drog|a f drug; **~aria** f chemist's, drugstore; **~uista** m, f druggist

dualismo m dualism

duas f of **dois**

dúbio doubtful, dubious

ducha f, **duche** m douche, shower

dúctil ductile

duelo m duel

duende m goblin

dueto m duet

duna f dune

duplic|ação f duplication; **~ar** v/t duplicate

duplo adj double

duque m duke; **~sa** f duchess

duração f duration

durante during

dur|ar v/i last; **~ável** durable

dur|eza f hardness, toughness; **~o** hard

dúvida f doubt

duvid|ar v/t, v/i doubt; **~oso** dubious; doubtful

duzentos two hundred

dúzia f dozen

E

e and

ébano m ebony

ébrio adj drunk

ebulição f ebullition

eclesiástico adj ecclesiastical; m ecclesiastic

eclipse m eclipse

eco m echo; **~ar** v/t, v/i echo

economia f economy; economics; **~s** f/pl savings

económico economic(al)

economizar v/t, v/i save, economize

edição f edition

edific|ação f edification; **~ar** v/t edify; build

edifício m building

edital m notice, order

editar v/t edit; publish

édito m notice, edict

editor m publisher

edredão m eider-down

educa|ção f education; **~dor** m educator; **~r** v/t educate; **~ti-**

vo educative

efe(c)ti|vamente in fact, really; effectively; **~vidade** f effectiveness; **~vo** adj effective

efe(c)tuar v/t effect(uate)

efeito m effect; **com ~** indeed

efémero ephemeral

efeminado effeminate

efervescência f effervescence

efic|ácia f efficacy; **~az** effective, efficient

efusão f effusion

egoísmo m egoism

egoísta m, f egoist; adj egoistical, selfish

égua f mare

eira f threshing-floor

eis here is, here are

eixo m axle; axis

ela she; it; her

elabor|ação f elaboration; **~ar** v/t elaborate

elasticidade f elasticity

elástico adj, m elastic

ele

ele he; it; him
ele(c)tricidade f electricity
elé(c)trico adj electric; m tram
ele(c)trifi|cação f electrification; ~car v/t electrify
elefante m elephant
eleg|ância f elegance; ~ante adj elegant
eleger v/t elect, choose
elei|ção f election; ~to adj elected, chosen; ~tor m elector; ~torado m electorate; ~toral electoral
elementar elementary
elemento m element
elev|ação f elevation; ~ador m lift, US elevator; ~ar v/t elevate; raise
elimin|ação f elimination; ~ar v/t eliminate
elo m link; bot tendril
elogi|ar v/t praise; ~io m praise; eulogy
eloqu|ência f eloquence; ~ente eloquent
elucidar v/t elucidate
em prp in; into; at; on; ~ casa at home
emagrec|er v/t, v/i lose weight, get thin; ~imento m emaciation
emanar v/i emanate from
emancip|ação f emancipation; ~ar v/t, v/r emancipate
emaranhar v/t entangle
embaciar v/t, v/i steam up; dull, dim, tarnish
embaixad|a f embassy; ~or m ambassador
embal|agem f crating, packing; ~ar v/t lull, rock; wrap, pack

embandeirar v/t flag
embaraçado embarrassed, ill at ease
embaraç|ar v/t embarrass; disturb; ~o m embarrassment; ~oso embarrassing; perplexing
embarca|ção f boat; ship; ~douro m landing-stage; ~r v/t, v/i embark
embargo m embargo; seizure; distraint; sem ~ nevertheless
embarque m embarcation
embasbacado gaping, aghast
embat|e m collision; impact; ~er v/i collide
embebedar v/t, v/r intoxicate
embebido drenched, soaked; fig enraptured
embelezer v/t embellish, beautify
embirrar v/i be obstinate, be stubborn; ~ com dislike
emblema m emblem
embocadura f mouth; mouthpiece
êmbolo m piston
embolsar v/t pocket
embora conj (al)though
emborrachar v/t intoxicate
emboscada f ambush
embranquecer v/t, v/i whiten; bleach; grow white
embravecer-se v/r get rough
embriag|ar v/t, v/r intoxicate; enrapture; ~uez f intoxication, drunkenness
embriagem f mec clutch
embrião m embryo
embroma m Braz humbug, cheating

embrulh|ada *f* imbroglio; mess; **~ar** *v/t, v/r* confuse; wrap up, pack; **~o** *m* parcel, packet

embuçar *v/t* disguise

embuste *m* artifice, trick

emend|a *f* emendation, amendment; **~ar** *v/t, v/r* amend, emend; improve

ementa *f* menu

emerg|ência *f* emergence; emergency; **~ir** *v/i* emerge

emigr|ação *f* emigration; **~ado** *m* émigré; **~ante** *m, f* emigrant; **~ar** *v/i* emigrate

eminente eminent

emiss|ão *f* emission; broadcast; **~or** *m* transmitter; **~ora** *f* broadcasting station

emitir *v/t* emit; broadcast

emoção *f* emotion, excitement

emocion|ante thrilling, moving, exciting; **~ar** *v/t, v/r* excite

emoldurar *v/t* frame, encase

empacotar *v/t* pack up, bale

empada *f* pie

empadão *m* pie

empalidecer *v/i* grow pale

emparelhar *v/t, v/i* couple, pair, match

empatado drawn

empat|ar *v/t, v/i* tie, draw; **~e** *m* tie, draw, dead heat

empe|cer *v/t, v/i* impede, hinder; **~cilho** *m* hindrance, snag

empeçonhar *v/t* poison

empedernir *v/t, v/i* petrify

empedr|ado *m* stone-pavement; **~ar** *v/t* pave

empenh|ar *v/t, v/r* exert oneself; pawn, pledge; mortgage; **~o** *m* pawn, pledge; mortgage; desire; diligence

empilhar *v/t* heap up; pile up

empinar *v/t, v/r* tip up, rear

emplast(r)o *m* plaster

empobrec|er *v/t, v/i* impoverish; grow poor; **~imento** *m* impoverishment

empola *f* blister

empolgar *v/t* grip; grasp, seize

empório *m* emporium; *Braz* grocer's (shop)

empossar *v/t, v/r* take possession (of)

empreend|er *v/t* undertake; **~imento** *m* undertaking, enterprise

empregada *f* **(doméstica)** maid, servant

empreg|ado *m* employee; clerk; **~ar** *v/t* employ; use; **~o** *m* use; employment; job

empreit|ada *f* piece-work; **~eiro** *m* contractor

empresa *f* undertaking, enterprise; firm, company

emprestar *v/t* lend, *US* loan

empréstimo *m* loan; borrowing

empunhar *v/t* grasp, grip

empurr|ão *m* push, shove; **~ar** *v/t* push, shove

emudecer *v/t, v/i* silence; become silent

enaltecer *v/t* extol, exalt

enamorar-se de *v/r* fall in love with

encade|amento *m* connection; chaining; concatenation; **~ar** *v/t* chain, link together

encaderna|ção *f* binding, bookbinding; **~dor** m bookbinder; **~r** v/t bind

encaixar v/t, v/i fit (in); pack; encase; enchase

encaixilhar v/t frame

encaixotar v/t pack; encase

encalhar v/t, v/i strand; run aground

encaminhar v/t, v/r make for; set on the right road; guide

encanar v/t canalize

encandear v/t dazzle

encantado delighted; enchanted

encant|ador m sorcerer; adj charming; **~amento** m enchantment; **~ar** v/t delight; enchant; charm; **~o** m enchantment; charm; spell

encapelado rough

encapotar v/t cloak; disguise; muffle

encarar v/t face; face up to

encarcerar v/t imprison, incarcerate

encardido soil

encarec|er v/t, v/i raise the price; enhance; exaggerate; **~imento** m enhancement

encargo m charge, office; order, commission

encarnado adj, m red

encarniçado bloodthirsty, fierce, relentless

encarregar v/t, v/r undertake; charge, entrust; order

encen|ação f staging; **~ar** v/t stage

encer|ado m oilcloth, linoleum; **~ar** v/t wax

encerr|amento m close; **~ar** v/t enclose; close

encetar v/t begin, start

encharcar v/t soak, drench

ench|ente f flood; highwater; **thea** full house; **~er** v/t, v/i, v/r fill

enciclopédia f encyclop(a)edia

enclausurar v/t enclose

encoberto adj overcast, dull; concealed, hidden

encobrir v/t hide, conceal

encolher v/t, v/i shrink; **~ os ombros** shrug one's shoulders

encolhido adj shrunk

encomend|a f order, commission; **~ar** v/t, v/r order, commission; entrust

encontr|ão m jostle; **~ar** v/t, v/i, v/r find; encounter, meet; **~o** m encounter, meeting

encorajar v/t encourage

encorpado substantial; bulky

encost|a f declivity, slope; **~ar** v/t, v/r prop (up); lean on; **~o** m prop; back

encrespado choppy

encrespar v/t, v/r ripple, get choppy; curl, crisp, frizzle

encruzilhada f crossroads

encurtar v/t shorten, curtail

encurvar v/t bend, arch

endereç|ar v/t address; **~o** m address

endiabrado devillish; mischievous

endinheirado well-off, rich

endireitar v/t, v/i, v/r straighten (up)

endividado in debt

endividar v/t, v/r run into debt

endoidecer v/t, v/i go mad

endoss|ado m endorsee; **~ante**
m endorser; **~ar** v/t endorse;
~o m endorsement
endurec|er v/t, v/i, v/r harden;
~imento m hardness
enegrecer v/t, v/i, v/r blacken
energia f energy
enérgico energetic
enevoado cloudy; foggy; misty
enevoar v/t dim, blur, cloud
enfad|ar v/t, v/r weary, annoy;
~o m annoyance; drudgery;
~onho troublesome, tiresome
ênfase f emphasis
enfastiar v/t, v/i, v/r weary,
disgust
enfático emphatic
enfeitar v/t embellish, adorn
enfeite m adornment, ornament
enferm|ar v/t fall ill; **~aria** f
ward, sickbay; **~eira** f nurse;
~eiro m male nurse; **~idade** f
infirmity, sickness, illness; **~o**
adj infirm
enferrujado rusty
enferrujar v/t, v/i rust
enfezado lean, rickety
enfiar v/t thread; slip on
enfim finally, at last
enforcar v/t hang
enfraquecer v/t, v/i weaken;
enfeeble
enfrentar v/t confront, face
enfurecer v/t, v/i, v/r infuriate, enrage; rage
engan|ar v/t, v/r deceive; be
mistaken; **~o** m deceit; mistake; trick; delusion
engarrafamento m congestion,
traffic jam

engarrafar v/t bottle
engasgar v/t, v/r choke; gag
engatar v/t cramp, couple
engelhar v/t, v/i, v/r wrinkle,
shrivel
engenh|aria f engineering;
~eiro m engineer; **~o** m talent, wit, skill; mill; **~oso** in-
genious, witty
engodo m allurement; decoy;
snare
engolir v/t swallow
engordar v/t, v/i fatten; grow
fat
engraçado pleasant; funny
engrandec|er v/t, v/i aggran-
dize; enlarge; **~imento** m ag-
grandizement
engraxar v/t black, polish
engrenagem f gear, gearing
engripado down with flu
engrossar v/t, v/i swell, thick-
en
enguia f eel
enguiç|ar v/t bewitch; **~o** m
bad omen, ill-luck
enigma m enigma, puzzle
enjeitar v/t reject; repudiate
enjoado seasick
enjoar v/t, v/i, v/r sicken, nau-
seate; be seasick
enjoo m seasickness
enla|çar v/t bind, entwine, en-
tangle; **~ce** m union, joining;
marriage
enlamear v/t splash, spatter
with mud
enlatar v/t can
enle|ado perplexed; **~ar** v/t
fasten, attach; perplex
enleio m perplexity

enlevar v/t, v/r charm; enrapture

enlevo m ecstasy, rapture

enlouquecer v/t, v/i madden; go mad

enobrecer v/t, v/r ennoble

enoj|ar v/t disgust; **~o** m disgust, nausea

enorme enormous

enquanto while; **por ~** for the time being

enraizar v/t, v/i, v/r root, take root

enrasc|adela f scrape, fix; **~ar** v/t ensnare

enredar v/t, v/i, v/r entangle, ensnare, embroil

enredo m intrigue; plot

enregelar v/t, v/i freeze

enrijecer v/t, v/i harden, stiffen

enriquecer v/t, v/i enrich; get rich

enrodilhar v/t twist

enrolar v/t roll up, wrap

enroscar v/t, v/r twist; coil up

enrouquecer v/t, v/i get hoarse

enrugar v/t, v/i, v/r crease; wrinkle

ensaboar v/t soap; fig scold

ensai|ar v/t rehearse; test; **~o** m essay; rehearsal; test; attempt

ensanguentado blood-stained

ensejo m opportunity

ensin|ar v/t teach, instruct; **~o** m instruction, teaching

ensopado adj drenched

ensopar v/t, v/r sop; drench

ensurdecer v/t, v/i deafen; grow deaf

entabular v/t start, open

entalar v/t stick, pinch

entalhar v/t, v/i carve, engrave

entanto meanwhile; **no ~** nevertheless

então int what!; well then; now then!; adj then

entardecer v/i grow dark

ente m being; creature

entead|a f stepdaughter; **~o** m stepson

entend|er v/t understand; mean; m opinion; **~ido** experienced, skilful; understood; **~imento** m understanding

enternec|er v/t, v/r move, touch; **~imento** m tenderness

enterr|ar v/t, v/r sink; bury, inter; **~o** m burial, interment

entesar v/t stretch, stiffen

entidade f entity

entoação f intonation

entoar v/t intone

entontecer v/t, v/i stun

entornar v/t, v/i, v/r spill; upset

entorpec|er v/t numb; **~imento** m torpor

entortar v/t, v/i, v/r twist; crook; **~ os olhos** (have a) squint

entrada f entry; entrance; entrance fee; beginning; first course

entranh|ar v/t, v/r penetrate; drive into; **~as** f/pl entrails, bowels

entrar (em) v/i enter, go in

entrave m encumbrance; trammels

entre among; between

entreab|erto ajar; **~rir** v/t open half-way; leave ajar

entrecosto m rib

entreg|a f delivery; **~ar** v/t, v/r deliver; give over/up to; hand over; **~ue a** delivered; given over to

entrelaçar v/t interlace

entrem|ear v/t intermingle, intermix; **~eio** m interstice; interim

entrementes adv meanwhile

entretanto adv meanwhile

entret|enimento m amusement, entertainment; **~er** v/t, v/r amuse, entertain

entrevado adj, m paralytic

entrever v/t glimpse

entrevist|a f interview; **~ar** v/t interview

entristecer v/t, v/i sadden

entroncamento m junction

entronização f enthronement

entrudo m Shrovetide

entulho m rubbish

entup|imento m blockage; **~ir** v/t block, stop up

entusiasm|ar v/t, v/r fill with enthusiasm; **~o** m enthusiasm

entusi|asta m, f enthusiast; adj enthusiastic; **~ástico** enthusiastic

enumer|ação f enumeration; **~ar** v/t enumerate

enunciar v/t enunciate

envelhecer v/t, v/i age, grow old

envenen|amento m poisoning; **~ar** v/t poison

envergadura f spread, span; scope

envergonh|ado ashamed; **~ar** v/t, v/r shame; be ashamed of

envernizar v/t varnish

enviar v/t send

envidraçar v/t glaze

envio m remittance, sending

enviuvar v/t, v/i become a widow(er)

envolver v/t wrap; involve

enxame m swarm; **~ar** v/i swarm

enxada f hoe

enxaguar v/t rinse

enxaqueca f migraine

enxergar v/t discern

enxerto m graft

enxofre m sulphur

enxotar v/t scare away, drive

enxovalhar v/t crumple, rumple

enxu|gar v/t, v/i dry; **~to** adj dry

épico adj epic

epidemia f epidemic

epidémico epidemic

epílogo m epilogue

episcopal episcopal

episódio m episode

epitáfio m epitaph

época f epoch

epopeia f epic

equador m equator

equil|ibrar v/t balance; **~íbrio** m balance, equilibrium

equipa f team

equipagem f crew; supplies

equipamento m equipment

equipar v/t equip

equiparar v/t compare

equitação f horsemanship, riding

equitativo equitable

equival|ência f equivalence; **~ente** adj; m equivalent; **~er a** v/i be equivalent to

equivocar v/t, v/r equivocate; be mistaken, make a mistake

equívoco adj equivocal; m ambiguity, equivocation

era f era

ere(c)ção f erection

erguer v/t, v/r rise; raise, lift; erect

eriçar v/t bristle, stand on end

erigir v/t erect

ermo adj retired, secluded, waste; m desert

eros|ão f erosion; **~ivo** erosive

erótico adj erotic

err|ante erring; wandering, errant; **~ar** v/t, v/i miss; err; wander; **~o** m error, mistake; fault; **~óneo** erroneous

erudi|ção f erudition; **~to** adj erudite

erupção f eruption

erva f grass

ervilha f pea

esbaforido panting, gasping

esbanja|dor adj extravagant; m spendthrift; **~mento** m squandering; **~r** v/t waste, squander

esbarrar contra v/i run into, dash against

esbelto slender, svelte

esboçar v/t sketch; draft

esboço m sketch; rough draft

esborrachar v/t crush, squash

escabeche m marinade; uproar

escabroso rough, rugged, craggy; coarse; difficult, ticklish

escada f staircase, stairs; **~ de**

caracol spiral staircase; **~ rolante** escalator, moving staircase; **~ria** f staircase

escala f scale; port of call; gamut; **em grande ~** on a large scale; **por ~** in rotation; **fazer ~ em** call at

escalar v/t scale, climb up

escaldar v/t, v/i burn, scald

escalfar v/i poach

escalope m cutlet

escama f scale

escancarar v/t throw wide open

escandalizar v/t, v/i, v/r shock, scandalize

escândalo m scandal; uproar

escandaloso scandalous

escandinavo adj Scandinavian

escangalhar v/t make a mess of; break up

escanhoar v/t shave

escapar v/i, v/r escape

escapatória f evasion, excuse, loop-hole

escape m escape, outlet; **~ de gases** exhaust (pipe)

escaravelho m beetle

escarlat|e scarlet; **~ina** f scarlatina; scarlet fever

escar|necer v/t, v/i scoff at; jeer; **~ninho** adj scoffing, jeering

escárnio m scorn

escarpa f slope; scarp

escarr|ar v/t, v/i spit; **~o** m spittle, phlegm

escass|ez f scarcity; **~o** scarce, rare; scanty

escavação f excavation

escavar v/t excavate

esclarec|er v/t clear up; enlighten; **~imento** m enlightenment

esco|amento m drainage; **~ar-se** v/r drain off/away

escocês adj Scottish, Scotch; m Scot, Scotsman

escol m élite, pick, cream

escola f school

escolh|a f choice; selection; **~er** v/t choose; select

escolho m reef

escolt|a f escort; **~ar** v/t escort

escombros m/pl rubbish, debris; havoc

esconder v/t, v/r hide; **~ijo** m hiding-place

escondidas f/pl hide-and-seek; **às ~** in secret, by stealth

esconjur|ar v/t exorcize; **~o** m exorcism

escopo m aim, object

escopro m chisel

escora f prop, support

escória f dross

escorregadi(ç)o slippery

escorregar v/i slip, slide

escorrer v/t, v/i drain, drip

escov|a f brush; **~ar** v/t brush

escrav|idão f slavery; **~izar** v/t enslave; **~o** m slave

escrev|er v/t, v/i write; **~inhar** v/t, v/i scribble

escrit|a f writing; **~o** m note, bill; **~or** m writer; **~ório** m office; study; **~ura** f deed, indenture; **~uração** f bookkeeping; **~urar** v/t keep the books

escrivaninha f desk

escrivão m clerk; scribe

escrúpulo m scruple

escrutinar v/t, v/i count (votes)

escrutínio m scrutiny, ballot

escudo m shield; escutcheon; escudo

escul|tor m sculptor; **~tura** f sculpture; **~tural** sculptural

escum|a f froth, foam, scum; **~adeira** f skimmer; **~oso** frothy, foamy

escuna f schooner

escuras: às ~ in the dark

escur|ecer v/t, v/i darken; become dark; **~idão** f darkness; obscurity; **~o** dark; obscure

escusado needless

escusar v/t, v/i have no need of, needn't; exempt

escutar v/t, v/i listen (to)

esfalfar v/t, v/r tire out, overwork

esfaquear v/t knife, stab

esfarrapado ragged, tattered

esfera f sphere

esferográfica f ball(-point) pen, biro

esfolar v/t flay, skin; strip; fleece

esfomeado hungry, famished

esforç|ado valiant; strong; **~ar-se** v/r try hard, strive

esforço m effort

esfregar v/t scour, scrub, rub

esfri|amento m cooling; **~ar** v/t, v/i grow cold, cool, chill

esganar v/t strangle

esganiçar v/t, v/r yelp, screech

esgar m grimace

esgaravatar v/t scratch, scrape

esgot|ado out of print; exhausted, worn out; **~ar** v/t, v/r exhaust; use up

esgoto m drain, sewer

esgrim|a f fencing; **~ador** m fencer; **~ir** v/t,v/i fence

esguelha f slant; **de ~** askance

esguich|ar v/t, v/i spurt, squirt; **~o** m jet, squirt

esguio thin, slender, lean

eslavo adj Slavonic; m Slav

esmagador adj smashing, crushing

esmagar v/t crush, squash

esmalte m enamel

esmeralda f emerald

esmerar v/t, v/r finish to perfection; take pains with

esmero m care, pains

esmiuçar v/t investigate minutely

esmo: a ~ at random

esmola f alms

esmorecer v/t, v/i discourage; lose heart

espaç|ar v/t extend, space out; **~o** m space, room; **~oso** spacious

espada f sword

espádua f shoulder-blade

espairecer v/t, v/i amuse

espaldar m chair back

espalhafato m fuss, bustle

espalhar v/t, v/r scatter, spread

espalmar v/t flatten

espanador m duster

espancar v/t spank, thrash

espanhol adj Spanish; m Spanish; Spaniard; **~ada** f swaggering, blustering

espantalho m scarecrow

espant|ar v/t, v/r frighten;

scare away; astonish; **~o** m fright; astonishment; **~oso** astonishing

espargo m asparagus

esparso sparse, scattered

espatifar v/t smash, shatter; squander

espaventoso ostentatious

espavorir v/t, v/r frighten

especial special; **em ~** specially; **~idade** f speciality; **~ista** m, f specialist; **~ização** f specialization; **~izar** v/t, v/r particularize; specialize

especiaria f spice

espécie f kind, sort; species

especific|ação f specification; **~ar** v/t specify

espe(c)táculo m spectacle; show, performance; **~aculoso** spectacular

espectador m spectator, onlooker

espe(c)tro m spectre

especul|ação f speculation; **~ar** v/i speculate

espelhar v/t mirror, reflect

espelho m mirror

esper|a f wait; delay; expectation; **à ~ de** waiting for; **~ança** f hope; **~ar** v/t, v/i wait; hope; expect

espert|eza f astuteness; sharpness; **~o** astute, sharp

espess|o thick; **~ura** f thickness

espetar v/t impale, spit

espeto m spit

espia m, f spy

espi|ão m spy; **~ar** v/t spy (on)

espicaçar v/t peck; prick

espichar v/t pierce

espiga f ear of corn; pin, bolt; drawback, snag

espinafre m spinach

espingarda f gun, rifle

espinh|a f fish-bone; backbone, spine, **~o** m thorn; prickle; trouble; **~oso** thorny; difficult, troublesome

espiolhar v/t examine closely

espionagem f espionage

espionar v/t, v/i spy

espiral f spiral

espírito m mind; spirit

espiritual spiritual

espirituoso witty; generous, full-bodied; spirituous

espirr|ar v/i sneeze; **~o** m sneeze

esplêndido splendid

esplendor m splendo(u)r

espoli|ação f spoliation; **~ar** v/t spoliate, despoil

espólio m spoils

esponja f sponge

esponsais m/pl betrothal

espon|taneidade f spontaneity; **~tâneo** spontaneous

espor|a f spur; **~ear** v/t spur (on)

espos|a f wife; **~ar** v/t marry; **~o** m husband

espraiar v/r expand, spread

espreguiçar-se v/r stretch, sprawl

espreitar v/t spy out; peep

espremer v/t squeeze (out)

espum|a f froth, foam; spray; **~ante** m sparkling wine; **~oso** frothy, foamy

esquadr|a f fleet; police-station;

~ilha f flotilla; squadron; **~o** m set square, US triangle

esquartejar v/t quarter

esquec|er v/t, v/r forget; **~imento** m forgetfulness; oblivion

esquel|ético lean; **~eto** m skeleton

esquem|a m scheme, plan; **~ático** schematic

esquentador m boiler, geyser

esquerd|a f left; **à ~** to/on the left; **~o** left

esqui m ski; **~ aquático** water skiing

esquiador m skier

esquife m bier; skiff

esquilo m squirrel

esquina f corner

esquisit|ice f eccentricity, oddity; **~o** exquisite; strange, odd

esquiv|ar v/t, v/r avoid, shun, disdain; **~o** coy; disdainful; intractable

essa pron that; **~ é boa!** that's a good one!

esse pron that

essência f essence

essencial essential

estabelec|er v/t, v/r establish; **~imento** m establishment

estabilidade f stability

estábulo m stable

estac|a f stake, prop, pole; **~ada** f stockade

estação f station; season; **~ de caminho de ferro** railway station; **~ dos correios** post office; **~ emissora** wireless station

estacar v/t, v/i stake; prop;

stop

estacionamento *m* parking

estacionar *v/i* stop; park

estad(i)a *f* stay

estádio *m* stadium

estad|ista *m, f* statesman; **~o**
m state; condition; **~o-maior**
m general staff

estaf|a *f* fatigue; **~ar** *v/t, v/i*
tire, weary

estágio *m* training, probation

estagn|ação *f* stagnation; **~an-
te** stagnant; **~ar** *v/i* stagnate

estala|gem *f* inn; **~jadeiro** *m*
innkeeper

estalar *v/t, v/i* crack, split;
crackle; break out

estaleiro *m* shipyard

estalido *m* crack(le)

estamp|a *f* picture, print; **~ar**
v/t, v/r print, stamp

estampido *m* crash, crack;
bang, report

estampilha *f* stamp; slap

estancar *v/t* staunch

estância *f* lit stanza; spa, resort

estanho *m* tin

estante *f* bookcase; bookshelf

estar *v/i, v/aux* be; **~ em/de
pé** stand

estático static

estatística *f* statistics

estátua *f* statue

estatuir *v/t* establish, decree

estatura *f* height, stature

estatuto *m* statute

estável stable

este *m* east

este *pron* this (one)

esteio *m* prop, stay

esteira *f* mat; wake

estender *v/t, v/i, v/r* extend,
stretch

estenograf|ar *v/t* take down in
shorthand; **~ia** *f* stenography,
shorthand

estenógrafo *m* shorthand typist, *US* stenographer

estepe *f* steppe

esterco *m* dung, manure

estéril sterile

esteril|idade *f* sterility; **~iza-
ção** *f* sterilization; **~izar** *v/t*
sterilize

estétic|a *f* (a)esthetics; **~o**
(a)esthetic

estibordo *m* starboard

esticar *v/t* stretch (out); **~ a ca-
nela/o pernil** kick the bucket

estilhaç|ar *v/t* splinter; **~o** *m*
splinter

estilo *m* style

estima *f* esteem

estim|ação *f* estimation; esti-
mate; esteem; **~ar** *v/t* estimate; esteem; **~ável** estimable

estimul|ação *f* stimulation;
~ante *m* stimulant; **~ar** *v/t*
stimulate

estímulo *m* stimulus

estio *m* summer

estiolar *v/t* wither

estipular *v/t* stipulate

estirar *v/t* stretch (out)

estirpe *f* stock, race

estofar *v/t* stuff; upholster

estofo *m* padding; **~s** *m/pl* upholstery

estoirar *v/t, v/i* explode

estojo *m* case, set

estômago *m* stomach, tummy

estontear *v/t* stun, astound

estopa *f* tow; oakum

estopada *f* drudgery

estorninho *m* starling

estorvar *v/t* hinder, encumber

estorvo *m* hindrance, encumbrance, trammels

estouvado heedless, rash, hot-headed

estrábico *adj* cross-eyed

estrabismo *m* squint

estrada *f* road, highway

estrado *m* dais, platform

estrag|ar *v/t* spoil, damage; waste; **~o** *m* damage, havoc

estrangeiro *m* foreigner; *adj* foreign; **no ~** abroad

estrangular *v/t* strangle

estranh|ar *v/t* wonder at; **~eza** *f* strangeness; **~o** *adj* strange

estrear *v/t*, *v/r* try on; make one's debut

estreia *f* first night; debut

estreit|ar *v/t*, *v/i*, *v/r* narrow, contract; **~eza** *f* narrowness; **~o** *adj* narrow

estrela *f* star

estrelado starry; fried

estrelar *v/t* star, stud with stars; **~ ovos** fry eggs

estremec|er *v/t*, *v/i* shake; frighten; shudder; love tenderly; **~imento** *m* shudder

estrépito *m* noise, din

estribo *m* stirrup

estridente strident

estrito strict

estrofe *f* strophe

estroin|a *adj* wild; hare-brained; **~ice** *f* folly, spree

estrondo *m* din, **~oso** noisy,

clamorous

estropiar *v/t* maim, cripple; mutilate; *fig* spoil

estrume *f* manure

estrutura *f* structure

estud|ante *m*, *f* student; **~ar** *v/t*, *v/i* study; **~ioso** studious

estúdio *m* studio

estudo *m* study

estufa *f* stove; hothouse, greenhouse

estufado *m* stew

estufar *v/t* stew

estupefacto stupefied

estupendo stupendous

estupidez *f* stupidity

estúpido stupid

estupor *m* stupor

esturrado scorched

esvaecer *v/i*, *v/r* vanish, disappear

esvaziar *v/t* empty

esvoaçar *v/i* flutter

etapa *f* stage

etern|idade *f* eternity; **~izar** *v/t* etern(al)ize; **~o** eternal

ética *f* ethics

etiqueta *f* etiquette; label

étnico ethnic

etnografia *f* ethnography

eu *pron* I

eucaristia *f* Eucharist

europeu *m*, *adj* European

evacu|ação *f* evacuation; **~ado** *m* evacuee; **~ar** *v/t* evacuate

evadir *v/t*, *v/r* evade; escape

evapor|ação *f* evaporation; **~ar** *v/t*, *v/r* evaporate

evasão *f* evasion; escape

eventual contingent; **~idade** *f* contingency, eventuality

evidência f evidence

eviden|ciar v/t, v/r show, make evident; **~te** evident

evit|ar v/t avoid; **~ável** avoidable

evocar v/t evoke

evolução f evolution

exacerbar v/t exacerbate

exa(c)t|idão f exactitude; **~o** exact

exager|ar v/t, v/i exaggerate; **~o** m exaggeration

exaltação f exaltation

exaltado adj exalted

exaltar v/t, v/r lose one's temper; exalt

exame m exam(ination)

examinar v/t examine

exarar v/t engrave; set down in writing

exasper|ação f exasperation; **~ar** v/t, v/r exasperate

exaurir v/t exhaust

exausto exhausted

exced|ente adj exceeding; m surplus; **~er** v/t, v/r exceed, surpass, excel

excel|ência f excellence; excellency; **~ente** excellent

excentricidade f eccentricity

excêntrico eccentric

exce(p)|ção f exception; **~cionalmente** exceptionally; **~to** except(ing), save; **~tuar** v/t except, exclude

excess|ivo excessive; **~o** m excess

excit|ação f excitation; **~ado** excited; **~ante** m stimulant; adj stimulating; exciting; **~ar** v/t excite; stimulate

exclam|ação f exclamation; **~ar** v/t, v/i exclaim

exclu|ir v/t exclude; **~são** f exclusion; **~sivo** exclusive

excremento m excrement

excret|ar v/t excrete; **~o** m excretions

excursão f excursion; outing

execu|ção f execution; **~tar** v/t execute; **~tivo** adj, m executive; **~tor** m executor

exempl|ar m model, copy; specimen; adj exemplary; **~ificar** v/t exemplify; **~o** m example

exéquias f/pl obsequies, funeral rites

exercer v/t exercise; practise

exerc|ício m exercise; **~itar** v/t exercise

exército m army

exib|ição f exhibition; **~ir** v/t exhibit

exig|ência f exigence; **~ente** exigent; **~ir** v/t exact, demand

exíguo exiguous

exilar v/t exile

exílio m exile, banishment

exímio eminent

exist|ência f existence; **~ente** adj existent; **~ir** v/t exist

êxito m success

êxodo m exodus

exorbit|ância f exorbitance; **~ante** exorbitant

exort|ação f exhortation; **~ar** v/t exhort

exótico exotic

expan|dir v/t, v/r expand; **~são** f expansion; **~sivo** expansive

expatriar v/t expatriate

expe(c)tativa *f* expectation

expedição *f* expedition; enterprise; dispatch

expediente *m* expedient; office hours; office papers

expedir *v/t* dispatch, forward; expedite

expensas *f/pl* expenses, costs; a ~ de at the expense of

experiência *f* experience; experiment; ~ente *adj* experienced

expiação *f* expiation, atonement; ~ar *v/t* expiate, atone for

expiração *f* expiration, expiry; ~r *v/i* expire

explicação *f* explanation; ~ar *v/t*, *v/r* explain

explícito explicit

explodir *v/i* explode

exploração *f* exploration; exploitation; ~dor *m* explorer; exploiter; ~r *v/t* explore; exploit

explosão *f* explosion; ~sivo *adj*, *m* explosive

expor *v/t*, *v/r* state; express; expose (to); expound

exportação *f* export(ation); ~dor *m* exporter; ~r *v/t* export

exposição *f* exhibition; exposition; exposure; ~tor *m* expositor, exhibitor

expressão *f* expression; ~ar *v/t*, *v/r* express; ~ivo expressive, significant

expresso *adj* express; *m* express (train)

exprimir *v/t*, *v/r* express

expropriação *f* expropriation; ~ar *v/t* expropriate

expulsão *f* expulsion; ~ar *v/t* expel

expurgar *v/t*, *v/r* expurgate

êxtase *m* ecstasy

extasiar *v/t*, *v/r* enrapture

extensão *f* extension; extent; ~ivo extensive

extenso long; extensive; por ~ in full

extenuar *v/t* extenuate

exterior *adj* exterior, outer; *m* exterior, outside; ~izar *v/t* exteriorize, express

exterminação *f* extermination; ~ar *v/t* exterminate

externo *adj* external; *m* day-boy

extinção *f* extinction

extinguir *v/t*, *v/r* extinguish

extirpar *v/t* extirpate

extorquir *v/t* extort

extra(c)ção *f* extraction

extra(c)to *m* extract

extradição *f* extradition; ~tar *v/t* extradite

extrair *v/t* extract

extraordinário *adj* extraordinary

extravagância *f* extravagance; ~ante extravagant

extraviar *v/t*, *v/r* lead astray; embezzle; mislay

extremidade *f* extremity, end; ~ista *m*, *f* extremist; ~o *adj* last, extreme; *m* extreme

extrínseco extrinsic

exuberância *f* exuberance; ~ante exuberant

exultação *f* exultation; ~ante exultant; ~ar *v/i* exult

F

fábrica f factory
fabric|ação f manufacture;
~**ante** m, f manufacturer;
~**ar** v/t manufacture; ~**o** m
manufacture
fábula f fable
fabuloso fabulous
faca f knife
façanha f deed, feat
fa(c)ção f faction
face f face; cheek; front; à/em
~ **de** in view of; **fazer** ~ **a**
face, meet
fachada f façade
facho m torch
fácil easy
facili|dade f facility; ~**tar** v/t
facilitate
fa(c)to m fact; deed; event; **de**
~ in fact; **ao** ~ aware
fa(c)tura f invoice; account;
~**ar** v/t invoice
facul|dade f faculty; ~**tar** v/t
facilitate; ~**tativo** adj op-
tional; m physician, doctor
fad|a f fairy; ~**ar** v/t destine;
~**ário** m fate, lot
fadiga f fatigue
fado m fate; popular song
fagulha f spark
faia f bot beech
faiança f faience
faina f task, work
faisão m pheasant
faísca f spark
faiscar v/t, v/i spark
faixa f band, belt; zone; ~ **de**
rodagem roadway

fala f speech; ~**dor** m chat-
terer; adj talkative; ~**r** v/t,
v/i, v/r speak, talk; ~**r de**
papo talk big; ~**r pelos coto-**
velos talk/speak nineteen to
the dozen, talk one's head off
falec|er v/i die, pass away;
~**ido** adj, m deceased; ~**i-**
mento m decease
falência f bankruptcy
falésia f cliff
falh|a f crack, flaw, blemish;
~**ar** v/t, v/i crack; split; fail;
miss
falir v/i go bankrupt
fals|ário m forger, counter-
feiter; ~**ear** v/t distort, misre-
present; ~**idade** f falsehood;
falsity; ~**ificação** f falsifica-
tion, forgery, counterfeit; ~**ifi-**
car v/t falsify, forge, counterfeit; ~**o** adj false
falt|a f lack, want, shortage;
fault, defect; **por** ~**a de** for
lack of; **sem** ~**a** without fail;
~**ar** v/i be lacking; fail; miss;
lack, need
fama f fame, reputation
família f family
familiar adj, m, f familiar;
~**idade** f familiarity; ~**izar**
v/t, v/r familiarize (**com** with)
faminto hungry, starving
famoso famous
fanfarr|ão m boaster, braggart,
bully; ~**onar** v/i swagger,
brag, boast
fanico m small piece; faint

fantasia *f* fancy; fantasy

fantasma *m* phantom; **~goria** *f* phantasmagory

fantástico fantastic

fantoche *m* puppet

faqueiro *m* knife-case

fard|a *f* uniform; livery; **~ar** *v/t* uniform

fardo *m* burden; bale

farejar *v/t, v/i* sniff, scent

farelo *m* bran; trifle

farináceo farinaceous

faringe *f* pharynx

farinha *f* flour, meal

farmacêutico *m* chemist, pharmacist

farmácia *f* pharmacy; chemist's (shop)

farol *m* lighthouse; headlight, headlamp; **~im** *m* beacon

farpa *f* banderilla; barb; splinter

farpado barbed

farrapo *m* rag, tatter

farrusco sooty

farsa *f* farce

fart|ar *v/t, v/r* satiate, sate; **~o** *adj* sated; full; fed up; **~ura** *f* plenty, abundance

fascin|ação *f* fascination; **~ar** *v/t* fascinate

fase *f* phase

fastio *m* loathing

fatal fatal

fatalidade *f* fatality

fatia *f* slice

fatig|ante tiring; **~ar** *v/t* fatigue, tire

fato *m* suit; *Braz* fact

faust|o *m* pageantry, pomp; *adj* lucky, happy; **~oso** luxurious,

gaudy

fava *f* broad bean

favela *f* *Braz* slum

favo *m* honeycomb

favor *m* favo(u)r; **por ~, se faz ~, faça ~** please; **a/em ~ de** on/in behalf of; **~ável** favo(u)rable; **~ecer** *v/t* favo(u)r

fazend|a *f* estate; farm; ranch; cloth, material; **~eiro** *m* farmer

fazer *v/t, v/i, v/r* do; make; be; become; **~ anos** celebrate one's birthday; **~ (as vezes) de** take the place of; **~ por** try to; **não faz mal** never mind; it doesn't matter

fé *f* faith

fealdade *f* ugliness

febra *f* fibre; lean

febr|e *f* fever; **~il** feverish

fechadura *f* lock

fech|ar *v/t, v/i* shut, close; **~ar à chave** lock; **~o** *m* bolt; end; **~o de correr** zip(per)

fecund|ar *v/t*, fecundate; **~o** fecund

feder *v/i* stink

feder|ação *f* federation; **~al** *adj* federal; **~ar** *v/t* federate

fedor *m* stink, stench

feição *f* form, aspect; **~ões** *f/pl* features

feijão *m* kidney bean; haricot bean; **~ verde** French bean

feijoada *f* beans dish

feio ugly

feira *f* fair, market

feiti|çaria *f* sorcery, witchcraft; **~ceiro** *m* sorcerer; *adj* bewitching; **~ço** *m* sorcery; fetish

feitio *m* temper, manner; shape, form; make

feito *m* feat, deed; *adj* done, made; **é bem ~** it serves you right

feixe *m* bundle, truss, sheaf

fel *m* gall; bitterness

feli|cidade *f* happiness; good luck; **~citações** *f/pl* congratulations; **~citar** *v/t, v/r* congratulate; **~z** *adj* happy; lucky, fortunate

felpudo shaggy

feltro *m* felt

fêmea *f* female

feminino feminine

fend|a *f* split, crack, rift; **~er** *v/t, v/r* split, crack

feno *m* hay

fenómeno *m* phenomenon

fera *f* wild animal

féria *f* weekly wage; **~s** *f/pl* holidays, *US* vacation

feriado *m* holiday

ferida *f* wound; sore

fer|imento *m* wound; **~ir** *v/t, v/r* wound; hurt

ferment|ação *f* fermentation; ferment; **~ar** *v/t, v/i* ferment; **~o** *m* ferment, yeast, leaven

fer|o wild; **~ocidade** *f* ferocity; **~oz** ferocious

ferradela *f* bite

ferra|dura *f* horseshoe; **~gem** *f* ironwork; hardware

ferramenta *f* tool

ferrão *m* sting

ferreiro *m* (black)smith

ferro *m* iron

ferrolho *m* bolt; latch

ferrovia *f* railway, *US* railroad

ferroviário *m* railwayman

ferrugem *f* rust

ferrugento rusty

fértil fertile

fertil|idade *f* fertility; **~izar** *v/t* fertilize

ferv|ente fervent; seething; **~er** *v/t, v/i* boil; seethe

fervor *m* fervo(u)r

fest|a *f* festival; feast; party; **~ança** *f* merrymaking, spree; **~as** *f/pl* caress; **boas-~as** Merry Christmas; Happy New Year; **~ejar** *v/t* celebrate; **~ival** *m* festival; **~ividade** *f* festivity; **~ivo** festive

feto *m* fern; *anat* f(o)etus

Fevereiro *m* February

fiador *m* bailsman; surety

fiambre *m* boiled ham

fiança *f* surety; bail, security

fiar *v/t, v/i, v/r* spin; trust

fibr|a *f* fibre; nerve; **~oso** fibrous

ficar *v/i* stay, remain; be; **~ com** keep; **~ bem** suit (well)

ficção *f* fiction

fich|a *f* counter; plug; card index; **~eiro** *m* filing cabinet

fictício fictitious

fidalg|o *m* nobleman, lord; *adj* noble; **~uia** *f* nobility

fidedigno trustworthy

fidelidade *f* fidelity

fiel *adj* faithful

fígado *m* liver

fig|o *m* fig; **~ueira** *f* fig tree

figura *f* figure

figurar *v/t, v/i* figure; depict

figurino *m* fashion plate

fila *f* file, rank, row
filatelia *f* philately
filete *m* fillet
filh|a *f* daughter; **~o** *m* son
fili|ação *f* filiation; **~al** *adj* filial; *f* branch
filiar *v/t, v/r* affiliate
film|agem *f* filming; **~ar** *v/t* film; **~e** *m* film
filtrar *v/t* filter, strain
filtro *m* filter
fim *m* end; aim; **a ~ de** in order to; **por ~** at last
finado *m* deceased; **dia m de ~s** All Souls' Day
final *adj, m* final
finalidade *f* purpose; finality
finanças *f/pl* finances
financeiro *m* financier
financi|amento *m* financing; **~ar** *v/t* finance
fincar *v/t* fix, drive
findar *v/t, v/i* end, finish
fineza *f* fineness; kindness
fingido *adj* feigned
fing|imento *m* feigning; pretence; **~ir** *v/t, v/i* feign, pretend
finito *adj* finite
finlandês *m* Finn; *adj* Finnish
fin|o fine; thin; shrewd; courteous; **~ura** *f* cunning; finesse; nicety; courtesy
fio *m* thread, yarn; wire
firma *f* firm; signature
firm|e *f* firm; **~eza** *f* firmness
fiscal *adj* fiscal; **~izar** *v/t* supervise, control
física|a *f* physics; **~o** *m* physicist; physique; *adj* physical
fisionomia *f* physiognomy

fístula *f* fistula
fita *f* ribbon; film; tape; scene
fitar *v/t* stare at
fito *m* aim, purpose; *adj* fixed
fivela *f* buckle
fix|ar *v/t* fix; affix; **~e** reliable; **~o** fixed
flagrante flagrant
flamante flaming; flamboyant
flanela *f* flannel
flauta *f* flute
flecha *f* arrow
flexibilidade *f* flexibility
flexível flexible
floco *m* flake
flor *f* flower; blossom; bloom; **~ação** *f* flowering, blossoming; **~eira** *f* flower-vase; **~escer** *v/t, v/i* flourish
floresta *f* forest
florir *v/i* flower, blossom
flu|ência *f* fluency; **~ente** fluent, flowing; **~ir** *v/i* flow; ooze
flutu|ação *f* fluctuation; **~ar** *v/i* fluctuate; float
fluvial fluvial
fluxo *m* flux; flow
foca *f* seal
focar *v/t* focus
focinho *m* snout, muzzle
foco *m* focus
fofo *adj* soft, puffy, spongy
fogão *m* stove
fogareiro *m* primus (stove)
fogo *m* fire; **~-de-artifício** fireworks
fogoso fiery; hot-tempered
fogueira *f* bonfire
foguete *m* rocket
foice *f* scythe

foicinha f sickle
fole m bellows
fôlego m breath; wind
folga f rest, repose; recreation
folgado f slack, loose
folgar v/t, v/i rest; rejoice; widen
folha f leaf; sheet; blade; ~do m puff pastry
folhagem f foliage
folhear v/t thumb through
folhetim m feuilleton, serial
folheto m booklet, leaflet
fome f hunger; famine
foment|ar v/t foment; ~o m fomentation
fonte f fountain; spring; source, origin; anat temple
fora prp except; int out! off!; adv abroad; outside; out; **lá** ~ outside; abroad; ~ **de si** beside oneself
foragido fugitive
forasteiro m stranger
forca f gallows
forç|a f force, strength; ~ar v/t force, compel; ~oso inevitable; necessary
forj|a f forge, smithy; ~ar v/t forge
forma f shape, form; **de** ~ **que** so that
forma f mo(u)ld, last; cake tin
form|ação f formation; ~ado adj, m graduate; ~al adj formal; ~alidade f formality; ~ar v/t, v/i, v/r graduate, take one's degree; shape, form; ~ativo formative; ~ato m format, size, shape; ~atura f formation; degree, graduation

formidável formidable, tremendous
formig|a f ant; ~ueiro m ant-hill; tingle, itch; swarm
formos|o beautiful; ~ura f beauty
fórmula f formula; form
formular v/t formulate
fornalha f furnace
fornec|er v/t, v/r supply, provide; ~imento m supply
forno m oven
forrar v/t line; cover
forro m lining
fort|alecer v/t strengthen; fortify; ~aleza f strength; fortress; ~e m fort; adj strong; robust
fortific|ação f fortification; ~ar v/t fortify
fortuito fortuitous
fortuna f fortune; chance
fosco dim
fósforo m match
fosso m ditch
foto f photo; ~cópia f photocopy; ~grafar v/t photograph; ~grafia f photography; photograph, picture; ~gráfico photographic
fotógrafo m photgrapher
fotómetro m exposure meter
foz f river mouth
fracass|ar v/i fail, collapse; ~o m failure
fra(c)ção f fraction; ~cionar v/t fractionate; ~cionário fractional
fraco adj weak, feeble, frail
fra(c)tura f fracture
frade m friar

fragata *f* frigate
frágil fragile
fragilidade *f* fragility
fragment|ar *v/t* fragment; **~o**
m fragment
fragor *m* noise, crash
fralda *f* nappy, *US* diaper; shirt-
-tail; foot of a hill
framboesa *f* raspberry
francês *m* French(man); *adj*
French
franco *adj* frank
franga *f* pullet
frangalho *m* rag, tatter
frango *m* cockerel; chicken
franja *f* fringe; tassel
franqu|ear *v/t* frank; stamp;
~eza *f* frankness, sincerity
franquia *f* postage
franzir *v/t* pucker, wrinkle;
fold; **~ as sobrancelhas**
frown
fraqueza *f* weakness, frailty
frasco *f* flask
frase *f* sentence; phrase
fratern|al fraternal; **~idade** *f*
fraternity
fraud|e *f* fraud, trick, guile; **~u-**
lento fraudulent
fregu|ês *m* customer; parish-
ioner; **~esia** *f* parish; cus-
tomers
freio *m* horse-bit; brake
freira *f* nun
freixo *m* ash(-tree)
frem|ente trembling, quiv-
ering; roaring; **~ir** *v/i* quiver,
roar
frêmito *m* trembling, quiv-
ering; roaring
fren|esi(m) *m* frenzy; **~ético**

frantic; phrenetic
frente *f* front; face; **à ~ de** at
the head of; **em ~ de** opposite
frequ|ência *f* frequency; **~en-**
tador *m* frequenter; **~entar**
v/t frequent; **~ente** frequent
fresco *adj* fresh; cool
frescura *f* freshness; coolness
fresta *f* cleft; slit
fret|ar *v/t* charter, hire out; **~e**
m freight; annoyance, trouble
fricassé *m* fricassee
fricção *f* friction
friccionar *v/t* rub
fri|eira *f* chilblain; **~eza** *f* cold-
ness; indifference
frigideira *f* frying-pan, *US* skillet
frígido frigid
frigorífico *m* refrigerator,
fridge, *US* ice-box
frincha *f* chink
frio *adj*, *m* cold; **está/faz ~** it's
cold; **tenho ~** I'm cold
frisar *v/t* frizzle, curl; emphasize, stress
fritar *v/t* fry
frívolo *adj* frivolous
frondoso leafy
fronha *f* pillow-case/-slip
front|al frontal; **~e** *f* fore-
head; front; **~eira** *f* frontier,
border; **~eiriço** bordering, adjacent; **~ispício** *m* frontispiece; façade
frota *f* fleet
frouxo *adj* slack, lax, weak
frugal frugal
fruir *v/t* enjoy
frustrar *v/t*, *v/r* frustrate,
thwart

frut|a f fruit; **~eira** f fruit bowl; **~eira** f fruit-bearing; fruitful; **~ificar** v/i fructify; **~o** m profit, advantage; fruit, fruits; **~uoso** fruitful, profitable

fug|a f flight; leak; **~az** fleeting; **~ir** v/i flee; **~itivo** m, adj fugitive

fulano m (Mr) so-and-so

fulgor m splendo(u)r, gleam

fulgurar v/i shine, flash, gleam

fuligem f soot

fulminar v/t fulminate

fum|aça f puff of smoke; smoke; **~ador** m smoker; **~ar** v/t, v/i smoke; **~e(g)ar** v/i fume, smoke; **~o** m smoke; **~oso** smoky

fun|ção f function; **em ~ção** in working order; **~cionamento** m functioning, performance; working; **~cionar** v/i function; work; **~cionário** m official, civil servant

funda|ção f foundation, establishment; **~dor** m founder

fundament|al fundamental; **~ar** v/t, v/r base on: establish; **~o** m basis; groundwork; fig kernel; foundation

fundar v/t found, establish

fundeadoiro m anchorage

fundear v/i cast anchor

fund|ição f smelting; foundry; **~ir** v/t, v/r fuse; cast; smelt

fundo adj deep; m bottom; **a ~** thoroughly; **no ~** at bottom, in essence; **~s** m/pl funds

fúnebre funeral; mournful

funeral m funeral

funesto baleful; fatal

fungar v/t, v/i sniff, snuffle

fungo m fungus; mushroom; toadstool

funil m funnel

fur|ador m awl, punch; **~ar** v/t bore, pierce, punch

furgão m luggage-van; **~oneta** f delivery van

fúria f fury; rage

furioso furious; fierce

furna f cavern, cave, den

furo m hole, puncture; loophole, way out

furor m rage, fury

furt|ar v/t, v/r escape, evade; steal, rob; **~ivo** furtive; **~o** m theft, robbery, larceny

fusão f fusion; union

fusco adj tawny; dusky

fusionar v/t amalgamate, fuse with

fusível m fuse

fuso m spindle

fuste m shaft

futebol m football, soccer; **~ista** m, f footballer

fútil futile

futilidade f futility

futura f fiancée

futurar v/t foretell; v/i conjecture

futur|idade f futurity; **~ismo** m futurism; **~o** m future; fiancé

fuzil m rifle; **~ar** v/t shoot dead; **~aria** f volley; fusillade; **~eiro** m fusilier

G

gabar v/t, v/r boast, brag; praise
gabardina f raincoat
gabarola m, f boaster
gabinete m cabinet; study; office
gado m cattle; livestock
gafanhoto m grasshopper
gag|o adj stammering; m stammerer; **~uejar** v/i stammer, stutter
gaiato m urchin; adj romping, boisterous
gaio m jay
gaiola f cage; jail
gaita f mouth-organ, harmonica; **~ de foles** (bag)pipes
gaiteiro adj smart, spruce; gay
gaivota f sca-gull
gajo m guy, type
galant|aria f courtliness, gallantry; **~e** adj gallant
galão m galloon; spring; glass of milky coffee
galego m, adj Galician; Braz Portuguese
galeria f gallery
galgar v/t, v/i leap over
galgo m greyhound
galheta f cruet
galheteiro m cruet stand
galho m twig, branch; antler
galhofa f fun; derision; **fazer ~ de** make fun of, laugh at
galinha f hen
galinheiro m hen-house
galo m cock
galocha f galosh, overshoe
galop|ar v/t, v/i gallop; **~e** m

gallop
gama f gamut; doe
gamela f trough
gamo m deer, fallow-deer
gana f desire, craving
ganância f covetousness
ganancioso covetous
gancho m hook; hairpin, hair grip
gangrena f gangrene
ganh|ar v/t, v/i earn; gain; win; **~o** m gain, profit
ganir v/i yelp
ganso m goose, gander
garagem f garage
garant|ia f guarantee, warranty; **~ir** v/t guarantee
garb|o m elegance, grace; **~oso** elegant, graceful
garça f zo heron
garção m Braz waiter
garço greenish-blue
gare f platform
garfo m fork
gargalhada f laughter; guffaw; chuckle
garganta f throat; gorge
gargarejar v/t, v/i gargle
garoa f Braz drizzle
garoto m urchin; lad; white coffee
garra f claw
garraf|a f bottle; **~ão** m demijohn
garrido stylish; bright, gay
gárrulo adj garrulous
gás m gas
gaseificar v/t gasify

gasolina f petrol, US gas(oline); m motor boat

gas|ómetro m gasometer, gasholder; **~osa** f (fizzy) lemonade, US lemon soda

gast|ar v/t, v/r spend; wear; waste; use; **~o** m expense, charge

gata f she-cat

gatilho m trigger

gato m cat; tom-cat

gatuno m pickpocket; pilferer

gaveta f drawer

gavião m sparrow-hawk

gazela f gazelle

gazeta f gazette, newspaper; **fazer ~** play truant/hook(e)y

gazua f picklock

geada f frost

gear v/t, v/i freeze; frost

gelado adj frozen; icy; m ice-cream

gelar v/t, v/i, v/r congeal, freeze (up)

gelatin|a f gelatin(e); **~oso** gelatinous

geleia f jelly

geleira f glacier; ice-box

gélido gelid, frozen

gelo m ice

gelosia f Venetian blind

gema f gem; bud; yolk

gémeo m twin

gemer v/t, v/i groan, moan; wail

gemido m groan, moan

general m general

generalidade f generality

generalizar v/t, v/i generalize

género m kind, type; gender; **~s** m/pl goods, products; **~s**

alimentícios groceries

generos|idade f generosity; **~o** adj generous

gengibre m ginger

gengiva f gum

génio m genius; temper

genital genital

genro m son-in-law

gente f people; **a ~** we, you, one

gentil adj kind; polite; **~eza** f kindness; politeness

gentio m, adj gentile; heathen

genuíno genuine

geografia f geography

geologia f geology

geração f generation

gerador m generator

geral adj general

gerar v/t generate

gerência f management

gerente m, f manager

gerir v/t manage, direct

germe m germ

germinar v/i germinate

gesso m plaster of Paris

gestão f management, administration

gesto m gesture

giesta f bot broom

gigant|e m giant; **~esco** gigantic

ginásio m gymnasium

ginástica f gymnastics

ginja f morello (cherry)

ginjinha f morello brandy

gira-discos m record player, US phonograph

girafa f giraffe

girar v/i gyrate, rotate, spin

girassol m sun-flower

giratório gyratory

gíria *f* jargon; argot

giro *m* rotation; turn; stroll, walk; *adj* funny, nice

giz *m* chalk

glacial glacial, icy

glande *f* acorn

glândula *f* gland

glicerina *f* glycerin(e)

globo *m* globe

glória *f* glory

glorifica|ção *f* glorification; **~ar** *v/t, v/r* glorify

glorioso glorious

glos|a *f* gloss, interpretation; **~ar** *v/t* gloss, interpret

glutão *m* glutton; *adj* gluttonous

goela *f* throat, gullet

goiaba *f* guava

gola *f* collar, neckband

gole *m* gulp, swallow

golfar *v/t, v/i* spout, gush

golfe *m* golf

golfinho *m* dolphin

golfo *m* gulf

golo *m* goal

golp|e *m* blow, knock, slash; **~ear** *v/t* strike, slash

goma *f* gum; *Braz* tapioca

gôndola *f* gondola

gorar *v/t, v/i, v/r* frustrate; addle; miscarry

gordo fat

gordura *f* fat; grease

gorduroso greasy

gorila *m* gorilla

gorjear *v/i* warble

gorjeta *f* tip, gratuity

gorro *m* bonnet, cap

gostar de *v/i* be fond of, like

gosto *m* taste; flavo(u)r, sa-

vo(u)r; relish; pleasure; **com muito ~** with great pleasure; **~so** tasty; pleasing

gota *f* drop; *med* gout

goteira *f* gutter

gotejar *v/t, v/i* drip, drop, trickle

gótico *adj* Gothic

governador *m* governor

governamental governmental

governante *adj* governing

governar *v/t, v/i, v/r* manage; govern

governo *m* government

gozar *v/t, v/i* enjoy

gozo *m* enjoyment

graça *f* grace; wit; **de ~** free, gratis; **~s a** thanks to; **~s a Deus** thank God

gracejar *v/i* joke, jest

gracios|idade *f* gracefulness; **~o** *adj* graceful; witty

grade *f* grating; harrow; railing; crate

grado *m* goodwill

gradu|ação *f* graduation; *mil* rank; **~al** *adj* gradual; **~ar** *v/t, v/r* graduate

gralha *f* rook; jackdaw; misprint

grama *f* gram(me)

gramado *m* *Braz* football field; lawn

gramática *f* grammar

grampo *m* cramp; clamp

granada *f* grenade

grand|e *adj* large; big; great; **~eza** *f* greatness; grandeur; size; **~iosidade** *f* greatness; grandeur; **~ioso** grand

granel *m* barn, cornloft; **a ~** by

heaps, in bulk
granito m granite
granizo m hail
granjear v/t win, get
grão m grain
grassar v/i spread
gratidão f gratitude
gratific|ação f gratuity, tip; **~ar** v/t tip; reward
grátis free, gratis
grato grateful; pleasing
gratuito gratuitous; free
grau m degree; rank, grade
grav|ação f engraving; recording; **~ador** m engraver; (tape) recorder; **~ador de cassetes** cassette tape recorder; **~ar** v/t engrave; record
gravata f tie
grave adj serious; grave; earnest
grávida adj pregnant
gravidade f gravity
gravidez f pregnancy
gravura f engraving
graxa f shoe-polish
grego adj, m Greek; **isso para mim é ~** it's all Greek to me
grelar v/i sprout
grelha f grill
grelhar v/t grill
grelo m sprout
grémio m guild; society
greta f crack, chink
gretar v/t, v/i, v/r crack, split; chap
greve f strike; **fazer ~** strike
grevista m, f striker
grilo m cricket
grinalda f garland; wreath
gripe f influenza, flu
grit|ar v/t, v/i shout; cry; yell;

scream; **~aria** f shouting; **~o** m shout, cry
grosseiro coarse, rude
gross|o adj thick, dense; **~ura** f thickness
grou m zo crane
grua f crane, derrick
grude m glue
grunhir v/i grunt
grupo m group
gruta f grotto
guarda f guard, watch; m guard, keeper, warden
guarda|-chuva m umbrella; **~-fato** m wardrobe; **~-lama** m auto mudguard, US fender; **~-livros** m book-keeper; **~napo** m napkin, serviette; **~-no-(c)turno** m night-watchman
guardar v/t guard; keep; watch over
guarda|-redes m goalkeeper, goalie; **~-roupa** m wardrobe; **~-sol** m sunshade; **~-vestidos** m wardrobe
guarida f den, cave; shelter; refuge
guarn|ecer v/t furnish, provide; garnish; **~ição** f garrison
guelra f gill
guerr|a f war; **~ear** v/t, v/i wage war; **~eiro** adj warlike; m warrior; **~ilha** f guerrilla war
guia f guide(-book); m guide
guiador m handle-bars; steering-wheel
guiar v/t, v/i, v/r steer; guide
guiché m counter; booking-office
guinada f swerve; sudden pain

hipismo

guincho m shriek, squeal
guindaste m crane
guis|ado m stew; **~ar** v/t stew, cook
guita f string, twine
guitarra f guitar
gula f gluttony

gulodice f titbit
guloso adj greedy; **ser ~** have a sweet tooth
gume m edge
guri m Braz child
gusano m (wood)worm
gustativo gustatory

H

hábil able, skilful, capable, clever
habilid|ade f ability, skill; **~oso** adj accomplished, dext(e)rous
habili|tação f qualification; **~tar** v/t qualify; enable
habit|ação f dwelling, residence; **~ante** m, f inhabitant; **~ar** v/t, v/i inhabit; **~ável** inhabitable
hábito m habit
habitu|al habitual; **~ar** v/t, v/r accustom, inure to
hálito m breath
harmonia f harmony
harmoni|oso adj harmonious; **~zar** v/t, v/i, v/r harmonize
harpa f harp
haste f staff; stem; **~ar** v/t hoist
haver v/t, v/aux there + be, exist; **lá** there is, there are; ago; **~ de** have to; will, shall; **~es** m/pl possessions
hebraico adj Hebraic; Hebrew
hectare m hectare
hediondo hideous, loathsome
hélice f propeller, screw
helicóptero m helicopter
hemorragia f hemorrhage

hemorróidas f/pl hemorrhoids
hepatite f hepatitis
hera f ivy
herança inheritance; heritage
herdade f farm, estate
herd|ar v/t, v/i inherit; **~eira** f heiress; **~eiro** m heir
hereditariedade f heredity
hereditário hereditary
here|ge m, f heretic; **~sia** f heresy
her|ói m hero; **~óico** heroic; **~oína** f heroine; **~oísmo** m heroism
hesit|ação f hesitation; **~ante** hesitant; **~ar** v/i hesitate
heterogéneo heterogeneous
hibern|ação f hibernation; **~ar** v/i hibernate
hidráulico hydraulic
hidroavião m seaplane
hidrogénio m hydrogen
hiena f hyena
hierarquia f hierarchy
higi|ene f hygiene; **~énico** hygienic
hilari|ante hilarious; **~dade** f hilarity
hino m hymn; **~ nacional** national anthem
hipismo m horse-racing

hipocrisia f hypocrisy
hipócrita m, f hypocrite
hipódromo m hippodrome; racecourse
hipopótamo m hippopotamus
hipotec|a f mortgage; **~ar** v/t mortgage
hipótese f hypothesis
hipotético hypothetical
história f history; story
historiador m historian
histórico historic(al)
hodierno present-day
hoje adv today; **~ em dia** nowadays; **de ~ em diante** from this day on
holandês adj Dutch; m Dutch; Dutchman
homem m man
homenagem f homage
homicídio m homicide, murder
homogéneo homogeneous
honest|idade f honesty; **~o** honest
honorário adj honorary; **~s** m/pl fees
honra f hono(u)r; **~dez** f honesty; **~do** honest; hono(u)rable; **~r** v/t hono(u)r; **~ria** f distinction, rank
honroso hono(u)rable, decorous
hóquei m hockey
hor|a f hour; time; **à última ~** at the eleventh hour; **a toda a ~** at all hours; **~s extraordinárias** overtime; **que ~s são?** what time is it?; **~ário** m timetable
horda f horde
horizont|al horizontal; **~e** m

horizon
horrendo horrid
horripilante horrifying
horrível horrible
horror m horror
horroroso horrible, dreadful, awful
hort|a f kitchen garden; **~aliça** f greens, vegetable(s)
hortelã f mint; **~ pimenta** peppermint
horticul|tor m horticulturist; **~tura** f horticulture
hosped|agem f lodging, accommodation; **~ar** v/t, v/r lodge, put up
hóspede m, f guest; host
hospital m hospital; **~eiro** hospitable; **~idade** f hospitality
hospitalizar v/t hospitalize
hostil hostile; **~idade** f hostility; **~izar** v/t bear ill will to
hotel m hotel
hulh|a f coal; **~eira** f coal-mine, pit
human|idade f humanity; mankind; **~o** adj human; humane
(h)umedecer v/t, v/i, v/r humidify; moisten
(h)umidade f humidity; dampness, moistness
(h)úmido damp, moist; humid
humil|dade f humility; **~de** humble
humilh|ação f humiliation; **~ar** v/t, v/r humiliate
humor m humo(u)r; temper
humorista m, f humorist
húngaro adj Hungarian

I

iate *m* yacht
ibérico *adj* Iberian
içar *v/t* raise, hoist
i(c)terícia *f* jaundice
ida *f* departure, going; **~s e vindas** comings and goings
idade *f* age
ideia *f* idea; **fazer ~** imagine, realize; **não fazer ~** have no idea
idêntico identical
identi|dade *f* identity; **bilhete** *m* **de ~dade** identity card/certificate; **~ficação** *f* identification; **~ficar** *v/t, v/r* identify
idílico idyllic
idílio *m* idyl(l)
idioma *m* language, idiom
idiota *m, f* idiot; *adj* idiotic
ídolo *m* idol
idoneidade *f* suitability
idóneo suitable
ignição *f* ignition
ignóbil ignoble
ignomínia *f* ignominy
ignominioso ignominious
ignor|ância *f* ignorance; **~ante** *adj* ignorant; **~ar** *v/t* to be ignorant of; ignore
ignoto unknown
igreja *f* church
igual *adj, m, f* equal; **~ar** *v/t, v/r* equalize; equal; **~dade** *f* equality
iguaria *f* delicacy, titbit
ilegal illegal
ilegítimo illegitimate

ilegível illegible
ileso unhurt, safe
ilha *f* island; Isle
ilharga *f* flank; slope
ilhéu *m* islander
ilícito illicit
ilimitado unlimited, illimitable
ilógico illogical
iludir *v/t, v/r* delude, trick, deceive
ilumin|ação *f* illumination; **~ar** *v/t, v/r* illuminate
ilusão *f* illusion
ilustr|ação *f* illustration; **~ado** illustrated; **~ar** *v/t* illustrate; **~e** illustrious
imã *m* magnet
imagem *f* image
imagin|ação *f* imagination; **~ar** *v/t, v/i, v/r* imagine; **~ário** imaginary; **~ativo** imaginative
imbecil imbecile
imbuir *v/t, v/r* imbue (**de** with)
imediato *adj* immediate; next, following
imens|idade *f* immensity; **~o** immense
imerecido undeserved
imergir *v/t* immerse
imersão *f* immersion
imigr|ação *f* immigration; **~ante** *m, f* immigrant; **~ar** *v/i* immigrate
iminente imminent
imit|ação *f* imitation; **~ar** *v/t* imitate
imobilidade *f* immobility

imoderado immoderate

imodesto immodest

imolar v/t immolate

imoral immoral; **~idade** f immorality

imortal immortal; **~idade** f immortality; **~izar** v/t immortalize

imóvel adj immovable; immobile; unmovable; motionless

impaciência f impatience; **~entar** v/t, v/r make/get impatient; **~ente** impatient

impagável unpayable; fig humorous, comic

ímpar odd; unmatched

imparcial impartial; **~idade** f impartiality

impasse m impasse

impassível impassive

impávido fearless, intrepid

impecável impeccable

impedimento m obstruction, impediment

impedir v/t prevent, obstruct, hinder, impede

impelir v/t impel

impenetrável impenetrable

impensado thoughtless; unexpected, unforeseen

imperador m emperor; **~atriz** f empress

imperceptível imperceptible

imperdoável unforgivable, inexcusable

imperecível imperishable

imperfeição f imperfection; **~to** adj imperfect, faulty

império m empire; dominion

imperioso imperious

impermeável adj impermeable; waterproof; m raincoat, mackintosh

impertinência f impertinence; **~ente** adj impertinent

imperturbável imperturbable

impessoal impersonal

ímpeto m impetus; violence

impetuoso impetuous

impiedoso pitiless

ímpio impious

implacável implacable

implantar v/t implant

implicar v/t, v/i pick a quarrel; implicate; imply

implícito implicit

implorar v/t implore

imponderado rash, thoughtless

imponente imposing

impor v/t, v/r impose

importação f importation; import

importador m importer

importância f importance; **~ante** adj important; **~ar** v/t, v/i, v/r concern oneself; import; matter; **não ~a** never mind; **que ~a?** what does it matter?

importunar v/t importune; **~o** adj importunate, irksome

impossibilidade f impossibility; **~ível** impossible

imposto m tax, duty

impostor m impostor; **~ura** f imposture

impotência f impotence; powerlessness; **~ente** adj impotent; powerless

impraticável impracticable

imprecação f imprecation

impregnar v/t impregnate

imprensa *f* printing press; press

impressão *f* impression; imprint

impress|ionar *v/t* impress; **~ionante** touching, moving; impressive; **~o** *adj* printed; *m* printed matter

impreterível indispensable

imprevidente improvident

imprevisto unforeseen; unforeseeable

imprimir *v/t* print

improbabilidade *f* improbability

improdutivo unproductive

impróprio improper; unsuitable

improvável improbable

improvis|ação *f* improvisation; **~ar** *v/t* improvise

imprud|ência *f* imprudence; rashness; **~ente** *adj* imprudent, rash

impudente impudent

impudor *m* impudence

impugnar *v/t* impugn

impulsionar *v/t* impel

impuls|ivo impulsive; **~o** *m* impulse

impune unpunished, with impunity

impur|eza *f* impurity; **~o** impure

imput|ar *v/t* impute to; **~ável** imputable

imund|ície *f* dirt, filth; **~o** dirty, filthy

imune immune

imutável immutable, changeless

inabalável unshak(e)able; inexorable

inábil unable; unskilful

inabordável unapproachable

ina(c)ção *f* inaction; sluggishness

inaceitável unacceptable

inacessível inaccessible

inacreditável incredible

ina(c)tividade *f* inactivity

ina(c)tivo inactive

inadequado inadequate

inadiável not postponable; unavoidable

inadmissível inadmissible

inadvertência *f* oversight

inalienável unalienable

inalter|ado unaltered; **~ável** unalterable

inapto inapt, unfit

inato innate

inaudito unheard-of

inaudível inaudible

inauguração inauguration

inaugur|al inaugural; **~ar** *v/t* inaugurate

incalculável incalculable

incansável tireless

incapaz incapable; unable

incauto unwary, careless

incendi|ar *v/t* set fire to; **~ário** *adj* incendiary

incêndio *m* fire, blaze, conflagration

incenso *m* incense

incentivo *m* incentive

incert|eza *f* uncertainty; **~o** uncertain

incessante incessant

incesto *m* incest

inchar *v/t, v/i, v/r* swell

incidência *f* incidence

incidente *m* incident
incinerar *v/t* incinerate
incipiente incipient
incisão *f* incision
incit|ação *f* incitement; **~ar** *v/t* incite
inclem|ência *f* inclemency; **~ente** inclement
inclin|ação *f* inclination; **~ar** *v/t, v/i, v/r* incline; bend down
inclu|ir *v/t* include; **~são** *f* inclusion; **~sive** inclusive(ly); **~so** included
incoerente incoherent
incógnito *adj* unknown, incognito
incolor colo(u)rless
incólume safe and sound
incombustível incombustible
incomensurável immeasurable
incomodar *v/t, v/r* put oneself out; bother; disturb; trouble
incómodo *adj* uncomfortable; *m* inconvenience
incomparável incomparable
incompat|ibilidade *f* incompatibility; **~ível** incompatible
incompet|ência *f* incompetence; **~ente** incompetent
incompleto incomplete
incompreen|são *f* incomprehension; **~sível** incomprehensible
incomunicável incommunicable; incommunicado
inconcebível inconceivable
incondicional unconditional
inconsci|ência *f* unconsciousness; **~ente** *adj* unconscious
inconsequ|ência *f* inconse-

quence; **~ente** inconsequent; contradictory
inconsiderado inconsiderate
inconsistente inconsistent
inconsolável inconsolable
incontestável incontestable
inconveni|ência *f* inconvenience; **~ente** *adj* inconvenient; improper, rude; *m* snag, handicap, nuisance
incorre(c)|ção *f* incorrectness; innacuracy; impoliteness; **~to** wrong, incorrect
incorrer *v/i:* **~ em** incur
incorrigível incorrigible
incorru(p)tível incorruptible
incrédulo incredulous
incremento *m* increment
incriminar *v/t* incriminate
incrível incredible
incrust|ação *f* incrustation; **~ar** *v/t* incrust
inculcar *v/t* inculcate
inculpar *v/t* accuse
inculto uncultivated; uncultured, uneducated
incumbir *v/t, v/i* charge, entrust
incurável incurable
incursão *f* incursion
incutir *v/t* inculcate, infuse
indag|ação *f* investigation; research; **~ar** *v/t, v/i* inquire into, investigate
indec|ência *f* indecency; **~ente** indecent
indecifrável indecipherable
indeciso undecided, indecisive
indecoroso indecorous
indefensável indefensible
indeferir *v/t* reject

indefeso undefended
indefin|ido indefinite; undefined; **~ível** undefinable
indelével indelible
indelicad|eza *f* indelicacy; **~o** indelicate
inde(m)niz|ação *f* indemnity, indemnification; **~ar** *v/t* indemnify
independ|ência *f* independence; **~ente** independent
indescritível indescribable
indesculpável inexcusable
indesejável undesirable
indeterminado indeterminate
indiano *adj, m* Indian
indic|ação *f* indication; **~ar** *v/t* indicate, point out
índice *m* index
indício *m* sign, token, hint
indiferen|ça *f* indifference; **~te** *adj* indifferent
indígena *adj* indigenous, native
indig|ência *f* indigence; **~ente** *adj* indigent
indigerível indigestible
indigest|ão *f* indigestion; **~o** undigested; indigestible
indign|ação *f* indignation; **~ado** indignant; **~ar** *v/t, v/r* shock, incense; **~idade** *f* indignity; **~o** *adj* unworthy
índio *adj m* Indian
indire(c)to indirect
indisciplinado indisciplined
indiscreção *f* indiscretion
indiscreto indiscreet
indispensável indispensable
indisponível unavailable
indispor *v/t* indispose
indisp|osição *f* indisposition;

~osto indisposed, ill
indissolúvel indissoluble
indistinto indistinct
individual individual
indivíduo *m* individual, person
indivisível indivisible
índole *f* character, temper, disposition
indol|ência *f* indolence; **~ente** indolent
indomável indomitable; untamable
indómito untamed
indubitável indubitable
indulgência *f* indulgence
indul|tar *v/t* pardon, forgive; **~to** *m* indult
indústria *f* industry
industrial *adj* industrial
industrializar *v/t, v/r* industrialize
induzir *v/t* induce
inebriar *v/t, v/r* inebriate
inédito *adj* inedited, unpublished
inefável ineffable
ineficácia *f* inefficacy
ineficaz ineffective
inegável undeniable
inepto inept
inércia *f* inertia
inerente inherent
inerte inert
inesgotável inexhaustible
inesperado unexpected
inesquecível unforgettable
inevitável inevitable, unavoidable
inexa(c)t|idão *f* inexactitude, inexactness; **~o** inexact
inexorável inexorable

inexperiente inexperienced
inexplicável inexplicable
inexpressivo inexpressive
infalibilidade *f* infallibility
infalível infallible
infame *adj* infamous
infâmia *f* infamy
infância *f* infancy, childhood
infantil infantile, childish
infatigável indefatigable
infe(c)ção *f* infection; **~cioso** infectious; **~tar** *v/t, v/r* infect
infel|icidade *f* unhappiness; **~iz** unhappy
inferior *adj* inferior; lower
inferir *v/t* infer
infern|al infernal; hellish; **~o** *m* hell
infi|delidade *f* infidelity; **~el** *adj* unfaithful, disloyal
infiltr|ação *f* infiltration; **~ar** *v/t, v/r* infiltrate
ínfimo lowest, meanest
infinidade *f* infinity
infinito *adj* infinite
inflação *f* inflation
inflam|ação *f* inflammation; **~ar** *v/t* inflame
inflexível inflexible
infligir *v/t* inflict, impose
influ|ência *f* influence; **~enciar** *v/t* influence; **~ente** *adj* influential; **~ir (em)** *v/i* influence
inform|ação *f* information; **~ante** *m, f* informant; **~ador** *m* informer; **~ar** *v/t, v/r* inform; inquire after
infortúnio *m* misfortune
infra(c)ção *f* infringement
infringir *v/t* infringe

infrutífero fruitless
infundado unfounded, groundless
ingenuidade *f* ingenuousness; naivety
ingênuo ingenuous; naive
ingerir *v/t, v/r* interfere, meddle
inglês *adj* English; *m* English; Englishman
ingrat|idão *f* ingratitude; **~o** ungrateful
íngreme steep
ingressar *v/i* enter, join
ingresso *m* ingress, entry
inibir *v/t* inhibit
inici|ação *f* initiation; **~al** *adj, f* initial; **~ar** *v/t* begin, initiate; **~ativa** *f* initiative
início *m* outset, beginning
inimigo *m* enemy
inimizade *f* enmity
ininterrupto uninterrupted
inje(c)ção *f* injection; **~tar** *v/t* inject
injúria *f* insult; harm
injuriar *v/t* insult; harm
injust|iça *f* injustice; **~o** *adj* unjust
inoc|ência *f* innocence; **~ente** *adj* innocent
inodoro odo(u)rless
inofensivo inoffensive
inolvidável unforgettable
inoportuno inopportune
inov|ação *f* innovation; **~ar** *v/t* innovate
inquérito *m* investigation; inquiry; inquest
inquiet|ação *f* uneasiness; unrest; **~ar** *v/t, v/r* worry; dis-

quiet; disturb; ~o uneasy; restless

inquilino *m* tenant

inquirir *v/t*, *v/i* inquire; interrogate

insaciável insatiable

insalubre insalubrious

insatisfeito displeased, dissatisfied

inscr|ever *v/t*, *v/r* register; inscribe; ~**ição** *f* inscription; registration

inse(c)ticida *f* insecticide

inse(c)to *m* insect

inseguro insecure

insensat|ez *f* folly, stupidity; ~o senseless, foolish

insens|ibilidade *f* insensibility; ~**ível** insensible

inseparável inseparable

inserção *f* insertion

insigne eminent

insignific|ância *f* insignificance; ~**ante** *adj* insignificant

insinu|ação *f* insinuation; ~**ar** *v/t*, *v/r* insinuate (into)

insípido insipid

insist|ência *f* insistence; ~**ente** insistent; ~**ir (em)** *v/i* insist (on)

insolação *f* sunstroke

insolente *adj* insolent

insólito unwonted, unusual

insolúvel insoluble

insónia *f* insomnia, sleeplessness

inspe(c)|ção *f* inspection; ~**cionar** *v/t* inspect; ~**tor** *m* inspector

inspiração *f* inspiration

inspirar *v/t* inspire

instabilidade *f* instability

instal|ação *f* installation; ~**ar** *v/t*, *v/r* install

instant|âneo *m* snapshot; *adj* instantaneous; ~**e** *m* instant; *adj* urgent

instar *v/i* urge

instável unstable

instigar *v/t* instigate

instin|tivo instinctive; ~**to** *m* instinct

institu|ição *f* institution; ~**ir** *v/t* institute

instituto *m* institute

instru|ção *f* instruction; ~**ído** learned; ~**ir** *v/t* instruct; teach

instrumento *m* instrument

insubordinado insubordinate

insuficiente insufficient

insult|ar *v/t* insult; ~**o** *m* insult

insuportável intolerable

insurgir-se *v/r* revolt

insurreição *f* insurrection

insuspeito unsuspected

insustentável untenable

inta(c)to intact

integral *adj* integral

integrar *v/t* integrate

integridade *f* integrity

íntegro entire; upright

inteir|ar *v/t*, *v/r* find out; complete; ~**eza** *f* entirety; ~**o** *adj* entire, whole

intele(c)|to *m* intellect; ~**ual** intellectual

intelig|ência *f* intelligence; ~**ente** *adj* intelligent

intempérie *f* inclemency

intempestivo unseasonable, untimely

inten|ção f intention; **~cional** intentional

intendente m manager; superintendent

intens|idade f intensity; **~o** intense

intent|ar v/t try, attempt; **~o** m intention

intercalar v/t intercalate

intercâmbio m interchange

interceptar v/t intercept

interdi|ção f prohibition; **~zer** v/t prohibit

interess|ado adj interested; **~ante** interesting; **~ar** v/t, v/i, v/r interest; concern

interesse m interest; concern

interesseiro adj self-seeking

interferência f interference

interferir v/i interfere

interino adj interim; provisional

interior adj interior; inner; inland; m interior

intermediário m intermediary; go-between

intermédio adj intermediate; m mediator; **por ~** through, by means of

interminável interminable

interno adj internal

interpor v/t, v/r interpose

interpretar v/t interpret

intérprete m interpreter

interrog|ação f interrogation; **~ar** v/t interrogate; **~atório** m cross-examination

interromper v/t interrupt

interrup|ção f interruption; **~tor** m elect switch

interurbano adj interurban; m

Braz trunk-call, _US_ long-distance call

intervalo m interval; pause

intervenção f intervention

intervir v/i intervene

intestino m intestine

intimidade f intimacy

intimidar v/t intimidate

íntimo adj intimate; m intimate

intolerável intolerable

intoxicação f intoxication

intraduzível untranslatable

intransitável impassable

intransmissível non-transferable

intratável intractable; coy; unsociable

intrepidez f intrepidity

intrépido intrepid

intriga f intrigue

intrínseco intrinsic

introdu|ção f introduction; **~zir** v/t, v/r introduce, bring in; insert

intrometer v/r interfere, meddle in

intrujão m impostor, swindler

intruso m intruder

intui|ção f intuition; **~tivo** intuitive

intuito m aim, purpose

inúmero innumerable, countless

inund|ação f inundation, flood; **~ar** v/t inundate, flood

inútil useless

inutilidade f uselessness

invadir v/t invade

inválido adj invalid; m disabled, invalid

invariável invariable

invas|ão f invasion; **~or** m invader, aggressor
invej|a f envy; **~ar** v/t envy; **~oso** envious
invenção f invention
invencível invincible
inven|tar v/t invent; **~to** m invention; **~tor** m inventor
inverno m winter
inverosímil improbable; unlikely
invers|ão f inversion; **~o** adj, m inverse
inverter v/t invert; reverse
investig|ação f investigation; **~ar** v/t investigate
invicto unconquered
invisível invisible
invoc|ação f invocation; **~ar** v/t invoke, call on
invólucro m covering, case
involuntário involuntary
iodo m iodine
iogurte m yogh(o)urt
ir v/i, v/r go; **~ a pé** walk; **~ a cavalo** ride; **~ buscar** fetch; **~ de carro** go by car; **~-se embora** go away
ira f anger
irlandês adj Irish; m Irishman
irmã f sister
irmão m brother

ironia f irony
irónico ironic
irra! damn!
irradiar v/t, v/i, v/r irradiate
irreal unreal
irrealizável impracticable, unfeasible
irreconciliável irreconcilable
irregular irregular; uneven
irremediável irremediable
irresoluto irresolute
irresponsável irresponsible
irrequieto restless; fidgety
irrevogável irrevocable
irrigar v/t irrigate
irrisório laughable
irrit|ação f irritation; **~ar** v/t irritate; **~ável** irritable
irromper v/t burst into, break into
isca f bait; fried liver
isen|ção f exemption; **~tar** v/t exempt; **~to** exempt
isol|ador m insulator; isolator; **~amento** m isolation; insulation; **~ar** v/t, v/r insulate; isolate
isqueiro m (cigarette-)lighter
isso that; **por ~** therefore
isto this
italiano adj, m Italian
itinerário m itinerary

J

já now; already; **até ~** cheerio, see you later; **~ agora** even now; **~ não** no longer, no more; **~ que** since
jacaré m alligator
jacinto m hyacinth

ja(c)to m jet
jamais never, at no time
Janeiro m January
janela f window
jangada f raft
janota adj chic, slick

jantar v/t, v/i dine; m dinner
japonês adj, m Japanese
jaqueta f jacket
jardi|m m garden; **~nagem** f gardening; **~neiro** m gardener
jarr|a f vase; **~o** m jug, US pitcher
jaula f cage
javali m wild boar
jaz|er v/i lie; **~ida** f resting-place; geol mineral deposit; **~igo** m tomb, grave; geol mineral deposit
jeit|o m manner; knack; **~oso** skilful, handy
jejum m fast
joalheiro m jewe(l)ler
jocoso jocose
joelho m knee
jog|ador m player; gambler; **~ar** v/i play; gamble; **~o** m game, play; gambling; **~uete** m plaything
jóia f jewel
jóquei m jockey
jornada f trip, journey; day's work
jornal m newspaper; daily wage; **~eiro** m day-labo(u)rer; **~ista** m, f journalist
jorrar v/i spout, gush out
jorro m gush
jovem adv young; m, f young lady; youth, young man
jovial jovial; **~idade** f joviality
juba f mane
jubileu m jubilee
júbilo m joy, jubilation

jud|aico Jewish; **~aísmo** m Judaism; **~eu** m Jew; adj Jewish; **~ia** f Jewess
judiciário judicial
jugo m yoke
juiz m (pl juízes) judge
juízo m judg(e)ment; opinion; common sense
julgar v/t, v/i judge; think
Julho m July
jumento m ass, donkey
junção f junction, joining
junco m rush, reed
Junho m June
junt|a f junta; anat joint; **~ar** v/t join, connect; **~o** adj joined, united; adv near; together; **juntura** f juncture
jur|a f oath; curse; **~ado** m juror; **~amento** m oath; **~ar** v/t, v/i swear
júri m jury
jur|ídico juridical; **~isconsulto** m jurisconsult; **~isdição** f jursidiction; **~isprudência** f jurisprudence; **~ista** m, f jurist
juro m interest
jusante f ebb, low tide
justamente exactly, just
justapor v/t, v/r juxtapose, place side by side
justeza f accuracy
justi|ça f justice; **~ceiro** impartial, severe; **~ficação** f justification; **~ficar** v/t justify
justo adj fair, just; exact; accurate
juven|il juvenile; youthful; **~tude** f youth, youthfulness

L

lá *adv* in that place, there

lã *f* wool

labareda *f* flame, blaze

lábio *m* lip

labut|a *f* hard work, drudgery; **~ar** *v/i* work hard

laca *f* lacquer

laç|ada *f* slipknot; **~o** *m* noose; snare; lasso, US lariat; bow, knot

lacónico laconic

lacrar *v/t* seal

lacrau *m* scorpion

lacre *m* sealing-wax

lacuna *f* gap, lacuna

ladeira *f* slope; hillside

ladino *adj* cunning, sly

lado *m* side; **ao ~ de** beside, next to

ladr|a *f* woman thief; **~ão** *m* thief, robber

ladrar *v/i* bark

lagart|a *f* caterpillar; **~o** *m* lizard

lago *m* lake

lagosta *f* lobster

lagostim *m* crayfish

lágrima *f* tear

lama *f* mud; **~çal** *m* slough; **~cento** muddy; slushy

lamb|areiro *adj* greedy; sweet-toothed; **~arice** *f* greediness, gluttony

lamber *v/t* lick

lambreta *f* motor scooter

lament|ação *f* lamentation; **~ar** *v/t, v/r* regret; lament; **~ável** lamentable; **~o** *m* lament

lâmina *f* blade

lâmpada *f* lamp; **~ elé(c)trica** light bulb

lampejar *v/i* flash, glitter

lampião *m* lantern; street-lamp

lanç|a *f* lance; spear; **~amento** *m* throwing; launching; dropping; *com* entry; **~ar** *v/t, v/r* throw, cast; launch

lance *m* event; **~ de olhos** glance

lancha *f* launch

lanche *m* afternoon tea; snack

lanço *m* bid; **~ de escadas** flight of stairs

lânguido languid

lanterna *f* lantern

lápide *f* tablet; tombstone

lápis *m* pencil

lapiseira *f* propelling pencil

lapso *m* lapse

lar *m* home; fireside

laranj|a *f* orange; **~ada** *f* orangeade; **~eira** *f* orange tree

larápio *m* pilferer

lareira *f* hearth; fireplace

largar *v/t, v/i, v/r* let out; let go, release; sail, put to sea

larg|o *adj* broad, wide; *m* square; **ao ~** aloof; **~ura** *f* breadth, width

laringe *f* larynx

larva *f* larva

lasc|a *f* splinter; **~ar** *v/t, v/i* splinter

lascivo lascivious

lass|idão *f* lassitude; **~o** weary;

loose, slack

lástima f pity; pitiful thing

lastim|ar v/t, v/r deplore; regret; **~ável** regrettable

lastro m ballast

lata f tin-plate; tin, can; cheek, impudence

latão m brass

latejar v/i throb

latente latent

lateral lateral

latifúndio m large estate

latim m Latin

latino adj Latin

latir v/i bark, yelp

latitude f latitude

lato extensive, vast

lavagem f wash

lava-louça m sink

lavandaria f laundry

lava|r v/t, v/r wash; **~tório** m wash-basin; US sink

lavável washable

lavor m needlework

lavoura f ploughing, farming

lavrad|eira f farmer's wife; **~or** m farmer

lavrar v/t plough, till; carve; plane

laxante m, adj laxative

leal loyal; **~dade** f loyalty

leão m lion

lebre f hare

le(c)cionar v/t, v/i teach

legação f legation

legado m legate; legacy

legal legal; Braz right, correct, o.k; **~idade** f legality; **~izar** v/t legalize

legar v/t bequeath

legenda f caption; key

legisl|ação f legislation; **~ar** v/t, v/i legislate

legitimar v/t legitimize

legítimo legitimate

legível legible

legume m vegetable

lei f law

leilão m auction

leitaria f dairy

leit|e m milk; **~eiro** m milkman

leito m bed; bedstead

leit|or m reader; lecturer; **~rado** m lectureship; **~ura** f reading

lebr|ança f remembrance, memory; keepsake; souvenir; **~ar** v/t, v/i, v/r recall; remind; remember

leme m tiller; rudder

lenço m handkerchief

lençol m sheet

lend|a f legend; **~ário** legendary

lenh|a f (fire)wood; **~ador** m woodcutter; **~o** m block, log

lente m lecturer; f lens

lentidão f slowness

lentilha f lentil

lento adj slow

leopardo m leopard

lepra f leprosy

leque m fan

ler v/t, v/i read

lesão f lesion, wound

lesar v/t hurt, damage

leste m east

lesto brisk, nimble

letra f letter; handwriting; **à/ao pé da ~** literally; **~ de câmbio** bill of exchange; **~s** f/pl letters, learning

letreiro m inscription, caption

leva f weighing anchor; levy

levant|amento m survey; insurrection; ~**ar** v/t, v/i, v/r lift, raise; rise, get up; ~**ar a mesa** clear the table; ~**ar voo** take off

levar v/t carry, bear, convey, take; ~ **a cabo** carry through; ~ **a mal** take amiss; ~ **em conta** take into account

leve light; slight

levedura f yeast

leveza f lightness

levian|dade f frivolity; ~**o** frivolous, inconsiderate

leziria f marsh

lhan|eza f plainness; sincerity; ~**o** plain; sincere

lhe to it; to him; to her; to you

liberal adj, m, f liberal; ~**idade** f liberality

liber|dade f freedom, liberty; ~**tação** f liberation; jur discharge; ~**tar** v/t, v/r liberate, set free; ~**tino** m libertine

libidinoso libidinous

libra f pound; ~ **esterlina** pound sterling

lição f lesson

licença f licence; permission; leave, furlough

licenci|ado m licenciate, graduate; ~**ar** v/t, v/r graduate; licence; ~**atura** f degree of licentiate

liceu m grammar-school, US high school

licitar v/t, v/i bid; auction

lícito lawful

licor m liquor; liqueur

lid|a f work, job, chore; ~**ar** v/i work; ~**ar com** deal with; ~**e** f fight, struggle; controversy

lido adj well-read

lig|a f league; alloy; ~**ação** f connection, link; ~**adura** f bandage; ligature; ~**ar** v/t bind; switch on

ligeir|eza f lightness; swiftness; ~**o** light; swift

lilás m lilac

lima f file; lime

limão m lemon

limar v/t file

limiar m threshold

limit|ação f limitation; ~**ar** v/t limit; ~**e** m limit; boundary

limítrofe bordering

limonada f lemonade, lemon squash

limpa-pára-brisas m windscreen wiper; ~**chaminés** m chimney-sweep(er)

limp|adela f cleaning; ~**ar** v/t, v/r clean; ~**eza** f clean(li)ness

límpido limpid, clear

limpo adj clean

lince m lynx

lindo pretty; fine; neat

língua f tongue; language

linguado m zo sole

linguagem f language, speech

linguiça f thin sausage

ling|uista m, f linguist; ~**uístico** linguistic

linha f line

linhagem f lineage

linho m linen; bot flax

liquid|ação f liquidation; ~**ar**

v/t, v/i liquidate

líquido *m adj* liquid

lírico *adj* lyric(al)

lírio *m* lily

lisboeta *m, f* native of Lisbon

liso smooth; lank

lisonj|a *f* flattery; **~eador** *m* flatterer; **~ear** *v/t, v/r* flatter; **~eiro** flattering

lista *f* list; menu; **~ telefónica** telephone directory

literal literal

liter|ário literary; **~atura** *f* literature

litig|ante *m, f* litigant; **~ar** *v/i* litigate, defend in court

litígio *m* litigation, lawsuit; contention

litro *m* litre

lívido livid

livrar *v/t, v/r* get rid of; free, release

livraria *f* bookshop, *US* bookstore

livre *adj* free; **~câmbio** *m* free trade

livreiro *m* bookseller

livrete *m* booklet

livro *m* book

lix|a *f* sandpaper; **~ar** *v/t* sandpaper

lixívia *f* lye

lixo *m* filth, dirt; garbage, litter

lobo *m* wolf

lobo *m* lobe

lôbrego dark, dismal, gloomy

local *adj* local; **~idade** *f* locality; **~izar** *v/t* localize

loção *f* lotion

locatário *m* lessee, tenant

locomo|ção *f* locomotion; **~ti-**

va *f* locomotive

locução *f* locution, idiom

locutor *m* announcer

lodaçal *m* puddle

lodo *m* mud, mire; **~so** muddy

lógic|a *f* logic; **~o** *adj* logical; *m* logician

logo *adv* presently; soon; immediately; *conj* therefore, so, then; **~ que** as soon as; **até ~** cheerio, see you later

lograr *v/t* get; succeed in

logro *m* fraud, hoax

loj|a *f* shop; **~ista** *m, f* shopkeeper

lomba *f* ridge, brow

lombo *m* loin; back

lona *f* canvas

long|e *adv* far; *adj* distant, far off; **ao ~e** in the distance; **~ínquo** distant; **~itude** *f* longitude; **~o** long; **ao ~o de** along

loquaz loquacious

lot|ação *f* capacity; **~ação esgotada** full house; **~ar** *v/t* allot

lotaria *f* lottery

lote *m* lot

louça *f* crockery, china

louc|o mad; **~ura** *f* madness

loureiro *m* bay; laurel

louro *m* laurel; *adj* fair, blond

lousa *f* slate; tombstone

louv|ar *v/t* praise; **~ável** praiseworthy; **~or** *m* praise

lua *f* moon; **~ de mel** honeymoon

luar *m* moonlight

lubrific|ação *f* lubrication; **~ar** *v/t* lubricate

lúcido lucid
lúcio *m* pike
lucr|ar *v/t, v/i* gain; profit by;
  ~ativo lucrative; **~o** *m* gain;
  profit
ludibriar *v/t* ridicule, mock
ludíbrio *m* mockery
lufada *f* squall, gust; **às ~s** by
  fits and starts
lufa-lufa *f* hurly-burly; **à ~** in a
  hurry
lugar *m* place; seat; spot, village;
  em ~ de instead of; **~ejo** *m*
  hamlet
lúgubre lugubrious; dismal
lume *m* fire; glow; light
luminoso luminous
lunar *adj* lunar
luneta *f* eye-glass
lupa *f* magnifying glass

lúpulo *m* hops
lusco-fusco *m* dusk, nightfall;
  ao ~ at twilight
lusitano, luso *m, adj* Lusita-
  nian, Portuguese
lustrar *v/t, v/i* glaze, polish
lustre *m* gloss, lustre; chandelier, sconce
luta *f* struggle; strife; wrestling
lutar *v/i* struggle; strive; wrestle
luto *m* mourning
luv|a *f* glove; **~as** *f/pl* gratuity,
  tip; **~eiro** *m* glover
lux|o *m* luxury; **~uoso** luxu-
  rious; **~úria** *f* lust; **~uriante**
  luxuriant, rank; **~urioso** luxurious
luz *f* light
luzidio glistening
luzir *v/i* shine, glow

M

má *adj, f, of* **mau** bad, evil
maca *f* stretcher; litter
maça *f* club; mace
maçã *f* apple
macacão *m Braz* overalls
macaco *m* monkey
maça|da *f* bore, nuisance;
  ~dor *adj* boring
maçar *v/t* bore; beat, pound
macarrão *m* mac(c)aroni
macela *f* camomile
machado *m* ax(e)
macho *m* mule; male
maciço *adj* massive; *m* massif
macieira *f* apple-tree
macio soft, smooth; mild
maço *m* mallet; packet; bundle
má-criação *f* ill-breeding; bad

  manners
mácula *f* stain
madeir|a *f* wood, timber; **~o** *m*
  trunk; beam; plank
madeixa *f* tuft, lock
madrasta *f* stepmother
madre *f* nun
madrepérola *f* mother-of-pearl
madressilva *f* honeysuckle
madrinha *f* godmother
madrug|ada *f* dawn; **~ador** *m*
  early riser; **~ar** *v/i* rise early
madur|ar *v/t, v/i* mature;
  ripen; **~o** *adj* ripe
mãe *f* mother
magia *f* magic
mágico *adj* magic(al)
magis|tério *m* teaching profes-

sion; **~trado** *m* magistrate; **~tral** *adj* masterly; **~tratura** *f* magistracy

magnânimo magnanimous

magnate *m* magnate

magnific|ência *f* magnificence; **~ente** generous

magnífico magnificent

mágoa *f* grief

magoar *v/t* hurt

magote *m* band, group

magr|eza *f* thinness, leanness; **~o** thin, lean

Maio *m* May

maiô *m* bathing suit

maionese *f* mayonnaise

maior *adj* of age; bigger, greater; larger; **a ~ parte** most; **~es** *m/pl* ancestors; **~ia** *f* majority; **~idade** *f* majority, coming-of-age

mais *adv* more; any more; *adj* more; **a ~** in excess, over; **~ too much; de ~ a ~** besides; **por ~ que** however much

maiúscula *f* capital letter

majest|ade *f* majesty; **~oso** majestic

major *m* major

mal *adv* badly; hardly; *m* evil; harm; illness

mala *f* suitcase; trunk

mal-agradecido ungrateful

malandro *m* scoundrel

malária *f* malaria

malcriado ill-bred; ill-mannered

maldade *f* wickedness

maldisposto ill-humo(u)red, cross; indisposed

maldito *adj* damned

maldizer *v/t, v/i* slander; curse

maleável malleable

maledicência *f* slander

mal|efício *m* evil; **~éfico** harmful

mal-educado ill-bred, impolite; **~entendido** *m* misunderstanding; **~estar** *m* indisposition

malevo|lência *f* malevolence, ill-will; **~lente** malevolent

malfadado ill-fated

malfeitor *m* malefactor

malga *f* bowl

malh|a *f* mesh; speckle; ladder; **~ado** *adj* speckled; **~ar** *v/t, v/i* thresh; beat

mal-humorado ill-tempered

mal|ícia *f* malice; **~icioso** malicious

maligno *adj* malignant

malmequer *m* daisy

malograr *v/t, v/r* frustrate; fail; upset

malogro *m* failure

malta *f* gang; mob; band

maltrapilho *m* ragamuffin

maltratar *v/t* maltreat; ill-treat

malu|co *adj* barmy; mad, crazy; **~quice** *f* madness, folly

malvad|ez *f* wickedness; **~o** *adj* wicked

mama *f* breast

mamã *f, Braz* **mamãe** mum, mummy, *US* mom(my)

mamão *m* papaya, pawpaw

mamar *v/t, v/i* suckle

mamífero *m* mammal

mana *f* sister

manada f herd, drove
manancial m spring, fountain; source
manar v/t, v/i flow; issue
mancar v/i limp
mancebo m youth
mancha f spot, stain, **~ar** v/t stain, soil, sully
manco m cripple
mandado m order; errand; writ; **~amento** m commandment; **~ar** v/t, v/i command; send; **~ar buscar** send for; **~atário** m attorney, proxy; **~ato** m mandate
mandíbula f mandible, jaw-bone
mando m command, power; authority
mandrião m sluggard, idler
mandriar v/i lounge, idle
manducar v/t, v/i chew, eat
maneira f manner, way; **de ~ nenhuma** not at all; in no way; **de ~ que** so that
manejar v/t, v/i handle; manage; **~o** m handling
manequim m model; dummy
maneta adj one-armed
manga f sleeve; bot mango
mangar v/t mock, joke
mangueira f hose; mango-tree
manha f craft, trick, cunning; bad habit
manhã f morning; **de ~** in the morning
manhoso crafty, artful
mania f mania; craze; **~íaco** m maniac; **~icómio** m mental hospital/home
manifestação f manifestation;

demonstration; **~ar** v/t, v/r manifest; demonstrate; **~o** adj manifest; m manifesto
manipulação f manipulation; **~ar** v/t manipulate
manivela f handle, crank
manjar m food; tidbit, delicacy
manjedoura f crib, manger
mano m brother
manobra f manoeuvre, US maneuver; **~ar** v/t, v/i manoeuvre, US maneuver
manquejar v/i limp
mansarda f garret
mansidão f meekness, gentleness; **~so** meek, gentle; tame
manta f blanket; rug
manteiga f butter; **~ueira** f butter-dish
manter v/t, v/r maintain; keep
manual m, adj manual
manufactura f manufacture; **~ar** v/t manufacture
manuscrito m manuscript
manutenção f maintenance
mão f hand; **à ~** at hand; **~-de-obra** f handwork
mapa m map
maquilhagem f make-up
máquina f machine; **~ de barbear** electric razor; **~ de costura** sewing-machine; **~ de escrever** typewriter; **~ de lavar (roupa)** washing-machine; **~ de lavar louça** dish-washer; **~ fotográfica** camera
maquinação f machination; **~al** mechanical; **~aria** f machinery; **~ismo** m machinery; **~ista** m, f machinist; engine-

-driver
mar m sea
maracujá m passion fruit
maravilh|a f marvel; **~ar** v/t, v/r marvel
maravilhoso adj marve(l)lous, wonderful
marc|a f mark; brand, make; **~ação** f demarcation; booking, reservation
marcar v/t mark; dial; fix; book, reserve
marceneiro m joiner
marcha f march
marchar v/i march
marco m landmark; mark; **~ postal** pillar box
Março m March
maré f tide; **~ alta** high tide; **~ baixa** low tide; **~ enchente** flood tide; **~ vazante** ebb tide
marechal m marshal
marfim m ivory
marg|em f bank; margin; **~inal** marginal
marido m husband
marinha f navy
marinheiro m sailor, seaman
marisco m shellfish
marítimo adj maritime
marmel|ada f quince jam; **~o** m quince
mármore m marble
maroto m rascal
marqu|ês m marquis; **~esa** f marchioness; couch
marr|ada f butt; **~ar** v/i butt, push with the head
martel|ada f blow with a hammer; **~ar** v/t, v/i hammer; **~o** m hammer

mártir m martyr
martírio m martyrdom
marujo m sailor, seaman
mas conj but
mascar v/t chew
máscara f mask
mascote f, m mascot
masculino adj, m masculine
másculo virile
massa f dough; mass; slang money
massacr|ar v/t massacre; **~e** m massacre
massag|em f massage; **~ista** f masseur; f masseuse
massudo massive
mastigar v/t chew, masticate
mastro m mast
mata f thicket, wood
mata-borrão m blotting-paper
mat|adouro m slaughterhouse; **~ança** f slaughter, killing, butchery; **~ar** v/t, v/r quench; kill; slaughter
matemátic|a f mathematics; **~o** m mathematician
matéria f material; matter; **~ prima** raw material
material m, adj material
matern|al maternal; motherly; **~idade** f maternity
matilha f pack
matinal morning, early
matiné f matinée
matiz m hue, nuance, tone
mato m undergrowth; jungle
matrícula f matriculation (fee); roll; list
matrim|onial matrimonial; **~ónio** m matrimony
matriz f matrix; womb; origin

menos

maturação f maturation
maturidade f maturity
matutino adj morning
mau adj bad, evil; naughty
mavioso tender, sweet; melodious
maxila f jaw
máxima f maxim
máximo m maximum; adj greatest
mazela f wound, sore; illness
me me; to me
meado m middle
mealheiro m money-box
mecânic|a f mechanics; ~o m mechanic; adj mechanical
mecanismo m mechanism
mecha f wick; haste; speed
medalha f medal
média f average
medi|aneiro m mediator; ~ano middling, medium
mediante prp by means of
medicamento m medicine
medição f measurement
med|icar v/t treat, doctor; ~icina f medicine
medicinal medicinal
médico m doctor, physician
medida f measure, size
medieval medi(a)eval
médio adj middle; middling, average; intermediary
mediocre adj mediocre
medir v/t measure
medit|ação f meditation; ~ar v/t, v/i explore
mediterrâneo adj Mediterranean
medo m fear
medonho frightful

medrar v/i thrive
medroso timid, fearful
medula f marrow; pith
meia f stocking
meia-lua f half-moon; ~-luz f half-light; ~-noite f midnight
meig|o mild, meek, gentle; ~uice f mildness, gentleness; ~uices f/pl caress
meio m middle, centre; adj half; ~-dia m noon, midday; south
mel m honey
melancia f water-melon
melão m melon
melhor adj better; best; ~a f improvement; ~amento m improvement; ~ar v/t, v/i get better; improve; ~ia f improvement
melindr|ar v/t, v/r hurt, offend; ~e m touchiness, sensitiveness; ~oso touchy, sensitive
melodia f melody
melro m blackbird
membro m member; limb
mem|orável memorable; ~ória f memory; record, report; ~órias f/pl memoirs
men|ção f mention; ~cionar v/t mention
mendicidade f begging
mendig|ar v/t, v/i beg; ~o m beggar
men|ear v/t shake; wag; ~eio m shaking; wagging
menin|a f girl; miss, young lady; ~o m boy; lad
menor adj less(er); smaller; younger; minor; m minor
menos prp but, except; adj, adv

~ **mal** so so, not too bad; **ao/pelo** ~ at least; **a** ~ **que** unless, except

mensag|eiro m messenger; ~**em** f message

mensal monthly

menstruação f menses, menstruation

ment|al mental; ~**alidade** f mentality; ~**e** f mind

mentir v/i lie; ~**a** f lie

mercado m market; ~**ria** f goods, merchandise

mercante adj mercantile, merchant

mercê f reward; mercy

merce|aria f grocery; grocer's shop; ~**eiro** m grocer

mercúrio m mercury

merda f shit

merece|dor deserving; ~**er** v/t deserve, merit; ~**ido** merited, deserved, just, due; ~**imento** m merit, worth

merenda f snack, picnic meal, light meal; ~**ar** v/i eat a snack

mergulh|ador m diver; ~**ar** v/t, v/i plunge, dip, dive

meridional adj southern

mérito m merit

mero adj mere

mês m (pl **meses**) month

mesa f table; ~ **de cabeceira** bedside table

mesada f monthly allowance

mescla f mixture, medley

mesmo adj same; self; adv even

mesquinho stingy, mean

mestr|a f mistress, teacher; ~**e** m master, teacher; ~**ia** f mastery

meta f limit, end; goal

metade f half

metal m metal; ~**urgia** f metallurgy

metamorfose f metamorphosis

meter v/t, v/r put, place, set ~ **o nariz em** poke one's nose into something; ~**se com alguém** provoke someone

meticuloso meticulous

método m method

metralhadora f machine-gun

metro m metre; tube

metrópole f metropolis

metro(politano) m underground, US subway

meu adj mine; pron (o) ~ my

mexer v/t, v/i, v/r touch; stir, move, shake

mexerico m gossip

mexilhão m mussel

miar v/i miaow, US meow

microfone m microphone

migalha f crumb, scrap

migração f migration

mil thousand

milagr|e m miracle; ~**oso** miraculous

milha f mile

milhão m million

milhar m thousand

milho m maize

milícia f militia

milionário m millionaire

militar military; m regular, professional soldier

mim me

mimo m caress, pat; ~**so** adj tender; soft; delicate

min|a f mine; ~**ar** v/t mine; undermine; ~**eiro** m miner, collier; **~eral** adj, m mineral

míngua f lack, shortage

minha f of **meu** my, mine

minhoca f earth-worm

mínimo adj least; slightest; m minimum

ministério m ministry

minist|ar v/t administer to; **~o** m minister

minoria f minority

min|úcia f minutia; **~uciosidade** f accuracy; **~ucioso** meticulous, detailed; **~úscula** f small letter; **~úsculo** minute, tiny

minuta f minutes

minuto m minute

miolos m/pl brains

míope adj short-sighted, US near-sighted; myopic

mira f sight; aim, end, goal

mir|ante m belvedere; **~ar** v/t, v/i, v/r aim (at); look (at)

mirim adj Braz small

mirrar v/t, v/i dry, wither

mirto m myrtle

miscelânea f miscellany

miser|ando pitiable, wretched; **~ável** adj miserable, wretched; niggardly

miséria f misery, wretchedness

misericórdia f mercy; compassion

mísero adj scarce; miserable, wretched

missa f mass

missão f mission

mister m need; duty function; **ser ~** be necessary

mist|ério m mystery; **~erioso** mysterious

místico adj, m mystic

mistificar v/t mystify

mist|o adj mixed; **~ura** f mixture; **~urar** v/t mix

mitigar v/t mitigate

mito m myth

miudeza f minuteness; **~s** f/pl giblets; odds and ends/sods, gewgaws, trifles

miúdo m boy, youngster; adj small, minute; petty; **~s** m/pl small change

mobília f furniture

mobilidade f mobility

mobilizar v/t mobilize

moça f young woman, girl; girl friend

moção f motion

mochila f rucksack

mocho m owl

mocidade f youth

moço m boy, young man; boy friend; servant

moda f fashion

modalidade f modality

modelar v/t model

modelo m model

moder|ação f moderation; **~ar** v/t moderate

moderno adj modern

mod|éstia f modesty; **~esto** modest

módico moderate

modific|ação f modification; **~ar** v/t modify

modo m way, manner, mode; **de ~ nenhum** not at all; **de ~ que** so that

moeda f coin

moela f gizzard

moer v/t, v/r wear out; grind

mof|a f mockery, banter; **~ar** v/t scoff at, mock at

mofo m mo(u)ld, mustiness

mogno m mahogany

moinho m mill

mola f spring; **~ real** mainspring

mold|ar v/t mo(u)ld; **~e** m mo(u)ld; model; **~ura** f mo(u)lding; picture frame

mole adj soft; indolent, inert

moleiro m miller

molestar v/t annoy, disturb; molest

moléstia f trouble

moleque m little Negro; Braz urchin

moleza f softness; slackness

molhar v/t, v/r (get) wet

molhe m mole, pier

molho m bundle

molho m sauce, gravy

moment|âneo momentary; **~o** m moment

monar|ca m monarch; **~quia** f monarchy

monástico monastic

mondar v/t weed, hoe

monetário adj monetary

monge m monk

monja f nun

mono m ape

monopólio m monopoly

monotonia f monotony

monótono monotonous

monstr|o m monster; **~uoso** monstrous

monta f amount; worth

montagem f erection; montage; fitting

montanh|a f mountain; **~oso** mountainous

montante m amount, total

montar v/t, v/i ride; mount; put up, set up; come to

montaria f hunting

monte m hill; heap

montra f shop-window, show-case

monumento m monument

mor|ada f address, residence; **~adia** f villa, house; **~ador** m resident, inhabitant

moral f, adj moral; **~idade** f morality

morango m strawberry

morar v/i live, dwell

mórbido morbid

morcego m bat

morcela f black pudding

mordaça f gag

mord|az mordant; biting; **~edura** f bite; **~er** v/t, v/i, v/r bite

moreno adj dark-skinned

moribundo adj moribund

morno lukewarm

moroso sluggish

morrer v/i die

morro m mound, hillock

mortal adj mortal; deadly; **~idade** f mortality; death-rate

mortandade f slaughter

morte f death

mortiço dull, lifeless

mortific|ação f mortification; **~ar** v/t, v/r mortify

morto adj dead; killed; estar **~** por be dying for/to; **~ de cansaço** fagged

mosca f fly

mosqui|teiro m mosquito

net; ~to m mosquito
mostarda f mustard
mosteiro m monastery
mostra f sample, specimen
mostrador m face, dial
mostrar v/t show; display
mote|ar v/t, v/i mock at, deride; ~o m jeer, banter
motim m mutiny; riot
motivar v/t motivate
motivo m reason; motive
motocicl|eta f motor-cycle; ~ista m, f motor-cyclist
motor m motor; engine; ~ exterior móvel outboard motor; ~ista m, f motorist
motriz adj motive, driving
mouco deaf
móveis m/pl movables; furniture
móvel adj movable, mobile; m motive; piece of furniture
mov|er v/t, v/i, v/r move; ~imento m movement
mucos|a f mucous membrane; ~o mucous
mud|a f change; moulting; ~ança f change; removal; ~ar v/t, v/i, v/r change; remove; moult; ~ável mutable; changeable
mud|ez f dumbness; ~o adj dumb, mute
mugir v/i bellow, low, moo
muito adj a lot of, much, pl many; adv very; much; too; too much
mula f she-mule
mulher f woman; wife
multa f fine
multicolor multicolo(u)red

multidão f crowd; multitude
multiplic|ação f multiplication; ~ar v/t, v/i multiply
múltiplo adj, m multiple
mundano worldly, mundane
mund|ial world-wide; ~o m world
mungir v/t milk
munição f (am)munition
municipal adj municipal; ~idade f municipality; township
município m borough
munir v/t, v/r provide
muralha f wall, rampart
murch|ar v/t, v/i wither, fade; ~o withered, faded
murmurar v/t, v/i murmur, whisper
murmúrio m murmur
muro m wall
murro m blow, punch
músculo m muscle
musculoso muscular, brawny
museu m museum
musgo m moss
música f music
music|al m musical; ~ar v/i make music; ~ata f brass band; piece of music
músico adj musical; m musician
mut|abilidade f mutability; ~ação f mutation
mutil|ação f mutilation; ~ado adj mutilated, disabled; ~ar v/t mutilate
mutismo m dumbness; muteness
mutuar v/t exchange
mútuo mutual

N

na *contr of* **em** *and* **a**

nabo *m* turnip

nácar *m* mother-of-pearl

nacional *adj* national; **~idade** *f* nationality; **~ismo** *m* nationalism; **~ização** *f* nationalization; **~izar** *v/t* nationalize

nada *adv, m* nothing; **de ~** not at all

nad|ador *m* swimmer; **~ar** *v/i* swim

nádega *f* buttock

nado *m* swim; **a ~** by swimming

namor|ada *f* girl friend; **~ado** *m* boy friend; **~ar** *v/t* court; **~i(s)car** *v/t, v/i* flirt; **~o** *m* courtship

não *adv* no; not

narciso *m* narcissus

narcótico *m* narcotic

nariz *m* nose

narr|ação *f* narration; **~ar** *v/t* narrate, relate; **~ativa** *f* narrative

nascente *f* source, spring

nasc|er *v/i* be born; arise; **~imento** *m* birth; origin

nata *f* cream

natação *f* swimming

natal *adj* natal, native; **♀** *m* Christmas

natalício *m* natal

natalidade *f* birth-rate

natividade *f* nativity

nativo *m* native, natural

natural *adj* natural; **~idade** *f* naturalness; nationality

naturalizar *v/t, v/r* naturalize

natureza *f* nature; **~ morta** still life

naufragar *v/i* shipwreck

naufrágio *m* shipwreck

náufrago *adj* shipwrecked

náusea *f* nausea

naval *adj* naval

navalha *f* razor

nave *f* nave

nave|gação *f* navigation; **~gar** *v/t, v/i* navigate; **~gável** navigable

navio *m* ship, boat

neblina *f* fog, mist

nebuloso *adj* nebulous, cloudy

necessário *adj* necessary

necess|idade *f* necessity; **~itar** *v/t* need

necrologia *f* necrology

nédio *adj* sleek, fat, plump

neg|ação *f* negation, denial; **~ar** *v/t, v/i, v/r* refuse; deny; **~ativa** *f* negative; **~ativo** *m, adj* negative

neglig|ência *f* negligence; **~ente** negligent

negoci|ação *f* negotiation; **~ante** *m, f* trader; businessman; **~ar** *v/i, v/t* negotiate; **~ável** negotiable

negócio *m* business; trade

negro *adj* dark; black

nela, nele *contr of* **em** *and* **ela, ele**

nem *conj* neither; nor; *adv* not **~ ... ~** neither ... nor; **~ sequer** not even

nené *m* baby

nervo *m* nerve; **~so** nervous

néscio *adj* ignorant, foolish

nesse, neste *contr of* **em** *and* **esse, este**

net|a *f* granddaughter; **~o** *m* grandson

neutral neutral

neutro *adj*, *m* neuter

nev|ada *f* snow-fall; **~ão** *m* snow-storm; **~ar** *v/i* snow; **~e** *f* snow

névoa *f* fog, mist

nevo|eiro *m* thick fog; **~ento** foggy, misty

nicho *m* niche

ninguém nobody, no one

ninho *m* nest

nisso, nisto *contr of* **em** *and* **isso, isto**

nitidez *f* clearness; sharpness

nítido clear; shining; sharp

nível *m* level; **~ de vida** standard of living, living standard

no *contr of* **em** *and* **o**

nó *m* knot; knuckle

nobre *adj*, *m* noble; **~za** *f* nobility

noção *f* notion

nocivo harmful

no(c)turno *adj* nocturnal

nódoa *f* stain

nogueira *f* walnut-tree

noite *f* night; **à/de ~** at/by night

noiv|a *f* bride; fiancée **~o** *m* bridegroom; fiancé

noj|ento nauseous, disgusting; **~o** *m* nausea; disgust

nom|e *m* name; **~eação** *f* nomination; **~eada** *f* renown;

~ear *v/t* nominate, appoint; name

nono *adj* ninth

nora *f* daughter-in-law

nordeste *m* north-east

nórdico *adj* Nordic

norma *f* norm, standard

noroeste *m* north-west

nort|ada *f* north-wind; **~e** *m* north

norueguês *adj*, *m* Norwegian

nos *pers pron* (to) us; (to) ourselves

nós we; us

nosso *pron*, *adj* ours

not|a *f* note; mark; **~ar** *v/t* note; observe; notice **~ário** *m* notary; **~ável** remarkable, notable

not|ícia *f* news; **~iciador** *m* reporter

noticiário *m* newscast

not|oriedade *f* notoriety; **~ório** notorious, well-known

noutro *contr of* **em** *and* **outro**

nova *f* news

nove nine

novela *f* novel, story

novelo *m* ball, clew

Novembro *m* November

noventa ninety

novidade *f* novelty

novilho *m* young steer; bullock

novo *adj* new; young; **de ~** again, anew

noz *f* walnut

nu *adj* naked, nude, bare

nublado *adj* cloudy

nuca *f* nape, scruff

núcleo *m* nucleus, kernel

nuclear nuclear

nulidade f nullity; invalidity; nonentity
nulo null, void
num, numa contr of **em** and **um, uma**
numer|ação f numeration; **~al** adj, m numeral; **~ar** v/t number
número m number

numeroso numerous
nunca never; **~ mais** never again
núpcias f/pl nuptials, marriage, wedding
nutr|ição f nutrition; **~ir** v/t, v/r nourish; **~itivo** nutritive
nuvem f cloud

O

o art the; pron it, him, he; the one; **~ que** what; he who, the one that
oásis m oasis
obcec|ação f obstinacy; **~ar** v/t blind, bewilder
obedecer v/i obey
obedi|ência f obedience; **~ente** obedient
obeso obese
óbito m decease
obje(c)|ção f objection; **~tar** v/t object
obje(c)tivo adj, m objective
obje(c)to m object
oblíquo oblique
obr|a f work; **~a-prima** f masterpiece; **~ar** v/t, v/i act; work; **~eiro** m workman, worker
obrig|ação f obligation; **~ado** adj obliged; int thank you; **~ar** v/t oblige; compel; **~atório** obligatory
obscen|idade f obscenity; **~o** obscene
obscur|ecer v/t, v/i, v/r darken; **~idade** f obscurity; **~o** obscure; dark

obséquio m favo(u)r, kindness
observ|ação f observation; remark; **~ador** m observer; **~ância** f observance; **~ar** v/t, v/r observe; remark; **~atório** m observatory
obsessão f obsession
obsoleto obsolete
obstáculo m obstacle
obstante hindering; **não ~** in spite of, notwithstanding
obstar v/i hinder, obstruct
obstin|ação f obstinacy; **~ado** obstinate; **~ar** v/t, v/r persist (**em** in)
obstru|ção f obstruction; **~ir** v/t obstruct
obtenção f obtainment
obter v/t obtain, get
obtur|ador m obturator, shutter; **~ar** v/t fill; plug, stop up
obtuso obtuse
óbvio obvious
ocasião f occasion; opportunity
ocasion|al occasional; **~ar** v/t occasion, cause
ocaso m setting; west; fig decadence, end
oceano m ocean

ocident|al western, occidental;
~**e** m west, occident
ócio m idleness, leisure
ocios|idade f idleness; ~**o** adj
idle
oco hollow
ocorr|ência f occurrence; ~**er**
v/i occur
oculista m, f optician; oculist
óculos m/pl specs, spectacles,
glasses
ocultar v/t, v/r hide
ocupa|ção f occupation; ~**do**
busy; occupied, taken; ~**r** v/t,
v/r occupy
odiar v/t hate
ódio m hate, hatred
odor m odo(u)r; scent
odre m wineskin
oeste m west
ofegante panting, breathless
ofegar v/i pant, puff
ofender v/t, v/r offend; insult
ofensa f offence; insult
ofensiva f offensive, attack
ofere|cer v/t offer; ~**imento**
m offering
oferta f offer; tender
oficial adj official; m officer; official
oficina f workshop
ofício m trade, craft duty, office
ofuscar v/t obfuscate; bewilder
oitava adj eighth
oitenta eighty
oito eight
oitocentos eight hundred
olaria f pottery
oleado m oilcloth, linoleum
olear v/t oil
oleiro m potter

óleo m oil; ~ **de fígado de
bacalhau** cod-liver oil
olfa(c)to m sense of smell
olha(de)la f glance, look
olhar v/t, v/i, v/r look (at); m
look, glance
olheiras f/pl shadows under
the eyes
olho m eye; **a ~ vistos** visibly;
até aos ~s to the teeth
olimpíada f Olympiad
olival m olive grove
oliveira f olive-tree
olmo m elm
ombro m shoulder
omeleta f omelette
omissão f omission
omitir v/t omit
o(m)nipot|ência f omnipotence; ~**ente** adj omnipotent
onça f ounce; zo lynx
onda f wave
onde adv where; ~ **quer que**
wherever
ondulação f undulation
oneroso onerous, burdensome
ónibus m bus
ontem yesterday; ~ **à noite** last
night
onze eleven
opaco opaque
opção f option
ópera f opera
operação f operation
operador m operator
operar v/t, v/i operate
operário m workman
opinião f opinion
opor v/t, v/r oppose
oportunidade f opportunity
oportuno opportune

oposição f opposition
oposto m adj opposite
opressão f oppression
oprimir v/t oppress
ó(p)tico m optician
o(p)timista m, f optimist
ó(p)timo excellent
opulento opulent
ora conj but; int well! oh!; adv now; ~ **bem** well now; ~ **essa**; why! the very idea!
oração f oration; prayer; clause, sentence
orador m orator
oral adj oral
orar v/i pray
orbe m orb, sphere, globe
órbita f orbit
orç|amento m estimate; budget; **~ar** v/t estimate
ordem f order; command
ordenação f ordination; ordinance; arrangement
ordenado m salary
ordenar v/t, v/i order, command; put in order, arrange
ordinário adj ordinary
orelha f ear
orfanato m orphanage
órfão m (f **órfã**) orphan
orgânico organic
organismo m organism
organização f organization
organizar v/t organize
órgão m organ
orgulhar-se v/r pride oneself
orgulho m pride; **~so** adj proud
oriental adj oriental, eastern
orientar v/t, v/r orient(ate); find one's bearings

oriente m orient, east
orifício m orifice, hole
origem f origin
original adj, m original; **~i-dade** f originality
originar v/t, v/r originate
originário de native of
orla f fringe, edge
ornamento m ornament; decorate; **~o** m ornament
ornar v/t adorn
orquestra f orchestra
orquídia f orchid, orchis
ortografia f orthography, spelling
orvalho m dew
oscil|ação f oscillation; **~ar** v/i oscillate
ósculo m kiss
osso m bone
ostensível ostensible
ostentação f ostentation
ostentar v/t, v/i show off
ostra f oyster
ou either; or
ouriço(-cacheiro) m hedgehog; **~-do-mar** sea urchin
ourives m goldsmith
ourivesaria f goldsmith's shop, jewellery
ouro m gold
ousad|ia f boldness; daring; **~o** daring, bold
ousar v/t dare
outono m autumn, US fall
outorgar v/t grant
outrem other people
outro adj, pron other; another
outrora formerly
outrossim likewise, also
Outubro m October

ouvido *m* ear; hearing
ouvinte *m*, *f* listener, hearer
ouvir *v/t*, *v/i* listen to; hear; ~
  dizer que be told that; ~ **falar**
  de hear of
ova *f* roe
ovação *f* ovation

ovelha *f* sheep; ewe
ovo *m* egg; ~ **escalfado** poach-
  ed egg; ~ **estrelado** fried egg;
  ~ **mexido** scrambled egg; ~**s**
  moles sweet eggs
oxalá! let's hope!, would that!
oxigénio *m* oxygen

P

pá *f* shovel, spade
pacato *adj* peaceful, placid
pachorrento sluggish
paciência *f* patience
paciente *m*, *adj* patient
pacific|ação *f* pacification;
  ~**ar** *v/t*, *v/r* pacify
pacífico *adj* pacific, calm
pacote *m* packet, parcel
pacto *m* pact
padaria *f* bakery
padec|er *v/t*, *v/i* suffer; ~**i-**
  mento *m* suffering
padeiro *m* baker
padrão *m* stone monument;
  pattern, sample; standard
padrasto *m* stepfather
padre *m* priest; Father
padrinho *m* godfather
padroeiro *m* patron saint
paga *f* pay; ~**mento** *m* payment
pagão *m* pagan, heathen
pagar *v/t*, *v/i*, *v/r* pay (for)
página *f* page
pai *m* father
painel *m* panel; painting
paio *m* thick sausage
pais *m/pl* parents
país *m* country
paisagem *f* landscape, country-
side
paisano *m* civilian
paixão *f* passion
palácio *m* palace
paladar *m* taste
palato *m* palate
palavra *f* word
palavrão *m* swear-word
palco *m thea* stage
palerma *m*, *f* simpleton, dolt
palestra *f* talk, chat
palha *f* straw
palhaço *m* clown
palhinha *f* straw
palhota *f* straw hut
paliativo *m* palliative
paliçada *f* palisade
pálido pale, pallid
palito *m* toothpick
palma *f* palm; ~**s** *f/pl* clapping
palmada *f* clap, slap
palmeira *f* palm-tree
palmo *m* span; ~ **a** ~ inch by
  inch; step by step
pálpebra *f* eyelid
palpit|ação *f* palpitation; ~**ante**
  thrilling, exciting; ~**ar** *v/i*
  palpitate; ~**e** *m* presentiment,
  inkling
palrador *m* chatterbox
palrar *v/i* chatter

pancada f blow, knock
pançudo pot-bellied
pândega f spree, frolic, revelry
panela f pot
panfleto m pamphlet
pânico m panic
pano m cloth; ~ **de fundo** back-drop, back-cloth; ~ **de boca** thea curtain
pântano m swamp, marsh
pantera f panther
pantufa f slipper
pão m bread; loaf; ~**zinho** m roll
papa m Pope; f pap
papá m dad(dy), US papa, pop-pa
papagaio m parrot; kite
papai m Braz dad, papa
papeira f mumps
papel m paper; thea role, part; ~ **higiénico** toilet paper; ~**ão** m cardboard; ~**aria** f stationer's (shop); ~**inhos** m/pl confetti; ~**-moeda** m paper-money
papoila f poppy
par m pair; adj even; equal
para for; to; towards; in order to; ~ **que** so that; ~ **quê?** what for?; **estar** ~ be about to
parabéns m/pl congratulations
pára-brisas m wind-screen; ~**-choques** m bumper, buffer
parada f parade; Braz bus stop
parafuso m screw
paragem f bus stop
paraíso m paradise
paralisar v/t, v/i, v/r paralyse
paralisia f paralysis
paralítico adj, m paralytic

parapeito m window-sill
pára-quedas m parachute
parar v/t, v/i stop, halt
pára-raios m lightning-conductor
parceiro m partner
parcial adj partial; ~**idade** f partiality; ~**mente** partly; partially
parco frugal, thrifty
pardal m sparrow
pardo adj grey
parecer v/i, v/r resemble, look like; seem, appear; m opinion; appearance
parecido similar, like, resembling
parede f wall
parelha f pair, couple
parente m relative
parentela f kindred
pargo m sea bream
parir v/t give birth to, bear
parlamento m parliament
parlapatão m braggart
pároco m parish priest
parque m park
parte f part
parteira f midwife
particip|ação f participation; ~**ante**, m f participant; ~**ar** v/t, v/i participate; announce
particular adj particular, peculiar, private
partida f departure; match, game; trick
partidário m partisan
partido m (political) party; adj divided; broken
partilh|a f share; ~**ar** v/t share

partir *v/t, v/i, v/r* break; divide; depart, leave; **a ~ de** from...on
parto *m* child-birth
parvo *adj* stupid
Páscoa *f* Easter
pasm|ar *v/t, v/i, v/r* astonish; **~o** *m* astonishment
passa *f* raisin
passadeira *f* zebra crossing; runner, stair-carpet
passado *m* past; *adj* passed; past, last
passador *m* strainer, colander
passageiro *m* passenger; *adj* transitory; passing
passagem *f* passage; passing; way through; fare
passaporte *m* passport
passar *v/t, v/i, v/r* happen; cross; pass; spend; **~ a ferro** iron, press; **~ por alto** overlook; **não ~ de** be no more than, be only; **~ sem** do without; **passou bem?** how are you?
pássaro *m* bird
passatempo *m* pastime, hobby
passe *m* pass, free pass
passear *v/t, v/i* walk, stroll
passeio *m* walk; pavement, *US* sidewalk; promenade
passivo *adj* passive
passo *m* pace, step, stride; passage; **ao ~ que** while
pasta *f* paste; brief-case; portfolio
past|agem *f* pasturage; **~ar** *v/t, v/i* graze
pastel *m* pie, pastry; pastel
pastelaria *f* confectioner's shop; confectionery
pasto *m* pasture; food
pastor *m* shepherd
pata *f* paw, foot; duck; **à ~** on foot
patamar *m* landing
patear *v/i* kick, stamp
patente *adj, f* patent
patentear *v/t* manifest
paternidade *f* paternity
patife *m* rogue, scoundrel
patim *m* skate; **~ de rodas** roller-skate
patinar *v/i* skate
pátio *m* yard, courtyard
pato *m* drake, duck
patrão *m* master, boss
pátria *f* mother country, fatherland
património *m* patrimony
patrocinar *v/t* sponsor, support
patrocínio *m* patronage
patrulha *f* patrol
patusco *adj* boisterous
pau *m* stick, pole; wood
pausa *f* pause
pauta *f* ruled paper; list
pavão *m* peacock
pavilhão *m* pavilion
pavimento *m* paving; floor, stor(e)y
pavor *m* dread; **~oso** dreadful
paz *f* peace; quiet
pé *m* foot; leg; **~ de vento** gust of wind; **a ~** on foot; **ao ~ de** near, close to; **de/em ~** standing
peão *m* pedestrian; pawn
peça *f* piece; play
peca|do *m* sin; **~dor** *m* sinner; **~r** *v/i* sin

pechincha

pechincha f bargain

peçonh|a f poison; **~ento** poisonous

peculiar peculiar, exclusive

pecúlio m savings, hoard

pedaço m bit, piece, fragment

pedido m request; *com* order

pedir v/t ask (for), request; **~ desculpa** apologize; **~ emprestado** borrow

pedr|a f stone; **~eira** f quarry; **~eiro** m stone-mason

pega f magpie

pega f handle; quarrel

pegada f footprint, trace

pegado stuck; near to

pegar v/t, v/i, v/r start; catch; grasp, seize; take root; glue, stick; **~ fogo a** set fire to; **~ no sono** get to sleep

peito m chest; breast; *fig* heart

peitoril m sill; parapet

peix|e m fish; **~eiro** m fishmonger

pejo m shyness, coyness

pela *contr of* por *and* a

pelar v/t, v/r skin; peal; **~se por** be very fond of

pele f skin; fur

peleja f fight; **~r** v/i fight

pelica f kid (leather)

pelo *contr of* por *and* o

pêlo m hair

peludo *adj* hairy

pena f feather; quill; punishment; grief, sorrow; pity; é **(uma) ~!** it's a pity; **ter ~ de** be sorry for

penal penal; **~idade** f penalty

penar v/i pain, grieve

pendente *adj* pendent; m pendant

pender v/i hang

pendor m slope; propensity

pêndulo m pendulum

pendurar v/t hang up

penedo m rock, boulder

peneira f sieve; **~r** v/t sieve

penetr|ação f penetration; sagacity; **~ante** piercing, penetrating; **~ar** v/t penetrate, pierce; **~ável** penetrable

penha f rock, crag, cliff

penhasco m cliff

penhor m pledge; security; token

penhora f seizure, distraint; **~r** v/t seize, impound, confiscate

península f peninsula

penitência f penance; penitence

penitenciária f penitentiary

penitente m, adj penitent

penoso irksome, laborious

pensamento m thought

pensão f pension; boarding-house

pensar v/t, v/i think; intend to

pensativo thoughtful, pensive

penso m bandage, dressing

pente m comb; **~ado** m coiffure; **~ar** v/t comb

penugem f down, fluff

penúltimo penultimate

penumbra f penumbra

penúria f penury

pepino m cucumber

pequeno *adj* small, little

pêra f (pl peras) pear

perante before, in the presence of

perceber v/t understand; perceive

percentagem *f* percentage

percepção *f* perception

perceptível perceptible

percevejo *m* bedbug; drawing--pin, US thumb-tack

percorrer *v/t* go through, travel all over

percurso *m* course; route

percussão *f* percussion

perda *f* loss

perdão *m* pardon; ~! I'm sorry!

perder *v/t, v/i, v/r* get lost; lose; miss; waste; ~ **de vista** lose sight of

perdido *adj* lost; ~ **de riso** beside oneself with laughter

perdiz *f* partridge

perdo|ar *v/t* pardon, forgive; ~**ável** pardonable, forgivable

perdulário *adj* wasteful; *m* spendthrift

perecer *v/i* perish

peregrin|ação *f* pilgrimage; ~**ar** *v/i* go on a pilgrimage; ~**o** *m* pilgrim

pereira *f* pear-tree

peremptório peremptory

perene perennial

perfazer *v/t* complete

perfeição *f* perfection

perfeito perfect

pérfido perfidious, treacherous

perfil *m* profile

perfilhar *v/t* adopt

perfum|aria *f* perfumery, perfumier's; ~**e** *m* perfume

perfurar *v/t* perforate, bore, drill

pergaminho *m* parchment

pergunta *f* question; ~**r** *v/t, v/i* ask, question

perícia *f* skill

perigo *m* danger, peril; ~**so** dangerous, perilous

periódico *adj* periodical; *m* newspaper

período *m* period

periquito *m* parakeet

perito *adj* skilful, able; *m* expert, connoisseur

perjúrio *m* perjury

perjuro *m* perjurer

permanecer *v/i* remain, stay

perman|ência *f* permanence; stay; ~**ente** *f* perm, US permanent; *adj* permanent

permissão *f* permission

permitir *v/t* permit

permut|a *f* permutation; ~**ar** *v/t* permute; exchange

perna *f* leg

pernicioso pernicious

pernoitar *v/i* spend the night

pérola *f* pearl

perpendicular *adj, f* perpendicular

perpetuar *v/t, v/r* perpetuate

perpétuo perpetual

perplexo perplexed

persa *adj* Persian

perscrutar *v/t* peruse, scan

persegu|ição *f* persecution; ~**ir** *v/t* pursue; persecute

persever|ança *f* perseverance; ~**ante** persevering; ~**ar** *v/i* persevere

persiana *f* Venetian blind

persist|ência *f* persistance; ~**ente** persistent; ~**ir** *v/i* persist

personagem *m, f* character,

personage
personificar v/t personify
perspe(c)tiva f prospect; perspective
perspic|ácia f perspicacity;
~az perspicacious
persuadir v/t, v/i, v/r persuade; convince
persuasão f persuasion
persuasivo persuasive
perten|cente belonging, appertaining; ~cer v/i belong; appertain to
pertin|ácia f pertinacity; ~az pertinacious, stubborn
perto adv close, near; ~ de nearly; nearby; de ~ intimately; closely
perturb|ação f perturbation; ~ar v/t, v/r disturb, perturb
peru m turkey
pesadelo m nightmare
pesado heavy
pêsames m/pl condolences
pesar v/t, v/i, v/r weigh; m sorrow, grief; regret
pesaroso sorry, sorrowful
pesca f fishing
pescada f zo hake, whiting
pescador m fisherman; ~ à linha angler
pescar v/t, v/i fish; ~ à linha angle
pescoço m neck
peso m weight
pesquis|a f search, inquiry; investigation; ~ar v/t search, investigate; prospect for
pêssego m peach
pessimista m, f pessimist
péssimo very bad

pessoa f person
pessoal adj personal; m staff, personnel
pestana f eyelash
peste f plague
petição f petition
petisco m titbit
petiz m child, nipper
petroleiro m oil tanker
petróleo m petroleum; paraffin
petulância f petulance
peúga f sock
pia f sink
piada f joke, wisecrack
piano m piano; ~ de cauda grand piano
piar v/i chirp, cheep
picada f prick; sting
picadeiro m riding-school
picante adj hot, piquant
picar v/t prick; sting
picareta f pickax(e)
pico m peak; e ~ odd, and a bit
piedade f piety; pity
piedoso pious; pitiful
piegas adj soppy, faint-hearted
pijama m pyjamas, US pajamas
pilar m pillar
pilha f pile; battery
pilhar v/t pillage; steal
piloto m pilot
pílula f pill
pimenta f pepper
pimento m paprika
pinça f tweezers
pincel m brush; ~ da barba shaving-brush
pinga f drop; wine
pingar v/i drip; trickle
pingo m drop
pingue-pongue m ping-pong

pinguin *m* penguin

pinh|a *f* pine-cone; crowd; ~al *m* pinewood; ~eiro *m* pine-tree; ~o *m* pine

pino *m* top; handstand; **a ~ per-pendicular**, upright; **no ~ do inverno** in the depth of winter; **no ~ do verão** at the height of summer

pinta *f* spot, mark

pintar *v/t, v/i* paint

pintarroxo *m* robin (redbreast)

pinto *m* chicken

pint|or *m* painter; ~ura *f* painting, picture

piolho *m* louse

pior *adj, adv* worse; ~ar *v/i* get worse

pipa *f* cask, barrel

pires *m* saucer; *adj* silly

pisar *v/t* tread, trample; bruise

pisca-pisca *m* indicator light

piscar *v/t* wink, blink

piscina *f* swimming-pool

piso *m* floor; ground; stor(e)y

pista *f* track; runway

pito *m Braz* pipe

placa *f* plaque; sheet

plácido *adj* placid

planalto *m* plateau

plane(j)ar *v/t* plan (out)

planície *f* plain

plano *m* plan; *adj* flat, level

planta *f* plant; sole; ~ção *f* plantation; ~r *v/t* plant

plataforma *f* platform

plátano *m* plane(-tree)

plateia *f thea* pit, stalls

plausível plausible

pleito *m* lawsuit

plenipotenciário *adj, m* pleni-potentiary

pleno full; absolute

pluma *f* plume

pneu *m* tyre, *US* tire

pneumonia *f* pneumonia

pó *m* powder; dust

pobre *adj* poor; ~za *f* poverty

poça *f* puddle

poço *m* well

poder *v/t, v/i* be able, can; may; *m* power; ~oso powerful

podr|e *adj* rotten; ~e de rico money-bags; ~idão *f* rotten-ness

poeir|a *f* dust; ~ento dusty

poente *m* west

poesia *f* poetry; poem

poeta *m* poet

pois *conj* for; then; as, since; ~ bem well then; ~ é that's it; ~ não of course, certainly; ~ sim oh sure; yes, that's right; ~ quê? why so?

polaco *adj* Polish; *m* Pole

polegar *m* thumb

polémica *f* polemic

polícia *f* police; *m* policeman

policial *m Braz* policeman

polid|ez *f* politeness; ~o *f* polite; polished

polir *v/t* polish

política *f* politics; policy

político *adj* political; *m* politician

pólo *m* pole; polo

poltrona *f* armchair

poluição *f* pollution

polvilhar *v/t* powder

polvo *m* octopus

pólvora *f* gunpowder

pomada *f* ointment

pomar m orchard

pomba f, **pombo** m dove; pigeon

pomp|a f pomp; **~oso** pompous

ponderar v/t, v/i ponder

ponta f point; tip; edge; stub; **nas ~s dos pés** on tiptoe

pontada f stitch, pain

pontapé m kick

ponte f bridge

ponteiro m hand; pointer

ponto m stitch; point, dot, spot

pontual punctual; **~idade** f punctuality

popa f stern, poop

população f population

popular adj popular; **~idade** f popularity

populoso populous

por for; by; through

pôr v/t, v/r put, set; lay; **~se de pé** stand up

porão m hold

porção f portion

porcaria f filth, rubbish

porcelana f porcelain

porco m pig

porém but, however

pormenor m detail

porquanto considering that, seeing that

porque because; why

porquê why

porta f door

porta|-aviões m aircraft carrier; **~-bagagens** m boot, US trunk

portador m bearer, holder

portagem f toll; tollgate

porta-moedas m purse

portanto therefore

portão m gate(way)

portaria f main gate; entrance-hall; decree, order

portar-se v/r behave, conduct

porte m postage; bearing

porteiro m porter, doorkeeper

portento m wonder; **~so** portentous

porto m port, harbo(u)r; **~ franco** m free port

português m, adj Portuguese

porventura by chance, perhaps

posição f position

possante powerful

posse f possession

possibilidade f possibility

possível adj possible

possuidor m possessor

possuir v/t possess

posta f slice; **~-restante** poste restante, US general delivery

postal m postcard; adj postal

poste m post

posteridade f posterity

posterior adj, m posterior

postiço false, artificial

postigo m peep-hole

posto m job, post; military rank; **~ que** although

póstumo posthumous

potável drinkable

pote m pot

potência f power; authority; potency

potente powerful; potent

pouco adj, adv little; **~s** few

poupar v/t, v/i, v/r save; spare

pousada f, inn, hotel

pousar v/t, v/i perch; put, set down

povo *m* people; ~ação *f* population; township

povoar *v/t, v/r* people

praça *f* square; market-place; ~ de touros bullring

prado *m* meadow

praga *f* curse; plague

praguejar *v/t, v/i* curse

praia *f* beach; shore; seaside

pranto *m* weeping, lamentation

prata *f* silver

prateado silvery

prática *f* practice

praticar *v/t* practise

prático *adj* practical

prato *m* plate; dish; course

praxe *f* practice, custom

prazer *m* pleasure; muito ~! how do you do?

prazo *m* period, term; a longo/curto ~ in the long/short term

pré *m* military pay

precário precarious

precaução *f* precaution

precaver *v/t, v/r* guard against

prece *f* prayer

precedência *f* precedence

preceder *v/t, v/i* precede

preceito *m* precept

precios|idade *f* preciousness; ~o precious

precipício *m* precipice

precipit|ação *f* precipitation; rashness; ~ado *adj* rash; *m chem* precipitate; ~ar *v/t, v/i, v/r* precipitate

precis|ão *f* precision, accuracy; ~ar *v/t, v/i* need; ~o necessary; precise

preço *m* price

precoce precocious

preconceito *m* prejudice, preconception

precursor *m* precursor

predestinação *f* predestination

predição *f* prediction

predile(c)ção *f* predilection

prédio *m* building

predizer *v/t* predict

predominar *v/i* predominate

predomínio *m* predominance

preencher *v/t* fill in/up

prefácio *m* preface

prefeito *m* prefect

prefer|ência *f* preference; ~ir *v/t* prefer; ~ível preferable

prega *f* fold, pleat

pregar *v/t, v/i* preach

pregar *v/t* nail; fix; ~ os olhos em fix one's eyes on; ~ uma partida play a trick; não ~ olho not to sleep a wink

prego *m* nail

preguiç|a *f* laziness; ~oso lazy, idle

prejudicar *v/t* damage, harm

prejuízo *m* prejudice; damage

preliminar *m, adj* preliminary

prelúdio *m* prelude

prematuro premature

premedit|ação *f* premeditation; ~ar *v/t* premeditate

premiar *v/t* reward

prémio *m* prize; premium

prenda *f* gift

prender *v/t, v/i, v/r* fasten; seize, grasp; arrest, capture

prenhe pregnant

prensa *f* press

prenúncio *m* presage

preocupação *f* worry; preoccupation

preocupar v/t, v/r worry; preoccupy

prepar|ação f preparation; **~ar** v/t, v/r prepare; **~ativo** m preparation; **~atório** preparatory

preponderante preponderant

prerrogativa f prerogative

presa f prey; talon; claw

prescrever v/t prescribe

prescrição f prescription

presença f presence

presenciar v/t witness, be present at

presente m, adj present

presentear v/t present

presépio m crib

preservar v/t, v/i preserve

presidente m, f president

presidir v/t, v/i preside (over)

preso m prisoner; adj captured, held

pressa f haste, hurry

pressão f pressure

pressentimento m presentiment

pressentir v/t surmise, have a presentiment of

prestação f instalment

prestar v/t, v/r give, render; be good; be suitable for; **~ atenção** pay attention; **~ juramento** take an oath; **não ~ para nada** be of no use

prestes adj ready

prestígio m prestige

préstimo m merit; utility

presumir v/t presume

presunção f presumption

presunto m ham, gammon

pretender v/t claim

pretens|ão f pretence; pretention; **~ioso** pretentious

pretexto m pretext

preto adj black

prevalecer v/i prevail

prevenção f prevention

prevenir v/t, v/r warn; prevent; provide against

prever v/t foresee

previdente farseeing

previsão f foresight; forecast

prezar v/t prize

prima f cousin

primário primary

primavera f spring; bot primrose

primazia f primacy

primeiro adj first

primitivo adj primitive

primo m cousin

principal adj main, principal

príncipe m prince

princip|ante m beginner; **~ar** v/t, v/i begin

princípio m beginning; principle

prioridade f priority

prisão f imprisonment; prison; **~ de ventre** constipation

prisioneiro m prisoner

privada f toilet, lavatory

privado adj private

privar de v/t, v/r deprive of

privilégio m privilege

proa f bow, prow

probabilidade f probability

probidade f probity

problema m problem

probo honest, upright

proceder v/i proceed from; act,

behave

procedimento m behavio(u)r; procedure

processo m process; lawsuit

procissão f procession

proclamar v/t proclaim

procura f search; demand

procuração f proxy

procurador m proxy

procurar v/t look for; try to

prodígio m prodigy

pródigo prodigal

produção f production

produtivo productive

produto m product; produce

produzir v/t produce

proeminente prominent

profan|ar v/t profane; ~o adj profane

profecia f prophecy

proferir v/t utter, pronounce

professor m teacher; professor

profissão f profession

profund|idade f profundity; depth; ~o adj profound; deep

profus|ão f profusion; ~o profuse

prognóstico m prognostic

progredir v/i progress

progresso m progress

proib|ição f prohibition; ~ir v/t prohibit, forbid

proje(c)tar v/t plan; project

proje(c)til m projectile

proje(c)to m plan, project

proje(c)tor m projector

prole f offspring

prolongar v/t, v/r prolong

promessa f promise

prometer v/t, v/i promise

promoção f promotion

promover v/t promote

pronto adj prompt; ready

pronúncia f pronunciation

pronunciar v/t pronounce; utter

propaganda f propaganda

propor v/t, v/i propose

proporção f proportion

proporcionar v/t give, afford

propósito m purpose; **a** ~ by the way; **de** ~ on purpose

proposta f proposal

propriedade f property

proprietário m proprietor, owner

próprio adj own; proper; self

propulsão f propulsion

propulsor adj propellant

próspero adj prosperous

prosseguir v/t, v/i pursue

protagonista m, f protagonist

prote(c)|ção f protection; ~tor m protector

proteger v/t protect

protest|ar v/t, v/i protest; ~o m protest

prova f proof; trial, try-out; test; **à** ~ **de água** waterproof

provar v/t prove; try; test; try on; taste

provável probable, likely

proveito m profit; ~so profitable

prover v/t provide, supply

provérbio m proverb

providência f providence

província f province

provir v/i proceed (**de** from)

provisão f provision

provisório adj provisional

provoc|ação f provocation;

~ar v/t, v/i provoke
proximidade f proximity
próximo adj near, next; m fellow-creature
prudência f prudence
prudente prudent
pseudónimo m pseudonym
psíquico psychic
publicar v/t publish
publicidade f publicity; advertising
público m, adj public
pudim m pudding
pudor m bashfulness, shame
pugilis|mo m boxing; pugilism; ~**ta** m, f boxer, pugilist
pujança f might; vigo(u)r
pular v/i spring, jump, leap
pulga f flea
pulmão m lung
pulo m spring, jerk
pulsação f pulsation
pulseira f bracelet
pulso m pulse; wrist
pulveriz|ador m sprayer; ~**ar** v/t spray; pulverize

punhado m handful
punhal m dagger
punho m fist
pun|ição f punishment; ~**ir** v/t punish; ~**itivo** punitive; ~**ível** punishable
pupila f ward; pupil
pupilo m ward
puré m puree; ~ **de batata** mashed potatoes
pureza f purity
purg|ante m purgative; ~**ar** v/t purge
purific|ação f purification; ~**ar** v/t purify
puro pure; mere, sheer
pus m pus
pústula f pustule
putrefa(c)|ção f putrefaction; ~**to** putrefied
puxa int why! now!
puxador m handle, knob
puxão m tug, pull, jerk
puxar v/t, v/i draw, drag, tug, pull

Q

quadra f square room; time, period; Braz block
quadrado adj, m square
quadril m hip
quadrilha f gang, band
quadro m picture, painting; table, list; black-board; tableau; staff
quádruplo m quadruple
qual pron which, that; int what; adj which
quali|dade f quality; ~**ficação**

f qualification; ~**ficar** v/t qualify
qualquer adj, pron either; any
quando adv, conj when; ~ **menos** at least; **de** ~ **em** ~ from time to time
quantia f sum, amount
quantidade f quantity
quanto adv how; adj, pron how many; how much; all that; ~ **a** as for/to; ~ **antes** as soon as possible; ~ **mais cedo, me-**

lhor the sooner the better; ~ **tempo?** how long?
quarenta forty
quaresma f Lent
quarta-feira f Wednesday
quarteirão m block
quartel m barracks
quarto adj fourth; m quarter; room; ~ **de casal** double room
quase almost, nearly
quatro four
quatrocentos four hundred
que pron who(m), which, that; conj that; than; as; int what a; how; **o** ~ what; he who; **os** ~ those who
quê m something; complication; pron what?; **não tem de** ~ not at all
quebra f rupture, breach; break-age; com bankruptcy
quebra|-gelo m ice-breaker; ~**-luz** f lamp-shade; ~**mar** m breakwater; ~**-nozes** m nut-cracker
quebrant|ar v/t break; weary; ~**o** m prostration; weariness; evil eye
quebrar v/t, v/i break, shatter, smash
queda f fall; downfall; ~ **de água** waterfall
quedar v/i, v/r remain
quedo quiet, still
queijada f cheese-cake
queijo m cheese
queima f burning; ~**dura** f burn; scorch; ~**r** v/t, v/i, v/r tan; burn; **à** ~**-roupa** point-blank

queix|a f complaint; ~**ar-se** v/r grumble; complain; ~**o** m jaw, chin; ~**oso** adj plaintive
quem who; **de** ~ whose; ~ **me dera** I wish I could; ~ **quer que** whoever
quente adj warm, hot
queque m small cake
quer conj either, or; whether
querela f plaint, suit; ~**do** m defendant; ~**nte** m plaintiff; ~**r** v/i sue
querer v/t wish, want; desire; ~ **dizer** mean
querido adj dear, beloved
quest|ão f question; ~**ionar** v/t dispute; question; ~**ioná-rio** m questionnaire
quiçá perhaps
quiet|ação f quietness; ~**o** quiet; ~**ude** f quiet(ude)
quilate m carat; fig excellence, quality
quilha f keel
quilo(grama) m kilo(-gram[me])
quilómetro m kilometre
quimera f chimera
químic|a f chemistry; ~**o** adj chemical; m chemist
quinhão m share, portion
quinhentos five hundred
quinquilharia f hardware
quinta f farm; estate
quinta-feira f Thursday
quintal m yard; quintal
quinto adj fifth
quintuplo adj quintuple
quinze fifteen
quinzena f fortnight
quiosque m kiosk

quisto *m* cyst
quite *adj* free; quits

quota *f* share; quota
quotidiano daily

R

rã *f* frog
rabanada *f* French toast
rabanete *m* radish
rabicho *m* pigtail
rabiscar *v/t, v/i* scrawl, scribble
rabo *m* tail; buttocks
rabugento morose, peevish
rabujar *v/i* be sullen; sulk
raça *f* race, breed
ração *f* ration, portion
rach|a *f* splinter; cleft, chink, slit; **~ar** *v/t, v/i, v/r* cleave, split
racioc|inar *v/i* reason, ratiocinate; **~inio** *m* reasoning
racional *adj* rational
racionalizar *v/t* rationalize
racionar *v/t* ration
radar *m* radar
radi|ação *f* radiation; **~ador** *m* radiator; **~ante** *adj* radiant; beaming
radic|al *adj, m* radical; **~ar** *v/t, v/i, v/r* root
rádio *m* radius; radium; radio set; *f* radio
radio|a(c)tividade *f* radioactivity; **~a(c)tivo** radioactive; **~grafia** *f* radiography; **~logia** *f* radiology; **~terapia** *f* radiotherapy; **~uvinte** *m, f* radio listener
ráfia *f* raffia
raia *f zo* ray, skate; line, stroke, streak

raiar *v/t, v/i* border on; streak, stripe; radiate
rainha *f* queen
raio *m* beam, ray; spoke
raiv|a *f* rage; **~oso** angry, furious
raiz *f (pl raízes)* root
rajada *f* squall, gust, blast
ral|ação *f* worry; **~ador** *m* grater; **~ar** *v/t* grate; vex
ralhar *v/i* scold, rebuke
ram|agem *f* foliage, branches; **~al** *m* branch railway, branch road; **~alhete** *m* bouquet, bunch; **~ificação** *f* ramification; **~ificar** *v/t, v/r* ramify, branch (out); **~o** *m* branch; bunch
rancho *m* mess; band, party; *Braz* shack
rancor *m* ranco(u)r
rançoso rancid
ranger *v/t, v/i* creak; gnash
ranho *m* mucus, snot
ranhura *f* groove, slot
rapar *v/t* scrape
rapariga *f* girl
rapaz *m* boy
rapidez *f* rapidity
rápido *adj* quick, rapid; *m* express train; rapid
rapina *f* plunder
raposa *f* fox
rapt|ar *v/t* abduct, kidnap; **~o** *m* abduction; kidnapping; rapture

raqueta f racket

raridade f rarity

raro adj scarce; rare

rascunho m sketch, draft

rasg|ar v/t, v/r tear, rip; ~o m burst; flight, flash; dash, stroke; **de um ~o** at/with one blow

raso adj level, even, flat

raspar v/t, v/r clear off; scrape, rasp, erase

rastejar v/i creep, crawl

rasto m track, trace, trail

ratazana f rat

ratific|ação f ratification; ~ar v/t ratify

rat|o m mouse; ~oeira f mouse-trap

ratoneiro m pilferer

razão f reason; sense; rate; **ter ~** be right

razoável reasonable

ré f culprit; naut stern

reabastecer v/t replenish

reabilit|ação f rehabilitation; ~ar v/t, v/r rehabilitate

rea(c)ção f reaction

reagir v/i react

real adj real; royal, regal, kingly

real|çar v/t, v/i set off; enhance; ~ce m, ~ço m lustre, distinction

realejo m barrel organ, hurdy-gurdy

realidade f reality

realiz|ação f realization, fulfilment; staging; ~ar v/t, v/r realize, achieve, fulfil; take place; ~ável realizable, feasible

reanimar v/t cheer up; revive

rearmamento m rearmament

reatar v/t tie again; reestablish; renew, resume

reaver v/t recover, get back

rebaixar v/t, v/r lower; demean, debase

rebanho m flock, herd

rebate m alarm; rebate; ~er v/t repel; confute; discount

rebel|de adj rebellious; m rebel; ~ião f rebellion

rebent|ar v/t, v/i burst, explode; break out; ~o m sprout, shoot

reboc|ador m tugboat; ~ar v/t tow

rebolar v/i, v/r tumble, roll

reboque m tow

rebuçado m sweet

recado m message, errand; **mandar ~** send word

reca|ída f relapse; ~ir v/i relapse

recalcitrante adj, m, f recalcitrant

recambiar v/t return, send back

recapitul|ação f recapitulation; ~ar v/t recapitulate

recat|ado retiring; ~ar v/t, v/r safeguard; hide; ~o m prudence, circumspection

recear v/t, v/i, v/r fear

receb|er v/t receive; ~imento m receiving, reception

receio m fear

receit|a f recipe; prescription; ~ar v/t prescribe

recém-nascido m, adj newly born

recense|amento m census; ~ar v/t take a census of

recente recent

receoso fearful, timid

recepção f reception

receptor m receiver

reche|ar v/t stuff, cram; **~io** m force-meat, stuffing

recibo m receipt

recife m reef

recinto m precinct

recipiente m receptacle

reciprocidade f reciprocity

recíproco adj reciprocal

récita f performance, recital

recit|ação f recitation; **~al** m recital; **~ar** v/t recite

reclam|ação f claim, demand; **~ar** v/t, v/i reclaim, claim; demand

reclame m advertisement; catchword

reclinar v/t, v/r recline

reclus|ão f reclusion; **~o** m recluse

recobrar v/t recover, regain

recolher v/t, v/i, v/r retire; gather, collect, assemble

recomend|ação f recommendation; **~ar** v/t recommend; **~ável** recommendable

recompens|a f recompense; reward; **~ar** v/t recompense; reward

reconcili|ação f reconciliation; **~ar** v/t, v/r reconcile

reconfortar v/t strengthen, soothe, relieve

reconhec|er v/t acknowledge; recognize; **~ido** acknowledged; grateful; **~imento** m recognition; acknowledge(e)ment; gratitude; reconnaissance

reconquistar v/t reconquer

reconstituir v/t reconstruct

reconstru|ção f reconstruction; **~ir** v/t reconstruct

record|ação f remembrance, recollection; souvenir; **~ar** v/t, v/r recall; remind

recorrer v/i have recourse; jur appeal

recortar v/t, v/r routline; cut out

recorte m outline; cut-out

recostar v/t lean, rest

recreio m recreation; playground

recruta m recruit

re(c)tidão f rectitude

re(c)tific|ação f rectification; **~ar** v/t rectify

re(c)to adj straight; right; m rectum

recu|ar v/t, v/i recoil; back; **~o** m recoil; retreat

recuper|ação f recuperation; **~ar** v/t recover; recuperate

recurso m recourse; jur appeal; **~s** m/pl resources

recus|a f refusal; **~ar** v/t, v/r refuse

reda(c)ção f editing; wording; editorial staff; composition

reda(c)tor m editor

rede f net

rédea f rein

redenção f redemption

redigir v/t draw up; edit

redobrar v/t, v/i redouble

redondeza f roundness; surroundings

redondo adj round

redor m circuit; **ao ~ de** around ...

redução *f* reduction

reduzir *v/t* reduce

reedição *f* new edition

reedificar *v/t* rebuild

reeducar *v/t* re-educate

reembolso|ar *v/t* reimburse; **~o** *m* reimbursement

refazer *v/t, v/r* remake; do again; restore, rally

refeição *f* meal

refeitório *m* refectory

refém *m* hostage

refer|ência *f* reference; **~ente** referring to; **~ir** *v/t, v/r* refer; relate

refinar *v/t* refine

refinaria *f* refinery

refle|(c)tir *v/t, v/i, v/r* reflect; meditate; **~xão** *f* reflection; **~xivo** reflexive; **~xo** *m, adj* reflex

reforçar *v/t* reinforce

reforço *m* reinforcement

reforma *f* reform; **~ção** *f* reformation; **~r** *v/t* reform

refrescar *v/t, v/i, v/r* refresh; cool

refresco *m* refreshment

refrig|erante *m* cool drink; **~ério** *m* comfort, relief

refugi|ado *m* refugee; **~ar-se** *v/r* take refuge

refúgio *m* refuge

refut|ação *f* refutation; **~ar** *v/t* refute

rega *f* irrigation; **~dor** *m* watering-can

regalar *v/t, v/r* regale (o. s.) on; delight

regal|ia *f* royal prerogative; privilege; **~o** *m* treat, feast

regar *v/t* irrigate, water

regatear *v/t, v/i* haggle; wrangle

regato *m* brook

regelar *v/t* congeal, freeze

regener|ação *f* regeneration; **~ar** *v/t* regenerate

reger *v/t, v/r* rule, govern; *mus* lead

região *f* region

regime *m* regime; diet; regimen

regis|t(r)ar *v/t* register; **~t(r)o** *m* registry; register

rego *m* furrow; rut

regozij|ar *v/t, v/r* delight, gladden; **~o** *m* rejoicing

regra *f* rule

regress|ar *v/i* return; **~o** *m* return

régua *f* ruler

regulamento *m* regulation, rule

regular *v/t, v/i* adjust; regulate; *adj* regular; normal; **~idade** *f* regularity

regularizar *v/t* regularize

rei *m* king

reimpressão *f* reprint

reinado *m* reign

reinar *v/i* reign, rule

reino *m* kingdom

reintegrar *v/t* reinstate

reitor *m* rector; headmaster

reivindic|ação *f* claim; **~ar** *v/t* claim

rejeitar *v/t* reject; refuse

relação *f* relation

relacionar *v/t, v/r* connect; become acquainted with

relâmpago *m* lightning

relampaguear *v/i* lighten

relat|ar *v/t* relate; **~o** *m* account; **~ório** m report

relaxar v/t, v/r relax, slacken

relevo m relief

religi|ão f religion; **~osa** f nun; **~oso** adj, m religious

relinchar v/i whinny, neigh

relógio m clock; watch

relojoeiro m watch-maker

relut|ância f reluctance; **~ante** reluctant

reluzir v/i gleam

relva f lawn; grass

relvado m lawn

remar v/t, v/i row

remat|ar v/t end, conclude; **~e** m end, conclusion

remediar v/t remedy

remédio m remedy

remend|ar v/t mend; patch; **~o** m patch

reme|ssa f remittance; shipment; **~tente** m sender, remitter; **~ter** v/t send, remit

remexer v/t stir again; rummage

reminiscência f reminiscence

remir v/t redeem; ransom

remo m oar

remoinho m whirl(pool)

remontar v/i go back to

remorso m remorse

remoto remote

remover v/t remove

remuner|ação f remuneration; **~ar** v/t remunerate

renascença f renascence, renaissance

renascer v/i be born again

renda f rent; income; lace

rend|er v/t, v/i, v/r subdue; produce; surrender; **~ição** f

surrender; **~ido** conquered; ruptured; **~imento** m income; profit; **~oso** profitable

renhido fierce

renit|ência f resistance; reluctance; **~ente** recalcitrant

renome m renown

renov|ação f renovation; renewal; **~ar** v/t renovate; renew

renúncia f renunciation

renunciar a v/t renounce

reorganiz|ação f reorganization; **~ar** v/t reorganize

repar|ação f reparation; repair; **~ar** v/t, v/i repair, mend; notice

reparo m attention, notice

repart|ição f distribution; department; **~ir** v/t distribute, share out

repatriar v/t, v/r repatriate

repel|ão m pull; push, shove; **~ir** v/t repel

repentino sudden

repercussão f repercussion

repertório m repertoire

repet|ição f repetition; **~ir** v/t, v/i, v/r repeat

repleto replete, full

réplica f retort, reply

replicar v/t, v/i retort, reply

repolho m savoy (cabbage)

repor v/t replace, restore

report|agem f report, reportage; **~ar** v/t refer to

repórter m reporter

reposição f restitution

reposteiro m hangings, US drapery

repous|ar v/i rest, repose; **~o**

m rest, repose
repreen|der *v/t* rebuke, scold; **~são** *f* rebuke
represa *f* dam
represent|ação *f* representation; performance, **~ante** *m, f; adj* representative; **~ar** *v/t, v/i* represent; perform
repressão *f* repression
reprimir *v/t* repress
reprodu|ção *f* reproduction; **~zir** *v/t, v/r* reproduce
reprov|ação *f* reproof; failure; **~ar** *v/t* fail; reprove; disapprove; **~ável** blameworthy
república *f* republic
rep|udiar *v/t* repudiate; **~údio** *m* repudiation
repugn|ância *f* repugnance; **~ar** *v/i* be repugnant
repulsa *f* repulsion; repulse
reputação *f* reputation
repuxo *m* jet, fountain
requeijão *m* curd
requentar *v/t* warm up/over
requer|er *v/t* require; **~imento** *m* request, application
requinte *m* refinement; acme
requisi|ção *f* requisition; **~tar** *v/t* requisition; **~to** *m* requisite
rés-do-chão *m* ground floor
reserv|a *f* reserve; reservation; **~ado** *adj* booked; reserved; **~ar** *v/t* reserve; book; **~atório** *m* reservoir
resfri|ado *adj* cooled; *m* cold; **~amento** *m* chill, cold; **~ar** *v/t, v/i, v/r* cool; catch (a) cold
resgat|ar *v/t* ransom; **~e** *m* ransom

resguard|ar *v/t* preserve; defend; protect; **~o** *m* protection; defence
resid|ência *f* residence; **~ente** *adj* resident; **~ir** *v/i* reside
resíduo *m* residue
resign|ação *f* resignation; **~ar** *v/t, v/r* resign
resina *f* resin
resist|ência *f* resistance; **~ente** *adj* resistant; **~ir (a)** *v/i* resist
resmungar *v/t, v/i* mumble, grumble
resolução *f* resolution
resolver *v/t, v/r* solve; resolve; decide
respe(c)tivo respective
respeit|ar *v/t, v/i* respect; concern; **~ável** respectable; **~o** *m* respect; **a ~o de,** **com ~o a** with respect to
respir|ação *f* respiration, breathing; **~ar** *v/t, v/i* breathe
resplandecer *v/i* shine, glow
resplendor *m* brightness; splendo(u)r
responder *v/i* answer, reply, respond
responsabili|dade *f* responsibility; **~zar** *v/t, v/r* be responsible for
responsável responsible
resposta *f* answer, reply, response
ressaltar *v/t, v/i* emphasize; jut out; rebound
ressentido resentful
ressentir *v/t, v/r* resent
ressequido parched, withered
ressurgir *v/i* reappear

ressurreição f resurrection

restabelec|er v/t, v/r re-establish; recover

restar v/i be left over, remain

restaur|ação f restoration; **~ante** m restaurant; **~ar** v/t restore

restitu|ição f restitution; **~ir** v/t give back

resto m rest, remainder; **de ~** besides

restrição f restriction

restringir v/t restrict

result|ado m result; **~ar** v/i result from/in; turn out

resum|ir v/t abridge, sum up, summarize; **~o** m summary

resvalar v/i slip, glide, slide

retalh|ar v/t shred; **~o** m shred, scrap; **a ~o** by retail

retardar v/t delay, retard

ret|enção f retention; **~er** v/t retain; withhold

retesar v/t stretch, tighten

retir|ada f retreat; withdrawal; **~ar** v/t, v/r withdraw; retreat

retocar v/t retouch, touch up

retomar v/t resume

retorcer v/t twist, wind; writhe, wriggle

retornar v/t return

retorquir v/t, v/i retort

retra|imento m reserve; retirement; **~ir** v/t, v/r retract, draw back, withdraw

retrato m portrait

retrete f lavatory, toilet

retribu|ição f retribution; **~ir** v/t reciprocate

retroceder v/i recede

retrógrado adj retrograde

retrospe(c)tivo retrospective

retumbar v/i resound

réu m accused, culprit

reun|ião f meeting; gathering; reunion; **~ir** v/t, v/r reunite, join, gather, meet

revel|ação f revelation; development; **~ar** v/t, v/r develop; reveal

rever v/t, v/r review, revise

rever|ência f reverence; **~ente** reverent

revés m setback, reverse; **ao ~** wrong way round; upside-down

revezar v/t, v/i, v/r alternate

reviravolta f turn, veering

revis|ão f revision; **~or** m ticket collector

revista f review; magazine; revue

revistar v/t search; examine

reviver v/t revive

revogar v/t revoke

revolta f revolt

revoltar v/t, v/r revolt

revolução f revolution

revolver v/t stir; spin, revolve; roll

revólver m revolver

rezar v/t, v/i pray

riacho m brook, stream

riba f cliff, high bank

ribalta f footlights

ribeir|a f riverside; riverbank; small river; **~o** m brook, stream

ribombar v/i thunder

rico rich

ridículo ridiculous

rifa f raffle

rifão *m* proverb, adage

rifar *v/t* raffle

rigidez *f* rigidity

rígido rigid

rigor *m* rigo(u)r, severity

rijo sturdy, hard

rim *m* kidney

rima *f* rhyme

rio *m* river

riqueza *f* wealth; riches

rir *v/i*, *v/r* laugh

risada *f* laughter

risca *f* parting, *US* part; stripe; **à ~** exactly

riscar *v/t* cross out/off, delete

risco *m* risk; stroke; streak

riso *m* laugh(ter)

risonho smiling, cheerful

ríspido harsh, severe

rival *m* rival; **~idade** *f* rivalry; **~izar** *v/i* vie

rixa *f* brawl, row

robalo *m* snook

robe *m* dressing-gown

robust|ecer *v/t*, *v/i*, *v/r* fortify; grow robust; **~o** robust

roçar *v/t*, *v/i* graze, skim

roch|a *f* rock; **~edo** *m* crag, cliff; **~oso** rocky

roda *f* wheel

rodagem *f* set of wheels; **em ~ auto** running in

rodar *v/t*, *v/i* roll; *m* rumbling, rattling, rolling

rodear *v/t* surround

rodopi|ar *v/i* spin; **~o** *m* spin

rodovia *f* high road, *US* highway

roer *v/t*, *v/i* gnaw, nibble

rogo *m* request, entreaty

rojar *v/i*, *v/r* trail

rol *m* list; **~ de roupa** laundry list

rola *f* turtle-dove

rolar *v/t*, *v/i*, *v/r* roll

roldana *f* pulley

roleta *f* roulette

rolha *f* cork

rolo *m* roll

romã *f* pomegranate

romanc|e *m* novel; romance; **~ista** *m*, *f* novelist

românico *adj* Romance

romano *adj*, *m* Roman

romântico *adj*, *m* romantic

romantismo *m* romanticism

romaria *f* pilgrimage; popular festival

romeno *m*, *adj* Rumanian

romper *v/t* break; burst

roncar *v/i* snore

rond|a *f* watch, patrol; **~ar** *v/t*, *v/i* pratrol; haunt; prowl, lurk

ros|a *f* rose; **~ário** *m* rosary

rosbife *m* roast beef

rosca *f* worm; coil

roseira *f* rose

rosnar *v/i* growl, snarl

rosto *m* face

rota *f* route, course

rotação *f* rotation

roteiro *m* guide-book

roto torn; broken

rotular *v/t* label

rótulo *m* label

rotura *f* breach; rupture

roub|ar *v/t*, *v/i* rob, steal; **~o** *m* theft, robbery

rouco hoarse

roupa *f* clothes; laundry, wash

roupão *m* dressing-gown

rouquidão *f* hoarseness

rouxinol _m_ nightingale
roxo _adj_ purple, violet
rua _f_ street
rubor _m_ blush; shame
rubrica _f_ rubric; caption; initials
rubricar _v/t_ caption; initial
rude rude, primitive, rough
rudimento _m_ rudiment
ruga _f_ wrinkle; crease
rugir _v/i_ roar
ruido _m_ noise; din
ruim bad, evil, wicked

ruína _f_ ruin
ruir _v/i_ collapse, crumble, fall in
ruivo _adj_ red-haired
ruminar _v/i_ ruminate
rumo _m_ direction, course
rumor _m_ rumo(u)r; noise; **~e-jar** _v/i_ rustle; babble; murmur
rural rural
rusga _f_ scuffle; roundup, mass arrest
russo _m, adj_ Russian
rústico rustic
rutilar _v/i_ shimmer

S

sábado _m_ Saturday
sabão _m_ soap
sab|edoria _f_ wisdom; **~er** _v/t, v/i_ know; know, can; taste; _m_ knowledge, learning; **a ~namely**
sábio _adj_ wise, learned
sabonete _m_ toilet soap
sabor _m_ flavo(u)r, taste; **~ear** _v/t, v/r_ taste; savo(u)r; relish; **~oso** tasty, savo(u)ry
sabotagem _f_ sabotage
sabotar _v/t_ sabotage
saca _f_ sack, large bag
sacada _f_ balcony
sacar _v/t_ draw, take out
saca-rolhas _m_ cork-screw
sacerdote _m_ priest
saci|ar _v/t, v/r_ sate, satiate; **~edade** _f_ satiety
saco _m_ bag
sacrificar _v/t, v/r_ sacrifice
sacrifício _m_ sacrifice
sacrilégio _m_ sacrilege
sacrílego sacrilegious

sacro holy, sacred
sacudir _v/t, v/r_ jolt; shake
sadio healthy, wholesome
safanão _m_ shove, jerk
safar-se _v/r_ clear off
sagaz wise, sagacious
sagrado _adj_ sacred
saia _f_ skirt
saibro _m_ gravel
saída _f_ way out; exit; departure; sally, quip
sair _v/i, v/r_ come out; take after; turn out; go out; leave; depart
sal _m_ salt
sala _f_ room
salada _f_ salad
salão _m_ saloon; salon
salário _m_ salary, pay
saldar _v/t_ balance, settle
saldo _m_ sale; balance, surplus
salgar _v/t_ salt
salgueiro _m_ willow-tree
salient|ar _v/t, v/r_ set off, enhance; stand out; **~e** salient

se

salitre *m* saltpetre
saliva *f* saliva
salmão *m* salmon
salmoura *f* pickle, brine
salpicar *v/t* spatter, splash; sprinkle
salsa *f* parsley
salsicha *f* sausage
saltar *v/i* jump, leap
saltitar *v/i* hop, skip
salto *m* jump, leap
salubre *adj* healthy, wholesome, salubrious
salutar salutary
salva *f* sage; salvo; salver
salvação *f* salvation
salva|dor *m* savio(u)r; rescuer; **~guarda** *f* safeguard; **~mento** *m* salvage; rescue; safety
salvar *v/t, v/r* save; rescue; salvage
salva-vidas *m* lifeboat; lifebelt
salvo *prp* except, save; *adj* safe; **a ~** in safety; **~ erro** if I'm not mistaken; **~-conduto** *m* safe conduct
sanção *f* sanction
sancionar *v/t* sanction
sandália *f* sandal
sanduíche *m* sandwich
saneamento *m* sanitation
sanear *v/t* cleanse; make sanitary
sangrar *v/t, v/i* bleed; **~ento** bleeding, bloody
sangue *m* blood; **~-frio** *m* sang-froid; **a ~-frio** in cold blood
sanguíneo *adj* sanguine
sanha *f* wrath
sanitário sanitary

sant|idade *f* sanctity, holiness; **~ificar** *v/t* sanctify; **~o** *m* saint; *adj* holy; **~uário** *m* sanctuary
são *adj* sane; sound, healthy, wholesome; *abbr of* **santo;** **~ e salvo** safe and sound
sapador *m* sapper
sapat|aria *f* shoe-shop; **~eiro** *m* shoemaker; **~o** *m* shoe
sapiência *f* wisdom
sapo *m* toad
saque *m* sack, pillage; *com* draft; **~ar** *v/t* sack, pillage
saraiva *f* hail; **~r** *v/i* hail
sarampo *m* measles
sarar *v/t, v/i* heal; cure
sarau *m* soirée, party
sarda *f* mackerel; freckle
sardinha *f* sardine
sargaço *m* seaweed
sargento *m* sergeant
sarilho *m* hubbub, mess
sarna *f* itch
satélite *m* satellite
sátira *f* satire
satisfa|ção *f* satisfaction; **~tório** satisfactory; **~zer** *v/t, v/i, v/r* satisfy
satisfeito satisfied
saturar *v/t* saturate
saud|ação *f* salutation, greeting; **~ade** *f* longing, yearning, nostalgia; **~ar** *v/t* greet; salute
saudável healthy
saúde *f* health
saudoso longing, yearning
sazonado ripe; experienced
se *conj* if; *pron* oneself; one; himself; herself; itself; themselves; yourself; yourselves

sé *f* cathedral; see

seara *f* corn field

sebe *f* hedge

sebento dirty, greasy

sebo *m* tallow

seca *f* drought

secador *m* hair-drier/dryer

secar *v/t, v/i, v/r* dry

se(c)ção *f* section

sécia *f* bot aster

seco dry

secreção *f* secretion

secretaria *f* office; secretariat

secretária *f* desk; secretary

secretário *m* secretary

secreto *adj* secret

se(c)tor *m* sector

secular *adj* age-old; secular

século *m* century

secundar *v/t* second

secundário secondary

secura *f* dryness

seda *f* silk

sedativo *m, adj* sedative

sede *f* thirst

sede *f* see; seat

sedentário *adj* sedentary

sedento thirsty

sedimento *m* sediment

sedoso silky

sedu|ção *f* seduction; allure; **~tor** *adj* seductive; **~zir** *v/t* seduce; entice

seg|a *f* reaping; harvest; **~ar** *v/t* mow, reap

segredar *v/t, v/i* whisper

segredo *m* secret; secrecy

segreg|ação *f* segregation; **~ar** *v/t* segregate

seguida *f* following; **em ~** afterwards, thereupon, next

seguinte *adj, m* following

seguir *v/t, v/i* follow; carry on, continue

segunda-feira *f* Monday

segundo *m, adj* second; *prp* according to

segur|ança *f* safety; security; assurance; **~ar** *v/t, v/r* insure; grasp, seize; secure; **~o** *adj* safe, secure; *m* insurance

seio *m* breast; bosom

seis six

seiscentos six hundred

seita *f* sect

seiva *f* sap

seixo *m* pebble

sela *f* saddle

selar *v/t* saddle; seal

sele(c)|ção *f* selection; **~cionar** *v/t* select; **~ta** *f* anthology; **~to** *adj* select

selim *m* (bicycle-)saddle

selo *m* seal; stamp

selva *f* jungle

selvagem *adj, m, f* savage

sem without

semáforo *m* semaphore; traffic light/signal

semana *f* week; **~l** *adj* weekly

semanário *m* weekly

semblante *m* countenance

semear *v/t* sow

semelhan|ça *f* resemblance; **~te** *adj* alike, similar, like; such a

sement|e *f* seed; **~eira** *f* seed-time; sowing

semestr|al half-yearly; **~e** *m* half-year

seminário *m* seminary; seminar

sêmola *f* semolina

sem-par matchless

sempiterno everlasting

sempre always; still; ever; ~ que whenever

senado *m* senate; ~r *m* senator

senão *conj* otherwise, or else; *prp* but; except; ~ quando all of a sudden

senda *f* (foot-)path

senha *f* password; voucher

senhor *m* master; lord; sir; mister, Mr.; o ~ you; ~a *f* lady; mistress; madam; Mrs.; ~ia *f* landlady; ~il ladylike; lordly; ~inha *f* miss; ~io *m* landlord; ~ita *f Braz* miss

senil senile; ~idade *f* senility

sensa|ção *f* sensation; ~cional sensational

sensat|ez *f* good sense; ~o sensible

sensibilidade *f* sensibility

sensibilizar *v/t, v/r* move, touch; sensitize

sensível sensitive; perceptible

senso *m* sense

sensual sensual

sentado sitting, seated

sentar-se *v/r* sit down

senten|ça *f* sentence, judg(e)ment; maxim; ~ciar *v/t, v/i* sentence

sentido *m* sense; meaning; direction; *adj* hurt, sensitive; sorrowful, grieved

sentiment|al sentimental; ~o *m* feeling; sentiment

sentinela *f* sentry

sentir *v/t, v/i, v/r* feel; sense; regret

separ|ação *f* separation; ~adamente separately; ~ar *v/t, v/r* part with; separate

sepulcro *m* sepulchre, tomb

sepult|ar *v/t* bury; ~ura *f* grave

sequência *f* sequence

sequestr|ação *f* sequestration; kidnapping; ~ar *v/t* sequestrate; kidnap

séquito *m* retinue

ser *v/i* exist, be; *m* being; ~ de belong to; come from, *US* hail from; be made of; a não ~ que unless

serão *m* soirée, party; overtime, night-work

sereia *f* mermaid; siren

serenar *v/t, v/i* calm

serenidade *f* serenity

sereno *adj* serene

série *f* series

seriedade *f* seriousness

seringa *f* syringe

sério *adj* earnest; serious

sermão *m* sermon

serpente *f* serpent

serpentear *v/i* meander, wind

serpentina *f* paper-streamer

serra *f* saw; mountain range

serralheiro *m* locksmith

serran|ia *f* ridge of mountains; ~o *m* mountain-dweller

serrar *v/t* saw

serrote *m* handsaw

sertã *f* frying-pan, *US* skillet

sertanejo *m* backwoodsman

sertão *m* backwoods; hinterland

servente *m, f* servant

serviçal *adj* obliging; *m* servant

serviço *m* service; **de ~** on duty
servidor *m* servant
servir *v/t, v/i, v/r* help oneself; use; suit; serve; avail o.s. of
servo *m* serf
sessão *f* session; sitting
sessenta sixty
sesta *f* siesta
seta *f* arrow
sete seven; **~centos** seven hundred
Setembro *m* September
setenta seventy
setentrional *adj* northern
sétimo *adj* seventh
seu, sua *adj, pron* his; her(s); its; your(s); their(s)
sever|idade *f* severity; **~o** severe
sexo *m* sex
sexta-feira *f* Friday
sexto *adj* sixth
sezão *f* intermittent fever
si *pron* himself; herself; itself; oneself; yourself; themselves; yourselves; you
sibilante sibilant; hissing
sibilar *v/i* hiss, whistle
siderurgia *f* iron and steel industry
sidra *f* cider
sifão *m* siphon
sigilo *m* secret; secrecy
signatário *m* signatory
signific|ação *f* significance; meaning; **~ado** *m* meaning; **~ar** *v/t* signify; mean
signo *m* sign
sílaba *f* syllable
silêncio *m* silence
silencioso silent

silhueta *f* silhouette
silvar *v/i* whistle; hiss
silvestre wild
silvicultura *f* forestry
sim *adv* yes
símbolo *m* symbol
similar *adj* similar
simpatia *f* sympathy
simpático *adj* nice, friendly
simpatizar *v/i* like, take to
simples *adj* simple
simplicidade *f* simplicity
simplificar *v/t* simplify
simulacro *m* sham, pretence
simular *v/t* simulate
simultâneo simultaneous
sina *f* fate, lot, destiny
sinal *m* sign; signal; **~ de alarme** alarm-signal; communication cord; **~ horário** time-signal; **~eiro** *m* signal-man; traffic warden
sinalização *f* traffic signals
sincer|idade *f* sincerity; **~o** sincere
síncope *f* syncope; faint
sindicalismo *m* syndicalism
sindicato *m* syndicate; trade/labour union
singel|eza *f* simplicity; **~o** single; simple, plain
singular *adj* singular; odd, strange; **~idade** *f* singularity
sinistro *adj* sinister; *m* disaster, accident; damage
sino *m* bell
síntese *f* synthesis
sintético synthetic
sintoma *m* symptom
sintonizar *v/t* tune in
sinuos|idade *f* sinuosity; **~o**

solicitar

sinuous

sismo *m* earthquake
siso *m* sense; judg(e)ment
sistema *m* system
sisudo *adj* sensible, judicious
sítio *m* place, spot; site; siege
sito *adj* situated
situa|ção *f* situation; **~ar** *v/t* situate
só *adj* alone; *adv* only; merely
soalho *m* floor
soar *v/t, v/i* sound
sob under, beneath
sobej|ar *v/i* be left over; **~o** *adj* excessive; **~os** *m/pl* left-overs
soberan|ia *f* sovereignty; **~o** *adj m* sovereign
soberb|a *f* pride; **~o** *adj* proud
sobra *f* excess, surplus
sobrado *m* floor
sobranceiro *adj* overlooking, overhanging; *fig* haughty
sobrancelha *f* eyebrow
sobrar *v/i* be left over
sobras *f/pl* left-overs, remains
sobre *prp* on, over, above
sobrecarga *f* overload
sobrecarregar *v/t* overload
sobreiro *m* cork-oak
sobremaneira *adv* excessively
sobremesa *f* dessert
sobrenome *m* surname
sobrepor *v/t* superimpose
sobrescrito *m* envelope
sobressair *v/i* stand out; overtop
sobressalt|ar *v/t, v/r* startle, frighten; **~o** *m* sudden fear, start
sobresselente *adj* spare
sobretaxa *f* surtax, surcharge

sobretudo *adv* above all, especially; *m* overcoat
sobrevir *v/i* occur
sobreviv|ente *m, f* surviver; **~er** *v/i* survive; outlive
sobriedade *f* sobriety
sobrinha *f* niece
sobrinho *m* nephew
sóbrio sober; frugal
social social
socialista *adj, m, f* socialist
socializar *v/t* socialize
sociável sociable
sociedade *f* society; **~ anónima** joint-stock company
sócio *m* associate, partner
sociologia *f* sociology
soco *m* blow, cuff, sock
soçobrar *v/t, v/i* overturn, capsize
socorr|er *v/t, v/r* rescue; resort to; help, aid; **~o** *m* aid, help, assistance
sôfrego greedy
sofr|er *v/t, v/i* suffer; **~imento** *m* suffering
sogra *f* mother-in-law
sogro *m* father-in-law
sol *m* sun; sunshine
sola *f* sole
solar *m* manor-house
solavanco *m* jolt, jerk, bump
soldado *m* soldier
soldar *v/t* solder
soldo *m* military pay
soleira *f* threshold
solen|e solemn; **~idade** *f* solemnity
soletrar *v/t, v/i* spell out
solh|a *f* flounder; **~o** *m* plaice
solicit|ação *f* solicitation; **~ar**

v/t, v/i solicit

solícito solicitous
solidão *f* solitude, loneliness
solidariedade *f* solidarity
solidário joint, common
solid|ez *f* solidity; **~ificar** *v/t* solidify
sólido *adj, m* solid
solitária *f* tapeworm
solitário *adj* solitary, alone, lonely
solo *m* soil
sol|-pôr *m*, **-posto** *m* sunset
solstício *m* solstice
soltar *v/t, v/r* let out; release; untie, loosen, set loose
solteir|ão *m* bachelor; **~o** *adj* single, unmarried; **~ona** *f* spinster
solto loose, free
soltura *f* freeing; looseness
solução *f* solution
soluçar *v/i* sob
solucionar *v/t* solve
soluço *m* sob
solúvel soluble
solv|ência *f* solvency; **~ente** solvent
solver *v/t* repay
som *m* sound
soma *f* sum
somar *v/t, v/i* add up, tot up
sombr|a *f* shadow; shade; tinge; **à ~ de** in the shade; under; **nem por ~s** not in the least; **~ear** *v/t* shade; **~inha** *f* sunshade; **~io** *adj* dark, shady; sombre
somenos of little worth
somente only
sonante sounding, sonorous

sond|a *f* probe; plummet; **~ar** *v/t* sound, probe, plumb
soneca *f* nap, snooze
sonegar *v/t* conceal
soneto *m* sonnet
sonh|ador *m* dreamer; **~ar** *v/t, v/i* dream
sonho *m* dream; fritter
sono *m* sleep; **com ~** sleepy
sonoro sonorous
sopa *f* soup
sopé *m* foot, base
sopeira *f* soup tureen; maid
soprar *v/t, v/i* blow
sopro *m* puff, blow
sórdido sordid
soro *m* serum, whey
sorr|idente smiling; **~ir** *v/i* smile; **~iso** *m* smile
sort|e *f* fate, lot; luck; **~ear** *v/t* raffle; draw lots; **~eio** *m* draw, raffle
sortido *m* assortment
sorver *v/t* sip
sorvete *m* ice-cream
sorvo *m* sip
sósia *m, f* double
sossegado quiet, calm
sossegar *v/t, v/i, v/r* quiet(en), calm (down)
sossego *m* quiet, calm, peace
sótão *m* garret, loft, attic
sotaque *m* accent
soterrar *v/t* bury
soturno *adj* sullen, morose
sova *f* beating, hiding
sovaco *m* arm-pit
sovar *v/t* knead; trash
soviético Soviet
sovin|a *adj* miserly; **~ice** *f* avarice, stinginess

sozinho alone
suar v/i sweat, perspire
suav|e suave; smooth, soft; gentle; mild; **~idade** f gentleness; mildness
suavizar v/t soften, soothe
subalterno m subaltern
subconsciente m subconscious
sú(b)dito m subject
subdivi|dir v/t subdivide; **~são** f subdivision
subentender v/t assume, understand
subida f ascent, way up; rise
subir v/i go up, climb up, mount, ascend; rise; raise
súbito adj sudden; **de ~** suddenly
subjugar v/t subjugate
sublev|ação f insurrection; **~ar** v/t, v/r raise, revolt
sublime adj sublime
sublinhar v/t underline
sublocar v/t sublease, sublet
submarino m, adj submarine
submergir v/t submerge
submeter v/t subject; submit
submissão f submission
submisso submissive
subordin|ação f subordination; **~ado** adj, m subordinate; **~ar** v/t subordinate
suborn|ar v/t bribe, suborn; **~o** m bribery; bribe
subscrever v/t, v/i subscribe
subscrição f subscription
subsequente subsequent
subsidiar v/t subsidize
subsídio m subsidy; allowance
subsistência f subsistence
subsistir v/i subsist
subsolo m subsoil
substância f substance
substancial adj substantial
substitu|ição f substitution; **~ir** v/t substitute
substituto m substitute
subterfúgio m subterfuge
subterrâneo adj underground, subterranean
subtil adj subtle
subtra(c)ção f subtraction
subtrair v/t subtract
subúrbio m suburb
subven|ção f grant, allowance; **~cionar** v/t subsidize
subversivo subversive
subverter v/t subvert
sucata f scrap iron
suceder v/i, v/r succeed; happen
sucessão f succession
sucesso m success; event, happening
sucinto succinct
suco m juice
suculento succulent
sucumbir v/i succumb
sucursal f com branch
su(d)este m south-east
sudoeste m south-west
sueco m Swede; adj Swedish
suficiente adj sufficient
sufoc|ação f suffocation; **~ar** v/t, v/i suffocate
sufrágio m suffrage
sugar v/t suck
sugerir v/t suggest
sugestão f suggestion
sugestivo suggestive
suicidar-se v/r commit suicide

suicídio *m* suicide
suíço *m, adj* Swiss
sujar *v/t, v/r* dirty, soil
sujeição *f* subjection
sujeitar *v/t, v/r* subject
sujeito *m gram* subject; chap, fellow, bloke
sujidade *f* dirt, filth
sujo dirty, filthy
sul *m* South, south
sulc|ar *v/t* plough, furrow; **~o** *m* furrow
suma *f* sum; **em ~** in short
sumarento juicy, succulent
sumário *m, adj* summary
sumir *v/t, v/r* vanish, disappear; sink; hide
sumo *m* juice
sumptuoso, *Braz* **suntuoso** sumptuous
suor *m* sweat, perspiration
superabundar *v/i* be superabundant
superar *v/t* surmount; surpass; overcome
superficial superficial
superfície *f* surface
supérfluo *adj* superfluous
superior *adj* superior; upper; **~idade** *f* superiority
superstição *f* superstition
supersticioso *adj* superstitious
supervisão *f* supervision
suplantar *v/t* supplant
suplement|ar supplementary; **~o** *m* supplement
suplente *m, f* substitute
súplica *f* supplication
suplicar *v/t* beg, implore, entreat
suplício *m* torment; torture

supor *v/t* suppose
suport|ar *v/t* support; put up with; **~ável** tolerable, endurable
suporte *m* support
suposição *f* supposition
suposto *adj* supposed; **~ que** supposing that
supremacia *f* supremacy
supremo *adj* supreme
supressão *f* suppression
suprimir *v/t* suppress
suprir *v/t* supply; make up for, do duty for
surdez *f* deafness
surdo *adj* deaf
surdo-mudo *adj* deaf and dumb; *m* deaf-mute
surgir *v/i* surge, arise; emerge, appear
surpreend|ente surprising; **~er** *v/t* surprise
surpresa *f* surprise
surra *f* thrashing
surtir *v/t, v/i* occasion; turn out, result; **~ efeito** take effect
susce(p)tibilidade *f* susceptibility
susce(p)tível susceptible, tender
suscitar *v/t* stir up, raise
suspeit|a *f* suspicion; **~ar** *v/t, v/i* suspect; **~o** *adj, m* suspect; **~oso** suspicious
suspender *v/t* suspend
suspensão *f* suspension
suspensórios *m/pl* braces, US suspenders
suspir|ar *v/t, v/i* sigh; **~o** *m* sigh; meringue
sussurrar *v/i* rustle; babble

tasca

sussurro *m* murmur, whisper
sustentáculo *m* prop, stay, support
sustent|ar *v/t, v/r* support, prop up; maintain; live on; **~o**

m maintenance; sustenance
suster *v/t* sustain; support; hold up
susto *m* fright
sutiã *m* bra

T

tabac|aria *f* tobacconist's (shop); **~o** *m* tobacco
tabela *f* list, table, schedule
tabelião *m* notary (public)
taberna *f* inn; bar
tábua *f* board; list, table
tabuleiro *m* tray; garden bed; landing
tabuleta *f* signboard
taça *f* wine-glass; cup
tacão *m* heel
tacha *f* tack, stud; blemish
tacho *m* pan
tácito tacit
taciturno taciturn
ta(c)tear *v/i* grope, fumble
tá(c)tica *f* tactics
ta(c)to *m* touch; tact
tagarel|ar *v/i* prattle; **~ice** *f* prattle, chatter
tal *adj, pron* such (a); like
talão *m* heel; counterfoil, stub
talento *m* talent; **~so** talented
talha *f* carving
talhada *f* slice
talhar *v/t, v/i* cut, carve, slice; curdle
talher *m* cover; place
talho *m* butcher's (shop)
talo *m* stem, stalk; shaft
taluda *f* top lottery prize
talvez perhaps, maybe
tamanco *m* wooden clog

tamanho *m* size
tâmara *f* date
também *int* really; *adv* as well, also, too; **~ eu** so do/did I; so am/have I
tambor *m* drum; eardrum
tampa *f* lid, cover
tampão *m* tampon
tanga *f* loin-cloth; **estar de ~** be broke
tangerina *f* tangerine, mandarin(e) (orange)
tanque *m* tank; pond
tanto *adj* as much, so much
tão so, as
tapar *v/t* cover, stop up, block up
tapeçaria *f* tapestry; upholstery
tapete *m* carpet
tapume *m* fence; hedge
taquigrafia *f* shorthand
tara *f* tare; derangement
tard|ar *v/t, v/i* linger, be tardy, be late; **sem mais ~ar** without delay; **~e** *adv* late; *f* afternoon; **~inha** *f* evening
tarefa *f* task
tareia *f* thrashing, flogging
tarifa *f* tariff
tarimba *f* bunk
tarraxa *f* screw
tartaruga *f* tortoise; turtle
tasca *f* pub, dive

tatuagem f tattoo
tauromaquia f bullfighting
taxa f rate; duty; **~r** v/t rate
táxi m taxi
te you, to you
tear m loom
teatro m theatre
tece|lagem f weaving; **~lão** m weaver; **~r** v/t weave
tecido m material, cloth; tissue
tecla f key; **~do** m keyboard
técnic|a f technique; **~o** m technician; adj technical
te(c)to m ceiling
tédio m tedium
teia f weft; web; plot; **~ de aranha** cobweb
teim|a f obstinacy; **~ar** v/t, v/i be obstinate, persist; **~oso** adj stubborn, obstinate
tela f linen; canvas
teleférico m funicular (railway)
telefon|ar v/t, v/i (tele)phone, ring up; **~e** m telephone; **~ema** m call; **~ia** f telephony
telegrafar v/t, v/i telegraph, wire, cable
telegrama m telegram
telescritor m teleprinter
televisão f television
telha f tile; **~do** m roof
tema m theme; exercise
temer v/t fear
temer|ário rash, foolhardy; **~idade** f temerity, rashness
temor m fear
têmpera f temper; tempera; distemper
temper|ado temperate; **~a-mento** m temperament; **~ança** f temperance; **~ar** v/t

temper; season; **~atura** f temperature
tempero m seasoning
tempest|ade f tempest, storm; **~ivo** seasonable, opportune; **~uoso** tempestuous, stormy
templo m temple
tempo m time; weather; gram tense; **há muito** ~ long ago; a ~ on/in time; **~rada** f period, while; thea season; **~ral** m storm; **~rário** temporary; **~rizar** v/t, v/i temporize
ten|acidade f tenacity; **~az** adj tenacious; f tongs, pincers
tenção f intention
tencionar v/t intend
tenda f tent; stall, booth
tendão m tendon; sinew
tend|ência f tendency; **~er** v/t, v/i tend
tenebroso dark, gloomy
tenente m lieutenant; **~-coronel** m lieutenant-colonel
ténia f tapeworm
ténis m tennis
tenro tender
tens|ão f tension; ~ **arterial** blood pressure; **~o** tense, tight, taut
tent|ação f temptation; allurement; **~ador** m tempter; adj tempting; **~ar** v/t tempt; attempt, try; **~ativa** f attempt, trial, try-out
tento m care, circumspection; Braz goal; **sem** ~ careless
tênue tenuous, thin
teor m course, tenor
teoria f theory
teórico adj theoretic(al)

tépido tepid

ter *v/t, v/i, v/r* have (got), possess; hold; get; ~ **de/que** have to; **ir** ~ **com** meet; ~ **cuidado** be careful, take care

terça-feira *f* Tuesday

terceiro *adj* third

terço *m* third (part)

terebentina *f* turpentine

termas *f/pl* spa, hot springs

termin|ação *f* termination, end; ~**ar** *v/t, v/i* terminate, end

término *m* terminus; termination, end

termo *m* limit, boundary; period; term, expression

termómetro *m* thermometer

tern|o *adj* tender; *m Braz* suit; ~**ura** *f* tenderness, affection

terra *f* earth, land

terraço *m* terrace

terremoto *m* earthquake

terreno *m* ground, terrain

terrestre terrestrial, earthly

terrina *f* tureen

território *m* territory

terrível terrible

terror *m* terror; ~**ismo** terrorism; ~**ista** *m, f* terrorist; ~**izar** *v/t* terrorize

tese *f* thesis

teso *adj* broke; stiff; inflexible

tesoura *f* scissors

tesour|aria *f* treasury; ~**eiro** *m* treasurer; ~**o** *m* treasure

testa *f* forehead

testament|eiro *m* executor; ~**o** *m* will, testament

teste *m* test

testemunh|a *f* witness; ~**ar**

v/t, v/i bear witness to; testify; ~**o** *m* testimony, evidence

testículo *m* testicle

teta *f* nipple, teat

teu *adj* your; *pron* o ~ yours

text|o *m* text; ~**ual** textual

texugo *m* badger

tez *f* complexion

ti *pron* you

tia *f* aunt

tibieza *f* lukewarmness; *fig* indifference

tíbio lukewarm; *fig* indifferent

tifo *m* typhus

tigela *f* bowl, basin

tigre *m* tiger

tijolo *m* brick

tília *f* linden, lime-tree

timbr|ar *v/t* stamp; ~**e** *m* crest; emblem; tone

time *m Braz* team

timidez *f* timidity; shyness

tímido *adj* timid; shy, bashful

tina *f* tub

tingir *v/t* tinge; dye

tinir *v/i* tinkle

tino *m* judg(e)ment, sense

tint|a *f* ink; paint; ~**eiro** *m* inkpot

tintim por tintim in minute detail

tinto dyed; red

tintur|a *f* dye; tincture; ~**aria** *f* dyer's

tio *m* uncle

típico typical

tipo *m* type; features; fellow

tipografia *f* typography

tique *m* tic, twitch

tira *f* strip

tiragem *f* drawing; printing

tirano *m* tyrant
tira-nódoas *m* stain remover
tirar *v/t, v/r* take off; remove; extract; draw, pull; print; deduce, infer; deduct; **~ uma fotografia** take a photograph
tiro *m* shot
tiroteio *m* volley, shooting
titubear *v/i* waver, stagger, hesitate
título *m* title
toa *f* tow-line; **à ~** at random
toada *f* tune, air, melody
toalha *f* towel; **~ de mesa** table-cloth
toar *v/i* (re)sound; fit
toca *f* burrow; lair
toca-discos *m Braz* record player
tocar *v/t, v/i, v/r* touch; play
tocha *f* torch
todavia *adv, conj* however, yet, nevertheless
todo *m* whole; *adj* whole; all, every; **em ~ o caso** in any case; **~s** everybody; all
toldo *m* awning; sun-blind
toler|ância *f* tolerance; **~ante** tolerant; **~ar** *v/t* tolerate; **~ável** tolerable
tol|ice *f* folly, stupidity; **~o** *adj* foolish, stupid
tom *m* tone
tom|ada *f* taking; seizure; socket; **~ar** *v/t, v/i* have; take; seize; capture
tomate *m* tomato
tomb|ar *v/t, v/i* throw down, knock down; fall down; **~o** *m* tumble, fall
tomilho *m* thyme

tomo *m* volume; tome
tonel *m* cask; vat
tonela|da *f* ton; **~gem** *f* tonnage
tonificar *v/t* invigorate, refresh
tont|o stupid; giddy, dizzy; **~ura** *f* giddiness, dizziness
topar *v/t, v/i* come across; find; **~ com** stumble across/on
tópico *m* topic
toque *m* touch
toranja *f* grape-fruit
torc|er *v/t, v/i, v/r* writhe; twist, wrench; distort; wring; turn; **~ida** *f* wick
tordo *m* thrush
torment|a *f* storm; **~o** *m* torment; **~oso** stormy, boisterous
tornar *v/t, v/i, v/r* come back, return; do again; become
tornear *v/t* turn; encompass
torneio *m* tournament
torneira *f* tap
torno *m* lathe; **em ~ de** *prp* around ...
tornozelo *m* ankle
torpe shameful, vile; torpid
torpedeiro *m* torpedo-boat
torpeza *f* baseness
torpor *m* torpor
torrada *f* toast
torrão *m* clod
torrar *v/t* toast; roast
torre *f* tower
torren|cial torrential; **~te** *f* torrent
torresmo *m* rasher, crackling
tórrido torrid
torta *f* tart
torto *adj* twisted, crooked; de-

formed; **a ~ ou a direito** by
hook or by crook

tortuoso tortuous

tortur|a *f* torture; **~ar** *v/t* torture

torvelinho *m* whirlwind; whirl
pool; eddy

tosar *v/t* shear; drub

tosco coarse, rough

tosquiar *v/t* shear

toss|e *f* cough; **~ir** *v/i* cough

tostão *m* 10 centavos

tostar *v/t* parch, toast

total *m, adj* total; **~idade** *f* totality

toucador *m* dressing-table

toucinho *m* bacon

toupeira *f* zo mole

tour|ada *f* bullfight; **~eiro** *m*
bullfighter, toreador; **~o** *m*
bull

tóxico *m* poison; *adj* toxic

trabalh|ador *m* labo(u)rer,
workman; *adj* hard-working;
~ar *v/i* work; **~o** *m* work

traça *f* moth

traç|ado *m*, outline, sketch,
plan; **~ar** *v/t* trace, outline;
sketch, draw

tra(c)ção *f* traction

traço *m* line; dash; stroke; trace;
~ de união hyphen

tra(c)tor *m* tractor

tradição *f* tradition

tradu|ção *f* translation; **~tor** *m*
translator; **~zir** *v/t* translate

tráfego *m* traffic

trafic|ante *m* trafficker; **~ar**
v/t, v/i traffic in, trade

tráfico *m* trade, traffic

tragar *v/t* swallow

tragédia *f* tragedy

trai|ção *f* treason; betrayal;
treachery; **~çoeiro** treacherous; **~r** *v/t, v/r* betray

traje *m* dress, garb

traje(c)to *m* way, route; tract

traje(c)tória *f* trajectory

tramar *v/t* plot

trâmite *m* path

trampolim *m* spring-board

trança *f* plait, *US* braid

trancar *v/t* bar, bolt

tranquil|idade *f* tranquil(l)ity;
~izar *v/t, v/r* tranquil(l)ize;
~o tranquil

transa(c)ção *f* transaction; **~to**
past, bygone; former

transfer|ência *f* transference;
~ir *v/t* transfer

transform|ação *f* transformation; **~ar** *v/t, v/r* transform

transgre|dir *v/t* transgress;
~ssão *f* transgression

transi|ção *f* transition; **~gente**
adj condescending, compliant;
~tar *v/i* travel, journey, pass
along

trânsito *m* transit; traffic; **em
~** in transit

transitório transitory

transmi|ssão *f* transmission;
~tir *v/t* broadcast; transmit

transpar|ência *f* transparency;
~ente *adj* transparent

transpir|ação *f* transpiration;
~ar *v/i* transpire

transplantar *v/t* transplant

transpor *v/t* transpose

transport|ar *v/t* transport; **~e**
m transport

transtorn|ar *v/t* upset; **~o** *m*

upset; inconvenience

transversal adj transversal, transverse

trapalhada f jumble, mess

trapo m rag

traquina(s) adj impish, naughty

trasbordar v/t tranship; transfer

trasbordo m transhipment; **fazer** ~ change trains

traseira f back part, rear

traseiro m buttocks, behind; adj back, rear

trasladar v/t transcribe; remove, convey

traste m piece of furniture; scamp, rogue

trat|ado m treaty; treatise; ~**amento** m treatment; ~**ante**, f swindler; ~**ar** v/t, v/i, v/r treat; deal with; ~**ar de** try to; ~**ar-se de** be a question of

trato m treatment; manners

trav|ão m brake; ~**ar** v/t, v/i engage in; brake; ~**ar conhecimento com** become acquainted with

trave f beam

travessa f lane, alley; railway-sleeper; dish, US platter

travessão m dash

travesseiro m bolster

travessia f voyage, crossing

travess|o naughty; ~**ura** f naughtiness; trick, prank

travo(r) m tartness; aftertaste

trazer v/t bring; wear; carry

trecho m period, interval; passage, extract

trégua f truce

treinar v/t, v/r train

treino m training

trem m carriage; Braz train

tremelicar v/i tremble

trem|endo tremendous; awful; ~**er** v/i tremble, quiver; ~**oço** m lupin; ~**or** m tremor, tremble, shudder; ~**or de terra** earthquake

tremular v/i wave; waver

trêmulo tremulous

trenó m sleigh, sledge

trep|adeira f bot creeper; ~**ar** v/t, v/i climb

trepidação f trepidation

três three

tresandar v/i reek of

tresloucar v/i become mad

trevas f/pl darkness

trevo m clover

treze thirteen

trezentos three hundred

triangular adj triangular

triângulo m triangle

tribunal m tribunal, court

tribut|ar v/t tax; pay tribute to; ~**ário** adj, m tributary; ~**o** m tribute

trig|o m wheat; ~**ueiro** adj swarthy

trilh|ar v/t thresh; tread; ~**o** m harrow

trimestre m term; quarter

trinado m warbling

trincar v/t crunch, munch

trincheira f trench

trinco m latch

trinta thirty

tripa f gut; tripe; entrails

triplo adj triple

tripulação f crew

triste *adj* sad; **~za** *f* sadness
triturar *v/t* grind, triturate
triunf|ar *v/i* triumph; **~o** *m* triumph
trivial *adj* trivial
triz *m* moment; **por um ~** by the skin of one's teeth
troar *v/i* thunder
troca *f* barter
troça *f* mockery, scorn, ridicule
trocar *v/t* barter, swap; exchange; change
troçar *v/t, v/i* mock, scorn, ridicule
troco *m* change; **a ~ de** in exchange for
troço *m* section; fragment
tromba *f* trunk; snout; **~ de água** waterspout
trombeta *f* trumpet; *m* trumpeter
trombone *m* trombone
tronco *m* trunk; stem
trono *m* throne
tropa *f* troop
tropeçar *v/i* stumble
trôpego hobbling, tottery
tropical tropical
trópico *m* tropic
trot|ar *v/i* trot; **~e** *m* trot
trovão *m* thunder
trovejar *v/i* thunder
trufa *f* truffle

trunfo *m* trump
truque *m* trick, dodge
truta *f* trout
tu *pron* you
tubarão *m* shark
tubo *m* tube
tudo everything, all
tudo-nada *m* iota, jot
tufão *m* typhoon
tufo *m* tuft
tulipa *f* tulip
túmido tumid; haughty
tumor *m* tumo(u)r
túmulo *m* tomb; tumulus
tumulto *m* tumult
túnel *m* tunnel
turbilhão *m* whirl; swirl
turbina *f* turbine
turbulento *adj* turbulent
turco *m* Turk; *adj* Turkish
turis|mo *m* tourism, travel; **~ta** *m, f* tourist
turma *f* class, group; *Braz* people
turno *m* turn; shift **por ~s** by turns
turv|ar *v/t* disturb, muddle, confuse; **~o** *adj* muddy, dim, troubled
tutela *f* guardianship, tutelage
tutor *m* guardian; tutor
tutoria *f* guardianship; tutorship

U

úbere *adj* fertile, abundant
ufan|ar-se *v/r* pride on; **~o(so)** proud, vain
uiv|ar *v/i* howl; **~o** *m* howl
úlcera *f* ulcer

ulmo *m* elm
ulterior ulterior; further
ultimamente recently
ultimato *m* ultimatum
último *adj* last; **por ~** at last

ultraj|ar v/t outrage; **~e** m outrage; insult

ultramar m overseas; **~ino** overseas

ultrapassar v/t surpass; overtake, outstrip

ulular v/i howl; wail

um, uma art a, an; one

umbigo m navel

unânime unanimous

unanimidade f unanimity

ungir v/t anoint

unguento m ointment, salve

unha f nail; claw

união f union

único single, sole, only; unique

unidade f unity

unific|ação f unification; **~ar** v/t unify

uniform|e adj, m uniform; **~idade** f uniformity

unir v/t unite

uníssono m unison

universal adj universal

universidade f university

universitário adj of a university; m university teacher

universo m universe

untar v/t grease; smear

unto m lard; fat; grease

urânio m uranium

urbaniz|ação f urbanization; **~ar** v/t urbanize

urbano adj urban; urbane

urbe f city

urdir v/t warp, weave; plot, contrive

urgência f urgency; emergency

urgente urgent

urgir v/i urge

urina f urine

urna f urn; ballot-box

urr|ar v/i roar, bellow; **~o** m roar, bellow

urso m bear

urtiga f nettle

urze f heather

usado used; worn out

usar v/t, v/r use; wear (out)

usina f Braz factory

uso m use; custom, usage; wear

usual usual, customary

usufru|ir v/t enjoy use of; **~to** m usufruct; **~tuário** m usufructuary

usur|a f usury; **~ário** m usurer

usurpar v/t usurp

utensílio m utensil, tool

útero m uterus, womb

útil adj useful

utilidade f usefulness; utility

utilizar v/t utilize, use

utópico utopian

uva f grape

V

vaca f cow

vacil|ação f vacilation; indecision; **~ar** v/i vaciIate

vacina f vaccine

vacin|ação f vaccination; **~ar** v/t vaccinate

vácuo adj void, empty; m vacuum

vadi|agem f vagrancy; **~ar** v/i wander, roam

vadio m vagrant; vagabond

vaga f wave; vacancy

vagão *m* railway carriage; **~-cama**, **~-leito** *m* sleeping-car; **~-restaurante** *m* dining/restaurant-car

vagar *v/i* be vacant; be idle; *m* leisure; **~oso** slow, leisurely

vagem *f* husk, pod

vagido *m* wail

vagina *f* vagina

vago vague; vacant

vaguear *v/i* rove, roam, ramble

vaia *f* hissing, hooting

vaidade *f* vanity

vaidoso *adj* vain

vaivém *m* fluctuation, coming and going

vala *f* ditch

vale *m* valley, vale; **~ postal** postal order, US money order

valent|e *adj* brave, valiant; **~ia** *f* valo(u)r

valer *v/t*, *v/i*, *v/r* be worth; **~a pena** be worth-while; **a ~ in** earnest, really; **~-se de** make use of; profit by

valeta *f* gutter

valia *f* value, merit

validade *f* validity

válido valid; robust

valioso valuable

valor *m* value, worth; stock, bond; **~izar** *v/t* increase the value of; **~oso** brave

valsa *f* waltz

válvula *f* valve

vampiro *m* vampire

vangloriar-se *v/r* boast

vanguarda *f* vanguard

vantagem *f* advantage

vantajoso advantageous

vão *adj* vain, futile

vapor *m* vapo(u)r, steam; steamboat

vara *f* rod, pole, stick

varanda *f* balcony; veranda(h)

varapau *m* cudgel

varar *v/t*, *v/i* strike, beat; pierce; run aground

vari|ação *f* variation; **~ar** *v/t*, *v/i* vary; **~ável** *adj* variable, changeable; **~edade** *f* variety

vários *pl* various, several

varonil virile; manly

varrer *v/t*, *v/i* sweep

vasilha *f* vessel; keg; barrel

vaso *m* flowerpot; vase

vassoura *f* broom

vast|idão *f* vastness, immensity; **~o** *adj* vast

vaticinar *v/t* prophesy, foretell

vau *m* ford

vaz|ante *f* ebb; **~ar** *v/t*, *v/i*, *v/r* ebb; empty; pour out

vazio *adj* empty

veado *m* deer, hart, stag

ved|ação *f* barrier, fence, enclosure; **~ar** *v/t* forbid; fence off

vedeta *f* thea star

veem|ência *f* vehemence; **~ente** vehement

veget|ação *f* vegetation; **~al** *adj*, *m* vegetable

veia *f* vein

veículo *m* vehicle

vela *f* candle; sail

velar *v/t*, *v/i* watch over; stay awake

veleiro *m* sailing ship

velejar *v/i* sail

velhac|aria *f* deceit; **~o** *m* rogue

velhice *f* old age

velho *adj* old; *m* old man

velocidade *f* velocity, speed; *auto* gear

veloz swift

veludo *m* velvet

vencedor *m* winner

vencer *v/t, v/i* conquer, defeat; win

vencimento *m, com* maturity, due date; salary

venda *f* sale; shop; blindfold

vend|er *v/t* sell; **~ível** sal(e)-able

veneno *m* poison; **~so** poisonous

vener|ação *f* veneration; **~ar** *v/t* venerate, revere

vénia *f* permission; bow

venta *f* nostril; **~s** *f/pl* nose

ventilação *f* ventilation

ventilador *m* ventilator

ventilar *v/t* ventilate

vento *m* wind; **~so** windy

ventoinha *f* fan

ventre *m* belly

ventur|a *f* luck; fate; **~oso** lucky

ver *v/t* see

veracidade *f* veracity, truthfulness

verão *m* summer

verba *f* item, clause; sum

verbal verbal

verbo *m* verb

verdade *f* truth

verdadeiro *adj* true; real

verde *adj* green

verdejar *v/i* grow green

verdura *f* greens; verdure

vereda *f* foot-path

verga *f* switch, shoot; yard-arm

vergar *v/t, v/i* bend, curve

vergonh|a *f* shame; **~oso** shameful

vergôntea *f* shoot, sprout; off-spring

verídico truthful

verific|ação *f* verification; **~ar** *v/t* verify; ascertain

verme *m* worm

vermelho *adj* red

vernáculo vernacular

verniz *m* varnish

verosímil probable, likely

verosimilhança *f* probability, likelihood

verruga *f* wart

verruma *f* gimlet

versado (em) conversant (with), versed (in)

versão *f* translation; version

verso *m* verse

vertente *f* slope

verter *v/t, v/i* leak; turn (**para** into); spill, pour

vertical *adj, f* vertical

vertig|em *f* dizziness, vertigo; **~inoso** dizzy

vesgo *adj* squint-eyed, squinting

vespa *f* wasp

véspera *f* eve; day before

vestiário *m* cloak-room, *US* check-room

vestíbulo *m* vestibule, hall; foyer

vestido *m* dress

vestígio *m* vestige, trace

vestir *v/t, v/i, v/r* put on; dress

vestuário *m* wardrobe, clothes, clothing

veterinária *f* veterinary medicine

vetusto ancient

véu *m* veil

vex|ame *m* vexation; **~ar** *v/t* vex, harass, annoy

vez *f* time; occasion; turn; **cada ~ mais** more and more; **de ~ em quando** now and then; **em ~ de** instead of; **uma ~** once; **às ~es** sometimes; **muitas ~es** often

via *f* way; road; **~ férrea** railway; **por ~ aérea** by air mail

viagem *f* journey, travel

viajante *m, f* trave(l)ler

viajar *v/i* travel

viatura *f* vehicle

víbora *f* viper, adder

vicejar *v/i* thrive

viciado *m* addict

viciar *v/t, v/r* addict; vitiate

vicioso vicious; corrupt

viçoso luxuriant, rank

vida *f* life

videira *f* vine

vidraça *f* pane

vidraceiro *m* glazier

vidro *m* glass; pane

viga *f* beam

vigarista *m, f* swindler

vigi|a *f* watch; vigil; porthole; *m* look-out; **~ar** *v/t, v/i* watch over; guard

vigilante *adj* vigilant

vigor *m* vigo(u)r; **~ar** *v/t, v/i* invigorate; be in force; **~oso** vigorous

vil *adj* vile, mean

vila *f* small town; villa

vinagre *m* vinegar

vinco *m* crease

vínculo *m* tie, bond

vinda *f* coming, arrival

vindicar *v/t* claim, vindicate

vindima *f* grape harvest, vintage; **~dor** *m* grape-picker

vindouro *adj* future, yet to come

ving|ança *f* vengeance; **~ar** *v/t, v/r* avenge; take vengeance on; revenge

vinha *f* vineyard

vinho *m* wine; **~ tinto** red wine

viol|ação *f* violation; **~ar** *v/t* violate

violência *f* violence

violent|ar *v/t* do violence to; **~o** violent

vir *v/i* come; **~ a ser** become

virar *v/t, v/i* turn; veer

virgem *f* virgin

viril virile, manly

virtude *f* virtue

virtuoso virtuous

visão *f* vision

visar *v/t* aim at

viscoso viscous

visibilidade *f* visibility

visita *f* visit; visitor; **~nte** *m, f* visitor; **~r** *v/t* visit

visível visible

vista *f* view; vista

visto *m* visa

vistoria inspection, survey

vistoso showy, flashy

vital *adj* vital; **~ício** lifelong, for life; **~idade** *f* vitality

vitela *f* heifer; veal

vítima *f* victim

vitória *f* victory

vitrina *f* shop-window; show--window; show-case

viúva *f* widow

viúvo *m* widower

vivacidade *f* vivacity

vivaz vivacious

vivenda *f* dwelling, home
viver *v/i* live
víveres *m/pl* provisions
vívido vivid
vivo lively; alive, living
vizinh|ança *f* neighbo(u)rhood; vicinity; ~o *m* neighbo(u)r; *adj* neighbo(u)ring
voar *v/i* fly
vocação *f* vocation
você you
vogar *v/i* row; sail
volante *m* steering-wheel; shuttlecock
voleibol *m* volley-ball
volta *f* turn; return; circuit; bend, curve; walk, stroll; **por ~ de** about
voltagem *f* voltage
voltar *v/i, v/i, v/i* come back, return; turn round
volume *m* volume; piece of luggage

volumoso voluminous
voluntário *adj* voluntary
voluntarioso headstrong
volver *v/t, v/i* turn, revolve
vomitar *v/t* vomit, throw up
vontade *f* will; wish, desire
voo *m* flight
vos *pron* you, to you
vós *pron* you
vosso *adj* your; *pron* yours
vot|ação *f* poll, voting; ~ar *v/i* vote; ~o *m* vote; vow; wish
vovó *f* granny, grannie
vovô *m* grandpa
voz *f* voice; ~earia *f* hullabaloo, clamo(u)r
vulcão *m* volcano
vulgar *adj* common, ordinary; ~izar *v/t, v/r* popularize
vulgo *m* populace, rabble
vulnerar *v/t* wound
vulto *m* countenance, mien; bulk; figure, form

X

xadrez *m* chess; *Braz* jail
xa(i)le *m* shawl
xairel *m* saddle-cloth
xarope *m* syrup

xeque *m* check; ~-mate checkmate
xícara *f* cup
xingar *v/t Braz* scold, rail

Z

zanga *f* anger; quarrel; ~do angry
zangar *v/t, v/r* annoy; get angry
zelar *v/t* watch over
zelo *m* zeal; ~so zealous; eager
zé-povinho *m* (the) Portuguese
zé-povo *m* (the) Brazilian
zero *m* zero; nil; nought

zomb|ador *m* scoffer; ~ar *v/i* jeer, scoff (**de** at)
zorro *m* fox
zumb|ido *m* buzzing, humming; ~ir *v/i* hum, buzz
zunir *v/i* hum, buzz; whir(r); whistle
zurrapa *f* rough wine
zurzir *v/t* thrash; cudgel; flog

Cardinal and ordinal numbers
Numerais cardinais e ordinais

0 nought *zero*	90 ninety *noventa*
1 one *um, uma*	100 a hundred *cem*
2 two *dois, duas*	101 a (one) hundred and one *cento e um/uma*
3 three *três*	
4 four *quatro*	200 two hundred *duzentos, -as*
5 five *cinco*	300 three hundred *trezentos, -as*
6 six *seis*	
7 seven *sete*	400 four hundred *quatrocentos, -as*
8 eight *oito*	
9 nine *nove*	500 five hundred *quinhentos, -as*
10 ten *dez*	
11 eleven *onze*	600 six hundred *seiscentos, -as*
12 twelve *doze*	700 seven hundred *setecentos, -as*
13 thirteen *treze*	
14 fourteen *catorze*	800 eight hundred *oitocentos, -as*
15 fifteen *quinze*	
16 sixteen *dezasseis*	900 nine hundred *novecentos, -as*
17 seventeen *dezassete*	
18 eighteen *dezoito*	1000 a thousand *mil*
19 nineteen *dezanove*	1000000 a million *um milhão*
20 twenty *vinte*	1st first *primeiro, -a*
21 twenty-one *vinte-e-um (-uma)*	2nd second *segundo, -a*
	3rd third *terceiro, -a*
23 twenty-three *vinte-e-três*	4th fourth *quarto, -a*
30 thirty *trinta*	5th fifth *quinto, -a*
40 forty *quarenta*	6th sixth *sexto, -a*
50 fifty *cinquenta*	7th seventh *sétimo, -a*
60 sixty *sessenta*	8th eighth *oitavo, -a*
70 seventy *setenta*	9th ninth *nono, -a*
80 eighty *oitenta*	10th tenth *décimo, -a*

Proper names
Nomes próprios

Africa ['æfrikə] África
America [ə'merikə] América
Angola [æŋ'ɡəulə] Angola
Antilles [æn'tili:z] Antilhas
Asia ['eiʃə] Ásia
Australia [ɔs'treiljə] Austrália
Austria ['ɔstriə] Áustria
Azores [ə'zɔ:z] Açores
Belgium ['beldʒəm] Bélgica
Biscay ['biskei] Biscaia
Brazil [brə'zil] Brasil
Canada ['kænədə] Canadá
Chile ['tʃili] Chile
China ['tʃainə] China
Czechoslovakia ['tʃekəuslə-'vækiə] Checoslováquia
Denmark ['denma:k] Dinamarca
Egypt ['i:dʒipt] Egipto
England ['iŋɡlənd] Inglaterra
Europe ['juərəp] Europa
Finland ['finlənd] Finlândia
France [fra:ns] França
Germany ['dʒə:məni] Alemanha
Gibraltar [dʒi'brɔ:ltə] Gibraltar
Great Britain ['greit'britn] Grã-Bretanha
Greece [gri:s] Grécia
Guatemala [ˌgwæti'ma:lə] Guatemala
Hungary ['hʌŋgəri] Hungria
India ['indjə] Índia
Irak [i'ra:k] Iraque
Iran [i'ra:n] Irão
Ireland ['aiələnd] Irlanda

Italy ['itəli] Itália
Japan [dʒə'pæn] Japão
Jugoslavia ['ju:gə'sla:vjə] Jugoslávia
Lisbon ['lizbən] Lisboa
London ['lʌndən] Londres
Luxemb(o)urg ['lʌksəmbə:g] Luxemb(o)urgo
Mexico ['meksikəu] México
Morocco [mə'rɔkəu] Marrocos
Mozambique [ˌməuzəm'bi:k] Moçambique
Netherlands ['neðələnds] Neerlândia
New York ['nju:'jɔ:k] Nova-Iorque
New Zealand [nju'zi:lənd] Nova Zelândia
Norway ['nɔ:wei] Noruega
Poland ['pəulənd] Polónia
Portugal ['pɔ:tjugəl] Portugal
Pyrenees [pirə'ni:z] Pirenéus
Rumania [ru'meinjə] Roménia
Scandinavia [ˌskændi'neivjə] Escandinávia
Scotland ['skɔtlənd] Esocócia
Sicily ['sisili] Sicília
Soviet Union ['səuviət 'ju:njən] União Soviética
Spain [spein] Espanha
Sweden ['swi:dn] Suécia
Switzerland ['switsələnd] Suíça
United States of America [ju:'naitid steits əv ə'merikə] Estados Unidos da América do Norte
Vietnam ['vjet'næm] Vietname